Praise for

THE MIDDLE KINGDOMS

A *Telegraph* (UK) Best History Book of 2023

"Rady deftly unravels the strands of a long and complex past to show Central Europe as both a battle zone of often hideous violence and a medieval cradle of Western democracy."   —*Wall Street Journal*

"A magisterial history."   —Peter Frankopan, *Spectator* (UK)

"This is a very impressive book, quirkily original but also scholarly and authoritative, to be read for pleasure and serious reflection."
                    —*Daily Telegraph* (UK)

"Popular academic history at its best."
                    —Ivan Krastev, *Financial Times*

"A masterly synthesis."   —*Times* (UK)

"Rady's history is full of stories and vignettes, personalities and ideas rather than grand theses. The result, built on a lifetime of scholarship and vast reading in multiple languages, vividly conveys the complexities and multifaceted nature of central Europe."
                    —*BBC History Magazine*

"A repeatedly rewarding study.... This book deserves attention."
                    —*New Criterion*

THE MIDDLE
KINGDOMS

THE MIDDLE KINGDOMS

A New History of Central Europe

MARTYN RADY

BASIC BOOKS
NEW YORK

Basic Books
Hachette Book Group
1290 Avenue of the Americas, New York, NY 10104
www.basicbooks.com

Printed in the United States of America
Originally published in hardcover and ebook by Basic Books in May 2023.
First Trade Paperback Edition: November 2024

Published by Basic Books, an imprint of Hachette Book Group, Inc. The Basic Books name
and logo is a registered trademark of the Hachette Book Group.

The Hachette Speakers Bureau provides a wide range of authors for speaking events. To find
out more, go to hachettespeakersbureau.com or email HachetteSpeakers@hbgusa.com.

Basic Books copies may be purchased in bulk for business, educational, or promotional
use. For information, please contact your local bookseller or Hachette Book Group Special
Markets Department at special.markets@hbgusa.com.

The publisher is not responsible for websites (or their content) that are not owned by
the publisher.

Print book interior design by Linda Mark.

The Library of Congress has cataloged the hardcover edition as follows:
Names: Rady, Martyn C., author.
Title: The middle kingdoms : a new history of Central Europe / Martyn Rady.
Description: First edition. | New York : Basic Books, 2023. | Includes bibliographical
    references and index.
Identifiers: LCCN 2022032147 | ISBN 9781541619784 (hardcover) |
    ISBN 9781541619777 (ebook)
Subjects: LCSH: Europe, Central—History. | Europe, Central—Civilization. | Europe,
    Central—Politics and government. | Europe, Central—History, Military. | Europe,
    Central—Foreign relations.
Classification: LCC DAW1038 .R337 2023 | DDC 943—dc23/eng/20220721
LC record available at https://lccn.loc.gov/2022032147

ISBNs: 9781541619784 (hardcover), 9781541619777 (ebook),
9781541606340 (paperback)

LSC-C

Printing 1, 2024

For Ann

Contents

List of Maps

A Note on Names

Generally, places are referred to by their modern-day names. The fortresses of the Teutonic Order are the exception, since they conventionally retain their German names. Königsberg, the city of Kant, self-evidently cannot be Kaliningrad, whose Soviet-era name recalls a mass murderer. Budapest was united only in 1873, so until this time it is referred to in the text as either Buda or Pest or as Pest-Buda. Bratislava has been thus for a century, although Germans have always called it Pressburg and Hungarians know it as Pozsony.

Personal names follow no scheme other than what tends to prevail in the English-language literature. Some names have been Anglicized, as in Frederick the Great, but Heinrich Himmler can never be Henry Himmler.

THE MIDDLE
KINGDOMS

Central Europe, the Dogmen, and the Oak Woods of Berehove

THE MEDIEVAL SCRIBES WHO ILLUSTRATED MANUSCRIPTS OFten added small sketches in the margins of pages, either to tantalize readers or as a relief from their own boredom. They drew winding vines, flowers, farmyard animals, and ordinary people, but they often also included fabulous creatures. These might be unicorns or mermaids, but there were monsters and monstrosities as well: flamespewing dragons, mossy wild men, and headless creatures with faces in their chests. A favourite was the 'dogman', or cynocephalus, who had a human body but a dog's head. Being social, as humans are, but only able to bark, the dogmen were frequently drawn gesticulating and pointing.

The dogmen were an idea taken from classical literature and they were thought to be real creatures, living on the edge of civilization in the same way they occupied the margins of manuscripts. Early Christian scholars debated the balance in dogmen of canine and human qualities, since if they were mainly human then it followed that they had souls and should be converted. But the dogmen were elusive, always keeping just beyond the reach of missionaries and of the warbands of Christian kings and rulers. Even so, stories kept on coming of what dogmen were doing just over the horizon—murdering priests, feasting on captives, and consorting with long-nailed female warriors or Amazons. No shaggy dogman was ever captured, but with unbelievers it was best to be on the safe side. One ninth-century account tells of how a missionary bishop in what is now Austria denied a place at the table to visiting pagan chieftains, instead laying out bowls on the floor.[1]

As the tide of religious conversion advanced eastwards, creating Christian kingdoms out of what had been pagan peoples, the dog-men were shunted out of Europe altogether and made to dwell on the world's edge. The late-thirteenth-century 'World Map' (*Mappa Mundi*) in Hereford Cathedral in England shows a group of dogmen in the far east being chased from the Garden of Eden by an angel. A second group are portrayed in their subsequent exile, gesturing on a promontory far in the north. They share the margin of the world with cave-dwelling troglodytes, headless men, and the one-legged monopods who sleep on their back in the shade of an overlarge foot. But, as it turned out, the banishment of the dogmen to the remote north would not be per-manent. Even by the time the monks of Hereford were drawing their World Map, the dogmen had returned to the European mainland in a new and more terrible form. This time, they were for real.

Central Europe rests on its western edge against the River Rhine, which joins the North Sea to the Alps, but its eastern boundary has no obvious physical marker. The Carpathian Mountains, which start northeast of Vienna, in modern-day Slovakia, curl around Hungary and Transylvania, forming a border in the southeast. But further north there is just open country. Northern Europe is flat, lying on the Great European Plain which reaches more than three thousand kilometres from the Low Countries to the Ural Mountains in Russia. On its southern flank, the Great European Plain blends into the steppe land or, as it was once known, the 'Wild Plain' that runs through modern-day Ukraine and Central Asia.

It was over the Wild Plain that the dogmen came, bursting out of Central Asia in 1241 and wasting Poland and Hungary. They called themselves Mongols and Tatars, and the second name betrayed (so it was thought) their origin in Tartarus, the classical name for the abyss of hell. Their leader, too, was self-evidently a dog, for he was known as a khan, a name that harked to the Latin word for dog (*canis*). The be-haviour of the Mongols confirmed the connection since, as one French witness related, 'they ate the bodies of their victims, like so much bread.' Believing all this, contemporary writers confidently reported that the Mongols were the dog-headed men of antiquity, belonging to the people of Gog and Magog whom Alexander the Great had once walled up in the Caucasus along with sundry giants, corrupt nations, and the unclean people who ate mice and flies. Evidently, something or someone had let them out.[2]

The Mongols were the dogmen of Tartarus or, in another description, the hounds of hell. Although the Mongol Empire rapidly fell apart, one of its successor states preserved the link. From the fifteenth century onwards, the Tatar khans of the Crimea launched successive raids on the Christian kingdoms to the west. They were looking for loot, in the form of slaves, and young ones in particular, whom they would sell in the Crimean port of Kaffa (now Feodosia), repurposed as either concubines or eunuchs. For centuries, the folklore of the peoples who lived around the Carpathian Mountains rehearsed the depravities of the 'dog-snouted Tatars', combining these with other tales involving devils and demons. In Hungarian accounts, the association of Tatars with dogmen was so complete that Tatars were seldom recorded before the twentieth century without the epithet of 'dog-headed'.[3]

It was not just the Tatars who were thought to be dogmen. From Anatolia, which is now mainland Turkey, the Ottoman Turks invaded and occupied the Balkan peninsula in the late fourteenth and fifteenth centuries, capturing Constantinople (modern-day Istanbul) in 1453. Less than a century later, they occupied central Hungary, raiding deep into the neighbouring countries. Unsurprisingly, the Turks were described as agents of Satan, with an insatiable thirst for blood. Western writers accused the Turks of all sorts of extravagances, including bestiality and sexual relations with fish, but from the very first they, too, were associated with the dogmen. According to the Protestant reformer Martin Luther, the Turks married dogs, generating hybrids from their union. Since the prophet Mohammed was also said to be a dog and was sometimes shown with a dog's head, it made sense to consider all Muslims as potential dogmen.[4]

The history of the dogmen embodies the predicament of Central Europe. Real and imagined, the dogmen are predatory and invasion is a recurrent theme in Central Europe's history. The list of would-be conquerors begins with the Goths and Huns in the fourth century, continues through the Avars, Slavs, and Hungarians in the seventh and ninth centuries, and goes on to include the Mongols and Ottoman Turks in the later Middle Ages. After 1500, the picture is more complicated, since invaders came from every direction—the French from the west, the Swedes from the north, and the Russians from the northeast. Of these, the Russians were the most tenacious, pushing into Central Europe in the late eighteenth century and occupying most of it after 1945.

But Central Europe has never been just a passive victim. Its kingdoms and empires have also been predatory, carving out spaces at the expense of their neighbours. Conflicts arising in the region have often spilled outwards as well. The Thirty Years' War fought in Central Europe between 1618 and 1648 engulfed almost the whole continent, with sideshows in Africa, the Caribbean, and even distant Taiwan. The seizure of Austrian Silesia in 1740 by Frederick the Great of Prussia led to more than two decades of war, which drew in Britain and France and, during the Seven Years' War (1756–1763), was partly waged in North America and the Indian subcontinent. German unification was made possible in 1871 only because the Prussian politician Otto von Bismarck had just defeated France and occupied Paris. In the twentieth century, Central Europe was the starting place of two world wars, and in the twenty-first century it was the site of the most destructive war waged in Europe for more than seventy years.

Central Europe has often been characterized by what it is not. The earliest definition of Central Europe, or 'Mitteleuropa', as it was known in German, was guided by the politics of the Napoleonic Wars. Published in Brunswick in 1805, Georg Hassel's 'Statistical Sketch of All the European States' (*Statistischer Umriss der sämtlichen europäischen Staaten*) was uncompromisingly exact. Central Europe was the part of Europe that was neither France nor Russia, so leaving just the lands belonging to the German rulers whom Napoleon had kept in power, Prussia, and the Austrian Empire. It was in the middle of Europe, not only geographically but politically too, and Europe's freedom from the double threat of French and Russian tyranny rested on its survival. The view that Central Europe lay in Europe's middle persisted through-out the nineteenth century in travel books and gazetteers, although to drum up sales, publishers of tourist guides to the region also added in excursions to London and Paris.

Political boundaries change, and with every alteration the idea of Central Europe changed too. Germany was always a part of it, but Central Europe's other members varied according to who was writing, and when, and where. So, Belgium was occasionally included, along with Alsace and Lorraine, and Poland either brought in or left out de-pending on whether the state of Poland actually existed at the time. Up to the Second World War, German geographers and historians were never less than ready to pronounce where the region was. But their definitions were often a cover for Germany rolling up the states to its east, either commercially or politically, on the dubious grounds that they had always been culturally German or produced goods that were particularly useful to the German economy. After 1945, 'Central Eu-rope' fell from use as a term, since Europe was now divided down the middle into West and East. Following communism's collapse, histori-ans and political scientists often referred to the former Eastern Europe as East Central Europe, although they seldom explained where West Central Europe might be.

This history of Central Europe is unique in combining the region's two halves, since historians usually discuss them separately as Germany and as East Central Europe, with Austria flitting uncertainly between the two. It does not foreground national histories but traverses the byways of the past, to kingdoms and duchies that were once great but whose memory has been squeezed out by histories that make the na-tion state their starting point. Broadly, the book covers the area now included in modern-day Germany, Poland, Hungary, Austria, Slove-nia, and western Romania or Transylvania, but its scope is as fluid as Central Europe's historical parts, venturing at times into the territory of today's Ukraine, Croatia, Switzerland, and the Baltic states.

This book aims to give a broad survey of Central European history, but it has another purpose too: to explore Central Europe's distinctiveness and to show it to be more than just a contested space. Central Europe's history has much in common with Western Europe's. The two regions shared the same medieval civilization. Like England and France, the kingdoms and duchies in Europe's middle had castles, knights, Catholic churches and monasteries, flourishing cities, and wealthy merchants. Central Europe experienced, too, the rediscovery of classical learning that is called the Renaissance, the struggle over religion during the Reformation, the growth of empire, the Enlightenment, Romanticism, modern nationalism, industrialization, and two world wars.

But Central Europe often embraced these larger movements differently, giving them a special twist or an unexpected intensity. Its knights were also colonizers, opening new spaces for settlement and founding villages and cities in the region's less populated eastern part. Across medieval Central Europe, noblemen, city folk, and villagers established parliaments, assemblies, and self-governing communities to a degree far greater than in most of Western Europe. Central Europe's Renaissance was influenced by what was going on in Italy, but it was infused, too, with a deep spirituality and a concern with death and redemption. Its Protestant Reformation threw up a medley of sects and denominations that survived into the seventeenth century in an atmosphere of relative toleration. Unlike France, Spain, and England, in most of Central Europe people were not burnt for their beliefs.

Conditions in the countryside differed too. Throughout Europe, the broad mass of the population comprised peasants who in return for their farms were obliged to pay rent to their lords, sometimes by working for them. But in much of Central Europe, particularly in its eastern parts, landlords' demands were more onerous and they frequently compelled peasants to labour in their fields for several or more days per week. On top of this, many peasants in the east of Central Europe were tied to the soil, in the sense that they could not quit their villages to escape their lords. In a large part of Central Europe, right through to the nineteenth century, a type of serfdom persisted that was mostly missing in Western Europe.

The modern state was born in Central Europe, where bureaucracy first fused with the early Enlightenment. So, whereas in England, France, and North America, the Enlightenment tended to promote individual liberty, in Central Europe the Enlightenment championed the state and the right of government to rule by decree. And, whereas in Western Europe, empires were built overseas, in Central Europe empires swallowed up the region, leading to a contest for hegemony fought out between the Austrian Habsburgs, Russia, and Prussia, which became the core of the new German Empire. At the end of the eighteenth century, the empires sliced up among themselves Poland and Lithuania. They then went on to fight among themselves, eventually destroying one another in the First World War. In the twentieth century, the fusion of nationalism with the pseudo-science of racial biology took destruction one step further, leading to the attempted elimination of whole peoples.

Central Europe's historical experience differs from Western Europe's. Its trends seem to replicate a good part of what was happening in Western Europe, but upon closer examination they pulse more vigorously or have a different quality, as if seen in a distorting mirror. Language makes Central Europe seem different too. The fictional Lorelei Lee, the narrator in Anita Loos's *Gentlemen Prefer Blondes* (1925), visited Central Europe in the 1920s. As she explains, Central Europe was 'where they talk some other kinds of landguages [*sic*] which we do not understand besides French.' (The 1953 screen version, starring Marilyn Monroe, leaves out this observation.) Language marks out Central Europe as difficult. German may be troublesome to the visitor on account of its habit of keeping the listener guessing what the operative verb is until the end of the sentence. But farther east, the languages spoken become baffling, written with an abundance of consonants, odd diacritical marks, and, in places, even a different alphabet.

Strip away the language or, better still, render it intelligible and we soon enter a world that, like Central Europe itself, reveals a mixture of familiarity and difference. So, from a fifteenth-century list itemizing a noble landowner's properties on the edge of the Carpathians, near today's city of Berehove:

> His oak woods, copses and orchards, beginning at the Ferry Water and going up to the road by the Eagle's Perch; next, his oak woods at Little Lapping, Little Mire, Round Lake, and Redoubt, along with the fish pond at Great Mastage and the wood called Elm Grove, beside the place where Great Owls Brook falls into the Black River, and going up to the road which leads from Mallards Meadow to the place and pasture called Long Sand . . .[5]

Once rendered in translation, Berehove's landscape and toponymy sound as if they could be somewhere in the French countryside. But Berehove is also a microcosm of the changes that have coursed through Central Europe over the last century. First mentioned in the 1240s, in the aftermath of the Mongol-Tatar invasion, Berehove was until 1918 a part of Hungary. At the start of the twentieth century, the city had a centre of monumental neo-baroque buildings with grand ornamental façades and tree-lined boulevards, set against a backdrop of rolling hills of oak and beech forests, cornfields, and vineyards. It had a mix of peoples too—Jewish shopkeepers and Hasidic rabbis, Gypsy musicians, and itinerant Turkish ice cream sellers, although the population was mostly Hungarian and Ukrainian.

After the First World War, Berehove became a part of Czechoslovakia, then briefly returned to Hungary in 1939 before being occupied by Germany in 1944. Nazi rule resulted in the murder of at least 3,600 Jews from Berehove and its immediate neighbourhood. At the end of 1944, Soviet troops conquered the city, which was soon afterwards swept into the Soviet Union. The Soviets completed the destruction of Berehove's Jewish culture, converting the main synagogue into a communist 'cultural centre'. To hide the Hebrew inscriptions and Jewish symbols on the building's exterior, they daubed it with thick cement. What had been one of Berehove's most imposing façades is now its ugliest. As for Berehove's countryside, the Soviets first plundered it and then carved it up into collective farms.

With every change of the map, Berehove's name changed too, from Beregszász to Berehovo, to Bergsass, to Berehovo again, and finally to Berehove. Together with the oak woods and elm groves of its countryside, Berehove now lies in western Ukraine, and beyond its horizon a new generation of dogmen prowl, this time armed with Kalashnikovs. They are the latest in a long line of invaders and conquerors who have broken into Central Europe over the course of two millennia and a fresh reminder of the vulnerability of its civilization. What follows is Central Europe's story, but it is also an exploration of the many little places like Berehove that belong both to Europe's middle and to its edge.

CHAPTER 1

The Roman Empire, the Huns, and the *Nibelungenlied*

THE POET OVID WAS UNLUCKY. AT THE START OF THE FIRST millennium, the emperor Augustus banished him from Rome for an unspecified crime. Ovid maintained that it was all a misunderstanding, but he was nevertheless sent to the Roman frontier city of Tomis on the Black Sea coast, which is now Constanța in Romania. In exile, Ovid complained of the cold in winter, which cracked vases of wine and froze their contents into icicles, and of the assaults on Tomis and its countryside by wild Sarmatian tribesmen. He described how their horsemen broke through the Roman defences, plundered farmsteads, and murdered indiscriminately with poison arrows. More accustomed, as he sobbed, to Cupid's darts, Ovid now had to dodge the venomous missiles of a savage people.

It was Ovid's misfortune to have been sent to one of the worst places on the Roman frontier, for otherwise the frontier was in the first centuries of Roman imperial rule generally quiet. At its greatest extent in the second century CE, the Roman Empire had a border that was five thousand kilometres long, enclosing five million square kilometres of territory. More than half a million soldiers were charged with its defence and with maintaining order in its hinterland. According to a list made about 300 CE, they faced no fewer than fifty hostile peoples, ranging from the Picts in the far north to the Armenians in the east and the Moors of Africa.[1]

In North Africa and the Middle East, the desert acted as a protective cordon. In Central Europe, the Roman frontier largely followed the line of the Rhine and Danube Rivers, but with salients that pushed deep into the territory beyond: most notably the Roman province of Dacia, which enclosed Transylvania and the eastern Carpathians, and the province of Upper Germania (Germania Superior), which included the triangle of territory between the upper reaches of the Rhine and the Danube. At its height, the Roman Empire occupied a large chunk of Central Europe, including what is now the Rhineland and western Germany, Switzerland, much of Bavaria and southern Germany, Austria, western Hungary, Slovenia, and western Romania. In the third century, the Romans abandoned Dacia and much of Upper Germany. Thereafter, the line of Central Europe's two main rivers, the Rhine and the Danube, marked the course of the frontier.

Roman patrol boats guarded the Rhine and the Danube. Jokingly called 'pleasure craft', or *lusoriae*, they were each manned by thirty soldier-oarsmen and attached to depots which doubled as memorials for the dead, where tablets listed the names of the drowned and slain. About a thousand warcraft plied the Danube in the second century. Defensive works—starting with clearings and watchtowers, and gradually augmented with ditches, palisades, stone walls, and towers—reinforced the natural geography of the frontier. Some sixty garrisoned blockhouses and forts ran along the southern bank of the Danube, from Passau to Vienna. Behind the Rhine and the Danube, on the Roman side, nestled a mix of the indigenous Celtic population, immigrant farmers who were often legionary veterans, and slaves captured in raids across the border.

Irrespective of their origins, the people living in Roman Central Europe were rapidly Romanized in their language, dress, and manners, soon adopting names like Julius, Tiberius, and Claudius. Their original tribal organizations vanished, only surviving in the names of the Roman provinces into which they were absorbed. The cities that clustered along the frontier mimicked Rome with amphitheatres, public baths, aqueducts, monumental buildings, square temples, and, from the early fourth century onwards, Christian churches. In the countryside, villas with mosaics and wall paintings were the centres of large

12

THE ROMAN EMPIRE c. 378 CE

agricultural, wine-producing, and herding enterprises. Archaeologists have identified the sites of some six hundred villas in the Roman province of Pannonia alone (roughly where western Hungary is today).[2]

Roman power did not stop at the border. The peoples who lived on the other side were often brought into the Roman political, diplomatic, and economic orbit. They traded amber, dyes, grain, and goose feathers to stuff pillows and provided recruits and even generals for the Roman legions, and their chief men were rewarded with lavish gifts and military protection. To make sure of the tribes' allegiance, legionary commanders dug forts deep in the Central European countryside, well beyond the shelter of the frontier. Roman troops also began the construction of a five-hundred-kilometre earthen rampart that looped around the edge of the Hungarian Plain, from Aquincum in the northwest (now a part of Budapest) to the fort at Viminacium, which lies east of today's Belgrade. Later called the Devil's Dyke, stretches of the earthwork are still there, although much eroded. Crossing modern-day Hungary, Romania, and Serbia, it was a military achievement comparable in scale to Hadrian's Wall in Britain.[3]

Peaceable relations on the frontier were achieved by exporting violence beyond it. The German tribes and Sarmatian nomads on the other side jostled for position, each seeking a place closer to the Roman Empire and thus easier access to its wealth. Shortly before 100 CE, the Roman historian Tacitus noted the inclination of the German tribes to violence and of their young men to fighting and looting. He listed the tribes, and historians have long puzzled over the names he gave them (Ubians, Cattans, Tencterians, and so on), for only a few reappear sixty years later in Ptolemy's great world map, which is actually a list of names and geographical coordinates. Some tribes can be tracked over several centuries, but most seem to have vanished almost as soon as Tacitus named them, most probably having been defeated and absorbed by rivals. As Tacitus wryly observed, 'Long, I pray, may foreign peoples persist, if not in loving us, at least in hating one another, for . . . fortune now has no better gift than the discord of our foes.'[4]

Tacitus's image of youthful tribes engaged in adolescent rivalry comported with Roman stereotypes of the peoples across the border, who were either hideous in their appearance or playful but wayward innocents in need of Rome's protection and example. For Romans, the Germans belonged to the second category. Living in rustic hamlets, they practised, so we are told, only a primitive agriculture, knowing neither proper government nor industry, nor even their own sexuality. So, both sexes bathed chastely together naked; the men could not be roused from their habitual indolence to undertake any craft, and they had no knowledge of money until introduced to it by the Romans. By contrast, the Sarmatians, whom Ovid encountered at Tomis, were, in one contemporary description, 'a robber horde . . . the most isolated of all the barbarous peoples in these regions'. Tacitus noted their double-handed swords and armour made of overlapping scales of iron and leather. Roman artists sculpted the Sarmatians as lizards.[5]

The same sense of difference also coloured the earliest descriptions of Central Europe's landscape beyond the Roman frontier. For Roman authors, Central Europe was a vast forest of oak trees, so dense that they made the climate colder, and whose colliding roots threw up archways wide enough to take a squadron of cavalry. Back in the first century BCE, Julius Caesar could find no one who knew the forest's true extent, but he thought it to be several months' march in breadth. A century later, Tacitus described Central Europe as distinguished by 'its misshapen landscape and harsh climate, wretched to live in or look on'. Its soil was too thin to support fruit trees, he explained, and the flocks and cattle there were underweight and ugly. Other writers stressed the rivers, mountains, and swamps that impeded travel and the lack of roads and stone buildings. For classical authors, the further northwards, the harsher the geography and climate became, until one arrived at the bleak Baltic Ocean, where the Finns lived, 'whose barbarism and baseness are sickening, beyond belief'.[6]

It was the Romans who first imposed on the peoples of Central Europe the label of German, for otherwise they had no word for themselves or any sense of a common identity—indeed, it seems doubtful that the dialects they spoke were mutually comprehensible, at least on first hearing. These early Germans lived in villages and kinship groups, which might or might not have been united in some sort of larger political confederation. Some of these tribal groups were ruled by kings, others by assemblies of headmen, and a few by priests. In several places, the inhabitants practised the head binding of infants, which resulted in the elongation of the skull in adulthood. Elsewhere, they were content with knotting their hair on the side of the head as a mark of belonging. Nevertheless, by favouring some tribes above others, Roman policy led to their political consolidation.[7]

The Roman Empire knew violence. Most of it was home-grown and caused by slave revolts, food riots, local uprisings, and civil wars caused by overambitious generals. Incursions across the border added to the mix. Towards the end of the second century, the German tribe of the Marcomanni burst through the Roman defences on the Danube, acting in concert with Sarmatian bands. They were repulsed, but not before they had raided northern Italy. In the middle decades of the third century, German tribes took advantage of prolonged periods of civil conflict in Rome to ravage across the frontier. But most incursions were small-scale and swiftly checked. In a famous illustration from the late third century, Roman patrol boats on the Rhine intercepted near Speyer a group of raiders which was returning home with several cartloads of plunder seized from a villa nearby. Upon being challenged, the robbers fled, leaving behind the silver plate, kitchenware, and farm implements they had stolen.[8]

Banditry gave way in the late fourth century to something altogether more serious. Instead of raiders looking for booty, the frontier was now assailed by whole peoples on the move, who brought with them their children, the sick, and the old. They were in flight for their lives, running from 'a race of men, which had never been seen before . . . which had arisen from some secret corner of the earth, and was sweeping away and destroying everything that came in its way.' Roman writers smugly rehearsed older stories about the peoples living north of the Black Sea, but the refugees insisted that they faced entirely new foes, born of the union of witches with the unclean spirits that dwelled in swamps. They called them the Huns.[9]

Classical authors were never discerning in their descriptions of the Huns, borrowing passages from earlier writers that related to quite different peoples, while adding their own rhetorical flourishes. So, we are told, the Huns, like Homer's Cyclops, ate roots and were wary of buildings; like centaurs, they were only half-human; and like the ancient Massagetae, they ate their old folk. Roman authors confidently concluded that the Huns were either descended from the primitive people described by the poet Virgil as springing from the trunks of trees or belonged to the Old Testament people of Gog and Magog. In fact, the people that Romans called the Huns were a mixed bag of tribes. The Hunnic core originated from what is now Kazakhstan and mainly comprised Turkic speakers, but the warrior elite also included members of previous bands that the Huns had defeated and even soldiers of fortune recruited from within the Roman Empire. A court jester of the Huns later kept his audience amused by gabbling, so we are told, in a mixture of Hunnish, Gothic German, and Latin.[10]

The Huns were nomads and pastoralists, but they needed sedentary populations both as tribute payers of gold and as suppliers of the manufactured goods that they lacked. The settled peoples west of the River Don were an obvious target. From the fourth century onwards, the Huns expanded westwards from their home in Central Asia along the steppe land. Having gathered allies on the way, they fell upon the Goths in the 370s. The Goths were a Germanic people, related linguistically to the Central European tribes. Divided into half a dozen separate groups, they occupied the space east of the Carpathians, in what is now Ukraine. The Gothic tribes living north and west of the Black Sea put up a futile resistance to the Huns. In vain, their last king sacrificed himself to the gods on his people's behalf. After a (literally) last-ditch attempt to halt the invaders failed, the Goths massed on the banks of the Danube, where they were joined by other tribes in flight from the Huns.

The Roman Empire was by this time divided into halves, with capitals at Rome and Constantinople (now Istanbul). The refugees petitioned the Emperor of the East, Valens, to give them shelter, since the Balkans south of the Lower Danube belonged at this time to the eastern half of the empire. Thinking them a potential source of manpower for the army, Emperor Valens agreed. But the settlement of the Goths was botched, and the Goths left starving and vengeful. Valens sought to reduce them to obedience by force, but the Goths destroyed his army at the Battle of Adrianople in 378 CE. The emperor either fell in the fighting or was burned to death in a cottage where he was resting to tend his wounds. In the wake of their victory, the Goths plundered the Balkans so thoroughly that, as Roman sources relate, nothing was left except for the horizon.

The Gothic leaders and Valens's successor, Theodosius, concluded a treaty in 382. Theodosius advertised it as the instrument by which 'an entire people of the Goths along with its king surrendered to the Romans', but the treaty was nothing of the sort. It let the Goths into the empire and exempted them from taxes, gave them land to farm, allowed continued governance by their own princes, and awarded them an annual tribute. Although the Goths were expected to serve in the Roman armies, they did so under the immediate command of their own chieftains. Unsurprisingly, when new bands broke into the Roman Empire, they pressed for the same extensive rights. The high point was reached on 31 December 406, when a mixed band of Germans, Sarmatians, and former allies of the Huns crossed the Rhine at Mainz and advanced into Roman Gaul. Four years later, a military confederation of Gothic tribes, called the Visigoths, seized and plundered Rome.[11]

From their encampment on the Hungarian Plain, Hun bands continued to raid Italy and the Balkans and to harass German tribes, pushing them across the frontier, while also offering their services as allies of the Romans. Most notoriously, the Roman commander Aetius enlisted the Huns of a chieftain called Rugila to crush the Burgundians, a German tribe that had occupied lands west of the Rhine around Worms. Rugila's massacre of the Burgundians in 437 CE was so complete that it passed into legend as a chilling example of the Huns' ferocity and of their readiness to wipe out whole peoples.[12]

But the Huns were not content to act as the Romans' gatekeepers. During the 440s, command of the Huns passed to Rugila's nephew, Attila. Attila welded the Huns and their allies into a confederation that was loyal to him, punishing the faithless with crucifixion and the errant tribes with extinction. Leadership among the Huns was customarily shared by twin kinsmen, but Attila would have none of this—he murdered his elder brother and co-ruler in 445, after which he assumed sole power. A contemporary description of him survives: 'Short of stature, with a broad chest and a large head; his eyes were small, his beard thin and sprinkled with grey; and he had a flat nose and swarthy skin, showing evidence of his origin.' Later accounts would give him a dog's head and describe his father as a greyhound, thus uniting him with the legend of the dogmen from the east.[13]

For the first few years of his sole rule, Attila was mostly active on the Danube frontier, waging a war of terror aimed at extracting loot from the East Roman emperors. But around 450 he turned his attention to the west. Behind the scenes, Attila had been negotiating with Honoria, the wily sister of the western emperor Valentinian III, and she had stirred an ambition in him to replace either Aetius as military commander in the west or even her own brother as emperor via an improbable marriage to herself. For Attila, both strategies made equal sense—no longer to press upon the empire from outside but to take it over entirely.

Attila began his campaign early in 451, when (in a contemporary description) 'suddenly the barbarian world, rent by a mighty upheaval, poured the whole north into Gaul', after which it descended on Italy. Attila's army was estimated at the time to be half a million men—an unlikely number, but testament to the panic it caused. Even so, it was clearly numerous, comprising a mass of German tribes. Among them were the remnants of the Gothic tribes, now welded together as the so-called Ostrogoths by a descendant of the Gothic king who had killed himself eighty years before. Also present were a section of the Franks, whose chieftains would ultimately inherit the power of the Huns in a large part of Central Europe.[14]

The end came swiftly. It may be that late in 452 Attila had a meeting with Pope Leo I, but it is unlikely that the saintly bishop of Rome convinced him to become a man of peace. Something earthlier forced Attila's withdrawal—a lack of fodder for his horses, brought on by a hot summer. Attila returned to his headquarters on the Hungarian Plain but died the next year, suffocated in his sleep by a nosebleed. His sons disputed their inheritance, prompting a civil war in the course of which Hun power both in Europe and on the Black Sea steppe collapsed. Historians today often exaggerate the strengths of the Huns and describe their empire as a state, but it was nothing of the sort. It was a loose assemblage of Hunnic, Germanic, and Gothic tribes, held together by a ruthless and ambitious ruler. Once he was gone, it fell apart.[15]

Even so, the Huns had remade Central Europe. By breaking its power, they had forced Rome to abandon its Central European provinces in what is now Germany, Austria, and Hungary. On the back of the Huns, German tribes took Rome's place in the southern and western parts of Central Europe. As the newcomers' leaders imposed their own taxes, apportioned land to their followers, and dispossessed the provincial Roman aristocracy, the marks of civilization contracted. Walled encampments and fortified hilltops took the place of country villas, and large agricultural estates went to ruin. As one Roman contemporary lamented, 'The flocks are gone, the seeds of the fruits are gone, and there is no place for vines or olive trees; destructive fire and rain have even taken away the buildings of the farms.' North of the Alps, hot running water as a household amenity disappeared for a thousand years. The Huns' legacy was also the cultural and economic impoverishment of a wide swathe of Central Europe.[16]

In the wake of the Huns' work of destruction, Gothic tribes pushed into the western half of the Roman Empire, carving out their own kingdoms. So, the Visigoths occupied southern France, and later

Spain, and the Ostrogoths took over Italy. In time, they would become linguistically acculturated so that the Latin-based Romance language of the majority prevailed in what would become France, Spain, and Italy. But in Central Europe, where the German settlement was denser, Latin was squeezed out and the region became mostly German-speaking. The Rhine, previously the Roman frontier, accordingly straddled two emerging linguistic zones, with German speakers to the east and Romance speakers to the west. As for the West Roman Empire, it ceased to exist in 476, when the last emperor abdicated in return for a pension from the Roman Senate and a palace in Naples.

After the fifth century, the originally German-speaking Franks, who had previously settled in northern France, extended their power across the old Roman province of Gaul and pushed eastwards across the Rhine. From the seventh century onwards, they were neighbours in Central Europe to Slavonic tribes. A new Central Europe was born under Frankish leadership. Frankish Central Europe was linguistically mixed, including both German and Slavonic speakers. To their number were added the Hungarians, with their unrelated language, who arrived in the Carpathians at the end of the ninth century. Over time, Franks, Germans, Slavs, and Hungarians adopted a common cultural code of kingship, Catholic Christianity, law, knighthood, and chivalry.

But curiously, that code was also infused with remembrance of the Huns. A common literary tradition united the different peoples of Central Europe, who looked back to the invasion of the Huns as a defining moment in their development. Greek and Roman writers had cast the Huns as villains, and most early Christian accounts did the same, piling on martyrs whose deaths were blamed on the Huns. But in Central Europe, a different dynamic was at work. Here, many of the German tribes had fought on Attila's side, and their descendants cultivated romantic tales about the Huns' exploits and the deeds done in their service. These legends took as their theme the last days of the court of Burgundy in Worms, before its destruction by the Huns in

437, and told of palace intrigues in the Huns' capital Esztergom (now
in Hungary), where Attila ruled under the name of Etzel in consort
with the Ostrogothic ruler Theodoric (Dietrich).

These historical fragments were overlaid by other stories—of the
deeds of the fabled Siegfried and of his murder, and of the vengeance
plotted by his Burgundian widow, Kriemhild, who became Attila's
fictional wife. Passed on in song and oral recitations, these tales later
fused in the epic poem known as 'The Song of the Nibelungs', or *Nibelungenlied*. More than two thousand verses long, the *Nibelungenlied*
achieved its final form only in the thirteenth century, thanks to an unknown poet from Passau in Bavaria. The *Nibelungenlied* is a tragedy
that describes the consequences of betrayal, jealousy, and grief, along
with dwarfs guarding treasure, cloaks of invisibility, dragon slaying, and
magic rings that turn people into dust.

The strands which contributed to the *Nibelungenlied*'s final form
were also woven into later Czech and Polish accounts (often via the
parallel 'Walther Legend'), some of which self-consciously modelled
themselves on the *Nibelungenlied*'s epic form. Again, many of these
celebrated the Huns' achievements and described a heroic contest between the Huns and their Roman adversaries. Others recast episodes
entirely, changing location and actors to fit their audiences while preserving the outlines of the plot—Tyrolean versions had a mountain-
ous backdrop, for instance, and Styrian ones added in ancestors of
the ruling ducal house in what is now Austria. Recollection of the
Huns also contributed to accounts of Hungarian origins which made
the Huns into the Hungarians' progenitors (the similarity of names
helped) and Attila into the forebear of the Hungarian ruling house.
Memory of the Huns and their empire worked its way into Central
Europe's first legends.[17]

But the *Nibelungenlied* was also typical of a larger European literary genre—its tropes of chivalric endeavour and vengeance, of courtly
ideals matched with martial vigour, and of a conflict of loyalties between kinsmen and lord are commonplaces in French epics, Scandi-

navian sagas, and Spanish and Provençal ballads. So too are the knight in search of a bride, ritual visits and exchanges of gifts, and the image of the careworn ruler (Attila-Etzel in the *Nibelungenlied*; King Arthur in the Round Table romances; King Mark in the Tristan legends, and so on). By embracing the *Nibelungenlied* and reworking its content, the fledgling societies of Central Europe also showed that they had become part of a larger cultural community, which was unmistakably Christian in character. How these societies became Christian in the first place and what types of Christianity they embraced are the subjects of the next chapters.

CHAPTER 2

The Franks and Charlemagne:
The View from Lake Constance

ROMAN CHRISTIANITY HAD NOT TAKEN CONVERSION SERIOUSLY. Christianity was a religion of the cities and the villas, and missionaries were slow to evangelize in the countryside. The same prejudice influenced bishops and popes in their dealings with the German tribes. It was only after a tribe or ruler had already converted that they sent in priests. The consequence was that the regions of the former Roman Empire settled by Germans either remained pagan or adhered to a heretical form of Christianity called Arianism. Named after the early-fourth-century theologian Arius (and so having nothing to do with the race theory of Aryanism), Arianism rejected the idea that Christ was of one being with the eternal God, arguing instead that God had created Christ and so 'there was a time when Christ was not.' Arians rejected the Trinity, proposing instead a hierarchy with God at the top followed by a created Christ and the angel that stood for the Holy Spirit.[1]

The conflict between Catholics and Arians was bitter and vicious, with Arian mobs running amok in Roman cities. But despite its apparent obscurity, Arianism was Central Europe's earliest Christian religion, adopted in the fourth and fifth centuries by most of the Goths and many of the German tribes. Only the Franks, Frisians, and Saxons, whose chieftains stuck to paganism, stayed outside Arianism's embrace. Arianism's appeal lay in its church services, which were held in the vernacular and not in the Latin favoured by Catholic priests. The first translation into German Gothic of the New Testament and of a part of the Old Testament was done by an Arian bishop, Ulfila (Little Wolf), in the middle of the fourth century in a script of his own invention. Importantly, too, the idea that there was a celestial hierarchy fitted in with older pagan beliefs that there were many gods but with a superior god on top.[2]

The Franks had originally comprised several tribes living close to the Middle and Lower Rhine, on both sides of the Roman frontier. Their first king of whom we have definite knowledge was Childeric (died 481 CE), who belonged to the line of so-called Merovingian rulers—they were named in honour of an eponymous sea serpent's brood. His extraordinary grave at Tournai bears witness to his double role as a tribal leader and Roman administrator, for Childeric was buried with the long shoulder-length hair that was the mark of Frankish royalty, his horse's severed head, a cloak bearing three hundred golden bees, and gifts that could only have come from the East Roman emperor in Constantinople. Under Childeric's son, Chlodwig or Clovis (lived 466–511), the Franks expanded from the northwest to take over most of the old Roman province of Gaul, while also vanquishing the region between the Upper Rhine and the Danube.

Catholic Christianity was lucky that around 496 Clovis converted from paganism to Catholicism, after which, we are told, many of his leading men also embraced the new faith. Clovis became a Catholic under the influence of his devious wife, who was already a Catholic, and because her God had helped him in battle. But conversion also made political sense since a good part of the Romanized population of Gaul were already either Catholics or followed a mixture of Catholicism and Roman pagan cults. Clovis was the first German ruler to embrace the faith of Rome, for which the East Roman emperor rewarded him with the rank of consul, even though the title was meaningless.

Despite the recency of his conversion, Clovis advertised himself as God's minister. It was a role that justified his wars against pagans and Arians and sanctioned his conquests. Even so, the pace of conversion in the Frankish countryside was slow. Older practices continued, which included not only, as one sixth-century law code complained, 'nights spent at Christmas and Eastertide in drunkenness, buffoonery, and song' but also human sacrifice and worshipping an image of Christ with an extended phallus. But the Frankish bishops were not drawn to missionary work. They kept to their dioceses, cultivating local saints and writing thoughtful sermons against Arianism and other varieties of misbelief. Frankish conquests east of the Rhine were not matched by the conversion of the population from paganism or of their chieftains from Arianism.[3]

Help came from an unusual quarter. The island of Ireland, or Hibernia, had never been part of the Roman Empire. But a zealous clergy, operating largely independently of Rome and the Catholic Church, had impressed Christianity there. Since Hibernia had no cities, it was hard to impose a network of bishops based upon urban centres. Monasteries took their place. But whereas monks elsewhere in Europe shunned the outside world, their Irish brethren actively sought it out, making popular conversion their vocation and, in the words of one bardic verse of the time, travelling 'eastward towards the Sun Tree, into the broad long-distant sea'. By the last decades of the sixth century, Irish monks were establishing monasteries on the Continent and inspiring a new generation of missionaries to press into what is now southern Germany. Among these was the combative St Columbanus (540–615), from what is now Leinster in Ireland, to whom an angel had revealed a map of the world and explained its conversion as the saint's vocation.[4]

Now in Switzerland, the abbey of St Gallen near Lake Constance has its origin in the life of St Gall, a follower of St Columbanus. Around 610, Columbanus had been journeying with his entourage to Bobbio in northern Italy to preach to the Arian Lombards there. Gall had fallen sick, so Columbanus had instructed him to stay by Lake Constance and set an example of piety. Gall made his home in a hut by a waterfall, from where he went to preach to the neighbouring German tribe of Alemanns. A small religious community gathered around the hermit's cell which survived his death in around 650. Over the next two centuries, the cell became a chapel and then a three-nave abbey church, and finally a monastic complex with dormitories, a school and infirmary, kitchens and gardens, a scriptorium for copying manuscripts, and a library which by the ninth century had about four hundred books, making it one of the largest in Europe.

St Gallen was one of a line of frontier monasteries founded in the Irish tradition that carried Christianity into Central Europe. Disciplined and hardy, the monks were not tonsured. Instead, they shaved the front of their scalps and let their hair grow in a mane behind, and they frequently tattooed their eyelids—a painful undertaking, but that was the point of it. They promoted as models not only Saints Columbanus, Gall, and Kilian, martyred at Würzburg in 689, but also more distant holy men and women in Ireland and on the island of Iona in the Scottish Hebrides. Notwithstanding the shattering of Irish monasticism by the Scandinavian Vikings in the ninth century, Ireland retained a fabulous reputation in German legend as the homeland of dragons, miracle-working queens, and dangerous love potions.

Monks schooled in the Irish tradition were the shock troops of Merovingian Christianity. But after Clovis, the Merovingian kings have a poor reputation. Doubtless some fitted one modern historian's description of them as rulers who 'performed no services . . . were utterly incapable of organizing anything . . . suspicious, cruel, capricious and selfish despots.' Even so, they built on Roman foundations, melding German practices such as the blood feud with courts of law and legal codes that copied the example of Rome. They had an effective tax system and a literate bureaucracy. Even the kings could read, and one wrote Latin poetry, albeit badly. However risible, the kings of the Franks saw themselves as the heirs of the Romans, even to the extent of building amphitheatres, presiding like Roman emperors over crowded 'spectacles' (usually horse races run around a circular track), and augmenting the list of their ancestors with Roman deities.[5]

The problems were several. First, the Merovingian line of kings was weakened by partible inheritance, which meant that sons divided up the kingdom among themselves on their father's death, and rulers diminished their authority still further by giving away the right to tax to private lords, mainly churchmen. Second, the Merovingian monarchs were held to be sacred beings, so much so that they added strands of their hair to the wax of seals, lending an almost magical power to their commands. As such, they stood aside from the daily routines of rulership, entrusting the business of government and warfare to a majordomo or 'mayor of the palace'. From the late seventh century, the office of mayor became hereditary. Historians call the dynasty of mayors the Carolingians. The name recalls the warlord and mayor Carolus, also known as Charles the Hammer or Charles Martel (lived c. 688–741). Bit by bit, the Carolingian mayors nibbled away at the royal power.

All of this was watched in St Gallen. The monks compiled annals, listing important events year by year. The names of kings barely feature in them; instead, it was the achievements of the mayors that they itemized—Charles the Hammer fighting the Frisians by the North Sea, fending off an Arabic attack from Spain across the Pyrenees, and pushing Frankish power eastwards. Next, they told of Charles's elder son and successor as mayor, Carloman, renewing the war against the Alemanns and in 747 going to Rome to become a monk. Then it is Pippin, Carloman's brother and successor as mayor, whose deeds the annalists related. But in a brief entry of just four words the St Gallen annals noted a sudden change in his rank. Under 751, the monastic compiler wrote: 'Pippin is made king' (*Pippinus in regem elevatur*).[6]

What the annals of St Gallen describe here was a coup d'état. For two centuries, the mayors had acted as de facto rulers. Now the mayor seized the royal office. Pippin justified his takeover of the kingdom on the grounds that 'it was better to call him king who had the royal power than the one who did not.' The transition was effortless, and the deposed king was shorn of his long locks and packed off to a monastery in an oxcart. To make sure of his new title, Pippin had himself anointed king first by the archbishop of Mainz and then by the pope, who in 754 travelled across the Alps to perform the rite. This was one of the first occasions when a European ruler was sanctified with oil. The ceremony of anointment, which drew on the Old Testament, placed Pippin in the same tradition as the biblical David, whom the prophet Samuel had anointed king in place of King Saul.[7]

The Merovingian rulers had extended their authority eastwards across the Rhine, but they had not consolidated their power there, treating the local tribes of Alemanns and Thuringians more as providers of tribute than as subjects to be governed. Under Charles the Hammer, policy changed, and the local German chieftains were subordinated to Frankish warlords. Frankish settlers also moved into the new space, which was divided up into counties, giving the name of Franconia to the region around the confluence of the Rhine and Main Rivers. The new regime was imposed ruthlessly. When the Alemanns rebelled in 746, Pippin's predecessor, the mayor Carloman, hauled their leaders before a court and condemned them to death. The scale of the slaughter, which may have included several thousand men, was even at the time thought excessive, and may have prompted Carloman's decision to become a monk.[8]

The tide of Frankish power sweeping eastwards across the Rhine is captured in the earliest of St Gallen's charters. As the monks' reputation spread, laymen gave over land to their monastery so that St Gallen soon owned a swathe of properties across what is now southern Germany and Switzerland. But land was vulnerable to depredation. To discourage raiding, the first charters conveying property to St Gallen, which the monks wrote on the donor's behalf, included clauses that told how God would take revenge upon anyone who tried to cheat the monastery out of its land. But during the course of the eighth century, the type of threat changed. New financial penalties were added, made payable to the royal treasury as breaches of the peace, and it was no longer just with God's vengeance that wrongdoers had to reckon but also with 'the anger of the king'.[9]

The protective embrace of Carolingian rule came at a price. Charles the Hammer and his heirs were wary of Irish monasticism, since without the supervision of bishops the monks tended to embrace unusual and even perverse schemes of belief. Complaints at the time included that the monks explained the Bible incorrectly, allowed polygamy, rejected the teaching of the Church Fathers, and (worst of all) held Easter on the wrong date by following the Jewish calendar. Their treatment of female supernumeraries was also perverse. Walled up in cells with only a small hatch through which to pass food, the women frequently went mad, at which point the monks scrutinized their ravings as divinely inspired visions.

Under the direction of St Boniface, the energetic archbishop of Mainz (in office 745–754), the task of evangelization was taken away from the monasteries and given to bishops. Henceforth, the monks were relieved of all pastoral responsibilities outside the monastery walls and told to dedicate themselves to prayer. Frankish officials followed up by reallocating some of St Gallen's estates to the nearby bishops of Constance and Chur. When St Gallen's abbot protested, he was arrested and exiled to an island on Lake Constance, where he soon died (in 747). It was more than a century before the properties were restored.

King Pippin died in 768 and was succeeded by his two sons, who divided the kingdom of the Franks between them. The elder, Charles, was almost from the first called 'Magnus' or 'Great' since this was a part of the royal style, and it is in the contracted form of Charlemagne that he was later known. Charlemagne immediately contested his brother's rights, and it was only his brother's early death in 771 that prevented them from coming to blows. For more than thirty years, Charlemagne was almost continually at war—in southern France, along the Pyrenees, in Central Europe, and south of the Alps, where he had himself crowned king of Italy in 774. All these places were traditional targets of Frankish expansion. But the scale of Charlemagne's interventions, his success in battle, his doubling of the size of the Frankish kingdom to a million square kilometres, and his ruthless determination mark him out (in one historian's estimation) as a military genius, almost without parallel in European history.[10]

Part of Charlemagne's success lay with the terror he caused. When thwarted, Charlemagne was violent. In his long war against the Saxons east of the Rhine, he deported swathes of the native population, enslaved women and children, and murdered the Saxons' leading men in a bloodbath that allegedly claimed 4,500 lives. The missionaries who

came in the wake of this slaughter brought a warning—either to convert or to face Charlemagne, 'who will invade your lands, plundering
and wasting them, exhausting you in battle; he will make you exiles,
take your lands or kill you, give your possessions to whomever he likes,
and you will be his slaves.' Single-minded in his dedication to war,
Charlemagne was the first European ruler to deploy a war elephant.
Originally a gift of the caliph of Baghdad, the poor beast perished in
804, during his master's campaign against the Danes.[11]

But behind the terror was organization. In the language of the time,
Charlemagne was not only a warrior (*bellator*) but also a commander
(*imperator*). He had Roman military manuals read to him, ordered
the drawing of maps and march routes, organized supply depots and
pontoon bridges, and instructed his generals to use the sun and stars
to plot latitude. It was entirely possible for him to accomplish pincer
movements over hundreds of kilometres of hostile terrain. All this was
sustained by lists—of taxpayers, of saints whose names might be invoked in battle, and of the counts and commissioners (*missi dominici*)
who executed his will in the Frankish countryside. One hundred and
twenty palaces, each with a great hall and church, were the economic
backbone of his rule, for the villages attached to each palace sustained
the king's mobile court, household, and armed retinue. Their contents
were catalogued too—how many peasant farmers, horses, and goats
they had. Charlemagne demanded conformity as well. Whereas the
laws of all the Merovingian kings amount in the standard edition to
just twenty-five pages of text, Charlemagne's run to several hundred.

Charlemagne never learned to read. We are told that he kept a wax
tablet and stylus beneath his throne and tried painfully to inscribe letters in his spare time, but the task was beyond him (rheumatism cannot
have helped). Even so, he had books read aloud to him and his aman-
uenses often wrote in the margins his critical comments on poems and
philosophy. His officers also reported directly to him, and some of his
injunctions to them survive—'this is what we want,' 'you should do as
the law says,' and even 'we've told you this before with our own mouth
and you have never understood.' List-making fitted in with the literary

THE EMPIRE OF CHARLEMAGNE 800 CE

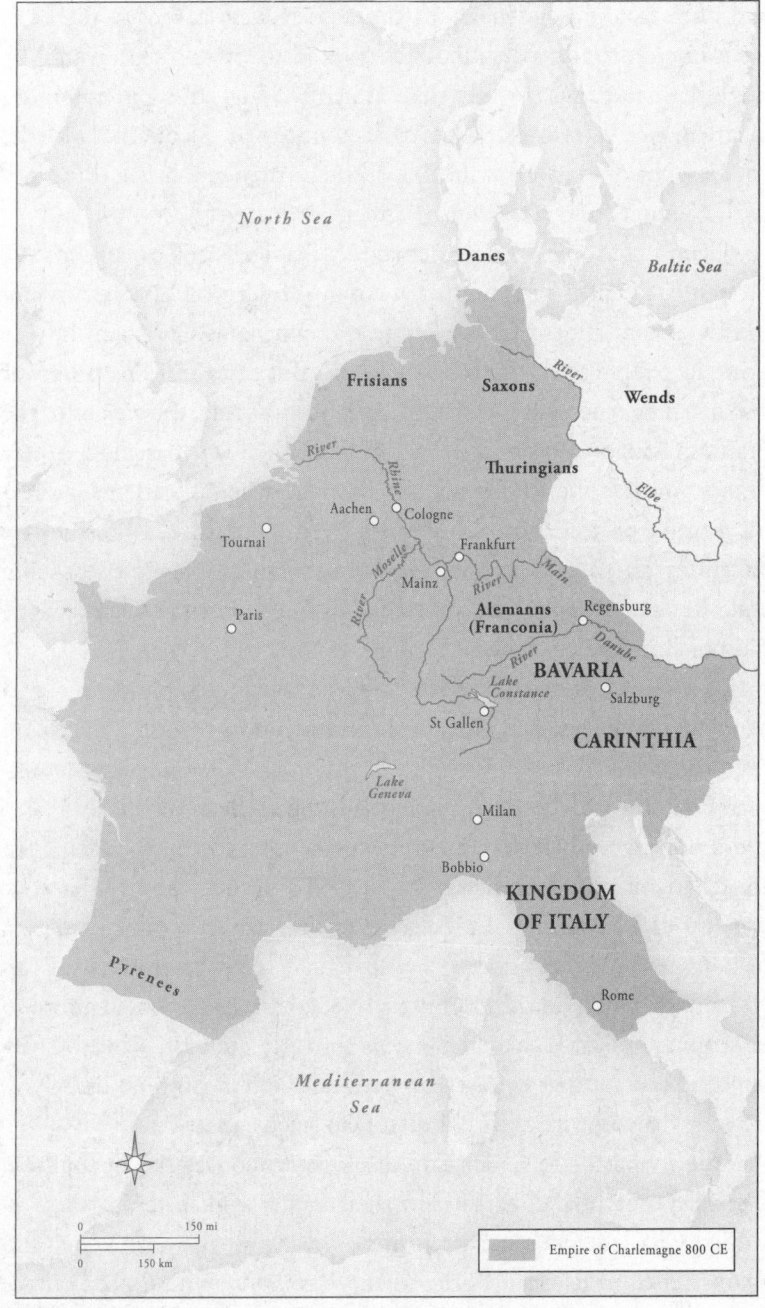

style known at the time as *congeries*, which was the piling on of words and phrases, and Charlemagne's court poets were never less than diligent in enumerating the king's virtues and the heroes with whom he might be compared. Greater than Hercules, Augustus, and Solomon, Charlemagne was (in the words of his top scholar, Alcuin of York) 'the golden light of the world, the salt of the earth, a safe haven, the glory of the Church, and a crown resplendent with jewels'.[12]

Central Europe was Charlemagne's main area of expansion. Although the Franks had eliminated Arianism, Central Europe was still mostly pagan, and so Charlemagne thought it his Christian duty to bring its people to the faith by conquest. But eastward expansion was also a strategic necessity. During Charlemagne's rule, the weight of the Frankish kingdom shifted from the interior of what is modern-day France towards the Rhine and the Moselle, where Charlemagne had his greatest palaces. But to the north lived the Saxons, who stuck by paganism and regularly trespassed into Frankish territory, sacking churches and stirring local resistance to Frankish rule. Charlemagne did not shirk the challenge.

In 771, Charlemagne ransacked the Saxon temple to the god Woden, felling its sacred grove and carrying off its treasure. The Saxon response was to invade immediately the Eder Valley north of Frankfurt. Only the sudden arrival of angels stopped the Saxon advance, but it did nothing to halt the war, which ground on for thirty years. Even so, Charlemagne's Franks had by the 790s pushed the frontier eastwards to the River Elbe. In the wake of their advance came churches, bishops, palaces, tax collectors, and brutal laws that forbade pagan worship on pain of death. But in victory, Charlemagne could afford to be magnanimous. If Saxon chieftains converted to Christianity, Charlemagne spared their lives, even restoring them to power, but only as his servants and with their children held as hostages.

The monks of St Gallen and of its sister monasteries in southern Germany watched all of this. In their annals and histories, they recorded Charlemagne's triumphs not only against the Saxons but also against enemies closer to home—the Bavarians, whose dukes, once subject to the Merovingian kings, had assumed an independent power; the Wends, who frequently fought beside the Saxons; and the nomadic Avars, who occupied what is now eastern Austria and Hungary. The monks wrote breathlessly, for Charlemagne's ambition and military deployments were, indeed, astonishing: so, for instance—

> 797: Charlemagne was once more in Saxony, whither he ferried ships overland and launched them on the rivers, and he built a castle, which hemmed the Saxons in well enough. And he sent his son Pippin against the Wends, another army against the Avars, and his son Louis to Spain. And he went to Aachen, and once more to Saxony, and wintered there.

The staccato itemization of campaigns was followed three years later by the following terse note, which records a turning point in European history—

> 800: Charlemagne held court in Mainz; from there, he went to Italy and arrived in Rome, where he was made emperor.[13]

The coronation of Charlemagne as emperor was performed by Pope Leo III, in St Peter's in Rome, on Christmas Day 800. We may safely disregard the comment by Charlemagne's earliest biographer that the crowning came as an unwelcome surprise to Charlemagne as well as the speculation that had he not had arthritis the king might have somehow dodged the pope as he brought the diadem to him. Negotiations over the coronation had been proceeding for several years and Charlemagne had taken his daughters to St Peter's to see the event.

Plainly though, the coronation meant different things to people at the time. For the pope, it signified the appointment of a new protector, in which respect it helped that Charlemagne's soldiers had recently rescued the unpopular pope from a vengeful mob in Rome. For the main Byzantine commentator of the time, who viewed the Byzantine Empire as Rome's true successor, the coronation was an absurdity, and the ceremony of anointing the new emperor carried out so inexpertly that his robes were drenched with oil. For Charlemagne's advisers, it signalled the rebirth of the Roman Empire and the foundation of a new Christian Europe under Frankish leadership—'renewal', 're-making', 're-creation', and 'renovation of the Roman Empire' were the words Charlemagne's scribes used in letters and on seals to describe the significance of their master's new title.[14]

Charlemagne never disclosed his own thoughts on the matter. But he plainly had an elevated view of his own kingship, being the first European ruler to use the formula *Dei gratia* (by grace of God) as part of the royal style. He also looked to Roman antiquity for inspiration, hauling Roman columns and stonework to Aachen as furniture for his palace and de facto capital—he was first buried in a second-century marble sarcophagus that rather randomly bore a relief of Pluto ravishing Proserpina. The polygonal chapel at Aachen was also modelled on a Roman design. But empire made sense too. By his conquests, Charlemagne had become a king three times over—king of the Franks, king of Italy, and, although never crowned as such, king of the Saxons. The imperial office brought together the separate realms of Franks, Lombards, and Germans in a new superstructure, headed by a super-monarch with a super title.[15]

Rules, writing, and Roman—the three Rs embodied Charlemagne's cultural legacy, but it was not only disseminated by the palace at Aachen and Charlemagne's team of churchmen and advisers. The so-called Carolingian Renaissance was polycentric and the monasteries were its hubs. St Gallen was in the forefront of rulemaking—laying down guidelines for musical notation, for the education of the young, and for Latin grammar and script. It was a literate community which insisted that its business be conducted in writing according to a standard format and that all its important records be stored in a dedicated archive with numbered drawers. Its monks were also at the forefront of preserving classical Roman texts, copying and crosschecking for errors some of the earliest editions of Caesar, Tacitus, Livy, Ovid, and Horace, and depositing their finished works in the monastery library.[16]

Charlemagne's courtiers extolled him as a poet-king, a second David, an exemplar of piety and moral worth. But Charlemagne never
lived up to the grand images that others thrust upon him. Despite the
penance he prescribed for violating God's commands, he kept concubines and was unsparing in his sexual quests. Even his daughters
seem to have shared his bed and borne him children. On his death,
few mourned him and there is only one contemporary lament of his
passing. Instead, writers told of the terror he had unleashed, rehearsed
how an angel had once presented Charlemagne with a scroll that announced his secret vice, and spoke of a visionary that had seen the
emperor suffering in the afterworld, with 'his privies being gnawed at
by some type of animal'. It was only later that Charlemagne's reputation recovered, when publicists made him into a paragon of moral and
martial worth to set against the shortcomings of his successors.[17]

Whatever his personal failings, it was under Charlemagne that
the Roman Empire was reinaugurated in Europe. For the next thousand years, there would be a Roman emperor in the west, governing
a large chunk of Central Europe. There would be gaps in the succession, and the title of 'Holy' would later be added to 'Roman Empire'.
What 'Roman' and 'empire' meant would vary over time as much as
the significance of Charlemagne's coronation differed in the minds of
contemporaries. Because the idea of empire was never defined at the
moment of its birth, later generations could bend its meaning to fit in
with their own fantasies and programmes. So, over time the renewed
Roman Empire might stand for a united Christian Europe, a mission
to defend the Catholic Church and convert the faithless, a stepping
stone to the Last Judgment, a worldwide scheme of conquest, a means
of bringing the whole earth into harmonious concordance with God's
grace, or just another way of saying Germany. All of these ideas would
be played out in the millennium that followed Charlemagne's coronation, and Central Europe would be their stage.

CHAPTER 3

Avars and Slavs: Destruction and Conversion

W EST OF THE RHINE, CHARLEMAGNE'S EMPIRE MOSTLY comprised the German tribes that either he or his Frankish predecessors had conquered—Alemanns in what is now southwestern Germany, because of which the French name for Germany is *Allemagne*; north of them, Thuringians, Frisians, and Saxons; and in the east, Bavarians. In the rest of Central Europe, Frankish influence was less pronounced and exercised indirectly through ceremonies when local chieftains paid homage, attending the Frankish ruler's court with gifts and tribute. Even so, there are some signs of Frankish settlement in areas otherwise remote from the centres of Frankish power. Byzantine accounts knew the region adjoining the Lower Danube in what is now northern Serbia as Frankochorion, pointing to some sort of Frankish presence there, and we know of confrontations between Franks and Bulgarians close to the western edge of Transylvania.[1]

East of the region of German settlement (and in places overlapping with it) lived the Slavs. By the seventh century, the Slavs occupied the vast space between the Baltic and the Aegean Sea, from what is now the southeastern corner of Denmark to the steppes and including most of the Balkans. The origin of the Slavs is entirely mysterious, for they are not mentioned by writers much before they are found occupying almost the whole of Central and Eastern Europe. One of the earliest accounts (550 CE) describes them as 'very populous' and occupying 'a great expanse of land' in what is now southern Poland. How the Slavs came there without anyone noticing cannot easily be explained.[2]

Historians have done their best with ambiguous archaeological remains and linguistic fragments. Because the early Slavs borrowed from German their name for beech tree, historians once hunted for a place where beech trees were missing and so made the Pripet Marshes that lie between modern-day Kyiv and Minsk the Slavs' original starting point. Alternatively, because the early Slavs were sometimes known as Wends, they were thought to be identical with the Venedi, whom Roman geographers had described living on the Baltic shore in the first and second centuries CE. Neither theory of Slavonic (or Slavic) origins now carries much scholarly weight, although historical atlases have been slow to catch up. Suffice it to say that early accounts of the Slavs put them between the Upper Vistula, the Lower Danube, and the Dnieper Rivers—a region large enough to accommodate most speculation. But just to confuse matters, some DNA research suggests a continuous Slavonic presence in what is now western Poland, thus implying that the Slavs did not migrate to Central Europe from anywhere further east but had been living in part of it all the time.[3]

Estimating population densities in the early Middle Ages is a fool's game, but sometimes the jester's cap is the only headwear on offer. Putting guesstimates together suggests that the eastern part of Central Europe (nowadays including the Czech Republic, Hungary, Poland, Romania, and Slovakia) had a population density in the first millennium of less than one person per square kilometre. By contrast, the area of modern-day Germany had perhaps as many as eight per square kilometre. We can double, halve, or treble the figures, but the implication amounts to the same—much of the eastern part of Central Europe was sparsely populated, and it would not take the movement of many people to change its complexion entirely. Instead of great waves of peoples rippling across Central Europe, it is probably more sensible to think of thinner, but equally decisive, population flows.[4]

By the end of the sixth century, Slavs predominated in the parts of Central Europe previously vacated by the Germans and Goths. Contemporary commentators all described the Slavs as made up of small tribes practising a primitive agriculture, living in squalid huts in the forests for safety, and having only the most primitive weapons—short spears, unwieldy swords, and poison arrows. In combat, we are told, they were disorganized, being unable to fight in close order, and they preferred—when not hiding in the woods—to run at the enemy in a disorganized mass. At the beginning of the eighth century, a band of Slav warriors near Friuli defended itself, according to one account, 'more with stones and axes than with weapons of war'.[5]

Unsophisticated militarily and politically disunited, the Slavs fell prey to more organized groups. One of these was led by a Frankish adventurer called Samo, who in the first half of the seventh century carved out a duchy that may have reached from modern-day Slovenia to southern Poland. Samo was a merchant and his principal cargo was slaves. It was during the seventh century that the names *Slav* and *slave* were first treated as synonymous both in Europe and in the Middle East. (The name *Slav* derives from *slovo*, or 'word', meaning 'the people who speak'.) Many male Slav slaves went to the castration factories of Lyons, Venice, and Verdun where they were prepared for onward consignment, to be sold as eunuchs. Doubtless some of the female slaves fed Samo's appetite for marriage and procreation—he had at least twelve wives and is said to have fathered twenty-two sons and fifteen daughters.[6]

Notwithstanding Samo's fecundity, his slave state did not outlive his death in 658. The Avar kingdom in Central Europe proved more enduring. Avar origins are as mysterious as Slav, although in the case of the Avars we do not even know what language they spoke. They were, like the Huns, pastoral nomads and stockbreeders from the steppe land who had been displaced and forced westwards, probably from Transoxiana in Central Asia. From the late sixth to the late eighth century, the Avars occupied the old Roman province of Pannonia and the neighbouring Hungarian Plain, but their influence also extended both westwards and southwards, into what is now Austria and eastern Bavaria, Transylvania, and the western Balkans. The Byzantine emperors relied for defence on a network of castles and walls reaching south of the Lower Danube, but the Avars still broke through. In their wake, tens of thousands of Slavs pushed into the Balkan peninsula, fundamentally changing its linguistic landscape. By the mid-seventh century, Thessaloniki was a mainly Slav-speaking city.

The Avars provided political organization. The disparate Slavonic tribes began to coalesce into larger, more stable groups. The Avar state was a tribute state, which survived by amassing booty through war raids, ransoms, and tribute. In the late sixth and early seventh centuries alone, the Byzantine emperor paid over to the Avars more than six million gold coins. The loot was then distributed to chieftains and headmen to keep them loyal. But the growing power of the Franks limited raiding opportunities in the west, while in the south a new state, populated by Slavs but led by an elite of former steppe nomads called Bulgars, prevented movement into the Balkans.

Deprived of booty, the power of the Avar chieftains or khans withered. In the mid-eighth century, the Bavarian dukes, who paid only a nominal allegiance to the Frankish ruler, pressed upon the Avars from the east and supported a rebellion among their Slavonic subjects in what is now northern Slovenia and southern Austria but which was then called Carantania. In the aftermath of the Bavarian victory, Irish monks from Salzburg set about the conversion of the Slavs in this corner of Central Europe. But Charlemagne resented the independence of Bavaria's rulers. Once he had made good his power in the west, Charlemagne crushed the Bavarians, condemning the last of their ducal line to death and only sparing him when he became a monk.

Now it was Charlemagne who led the war against the Avars in a series of campaigns during the 790s. The Avars had reinforced their land with elaborate circles of earthworks, brushwood, and logs, but Charlemagne's troops punched through these and captured what was left of their treasure. As one monk reported from St Gallen, 'All the booty of the Avars, which Charlemagne found in Pannonia, he divided most liberally among the bishoprics and the monasteries.' Evidently, not all of it went to the Church, for another account tells of how Avar loot transformed the fortunes of the Frankish chieftains and warriors, who 'until that time had seemed almost paupers'. Charlemagne not only took the Avars' gold but also destroyed their leading men. A few became his vassals, ruling in his name over shadowy dukedoms, but otherwise we are told 'the whole nobility of the Avars perished and all their glory ended.' After more than two centuries' sojourn in Pannonia, the Avars simply disappeared from the historical record. As an old Russian saying once put it, 'They have perished like the Avars.'[7]

The list of Central Europe's invaders and occupiers between the fifth and the ninth century is a long one—Huns, Ostrogoths, Slavs, Avars, Samo's slavers, Bavarians, and Franks. But among these the Avars were not just one in a line of conquerors who came and went, leaving little trace. They were predatory, but to exploit their subject peoples they marshalled them into groups and consolidated them—perhaps, after all, there is not so much difference between shepherding flocks and shepherding peoples. The Avars brought innovations too. The stirrup was their contribution to technology in Europe, and with it the means of riding against the enemy at full tilt without being tossed off on impact. Less happily, the Avars also brought to Europe a new strain of leprosy that was considerably more virulent than its predecessors. Following the Avars' arrival in Central Europe, as many as a quarter of male skeletons excavated in parts of the region show evidence of infection from leprosy. As well as its monastery, school, and scriptorium, the abbey of St Gallen also had a *leprosarium*, or hospital for lepers, founded at some point in the eighth century.[8]

Perhaps on account of their background as nomads, the Avars prized portable works of art. In all of continental Europe, the greatest find from the first millennium is surely theirs—the treasure unearthed in 1799 at Sânnicolau Mare (Nagyszentmiklós), which lies today on the Romanian side of the border with Hungary and is otherwise famous as the birthplace of the composer Béla Bartók. Made in the eighth century for a nameless Avar chieftain, the hoard comprises twenty-three gold vessels—tureens, bowls, and ewers, each ornately engraved with images and pattern work. The repertoire of designs draws on late Roman and Byzantine motifs, Catholic religious iconography, and Central Asian and Persian motifs, including lions, sea griffins, and leopards.

Several inscriptions are written in Greek letters but an unknown language. Only two words are decipherable—'zoipan', or *župan*, which is Slavonic for 'chieftain', and 'Boila', which is a common enough Turkic word, usually translated as 'noble', although it may also be a proper name. The Sânnicolau Mare hoard bears witness not only to the wealth of the Avars but also to their curiously hybrid culture, with its mix of Asiatic and Slavonic languages and fusion of Byzantine, Oriental, and continental European designs. Forgotten in the ebb and flow of conquest, the Avars deserve to be better known.[9]

Slavonic dukedoms replaced the Avar khanate, forming a patchwork along either side of the Danube. But the big players in the region were the Franks of Charlemagne and his successors and, further east, the Bulgarians whose Bulgar chieftains pressed into Transylvania and along the waterways of the Hungarian Plain with the aim of capturing the salt mines and trade routes. In 822, envoys from half a dozen Slavonic tribes came to Frankfurt bearing gifts for Charlemagne's son and successor Louis the Pious and asking for help against the Bulgarians. Four years later, Louis and the Bulgarian Khan Omurtag agreed on a common border between their two realms that ran through the Hungarian Plain, after which Louis organized the border region into marchlands. It was the first major international partition of Central Europe's space.[10]

North of Pannonia and the Hungarian Plain lay a confusing medley of Slavonic groups and statelets. Around the year 900, a nameless monk known to historians as 'the Bavarian Geographer' compiled a list of some sixty peoples in Central Europe, including many who belonged to these early political formations, and he counted the fortified places each had. A few of the tribes on his list had names that would endure—Bohemians, Moravians, Sorbs, and so on. But the majority of names are the only relic of shadowy principalities that rose and fell without leaving any trace—'The Thadesians with more than two hundred forts, the Goplans who have four hundred forts or more, the Zeurians with three hundred and twenty-five forts,' and so on. We do not know what happened to these people or where they lived, and their so-called forts were probably no more than hilltops circled with earthen walls. It was these minor political groupings in Central Europe that now became targets of Frankish expansion and evangelization.[11]

The contest, however, was not just between Christianity and paganism. There were rival Christianities—the Catholicism of Rome and the Orthodoxy of Constantinople, both of which were interested in the spiritual colonization of Central Europe but increasingly estranged. And there were rival bishops, too, each anxious to implant their priests and to enlarge the extent and prestige of their dioceses. So, the archbishops of Mainz in the Rhineland competed for souls and patronage with the missionary Bavarian sees of Salzburg, Regensburg, and Passau, with Würzburg in Franconia, and in the tenth century with the archbishops of Magdeburg in Saxony. The popes in Rome also watched the growing influence of the independent-minded German bishops with alarm and worked to hinder their endeavours. Conversion was never only about *to what* but also *to which* of a variety of religious competitors.

The religious battleground was Pannonia and the rim of the Carpathian Mountains to the north. In the aftermath of the Avars' defeat, new Slavonic rulers carved out semi-independent principalities. We know of at least four of these, reaching from the shelter of the Little Carpathians north of modern-day Bratislava to what is now Croatia on the Adriatic coast, where corsairs were busy becoming princes. Some of these early formations were of Avar origin, set up to facilitate tribute payment, but others were Frankish marcher lordships, under Slavonic leadership. Historians seek to plot their location on maps, but they are better thought of more as dukedoms than as duchies—as groups of people who acknowledged an overlord and duke, and not as defined spaces with fixed borders.

During the first decades of the ninth century, missionaries described at the time as 'Italians, Greeks, and Germans', were active among the Slavs of Pannonia and the northern Carpathians. Among these, the rival sees of Passau and Salzburg took the lead, but Passau

won an early advantage when in the 830s its protégé, Mojmir, overthrew Salzburg's man, Pribina, and seized his lands, which lay around
Nitra, now in western Slovakia. Mojmir called himself Duke of the
Moravians, and his power base seems to have lain in what is now the
eastern part of the Czech Republic, which is still called Moravia today. Mojmir was succeeded in 846 by his nephew Rastislav, who was
plainly dissatisfied with Passau's priests. Accounts tell of how they had
betrayed their mission, preaching that 'Beneath the ground live people
with huge heads; and all reptiles are the creation of the devil, and if
someone kills a snake, they will be absolved of nine sins.' But politics
also had something to do with it, since the German clergy stood close
to the Frankish bishops and promoted their interests.[12]

In 862 Rastislav made an extraordinary move. He sent an embassy
to Constantinople to ask the Byzantine emperor to send him priests,
'who can explain to us in our own language the true Christian faith'.
But there was a hint in Rastislav's overture that something more was
afoot—'so that other countries which look to us might emulate us'. At
this time, Constantinople and Rome were sparring over Bulgaria and
whether it should be subject to the Byzantine patriarch or to the pope.
Rastislav was effectively promising to bring his people over from the
Catholicism of Rome to the Orthodoxy of Byzantium, and he knew
that by opting for one side or the other he could tilt the religious balance in the Balkans.[13]

In Constantinople, Emperor Michael III understood what Rastislav meant and he knew just the man to lead the expedition: St Cyril
of Thessaloniki. (In fact, St Cyril's baptismal name was Constantine,
and he chose to be called Cyril only on his deathbed, when he became
a monk, but he is generally known as Cyril.) Cyril had proven credentials in the mission field, having preached to both Muslims and Jews
in the Middle East and the Caucasus. Like his brother Methodius,
an abbot on Mount Olympus and provincial administrator, he was
a thoroughly seasoned diplomat. Cyril had recently won plaudits in
Constantinople for identifying a chalice as belonging to the time of
the Old Testament King Solomon on the basis of its inscription of

'999 BC' (Before Christ). Cleverly, too, having recovered under divine direction the body of the first-century pope and saint Clement, Cyril had kept the saint's body parts as a bank of relics to exchange for political favours.

Cyril and Methodius already knew Slavonic from living in Thessaloniki, and we must imagine that at this time the Slavonic spoken in the Balkans was still close to the language used by Rastislav's subjects. Cyril accordingly devised an alphabet whereby Slavonic might be written down as the first step to producing a Bible, liturgy, and manuals of religious instruction. This alphabet, which was later called Glagolitic, roughly meaning something to be spoken, was partly based on Greek lowercase letters with additional sounds rendered in Syriac, Hebrew, and possibly Armenian characters. The individual letters, of which there were no fewer than forty-one, were further ornamented with religious symbols—a circle standing for eternity, a triangle for the Trinity, and so on. It was not an easy script to master.

Cyril and Methodius's mission, which reached Moravia in 863, was guaranteed to face hurdles, for too much rested on Rastislav, and the chieftain's political position was never secure. He was eventually overthrown in 870, following a bungled attempt to strangle his main rival. But the two brothers found an unexpected ally in Pope Adrian II (ruled 867–872). Pope Adrian approved the mission and religious texts translated into Slavonic with the Glagolitic alphabet, made Methodius bishop of the Slavs of Moravia and Pannonia, and received in return what was left of St Clement's corpse. Adrian plainly intended to turn Methodius into his own creature. But, upon returning to Moravia in 870, Methodius was promptly arrested by the new pro-Frankish ruler of Moravia, Svatopluk, who handed him over to trial and imprisonment by his ecclesiastical enemies on the grounds of usurping episcopal authority. (Cyril had meanwhile died, in 869.)[14]

We do not know whether papal pressure or a change in political direction prompted the rapprochement between Methodius and Svatopluk which followed the saint's release from confinement in 873.

For the next dozen years, Methodius trained priests in the Slavonic liturgy, translated Greek religious texts into Glagolitic, and celebrated the mass in Latin, Greek, and Slavonic. He also sent out clergy into the mission field, preaching in Bohemia and what is now southern Poland. But the Frankish clergy in Svatopluk's court never ceased to mount objections to Methodius's presence, accusing him of heresy for delivering the mass in Slavonic and not in Latin. His life ended in 885 amidst turmoil—his bitter excommunication of his adversaries, a revised papal verdict that banned celebration of the mass in Slavonic, and shortly after his death, Svatopluk's expulsion of Methodius's followers from Moravia.

Cyril and Methodius's legacy endured. The Orthodox Church headed by the patriarch of Constantinople embraced their linguistic innovations. The outward form of Church Slavonic changed, modified by the saints' students into the more manageable alphabet based on Greek uppercase letters that, in Cyril's honour, is still known as Cyrillic. It was with this alphabet that the Serbs, Russians, and Bulgarians were eventually educated in Christian doctrine and brought to knowledge the Christian faith. But in Central Europe, Latin prevailed as the language of the liturgy and of church services, and with it the Catholic faith that looked to Rome. Only in Dalmatia, a part of Croatia, did the Slavonic mass survive. But except as a curiosity, the Slavonic mass and adherence to the Orthodox faith failed in Central Europe. So, the Czech composer Janáček's eerie 'Glagolitic Mass', first performed in Brno in Moravia in 1926, is thoroughly Catholic in its setting and composition—it just happens to be sung in a mix of old Slavonic languages.[15]

The Catholic mission would continue to prosper in Central Europe. Bohemia and Croatia were brought into the Catholic fold in the ninth century, and Poland and Hungary in the century after. In all these countries, Latin became the language of the mass and of divine worship. Because the Catholic clergy provided most clerks, administrators, and teachers, the Latin language also became the language of government, legislation, literature, and learning, right through to the eighteenth century. By contrast, in Russia and most of the Balkans, it was the Orthodox religion and the Slavonic liturgy that flourished, and with them a quite different religious culture and intellectual landscape. In time, the use of the vernacular in church services would produce national churches that intensified religious allegiances by their patriotic appeal—a Bulgarian Orthodox Church, Russian Orthodox Church, and so on.

At the same time, Orthodoxy was founded on quite different principles to the Catholic faith of Rome. Owing to the primacy of the Greek language, the Orthodox intellectual tradition diverged from Latin-based Roman Catholicism, focusing on ancient Greek metaphysics, the writings of the early Greek Fathers (from the first centuries CE), and the critical interpretation of biblical and Greek religious texts. The newly converted Slavs joined in this inheritance, mediated through Greek texts translated into Church Slavonic. They also shared with their Greek counterparts a distrust of Catholic Christianity, partly arising from different theological stresses, but also fuelled by a sense of superiority that regarded users of Latin not only as 'men of a different language' but even as 'men of another race'.[16]

These different religious and cultural trajectories were decisive in Central Europe's development. The Orthodox religion emerged out of the Byzantine Empire, whose rulers governed with an almost unlimited power as both the servant and image of God. Orthodoxy embraced this ideal, emphasizing in its rituals and ceremony the authority of the monarch, whose power came directly from God. In Byzantium, representative institutions and assemblies were missing, for with an all-powerful sovereign there was simply no room for them.

Catholic and Western scholars often describe Orthodox Christianity as conservative, insular, and traditional, whereas in reality it was just different. But for Central Europe this difference mattered. Having been brought into the fold of the Catholic Church, Central Europe would share in the fruits of its civilization, experiencing the same impulses and movements that guided Catholic and, later, Protestant Europe.

Universities, parliaments, the Renaissance, Reformation, and Enlightenment were not missing in Orthodox Europe, but they only appeared there in shadowy and attenuated forms. By embracing Catholicism and rejecting Orthodoxy, Central Europe was drawn culturally westwards. Russia and the Balkans went off in a quite different direction. Notwithstanding the common origin of the Slavs and their related languages, the Slavonic world was split in two.

CHAPTER 4

The Return of the Huns, Slave States, and the Shaping of Central Europe

THE EARLIEST HISTORIES COMPOSED IN CENTRAL EUROPE considered its countries as homes gifted by God to the peoples who lived in them. Medieval chroniclers spoke of their own people as wandering across the face of the earth until guided by a patriarch, who like the Old Testament Moses led them to the place promised by the Almighty and installed their first rulers. The land given them was invariably abundant in all things, with plentiful pastures, clear streams, and riverbanks studded with gems. Variations on this theme added in how the chronicler's people had come from Troy or once fought along-side Alexander the Great, and writers wove in fabulous etymologies, tricky prophetesses, and hostile dragons. Even so, the presumptions of the earliest chroniclers were largely the same. The nations they de-scribed had always existed and providence had ordained the territories they would occupy and their earliest leaders. Rulership, people, and land converged as part of a divine plan.[1]

In reality, boundaries were fluid, rulership was contested, and what constituted a people was still uncertain. The prevailing pattern was one of consolidation, disintegration, and the reassembling of the parts into entirely new configurations of territory, people, and power. Be-tween the ninth and eleventh centuries, Central Europe was repeat-edly pulled apart, reorganized, and then dismantled again. Even at the time, contemporaries lamented the many kinglets that sprang unin-vited from the bowels of the earth (intestinal analogies were much the fashion), and how 'all were driven by greed, and sought only their own advantage.' Gradually, however, the pieces stabilized. The map of

Central Europe round about 850 shows a medley of minor principalities and dukedoms—some with familiar names, but likely as not in unusual places. A century and a half later, the lines and labels are more recognizable and the political boundaries more fixed.[2]

The Frankish Empire was the first great power to fall apart and be rebuilt. Its disintegration began almost immediately after Charlemagne's death. Charlemagne's sole surviving heir was Louis, known even in his own lifetime as 'the Pious' (ruled 814–840). It was a sobriquet that he chose, signing himself 'Louis the most pious emperor'. But at the time piousness had nothing to do with saintliness. Instead, it meant a readiness to set aside personal interests, friends, and family for the sake of the public good. Louis was conspicuous in not doing this. Although Louis had already been crowned co-emperor, upon hearing of his father's death in 814 he raced to his father's old palace in Aachen to be crowned there again—a third coronation by the pope in Rheims followed the next year. Despite these grand ceremonies, contemporary commentators were swift to point out that Louis had little of his father in him, that 'he never showed his white teeth in a smile', and foretold that he would squander his inheritance.[3]

Following Frankish tradition, Louis planned that the Frankish Empire should be divided after his death among his three sons. But he treated his legacy like a caricature aunt rewriting her will, except that the consequences were bloodier. In the partition that he devised in 817, he left out his nephew, whom Charlemagne had already made king of Italy, so the nephew promptly rebelled. Louis ordered him blinded, but the punishment was botched and the nephew left to die in agony. Then, upon the death of his first wife, Louis took a second, whom he chose at a beauty pageant of potential spouses.

Louis's new wife, Judith of Bavaria, had a reputation for promiscuous living and consorting with sorcerers. In 823 she threw Frankish politics into turmoil by bearing Louis a son, which meant that the scheme of succession had to be adjusted. It did not help that the son's paternity was in doubt. Since the elder three sons must lose out if a dubious fourth was added to the arrangement, they went to war against their father. Louis attempted to placate each in turn, at which point the others allied to overturn whatever had been agreed. In the mayhem, Louis was twice deposed and had to go through several ceremonies of public penance at which he confessed to betraying the royal office, his own uselessness, and being responsible for 'murder, perjury, sacrilege, adultery, pillage, the arson of churches and other places, and robbing and oppressing the poor'.[4]

Shortly before his death in 840, Louis left it to his surviving three sons (one had died in the meantime) to divide up the empire as if it were a children's cake so that the one who did the slicing had the last pick. In fact the brothers did a reasonably good job, balancing out land and income. The Frankish Empire was accordingly divided into three kingdoms, along lines that ran north–south. To the west was a portion that took in much of modern-day France. In the east lay a crescent-shaped part that reached from what is now Denmark to the Alps but running southeastwards across Bavaria to the Hungarian Plain. Between the two was 'Middle Francia', which was the premier of the three kingdoms because it included Rome and Charlemagne's premier seat of Aachen. This went to Lothar I, the eldest of the three sons, along with the imperial title.[5]

With the passage of generations, further divisions followed. Middle Francia was repeatedly partitioned between heirs and its fragments fought over. By the end of the ninth century, it had dissolved into separate realms—Italy, Provence, Upper and Lower Burgundy, and Lotharingia, which was itself partitioned after 870. Called after Louis the Pious's grandson Lothar II, Lotharingia became in time the much smaller Lorraine, and thus a contested space right through to the twentieth century. West and east of Middle Francia, the separate language communities hardened: a Romance-speaking region on the one side and a Germanic-speaking one on the other. So, when in 842 Louis the German and Charles the Bald, kings respectively of eastern and western Francia, swore to join arms against their older brother, the Emperor Lothar I, they concluded their treaty in both Old French (or Gallo-Romance) and Old High German.

Charlemagne's line withered. What had once been a thriving enterprise with too many sons faltered in the last decades of the ninth century on account of childlessness and premature deaths. The idea of empire seemed on the edge of extinction too. Since emperors needed to be crowned by the pope in Rome, the title came easiest to whoever had the advantage in Italy and could force the papal hand, by storming the Holy City if need be. So, a succession of minor princelings had themselves crowned by popes, culminating in the elevation in 915 of the obscure Berengar of Friuli, of whom nothing good has been written. On his death in 924, Berengar crowned his disservices by leaving only daughters. Since no one stepped forward as his successor, the office and title of emperor languished.

The Hungarians changed everything. Hungarian origins are almost as obscure as Slavonic. The linguistic, literary, archaeological, and DNA evidence is all contradictory, which has given room for fanciful speculations. The broad consensus among scholars is that the Hungarians originated in western Siberia, speaking a language distantly related to Finnish. Over several millennia, the Hungarians moved into and across the steppe land, but it is impossible to say whether they were sedentary agriculturalists or had 'nomadized', becoming herders and migrating between summer and winter pastures. It was on the edge of the steppe land, not far from the Crimea, that St Cyril encountered the Hungarians around 860, when they fell upon him, howling like wolves. Abashed by his holiness, they left Cyril unscathed.[6]

While on the steppe land, the Hungarians were taken over by successive tribes of Turkic nomads, one of which, called Onogurs, gave their name to the people over whom they ruled—whence 'Hungarian'. The Turkish element was swiftly assimilated into the majority linguistic population, who spoke an early version of what is called today Magyar or Hungarian. Even so, there are still about three hundred Old Turkic loan words in modern Hungarian, starting with the word for Sunday, which is *vasárnap*—'shopping day', a word having its root in the Turkic *vasar* meaning 'a market or bazaar'. All of the earliest Hungarian leaders, right through to the eleventh century, bore

Turkic names. They looked Turkic too, wearing caftans, carrying long scimitars, and braiding their hair.[7]

Hungarian chroniclers would later tell of the victorious entry of the Hungarians into the former Roman province of Pannonia in 895 or 896 and their scattering of the Slavs and Bulgarians they found living there. In fact, the Hungarians crossed the Carpathians in flight, having been thrown off the western steppe by another group of Turkic nomads called Pechenegs. When the earliest Hungarian historians came to describe this event, they were evasive, describing the Pechenegs instead by their totem, the eagle, and telling of the convocations of eagles which had swooped down upon the Hungarians from their eyries and fastnesses in the Carpathians. Evidently, too, the Hungarians came in waves, since as early as the 860s Frankish and Moravian leaders were using Hungarians as auxiliaries in their wars. Some were surprisingly early converts to Christianity.[8]

The Hungarian settlement in Central Europe was accompanied by extensive raiding. Hungarian attacks intensified at the start of the tenth century, ravaging Moravia, after which the newcomers overran large parts of Central Europe, also sending warbands as far afield as Spain and Italy. A chronicle of the time reported the Hungarians' annual incursions:

907: The Bavarians fought the Hungarians, and many were cut down with great slaughter.

908: The Hungarians came across the frontiers again, and devastated Saxony and Thuringia.

909: The Hungarians entered Alemannia.

910: The Franks fought the Hungarians on the frontier between Bavaria and Francia, and pitiably they either fled or were defeated.[9]

When describing the Hungarians, contemporary writers mostly borrowed from earlier accounts of the Avars or, more usually, of the Huns. The similarity of name helped—hence, 'the Hungarians, that is to say the Huns', 'the Huns who are also called Hungarians', and so forth. So, like the Huns, the Hungarians were described as the people of Gog and Magog, whom Alexander the Great had enclosed in the Caucasus. And, like the Huns too, 'they eat their meat raw, drink blood, chop up the hearts of captives and swallow them bit by bit as if they were medicine.' Gradually, Huns and Hungarians merged together into a common story so that, in one later Croatian account, they were both in origin Massagetae people who ate their parents. The earliest Hungarian chronicles developed this theme, casting their first leader, Prince Árpád, as Attila's heir and plundering older accounts of the Huns to flesh out their texts. But these descriptions were primarily literary exercises in which the writer showed off his knowledge of classical authors. Relations on the ground were clearly more complicated. In a curious episode in 903, Bavarian chieftains invited the Hungarian leaders to a feast, during the course of which they murdered them. Despite its grisly ending, a shared meal hardly suggests wholly insuperable cultural differences.[10]

East Francia was in no position to meet the Hungarian challenge. Central authority had perished there, leaving the initiative with local strongmen. Originally military leaders, appointed by the ruler, German dukes carved out regional power bases. They sealed alliances with marriage, gift giving (relics were especially prized), and pacts of friendship and remembrance by which groups of leading men vowed to arrange masses for each other after death. Where institutions to broker relationships of power were missing, tokens of affection and ceremonies of solidarity filled the gap. The East Frankish duchies differed in the extent of their political integration—some, like Franconia and Swabia, both of which had once been the home of the Alemanns, were loose associations of chieftains; others, like Saxony and Bavaria, were united beneath a duke drawn from the premier family there.

With the extinction of Charlemagne's heirs, the dukes increasingly demanded a say in who the kings of East Francia should be. There were no fixed rules of succession. For any prospective ruler, nomination by his predecessor, the vote of the dukes and great men, and acclamation by a warband were equally good routes to the royal diadem. But much depended on who was in physical possession of the crown and corona-tion robes. After a miserable reign, the heirless King Conrad I (ruled 911–923) chose on his deathbed his main adversary, Duke Henry of Saxony, to be his successor, sending him the royal wardrobe and jewels. Even so, Henry presented himself before the great men of East Francia so that they might acclaim him and affirm his kingship.

Powerfully built, Henry of Saxony conveyed a natural authority, so much so that few dared to respond in kind to his playful jibes. He did everything expected of a warrior—leading from the front, distributing booty in equal measure, and excelling in the hunt. Little more than a century before, his ancestors had been pagans, and Henry retained a hearty dislike of priests, on which account he refused a coronation, since he had no wish to have a churchman crown him. For the same reason, he made do without a writing office since he was unwilling to rely on the clergy for scribes. Letters from his reign are scarce, but chronicles survive. They tell of Henry's tireless battles against the Hun-garians and his defeat of their warbands, his building of earthwork cas-tles to act both as refuges and centres of resistance, and the armoured knights that he deployed against the enemy line.[11]

But it was Henry's son and successor Otto I (ruled 936–973) who accomplished the Hungarians' greatest defeat. In 955 Otto trapped the Hungarian army near Augsburg, by the confluence of the Danube and the Lech. On the watery and wooded Lechfeld, the Hungarians were unable to complete their usual tactic of outflanking the enemy and harrying its ranks with arrows. As the Hungarians dallied to plunder the dead, Otto's armoured cavalry rode them down and forced the Hungarians to engage at close quarters. In hand-to-hand fighting, the lightly equipped Hungarian horsemen were no match for the iron-clad German knights. They tried to withdraw, but Otto's troops blocked their retreat and captured the Hungarian commander and several other princes. Otto had them hanged. Otto's ally, the bishop of Cremona, crowed that the victory on the Lechfeld had cowed the Hungarians so completely that they did not now dare even to mutter. In fact, it was as much the Byzantine advance northwards through the Balkans in the late tenth century that prompted the Hungarian leaders to make peace with their neighbours and to embrace Christianity.[12]

Notwithstanding the Hungarians' defeat, their onslaught over the previous half century had changed the map of Central Europe. Destroyed by the Hungarians, Moravia disappeared as an independent state, with much of its territory being taken by a new creation, Bohemia, centred on Prague. Here a new dynasty of rulers, the Přemyslids, gradually erased the duchies of their rivals. (The Přemyslids owe their name to their mythical progenitor, the ploughman Přemysl.) During the tenth century, too, Croatia advanced northwards from the Adriatic coast to take the space of the Pannonian dukedoms which the Hungarians had previously destroyed. After 925, the Croatian ruler Tomislav, already a Catholic, adopted the title of king. Bavaria also expanded eastwards, incorporating Carinthia, Carniola, and Istria. A part of this new territory was subsequently reorganized to make the Eastern March or Ostmark, the kernel of the future Austria. (Austria was originally the Latin name for Ostmark.)

In the north, an entirely new principality emerged, possibly based upon a land or people called Polanie. Nothing is known of Polanie before the tenth century, except that the people there built large mounds, but it was the starting point for what became Poland. Medieval Poland's earliest known ruler, Mieszko (lived c. 930–992), pushed the boundaries of his duchy in all directions, taking over almost the entire space between Gdańsk (Danzig) on the Baltic and the Carpathians. Mieszko's family claimed descent from a mythical wheelwright called Piast, but where the family originated is uncertain—Gniezno, now in central Poland, is its most likely home. Mieszko's advance southwards into the Cracow region and his son and successor Bolesław the Bold's occupation of northern Moravia were aided by the general dislocation that followed the Hungarian invasion that had rendered these territories leaderless.[13]

But the sudden appearance of new political units in Central Europe was due to more than the political mayhem caused by the Hungarians. The development in the ninth and tenth centuries of commercial routes between the Baltic and the Black Sea transformed the economy of the whole region. The main intermediaries in the new trade were the Scandinavian Vikings, who besides plundering Europe's coastal parts also opened up its riverways to long-distance commercial traffic. The merchants who came in their wake dealt in silver and they were looking for slaves, partly for onward shipment to Central Asia and the Middle East but also to satisfy domestic demand in Catholic Europe, where even Rome had a slave market that sold Christian captives. The profits to be made from the traffic in humans were substantial. A slave bought in ninth-century Europe for the equivalent of thirty-five grams of gold might realize around one hundred and fifty grams in Baghdad.[14]

Mieszko's Poland is home to some of the densest concentrations of Arabic coin hoards found in Europe outside Scandinavia. The urge to accumulate silver, either for exchange, gifts, or display, drove Mieszko's conquests. Beyond Mieszko's core territory around Gniezno and Poznań, the neighbouring peoples were rounded up, herded into earthen holding pens, and sold off in shackles to Viking, Arab, and Jewish merchants. Rural depopulation was a feature of these wasted parts right through to the eleventh century. Neighbouring Prague, by contrast, counted more as a trading hub. Spain was one of the main destinations for Prague's slave trade and it is from a Spanish Jewish traveller that we have the earliest description of the city, written around 960—

The city of Prague is built of stone and lime and it is the greatest commercial centre in that land. Vikings and Slavs come to it from Cracow with their wares, and from the lands of the Turks come Muslims, Jews, and Turks, also with their wares and currency, and buy slaves, tin, and pelts.[15]

But the East Frankish lands were also a reservoir of bodies for trafficking. As one late-eighth-century writer explained, Central Europe south of the Baltic was called 'Germania' because it 'germinated' so many people: 'And this is why the countless crowds of slaves are frequently driven down from this populous Germania and sold to southern peoples.' Even so, the Frankish and German rulers themselves seem generally to have eschewed both the trading and purchase of slaves. At most, they may have owned a handful of slave women, some of whom doubled up as concubines.[16]

With the crushing of the Hungarians at the Lechfeld, the East Frankish kingdom had become the big player in Central Europe. Rulers hastened to come to terms with Otto I, even if it meant forsaking paganism. The first was the Polish Mieszko, who was baptised in 966. In the south, Mieszko also faced the Bohemians, whose dukes had become Christians probably at the time of Methodius's mission in Moravia (or even before), and they were for long periods Otto I's allies. It helped that Mieszko's wife was a Bohemian Christian, who denied him her bed until he promised to convert. Prince Géza of Hungary, a descendant of the legendary Árpád who had led the Hungarians into Pannonia, also turned to Catholicism in the 970s. But he was an unenthusiastic convert, who explained his wealth and power by his devotion to many gods. It was not until the reign of Géza's son, Vajk, who became St Stephen (ruled 997–1038; canonized 1083), that Christianity was planted firmly in Hungary.

For slaves, it mattered not a jot that the rulers of Bohemia, Poland, and Hungary had embraced Christianity. The trade in human cargoes persisted and a lively market in Greek and Slav women and children carried on in Hungary until at least around 1200. Right through to the 1240s transactions were recorded in Poland that included 'girls and cattle'. This is unsurprising. The new states of Central Europe depended on the slave trade, and their rulers were loath to give up the material basis of their power. As the coin hoards attest, slaves meant money. Money lubricated production and exchange, so much so that Arab dirham coins were forged in Polish mints. For rulers, money was a resource that was more easily taxed than grain and herds of cattle: the more energetic the slave trade, the more cash rolled into royal and princely treasuries. Across a wide swathe of Central Europe, state formation and slavery went hand in hand.[17]

The main beneficiary of the Hungarian irruption were the Saxon kings. Chronicles tell that Henry's warriors proclaimed him an emperor after he had won a battle against the Hungarians in 933, but Henry was never crowned in Rome. Beginning with his son Otto, Henry's successors were, thus renewing the tradition of papal coronation begun by Charlemagne. The link to the Hungarians was decisive. In the first decade of Otto I's rule, several dukes had plotted his overthrow. But after Otto I's victory at the Lechfeld, the grumbling stopped, and the leading men of the kingdom fell into line, leaving Otto free to journey to Rome and to his coronation there in 962, after which he took the opportunity to extend his influence into southern Italy. It was a mark of Otto's international prestige that the Byzantine emperor agreed to Otto's son, the future Otto II, marrying his niece Theophanu.[18]

But the high point of Otto I's reign came in 973, at the very end of his reign. Celebrating Easter at the fortress of Quedlinburg in Saxony, Otto received delegations from all the neighbouring countries, which came to acknowledge his fame. Contemporary accounts tell how the envoys and leaders of the Bohemians, Poles, Hungarians, Danes, and assorted Slavonic tribes resolved their differences with him and received in return handsome gifts. But this was no peace conference of equals. In terror of Otto, Mieszko of Poland sent his son to represent him instead, and the Danes came bearing a backlog of tribute payments. During the proceedings, Otto mapped out the future of Central Europe as Catholic and Christian, instructing the foundation of bishoprics in Prague and in Esztergom in Hungary, which was the seat of the slippery Prince Géza. After the Lechfeld and his coronation in Rome, Otto I was indeed, as one of his scribes described him, 'lord of almost all Europe'.[19]

Otto's son and grandson, Otto II (ruled 973–983) and Otto III (ruled 983–1002), were both crowned in Rome and increasingly drawn into Italian politics. The peninsula was wealthy and, at a time when the leading men of East Francia were also warriors, it made good sense for rulers to have them fight abroad rather than at home. The chaos of Roman and papal affairs additionally meant that military interventions were needed to keep order in the Holy City. On top of this, Italy's classical stonework might be taken to grace buildings north of the Alps and the peninsula had a plentiful supply of saintly body parts for distribution as relics. But for Otto II and Otto III, Italy was more than just a place for battle and collecting furniture and bones. Rome was the 'head of the world' (*caput mundi*) and its landscape was the theatre in which to perform as world rulers and as heirs to the emperors of antiquity.

From 979 until his death four years later, Otto II lived and fought in Italy, administering his empire from Rome. His son, Otto III, went even further. He made his palace in the fortified Septizonium on the Palatine Hill in Rome and, after reaching his majority in 994, spent nearly all his reign in Italy. He not only protected the popes but also made and unmade them, deposing and mutilating one and imposing another. His seals bore after 998 the grand inscription 'Renewal of the Roman Empire', and he styled himself 'Consul of the Senate and People of Rome'. To add to his Roman and imperial credentials, Otto borrowed from the rituals of the Byzantine Empire, imagining these to be closest to the practices of ancient Rome. At the end of his life, he was about to be wed to the most eligible of Greek princesses, but his death in 1002 left her literally waiting at the quayside.

Otto III was still a Frank as much as a Roman. Visiting the German lands in the year 1000, he hastened to Charlemagne's tomb in Aachen. Opening the vault, Otto found the corpse of the emperor intact except for a piece of nose that had fallen off. Otto had it repaired with gold and pocketed one of Charlemagne's teeth, but he made sure that his scribes described the incorruptibility of the emperor's body and the sweet smell that emanated from his tomb, for these were the marks of sainthood. Doubtless, Otto intended Charlemagne's canonization and to build Charlemagne's legacy into his own capacious idea of empire, but he did not live long enough to see it through.[20]

Otto III's idea of empire was a blend of Roman, Frankish, and Byzantine ideas and motifs. But he had no doubt that as emperor he stood at the centre of the Christian world. A remarkable illumination included in a manuscript book of the gospels gives a glimpse of his vision and of the new Central Europe that was emerging. Completed in the abbey of Reichenau on Lake Constance around the year 1000, the gospel book shows Otto enthroned, wearing a crown and holding the imperial staff and, unusually at this time, an orb inscribed with a cross, signifying the global reach of his and God's power. Before him stoop four women, bearing gifts. The artist names them—France, Italy, Germany, and Sclavinia, meaning the land of the Slavs. Probably commissioned by Otto personally, the gospel book's illumination announces that the Slav realms of Central Europe had been brought into his renewed Roman empire and that they had now joined the concert of nations that made up the Catholic Christian world. If regions can have birth certificates, Central Europe's is the gospel book of Otto III.

In the first years of the eleventh century, and the last years of his life, Otto translated this message into practical politics. Touring Central Europe in 1000 and 1001, Otto visited Bolesław the Brave of Poland (ruled 992–1025), who had succeeded Mieszko as ruler ten years before. With the agreement of the pope, Otto made Gniezno an archbishopric. We do not know for sure what happened between Otto and Bolesław, except that the Polish ruler gave the emperor a camel and in return received a copy of the Holy Lance. Some later accounts suggest that Otto gave Bolesław a crown, but it is more likely that he simply extended friendship to him. With Hungary, it was different, for Otto sent its ruler a circlet of some sort. At this time, the Hungarian ruler Stephen was barely able to keep Hungary Catholic and Christian, for he was assailed on all sides by rival chieftains who either stuck to paganism or had adopted Orthodoxy. By giving the future St Stephen a crown, Otto helped keep him in power and the new kingdom in the Catholic fold. Stephen did the rest, burying his main adversary alive to ease his passage to the afterlife.[21]

Historians talk of the tenth century as either 'calamitous' or the 'crucible of Europe', but these are not mutually exclusive descriptions. Out of the disintegration of the Carolingian Empire and the eruption of the Hungarians, a new Central Europe was born, underpinned materially by the trade in slaves. Just as it had been the Huns that redrew the map of Europe by bringing down the Roman Empire, so their Hungarian namesakes transformed the political geography of Central Europe. By their destruction and the responses it provoked, the region began at this time to acquire its distinctive historical shape. To the west lay the German lands, now making up the bulk of the Roman Empire, renewed by Otto I and his heirs. To their east stood the emerging kingdoms of Poland and Hungary and the duchy (later kingdom) of Bohemia, all of which had been brought into the fold of Catholic Christendom. However much these boundaries would twist and turn in the centuries to come, the basic outline of Central Europe was in place.

CHAPTER 5

The Making of the Holy Roman Empire and Central Europe's Wild East

THE KINGS OF GERMANY WERE ALSO KINGS OF ITALY. Their Italian kingship conveyed little real power, but there was a coronation in Pavia or Milan with the so-called Iron Crown of the Lombards. Made of gold and silver, the crown had within it a flattened and bent iron nail allegedly taken from the True Cross. But apart from the pageantry, coronation with it counted for little. Far more important was the title of emperor, which transformed the German monarch into a super-ruler and the supposed head of the Christian world. But the rulers of East Francia, or the German lands, as East Francia was increasingly known, only counted as emperors once the pope in Rome had crowned them with the imperial tiara. So, to achieve the top office, they had to cross the Alps into Italy, and most of them did. Of the ten kings who ruled the German lands in the eleventh and twelfth centuries, only one did not make the journey south of the Alps to become an emperor.

A line of monasteries provided lodgings for the German rulers and the monks took care to keep the roads repaired, but would-be emperors seldom came without entire armies. Once in Italy, they adjudicated disputes among the prosperous cities of the plain, fined wrongdoers, extracted taxes, and imposed placemen where they could. Once crowned, emperors were expected to defend the popes and maintain them in power against rival families in Rome who also vied to control the Holy See. Half a dozen anti-popes were falsely elected during the eleventh century and a further ten in the century following. Not a few of these were creatures of the emperors, pointing to the complexity of papal politics at this time.

On Otto III's death in 1002, the royal title passed to his closest kinsman, his uncle Henry II, but Henry died childless in 1014 and the Saxon dynasty of German rulers came to an end. The power of the Saxon kings had partly rested on the duchy of Saxony, where they had the bulk of their estates. Their successors, whom later chroniclers called the Salians (a nonsense name intended to evoke an ancient ancestry), had fewer lands of their own, mostly in Franconia and the Rhineland. Even so, the other resources available to German kings were formidable. Across the German lands lay a network of about a thousand manors, estates, and villages that belonged to the king by virtue of his office. Taken together, these accounted for perhaps as many as half a million people in a population of under four million. Even a conservative estimate suggests an annual profit from these places of more than twenty thousand tons of grain, an equal number of cartloads of wine, more than a hundred thousand pigs, and one and a half tons of silver.[1]

The German rulers could also count on the Church. The itinerant court of the ruler included his chapel. Although often given choice canonries in cathedrals, the chaplains travelled with the monarch. They conducted religious services, cared for the royal cabinet of relics, and prayed for the souls of the dead on the battlefield. But they were also the king's administrators, who composed letters for him, undertook diplomatic tasks, and advised on policy. Having won the royal trust, most chaplains went on to become bishops and abbots and thus great landowners. Even after they had been promoted out of the chapel, kings still considered them part of the apparatus of royal rule. On the king's behalf, they founded cities, led missions across the frontier, and maintained order in the countryside.

Churchmen were warriors too. Bishops were expected to defend their dioceses militarily and abbots their monasteries, providing armed retinues which joined the monarch on campaign. A list drawn up at the end of the tenth century, probably for Otto II, shows the weight of the Church's contribution. The register specified the provision of just under two thousand armoured knights for the next expedition. Of these, a handful of dukes and counts were expected to furnish just over five hundred, with the remainder of fifteen hundred horsemen coming from the bishops and abbots. Churchmen also led their contingents into battle and fought and died on the field. Campaigning in Italy, one archbishop of Mainz slew eight of the enemy with his three-bladed battle axe, after which he used a stone to smash the skulls of several dozen highborn prisoners.[2]

Rulers rewarded loyalty, giving away large tracts of estate to churches and abbeys, with the added benefit that their gifts would count in the afterlife. The consequence was that the material basis of royal power became dangerously depleted, but monarchs did not see gifts to the Church as a problem. Church and state were so interwoven that rulers viewed grants of land to churchmen not as a loss but as a simple re-allocation of resources, akin to giving property to trusted retainers. It was the same with the empire's great men and other landowners. They gave a portion of their wealth to found churches and monasteries, but they still expected to appoint the priest or abbot, to enjoy a share of the income, and to have masses said for their soul. The churches were theirs, as much as any of their castles, villages, or watermills.[3]

The foundations of the German monarchy were shaken in the 1070s in a drama known as the Investiture Conflict. At the heart of the contest lay the management of the Church and the way clergy-men were appointed to office, or invested. The German rulers treated the clergy and priesthood as a private asset and the churches they had endowed as their own, so they thought nothing wrong with deciding which priests served where. It was the same with popes, over whom the emperors had assumed an upper hand, appointing and dismissing them at will. In just one year, in 1046, Emperor Henry III forced three popes from office—one for 'many loathsome acts of adultery and murders done with his own hands', another for having bought the title, and the third for being the tool of a hostile Roman clique. In their place, Henry III elevated four popes over the next ten years, all of them Germans.[4]

Henry III's popes were not puppets but energetic and independently minded reformers. Their main concern was to crack down on priests taking wives and on churchmen buying offices, but the movement they launched soon snowballed. Renewal of the Church meant restoring its practices to legality, which led in turn to having all appointments made properly. Allowing rulers to choose bishops, abbots, and even popes contradicted this principle. Most objectionable was the ceremony of investiture whereby, after a brief discussion with the cathedral canons (and sometimes not even that), the king or emperor decided on the new bishop and handed to him the ring and staff of office. Reformers demanded instead that all bishops be properly elected by their cathedral chapters and that a firm line be drawn between Church and state.

Emperors did not see it that way. In their view, they were as good as popes and bishops and had an equal right to administer church affairs. The imperial coronation in Rome signified as much. Although the pope did the crowning, the emperor wore beneath the diadem a bishop's mitre, the same red leather shoes as the pope (the colour signifying Christ's blood), and a bishop's ring. He was, his propagandists explained, a reincarnation of the Old Testament Melchizedech, who was both priest and king. On this account, emperors would in the twelfth century add the adjective 'sacred' and even 'most sacred' to the name of Roman Empire, after which historians have called it the Holy Roman Empire. The name has stuck, even though right through to the early nineteenth century most people still called it just the Roman Empire. But there was more to it than ceremony and words. Archbishops, bishops, and abbots were a part of royal government. They made it work. If the monarch lost the right to appoint churchmen, then he gave up his means to rule.

The crisis came to a head during the reign of Henry III's son, Henry IV (ruled 1054–1105). Although personally devout, Henry IV continued to appoint his men to the wealthiest of church offices, including to the sees of Milan and Constance, and he disregarded papal protests. Coinciding with a rebellion in Saxony, the consequences were severe. In 1076, the pope Gregory VII excommunicated Henry and declared his subjects free of their allegiance to him, thus rekindling and widening the Saxon revolt. In response, Henry tried to buy time.

In January 1077, he presented himself in the inner courtyard of the mountain castle of Canossa, where the pope was staying, and pleaded for forgiveness. After several days' delay, the pope brought him into the warmth of his embrace and forgave him his sins. (The story that Henry waited barefoot in the snow for three days, clad only in a chemise, was exploded 150 years ago, but lingers on in textbooks.)[5]

Despite Henry's penance, the issues had not been resolved. Henry continued to appoint churchmen to office and bore down on the pope's German supporters. Meeting at Forchheim in 1077, the Saxon rebels elected a rival or 'anti-king', the first in German history. When Pope Gregory threw in his lot with the pretender and excommunicated Henry for a second time, Henry had the German bishops declare Gregory deposed and then held a Church Council which elected a new pope. It was this anti-pope, Clement (III), who crowned Henry emperor in Rome in 1084. It was by all accounts a glittering ceremony, marred only by a bungled assassination attempt, for which contemporaries blamed Pope Gregory.[6]

The conflict between Henry and Gregory VII and his successors continued into the twelfth century. Henry remained excommunicated and took his revenge by appointing a line of anti-popes. On both sides, pamphlets, sermons, and songs circulated that accused pope and emperor in turn of madness, usurpation, conspiracy with the devil, depraved couplings with nuns, necromancy, murder, and much else. It was the first propaganda war in Central Europe. Eventually, a compromise was found under Henry IV's son and successor, Henry V (ruled 1105–1125), which allowed the ruler to be present when bishops and abbots were elected, but which denied him the right to hand over the staff and ring of office.

Not much seemed to have changed, for monarchs were still able to influence church appointments, albeit more remotely. Yet, the rulers' power had suffered. There had been plenty of rebellions before, but it was only in the 1070s that leading men in the German lands rose up to overthrow the sovereign. They had gone further, for by electing an anti-king they gave life to the electoral principle which the steady succession of sons over the preceding 150 years had done much to eclipse. To keep himself in power, Henry IV also gave away royal lands as rewards and inducements, thus further weakening the material basis of his power. Many of these properties became the cores of new lordships, crowned with square stone keeps and adorned with heraldic shields.

Henry IV had distributed grand titles, too, and let others assume them with neither permission nor rebuke. Whereas before, the title of count once signified some sort of public office, now it became largely honorific and hereditary. Variations on the title of count added lustre to the holder, so he might aspire to be a margrave or marcher count, even though his lands were distant from the frontier marches, or a count palatine, despite having no royal palace to guard. Whatever the title great men took, the outcome was much the same: the powers that counts, margraves, palatines, and so on had previously discharged on behalf of the ruler became their own, exercised (in one description of the time) by virtue of their 'own authority'.[7]

A typical way by which lords built up their power was to promise 'protection', usually to churches and monasteries. In many cases, the protection given was genuine enough, but in others the word 'racket' might be added. Warrior prelates like the skull-crushing archbishop of Mainz could fend for themselves, but most churchmen needed help. Their lands were often scattered and vulnerable to theft. On top of this, they had limited powers over their tenants, since, for religious reasons, they were unable to hold courts that gave out the death penalty or amputated hands. A protector who did the dirty work of administering tough justice, enforcing taxes, and leading a warband made sense. So, too, did his construction of castles, the better to defend beleaguered religious communities.

In return, protectors, or *Vogts* (from the Latin *advocatus*, meaning 'a person who gives aid'), kept back a portion of fines and taxes and helped themselves to a swathe of other revenues, from the right to seize straying cattle to the emolument owed to the church's bell ringer. But they also appointed their retainers as sub-Vogts, with an equal call on church revenues. Over time, lords bought and sold the office of protector, accumulating as many as four hundred churches, abbeys, and convents apiece, which they treated as part and parcel of their own private lands. Getting rid of a Vogt once he was in place was difficult, particularly since most lords regarded the office as hereditary and as a benefit to be passed on to their heirs.[8]

Vogts were just one type of power, since lords also built up their own personal apparatus of control. Increasingly, they relied on the people they knew best, their household servants. Energetic bodyguards and cost-conscious cellarers counted among the brawniest and brainiest of their staff, so they were re-deployed as warriors and estate administrators. These servants were at the time known as 'ministerials' (*ministeriales*), but the term was broad enough to include both the checker of weights in the marketplace and the helmeted thug who enforced his lord's will. Many ate at the lord's table and shared in the distribution of booty, but their masters often gave them a slice of land as a reward for good service or in lieu of salary. As son succeeded father in the lord's service, the ministerials' lands became hereditary, and they began to recruit their own ministerials. Many also copied a noble style, building their own castles, giving themselves the prefix of *von* (of) followed by the name of their main seat, adopting coats of arms, and feuding with their neighbours.

The ministerials were a new nobility. Ever conscious of their humble origins, ambitious ministerials commissioned epic poems and new versions of the Arthurian romances that pointedly taught how esteem had to be earned rather than coming from birth. Over time, some made it into the aristocracy of greater nobles, distinguished by their extensive lands, exalted marriages, and political influence. Many of the flower of Central European nobility were of humble ministerial origin, with ancestors who were cooks, stablemen, and carters. A few, like the princes of Liechtenstein, made it to the very top, hiding their obscure origins and lack of pedigree behind tall stories of ennoblement by Charlemagne or Julius Caesar. Others moved into the cities, using their landed income to buy the chief posts in urban government and the best houses.

Monarchs used ministerials too, as warriors and administrators, also rewarding them with slices of land and choice offices: one became the duke of Ravenna and regent of Sicily, another the archbishop of Hamburg-Bremen, and one more the commander of a band of a thousand soldiers. The royal lands in Saxony were critical to the rule of the Salian emperors, constituting, in one contemporary description, 'the emperor's kitchen'. Henry IV imposed several hundred ministerials to administer his estates there, ousting the local noblemen from influence and driving them into revolt. But it was under the Hohenstaufen emperors, who replaced the Salian line of rulers in 1138, that the ministerials had their heyday. More than a thousand ministerials made up the backbone of Hohenstaufen rule, enforcing the imperial will in the countryside and recruiting military contingents to back up their master's instructions with force. Ministerials took charge of a stretch of royal estate, concentrated mostly in Swabia, transforming the southwestern parts of the German lands into a Hohenstaufen fortress.[9]

There were in the Holy Roman Empire about twenty duchies around 1150. Some, like Franconia, were just empty shells, whose lands the Saxon and Salian rulers had given away to churchmen. Others, like Lorraine, had been partitioned among heirs. But in a handful of duchies, the dukes had built up a strong regional power, making the local counts into their men, controlling monasteries and churches through their own appointed Vogts, and imposing their will through their ministerials. The most important of these duchies were Saxony, Swabia, and Bavaria, and around these clustered a string of lesser duchies like Brabant, Carinthia, and Austria. The office of duke lay in the royal gift and was a mark of prestige and, from around 1200, carried the rank of prince. In return for the ducal title, monarchs expected loyalty. The cost of denying the ruler the devotion that he felt was his due could be high. Henry the Lion would learn this in his quarrel with Emperor Frederick I (ruled 1152–1190).

The Hohenstaufen emperor Frederick I Barbarossa, or 'Red Beard', was hard up. On paper, the income of Frederick's court looks impressive. Gathered not in money but in kind, the annual take amounted to 1,770 cows, 16,590 hogs, 2,802 suckling pigs, 5,160 geese, 28,500 chickens, 75,750 eggs, 46,440 cheeses, more than 2,000 cartloads of beer, and at least 400 cartloads of wine. But Frederick travelled with a retinue of about a thousand men, which works out at one egg per man every five days and a chicken a fortnight, although washed down with five litres of beer daily. Plainly, the list is incomplete, but it suggests how much it cost Frederick just to keep his retinue fed. Frederick looked to Italy for funds, mounting five expeditions in pursuit of the loot of its cities. When in 1174 Duke Henry the Lion of Saxony failed to send a contingent to back Frederick in Italy, the emperor turned on him.[10]

Named after the device on his coat of arms, Henry the Lion was a threat to everyone. As duke of Saxony, he had antagonized the local nobility by demanding that they convert their freehold estates into land held from him as their overlord, which meant he could dispossess them at will. But Henry was not just duke of Saxony. Through his father, he was the duke of Bavaria too, so the empire's other great men were wary of him. Summoned to court to explain his disobedience, Henry found he had no backers and so stayed away, compounding his crime. In 1180, the court stripped Henry of his lands for the crime of high treason. Frederick duly handed Bavaria over to the Wittelsbachs, hitherto a family of Bavarian counts, but he broke up Saxony. Although he allowed Henry to keep the area around Brunswick and Lüneburg, Frederick gave most of Saxony to the archbishop of Cologne and to Henry's neighbour Bernhard of Anhalt.

Saxony was not destroyed, but it was much diminished. The duchy that took its place under the descendants of Bernhard of Anhalt now mostly lay east of the Elbe River, eventually splitting in two halves centred upon Wittenberg and Lauenburg. But the fall of Saxony was as nothing compared to the collapse of Swabia less than a century later. Emperor Frederick I Barbarossa died in 1190 in Anatolia (modern-day

Turkey) while on crusade. His son Henry succeeded as emperor, being crowned the next year in Rome. Henry VI (ruled 1190–1197) spent most of his reign fighting in Italy, trying to make good his wife's claim to the kingdom of Sicily. His premature death, at the age of just thirty-two, plunged the empire into civil war, with one faction backing Henry's son Frederick, another supporting Henry's brother, Philip, and a third championing the son of Henry the Lion, Otto of Brunswick. Almost two decades of warfare followed, until the murder of Philip in 1208 and the deposition of Otto in 1215 left the way for Frederick to become emperor.

Swabia was the Hohenstaufen heartland, where the Hohenstaufen rulers had the bulk of their estates, castles, and ministerials. In the long civil war, Frederick II gave away vast chunks of land to buy support. He continued this policy once in power, for he was ready to sacrifice his possessions north of the Alps in order to rebuild Hohenstaufen power in Italy and Sicily. But Frederick's grandiose ambitions died with him in 1250. His son Conrad outlived him by just four years, and his grandson Conradin was never able to make good his claims to power in the German lands. Betrayed to his enemies in southern Italy, he finally perished on the executioner's block in Naples in 1268. In the chaos, avaricious lords seized what remained of the Hohenstaufen and imperial lands in Swabia, while the duchy's now lordless ministerials set themselves up as independent knights, surviving off what were often trifling properties guarded by tumbledown castles.

After Lorraine, Franconia, and Saxony, Swabia was the last great duchy to fall. Across the Holy Roman Empire, land and power were unpackaged, leaving behind just splinters of territory. The owners of these shards treated them as family possessions, dividing their lands between their heirs. So, what had once been Swabia was by the last decades of the thirteenth century a divided space, shared and fought over by several dozen counts, bishops and abbots, and a host of minor lords and knights. But irrespective of rank, the new owners exercised an almost complete authority within their domains, holding law courts, taxing, summoning assemblies of their chief men to discuss policy, and fielding their own armies. The loser in all this was the monarch, whose nominal subjects pillaged his lands, power, and authority. In one vivid description from the late thirteenth century, the emperor was shown no longer as the eagle that he bore on his coat of arms but as just a woodpecker tapping a rotten tree.[11]

Whereas in England, France, and much of thirteenth-century Europe, power was becoming increasingly concentrated at the top, in the Holy Roman Empire it was passing downwards. Rights that elsewhere belonged to monarchs became the personal prerogatives of local lords. The consequence is visible on any map illustrating the Holy Roman Empire's internal arrangement. If detailed enough, the map will show a mosaic of a thousand or so separate statelets—duchies, principalities, lordships, and petty dominions, sometimes just a few kilometres across. Giving a precise figure to these political units is impossible since, month by month, death and division added to their number or the expiry of a family suddenly rubbed a territory off the map, swallowed up by its neighbours. Most of these statelets had at least one castle, thrown up by their owners as a mark of prestige and as a stronghold. Within the territory of modern-day Germany, historians reckon on about twenty-five thousand stone castles surviving from the Middle Ages, but a systematic counting has only just begun.[12]

Yet something was happening in the east. On the fringes of the German lands, ambitious men were carving out their own spaces and founding new principalities at a distance from the traditional centres of royal power. The Holy Roman Empire had no capital city. Instead, the monarch and his retinue journeyed from place to place, eating up the local landscape before moving on. In the twelfth and early thirteenth centuries, kings and emperors increasingly stuck in their travels to the Rhineland and Franconia, where there was the greatest abundance of welcoming abbeys, and to Swabia, where they had their private estates. Except for the imperial palace at Goslar, most of Saxony was outside their orbit. Coronation in Rome and the wealth of the Italian cities also drew them dreamily southwards. The Slavonic

'Wild East' was remote from their vision and itinerant kingship. It was ready for the taking.

The lands east of the Elbe and running south of the Baltic Sea to the Polish frontier had been settled by Slavs in the seventh century. This vast swathe of territory, reaching more than six hundred kilometres from Kiel to the Polish port of Gdańsk, was sparsely populated, intersected by sluggish rivers, and a mix of forest, marshland, and sandy heaths. Travellers crossing its terrain complained of the mire that swallowed up horses, the monstrous snakes, and the flapping and croaking of the cranes. Back in the ninth and tenth centuries, Charlemagne and, later on, the first Saxon rulers had punched into this space, founding shadowy marcher lordships or margraviates that may have reached as far eastwards as the Oder River. But the land had been lost in a series of Slav uprisings beginning in the 980s that had pushed the conquerors back to where they had started. As one chronicler reported, all that was left were broken walls and fallen embankments.[13]

German chroniclers were dismissive of the Slavs, but foreign travellers were more discerning. Around 960, the Spanish Jewish merchant Ibn-Yaqub recorded the might of the Slav Abodrite realm, describing its walled capital and sanctuary at Gorod (now Mecklenburg), its abundance of horses, and its warriors' iron mail and weapons. Others reported the magnificence of the temple at Arkona on the Baltic island of Rügen, with its purple roof and supersized carving of their four-headed god, from whose drinking horn priests divined the future. Further east, pagan Pomerania sustained a lively commerce in amber, slaves, and fur that drew in merchants from as far as the Balkans. Indeed, so many Greeks were trading on the Pomeranian coast that one otherwise knowledgeable contemporary thought that the Baltic Sea must loop round to join the Black Sea. Pomerania's trade with the far north brought the Pomeranian dog to Central Europe. Originally a powerful sled dog akin to a huskie, the Pomeranian has since been cruelly miniaturized by breeding.[14]

German bishops looked eastwards to harvest souls. But they knew that conversion depended on military muscle and on inducements that were more than just spiritual. In 1108, a letter written on behalf of the archbishop of Magdeburg and the leading frontier bishops appealed for help:

> These unbelievers are the worst of men, but their land is the best for meat, honey, grain, and wild fowl, and if it were properly cultivated there would be an incomparable abundance of all sorts of produce—so say those that know. So, you Saxons, Franks, Lorrainers, and Flemings, most famed conquerors of the world, you can save your souls and, if you want, have the best land to live in.[15]

But on the other side of Central Europe, the Poles were busy too. Early in the twelfth century, the Polish king Bolesław the Wry-Mouthed (he had a twisted lip) asserted his right to Pomerelia in eastern Pomerania, which lay south of the port of Gdańsk. From there, he pushed westwards, capturing Szczecin on the Oder in 1121. The Pomeranian ruler Wartislaw promptly surrendered, dismissed his twenty-four wives, and embraced Christianity, after which Bolesław recruited Bishop Otto of Bamberg to convert his people. Bishop Otto did so with gusto. To impress the Slavs, he decked out his priests in the costliest robes and won over their leaders with expensive gifts. Otto's biographers duly noted the tally of converts: twenty here, seven thousand there, and in the Pomeranian capital of Wolin no fewer than 22,156 souls. They listed, too, the temples demolished, sacred groves felled, and idols destroyed.[16]

The pace of conquest and conversion accelerated in the middle of the twelfth century. In 1147, Pope Eugenius III launched the Second Crusade. The crusade came in two parts. While the main Christian army went to Palestine to shore up the crusader kingdom of Jerusalem, Eugenius directed a second army to make war on the pagan Slavs, and he promised that the northern crusaders would receive the same spiritual benefits and forgiveness of sins as their counterparts fighting in the Middle East. Although a crusade against pagans rather than

Muslims, the distinction between the two may not have been obvious to the participants. In Central Europe in the twelfth century, all non-Christians counted equally as *saladinistas*, or followers of the Turkish Sultan Saladin.[17]

The Christian forces pushed eastwards, with their principal host under the command of Albrecht the Bear of Anhalt—so named after the device on his shield. Albrecht led his army to Szczecin, unaware that the Pomeranians there were already Christians. But he was not to be thwarted. Pribislaw, the ruler of the Hevellian Slavs, had long been a Christian and was godfather to Albrecht's son, although he had done nothing to convert his subjects, reckoning his power too weak. On his deathbed, he renewed an earlier promise to Albrecht to leave him his territories, for he had no sons of his own. On news of Pribislaw's death in 1150, Albrecht smartly overran the Hevellian territories, although it took him several years to capture the main redoubt at Brandenburg.

Albrecht thought to set himself up as an independent prince, adopting the title 'Albrecht by grace of God margrave in the north', but it was an impossible ambition. His territories west of the Elbe were held, at least in theory, from the ruler and he could not extricate himself from the bonds that tied him to the Holy Roman Empire. Instead, he took the plainer title of margrave of Brandenburg and began the region's cultivation, on the edge of which he built the fortress of Spandau. To tame the landscape, he called in immigrants, mainly from the Low Countries as they were skilled in irrigation. He authorized the building of settlements, recruited farmers, whom he lured there with promises of tax relief, and attracted knights to his service. His descendants would continue his work, establishing monasteries and churches, founding the city of Berlin, and pushing onwards to the Oder River. In the twelfth century alone, they and their fellow frontier lords settled perhaps as many as two hundred thousand Germans east of the Elbe River, and a similar number in the century following.[18]

Brandenburg was Albrecht's creation, but it came at a cost to the native population. As one chronicler approvingly noted:

Now, however, because God gave plentiful aid and victory to our duke Albrecht and to the other princes, the Slavs have everywhere been crushed and driven out. A people strong and without number have come from the bounds of the ocean and taken possession of the territories of the Slavs. They have built cities and churches and have grown in riches beyond all estimation.[19]

In fact, the Slavs were not extirpated. Deprived of their religion and with their villages reorganized or uprooted, they found a new identity as Germans, although often speaking curious hybrids of German and Slavic. Even so, some fifty thousand Slav-speaking Wends (or Sorbs) survive to this day between the Elbe and Oder Rivers.

Albrecht was far from unique. Across Central Europe, German lords were pushing eastwards, founding churches, imposing unfamiliar taxes, and building new villages for migrants whom they recruited from the west. The lands they took were welded into the Holy Roman Empire, so the old Abodrite realm became the duchy of Mecklenburg, and the mainly Slav marchlands in the southeast, the duchies of Styria, Carinthia, and Carniola. Pomerania, too, became a part of the empire when in 1181 Wartislaw's son and successor, Bogusław I, threw off Polish overlordship for the title of Duke of the Empire. The power of the emperors may have been waning, but the Holy Roman Empire was not. Its princes and great men were busy thrusting its boundaries outwards and building cities, villages, and abbeys in what had been the Wild East of Slavonic settlement.[20]

CHAPTER 6

The Mongol-Tatars, New Cities, and New Knights

I N CENTRAL EUROPE, THE FURTHER EASTWARD THE TRAVELLER went, the more frustrating the journey. Once across the Rhine or Danube, the Roman roads petered out, to be replaced by trackways, marks cut into trees, and causeways built of roughly hewn logs. In Central Europe's interior, the forests seemed endless, much the same as Julius Caesar had described them more than a millennium before. Pushing into western Bohemia, an eleventh-century German army was outfoxed by their density, for every ridge yielded a new treescape stretching to the horizon. The exhausted troops cast off their armour and so proved easy prey for the Czechs, who cultivated the forest precisely as a defence. But once through the trees, travellers to the eastern parts of Central Europe invariably remarked on the abundance of cornfields and pastureland, the rivers teeming with sturgeon, catfish, and pike, and in Bohemia the wealth of the mines.[1]

Even so, right through to the thirteenth century the people living in the eastern half of Central Europe were thought to be awful. Bishop Otto of Freising, who crossed Hungary in the 1140s, described its inhabitants as being 'of disgusting aspect, with deep-set eyes and short stature . . . barbarous and ferocious in their habits and language . . . caricatures of men'. As for the Poles, they were 'practically barbarous and very warlike . . . and devour one another in time of famine'. Writing more than a century later, an anonymous French geographer concurred. By his reckoning, the Hungarians were small, solidly built, dark-skinned, and bellicose; the Poles, although more beautiful in appearance, shared their land with monstrous creatures like unicorns,

centaurs, and tigers; and the Czechs were thieves. Perils lurked below
ground too, in the subterranean chambers of Central Europe's dwarf
kings. As one French monk assures us, in Transylvania in 1235, the
stunted denizens of the underworld suddenly burst from their cav-
erns, riding in the open on scarlet steeds and staining red anyone rash
enough to take hold of them.[2]

Western visitors considered the eastern lands economically backward. They were probably right. Traversing the German lands, travellers
saw cities in abundance—Cologne, Worms, Würzburg, Regensburg,
and Passau. But from the Bavarian border, they found little of worth.
A French monk who joined Louis VII of France marching through
Central Europe at the time of the Second Crusade in 1147 wrote of
Esztergom in Hungary as a 'noble city' but saw little else to praise until
he was well into the territory of the Byzantine Empire. Otto of Freising was shocked by what he saw in Hungary—hovels built of reeds,
and rarely even of wood, and in the summer simple tents. The French
geographer was less critical, counting nine cities in Hungary, but even
he considered the number small given the kingdom's size.[3]

But what most offended Western commentators was that much
of Central Europe did not conform to their understanding of how
societies should work. In particular, the new kingdoms on the eastern side of Central Europe lacked what were thought at the time
to be the common denominators of civilization: noblemen with es-
cutcheons, a culture of knighthood with all its chivalric display, a
lavish royal household with a welcoming monarch, a merchant class
of wealthy urban patricians, councils of great men, courts of law
staffed by learned judges, and infant institutions that hemmed in the
ruler. Otto of Freising put the contrast starkly in his description of
the Hungarians:

> They all render such obedience to their prince that every man re-
> gards it as wrong, I will not say to enrage him by open contradic-
> tion, but even to annoy him by secret whisperings. . . . If anyone
> of the rank of count has even in a trivial matter offended against

the king, an emissary from the court, though he be of very lowly station and unattended, seizes him in the midst of his retinue, puts him in chains, and drags him off to various forms of punishment. No formal sentence is asked of the prince through his peers, as is the custom among us, no opportunity of defending himself is granted the accused, but the will of the prince alone is held by all as sufficient.[4]

Hungarian countryfolk were different too, and Otto noted their servility. He was right to the extent that the monarch allocated compulsory manufacturing, military, and provisioning tasks to large swathes of the population. After all, they were his people, living on his land, and he could do with them as he chose. Villages of cooks who served the royal household in rotation continued in Hungary through to the sixteenth century. This was not just a feature of Hungary but also widespread throughout Poland and Bohemia, where there were service villages whose inhabitants the ruler had assigned to cattle rearing, saddle making, smelting, the production of shields and weapons, exercising his dogs, and so on. As one early Czech chronicle observed, the ruler had the right to dispose of people as he wanted, making them serve him as millers, bakers, smiths, furriers, and so forth. Examples from Poland suggest that rulers might move service peoples from one village to another, according to their needs.[5]

The coercive organization of large parts of the Central European countryside explains how earthworks were so rapidly erected there, long ramparts and wastelands created to deter invaders, military roads driven through the forests, and complex irrigation channels dug that were over several thousand kilometres long. This type of top-down social and economic administration was completely missing in the German lands to the west except in a few places around rivers, where fishing rights were tied to the maintenance of the stream. It is perhaps the most important feature of the internal arrangement of Bohemia, Hungary, and Poland before the thirteenth century and a common denominator in their development that is unique.[6]

All this would change in the thirteenth century. Central Europe became more Western and absorbed its culture and civilization. The process was a long one, but it was hastened by the arrival of a new and unexpected foe from the east—the Mongol-Tatars. Like the Huns and the Hungarians before them, the Mongol-Tatars would transform Central Europe.

The Mongol-Tatar Empire was built by Genghis Khan (lived c. 1160–1227). Having overrun northern China, Genghis Khan pressed westwards. Like its Hun predecessor, the Mongol-Tatar Empire was designed to extract tribute from subject peoples and it rested on horsepower. To sustain their war machine, the Mongol-Tatars deployed about half the world's total horse population of twenty million, for each warrior came equipped with a small herd of fresh mounts. Mongol-Tatar warriors were only lightly equipped, but horsepower gave them speed and they were able to move at twice the pace of their sedentary foes. Their Blitzkrieg tactics were matched in victory by an equal ferocity. Defeated peoples were frequently massacred entire. Only a few, like the original Tatars, were recruited as equals into the Mongol-led army.[7]

The Mongol-Tatars sacked the great Central Asian cities of Tashkent in 1219 and Samarkand the next year. Genghis Khan died in 1227, but expansion continued under his son and successor, Ogedei Khan. Ogedei instructed his nephew Batu, who ruled the Mongol-Tatar Empire north of the Black Sea, to press further against the western kingdoms. Batu's forces devastated the Russian principalities, sacking Kyiv in 1240 so completely that, we are told, only its owls survived. On this occasion, the Mongol-Tatars proved adept at siege warfare, bringing up rams and catapults to break the city's walls. Since it was a Mongol-Tatar tradition that the blood of princes should not be spilled, Batu Khan crushed to death the Kyivan ruler and his family beneath a platform on which he feasted with his chief men.

The irruption of the Mongol-Tatars put to flight a nomadic Turkic tribe called the Cumans, who had previously been living between the mouth of the Danube and the Crimean Peninsula. Groups of Cumans now pushed into Hungary, where King Béla IV (ruled 1235–1270) gave them a reluctant welcome. But Batu regarded the Cumans as his servants, for they too were, he said, 'people who lived in felt tents' and so automatically his subjects. He demanded through messengers (one of whom was apparently an English adventurer) that Béla give up the Cumans and submit to him. Béla was unskilled in diplomacy and he lacked the ready wit of Emperor Frederick II who, on being asked by Batu's envoys to submit and take a title from their master, had replied that he was only qualified to be a falconer. Instead, Béla refused to answer Batu's letters and he slew the khan's emissaries.[8]

Béla did not know that, in 1219, when the shah of the Persian Khwarezmid Empire had executed Mongol-Tatar envoys, Genghis Khan had destroyed his lands in revenge. Now, Batu Khan did the same, launching an immediate attack even though it was the spring—the Mongol-Tatars preferred campaigning in the winter when the ground was hardened by frost. Three armies broke into Hungary in 1241, destroying a Polish army on the way and sacking the Polish cities of Cracow, Sandomierz, and Wrocław. Once in Hungary, they made short work of Bela's army at Mohi (Mohu). Having routed the Hungarians, Batu ordered a detachment to hunt down the king, forcing him to flee all the way to the Dalmatian island of Trogir.[9]

For a year, the Mongol-Tatars occupied Hungary, ransacking and slaying its people. A surviving witness recounted long periods of hiding in woods, the destruction of villages and towns, the ruses that the Mongol-Tatars employed to trick people into coming into the open, and the famine. As many as a third of the population may have died of starvation and the sword. The consequences are etched in the archaeological record. Rescue excavations undertaken in Hungary over the last twenty years in the course of motorway construction have brought to light from the time of the invasion buildings burnt down along with their inhabitants, pathetic hoards of farm implements, and what archaeologists intriguingly call 'deviant burials'—corpses thrown into ditches or left where they fell, and pits full of body parts. The gnawed bones of the dead are grisly testimony to the famine that accompanied Hungary's occupation. A Bavarian chronicler summed up the cataclysmic outcome of the Mongol-Tatar invasion—'In this year (1241) the kingdom of Hungary, which had existed for 350 years, was destroyed by the nation of the Tatars.'[10]

Their punishment delivered, the Mongol-Tatars departed in 1242 as swiftly as they had come, and Béla IV was left to rebuild his shattered kingdom. Béla feared the invaders' imminent return, but he had seen how stone defences had thwarted them—the walls of the archbishop's fortress at Esztergom had held despite a barrage of catapult fire; likewise the fortified monasteries at Tihany and Pannonhalma. So, Béla ordered the construction of new royal cities encircled with stone walls. The population of Pest, which lay exposed on the edge of the Hungarian Plain, had been easy prey for the Mongol-Tatars. In the 1240s, Béla accordingly moved the survivors across the Danube to the Buda hill opposite and he recruited a consortium of merchants and minters to build a new city and gird it with a five-kilometre-long stone wall, much of which is still standing. Elsewhere, Béla instructed that Gradec, the future Zagreb, be given a wall, and he moved the citizens of Esztergom and Székesfehérvár into the shelter of the existing stone ramparts. Over the next few decades, most of Hungary's cities were enclosed with walls.

To repair the population, Béla encouraged the immigration of German settlers, and he granted the newcomers extensive rights of self-government and temporary freedom from taxation. He designated land for settlement on which they either built new cities, often from scratch, or founded villages in what had previously been wilderness. Many of the newcomers moved to Transylvania, turning what had been a trickle of German immigration in the twelfth century into a flood. On the rim of the Carpathians in the southeastern corner of Transylvania, they established the so-called Saxon Land. Specially appointed agents (or *locatores*) recruited settlers, mostly from northern Germany and the Low Countries, and they advertised the opportunities available there. Later generations would talk of a Pied Piper whose music had lured German children eastwards to make their home in the Carpathian Mountains.

Béla had also seen that armoured knights could crush light horsemen, driving them from the field by the sheer weight of their armour and steeds. Indeed, at Mohi, heavily armoured knights, drawn from the religious order of the Templars, had scattered the Mongol-Tatars' ponies and might have won the day had they not been halted by concentrated catapult fire. Béla accordingly started converting Hungarian landowners into heavy horsemen, equipped with chain mail and plated armour. Royal grants of land now came with military service assumed and a new literary genre extolled martial and chivalric virtues. Leading Hungarians began to give their children names borrowed from the knightly romances, christening them Achilles, Hector, Tristan, and Lancelot. They invented illustrious pedigrees, adopted heraldic devices, and dressed in the latest courtly fashions.

Warriors built castles too, breaking with the tradition that only the king had the right to do so. In the eighty years following the Mongol-Tatar invasion, about two hundred new stone castles were thrown up in Hungary, mostly by members of the new military elite that Béla had called into being. Some were simple towers, but others included a great hall, chapel, and living quarters and were surrounded by large earthwork embankments or curtain walls that created courtyards for the new sport of jousting. Villages of peasant tenants provided the resources from which the warriors drew their wealth and bought their armour. As they became acculturated into the mainstream of European knighthood, the warriors assumed the name of noblemen—a title seldom used in Hungary before the mid-thirteenth century. Noble rank was prestigious and hereditary, and at least in theory could only be bestowed by the king.[11]

To maintain the new noble class, Béla allowed the old service villages to fall into disrepair. Many royal servants were downgraded to tenant farmers, now providing for an armed knight rather than the king. The royal lands on which they worked were in effect privatized, with the king allocating them to local champions along with their villages. Others were simply seized by strongmen. Some former royal servants managed to make a dubious leap into the new elite, calling themselves noblemen and trusting that no one would challenge their rank. Generations later, their descendants would find that they had no written record of their nobility, in which case they would petition the king for a charter to replace the 'lost' original. These so-called titles of new donation, backdating the grant of noble status and the lands attached, are commonplace in the fourteenth century.[12]

Out of the ruin of the Mongol-Tatar invasion, Béla IV made a new kingdom that had walled cities, German settlers, and a castled knighthood resting upon an elite of noblemen with dependent villages. Although the circumstances that gave rise to this transformation were exceptional, the same pattern of change may be observed elsewhere in Central Europe. Though taking place less rapidly, it was hastened by the menace from the east and the ever-present fear of a new Mongol-Tatar attack. In Poland, Bohemia, and the German lands, as well as in Hungary, society was becoming 'feudal'—an ugly but useful word that sums up the way land and power were parcelled up and distributed downwards.

Throughout Central Europe, kings and rulers seldom rested easily in their beds, for brothers and sons vied for their thrones and were often ready to use violence. In place of an orderly scheme of succession was a body of conflicting principles to any of which a claimant might appeal—the support of the great men or of the church hierarchy, primogeniture (the superior right of the eldest son), seniority within the family, and self-promotion on the grounds of being the most suitable. In pursuit of their alleged rights, pretenders frequently appealed to neighbouring rulers, who then set about plundering in their name. Between 1140 and 1198, Bohemia had ten separate periods of rule, shared among eight dukes (several ruled twice), of which no fewer than six ended in either deposition or abdication.

Poland was most affected by the lack of clarity in the succession, which resulted in bouts of civil war and foreign intervention throughout the eleventh, twelfth, and thirteenth centuries. The kingdom fell apart, eventually into nineteen separate duchies by the 1280s, and the title of king was abandoned. Fragmentation had important economic and cultural consequences. Military competition encouraged rival Polish dukes and warlords to expand their material resources. They did this using the same strategies as Béla IV in Hungary, populating the land with immigrants mainly drawn from established communities in the west and luring them eastwards with promises of tax breaks and large farms. The newcomers brought with them technological innovations—crop rotation, water mills, and the heavy plough, or *carruca*, which cut deep furrows and turned the soil, making it more productive than the stick plough that just scratched the earth. They organized their villages to be agriculturally efficient, with uniform plots that they arranged in patterns according to the landscape. So, in upland areas the plots were long strips that often extended several kilometres as the scrub behind was cleared, whereas in the lowlands the villages had room for a central square.

A Flemish verse survives that tells of the new settlers' hopes:

> *We want to ride to the Eastland,*
> *We want to go to the Eastland,*
> *All over the green heaths,*
> *Briskly over the heaths.*
> *It's better there.*

The verse goes on to promise a hearty welcome, big houses to live in, and the chance to drink beer and wine morning and night.[13]

Despite these inducements, annual migration to Poland probably numbered only several thousand persons, but it was concentrated mostly in the western parts and transformed the linguistic character of much of the countryside, switching it from Polish to German with an intermediate dialect made up of both languages. To encourage more settlers on their estates, landowners extended the same privileges to anyone belonging to the native population, effectively stealing their neighbours' tenants by offering better terms. The Black Death and attendant epidemics, which swept through Central Europe from the 1350s and which may have reduced its population by up to a third, would later prompt a similar competition between landowners and further concessions to the rural workforce. Across Poland, therefore, Polish and German villagers alike shared the benefits of the so-called German law—much reduced taxes, self-government under hereditary headmen, and the right to frame their own bylaws.[14]

The same principles applied to urban centres, except that their self-government was more complete, since city councils were elected and foundation charters itemized the citizens' rights and freedoms. By the end of the thirteenth century more than a hundred chartered cities existed in the Polish province of Silesia alone. These often borrowed their local laws from cities further west, thus replicating the legal arrangements of Magdeburg, Nuremberg, and Vienna. Law codes were not just sets of rules but also guides to how a citizen should behave, to the ceremonies which punctuated city life and made for a sense of civic solidarity, and to the geography of settlement, with each city having a large central piazza around which the wealthy had their homes. The new cities of Central Europe were smaller and poorer than their counterparts in the West, but in their layout and in the manner of their self-government, they were identically fashioned.[15]

Above all, the Polish dukes needed knights. Accordingly, the dukes allocated land to warriors, and they in turn recruited settlers to cultivate the soil. There were plenty of impoverished foreign knights eager for estates. The earliest German courtly romance, from around 1050, tells of the knight Ruodlieb, who, because his lord had not rewarded his loyalty, forsook his homeland to seek his fortune at a distant court. Grants of land, or fiefs, brought wealth and prestige. The Austrian troubadour Walther von der Vogelweide (died c. 1230) recorded in doggerel his delight at eventually receiving one:

> *Hey, everyone, I have my fief!*
> *For my toes in winter, it'll be a relief.*
> *No more over nothing to be bossed about,*

For the great noble king has now helped me out.
Above all my neighbours he's had me raised.
It's why I'm now singing that he should be praised.[16]

In Silesia in western Poland, more than four hundred German knights settled and received grants of land, mostly in the later thirteenth century, and they went on to found villages, churches, and castles and to marry into Polish families, with their children assuming a Polish identity. But it was not just Germans that Poland's dukes recruited as knights. Poles, too, were awarded land. Many of these grants were originally fiefs, in the sense that they could not be sold and that they reverted back to the ruler if the holder had no heirs. But over time their origins were often forgotten, and they were treated like freeholds that might be sold or exchanged without the ruler's permission.[17]

The Domesday variety of feudalism in Norman England describes a type of organization where the king distributed land to his barons in return for their military support and loyalty, and the barons in turn apportioned it to tenants, and they to individual knights. By contrast, hierarchies in Poland and much of Central Europe were typically flatter, with the ruler at the apex or, in the German lands, the duke, count, or margrave and below him just a single layer of landowning noblemen. Although some gradations applied, the nobles generally considered themselves equal because each stood in the same direct personal relationship to the ruler, which was understood in terms of faithfulness or fidelity (*fidelitas*), good companionship, a seat (at least in theory) at the ruler's table, and even his affection. More practically, noblemen were expected to serve on campaign, and they in turn anticipated that deeds of valour done on the ruler's behalf would result in further rewards. Land, knight service, and faithfulness constituted in Central Europe the marks of nobility, just as they did throughout much of Western Europe.

One of the most remarkable finds to come from medieval Central Europe is also one of the smallest, being just seven centimetres long. Dating from around 1290, it is a gold plate attached to a belt buckle that was found two hundred years ago in a field at Kigyóspuszta on the Hungarian Plain. On the plate four knights, bearing shields and lances and with cylindrical helmets, clash in a tournament while musicians blow trumpets and beat tambourines. The representations on the plate are testimony to the rapidity with which Hungary's emerging nobility embraced the common code of European knighthood. But there is more to the plate than that, for it comes from the grave of a Cuman chieftain, whose forebears had half a century before fled to Hungary for fear of the Mongol-Tatars and settled there. Acculturation into the European mainstream of courtly fashion and chivalric display was a process powerful enough even to accommodate the recent offspring of a Turkic nomad.[18]

CHAPTER 7

Dynastic Change, Charles IV of Bohemia, and the Prophets of the Antichrist

O N AVERAGE, DYNASTIES HAVE A 15 PER CENT EXPIRY RATE every twenty-five years, which means that more than half will fail every century, mainly through lack of sons. (Those that permit female succession will last longer.) But the dynasties of Central Europe's earliest rulers often survived for centuries. The line of St Stephen in Hungary, which went back to the ninth-century Prince Árpád, lasted for four centuries; so too did the Bohemian Přemyslid dukes and kings and Mieszko's heirs in Poland. The Babenberg family, whose members were first appointed margraves of Austria in the 970s, survived almost three centuries. Although members of the same dynasty frequently fought each other, a long period of rule by one family made for territorial cohesion. Since dynasties often generated saints, an aura of sacredness and of divine approval also attached to their rule.[1]

All this changed in the thirteenth and early fourteenth centuries, when the biological good luck of Central Europe's governing dynasties ran out. One by one, they fell. The Hungarian heirs to St Stephen died out in 1301, and the Bohemian Přemyslids in 1306. The Polish descendants of Mieszko temporarily defied the trend but eventually expired in 1370. The same dissipation happened in the Holy Roman Empire. The Babenbergs of Austria came to an end in 1246; the Hohenstaufens, who had governed the empire since 1138 but had a pedigree going back to the tenth century, finally gave up the ghost in 1254, and the main line of Albrecht the Bear's descendants in Brandenburg faltered in 1320.

Newcomers took their place: Bavarian Wittelsbachs, the Habsburgs from southern Swabia (now Switzerland), and the Luxembourg family from the western edge of the empire. Complete outsiders came too, most notably the Angevins of Naples, who at the beginning of the fourteenth century captured the kingdom of Hungary. Between them, these new families scythed up Central Europe.

After the death in 1254 of the last Hohenstaufen, Emperor Frederick II's son Conrad, the empire went through a painful interregnum, when unlikely candidates vied for the imperial throne—Count William of Holland, the Spanish Alfonso X of Castile, and the son of King John of England, Richard of Cornwall. In the attending chaos, order broke down, as the rival candidates' supporters plundered the Hohenstaufen and royal estates and then turned on each other. 'The days of evil approach, and the evil is growing,' wrote one chronicler about 1270. Others recorded the passage of comets in the sky, a woman giving birth to quadruplets, and the discovery of a giant's bones as portents of gloom. Across the pillaged countryside, processions of penitents moved, whipping themselves to appease God's wrath and rehearsing older heresies.[2]

Over the previous centuries, the idea that the empire's great men should have a voice in deciding who the next ruler should be had given way to dynastic succession so that the most suitable of the previous monarch's kinsmen generally followed on the throne. The death of the last Hohenstaufen in 1254 without an obvious heir breathed fresh life into the electoral idea, although it was not yet clear who the electors were, other than they should include 'the best men and princes of the empire'. This imprecision allowed the ambitious Rudolf of Habsburg to fix the vote by assembling a handful of loyal princes to elect him king in 1273, rewarding several on the spot with his daughters in marriage.[3]

Rudolf went on to seize the Austrian lands from their illegal occupation by the Přemyslid Ottakar II of Bohemia, transforming the Habsburg family's status and fortunes. That was the problem. Once in place, rulers might use what remained of the prestige of their office to build up a strong regional power. So, on Rudolf's death in 1291, the churchmen, dukes, and margraves who claimed the right to elect the ruler began to alternate the royal title among the other families of the empire, even if that meant occasionally appointing a weakling, and to gradually fasten down their number. From 1298, just seven princes did the electing: the archbishops of Mainz, Trier, and Cologne; the duke of Saxony; the count palatine of the Rhine; the margrave of Brandenburg; and the king of Bohemia. They alone made the German king (or King of the Romans, as he was also known), who was crowned in Charlemagne's old chapel in Aachen. Only if he made it to Rome for coronation by the pope did the king become emperor.

The electors chose as Rudolf's successor the minor princeling Adolf of Nassau, whose rule proved so dismal that after six years in office (1292–1298) they deposed him, replacing him with Rudolf's son Albert 'the One-Eyed' (so-called because he was, as the result of a botched operation). But the Habsburgs disgraced themselves with a family feud that led to Albert's murder in 1308. Although the family held onto some semblance of the royal title by promoting their own anti-king, their reputation had suffered. It would not be until 1438 that the electors chose another Habsburg as ruler. The Habsburgs' diminished stock was nowhere clearer than on the marriage market. Whereas under kings Rudolf and Albert, the Habsburgs had married into some of Europe's principal royal houses, they now had to make do with minor German duchesses and obscure Polish dukes.

This was exactly the wrong time for the Habsburgs to have been wrong-footed, for it allowed a new dynasty to install itself in Central Europe and to roll up both the royal title and the crown of Bohemia. This was the house of Luxembourg, and for the next 130 years it would dominate Central Europe. The Luxembourgers' rise was unexpected, since they had in the thirteenth century been only minor counts, living on the western fringes of the Holy Roman Empire. But on Albert's death in 1308, the archbishop of Trier convinced his fellow electors that his brother, Count Henry of Luxembourg, was the best of a bad lot of candidates.

No sooner had he been elected than Henry announced his intention to go to Rome to receive the imperial crown, which no German ruler had sought for over sixty years. As it turned out, Henry's descent into Italy was a fiasco, for he had insufficient troops and cash, and so resorted to selling offices to the highest bidders. His progress southwards was blocked by the cities of Lombardy and it was not until 1312 that he managed to have himself crowned in Rome. The following year, Henry died of malaria. For the next three decades, Austrian Habsburgs and Bavarian Wittelsbachs fought over who should succeed Henry, dragging the empire down in yet another round of civil war.[4]

The Italian poet Dante lamented Henry's death—'imperial in the world . . . he came to rule an Italy that was still unready for him.' But it was not Italy where Henry's successors would make their mark but Bohemia. Taking advantage of the confusion that attended the extinction of the Přemyslid dynasty in 1306, Henry had just before his death arranged the marriage of his son John to the Bohemian princess Elizabeth, the sister of the last Přemyslid king of Bohemia. With ridiculously small forces, Henry had prised John into power, scattering his rivals, who had worn themselves out by fighting each other. In 1311, John was crowned king of Bohemia. The Luxembourg dynasty would rule Bohemia for the next 130 years.[5]

Bohemia's status was never certain. Its rulers had in the eleventh and twelfth centuries mostly been dukes, and they are occasionally mentioned as vassals of the German kings and emperors. In token of their lowlier office, the Bohemian rulers did not wear a crown but instead a ring of peacock feathers. Only a handful had the title of king, which was an honour bestowed by the emperors and not treated as hereditary. It was not until 1212 that Emperor Frederick II formally allowed Bohemia to have its own hereditary king, a reward (he explained) for the faithfulness displayed by its people and ruler to the Holy Roman Empire. Textbooks always draw a thick line around Bohemia to indicate that it was a part of the empire, but it never was completely. Like Switzerland and the Low Countries, Bohemia lay outside the empire's developing fiscal, judicial, and military structures and would remain a semidetached part of it right through to the nineteenth century.[6]

King John of Bohemia is the stuff of legend. An adventurer and warrior, he died heroically in 1346 on the field of Crécy, fighting with his French ally against the English. By this time completely blind, John instructed several of his knights to tie the bridles of their horses to his charger and lead him where the battle was most furious. Striking out in all directions, he raced into the enemy line, and was promptly shot to pieces with arrows, perishing along with all the knights to whom he had been tethered. But in respect of Bohemia, John's legacy is less glorious than his death. To pay for his campaigning, he sold off great chunks of the royal lands, robbed churches and tombs, and made concessions to the nobility that effectively put the kingdom's government in their hands. His son Charles was later to lament the destitution he inherited, where all the royal castles had been sold off and the palace in Prague so ruined that he was obliged to live at first in an ordinary house.[7]

Charles had fought at Crécy but had avoided his father's fate. Succeeding as king of Bohemia in 1346, he was soon after elected king of Germany. Worn out by three decades of conflict over who should rule in the empire, the electors were happy to renew the Luxembourg connection and crown Charles German king in Aachen. But Charles liked coronations, loading himself not only with the imperial crown, obtained in a lightning dash to Rome in 1355, but also with the crowns of Italy and Burgundy, neither of which conveyed any real power. For good measure, he also remodelled the Bohemian crown to make it more spectacular, adding sapphires, emeralds, and pearls, and at the top a cross containing a thorn from Christ's own crown, worn at His Crucifixion.

Charles prized relics almost as much as crowns. In a lifetime of travelling, he broke into tombs and extracted bones and mummified body parts from across the empire. In St Gallen, he had the monks open up the grave of St Gall itself and went off with a part of the skull. When he found the head of St Gallen's first abbot, St Othmar, to be stubbornly intact, he ordered the portion he wanted to be sawn off, along with chunks of the ribcage. In his zeal for a piece of St Nicholas, whose body was kept in a Prague convent, Charles cut off the saint's desiccated finger, but when it miraculously bled he decided not to keep it. Foreign rulers pandered to Charles's acquisitiveness. From the Byzantine emperor in Constantinople, he received portions of the bodies of the Old Testament patriarchs Abraham, Isaac, and Jacob, and from the king of Hungary, the tablecloth from the Last Supper.[8]

Relics provided a shortcut to salvation for those who prayed next to them or were present when they were publicly displayed. Popes listed the years off in Purgatory that came with their veneration. Charles gave most of his collection away, thereby distributing God's grace to the community of the faithful. To house his relics, he built or enlarged churches and chapels in Prague and elsewhere in Bohemia and commissioned expensive monstrances and caskets in which to display them. He diligently cultivated the saints whose bones he had amassed, promoting traditional Bohemian saints, saints associated with the line of Přemyslid rulers, and Charlemagne, who although never canonized was revered at the time as if a saint.

These choices were conventional enough, but Charles tweaked the selection. He added to his repertoire of favourite saints St Sigismund, an otherwise undistinguished king of Burgundy back in the sixth century who had a reputation for healing. Charles snatched most of the saint's corpse from the monks of Agaune (now in the Swiss Valais), who had tried to hide it on news of his arrival, and took it back to Prague. The only link between Charles and St Sigismund was the kingship of Burgundy, but Charles feted Sigismund as an ancestor, thereby giving himself a saintly forebear.

Charles also honoured Saints Cyril, Methodius, and Jerome, the last of whom was by this time wrongly credited with the invention of the first Slavonic or Glagolitic script. In a tribute to his Slavonic past, inherited through his mother, Charles founded the Emmaus Church in Prague, dedicating it to 'the Slavonic patrons', as he called them, who had brought literacy to the Slavs. To magnify the Slavonic connection, he imported monks from Dalmatia to sing the Slavonic mass in the church and to produce liturgical and religious texts written in the Glagolitic script. The monks repaid Charles's patronage by forging a charter, allegedly composed by Alexander the Great back in the fourth century BCE, in which he bequeathed all his worldly conquests to the Slavs and thus by implication to their latest champion, Charles IV.[9]

But Charles cannot be dismissed as a royal magpie and the undiscriminating gatherer of crowns, relics, and saints. He had a purpose and it can be glimpsed in some of the works of history he commissioned. Most of these were revisions of older accounts that their authors slanted to emphasize the king's own descent and the unbroken continuity of Bohemian rulers, of which he was the latest. Others heaped praises on Charles, extolling how he had overcome an assassin's poison, how angels had given him advice, and how he had confounded theologians with his biblical knowledge. The exception is Giovanni de' Marignolli's *Chronicle of the Bohemians*, completed around 1360. In it, the author sandwiched a conventional enough history of Bohemia between an abbreviated history of the world, starting with the Old Testament book of Genesis, and an account of the origins and development of the Bohemian Church.

The book was badly done. A papal envoy before moving to Prague, Marignolli could not resist showing off his familiarity with exotic places. Even so, his message was clear. 'Bohemia is a part of Germany in Europe,' Marignolli explained, but in respect of its kings, their descent from biblical forebears and classical heroes, and of its bishops, whose line he imaginatively fused with the New Testament apostles, Bohemia was destined to lead Christendom. The three divisions of Marignolli's history—divinely ordained government, royal rule in Bohemia, and the Bohemian Church—fused together in an evocation of dynasty, leadership of the Slavonic people, the Bohemian church hierarchy, and the world stage on which Charles was preordained to rule. Uniting the Christian world, Marignolli explained, Charles would make Bohemia its centre, usher in a reign of peace, and ascend the throne of Jerusalem, as foretold in ancient prophesy.[10]

Charles was unhappy with Marignolli's account, which he regarded as too fabulous, but it nonetheless discloses a political programme of sorts—to refashion Christendom and the Holy Roman Empire with Prague at their heart. The year after his coronation in Rome in 1355, Charles issued a constitution for the Holy Roman Empire, which among much else defined the manner of the election of its king. In the so-called Golden Bull of 1356, he listed once more who the seven electors were and explained the manner in which they should conduct the voting. But Charles laid down, too, that the most important of the seven was the king of Bohemia, who was to be the first in processions and in the order of seating, and whose Czech language the other electors were now required to learn. (The word 'bull' derives from the Latin *bulla*, meaning 'a large hanging seal'.)

Charles knew what he was doing, and he included in the Golden Bull provisions that maintained Bohemia as an independent kingdom within the Holy Roman Empire. By so doing, Charles aimed to square the circle, giving the Bohemian king a prominent role in the empire, yet leaving him and his kingdom at one remove from it. Despite this ambiguity, the Golden Bull was a remarkable achievement, enduring until the Holy Roman Empire's dissolution in 1806. The Golden Bull was the first document in European history to regulate the royal succession, and it lasted as a constitution almost twice as long as its nearest rival, the still current Constitution of the United States.[11]

Presence and power buttressed Charles's innovations. He was a tireless traveller, who over the course of his reign made no fewer than 1,227 attested stays at 438 different locations, ranging from Wrocław in Silesia to Luxembourg and Cologne, with a magnificent state visit to Paris in 1378. In the Golden Bull, he spoke in the language of a Roman emperor, publishing decrees from 'the fullness of our imperial power, sitting on the throne of our imperial majesty, adorned with the imperial bands, insignia and diadem', but he had real force behind him. Charles seldom resorted to arms, for war was costly. Marriage, purchase, and diplomacy were his preferred methods. Bit by bit, he ate his way into the heart of Central Europe, with the aim of building a land corridor

THE HOLY ROMAN EMPIRE c. 1378

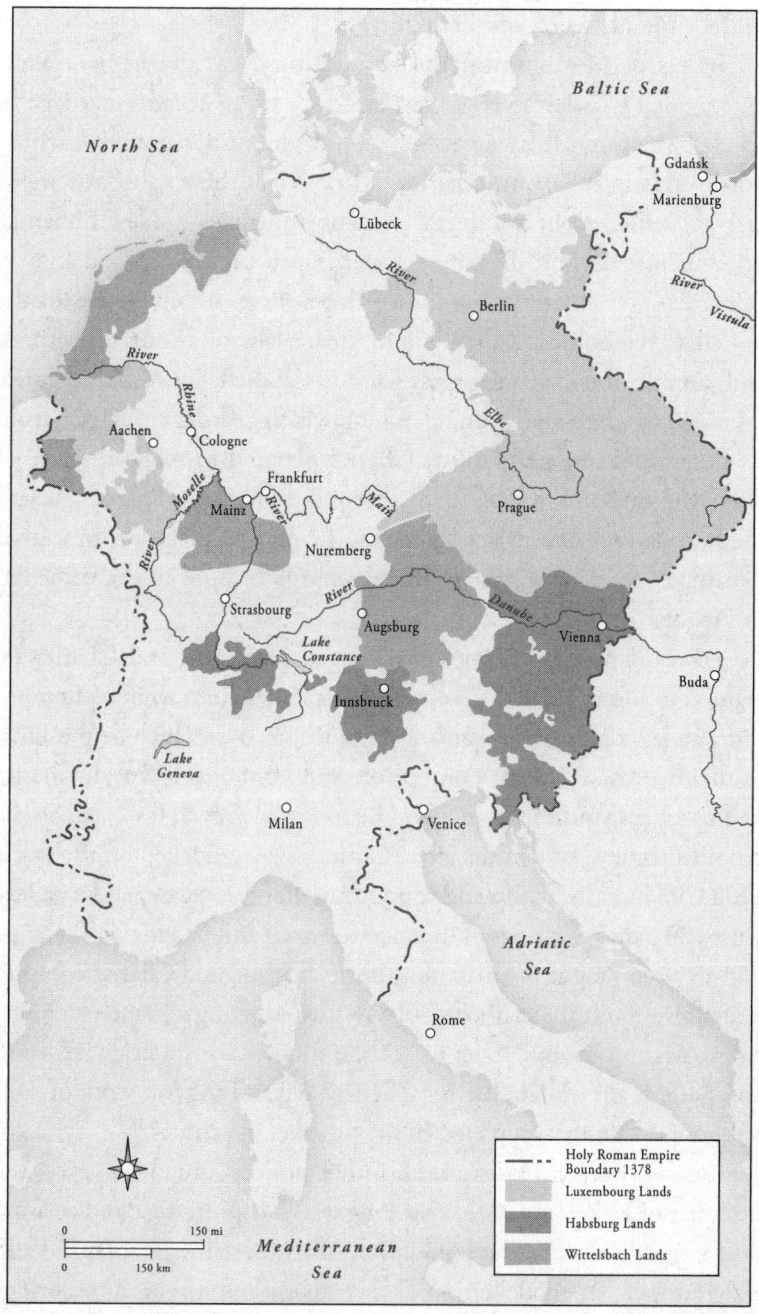

Baltic Sea

North Sea

Gdańsk
Marienburg

Lübeck

River

Berlin

River
Vistula

Elbe

River

Aachen
Cologne

Moselle
River

Mainz
Frankfurt
River

Main

Prague

Nuremberg

Strasbourg
River

Danube

Augsburg

Vienna

Lake
Constance

Buda

Innsbruck

Lake
Geneva

Milan

Venice

Adriatic
Sea

Rome

Mediterranean
Sea

0   150 mi
0   150 km

| | Holy Roman Empire Boundary 1378 |
| Luxembourg Lands |
| Habsburg Lands |
| Wittelsbach Lands |

that linked Bohemia to the confluence of the Rhine and the Main and to the cities of Mainz and Frankfurt.[12]

In his drive westwards, the key territory was the Upper Palatinate, which Charles obtained as the dowry of his second marriage in 1349, but around it lay a constellation of minor possessions reaching northwards into Saxony. Charles did not treat these gains as temporary acquisitions but as integral parts of Bohemia—a 'New Bohemia' or 'Bohemia beyond the forest' (referring to the thick woodland on Bohemia's western rim). He built palaces there, set up statues of the lion that symbolized Bohemia and great walls of armorial bearings, and commissioned stained glass windows and effigies of his favourite saints. It was the same in Brandenburg, which he bought in 1373 from its bored and neglectful ruler. Charles planned to make the city of Tangermünde on the Elbe River a second capital after Prague. He laid the foundations of a palace there, and he pressed the pope, in vain as it turned out, to subordinate Brandenburg's bishops to the cathedral of Prague.[13]

Power in Central Europe had moved eastwards, and Charles IV wanted to show it. He did so by making Prague into what contemporaries called a New Jerusalem and New Rome, over which he presided, in their words, as a New Constantine and Lord of the World. Charles had spent his youth in France and he followed French fashions. So, he rebuilt Prague Castle in the latest Gothic style, modelled on the Palais de la Cité in Paris, with wide windows, a grand staircase, and a gallery with 120 panel paintings of his ancestors, real and imagined. The pope had elevated Prague to an archbishopric in 1344, and Charles comprehensively rebuilt the Cathedral of St Vitus, bringing a French architect from Avignon to undertake its refashioning as a royal crypt, place of coronation, and storehouse for Charles's relics. The great work of construction was only completed in the nineteenth century.[14]

Charles was easily distracted. Other projects caught his eye—the building of Karlštejn Castle near Prague as a country seat and treasure house for his crowns; the foundation of a university, the first in Central Europe, but modelled on French lines; and a new stone bridge across Prague's Vltava River. Even today, Charles presides in effigy on the gateway of the bridge named in his honour, flanked by saints and dressed as the Roman emperor and bridge builder Vespasian. But Charles's greatest achievement was the construction of Prague's New Town. Running south of the existing city (Prague's Old Town), the New Town encompassed an area of seven and a half square kilometres. Previously made up of hamlets and residential overspill, Charles flattened it all except for the churches and mapped out a new metropolis organized on a grid plan. With a three-and-a-half-kilometre wall, interspersed with monumental gateways, Charles transformed Prague into a city with more than forty thousand inhabitants, making it the fourth most populous urban centre north of the Alps after Paris, London, and Cologne.[15]

The massive expansion of Prague had an unexpected consequence. The brothels that had nestled at the city's edge now found themselves close to the centre. None were more notorious than the brothels of the so-called Venice Street (named after the love goddess Venus), described in one contemporary account as Prague's 'worst and most horrible neighbourhood', where prostitution combined with gambling and cheap student accommodation. Some of the prostitutes belonged to brothels sanctioned by the city council and wore distinctive yellow or striped dresses, but most were freelancers operating out of private homes. Surviving reports suggest that many of their clients were clergy and that some priests had even built wooden shelters in their churchyards to facilitate the clandestine trade. The New Town needed cleaning up.[16]

Charles had an ally in the preacher Jan Milíč of Kroměříž. Charismatic and energetic, Milíč fastened his attention on reforming the prostitutes of Venice Street. Turning prostitutes away from their life of sin was holy work—marrying them even more so, for it bought time off in Purgatory, but Milíč never went this far. Instead, he began buying up the houses on Venice Street, turning them into homes for a religious community of former prostitutes, where dressed in nuns' habits they dedicated themselves to religious devotions. In 1372,

Charles speeded up Milíč's efforts, closing down the main brothel and converting it into a chapel called Jerusalem, which he assigned to the preacher. Venice became Jerusalem—the refuge for fifty or more women at any one time, which also served as some sort of school, with priests on hand to hear confessions. It was an experimental community and did not survive Milíč's death in 1374, after which Charles assigned Jerusalem to Cistercian monks. As with much else, Charles had lost interest.[17]

We do not know what happened to the women. Doubtless, some resumed their old life. But by dallying with Jan Milíč of Kroměříž, Charles was playing with fire. Milíč was a fanatic, who was never far away from heresy. In his sermons, he inveighed against the greed and corruption of the clergy, denounced the luxurious lifestyle of the bishops, and condemned the friars for betraying their vows of poverty. He foresaw the imminent arrival of the Devil's apprentice, the Antichrist and Man of Sin, and the final apocalyptic showdown between the forces of Heaven and the 'abomination of desolation', foretold in the Old Testament Book of Daniel. To tilt the balance in favour of the angels, Milíč recommended frequent communion, the appointment of an army of preachers, the comprehensive cleansing of the clergy, and the renewal of the Church under the joint leadership of pope and emperor.[18]

Milíč's Antichrist theology was the stock in trade of religious firebrands. The Black Death had swept through Central Europe in 1348, hitting Bohemia badly. Europe's largest plague pit, a mass grave for victims of the Black Death, is in the Bohemian city of Kutná Hora. Possibly as much as a third of the Bohemian population perished in this and subsequent epidemics, intensifying religious radicalism. On top of this, a flood of heretical literature, mostly of English provenance, flooded Bohemia. Some of these so-called Wyclifite works, inspired by the English theologian John Wyclif, only survive in Czech copies. The university in Prague was a hotbed of religious dissent and the main channel through which this literature arrived in Bohemia. The Czech masters in the university were engaged in a bitter dispute with their German counterparts and ready to enlist distinguished foreign authors to their cause. The debate was theological, but it had an increasingly national content, pitting Czech reformers against German traditionalists.[19]

Out of these cross currents and arguments sprang Jan Hus (1372–1415). Hus was preacher at the Bethlehem Chapel, close to Jan Milíč's former Jerusalem, and he stood in Milíč's tradition. He was relentlessly anticlerical, condemning the avarice of churchmen and anticipating the Antichrist's imminent arrival. But Hus took everything further, denouncing the pope as the agent of Satan, recommending a return to the communal egalitarianism described in the New Testament, and making the Bible the test of authority, on which account he translated all or most of it into Czech. Bit by bit, he rejected the division between priests and laymen, appealing to a comprehensive 'Church of the Elect', meaning all those whom God had selected for salvation. From this premise, he concluded that clergy and laymen alike should partake at the mass in the bread and the wine of Christ's sacrifice, by which God's grace was communicated. (Catholic practice at this time generally reserved the wine for the clergy.)[20]

The Church Council that was meeting at Constance condemned Hus's teachings and he was burnt at the stake there. Bohemia fell into chaos. On his death in 1378, Charles IV had been succeeded in both Bohemia and the Holy Roman Empire by his son Wenceslas IV. Known by contemporaries as 'the Idle', Wenceslas's sole achievement was to commission a lavishly illustrated Bible, replete with erotic imagery and portraits of naked courtesans. In 1400, the electors deposed him, describing Wenceslas as 'useless, sluggish, and negligent, a wrecker and most unworthy of office'. By this time, Wenceslas had in an alcoholic haze assigned control over most of Bohemia's government and judicial organization to the nobility. The nobles were convinced that Hus's death was an insult to the Czech nation, on account of which they took over the management of religious affairs as well. The overwhelming majority of noblemen sided with a programme of reform, ejecting priests from their churches and suppressing monasteries.[21]

The movement soon split into moderate and radical wings, prompting civil war, foreign intervention in the form of papal crusades against heresy, retaliatory expeditions, and intercommunal violence as Czechs fought Germans for control of cities and churches. Hussite armies recruited in Bohemia were among the first in Europe to deploy mobile forts made up of wagons, supported by artillery and troops bearing small handheld cannons. The words for 'howitzer' and 'pistol' entered the English language from the Czech *houfnice*, meaning 'a short piece of ordnance', and *píšťala*, a type of flute, since the weapon made a high-pitched noise when fired. The architect of Hussite battle tactics Jan Žižka was, at his own request, flayed after his death in 1424 and his skin used to make a drum. Žižka's drum, we are told, made the Czech Hussites invincible.[22]

But Hussitism was also an international movement that inspired followers across Central Europe. Even before Hus's execution, Hussite manifestos and wandering preachers were circulating in the Palatinate and Franconia, where their teachings fused with older heresies and challenges to the established Church. The movement grew powerful enough to prompt city magistrates to force citizens to swear oaths condemning Hussitism. In Würzburg alone, several hundred Hussites were put on trial for their lives in the 1440s. The surviving records suggest that these were just the tip of a larger movement that also won souls in the Black Forest, Lower Austria and Vienna, Pomerania, Saxony, Hungary, and Croatia. Hussitism even reached the Romanian principality of Moldavia, where a Hussite community lingered on until the seventeenth century, under the unlikely protection of the English ambassador in Istanbul.[23]

Hussitism was a Central European phenomenon and not a narrowly Czech and Bohemian one, as Czech nationalist historians constantly aver. But it wrecked the Bohemia of the Luxembourg kings. After Wenceslas IV's death in 1419, his brother Sigismund followed him on the Bohemian throne. Sigismund was already king of the Holy Roman Empire and of Hungary, and his reign should have been a glorious one. But much of it was spent at war with the Hussites, and

Sigismund was only formally acknowledged as king of Bohemia in 1436, the year before his death. Under Charles IV, Bohemia had been at the cultural forefront of Central Europe. Now, its churches were neglected, stripped of their relics and of the paraphernalia of Catholic worship. For several decades, the royal palace lay empty and the cathedral had no archbishop until 1561. The university became an academic backwater, where the masters debated theological points in their own intellectual cocoon. A papal embargo on trade with heretical Bohemia completed the kingdom's isolation.[24]

The wasting of the Luxembourg inheritance left room in Central Europe for other dynasties to recover or consolidate their influence— the Habsburgs, who were busy expanding in the south of the empire and towards the Adriatic coast; the Bavarian Wittelsbachs, who also controlled much of the Rhineland; and in the far north, the Jagiellon rulers of Lithuania, who at the end of the fourteenth century became kings of Poland. Central Europe's internal divisions were once more about to be rearranged to accommodate the new dynasties that emerged in the later Middle Ages. Even so, the impression that dynasties floated on the top of kingdoms, acquiring and exchanging territories among themselves, heedless of the people that actually lived there, is a false one. As the Luxembourg experience in Bohemia showed, rulers and dynasties had to fit in with what great men, nobles, and city magistrates wanted and expected, for the obedience of subjects was never unconditional. The next chapters will explain this.

CHAPTER 8

Councils, Diets, and the Confusion of the Laws

RULERS HAVE ALWAYS HAD COUNCILS MADE UP OF THEIR LEAD-ing men. For most of the Middle Ages, government was still small, and so kings and princes had to involve influential people in discussions simply to make things happen. Since the ruler counted as the highest judge in the land, councils also had a judicial function, acting as the final arbiter in matters of law. Until the thirteenth century, and even later in some places, the council overlapped with the ruler's court, household, and chapel—the last necessarily so, since at a time of widespread illiteracy its clergy provided the main reservoir of people who could write and knew how to keep records.

Throughout Central Europe, councils stood at the apex of government, but their membership was fluid. A council generally comprised the sovereign's office holders and household staff, leading churchmen, and important visitors. Sometimes unimportant ones joined in too—noblemen from the countryside who just happened to be nearby or a castellan with urgent advice. The council thinned out whenever the ruler was travelling, for few of his great men or officers had time to keep him company. The duke of Cracow was premier among the rulers of thirteenth-century Poland. When his council met in Cracow or San-domierz, it usually comprised a dozen or more lords and clergy, but when he was travelling he had with him a large entourage but only a handful of trusted officers and scribes. It was from these few that he took advice and whom he named as witnesses to the judgments he made.[1]

For most of the Middle Ages, rulers and councils generally avoided making definitive statements about the law's content. After a flurry of legislative activity aimed at eliminating pagan practices, rulers stopped making law in this way. Legal judgments and decisions became instead makeshift, designed to meet specific circumstances. General statements about the law's content were rare and unwelcome, for they imposed obligations that might later prove inconvenient. Rulers were happier to keep matters slippery. As Emperor Henry III observed around 1040: 'the law, as is commonly said, has a nose of wax, and the king has a long arm of iron so that he can bend it whichever way he pleases.'[2]

But by the thirteenth century, subjects were no longer content to operate in a legal void. Central Europe was changing on account of the inflow of settlers from the west, the emergence of knighthood and nobility, the ebb and flow of dynasties, and the founding of new castles and cities. Leading men in the countryside as well as the great men who served in the council demanded guarantees that their rights would not be infringed and that they be put in writing lest they be forgotten—in the expression of the time: 'mortal memory is short, but letters live on.' The earliest of these charters of liberty is the so-called Styrian Magna Carta, or Georgenberg Privilege of 1186 (named after its place of issue). In it, Ottakar IV of Styria confirmed that the duchy's knights had the right to settle disputes in court and not in combat, to leave their wealth to their heirs, and not to be harmed by the conduct of his officials.[3]

From this point onwards, written guarantees became increasingly common in Central Europe. In Hungary (1222), Bohemia (1229), the Tyrol (1289), and Bavaria (1293), rulers published laws that itemized the traditional rights (or what were said to be) of the emerging class of noblemen—their freedom from onerous taxation and arbitrary arrest, their exemption from trial by ordeal, their right to pass on their land to kinsmen, and so on. In the Holy Roman Empire, emperors and individual lords mostly issued generalized 'peace charters' which sought to smooth the most frequent causes of conflict, outlined how the courts should function, and promised 'to maintain all in their rights, ranks, freedoms, and honour'. Even so, in 1231 and 1232, Emperor Frederick II and his son King Henry issued the Statute in Favour of the

Princes. The statute did exactly as it said, affirming a whole series of rights claimed by the lords and dukes of the empire and giving them a free hand to carve out their own self-governing principalities within the empire.[4]

Not only were written laws now being made, but how they were made was also changing. Emperor Frederick II might well publish his statute for the princes in the form of a decree, issued 'from the high seat of empire', and write that 'to dispute the judgments, plans, and undertakings of the king is comparable to sacrilege', but even his son was unconvinced. In a sister charter to the statute, King Henry declared that 'none of the princes nor anyone else can make legislation or any laws whatsoever unless they have first obtained the consent of the good and the great of the land.' It was an injunction that applied as much to the emperor as to anyone else. Government at every level had been put on notice to consult and not to proceed on the ruler's whim.[5]

Of course, having been granted almost full control of their territories, lords and dukes might ignore with impunity the requirement to consult, but the principle that Henry had laid down gained ground. Subsequent laws rehearsed it and the agreement of 'the good and the great' was from now on used to describe how the principle of consent should be built into decisions. But there was more at work. Participation, consultation, and consent were part of a new political vocabulary that spoke of political communities as organic bodies made up of interrelated and mutually dependent parts. As King Rudolf put it in 1274, it was 'not in the nature of things that the whole body can be ruled by the head without the help of the limbs.' Others invoked the principle culled from Roman legal texts that 'what affects everyone should be approved by everyone.' Either way, power was no longer thought to be the exclusive right of rulers but something that rulers were expected to share.[6]

In Central Europe, an added twist was given by the idea of the nobleman. As charters repeatedly spelled out, the nobleman was a part of the ruler's household or family, even to the extent that (as one charter explained) he might be invited into his lord's 'home and daily life, sharing his table'. The nobleman gave his lord help and advice, and in return expected protection and preferment. It followed that he was entitled to be listened to, and this was one of the earliest demands of noblemen across Central Europe—that their concerns merited special consideration and a direct channel to the ruler. In this respect, they found it particularly irksome when rulers required them to put their requests in writing. Ordinary noblemen, often suspicious of the great lords who had the ruler's ear, demanded that they should be heard too.[7]

One of the earliest examples in this story comes from thirteenth-century Hungary. In 1222, disaffection among the emerging nobility led to a riot in front of the king and to the presentation of a petition which included a whole range of grievances, from the employment of Jews and Muslims in the royal mint to the hospitality demanded by the king's grooms, houndsmen, and falconers. The nobles averred that their rights were grounded in liberties originally conveyed by Hungary's first king, St Stephen (ruled 997–1038), among which was their right to assemble annually with the monarch. King Andrew II gave way, publishing a charter that enumerated the nobility's rights. It was the first of half a dozen charters of liberty from thirteenth-century Hungary that established the principle of consultation and consent as fundamental to royal government.[8]

Elsewhere, rulers did not have to be forced. They willingly conceded a share in government, reckoning that they could use the ordinary nobles as a counterweight to the great lords who often defied them, even in meetings of the royal council. Discussions in the Polish king's council were particularly fraught as quarrelsome churchmen and others bore down on the ruler, accusing him of negligence, indifference to established rights, and the promotion of unworthy officers. It was much the same in Hungary, where the king was periodically reduced to tears by the actions of the great lords, or in one case was prompted to violence, smashing a prelate in the face. Where the local ruler was a bishop, then he might use the knights in his service to block the cathedral chapter should it oppose his decisions. Broadening participation often made sense.[9]

How matters turned out followed no fixed rule. In a few places, no-blemen joined the ruler's council and became part of his government, but mostly they kept their distance, meeting in their own assemblies. These assemblies were often held simultaneously with gatherings of churchmen and townsfolk, with all three either attending their own meetings, often grandly known as curias, or else joining together but deciding separately. Elsewhere, nobles divided into great lords and knights so that there were four curias altogether. In Hungary and Po-land, the royal council was by degrees transformed into an upper house of great lords and royal office holders, while the assembly of the nobles became the lower house.

The names given to these assemblies varied. They could be called a general congregation or solemn gathering (*conventio solempnis*), a col-loquy, a meeting or matter of the country (*Landschaft, Landding*), a pleading (*placita*), a place of speaking or 'parliament', or more com-monly 'a day' (*Tag*), since the participants were invited to join together on a certain day—it is from the Latin *dies* or 'day' that the name *dieta* or diet derives. In Bohemia and Poland, assemblies were also called Sněms or Sejms, meaning 'a convocation' or 'a summons'.

Diets, as we shall now call them, eventually became legislative bod-ies, but making law was only a small part of what they originally did, and rulers often continued to issue statutes without bothering to con-sult them. Settling cases mostly about land and inheritance was their main activity, but it was interspersed with flighty oratory, quarrels over the correct order of seating, and excessive drinking. Dances and tour-naments livened up the proceedings, as did the occasional execution of an illustrious malefactor. Diets were a place to settle business, but they were also about exhibiting power, hierarchy, and friendship. It was thus a great insult for anyone to quit them early or for the ruler to arrive late, since it upset the solidarity that the diet's ceremonies were intended to impress.

Even so, diets had a double role. On the one hand, they stood for the kingdom, duchy, or territory, on which account they might inter-vene to prevent its partition between the ruler's heirs, insist on a role in determining the succession if this was disputed, or decide on the guardian when the heir was a minor. Bit by bit, they also took control of appointments to high office and of the right to authorize taxes. In Bohemia, the diet had accumulated these powers by the mid-fourteenth century; other kingdoms were soon to follow. As the financial needs of rulers exploded in the fifteenth century because of the increasing costs of warfare, diets also asserted their right to be consulted in matters of taxation, on which account they met more frequently to vote (or sometimes refuse) subsidies. In the expression of the time: 'Diet days are tax days' (*Landtage sind Geldtage*).

But on the other, diets were primarily gatherings of the ruler's vassals. All noblemen and knights who held their land directly from the ruler were his vassals and so entitled to meet with him. Cities were also part of the ruler's domain, having rights bestowed by his charters, so they also merited a place. And churchmen, although important in their own right as bishops and abbots, also held land directly from the ruler, so they likewise counted as his vassals. In the Tyrol, many small farmers were freemen, cultivating their own plots. They had no superior other than the duke, so they too were invited to attend the Tyrolean diet, making up a curia of their own. It was the same in the principality of Kempten (now in Bavaria), where the ruler was the abbot of Kempten's monastery. By the fifteenth century, the abbot's knights had mostly quit his service to seek their fortunes elsewhere, leaving the diet in the hands of the abbot's peasant tenants.[10]

In Central Europe, the feudal pyramid was a simple one. Most landowners stood in a direct relationship to the ruler of the territory, holding their land from him without going through the intermediaries known elsewhere as tenants-in-chief and 'mesne' or middle lords. Whenever a new ruler took over, his vassals were expected to go through a solemn investiture, swearing an oath of loyalty and clasping his hand. Often held at the diet, in its opening session, and repeated every time the property passed to an heir, this was an act of high ceremony and virtually the only time an artist captured the proceedings—the seated ruler surrounded by his children and favourite dog, with his lords crowded around, repeating an oath that was read out to them. Carinthia had the most theatrical version. There the new duke was installed in a ceremony that involved much processioning, face slapping, and switches of clothing, after which he moved to a carved stone seat to receive his vassals' oaths of allegiance and confirm them in their lands.[11]

Since most nobles were vassals of the ruler, they all might attend the diet. So, in Bohemia and Bavaria, a thousand nobles had the right to be present, but only a few hundred at a time actually did so. In Hungary, where the nobility was more numerous, over ten thousand or more noblemen might attend, and in the late fifteenth and sixteenth centuries many thousands sometimes turned up, placing an intolerable strain on political management. When Hungary's mass diets met, they did so out of doors in a fenced-off area, which was patrolled by armed men. To add to the impression of a modern-day pop concert, the king and council occupied a wooden stage at the front of the arena, while the noblemen hurled insults and complaints from the floor, occasionally erecting a gallows or executioner's block as a warning to traitors. These rowdy Hungarian diets, which were usually held on the Rákos Plain next to Pest, introduced a new word to the Polish lexicon—*rokosz*, meaning a violent insurrection of the nobility.[12]

But most diets embraced some form of representation, with clusters of noblemen appointing several or more of their number to act on their behalf. Cities sent their chief magistrates, and peasants delegated village elders. Bishops and abbots represented themselves. The exception was the imperial diet, or Reichstag. The diet of the Holy Roman Empire emerged only in the late fifteenth century out of meetings of vassals at the king's or emperor's court. Since it was considered 'his' assembly, it was up to him to choose who to invite, but to turn down an invitation was the gravest of insults, tantamount to heresy since it offended his divinely ordained majesty. Attendance varied according to the ruler's will, from almost five thousand in 1397 to fewer than a hundred in 1431.[13]

A series of reforms at the end of the fifteenth century made the imperial diet more sophisticated in its operation, with a fixed membership of about three hundred, set procedures for arriving at decisions, and an agenda agreed in advance. When controversial matters came up, the ruler and electors who controlled the flow of business usually hived them off to committees. But despite its claim to stand for the empire, German nation, and indeed all Christendom, the imperial diet never lost its original character as an assembly of vassals, consisting only of the several hundred dukes, counts, churchmen, and cities that happened to stand in a direct relationship to the king or emperor. So, noblemen in the Austrian lands were not entitled to attend the imperial diet because they held their estates from the dukes of Styria, Carinthia, the Tyrol, and so on, rather than from the king or emperor. It was the same with noblemen who had received their land from the dukes of Pomerania, Mecklenburg, Saxony, and so on, since they did not constitute imperial vassals but instead ducal ones.[14]

Even so, there was no great consistency. The imperial knights who held fragments of land mainly in Franconia, Swabia, and the Rhineland were the emperor's vassals, but they were by the fifteenth century excluded from the imperial diet. They were too numerous, and most served greater lords and churchmen anyway, thus compromising their standing. The noblemen attending the imperial diet generally treated the cities with disdain, even though these had received their foundation charters from the emperor and shouldered the greatest burden of taxes. The imperial diet comprised three curias—a curia for the lords, for the churchmen, and for the cities—which met together but cast a separate and unequal vote. The vote of the cities counted only as consultative and their deputies were unable to block decisions made by the other two curias even if injurious to their interests. The imperial diet also excluded entirely the hundred or so imperial villages (*Reichsdörfer*), which had no lord save the emperor.[15]

Diets were only the head of a hierarchy of assemblies that drilled down into Central European society. From the twelfth to the fourteenth century, Poland was divided into separate and competing dukedoms. Some consolidation took place at the end of the thirteenth century under Władysław the Elbow-High (so-called because he was), who by outliving his rivals extended his power from Kujavia in north-central Poland to Greater and Lesser Poland, based around Gniezno and Cracow, respectively. His son Casimir went on to add Lviv and Red Ruthenia, which now straddles western Ukraine and southeastern Poland. But the legacy of the 150 years of division was to reinforce local identities which expressed itself in the holding of between thirty and forty district and provincial assemblies of noblemen and clergy, called Sejmiks. These substituted for the lack of an overall Polish diet or Sejm, meaning that the ruler had to negotiate with each.[16]

Sejmiks sent delegates to each other's meetings so that they could agree among themselves to taxation, royal proposals, and what they saw as the infringements of traditional liberties. But the existence of so many Sejmiks was a messy arrangement. It hindered collective responses to royal demands and allowed an unscrupulous monarch to pursue a policy of divide and rule. It also created problems for the monarch since the Sejmiks often challenged his instructions and frustrated the coordination of policy. A single Sejm that brought together delegates from the local Sejmiks made sense for both sides and was increasingly summoned during the second half of the fifteenth century, usually meeting every year. Although the Sejmiks continued to have a strong local power, frequently (and sometimes violently) resisting the decisions of both ruler and Sejm, Poland was becoming joined up.

The same sort of complexity was evident in Bohemia, where separate diets met in Bohemia proper, Moravia, Silesia, and Upper and Lower Lusatia (now split between Germany and Poland), only occasionally joining together in a single body. Beneath these were regional assemblies, or 'dietines' (*sjezdy*), which had responsibility for peace-keeping, tax collection, and appointing deputies to the diets. The Bohemian diet claimed the privilege to choose the monarch, and indeed Charles IV had written the right into the Golden Bull of 1356. This allowed the diet in advance of an election to hem in a prospective ruler with all sorts of preconditions that made him its puppet. As the Czech nobles reminded King Wladislas (ruled 1471–1516), 'You are our king, but we are your masters.'[17]

Although often competing with the ruler, diets and assemblies of noblemen contributed to the solidity of kingdoms and duchies. Either directly or through representatives, diets brought together the political community in a given territory, conveying an idea of its space. They defined the physical boundaries in which power was exercised, but they shared in power too, since they contributed to the decisions reached. Despite the bravado of the Czech nobles, politics was becoming less personal and more organized. Whereas previously everything had hinged on the bond of affection and loyalty between ruler and vassal, diets with their increasingly elaborate procedures turned individual relationships into institutional ones. Despite the conflicts and rivalries that attended their meetings, diets were part of the glue that kept kingdoms and duchies together.

Even so, there was always a tension in Central Europe between the diets' role as assemblies of royal vassals and their claim to stand for the kingdom. Language did not help, for the word for kingdom, in Latin *regnum*, was slippery, meaning anything from the royal entourage to the physical extent of the ruler's territory. For most of the Middle Ages, diets were principally concerned with describing relations between the monarch and his vassals—the procedures to be followed in royal courts, to which only nobles and clergy had personal access, the taxes and troops that nobles were expected to cajole from their tenants, and the basic rights belonging to noblemen. At times, diets' understanding of *kingdom* could broaden out to include either its geographical bounds or its overall defence or the preservation of order within it, but only to the extent that these matters touched upon the nobility and their obligations.

Procedure in diets was much the same across Central Europe. The ruler laid out his propositions to churchmen, lords, and noblemen. Either in a single session or in curias, they debated the sovereign's text and presented their own counterproposals (quaintly called 'grievances'). Committees, spokesmen of the diet, influential courtiers, the royal council, and chancellery clerks then worked behind the scenes to hammer out a compromise, with business often returning to the diet for renewed consideration and bargaining. With the text settled, the chancellery wrote it up, fastening the royal seal and occasionally slipping in items that had not been agreed. The final document was invariably a hodgepodge, mixing taxation and the nitty-gritty of supplying garrisons with changes to the judicial administration and such minor matters as the debt owed to a worthy widow.[18]

There was little consistency in terminology even within duchies and kingdoms, and so the final document might be known as a decree, statute, constitution, or simply an agreement. But it is best thought of as a treaty—the product of negotiation between the ruler and his subjects as represented in the diet. Both sides regarded themselves as equally empowered and having equivalent rights. But as the leading Hungarian jurist of the sixteenth century explained, the ruler and the nobility as represented in the diet also had mutual and interlocking obligations, for they 'depend upon each other so closely that neither can be separated and removed from the other and neither can exist without the other.' It was out of their interaction that law derived.[19]

But the law that emerged was very unlike what we imagine the law to be today. Unlike a modern statute, the treaty agreed by ruler and diet did not constitute a set of binding obligations. In order for the contents to be persuasive, they had to be followed and so enter into everyday practice, because only customary law or the law as it was actually observed was considered compelling. This will sound very unfamiliar to readers today and even perverse, but it made sense. Before the age of printing, all legislation had to be copied out by hand, after which it was sent to the principal churches, cities, and royal officers in the countryside. Sometimes the recipients made distillations which they circulated at a price, but they were equally likely to file their copy away, particularly if the contents were burdensome. So, the majority of subjects had no idea what ruler and diet had settled on. They carried on in their usual manner until compelled to act otherwise, at which point their behaviour conformed to the legislation and so became the custom.

With limited circulation, previous laws were soon forgotten. Or they might be overtaken by decrees issued by the ruler without reference to the diet. There was no consensus on how far royal power extended and what the king might do by his own authority. In 1505, the Polish Sejm attempted to curb the royal right to make laws unilaterally. In the famous clause *Nihil novi* (Nothing new), the Sejm laid down (among much else) that the king should make no innovation without its consent. But the Sejm had no idea what an innovation was since there was no record of what it had in the past agreed with the king. So, the royal chancellor was deputed to find what he could and have these printed as the kingdom's laws, but he was as vague in his understanding of the law as the law itself was uncertain. What Poles called at the time the 'confusion of the laws' was evident in the chancellor's resulting compilation, which included old statutes that were no longer relevant, provisions of a doubtful legal character, and, in an annex, law codes that had been drawn up elsewhere, including a thirteenth-century Neapolitan text.[20]

The confusion of the laws was typical of a large part of Central Europe, but it should not obscure the region's political complexity. However much dynasties swapped crowns and kingdoms, power never belonged to monarchs alone. It was instead distributed and shared with a nobility that expected to be involved in the making of decisions. Central Europe had in the Middle Ages a vigorous political life, articulated through diets and assemblies that regarded their power as both the complement and counterpart to the ruler's own. Even so, institutions of noble power were just the tip of an iceberg of communal organization and popular participation that extended throughout Central European society. Medieval society was never democratic, but in a large part of Central Europe popular participation in adjudication, law making, and the local workings of government was both widespread and intense. The next chapter will explain this.

CHAPTER 9

Cities, Villages, and Freedoms: From Frisia to Transylvania

D IETS HELPED TO BUILD KINGDOMS AND DUCHIES. EITHER BY personal attendance or through representatives, diets brought together the political community in a given territory, conveying an idea of its space. They defined the physical boundaries in which power was exercised, but they shared in power, too, deciding taxation, the appointment of officials, and (when it was contested) even the identity of the ruler. Politics was becoming less personal and more formal. Whereas previously everything had hinged on the bond of affection and loyalty between ruler and vassal, institutions increasingly mediated relationships. Structures were hardening and the state was becoming more visible. For all the conflicts and rivalries that attended their meetings, diets were becoming part of the organizational fabric that kept kingdoms and duchies together.[1]

The processes at work here were common enough in western Christendom, from Scandinavia to Sardinia. But by concentrating on diets, we will miss some of the exceptionalism of Central Europe. The diets in Central Europe were dominated by the privileged orders and the vassals of rulers. They were mostly interested in their own affairs and in establishing the mutual rights and obligations they shared with the ruler. So, there was room for other groups lower down the social hierarchy to carve out their own spheres, to organize themselves in associations and assemblies, and to establish almost independent powers. Medieval Central Europe was the home of communal government, of republican experiments, and of initiatives from below that stand at odds with the story of state formation from above and of the consolidation of territories.

Throughout Central Europe, cities and citizenship went together. Every year, citizens in a thousand or more urban centres elected councillors and magistrates, normally in open-air meetings held on the main square, followed by the taking of oaths, the ceremony of handing over the staff of office, and a procession through the streets. But elections were not 'one man, one vote' occasions. Citizenship usually depended on owning a house and so being, in one contemporary description, among the 'well possessed and propertied, sensible people', while in most cities urban office was reserved to a small group of oligarchs known as patricians. In Nuremberg, it belonged only to members of the several dozen families who had the right to dance in the city hall. Elsewhere, eligibility depended on conspicuous wealth, marriage, a house that fronted onto the main square, and even a coat of arms and membership of the right drinking society or 'Rich Men's Club' (*Richerzeche*).[2]

Urban patricians were usually wholesale merchants or lived off rents. They were in the expression of the time *Müssiggänger*, or 'idlers', who had the time for council duties. Their rivals were the guildsmen, who were mostly retailers and so often at odds with their suppliers. Conflict was frequent, prompting uprisings in which the guildsmen enlisted the urban poor. But the guilds were associations too, with elected leaders, their own rules, and civic rituals, which were often linked to the veneration of particular saints or to the defence of a section of city wall. Urban society was shot through with bonds of belonging and communal organizations. Prostitutes, too, formed their own sisterhoods, taking part in processions often under the banner of the harlot saints, Mary Magdalene and Afra. After all, they too were practising a craft.[3]

To facilitate commerce and for physical protection, cities founded leagues. The earliest date from the mid-thirteenth century and regularly included lords and bishops with a similar interest in maintaining order. In the 1250s, the Rhineland League included a hundred cities, reaching from Aachen to Zurich as well as the archbishops of Mainz, Trier, and Cologne. With its own coordinating committee, the league launched on the Rhine some six hundred armed vessels to protect against piracy and suppress illegal toll stations. No less numerous was the Swabian League, founded in 1487. With more than five hundred members of knights, cities, and churchmen, mainly in the south and southwest of the empire, the Swabian League had an assembly of city delegates and local lords, as well as a standing committee to act as its government and a court for adjudicating members' disputes.[4]

On top of this, cities across Central Europe gathered together in legal unions. They borrowed codes of law from one another and adopted them either fully or in part as their own. The law of Lübeck was the most widespread and covered most aspects of city life, from the form of government to inheritance, weights, measures, and tolls. It was used by about a hundred cities, mostly on the Baltic shore as far east as Tallinn (formerly Reval, now the capital of Estonia) and Novgorod in Russia. The law of Magdeburg was also widespread, embraced by about eighty cities in the empire, as well as influencing urban law in Poland, Hungary, and Transylvania. Even distant Kyiv adopted it in the 1490s—a nineteenth-century monument in the form of a white pillar overlooking the Dnieper River commemorates the event. Smaller clusters of law developed around Ulm, Ingelheim, Cologne, Brno in Moravia, and Buda in Hungary.[5]

From this, it followed that when city magistrates confronted controversial or difficult cases, they might seek the advice of the mother city from which they had borrowed their laws. Either the council of the mother city or, more usually, a bank of experts attached to the council (called *Schöffen*, or assessors) examined the case and gave an opinion, usually in the presence of the magistrates of the daughter city and the parties to the suit. Inheritance and property law feature most frequently in the tens of thousands of opinions (*Schöffensprüche*) that survive. In the sixteenth century, urban magistracies and litigants often also referred to the law faculties of universities for a considered opinion.[6]

The Swiss Alpine valleys and the rolling meadows to their north were home to the best-known leagues—communities that were bound together in treaties of mutual support but which had by the fifteenth century merged into a loose confederacy. At the confederacy's heart lay the imperial cities between Lake Geneva and Lake Constance: Lucerne, Berne, and Zurich, which straddled the overland route between Italy and the merchant fairs of France and Flanders. In the mid-fourteenth century, these three allied with five of the self-governing rural communities of the forest valleys, which had previously thrown off the rule of their moderately oppressive counts. Their treaty was unusual since, in its own words, it brought together 'cities and countryside, citizens and rustics,' but it prospered. As much by conquest as by persuasion, the original eight signatories accumulated new allies and folded into their loose organization other leagues of cities and countryfolk.[7]

The confederacy's structure was complicated, but this was a strength, for it gave flexibility. By around 1500, the core of the league comprised thirteen 'places' (*Orte*) or, as they were later known, cantons. A dozen or more treaties and hundreds of written agreements over common issues united them, although the first in which they were all co-signatories dates only from 1513—the rest were just between groups of individual cantons or even parts of cantons. On top of this, there were 'common lordships' where several or more cantons governed a territory that they had either bought or conquered, and there were territories that had only allied with one or more of the cantons—the Graubünden or Grisons in the east and Geneva in the west fell into this category, and so too the ancient abbey of St Gallen.

From the mid-fourteenth century, a central diet brought together representatives of the cantons, each having an equal vote, but the cantons varied in their political composition. In the rural cantons, popular assemblies held ostensible authority, but they were mostly events that a handful of wealthy families choreographed. In the cantons where cities predominated, power rested either with wealthy merchants or with guildsmen. Villages, market towns, and valleys also had their own assemblies, at which there typically gathered 'the whole community of companions and freemen, and many people of property'. Mostly they met to approve the verdicts of courts, treaties of alliance, and decisions of the cantons, but they also affirmed that agreements were in keeping with their own traditions. Even so, this was not peasant democracy in action—smallholders were routinely excluded from village assemblies and the opinion of the wealthiest usually prevailed.[8]

Switzerland has its closest parallel in Transylvania. Both were land-locked, a mixture of mountains and pastures, and both stood astride commercial highways. Switzerland and Transylvania were similarly vulnerable to invasion, and they each preserve extraordinary military architecture. In Switzerland, it consists of the dense network of cas-tles on its rim, in the Aargau, Vaud, and Graubünden. Originally the homes of knights, they became in the fourteenth and fifteenth centuries outposts of the Swiss cities or the grand homes of wealthy merchants. In Transylvania, it is visible in the 150 fortified churches, behind whose thick walls communities sheltered at time of invasion. Fear of Turkish and Tatar raiders cut so deep in Transylvania that as late as the 1930s the larders in church battlements were still kept stocked with cheeses and hams.[9]

Transylvania was in the Middle Ages a part of Hungary but with its own government, headed by a voivode, who was a royal appointee, and with a landed elite of mainly Hungarian noblemen. Transylvania was notably diverse in terms of its populations and their privileges. In the twelfth and thirteenth centuries, successive Hungarian kings had settled Germans, generically called Saxons, in its southern part, where they went on to found farmsteads and small cities. The most import-ant of these gave Transylvania its German name: Siebenbürgen, or the Seven Cities, centred upon Sibiu (Hermannstadt). To the east of the main area of Saxon settlement lay a quite different population called the Székely, or Seklers. The Seklers provided light horsemen, who acted as border guards, and had collective privileges allowing them their own government and laws. Although Hungarian speakers, the Seklers' or-igins are obscure, but tradition held that they were a remnant of At-tila's Huns. To add to their mystery, right through to the eighteenth century, some Seklers continued to use their own runic script. Recently revived by enthusiasts in parts of Transylvania, signs written in Sekler runes now tell motorists the names of the villages through which they are passing.

The Hungarian nobility dominated the rest of Transylvania, meeting in their own county assemblies. On top of this, the voivode held a diet that met at least once a year, mostly to hear complex legal cases involving property and to draw up lists of outlaws—the forests of Transylvania were notorious as the haunts of robbers and highwaymen. The diet was made up of elected deputies from the counties and any nobleman who could be bothered to attend. But its membership was loose and by no means confined to the nobility. Leaders of the Saxon and Sekler communities might be there too, and until the fourteenth century the headmen of Romanian Orthodox villages. By the close of the Middle Ages, Romanians were probably the most numerous part of Transylvania's population and certainly its oldest, since they were descended from the legionaries who had settled in the old Roman province of Dacia back in the second and third centuries CE. But as Orthodox believers, they were subsequently excluded from a share in Transylvania's government on account of their different religion.[10]

Even so, there was no bar to Romanians once they had converted to Catholicism, and many of the greatest Transylvanian noble dynasties were of Romanian origin—the Hunyadi family, from whose line King Matthias Corvinus of Hungary descended (ruled 1458–1490), is the most notable. Additionally, many Romanians performed a military role as warriors attached to castles. Their privileges entitled them to have their own courts and local assemblies, and to administer affairs according to their own laws under the oversight of their castellans. There were several dozen districts of this type across Transylvania. In the countryside, Romanian enterprisers also founded villages and administered them as hereditary chieftains, or *cnezes*. They often joined together to appoint local leaders or voivodes, who coordinated military and fiscal policy and adjudicated cases that crossed village boundaries, giving their verdicts in the name of 'the community of the rich and the poor'.[11]

In 1437, a massive uprising swept Transylvania, which brought together peasants and petty noblemen, Hungarians and Romanians alike.
Its causes were the bishop of Transylvania's demand for increased tithe
payments and heavy-handed attempts to convert Orthodox Romanians to the Catholic faith. As it was, religious life in Transylvania was
at a low ebb. Contemporary accounts tell that many priests had abandoned their churches to pass the days in gambling, country pursuits,
and debauched living, and that their neglected flocks had embraced
radical beliefs, including the Bohemian heresy of Hussitism. But the
insurgents' demands spilled over to include the general alleviation of
peasant burdens, in pursuit of which they burned down noble homes
and occupied the city of Cluj (Klausenburg) in central Transylvania.[12]

In terror for their lives, the leaders of the Seklers, Saxons, and nobles forged in the same year a military alliance and 'brotherly union'
against the rebels. Their combined forces soon prevailed, and the rebel
leaders suffered the usual penalties—torture, death, mutilation, and
blinding. Its purpose achieved, that should have been the end of the
brotherly union, but instead it persevered. By the middle years of the
century, the Turks were pressing into Transylvania and royal demands
for taxation were increasingly oppressive, so a renewed alliance made
sense. In a new treaty concluded in 1459, the three groups stressed
that they now constituted 'a comprehensive and united community'
(*universitas et communitas adunata*).[13]

Over the succeeding decades, the league, or 'union of the three nations', as it was called, took over from the voivode's assembly to become
the diet of Transylvania, with Seklers, Saxons, and noblemen sharing
power through appointed delegates. By the beginning of the sixteenth
century, representatives of the union had also obtained permanent
seats in the voivode's judicial court. But each community continued
to maintain its own assemblies and, beneath these, smaller gatherings
for the cities and the individual Sekler clans and for noblemen in the
counties. The three nations also sent delegates to attend the Hungarian
diet since, as the royal letters of invitation explained, they too were
limbs of the kingdom and had better know what was decided.[14]

Although both lay on the edges of Central Europe, Transylvania and Frisia could not be much further apart or physically more different. The main part of Frisia, Great Frisia, lay on a long coastline that reached from the Zuider Zee in what is now the Netherlands to the estuary of the Weser River, north of Bremen. There was a second concentrated area of settlement on the west coast of Jutland, which included the Heligoland archipelago, lying fifty kilometres from the coast in the German Bight in the North Sea. The two population groups shared the same Frisian language, which even today is closer to English than to German or Dutch and, in some situations, even intelligible to English speakers. Sadly, for most British travellers, Frisia remains a nameless 'flyover country'.

Starting from artificial mounds dug in the marshland, Frisians had over centuries reclaimed the seabed to make fields for cattle and cabbages. This did not prevent periodic famines. The written customs of Frisia, dating from around the thirteenth century, include heart-breaking provisions for the care of starving children. But most Frisian law was about compensation for injuries, without which blood feuds could go on between families for generations. In cases of murder, the unavenged corpse of the slain man stayed mummifying in a corner of the family home as a reminder that there was a score to settle. Frisian law recognized over four hundred possible wounds, ranging from the amputation of a fingertip to an alarming set of injuries that might be done to male genitals.[15]

Frisian customs affirmed that 'all Frisians may compensate their breaking of the peace with their money and goods,' but not all could because they were too poor. On top of this, there were crimes which were considered unredeemable—arson done under cover of darkness, robbery, and the desecration of churches. In these cases, the culprits were mutilated, hanged, and their corpses mounted on wheels attached to the ends of upright poles. Executed criminals strapped to wheels are features of the art of Hieronymus Bosch and Pieter Bruegel the Elder, who worked in the Low Countries in the fifteenth and sixteenth centuries, respectively. More than three dozen of these gallows wheels were recorded in just one forty-kilometre stretch in Great Frisia, mostly set up at crossroads as a grisly warning to passers-by.[16]

By the thirteenth century, rule by hereditary counts had collapsed in Great Frisia. The counts had either been driven out or had sold off their rights to the rulers of Holland or to the bishops of Utrecht, whose rivalry cancelled each other out. In the gap, self-governing re-publics, or 'sealands', wielded an almost complete power. Claiming an authority that originated in a special concession given by Charle-magne, they vaunted, in the words of one thirteenth-century chroni-cle, 'the liberty of the Frisians that until now they have had, from the time of the Roman Emperor Charlemagne', and struck coinage with the inscription 'Money of Frisia's Liberty'. In Jutland, where Frisian independence was challenged by the Danish kings, the idea of liberty was preserved in the legend of the Frisian pirate Pidder Lüng (Tall Peter), with its stories of a Danish tax collector drowned in cabbage soup, songs extolling the freedom of the seas, and the recurring motif of the gallows and wheel.[17]

Judicial decisions were taken in Frisia by local assemblies of the village or parish, or by groups of them in districts, and, above them, by several dozen councils of so-called consuls that doubled up as courts of appeal. The councils also had the power to judge the most serious crimes and impose the death sentence. For short periods in the thir-teenth and fourteenth centuries, an annual meeting of consuls from the west of Frisia gathered beneath a spreading tree at Upstalsboom to administer common business. Split by rivalries, the institution soon withered, leaving the conduct of affairs with parishes, districts, and councils. Even so, the Upstalsboom keeps to this day a special place in the Frisian imagination as a symbol of popular freedom and of a historic Frisian exceptionalism now squeezed by competing Dutch and German identities.

As in the Swiss Confederacy and Transylvania, Frisian self-rule rested on inequality. Most Frisians were freemen, cultivating their own fields, but the larger landowners monopolized power, since they merited additional votes in the assemblies on account of their more extensive holdings. By the fourteenth century, some of these had taken the hereditary title of *haudling*, or captain, and aped a noble style, with coats of arms and turreted manor houses. Captains built up their own networks of clients and worked their estates with landless labourers and a servile workforce. By the fifteenth century, social relations in much of Frisia had degenerated into an anarchic struggle between the Fats and the Greys (referring, respectively, to well-fed cattle and rough, homespun clothes). Civil strife provided the entry point for foreign intervention and for Duke Albrecht III of Saxony's eventual smashing of the remains of Frisian independence at the end of the fifteenth century.[18]

Frisian liberty, while it lasted, was freedom from external control and from the rule of counts and dukes. In its rhetoric, it borrowed from the republicanism of the North Italian city states and of classical Rome. Cicero and Sallust were educated Frisians' favoured texts—thanks to a proliferation of monastic schools, Frisia was a surprisingly literate society. But Frisia was exceptional only in the degree of its self-government and its clever publicity. Across Central Europe, popular institutions of rule were the norm. Villages and districts were administered by elected councils drawn from the local community. They apportioned grazing rights, chose which household should bear the temporary burden of a bull (an expensive but intermittently necessary item), decided on crop rotation in communally farmed fields, and judged infractions. Councils met weekly or fortnightly and reported to communal assemblies that convened at least annually.[19]

Assemblies in Central Europe were held in the open air or in churches, barns, and dance halls. Announced by the ringing of church bells, they were often festive events, with drummers and trumpeters playing. With so much alcohol swilling about, they could be violent occasions, so weapons were routinely banned, and harsh penalties were laid down for troublemaking. But most village assemblies were dull affairs, where the headman announced the latest property exchanges, communicated new regulations, supervised elections to office, and gave an account of the village finances. Given the tediousness of the business, it is unsurprising that attendance had in places to be rewarded with half a barrel of beer.[20]

One of the headmen's main tasks was to announce judgments given in disputes, since they might provide precedents in similar cases. Weighty decisions were made conjointly with the council and with assessors who were thought to know the law. In difficult cases, headmen might refer to neighbouring city magistrates, or *Schöffen*, for instruction. The law of the community was expected to conform to traditional norms and so to be customary. But there was always slippage, forgetfulness, and deliberate lapses of memory as communities grappled with unforeseen contingencies and strove for a just outcome. So, the law spoken in village and local courts was in a constant state of renewal—it was, in the words of one historian, 'a primaeval forest which is constantly rejuvenated, and in a hundred years will be another forest altogether, although outwardly it remains the same old wood'.[21]

Even so, some important differences may be observed early on across Central Europe. Self-government was more entrenched in the western parts, where villages were older and had often been founded by peasant initiatives. Here, district headmen were generally elected, and corporate identities more deeply impressed, even to the extent that some villages had their own seals and chose their own priests. But society east of the River Elbe was rooted in colonization. Led by men like Albrecht the Bear, noble adventurers and pioneering abbots had invited enterprisers onto their land to recruit settlers, giving them in exchange hereditary leadership of the villages, a large plot of their own, and a slice of the fines paid for infractions. Even when villages had not been founded in this way, they were frequently put under the same arrangements, with the landowner appointing a headman of his own choosing.[22]

From the very start, village institutions of self-government were weaker in the eastern half. Many enterprisers went on to found other settlements, after which they sold on the office of headman, severing entirely their links with the community that they had built. In large parts of the region east of the Elbe, landowners simply appointed the village and district magistrates, without regard for the wishes of their communities, often for life terms. From the fifteenth century onwards, landowners increasingly reserved all but the least important cases to their own manor courts so that they might sweep up the fines, leaving the village authorities with only minor duties—chasing up debts, recording transactions, maintaining roads, and catching poachers.

East of the Elbe, communal government survived into the early modern period only in an attenuated form and often as just an administrative convenience, doing work that the lord's manor court considered trivial. As one lord in northern Bohemia laid down at the beginning of the seventeenth century, the village headman and council should attend to 'wrong dealings and conflicts which are of no importance' and so spare the lord's court from having 'to wait upon a few unimportant persons, so that in the meantime other things can be carried out'. The fictional lament of a curmudgeonly Polish farmer in Władysław Reymont's Nobel Prize–winning *The Peasants* (*Chłopi*, Warsaw, 1904–1908) vividly sums up the reduced and subordinate role of the village headman, or *sołtys*:

And if the taxes are unpaid, or a bridge is out of order, or if a dog hit by a cart goes mad, who is to blame? Why, the *sołtys* always! And the profit? How many a fowl and goose and score of eggs have I not had to send to the clerks and the district officials![23]

Nowhere is the difference between communal institutions west and east of the Elbe more pronounced than in local legislation. Across Central Europe, communities heeded the traditional or customary law. But west of the Elbe it was more firmly fixed. In Frisia, its contents were first committed to alliterative and repetitive verse by poets who doubled up as authorities in the law in court sessions. (There is nothing unusual in this: the same happened in Ireland.) When later put into writing, the texts of the law betray their origins in versified speech—hence one Frisian definition of paralysis caused by a blow to the body: that the victim 'cannot be in bath or in bed, on cob or on cart, on pathway or pond, or on slippery ice, in his house or in God's house, at his hearthside or at his wife's side'.[24]

The great period of Frisian compilation was the late thirteenth century, when oral declarations were put into writing in voluminous texts that included portions of the Bible, riddles, and lists of the sums due for inflicting wounds.[25] From the fourteenth to the sixteenth century, other communities across a wide swathe of Central Europe did the same, converting oral traditions into written memorials. Often known as *Weistümer*, or collections of rules, these were miscellaneous bodies of laws that were said to be traditional and that regulated the legal and economic life of the community. Most come from the western and southern parts of the empire, and they are almost entirely from west of the Elbe. Very many of them survive. In the nineteenth century, Jacob Grimm (otherwise famous for his children's tales) collected several thousand, which he published in a seven-volume edition. Since then, thousands more have come to light—almost eight hundred from Lower Austria, six hundred from Alsace, and so on.

Jacob Grimm saw the *Weistümer* as embodying ancient folk traditions and, although some of the Alsatian ones were composed in French, what it meant historically to be German. In fact, the provisions included in the *Weistümer* were seldom rooted in antiquity but were the product of negotiation between villages and their lords, aimed at avoiding future conflicts. The *Weistümer* were often composed on the basis of questions and answers, usually framed by the lord, with reputedly knowledgeable villagers sharing their beliefs on elections to office, inheritance, grazing on the commons, the gifts owed to the lord at Christmas, the siting of watermills, and so on. Their answers were recorded and provided the basis of the village's customary rights, mostly being rewritten to make them memorable, and often read out or even sung every year at the village assembly.[26]

The final redaction was a bargain between lord and community, but it codified their relations. As with any law, its terms might be superseded by new practices or agreements, but the *Weistümer* stabilized arrangements and provided a line of legal defence against lordly encroachments. Importantly, too, behind the thicket of often trivial injunctions lay the principles that the community should be largely self-regulating, that decisions should be reached by negotiation, and that the lord's power was subject to communal constraints. The *Weistümer* were emphatically not imposed on communities by their lords (as an older generation of historians once claimed) any more than they recollected an ancient folk memory. They were statements describing how power should be shared.[27]

In the sixteenth and seventeenth centuries, the Central European peasantry split down the middle, roughly along the course of the River Elbe and along the line of the *Weistümer*. To the west, a largely free peasantry emerged, having the right to move and to buy and sell land with minimal constraints, and paying cash rents to their lords. To the east, it was different. Lords tied peasant farmers to the land, forbidding them to move, and they obliged them to perform onerous services on their fields. They routinely conscripted peasant children as household servants. Although there were regional variations and local exceptions, across Eastern Holstein, Mecklenburg, Pomerania and the east Baltic shore, Saxony, Brandenburg, Prussia, Poland, Hungary, Transylvania, and large chunks of Bohemia, peasants and their families became more like serfs. In one description of the time, they were *Leibeigenen*—peasants whose lives were owned by their lords. The term is an exaggerated one, but lords could at the very least eject peasants from their plots and annex their farms (as they did in Mecklenburg) or make them serve in small industrial enterprises attached to the lord's manor.[28]

Across Central Europe, communal activity was intense in the Middle Ages. It generated not only self-rule in cities and villages but also urban leagues and families of law, new structures of governance, almost independent republics, and even new countries—by 1500, both Switzerland and Transylvania were moving towards separate statehood. But in the countryside, the foundations differed. East of the Elbe, rural self-government was historically weaker, while the absence of *Weistümer* left the peasantry there without the legal protections that benefited rural folk in the west. The full consequence of these differences would only become clear in the sixteenth and seventeenth centuries, when serfdom began, and the reach of the state became more extensive, but its causes lay deep—reaching right back to the time when the region had first been settled.

Old Prussia, the Adventures of Henry Bolingbroke, and the Union of Poland and Lithuania

*T*HE *TRAVELS OF SIR JOHN MANDEVILLE* WAS ONE OF THE MOST popular books circulating in Central Europe in the Middle Ages. Composed around the middle of the fourteenth century in either English or French (historians are unsure which was first), it had within a few decades been translated into German and Czech, with some fabulous illustrations made by an unknown artist in Prague. The author is a mystery. He may have been, as he says, a knight from St Albans in England, but he is just as likely to have been a Frenchman. One thing is certain—he had never visited most of the places he claims to have been but took his descriptions from older works and from his own fecund imagination.[1]

'Sir John' out-polos Marco Polo. He has been everywhere, he tells us, from the Tower of Babel and China to the legendary kingdom of Prester John, encountering on the way dog-headed men, centaurs, monopods, and griffins. He has been to the north of Europe as well, he says, to Russia, Lithuania, and Lithuania's Baltic neighbour, Livonia. His geography is sketchy, but he knows that east of the Baltic Sea the ground is marshy and that it is best to wait until snowfall so that travel may be done by sleigh. He thinks, too, that the people there are not Christians, which was partly correct at the time he was writing. But he goes on to describe them as Saracens: in other words, Muslim Turks, which the people were surely not.[2]

The same sort of muddle influenced the idea of crusade. Crusades to the Middle East were straightforward enough: they were intended to free Jerusalem and the holy places from Muslim rule. But by the thirteenth century, the crusade against the unbeliever in the land of Christ's birth had broadened to include supposed heretics in southern France and Bosnia, England's troublesome King John, and the popes' political enemies. The Baltic 'saracens' on Central Europe's edge were an obvious target, and Pope Celestine III proclaimed the first crusade against them in 1195. It was the start of more than a dozen expeditions over the next two decades that the popes either initiated or blessed. In anticipation of bringing this northern space into the Christian fold, Celestine's successor, Pope Innocent III, consecrated the region around the Gulf of Riga to Christ's mother, giving it in 1215 the name of 'the Land of Mary' (*Terra Mariana*).

But the Land of Mary was just one part of a vast area of pagan belief. From the mouth of the Vistula River eastwards, pagan tribes occupied a space five hundred kilometres wide, which eventually blurred into territories ruled by Russian princes where the Orthodox religion prevailed. It was difficult terrain, which explains why paganism had held out here. Forests of birch and spruce were intersected by marshes, sandy heaths, and peat bogs and were the home of lynxes, wolves, and bison. Bears had by the thirteenth century been hunted almost to extinction, for the people of the forest considered their roasted paws a delicacy. Foreign travellers found instead wolverines. Described at the time as half cat and half dog, the wolverine defied conventional categories.[3]

Even at the time, outsiders described the mass of tribes living around the eastern Baltic in umbrella terms—as Prussians, Livonians, Lithuanians, and so on, disregarding their political disunity. Many spoke languages that belong to the Baltic family, and most of these languages are now extinct. Only one short piece of Old Prussian survives that is not a religious text. Written down on a school textbook in Prague by a student sometime in the later fourteenth century, it is unsurprisingly about beer—'*Kayle rekyse, Eg koyte poyte*' (Hey, sir, do you want a drink?), but it goes on to warn that the bill will be split. Hollywood casts Prussians as the most bone-headed of Germans, but the first Prussians were not German speakers at all.[4]

The Old Prussians lived mostly in hamlets, often surrounded by fences mounted with animal skulls to ward off evil spirits. They venerated groves and oak trees and imagined gods who visited them in the guise of fire, thunder, snakes, and spectral shapes in the forests. But they practised human sacrifice too and enjoined the widows of slain warriors to hang themselves. As part of their death rituals, they buried horses alive or consigned whole stables to the flames. Even hardened knights, coming fresh to Prussia from the battlefields of the Holy Land, were shocked by what they saw. In one of their descriptions, Old Prussia was 'a land of horrors and wildernesses'.[5]

Single expeditions, as crusades conventionally were, seldom accomplished much. Once the troops had gone home, the Prussians ransacked the churches, cut down their bells, and murdered the priests. The crusaders, too, were frequently unreliable, and undiscerning when it came to varieties of belief. One account from the early thirteenth century tells how after capturing the Livonian town of Kokenhusen (now Koknese, in Latvia), the crusaders 'collected much booty from all its corners: clothes and silver and purple cloth and many flocks. They carried away with them the bells, icons, other ornaments, money, and large amounts of property which they took from the churches and they blessed God.' They had, of course, just ransacked an outpost of Orthodox Christianity.[6]

Discipline and long-term commitment were needed if the work of conquest and conversion was to prosper. The military orders brought this, for they comprised monks whose idea of service to the faith was to make continuous war against the unbeliever. Once they had crushed the pagans in battle, they could leave the completion of God's work to the priests. Although not tonsured, the knights of the orders were indeed monks. They lived communally, eating in refectories and sleeping in dormitories; had taken the monastic vows of poverty, chastity, and obedience; and wore habits over their chain mail. They even kept the divine offices, muttering Pater Nosters as they patrolled on horseback.

The emblems of the first military order to set foot on the Baltic shore were a red sword and cross, demonstrating the fusion of knighthood with Christian mission. The Brothers of the Knighthood of Christ in Livonia, more usually known as the Swordbrothers, were German knights whom the bishop of Riga recruited around 1201 to aid in the conversion of the Livonians. They were astonishingly successful, so much so that in 1213 the Polish duke, Conrad of Masovia, attempted to emulate them with his own military order, the Brothers of the Army of Christ, to fight the pagan Prussians on the edge of his duchy, but there were never enough of them to make a difference. When in the early 1220s, the Prussians sacked the Masovian Chełmno Land (Kulmerland) and advanced on Conrad's principal redoubt at Płock, Conrad embarked on a course that would reshape Central Europe—he invited the assistance of the Teutonic Knights.

The Teutonic Knights, or to give them their full name, the Order of Brothers of the German House of Saint Mary in Jerusalem, were founded in a hospital ship moored outside the city of Acre during the Third Crusade (1189–1192). (Acre is now Akko in northern Israel.) Although the order swiftly militarized by adopting the statutes of the Knight Hospitallers, it never forgot its original vocation of caring for the sick and wounded. But as the Muslim Turks slowly squeezed Christians out of the Middle East, it sought a new mission. After an abortive attempt to set up a statelet in Cilician Armenia (now in southern Turkey), the knights' commander, or grand master, looked to the edges of Central Europe for a new home.[7]

The order's first stop in Central Europe was on the edge of Transylvania, in the so-called Burzenland (around what is now the city of Braşov in Romania). In 1211, Andrew II of Hungary allowed several dozen Teutonic Knights to build fortresses there to defend Transylvania against the nomadic Cumans. The knights brought in settlers and threw up half a dozen strongholds of wood and stone. But Andrew soon changed his mind and decided to send friars to convert the

Cumans peacefully, making the knights' presence superfluous. Relations deteriorated badly, with Andrew claiming that the knights had deceived him and had sought to carve out an independent principality. As Andrew's emissaries complained to the pope, the knights were 'like coals on the chest, a mouse in the pocket, and a snake around the loins'. By 1225, the knights were gone, but not before they had presented Andrew with a large expense claim.[8]

The grand master, Hermann von Salza, was not going to repeat his mistake. So when, after much preliminary negotiation, Conrad of Masovia's formal invitation arrived in 1226, Hermann ensured that the knights had guarantees against a future change of heart. By agreement with Conrad, they were to receive the whole of the Chełmno Land and might keep any territory they captured. On top of this, Hermann extracted written promises from both pope and emperor that the order was subject to the authority of none save the grand master, who was now raised to the rank of Prince of the Empire. Emperor Frederick II's assurance, given in the 1226 Golden Bull of Rimini (called after its place of issue), scarcely runs to two dozen lines of text. More important were the witnesses—twenty of the empire's leading lords and churchmen, whose influence might be brought to bear should Conrad cause difficulties.[9]

The first knights arrived in the Chełmno Land in 1228 and began at once the construction of wooden strongholds along the Vistula River. They were later replaced by the order's characteristic red-bricked fortresses: most spectacularly at Marienburg (Malbork), Marienwerder (Kwidzyn), and Königsberg (Kaliningrad), and subsequently Gdańsk. By 1300, the knights had no fewer than twenty-three of these strongholds in Prussia. Since most of the order's resources were still in the Holy Land, there were to begin with no more than a few dozen knights, so they relied heavily on Polish troops and on volunteers who joined them on campaign. The fighting was at first easy. The Prussians were swiftly driven from the field by the armoured knights and their crude defences broken by catapult fire. But the Prussians used the forests as cover and soon learned how to build siege artillery of their own and to use crossbows. Even areas that had been pacified burst periodically into uprisings, with forts and villages overrun and captured knights roasted alive in their chain mail.

Even so, by 1273 Prussia was subdued and the last of its pagan leaders, Herkus Monte, hanged from a tree. From then on, the knights were in undisputed control. They divided up the land into uniform parcels, recruited agents to find German settlers, and lured newcomers with the usual promises of farmland, tax freedoms, and limited self-government. Noble immigrants received estates, performing in return military services for the order. Around the order's forts, new cities sprang up, again with imported settlers, who lived under a version of Magdeburg law (known as Chełmno or Kulm law). They mimicked the architecture of the German cities to the west, except due to the absence of stone, these too were made of red bricks. There were new bishoprics too, with their cathedral chapters stuffed full of knights to ensure that the right bishops were elected. Churches, monasteries, processions bearing relics (the order had an armful of pieces of the Holy Cross to distribute), and pilgrimage sites made sacred a formerly pagan landscape.[10]

Germanization followed. It was not deliberate, since the order allowed Prussian villages to remain under their own elders, following their own laws, and it dissuaded intermarriage. But the scale of immigration overwhelmed the native Prussians. One tale tells how the last Prussian bard sang at the grand master's court in the 1350s, but that there was no one left who could understand him and so he was dismissed with a plate of mouldy walnuts. A story is all it is—right through to the sixteenth century, the knights needed interpreters to communicate with the Prussians. But the Old Prussians' language and lore were lost soon afterwards. All that survives of the Old Prussians today are their strange stone statues of forgotten warriors, bearing swords and drinking horns, which stand a metre or so tall in fields and beside country lanes. (Most have now been moved to museums.)[11]

In 1239, the original Swordbrothers' order collapsed. Defeated by an alliance of Baltic tribes and at odds with its nominal superior, the bishop of Riga, the order merged with the Teutonic Knights. Although the Swordbrothers remained a separate fighting unit, they now came under the overall command of the grand master. Even so, the Teutonic Knights maintained the traditional expansionist ambitions of the Swordbrothers, aiming at the Russian principalities to the east and at the wealthy city of Novgorod. Alexander Nevsky's defence of Novgorod and defeat of the knights on the frozen Lake Peipus in 1242 put an end to their ambitions. (The so-called Battle on the Ice is famously the highpoint of Sergei Eisenstein's 1938 film *Alexander Nevsky*.) The Narva River, which joins Lake Peipus to the Gulf of Finland, marked the limit of Catholicism's eastward movement from the Baltic coastland.

To the east, the lands of the Teutonic Knights and of the Swordbrothers both bordered on the Lithuanians. The Lithuanians were the last of the Baltic tribes to convert to Christianity. In the imagination of contemporaries, they not only were Saracens but also fought with the Star of David on their shields, so they were thought to be tainted by Judaism too. The problem was that Lithuania was the premier of the Baltic states. It was ruled by a single house, led by a grand duke, who appointed his kinsmen to govern its parts. In the wake of the Mongol destruction of the Russian principalities, the grand dukes had rolled up huge parts of the region. By the middle years of the fourteenth century, they had occupied what is now Belarus and the north of Ukraine and were pressing hard against Smolensk and Kyiv. By 1375, Lithuania occupied a space of no fewer than seven hundred thousand square kilometres, making it by far the largest state in Europe.

The grand duchy of Lithuania also had the sparsest population density in all Europe—roughly two persons per square kilometre. Expansion had brought with it a significant Orthodox and Russian- and Ukrainian-speaking population. The grand dukes shrewdly embraced the West Russian language, written in modified Cyrillic characters, as their means of communication and they protected Orthodox congregations. (We use the term 'West Russian' advisedly: even today, it is variously called Ukrainian, Belarusian, and Ruthene, depending upon which nationalist axe is being ground.) They were indulgent to Catholicism too, permitting a church and Franciscan friary to be built in the Lithuanian capital Vilnius, and regularly putting their hastily converted daughters onto the marriage market in Poland, Bohemia, and elsewhere. In 1382, a part-Lithuanian princess, Anne of Bohemia, even became the queen of Richard II of England, to the consternation of church lawyers.[12]

In 1291, the Teutonic Order lost its final outpost in the Holy Land, after which it moved its headquarters to Marienburg in Prussia. The order now committed itself fully to crusading against the Lithuanians, in a war that would go on for 130 years. But the order's numbers were small—at most, it had a thousand or so knights in Prussia and Livonia, most of whom manned garrisons. So, it depended on a steady flow of volunteers from the west, who came for a season to fight in what the knights called 'the Wilderness'. There was no lack of them. Princes and kings were among the first to enlist, including King John of Bohemia—it was probably the ultraviolet light reflected off the snow that caused John to lose his sight. Tens of thousands of humbler knights, squires, and adventurers followed in their wake.[13]

Lithuania was the first international hunt, and the 'expeditions', or *Reysen*, were after big game—pagan princes who thought nothing of feasting for twelve hours or bagging a hundred bison in a single day. The rewards were not only spiritual. A tour in the Wilderness guaranteed new friendships and the chance to live out fantasies of knightly romance. True, women were in short supply, for the order was sworn to celibacy and its knights betrothed to the Virgin Mary. Even so, mealtimes could be lavish affairs, where to the sound of minstrels knights told stories of derring-do and poets recited tales of King Arthur and old German legends, reimagining Livonia as 'Nieflant', or the Land of the Nibelungs.[14]

Henry Bolingbroke, the future King Henry IV of England (ruled 1399–1413), was a latecomer to Lithuania, venturing there in 1390 and 1392. His account books survive, and they tell of the enormous personal wealth that well-heeled warriors disbursed during their stays

POLAND AND LITHUANIA AT THE END OF THE FOURTEENTH CENTURY

with the knights, much of which found its way into the order's coffers. Altogether, Henry spent on his first trip more than 4,300 pounds, which in the money of the time translates into several thousand or more good horses. His father, John of Gaunt, had to help him out on his return to England, but the duchy of Lancaster had deep pockets.[15]

Henry arrived in Gdańsk with almost a hundred men, including thirteen knights, eighteen squires, six minstrels, and a trumpeter. Within a month, he was outside Vilnius, the Lithuanian capital, where he helped in the storming of the city and the siege of the castle, until sent packing by a Lithuanian relief force. Having paid the ransom for several of his men who had been captured, Henry rode to the safety of Königsberg castle, where he spent the next few months hunting, riding in tournaments, and exchanging lavish gifts. All the while, his household staff were spending prodigious sums on food, fuel, fodder, beer, wine from Gascony and the Rhineland, sugar, pelts for Henry's wardrobe, and the upkeep of several Lithuanian boys whom Henry had adopted. Throughout his stay, Henry was expected to pay for his own and his retinue's accommodation and for their transportation by ship as well as boat repairs. Living out an Arthurian fantasy did not come cheaply.[16]

We do not know what Henry thought of the Lithuanians he fought. But by the late fourteenth century, they had lost much of their earlier menace. The Lithuanian dukes and nobles were in their dress and manner almost indistinguishable from their German counterparts. Their underlings were seen no longer as vicious pagans but as comparable to humble folk throughout Europe. In the words of a French knight, who fought with the order a decade after Henry, Lithuanian men were marked by their shoulder-length hair and their womenfolk by their simple homespun dress—so much so that they resembled the French peasants of Picardy. But, as the Frenchman's description of Lithuania's bishops and new brick churches makes clear, the Lithuanians were by the time he was writing also Christians.[17]

One of the most extraordinary aspects of the Lithuanian crusade is that it continued even after the Lithuanian ruling house had embraced Catholicism. Lithuania's grand duke did so for good political reasons. In the past, paganism had made sense, for it had allowed the Lithuanians to play their Catholic and Orthodox neighbours against one another. But by the late fourteenth century, both sides threatened to squeeze Lithuania. Moscow in the east had not only thrown off its subjection to the Tatars but was also expanding rapidly. To the west, the Teutonic Order was pressing forward with new vigour, mounting in the middle decades of the fourteenth century more than a hundred incursions into Lithuania in less than forty years. Christianity was inevitable, and Catholicism made more sense than Orthodoxy, for it would win allies against Moscow and embarrass the order.

But the initiative came from Poland. In the first decades of the fourteenth century, Władysław the Elbow-High (ruled 1306–1333) had restored the Polish monarchy, taking possession of the Polish duchies when they became vacant due to a lack of heirs and fomenting rebellions in the rest so as to drive out their rulers. His son Casimir the Great (1333–1370) continued the task of rebuilding the kingdom, shrewdly abandoning the Polish claim to Silesia as too hard to make good. He recaptured lost royal estates, filled up the kingdom's empty spaces by promoting immigration and giving settlers the same rights as they enjoyed further west, and reinvigorated the Polish cities by admitting Jews and Armenians. He ordered the construction of forty castles and stone city walls and founded in Cracow the second oldest university in Central Europe (after Prague).

But in one crucial respect, Casimir failed to fulfil his royal vocation, for he sired no male heir. It was not for want of trying, for Casimir discarded two wives when he thought them to have failed him. Not bothering with legal divorces, the king was a bigamist twice over. But his trespasses bore no fruit. On his deathbed, Casimir still only had five daughters. By previous agreement, the crown accordingly passed to his nephew, the Angevin king Louis I of Hungary. Yet, like Casimir, Louis too failed in the fundamental business of leaving a male heir, having only two daughters at the time of his death in 1382. The danger was that without a legitimate ruler, illegitimate ones would step into the void, dividing the kingdom up between them.

The lead was taken by a group of nobles from Lesser Poland around Cracow, boldly acting in the name of 'the community of lords and citizens'. There was no lack of unsuitable candidates for the throne of Poland—a Habsburg, Luxembourger, and several Polish lords with ambitions above their station. But King Louis's daughters had the most obvious biological claim and the younger, the eleven-year-old Jadwiga, came without the encumbrance of a spouse. So, she was crowned 'king' in 1384: like the English Channel Islands, where the late Queen Elizabeth II was styled a duke, Poland's law did not acknowledge the possibility of a female sovereign. But finding Jadwiga a husband just took the problem back to the start. The Polish lords reckoned well enough that Jadwiga would fall into line with whomever they chose for her, but they knew that the man would inevitably exercise the royal prerogatives on the girl's behalf.

We do not know who first had the idea that Jadwiga should marry the Lithuanian Grand Duke Jogaila, but it made sense. The Lithuanians were looking for a way out of their strategic impasse. The Poles, too, had suffered at the hands of the Teutonic Order. In 1311, the knights had seized the city of Gdańsk and the surrounding region of Pomerelia, after which border wars had repeatedly flared. Surviving accounts tell of the order's knights destroying churches, burning villages, chopping off heads and fingers, and raping Polish women and girls. A full-blown war fought in the late 1320s and 1330s saw the knights sack Gniezno, although sparing the cathedral. Even after peace was made in 1343, the order continued to stir up trouble by allying with disaffected Polish lords. Under continued pressure from the order, Polish interests now converged with those of their Lithuanian neighbours.[18]

The deal was done at the Lithuanian stronghold of Kreva in 1385. Jogaila agreed to convert to Catholic Christianity and to baptise his subjects. In return, the Polish lords would choose him as king and he would wed Jadwiga. Early the next year, Jogaila went through the three ceremonies—baptism, marriage, and coronation. Historians often describe

Jogaila as hairy, but he was only so to the extent that he wore his locks long, as was the Lithuanian custom. Even so, he sought to assuage Polish fears about pagan bodies, so before marriage he invited Jadwiga's chamberlain to interview him in his bath. The chamberlain was able to report back that Jogaila was 'graceful and well-shaped, has a merry expression, and a long face without trace of disfigurement'. As for Jadwiga, she proved after marriage a spirited companion, leading an army into the disputed frontier province of Red Ruthenia. But she also endowed the new university of Cracow, giving it a proper building instead of a handful of rooms, and engaged in conspicuous acts of piety until her early death in 1399.[19]

The constitutional relationship between Poland and Lithuania was unclear. The Kreva agreement spoke of the two countries as committed 'to join permanently together' (*perpetuo applicare*)—an unusual formulation that was perhaps deliberately vague. In fact, the union of Poland and Lithuania endured for four hundred years, proving Napoleon's dictum that the best constitutions are short and ambiguous. But there can be no doubt that the losers were the Teutonic Knights. The Kreva agreement had specified that Jogaila should recapture the lost parts of Poland and Lithuania, but he bided his time. It was only in 1409 that he took up arms, pushing into Prussia, putting Marienburg under siege, and smashing the order's knights at the Battle of Grunwald or Tannenberg (1410), after which the knights were obliged to sign a humiliating peace.

The Christianization of Lithuania had followed immediately upon Jogaila's baptism. First, he brought the chief men and Lithuanian nobles (or boyars) to the font. Then, the pagan temples were destroyed and the great shrine in Vilnius replaced by a cathedral. Parishes and bishoprics followed. Of course, in many cases conversion was only skin deep, as indeed it may have been with Jogaila. Although taking the name of Władysław at his baptism, Jogaila kept up, in one contemporary account, 'the old pagan custom that he had observed all his life, going into the forest to listen to its magic sounds and hear the song of the nightingale.' Jogaila's communing with nature eventually killed him, since in 1434 he contracted pneumonia after a night spent alone in the woods. But, on his deathbed, he made confession, heard the last rites, and commended his soul to the Christian God.[20]

The Teutonic Knights made much of such religious ambiguities. To justify their continued crusade against the Lithuanians and to win volunteers like Henry Bolingbroke, they postulated that the Lithuanians' conversion was a fraud and that they still fought alongside unbelievers and Muslim Tatars recruited from the steppe. The order's spokesmen maintained that by their association with the Lithuanians the Poles were pseudo-Christians too, and that they had demonstrated their unbelief by killing prisoners, raping and pillaging, burning down churches, and trampling the sacraments underfoot. Jogaila denied all this—he was, he averred, a good Christian and, indeed, 'Christ's champion' (*athleta Christi*), without whom the Lithuanians would never have been brought to the Catholic faith.[21]

The order took its complaints to the emperor and in 1415 to the Church Council meeting in Constance. There had been occasions in the past when Central European rulers had drawn attention to their role in the defence of Christianity. Back in the mid-thirteenth century, King Béla IV of Hungary had advertised Hungary as a gateway that must be kept closed to protect Christendom from the Mongols. A century later, Casimir the Great of Poland justified his capture of Red Ruthenia on the grounds that it was necessary for the protection of his kingdom, perched as it was on the edge of the Christian world. But under the influence of the Teutonic Order, the rhetoric used to describe the imperilled Christian frontier dramatically changed.[22]

At Constance, the knights' spokesmen militarized the language in which the frontier was described. Catholic Christianity was a fortress, they explained, and the knights were its walls, moat, and bastion: they were 'a tower of strength in the face of the enemy, and a wall of crystal with firm redoubts' that had held back the faithless hordes that gathered to overwhelm Christendom. Jogaila replied in writing. No, he declared, the knights were not the true guardians of Christendom, for they had turned their swords on the faithful. It was instead the Poles who were its protectors, and he also, for was he not 'the truest and firmest defender and most doughty shield of the Catholic faith'?[23]

The debate about which side was truer in its defence of Christianity dragged on for two years without the Church Council arriving at any firm conclusion. But it had revolutionized the way that Poles thought of themselves. Adopting the language of the knights, they too began to speak of Poland as a redoubt and rampart—in the language of the time, an *antemurale*. From then on, Polish diplomats increasingly inserted into their speeches references to Poland as a bulwark. Situated at the edge of Christian Europe, the kingdom was a citadel and rampart that prevented the tides of Tatars and Turks from overrunning all of Central Europe. But Poland had halted the Russians of Moscow too, they explained, blocking the way westwards of a ruler who was no true Christian but an Asian tyrant, blasphemer, and unbeliever (although in fact he was an Orthodox Christian). In short, Poland was necessary for Christendom's survival.[24]

The idea of Poland as an armed border and *antemurale* dug deep and wide. Foreign poets extolled Poland's defence of Christendom and, as early as the 1460s, papal envoys spoke of Poland in the same terms, as a 'wall and bastion of the Christian faith'. In similar vein, the Dutch scholar Erasmus celebrated in the 1520s the energy of Poland's king in defending a space that ran from the Baltic to the Carpathians and praised his victories that had 'protected the boundaries of Christendom'. Around the same time, the Italian diplomat and historian Niccolò Machiavelli similarly explained that the Poles along with the Hungarians

form a bastion which prevents the Scythians who live on their borders from attempting either to conquer them or to pass through them . . . and it has often been their boast that, if it had not been for them, Italy and the Church would on many occasion have felt the weight of Tatar armies. [Scythian is a classical catch-all name for a mounted raider.][25]

The language of the rampart, or *antemurale*, intensified with the Turkish advance in the Balkans and had by the sixteenth century become a common trope throughout much of Central Europe. It took root in Hungary, where the nobility saw themselves as keeping 'the rest of Christendom safe and unharmed at the cost of their blood, life, and wounds'. But it struck chords in what is now Slovenia and in Croatia and Austria too. By the close of the Middle Ages, rulers and their subjects were increasingly imagining Central Europe as a world of frontier fortresses, whose inhabitants were engaged in an incessant war of defence against an enemy that was as perennial and encircling as the dog-headed men of medieval legend and John de Mandeville's Saracens.[26]

CHAPTER 11

Merchants, the Hanseatic League, and the Fuggers

MERCHANTS WERE VULNERABLE. ON THE MOVE, THEIR WARES were strung out on lines of mules and packhorses—it took seventy of the beasts to carry the contents of a modern midsize truck. Ambushes of exposed convoys were frequent. Despite an escort of 150 men, a shipment of coin from Poland to Rome was looted near Pavia in 1328, with half the bullion stolen. Without the protection of an armed escort, robbery was certain. One wayfaring German knight baked his valuables in a loaf of bread to hide them from sight. Another wore a reversible jacket with a camouflage lining to confuse the bandits of the Tyrol. Even the helpless might expect no mercy: in some years, as many as a half of all pilgrims to Rome were murdered on the way.[1]

Cargoes were equally at risk on the high seas. The Danish straits between Jutland and Sweden were in the fourteenth century infested by several hundred pirate ships. Pirates also took over the island of Gotland in the Baltic, using it as a base to rob shipping, until ejected by the Teutonic Knights in 1398. There was state-sponsored piracy too. In just one decade in the late fourteenth century, German seafarers from Prussia claimed to have been wronged twenty-two times by Englishmen, including six cases of piracy and four occasions when their ships had been seized by agents of the English king. In retaliation, the cities of Prussia confiscated the goods in port of English merchants, bagging their cargoes. Under Duke Barnim VI (ruled 1394–1405), Pomerania became a haven for corsairs, whose plundering of the Baltic trade and coastline helped fill the ducal coffers.[2]

Depredation might also be done legally, through tolls. By the mid-fourteenth century, the main thoroughfares in Central European cities had been paved, cobbled, or given planked sidewalks, but in sub-urbs and villages they were seas of mud in winter. Wooden pattens that elevated the feet were usual. In the countryside, the condition of roads was often indicated by their names—'clay road', 'earthen road', 'grassy road', 'stony road', and so on. Landowners routinely charged tolls for the upkeep of roads and bridges, while neglecting to do any repairs. Even trackways had tolls—there were at least forty in the mountain-ous Vorarlberg east of Lake Constance. In the neighbouring Tyrol, toll stations were set up every ten or twenty kilometres on the roads. To add to the burdens of the travelling merchant, many of these stations doubled up as staples, where traders had under pain of fine to put their cargoes up for sale.[3]

Rivers were seldom canalled and embanked before the nineteenth century. They were sluggish, broad, and fouled by the dumping of of-fal from slaughterhouses upstream. At Vienna, the Danube comprised a shifting network of channels and mudbanks, six kilometres broad. The slough swallowed up whole the neighbouring Roman city of Car-nuntum following its abandonment in the fifth century. Fish weirs and floating watermills were an additional impediment to navigation. To power mills behind the riverbank, landowners frequently diverted the flow, thus rendering the river unnavigable. In the 1590s, one am-bitious enterpriser drained overnight an entire stretch of the Bodrog River in northeastern Hungary, leaving its bed exposed.[4]

Rivers also had their toll places, which were enforced by patrol boats and chains that ran from bank to bank. There were in the mid-thirteenth century twelve stations on the 180-kilometre stretch of the Rhine between Mainz and Cologne, to which we may add the illegal tolls gathered by the robber barons whose broken castles still overlook the river. It was later reckoned that one-third of the value of a cargo might be lost to tolls in just the seventy kilometres between Bingen and Mainz on the Rhine. Traffic on the Danube was similarly impeded by toll places, of which there were in the late fifteenth century no fewer than seventy-seven in Lower Austria alone. The bishops of Passau were the main beneficiaries.

Merchants formed alliances to bargain with rulers and lords over toll places and measures against brigandage and even to build new cities. Many of these became societies or guilds in which the members swore solemn oaths to support one another, to help each other out in time of need, and to honour their contracts. Where even the most basic means of enforcing obligations were missing, institutions of social solidarity had to take their place. Most Central European cities had merchant guilds, which restricted membership to the wealthy wholesale suppliers. Some managed to be both a guild and an organization for having masses said, as for instance the Society of the Holy Trinity in Lübeck, which for good measure also asserted an exclusive right to office in the city council.[5]

It was only a short step before some merchant societies became enterprises in their own right, with their members investing capital and taking a share of the return. The Great Ravensburg Company, founded in southern Swabia in the late fourteenth century, had up to ninety members who invested in enterprises as far afield as Antwerp, Barcelona, Milan, Vienna, Buda, and Wrocław. Its principal trade was in spices, wine, olive oil, paper, and metal ores. It also gave interest-free loans to its own members, and high-interest ones to churchmen. The annual return to investors averaged about 7 per cent. Other merchant societies dealt in the bulk supply of cloth and ore, and most fought to take control of their respective city councils with the aim of regulating their competitors out of business. But they did at least enjoin good conduct among the members, forbidding them (as in Gdańsk) from abusing bartenders, drawing knives in an argument, and throwing glasses and jugs at mealtime.[6]

The Hansa or Hanseatic League started off as a merchant society but became an alliance of cities. (In German, *Hansa* simply means an association or fellowship.) At its height in the fourteenth and fifteenth centuries, it dominated commerce in northern Europe, mostly along the Baltic shore and what is now northwestern Germany, but with outposts in England, Norway, Novgorod in Russia, and Iceland (for its hawks). But its organization was opaque. As the league's envoys explained in 1469 when pressed by an English court to describe the league's constitution, it was neither a company, nor a partnership, joint venture, or corporation, but instead 'an agreement and alliance of many cities . . . a firm confederation of many cities, towns, and communities for the purpose of ensuring that business enterprises by land and sea should have a desired and favourable outcome.'[7]

In fact, the Hanseatic League was a business lobby, with gunships. Depending on when and how we count them, the league had anywhere between seventy and two hundred member cities, but some were full participants in its organization while others enjoyed the benefits of belonging without contributing to the costs. Even the Hansa's chief officers claimed they could not list the league's members. Nonetheless, the league took on kingdoms and duchies, forcing through advantageous commercial agreements for its members under threat of blockade. Its navy, mainly supplied by the chief city of Lübeck, fought against Denmark in the 1360s and against England in the 1470s. On this occasion, the league blockaded the English coast until King Edward IV backed down and gave the league extensive concessions.

The league negotiated with kings and rulers to obtain reductions in customs duties, for legal exemptions for merchants, for rights of salvage and wreck, and for permission to set up 'factories' or bonded warehouses, where goods could be stored for onward shipment without payment of tariffs. Typical of these was the London Steelyard. (The name derives from *Stahlhof* or *Stapelhof*, meaning a depot where goods were exchanged.) Now covered by Cannon Street railway station, the Steelyard had its own warehouses, great hall, and accounting offices, as well as kitchens and accommodation. Occupying a site 50 by 150 metres next to the River Thames, the Steelyard operated according to the practices and regulations of the Hanseatic League, disregarding the English Common Law.[8]

By the fourteenth century, the Hanseatic League had its own diet (Hansetag), which usually met in Lübeck. The diets were supposed to gather every three years, but they often assembled more frequently. The diets levied taxes on the Hanseatic cities, decided on blockades and military action in support of the league, ruled on the admission of new members, and arbitrated disputes. The diet's decisions were binding and made by a supposedly unanimous vote, but they were usually judged inapplicable to cities that had not sent delegates. So, many cities stayed away, preventing common action. Nor did the league ever establish a single body of maritime law. Cases were instead adjudicated according to the law of the city where the dispute originated. In this respect, the league was never more than the sum of its parts.[9]

Instead, the league was a facilitator. It created the conditions for trade and for the prosperity of its members. But it also fostered a sense of common identity. Its cities emulated Lübeck, building brick churches that were inspired by Lübeck's St Mary's and tall gabled houses that were large enough to include a warehouse. Lübeck's almond-rich marzipan was famous, and its recipe copied across the Baltic. The league's merchants, ever anxious for social respectability, aped the nobility, inventing their own fabulous Hanseatic lore that wove together Arthurian romance, epic tales, and stories about their own families and cities. Knights' Halls, new coats of arms in sticky stucco, and oversize statues of Charlemagne's legendary companion Roland of Roncesvalles were as much features of these early centres of capitalist endeavour as the country-club memberships and manor houses to which today's wealthy businessmen aspire.

But the league's greatest achievement was more practical—a solid body of technical knowledge for navigating the northern seas that its members exchanged and refined. Manuals and guidebooks listed the landmarks to be followed, the prevailing winds, the right nautical bearings, and the depth of the sea. By using a plumb line, the mariner could follow the lie of the seabed to reach his destination, plotting his course by reference to the submarine mounds and gullies. In addition, by coating the lead weight of the plumb line with wax or glue, Hanseatic skippers could tell from the mix of sand and soil how close they were to estuaries or landfall. As Fra Mauro, the greatest of fifteenth-century cartographers, observed of the Baltic, 'In this sea, one navigates neither by chart nor by compass, but by the lead.'[10]

The main trade of the Hansa was west–east. Although they also traded luxury goods, like amber, spices, and ermine fur, the league's members mostly dealt in bulk: timber, ores, beer, textiles, barrelled herring, and salt. The axis of Hanseatic trade ran roughly from Novgorod in Russia to Lübeck, Hamburg, Bruges, and London. But by the fourteenth century, the Hanseatic trade route was under pressure from a second axis, further to the south, that linked Cracow and Wrocław to Leipzig and the cities of southern Germany, pre-eminently Nuremberg and Augsburg. The merchants involved in this trade were also bulk carriers, bringing cloth from the Low Countries and England. They were the league's competitors and what they were after was metal ore.

The Carpathians were rich in precious metals. Hungary was the main producer, accounting in the fourteenth century for two-thirds of the world's gold. Its silver deposits were second in Europe only to Bohemia's. Hungary's kings made their trade a royal monopoly. Base ores were unaffected, even though these too often had a high value. Copper was in increasing demand in manufacturing and roofing, and later for shipbuilding. When mixed with tin, it made the bronze for cannons and bells. Copper was also a valuable export item, feeding the Middle Eastern markets, where it was minted for everyday coinage.[11]

By the early fourteenth century, Central Europe's traditional source of copper in the Harz mountains had dried up as a result of exhaustion and of rainwater seeping into and eventually flooding the mine shafts. Merchants from the south German cities accordingly reoriented their trade towards Hungary, buying up copper ore and selling it on for domestic manufacture or for export via Venice. To begin with, they faced competition from Hanseatic merchants selling to the Teutonic Order and from the Medici family in Florence. But by adept political manoeuvring and the sheer weight of their capital, merchants from Nuremberg were able to oust their rivals and build a cartel that dominated the Hungarian copper trade. They reinforced their control by also having copper declared a royal monopoly, in the transport of which they had exclusive rights.[12]

Hungary had an infant industry that mined copper, mostly in the mountains to the north in what is now central and eastern Slovakia, but it was underresourced. To prosper, it needed investment. Drainage equipment was prohibitively expensive—likewise, the cost of digging sluices to carry off the water. On top of this, timber, winches, and industrial hammers had to be bought, and wooden railways and trucks built for the galleries. The Nuremberg merchants provided the money for all this, and from roughly 1390 to 1440 Hungarian mining flourished. Sometimes, the merchants took over the mines and worked them directly, but more usually they invested capital in return for a portion of the ore extracted. They could afford to, for they shared a secret.

The secret was that Hungarian copper was argentiferous, or silver bearing, and from no later than 1400 the Nurembergers knew how to break it down into its elements. Smelting was not enough to separate copper and silver. Instead, a special furnace was needed that alloyed lead and argentiferous copper, after which the alloy itself was remelted, or 'liquated', so that the lead carried off the silver. The process had to be repeated several times to extract all the silver from the copper and have it bond to the lead. At that point, it was easy to separate the silver and lead by melting the new compound in a cupellation furnace (really, a large crucible) and oxidizing the lead. Liquation and cupellation meant that the copper was purer and that it came with the bonus of a small but valuable quantity of silver.[13]

Liquation was arduous and closely guarded. Outside the south German cities and a few places in northern Italy, no one knew how to do it. Business partners admitted to the confidence had to swear oaths of secrecy, while manuals for the recently initiated hid the techniques behind alchemical symbols and Hebrew letters. This is unsurprising, since liquation yielded spectacular returns. In just thirty years in the sixteenth century, one operator in northern Hungary refined

fifty thousand tonnes of copper, yielding five hundred tonnes of silver.
A Nuremberg merchant acquired in the 1520s a consignment of Bohemian copper that after liquation was worth more than forty times
the cost of purchase.

But, by the mid-fifteenth century, the heyday of the Nurembergers
had passed. The Hungarian diet ordered the breakup of their monopoly at exactly the time the Saxon Mansfeld and Tyrolean copper mines
were being opened up. The Nurembergers' place in Hungary was taken
by local entrepreneurs, but none of these had the financial wherewithal
to fund development. Formerly prosperous mines fell into disrepair
and the pitheads were abandoned, absorbed into agricultural land. Tax
holidays and other reliefs brought no change in fortune. It was the
same in the gold mines, where the most productive seams had been
worked out. By the 1490s, most of Hungary's mining industry was in
ruins.[14]

The Hansa and the south German merchants were old-fashioned
venturers, exchanging goods for ready cash, which they then invested
in new cargoes or enterprises. But by the fifteenth century, the bankers and accountants were moving in—they knew how to keep books,
how to move money on paper bills rather than in sacks of coin, and
how to negotiate and sell on commercial debt. The Medici family in
Florence was at the forefront of innovation, grafting banking and exchange onto international trade, and with commercial connections
that reached north of the Alps, to Buda and Cracow. But the Medici
mostly conducted their affairs through temporary partnerships and
not as a consolidated business or even as a family enterprise. Medici
financial methods and accounting were also sloppy, with theft and
mismanagement commonplace, while the Medici frequently paid the
interest on debt they owed by the dangerous remedy of taking on new
debts. A desperate raid on bridal dowries deposited for safe keeping
presaged the Medici bank's collapse in the 1490s.[15]

In Central Europe, the principal financiers were the Fugger family, based in Augsburg. They did not make the same mistakes as the
Medici. First, they ran the family enterprise as a unit, with brothers

and nephews all investing. As they contracted not to trade under their own private accounts, the profits came back into the business. This made for a concentration of capital, which the Fuggers used to monopolize the market in loans and metals. By the end of the fifteenth century, they were the bankers of both emperors and popes, and the largest dealers in copper and silver in the world. The copper ingots they exported on galleons that shipwrecked off the African coast still lie on the shores of Namibia and Mozambique today.[16]

Secondly, the Fuggers had as their accountant one of the sharpest and most original minds of the day, Matthäus Schwarz (1497–c. 1574). Schwarz was a dandy who employed an artist to keep a record of the hundred or more outfits he bought in his lifetime, each of which could cost as much as five times a servant's annual wage. Schwarz's clothes were wonderful assemblages of coloured silk hosiery, garters, fur-lined cloaks, and doublets that had been tailored with slashes to show off their expensive lining. Schwarz was among the first in Europe to celebrate his birthday since it increased the number of occasions on which he might parade in his latest dress. (Hitherto only name days had been celebrated.) He marked the turning points in his life with portraits too—of him stamping on his textbooks when he left school, riding in the sleigh he crashed in the marketplace, and recovering in bed from a stroke.[17]

Schwarz only joined the Fuggers in 1516, but that makes his achievement all the greater, for he was taking on a business at its height with its own conventions and ways of adding up. Schwarz's oversight extended to forty branches of the Fugger bank that straddled Europe. Schwarz was a masterful bookkeeper, versed in the different regional accounting methods. A further passion of his was to describe these in a manuscript for private circulation that he periodically updated called *On the Three Ways of Bookkeeping* (*Von Dreierlay Buchhaltung*). Schwarz explained the Italian and German techniques of accounting and how the Fuggers' head office in Augsburg kept track of its own business in local branches.[18]

Schwarz was not the first bookkeeper north of the Alps to use double entry, where every transaction is recorded twice, as both a debit and a credit. But he refined it and established the language of the journals or day books that made it possible to see the relevant figures at a glance so that they might then be added to the ledger. Schwarz was crusading in his advocacy of record keeping and dismissive of merchants who 'confine everything to memory or to piecemeal scraps of paper . . . such people soon go bankrupt and, what is even worse, do not know why it has happened.' As he urged his readers in the *Three Ways of Book-keeping*, 'Don't forget anything, and write everything down!' By his cajoling and example, Schwarz gave the Fuggers an integrated system for calculating assets, debts, and profits, and a means of auditing the performance of local branches. He gave Central Europe its first taste of modern financial management.[19]

The Fuggers were parvenus. Only two generations before, they had been poor immigrants from the countryside who had come to Augsburg looking for work—one had ended up a servant with criminal connections. Originally weavers, the Fuggers had moved into commerce so that by the 1470s they already counted as one of Augsburg's premier families, conducting in one description of the time an 'enormous trade, with spices, silks and woollen cloth'. But they were also moving into finance, transferring funds across Central Europe on behalf of clients and lending to churchmen as far afield as Rome and Pomerania.[20]

By the beginning of the fifteenth century, Jacob Fugger was head of the family. His brothers were dead and his cousins, having tried to do business on their own, were bankrupts. From the very first, Jacob was alert to the perils of insolvency. His earliest loans were to Sigismund of the Tyrol, a Habsburg archduke who owned the fabulous wealth of the Schwaz silver mines. Sigismund spent his fortune on mistresses (they bore him no fewer than fifty bastards), lavish entertainments that involved small people leaping out of pies, and the hunting lodges where he kept his trophies. The rest he squandered.[21]

Jacob knew Sigismund's reputation, but he made the decision that the Fuggers should move from commerce into 'larger and more profitable enterprises, namely exchange and mining'. In return for his loans,

Jacob took not an empty promise of repayment but almost the whole Schwaz mining industry as collateral as well as the sole right to sell silver to the Tyrolean mint. In other words, he acquired the monopoly in both the purchase and sale of Tyrolean silver. Within ten years of the first loan in 1485, Jacob had made a profit from Sigismund of 400,000 florins. (Although comparisons are misleading, the gold equivalent in modern-day terms is about US$70 million, but for purchasing power we should probably multiply that by ten.)[22]

Jacob Fugger was a good judge of men. He spotted Schwarz and throughout his life Jacob was either the employer or the benefactor of some of the greatest scholars and artists of the early sixteenth century. He was the patron of both Albrecht Dürer and Hans Burgkmair. Dürer not only painted Jacob's portrait but also designed the Fugger burial chapel in Augsburg's Carmelite chapel, one of the earliest examples of Renaissance architecture in Central Europe. Burgkmair went to work on the frescoes that decorated the façade and main rooms of the Fugger Palace (Fuggerhäuser) in Augsburg—otherwise, a gaudy assemblage of gold stucco work and marble floors on whose ice-like surface the unwary visitor could slip. But Jacob's most enduring monument was the work of an Augsburg mason, Thomas Krebs. Krebs designed and built the almshouses at Fuggerei, then on the outskirts of the city. With more than a hundred dwellings, it was at the time the largest complex of its type in Europe. Still in operation today, the Fuggerei's occupants are enjoined to pray thrice daily for Jacob's soul.[23]

Jacob was drawn to the Hungarian foundry owner and entrepreneur John Thurzó. Thurzó came from the mining districts of northern Hungary but had moved in the 1460s to Cracow to oversee his family's trade in ores. From 1488 onwards, Thurzó began buying up mines around Banská Bystrica (Neusohl) in what is now central Slovakia. In 1494, he entered into a partnership with Jacob Fugger. In return for capital investment and a 50 per cent share of the profits, Thurzó agreed to expand his operation to include the entirety of Banská Bystrica's production. Within ten years, Jacob Fugger had ploughed a million florins into the enterprise, most of which he had borrowed. It was, as Jacob realized, thoroughly risky. As he wrote: 'No business can fall apart more quickly than mining. Most of the time ten perish before one gets rich.'[24]

A vast industrial operation underpinned the trade in Banská Bystrica's copper. Liquation foundries outside the city processed much of the copper ore, which was then sent northwards to the Baltic for onward shipment to the Low Countries. The rest was sent as unrefined ore through Leipzig for liquation at Hohenkirchen in Thuringia or across Hungary to Villach in Carinthia, where a third liquation plant operated. To make sure that he controlled the supply, in 1498 Jacob Fugger dumped copper onto the Venetian market at rock-bottom prices to bankrupt his south German competitors, who mostly traded through the Rialto. Even at the time, Jacob's methods were denounced as 'unbrotherly and unchristian'.[25]

Thurzó died in 1508 and Jacob Fugger in 1525, but the partnership endured, being continued by their heirs, who soon intermarried. Its profits are disputed, although it is suggestive enough that historians argue over millions. Suffice it to say that the Fugger balance sheet for 1546 indicates a gross profit over the previous seven years of 1.25 million florins from Hungarian mining. By this time, the Fuggers were winding down their operations in Hungary since the kingdom had become a war zone and were making money instead by lending to the Spanish treasury. Even so, the profits still coming from their mines and foundries in northern Hungary compare favourably with their Spanish business over the same period.[26]

Thurzó was an engineer. He was to machinery what Matthäus Schwarz was to accountancy, and it is no accident that Jacob Fugger should have teamed up with him. The principal problem that mining faced was the flooding of the shafts by rainwater. Building on established Hungarian technology, Thurzó introduced pumping gear of increasing sophistication, most of which worked by harnessing over-ground streams to drive waterwheels. Chief among these was the *Kehrrad*, a massive waterwheel that could be rotated in both directions to pull up water in great hoppers from a depth of several hundred metres. It was, according to one knowledgeable commentator, 'the largest machine of all those that draw water'. Thurzó's son George later installed engines of this type in Baia Mare (now in Romania), where he was digging for gold. George marvelled at the *Kehrrads*—with their 'unbelievably big hoppers . . . nothing like them has ever been seen in all the Christian world.' A precedent of sorts had been set—two centuries later, around 1720, engineers introduced into the north Hungarian mines the first Newcomen steam pump on the continent.[27]

As the example of Thurzó suggests, there was nothing technologically backward about the Hungarian mining industry. What it lacked was capital. Hungary's predicament typifies a large part of Central Europe. Merchant capital needs cities, and cities in turn need a populous hinterland. The western part of Central Europe had always had a denser population. This cannot be an exact statement since there are different ways of calculating populations and strong local variations. But overall the German lands probably averaged about twenty persons per square kilometre in 1500. For Poland and Lithuania, the combined figure was about six or seven, although Poland was probably twice as populous as Lithuania. In Hungary, the population density was about ten persons per square kilometre.[28]

The cities in the western half of Central Europe were more numerous and larger too. Around 1500, Cologne had over 40,000 inhabitants, Vienna and Nuremberg about 25,000 thousand each, Ulm, Würzburg, and Augsburg just under 20,000 apiece, and so on. But east of Vienna, there were few cities with a population larger than 10,000. Cracow and Prague always poke out of historical atlases, showing populations of between 30,000 and 40,000 persons around 1500. But both were centres of consumption, catering to large and extravagant courts. They were not hubs of manufacturing, with concentrations of capital looking for places to invest.[29]

Merchant venturers like the Fuggers and the great south German metal merchants brought capital eastwards. But they were mainly interested in raw materials. Later on, in the sixteenth and seventeenth centuries, merchant companies would be looking for grain to feed a burgeoning population. The consequence was to lock the eastern part of Central Europe, predominantly Hungary and Poland and Lithuania, in a condition of almost colonial dependency, as a source of primary products for shipment to the west. Like the plantations of Latin America, they too became the providers of cash crops for export. The imbalance between the western and eastern halves of Central Europe would widen after 1500 as merchants exploited price differentials to buy up the east's raw materials. By so doing, they would contribute to the trend that led to the conversion of a large part of Central Europe's population into a coerced workforce of serfs.

CHAPTER 12

The Dragon in the China Shop
and the Habsburg Imagination

THE HOUSE OF LUXEMBOURG HAD FLOURISHED UNDER EM-
peror Charles IV but had been brought low by the drunkenness
and lethargy of his eldest son, Wenceslas the Idle (ruled in Bohemia,
1378–1419). Deposed as ruler of the empire in 1400 because of his
sloth, Wenceslas held onto power in Bohemia because his inactivity
suited the kingdom's nobility. The last years of his reign saw Bohemia drift into chaos as Hussite groups seized churches, demanding
the right to preach 'God's Law'. When in July 1419, the council of
Prague's New Town ordered the churches in its part of the city to be returned to Catholic worship, a mob stormed the town hall, threw seven
magistrates out of an upper-storey window, and hacked them to death
in the street. News of the slaughter proved too much for Wenceslas,
who had the first of several strokes. He died a fortnight later.[1]

The Luxembourgs' fortunes were saved by Wenceslas's younger
brother Sigismund. Sigismund became ruler of Hungary in 1387, was
elected king of the empire in 1411, succeeded his brother as king of
Bohemia in 1419, and eventually made it to Rome to be crowned emperor there in 1433—almost eighty years after his father, Charles IV,
had received the imperial diadem. Yet as his childhood nickname of
'the Ginger Fox' suggests, Sigismund was never less than ambiguous.
He was, in one description of the time:

> Of noble, kingly, and lordly appearance, but he had a false heart and
> did many ignoble things. . . . His words were emollient, soothing,
> and fair, but his deeds were short, paltry, and small. As a monarch,

161

he was a master of good words, who said what everyone wanted to hear; he spoke, gave, talked, and unashamedly promised much that he did not do.[2]

In Sigismund's defence, he had spent his early years in the hard school of Hungarian politics, where deception was vital to survival. In 1385, when he was seventeen, Sigismund had married the reigning Queen Mary, daughter and heir to King Louis I of Hungary. Like her sister, Jadwiga, who had become 'king' of Poland the year before, Mary faced opposition on account of her sex. The arrival of a Neapolitan pretender with some semblance of a claim to the throne pushed Hungary into civil war and left the royal couple in fear of their lives. Even so, Sigismund managed to convert his status as husband and 'first man' (*antecessor*) to that of king. After his coronation in 1387, he turned on Mary's opponents, using unusual methods of execution (involving red-hot pincers) and indiscriminate slaughter to impress his and Mary's joint rule as Hungary's sovereigns.[3]

Mary died ten years into the marriage from a riding accident. Her passing made Sigismund politically vulnerable. For a short time in 1401, he was even deposed and imprisoned while a council made up of his enemies ruled the kingdom, bizarrely issuing instructions in the name of Hungary's Holy Crown. But Sigismund was shrewd and determined. He continued after his release to build a loyal body of supporters by the simple expedient of giving them the bulk of the royal lands. He also recruited foreign knights, military experts, and financiers who were beholden to him and took no revenge on the lords who had deposed him but let them fester instead in their castles.

In 1405, Sigismund remarried, wedding Barbara of Cilli (Celje, now in Slovenia), the daughter of one of his most powerful and ardent supporters. Barbara's pregnancy and an illness that he had recently contracted on campaign made Sigismund concerned about the future. In an unexpected move, in December 1408, Sigismund founded a new chivalric order. Named the Order of the Dragon, after the mythical serpent slain by St George, it purported to be dedicated to the defence of Christendom. But as its charter of foundation explained, the order's main purpose was to protect Sigismund and, in the event of his death, his widow and any children he might have. The founding members, of which there were twenty-one, are a roll call of all the most important Hungarian lords of the time. These now came together to constitute a society, promising always to defend the royal family, say masses for dead companions, sport the badge of the order on their shoulders, and give glory to Christ.[4]

Sigismund always aimed to be more than just king of Hungary. With the Turks pressing against southern Hungary, he had in 1395 thrown his weight behind an international crusade that had gathered together the flower of Christendom's chivalry. The campaign had ended miserably on the field of Nicopolis (now Nikopol, in Bulgaria), after which the Turkish sultan had feasted in Sigismund's abandoned pavilion. But in 1410, the kingship of the Holy Roman Empire became unexpectedly vacant. Sigismund presented himself as a candidate, but it was not until the next year, after much wrangling and false starts, that the electors appointed him king.

Sigismund now had the stage he sought. He could put Hungarian politics behind him and become the lord of all Christendom or, as contemporaries put it, 'the light of the world' and even 'a world monarch'. He pursued this goal relentlessly, travelling across Europe, from the Pyrenees to Lutsk in Lithuania (now in Ukraine) and from London to Constantinople, via the Mediterranean island of Rhodes. Indeed, he was difficult to keep up with. One mission sent by the electors struggled across Hungary to find Sigismund—after several weeks they finally caught up with his entourage, only to find that he was out hunting and that they should wait another day.[5]

In 1412, just a year after his election as emperor, Sigismund hosted a grand gathering at Buda. Glumly called a congress by historians, it is better thought of as being, in Sigismund's own description, 'a special occasion for dances of fun and joy'. The main purpose of the event was to advertise Sigismund before an international audience, on which account he invited the kings of Poland and Bosnia, the despot or ruler of Serbia, and a further nineteen princes, three archbishops, eleven bishops, counts, and lords, and more than a thousand knights. To the consternation of the partygoers, there were also Jews from Jerusalem and even, according to one account, some 'frightful pagans with long beards, fat bellies, and tall hats'.[6]

In the wake of the dancing, Sigismund reorganized the Order of the Dragon. He started admitting new members from abroad, including the kings of Aragon and Naples and the Romanian prince of neighbouring Wallachia. The last of these was so pleased with his investiture that he took the name of 'Dragon', or *Dracul* in Romanian, which his son Vlad III, nicknamed 'The Impaler' (lived c. 1430–1476), later adopted in the form of Dracula. Sigismund gave each new member dozens of badges for them to distribute as rewards. Clearly, the dragon insignia meant something. Across Central Europe, there are marble sarcophagi and coats of arms that display the mark of the dragon, even though the bearers are not otherwise known to have been admitted to membership.[7]

Sigismund would later dedicate the Order of the Dragon to the liberation of the Holy Land, on which account he won from the pope the promise that all members of the order who fought against the Turks should have full remission of sins, thus speeding their souls through Purgatory. To begin with, though, the purpose of the enlarged order was to magnify Sigismund. As he explained, the more numerous the order was, the more majestic his throne and the more glorious his rule as monarch of the Holy Roman Empire. A cosmopolitan society of knights that looked to him as its head emphasized the international character of the imperial office which he now held.[8]

In his understanding of what his kingship involved, Sigismund imagined himself as a supermonarch, set above all other rulers and princes. But Sigismund's personal diplomacy was seldom other than shambolic: in the words of one historian, he was in matters of state 'a dragon in the china shop'.[9] He was needlessly rude, frequently drunk in public, and presumptuous with other men's wives. A sixteenth-century Hungarian verse sums up his posthumous reputation:

Many a wench adorned with long tresses,
Sweet maidens and damsels, all in fine dresses—
Sigismund has measured each waist and breast,
Listed vital statistics and what they do best.[10]

It did not help that Sigismund spoke six languages fluently, since it only multiplied the opportunities he had to offend. His visit to Paris in 1416 was a typical disaster. He spoiled a feast held in his honour with drunken singing, although on this occasion he managed not to strip off in public. (He did so later in Strasbourg.) Then, upon visiting the law court of the Paris Parlement, he gave full rein to his belief in the superiority of his office. He sat in the royal chair, interfered in the judicial proceedings, and when he found that a litigant was disadvantaged because he was not a full nobleman, dubbed the man a knight on the spot. It was an egregious breach of protocol, but typical of Sigismund's conviction that as ruler of the empire he was above all other monarchs. Unsurprisingly, upon arriving on the English coast, he was greeted at Dover by the Duke of Gloucester, who demanded that before he land, Sigismund should renounce all imperial claims over English soil.[11]

As it turned out, Sigismund's visit to England was a diplomatic triumph. King Henry V of England was lavish with his hospitality and supply of well-dressed ladies, and he invested Sigismund a Knight of the Garter in St George's Chapel at Windsor. In return, Sigismund made Henry a dragon knight and presented him with a sword and scabbard bearing the order's insignia. (It is now in the Mansion House at York.) Sigismund then tried to broker a peace between England and France but settled instead for a treaty with Henry V that did much to weaken French influence on the Continent. Two decades later, Sigismund was still recalled fondly in England. On news of his death in 1437, requiem masses were said for his soul in every English cathedral.[12]

Sigismund's negotiations for a peace between England and France reflected his conviction that the imperial title was more than just a German office but made him the leader of Christendom. In token of his high rank, he presided over the Church Councils that met at

Constance (1414–1418) and Basle (1433–1437) to resolve which of several popes was the true successor to St Peter and to promote the union between the Catholic and Orthodox Churches. He coordinated the international defence of the Danube, promoted himself as champion of the faith against both Turks and Hussites, deposed the troublesome king of Bosnia Tvrtko II, and planned to make the grand duke of Lithuania into a king. When challenged over this, he replied that he had the power to elevate the Lithuanian ruler because he was monarch of the Holy Roman Empire.[13]

In May 1433, more than twenty years after his election as German king, Sigismund was crowned emperor by the pope in Rome. Shortly afterwards, he minted a new seal that he had first planned almost twenty years before. On the front side, it showed him seated on a throne, surrounded by the arms of the Holy Roman Empire, Luxembourg, Bohemia, and Hungary. On the reverse was the double-headed eagle—a common enough heraldic device at the time, which Sigismund now made the symbol of the empire. But seals were not just instruments that validated deeds but also a way of advertising the owner and his power. Every charter and privilege issued in Sigismund's name bore the tokens of his rulership and his distinctive forked beard. In woodcuts, frescoes, and illuminated manuscripts too, his carefully crafted portrait was reproduced and circulated, making his face the best known in Christendom.[14]

There are occasional glimpses of deeper currents in Sigismund's thinking of what rulership involved—most tantalizingly in the mysterious inscription around the eagle on his seal: 'Ezekiel's eagle is the bride sent from heaven. It soars unrestrained, higher than seers and prophets.' (Or it may just be lines from a hymn that Sigismund liked.) Others read all sorts of fantastic meanings into Sigismund's rule— that he was destined to cleanse the Church, battle with the devil, restore the unity of Christendom, and so on. But from Sigismund himself we learn little. He had ideas about the power he wielded, as he showed in the Paris Parlement, but these were roughly hewn and unrefined.

Sigismund died after a long illness, leaving only a daughter. She was married to Albert of Habsburg, the foremost warrior of the day, an egregious persecutor of Jews, and the emperor's chosen successor. Albert was happy enough to press his claim through his wife to the crowns of Bohemia and Hungary, but he baulked at succeeding Sigismund as ruler of the Holy Roman Empire. The electors chose him anyway, and the first Albert knew about it was the arrival of a slew of paperwork. But within eighteen months of his election in 1438, Albert was dead of dysentery, contracted on campaign in Hungary. He never made it even to Aachen to be crowned German king, let alone to Rome to be made emperor.

Not to be thwarted, the electors unanimously chose as Albert's successor the next best Habsburg, who was Frederick of Styria. As ruler of the Holy Roman Empire, Frederick III (ruled 1440–1493) looked the part. With long blond hair, he had inherited the good looks of his mother, the half-Polish and half-Lithuanian Cymburga, together with her reputation for driving nails bare-fisted into oak tables. He had also done all the right things, including joining the best chivalric societies, going on pilgrimage, and being dubbed a knight on the Mount of Olives outside Jerusalem. His name was the right one too, for prophecies foretold that it would be an emperor called Frederick who fought the Antichrist in the Holy Land and ushered in the Day of Judgment.

With so much expected of him, Frederick was bound to disappoint. He guessed as much himself, taking two months to decide whether to accept the office of sovereign. Unlike his predecessor, Frederick was not a warrior at all, but reclusive and conciliatory by nature—for twenty-seven years he did not stray beyond the Austrian cities of Vienna, Wiener Neustadt, and Linz. Penny-pinching and superstitious, he also travelled with his own hen coops (to avoid having to buy eggs), bought from market stalls in disguise (so as not to be overcharged), and scrutinized mouse droppings in the way later generations would consult tea leaves. One ambassador reviled him at the time as 'indolent, morose, brooding, sulky, melancholy, miserly, frugal, and troubled', and historians habitually describe him as a shiftless dreamer.[15]

But Frederick understood power in a way few others did. Together with his son, Maximilian (ruled 1493–1519), he remade the Holy Roman Empire and fused it with the mystique of the Habsburg dynasty. To begin with, he had a grasp of how bureaucracy worked. At a time when other rulers confused government with jousting, Frederick promoted new ways of projecting his authority, but instead on paper and by delegation. Secondly, he recognized that the power of monarchy worked by charisma. Since he lacked this (painfully so), he enlisted his forebears, both real and mythical, to stand in for him. Charles IV of Bohemia had done much the same a century before, but Frederick put his descent squarely at the centre of his propaganda. His son Maximilian went one stage further—mythologizing his ancestry with fantastic conceits and fashioning an equally fanciful mythology about himself.

None of this was done well. Maximilian's fantasies were often comic (not least, his plan to make himself pope), and Frederick's administrative improvements incomplete. But Frederick had a real problem—the scourge of private feuding and local warfare that made conditions intolerable for the majority but yielded abundant opportunities for the few. In a feud, whether it be over land, a dowry, or some imagined slight, there were rules that the parties were expected to follow—due notice, days off for prayer and penance, and not killing captives. But the robber knights and mercenaries employed to do the intimidation had little time for etiquette. The one-eyed warrior, diplomat, and last of the German troubadours, or Minnesinger, Oswald von Wolkenstein (died 1445) was typical of them. His poems gruesomely celebrated the mayhem he had caused while feuding: the marrow oozing from smashed limbs, the whoosh of arrows, and the mice roasting in the timbers of scorched homes.[16]

For more than three centuries, monarchs had sought to limit feuding by instructing local committees of dukes and counts to keep the peace. Frederick now lifted the main business of law enforcement into the courts and the royal administration. Whenever alerted to a dispute, he appointed commissioners drawn from the region where it had flared whose task was to force a settlement either by negotiation or by law. Over the course of his reign, some three thousand of these commissions were dispatched. Troublemakers who ignored the commissioners or their judgments faced an escalating scale of penalties that ended with military intervention and the confiscation of goods. Aggrieved parties might take their cases to the ruler's appeal court, the Chamber Court, but it generally upheld the commissioners since their decisions were considered 'as if our most gracious lord the Roman emperor had made them'.[17]

The commissioners and the Chamber Court impressed their will unevenly. Most of their interventions were in the south and southwest of the empire, but they were active too in resolving disputes on the Baltic shore, in Mecklenburg and Pomerania, and even in far off Livonia, where on account of distance the ruler's power had always been thin. Importantly, too, the commissioners and Chamber Court judged by a single law and they disregarded local customs and procedures. As far as it affected great men, landowners, and city magistrates, the law of the Holy Roman Empire was becoming increasingly unified. And at the top of the hierarchy of courts and commissioners was Frederick III. Altogether in a reign of just over fifty years, Frederick's chancellery issued some fifty thousand letters and charters, of which many bore the *p* mark indicating that they had been composed on Frederick's personal instruction.[18]

The Austrian lands were the home of fable. Not only were some of the earliest versions of the *Nibelungenlied* composed there, but also a burgeoning chronicle literature told of how Austria had been singled out in antiquity to bear the inheritance of Rome. Much of this originated with the Habsburgs' predecessors, the Babenbergs, who had ruled Austria from the tenth to the thirteenth century. The Babenbergs had married into the lines of both Byzantine and Holy Roman emperors and saw themselves as destined to greatness. The Habsburgs built on their myth-making—inventing stories that told of their own illustrious pedigree, blurring their line into the Babenbergs so as to capture their predecessors' saints and champions, and forging charters that told how Julius Caesar and Nero had declared Austria to be the most splendid of all their lands. It was on the basis of these and similar fakes that the Habsburgs claimed to be 'archdukes', with the right to wear coronets.

Frederick III believed in all this. Historians have drawn attention to his monogram, the AEIOU acrostic, which he chiselled into walls and inked into books. The acrostic has several hundred possible meanings in both Latin and German—hence 'The chosen eagle rightly conquers all' (*Aquila Electa Iuste Omnia Uincat*) or 'All glory belongs to Austria' (*Aller Ehren ist Österreich voll*). Of these, the predominant solution was the grandiose 'Austria is to rule the whole world' (in Latin, *Austria Est Imperare Orbi Universae*, and in German, *Alles Erdreich Ist Österreich Untertan*). But behind the bravado lay a subtler symbolism that was embedded in heraldry and genealogy.

In the 1440s, Frederick commissioned a heraldic manuscript, which bears his acrostic. At first sight, the manuscript looks like any other collection of painted coats of arms, but on closer inspection it is obvious that most of the devices are imaginary. The illustrator tells us that these are 'the old coats of arms of the Land of Austria that its Pagan, Jewish, and Christian Princes bore'. Of course, Austria had never been ruled by Jewish princes, let alone ones with their own coats of arms. But this fantastic make-believe was not confined to a library, to be scrutinized only by heralds and antiquarians. Around 1450, Frederick commissioned an architect to build a 'Heraldic Wall' (*Wappenwand*) on the west face of St George's Chapel, next to his palace in Wiener Neustadt, that reproduced these coats of arms. Below them, Frederick instructed an effigy of himself, with angels bearing the AEIOU acrostic.[19]

The heraldic book and the wall in Wiener Neustadt hark back to one of the most extraordinary manuscripts of the later Middle Ages. Composed shortly before 1400, the *Chronicle of the Ninety-Five Lords* was a nonsensical history of Austria. Starting with the Flood and the fictional Abraham of Temonaria, who came to Austria from Wonderland (*Terra Amirationis*), the chronicle listed Austria's earliest rulers, including twenty-six Jewish dukes and duchesses, who reigned in the first centuries before Christ. Thereafter, the chronicle interwove histories of the popes and emperors with mostly fictional biographies of each of the remaining ninety-five rulers of Austria, lovingly describing their coats of arms and rehearsing prophecies. Despite (or because of) its weird contents, the chronicle was popular. Some eighty manuscript editions survive.[20]

The AEIOU acronym and the *Chronicle of the Ninety-Five Lords* spoke to the same theme. Austria was not just a place but a land whose rulers and people were preordained for greatness. Indeed, Austria was not really a land at all, but a learned construction that united empire, inheritance, and destiny. Other rulers might call themselves after their principal territory—the House of Brandenburg, the House of Saxony, and so on. But Austria was different, for it signalled a set of beliefs that stood apart from geography. When Frederick mused that Austria would rule the whole world, he was not thinking of Austria engaging in a war of conquest but of his family's fame, its worldwide reputation, and its continued hold on the imperial office, which put the Habsburgs above all other earthly rulers.

It was left to Frederick's son Maximilian to make sense of these riddles and allusions. Elected in 1486 German king and co-ruler with his father, Maximilian moved effortlessly into power on Frederick III's death in 1493. Unlike Frederick, Maximilian was always on the move, scarcely staying in any one place for more than three weeks. Maximilian's style of government depended on presence and, since he could not be everywhere at once, on the projection of his image through portraits and the new medium of printing. Artists were commissioned to communicate Maximilian's image and achievements in ever more dramatic ways. Albrecht Dürer and Albrecht Altdorfer were among the engravers who designed the two massive woodcut series, the 'Triumphal Procession' and the 'Triumphal Gate', which advertised Maximilian's ancestry and accomplishments. Made up of interlocking printed sheets, they were intended to be pasted onto the walls of palaces and city halls.

At a time when all ruling families cultivated ambitious genealogies, Maximilian was determined to have the most impressive. He chased his own descent back to Noah and, building outwards, linked the Habsburg family tree to prophets, Greek and Egyptian demi-gods, popes, over two hundred saints and martyrs, and all of Europe's ruling families. His mausoleum in Innsbruck, planned during his lifetime, had his tomb reverentially surrounded by his forebears, assorted Frankish kings, the first crusader king of Jerusalem, and the English King Arthur. A further dozen bronzes, thirty-four busts of Roman emperors, and a hundred statues of saints were planned, but only a handful were ever executed. To make himself the epigone of chivalry, Maximilian became master of the Burgundian Order of the Golden Fleece, which was the premier noble society in all of Christendom. The emblem of the dead sheep replaced the dragon as the must-have badge of Central European knighthood.[21]

In practical politics, Maximilian was less successful. Although he surrounded his tomb in Innsbruck with reliefs depicting his military victories against the French, Low Countries' militias, Hungarians, and Venetians, most of these were inconsequential in the long term. In the empire, he had to face the concerted resistance of dukes, counts, and cities to his own and his father's rule. Frederick's commissions and the Chamber Court had been too successful and threatened to tilt the administration of justice in favour of the ruler. Maximilian was obliged in 1495 to make the court an instrument of the diet, which from now on had a voice in the appointment of its judges. In response, Maximilian established a separate court in Vienna which adjudicated disputes arising among the cities and great men of the empire.

In fact, the two separate courts worked together rather than in competition. Importantly, too, they usually judged by the same law, so contributing to the empire's legal integration. It was the same with the diet. Reformers pushed through its thorough reorganization, making an institution in place of an event, with set procedures, regular meetings, a fixed membership, and committees to handle difficult business. This suited Maximilian, since it provided a single forum for negotiation and display. His main objection was that the streamlining of the diet's administration did not yield the revenues he needed to sustain his wars. He also had no time for what he saw as the diet's trespassing into his sphere of authority. A council of government tasked by the diet in 1500 with 'negotiating and coming to decisions' lasted only two years before Maximilian closed it down.[22]

Maximilian's achievement was to translate the idea of Austrian and Habsburg leadership into marriage, scooping up territories and kingdoms on the way. In 1477, following the death and defeat of Charles of Burgundy, Maximilian hurried to the defence of the duke's beleaguered daughter, married her, and took the wealthy Burgundian lands in the Low Countries. For his children by Mary, he organized several double marriages, where a brother and sister married a sister and brother. The first of these, with the ruling Spanish house of Trastámara, was cemented in 1496–1497 when his son Philip married the infanta, Princess Juana of Spain, and his daughter Margaret married Juana's brother Prince Juan. The second union did not prosper, for Juan soon died, worn out (we are told) by the amorous attentions of his bride. But the first, between Philip and Juana, yielded no fewer than six grandchildren for Maximilian. When the ageing King Ferdinand of Aragon died in 1516, it was Maximilian's eldest grandson, Charles, who became the next king of Spain, side-stepping his mother who had lapsed into insanity.

Double marriages were a two-edged sword. Had it been Maximilian's heirs who perished first, and had Ferdinand of Aragon been blessed with a living male heir, then the house of Trastámara might have swallowed up the Habsburg possessions and become a Central European power. But Maximilian was a gambler. He had won the round, so he continued to roll the dice. During the last years of his life, he negotiated a second double marriage with the junior branch of the house of Jagiellon, which ruled Bohemia and Hungary. (Named after Jogaila of Lithuania; the senior branch continued to reign in Poland and Lithuania.) His grandson Ferdinand was betrothed to the Jagiellon princess Anne, and his granddaughter Mary to the young

Jagiellon king of Hungary and Bohemia, Louis II. The engagements were only converted into marriages several years after Maximilian's death in 1519. But it was through this route that, upon the death in battle of King Louis II in 1526, the Habsburgs swallowed up Bohemia and Hungary, forging a union that would last until 1918.

Maximilian long intended to be crowned emperor in Rome, in imitation of his father who had received the imperial diadem in 1452. Maximilian began his journey there in 1508 but was blocked by his Venetian foes. Not to be outdone, he proclaimed himself emperor in Trento Cathedral, and extracted the pope's agreement to the arrangement. From now on, rulers of the Holy Roman Empire were automatically emperors as soon as they were crowned in Aachen (after 1531 Frankfurt). As an added benefit, the emperor could in his own lifetime have the electors appoint a king, who would effectively become the emperor-in-waiting. This now became the means whereby the Habsburgs held onto power in the Holy Roman Empire, with each emperor bribing, cajoling, or manoeuvring the electors to elevate his son or heir in advance to the supreme office.

The meaning of the imperial office was never clear. It carried prestige, which was why so many German kings had gone to Rome to be crowned. Commentators all had their own views as to what empire involved, including that it was worth very little—in one verdict of the time, it was 'either a nothing or a trifle, depending on how you looked on it'. Most late medieval monarchs had regarded it, at best, as an extra—something to be added to their existing titles as a way of magnifying their existing authority. So, for Charles IV, empire was enlisted as a way of augmenting the territories and greatness of Bohemia. For Sigismund, it implied some sort of priority over other kings and a license for bad behaviour, but for his down-to-earth heir, the uncrowned Albert II, the title of emperor seemed hardly worth the effort.[23]

Frederick III and Maximilian restocked the imperial idea. By blending empire with the mystique of the House of Austria, they anchored emperorship to dynasty and made the Habsburgs the natural inheritors of the Roman crown. Their vision was embedded in acrostics, fraudulent genealogies, ancient prophecies, and mysterious allusions. It was less a programme than a series of high-flown conceits and aspirations. But that made its dreamy message all the more persuasive, for it allowed others to read in what they chose—and Habsburg apologists were never less than expansive when ruminating on the rights and reach of the imperial office. For four centuries to come, Central Europe would have to live with this reinvigorated idea of empire and with the Habsburgs.

CHAPTER 13

Central Europe's Renaissance, Roman Law, and the Library of the Raven King

M OST MONARCHIES START OFF BY CHOOSING RULERS THROUGH some form of election but become hereditary. Hungary (and later Poland) went in the other direction. Hungary's monarchy was hereditary until the late fourteenth century but thereafter became elective. This was because from 1382 to 1506, only one Hungarian king left a living male heir, so the diet was increasingly called upon to decide who should be ruler or regent. The exception was Sigismund's son-in-law Albert II of Habsburg (ruled 1438–1439), but the child he sired died prematurely in 1457, again without an heir. The diet once more stepped in, appointing as king the son of John Hunyadi (lived c. 1406–1456), the formidable military commander who just a year before had defeated the Turks outside Belgrade. The son is known to history as Matthias Corvinus (ruled 1458–1490) or Matthias the Raven, from the device on his crest.

Matthias was an upstart. His father was of Romanian origin and had achieved fame by his prowess on the battlefield. Although his tame scribes claimed Matthias to be descended from the Corvini family of ancient Rome, even within Hungary Matthias was looked down upon as a 'Romanian princeling' and disparaged on account of his humble background. Neither Emperor Frederick III nor the Polish king Casimir IV (ruled 1447–1492) would consider providing him with a bride. Instead, they intrigued with factions in the kingdom to overthrow Matthias so that they might replace him with a Habsburg or a Pole. As the contemporary historian Antonio Bonfini explained, throughout his life Matthias made war abroad as if the Hercules of his age, but only that he might live unvexed at home.[1]

Matthias's military strength rested on a large mercenary army of mostly Germans and Czechs, which furnished some twenty thousand horsemen and eight thousand infantrymen, supported by a large artillery train. With this muscle behind him, Matthias overran the Bohemian lands in the 1470s, defeated its recently elected Polish king, Wladislas Jagiellon (the son of Casimir IV), and took Moravia, Lusatia, and Silesia as well as the title of king of Bohemia. Then, he turned on Frederick III, who was constantly intriguing against him. He ousted the emperor from the Habsburg heartland of Styria and Lower Austria, capturing Frederick's twin capitals of Vienna and Wiener Neustadt. By the time of his death in 1490, Matthias Corvinus held a large chunk of Central Europe, from the Brandenburg border, just fifty kilometres south of Berlin, to the Adriatic coast and running more than a thousand kilometres eastwards to Transylvania.

Such an army had to be paid for. Matthias upped fivefold the taxes that fell on the peasantry and confiscated the property of rebels and heirless landowners: he was fortunate that some of the wealthiest Hungarian families died out during his reign. Additionally, he masterminded a scheme whereby he would borrow money against a pledge in land and then sell on the right of redemption, yielding a further sum. (It is doubtful whether the parties who agreed to these transactions did so willingly.) Matthias played fast with the cities too, renaming taxes from which they had previously bought exemptions so that they would have to buy them for a second time. At the height of Matthias's reign, the royal revenues in Hungary amounted to more than 600,000 florins a year, of which about two-thirds went on sustaining the king's mercenary army.

The problem was that Hungary's southern neighbour was the Ottoman Turkish Empire, whose sultan had an income in excess of 3 million florins and an ambition for conquest that matched his wealth. Matthias's solution was to avoid warfare with the Turks as much as possible. He took no action when the Turks overran the defensive cordon established by Sigismund in the Balkans, building up instead a line of fortresses along the Danube. But he was happy enough to let Turkish troops cross Hungary unimpeded in order to raid the Austrian lands, while simultaneously advertising Hungary and himself as the bulwark, defence, and shield of Christendom.[2]

Matthias had been educated in childhood by one of Hungary's greatest scholars, John Vitéz, who went on to become bishop of Oradea (Nagyvárad) and later the primate of all Hungary. Vitéz was a classicist, mathematician, alchemist, and astrologer. In Oradea, he built a new episcopal palace, decked out in marble in the latest Renaissance design, which owed its inspiration to the styles of classical antiquity. With an observatory and extensive library, and grounds furnished with elaborate water features and terraced hanging gardens, the palace also had hot running water in the bishop's private apartments—the first in Central Europe since the Romans.[3]

Matthias copied Vitéz, first gathering his own library, and then in the 1470s rebuilding the royal palace in Buda. The royal residence at Buda was already impressive, since Sigismund had furnished it with the hall that bore his name. Measuring seventy metres by eighteen, the Sigismund Hall was larger than London's Westminster Hall. To its south lay the Stephen Tower. Put up in the mid-fourteenth century, it was a stone keep thirty metres high, surmounted with turrets, spires, and finials. It was between these two landmarks that Matthias built his new palace.

Matthias's palace no longer exists, since it was built over in the eighteenth century to make way for the present Baroque one. Little more than its foundations survive, but the Italian Bonfini gives us a contemporary description:

> Matthias rebuilt the castle of Buda, especially the inner palace, where except for Sigismund's grand buildings, there had been nothing of note. He built a chapel overlooking the Danube with a water organ and a stoup of silver and marble. Above it he built a library,

amply stocked with books in Latin and Greek, most luxuriously presented. In front of it, and facing southwards, was a hall with a curved ceiling, on which the whole heavens might be discerned. Such palaces he built, without equal except for the sumptuousness of the Romans. There were spacious halls for feasting, the most magnificent reception rooms and bed chambers, with variously panelled ceilings everywhere, adorned with contrasting gilded blazons. The casements of the doors were made of marquetry, and the stoves were furnished on their four sides with depictions of the ancients of the Romans.[4]

With its gardens, arcades, fountains, painted ceilings, and red marble furnishings, Matthias's palace outdid Vitéz's Oradea in both size and splendour. But Vitéz betrayed Matthias, turning against him in 1471 when the king confiscated part of the wealth of the Church in Hungary to pay for his wars. Matthias pardoned his rebellion but helped himself to Vitéz's goods, including his books. To these he added manuscripts illuminated either by miniaturists in Florence or in the royal workshop of Buda. Matthias's marriage to the Italian princess Beatrice of Naples, in 1476, intensified cultural connections between Hungary and Mediterranean Europe.[5]

With between 2,000 and 2,500 manuscripts by the time of his death, Matthias's collection counted at the time as the second largest library in Christendom (after the Vatican's). It was, as Matthias explained, intended for the pleasure of the mind and for the glory of the kingdom, being both comprehensive and, visible from the throne room, the backdrop to court ceremonies. It was also a working library. In discussions with his chief men, Matthias might indicate the volumes in which information on a point might be had, and he upbraided the attending nobles for their ignorance and boorishness. Display mattered too, for it communicated Matthias's international prestige. As visiting Italian scholars reported, Matthias ranked equal to the greatest collectors of antiquity, demonstrating a magnificence 'following that of the Roman emperors'.

Matthias had no legitimate heirs. Even so, he hoped that his bastard son John Corvin might succeed him, and he bound the chief men of the kingdom to support John's succession. But, as he disclosed to his brother-in-law, the duke of Calabria, in 1489, 'the power to choose the king belongs to the people of the kingdom and they may happen to select someone other than whom we hope and desire, for only God knows what moves in the hearts of subjects.' Matthias's forebodings came true. On his death, the kingdom's barons stripped the young John of his wealth and isolated him politically. Instead of John, they convinced the diet to choose King Wladislas (Jagiellon) of Bohemia as Hungary's ruler, since in their estimation, he would be 'a king whose braids they could hold in their fists'.[6]

Wladislas neglected Matthias's library. He gave away manuscripts as gifts to diplomats; others he lent, but never troubled to have returned. The royal librarian Taddeo Ugoleto, who had been in Italy buying books when Matthias died, returned to find the collection already dissipated—in despair, he went home to Parma and was not replaced. Without a custodian, the books were stolen, left in such a muddle that individual items could seldom be found, and nibbled away by mice and worms. The Ottoman capture of Buda and the sack of the palace in 1526 marked the library's definitive end. What was not destroyed by the plundering soldiers was packed up and sent to Istanbul as a gift to the sultan. Little more than two hundred volumes survive today.[7]

Historians often present the decay of Matthias Corvinus's library as emblematic of Hungary's cultural retardation—as an 'isolated initiative amidst circumstances of relative backwardness'. So, when the king died, the arts and learning perished with him. This is unfair, for the Renaissance in Hungary was not a phenomenon confined to the royal court. Matthias's library was founded on earlier collections in Hungary, which it absorbed—the fate of Vitéz's library is just one example. We know, too, of other extensive collections, not least the library of George Handó (c. 1430–1480), archbishop of Kalocsa, which numbered some three hundred books and included works by Plato, Catullus,

Horace, Livy, and Vitruvius. Matthias's library was exceptional in Hungary not so much for its contents as for its scale and luxury.[8]

The Renaissance style of Matthias's palace was imitated as well. The palace's red marble sculptures inspired monumental tombstones across Hungary and the dazzling domed chapel of Archbishop Thomas Bakócz in Esztergom. Begun in 1506, the Bakócz Chapel is the first building north of the Alps to have been planned in its entirety in the Renaissance style. Elsewhere, aristocratic patrons and urban councils commissioned architects to put Renaissance-style frontages onto castles and city halls, specifically requiring that new 'Italian windows' be included. In humbler fashion, the green and polychrome glazed tiles used on stoves in the royal palace were copied and sold, influencing tile design throughout the kingdom, from Transylvania to Croatia.[9]

Italianate designs flourished side by side with traditional Gothic architecture. Matthias's summer palace at Visegrád, built in the 1470s, featured typically Renaissance loggias and arcades but with pointed arches and lancet windows. It was the same in Poland, where the royal court provided opportunities for Italian architects and sculptors left unemployed after Matthias's death. Francesco Fiorentino moved from Buda to Cracow in the 1490s to rebuild the courtyard of the Wawel Palace. The palace's three-storey arcade with rounded arches is thoroughly Italianate, but it is surmounted by the steep overhanging roof typical of late Gothic architecture north of the Alps. Inside the cathedral next door to the palace, the sepulchre for King Jan Olbracht of Poland (ruled 1492–1501) brought the two styles together. Fiorentino's setting, with its triumphal arch, pilasters, and coffered ceiling, is thoroughly Italianate. But the red marble tomb, with its stylized armour and ornamentation, belongs to the late Gothic and is almost certainly the work of a second sculptor, schooled in an older craftsmanship.

The mixing or 'hybridization' of Renaissance and Gothic styles is everywhere in Central Europe, with individual regions having their own distinctive blends. In Lithuania and along the Baltic coast, the so-called Brick Renaissance combined Italianate designs rendered in brickwork and terracotta with the tall chimneys and steep roofs needed in a colder and wetter climate. The Weser Renaissance in the north-west of the Holy Roman Empire favoured symmetrical façades, with high gables, often ornamented with stone or brick semicircles and half-timbered fronts. In sculpture, there was Tuscan influence from Italy, but some artists, like Tilman Riemenschneider from Nuremberg, developed traditional forms to the exclusion of all else. Even so, the south German sculptors produced limewood figures of exquisite pathos, with their detail often enhanced by not painting the statues but giving them instead a plain brown wash.[10]

The stylistic eclecticism and Italian borrowings of Central European Renaissance design is sometimes dismissed by art historians as a superficial bricolage, where 'forms created to express a certain content are taken over in a milieu where acquaintance with the original content has been lost.' Some of it was. But the contrast between Gothic and Renaissance was never clear-cut. What has been called 'the great collision' of styles also involved accommodation, appropriation, and ultimately a fusion that produced something quite new and distinctively Central European.[11]

Central Europe had already embraced naturalism and realism in art well before it encountered the Italian Renaissance. First evident in the altarpieces and portraits of the Flemish Jan van Eyck and Rogier van der Weyden, faces and drapery were no longer painted as if on stylized icons but as though the subjects were real people. It was the same with nature, where forests and the countryside were reproduced with often startling attention to detail. Ultimately, these led to the genres that make Central European art distinctive—the landscape picture, the still life, and the studio portrait. Their visual power was magnified by the pioneering use of oils in Central Europe which yielded stronger colours and allowed more precise brushwork.

Engraving and the printing press were first developed in Central Europe and they provided the means by which its styles and genres were circulated internationally. Among the first artists to exploit the new media was Albrecht Dürer (lived 1471–1528). Originally from

Nuremberg, Dürer visited Italy and brought back the techniques of composition, proportion, and perspective that he had learned there. But though Dürer's aesthetic reconciles Italian with Gothic styles, his content is emphatically Central European. The grotesque characters, the twisted and wounded images of humanity, and the apocalyptic visions are partly taken from altarpieces north of the Alps. In the woodcuts and engravings he executed for Emperor Maximilian, he conveys the triumphalism and monumental forms of Milan and Mantua, but he can give us, too, the blades of grass on a piece of turf, the whiskers on a hare's nose, and dark forebodings of ruin and death. His art is microscopic in its attention to detail, but universal in the way it communicates humankind's fall from grace, the imminence of God's Judgment, and the daily perils that menace the soul.

The big themes that characterize Dürer's work are frequent in Central European art, reproduced in the mountain and forest landscapes of Albrecht Altdorfer and in the work of Dürer's pupil Hans Baldung Grien, with his woodcuts of cavorting witches, frenzied horses, and deadly enchantments. Religious themes predominated, so even the artists of the mass-market Antwerp School (a misnomer since it included several hundred painters from the Rhineland, Holland, and Picardy in France) specialized in devotional themes, often reproducing almost identical items for undiscerning buyers. The Adoration of the Magi was a favourite since it allowed the painter to show off his skill in portraiture, drapery, landscape, and ruins. Antwerp School nativities are still the stock in trade of upmarket Christmas cards today.[12]

Death imagery was familiar enough throughout Christian Europe, not only as a means of commemoration but also as a way of cementing the idea of the dynasty and of its existence through time. In the Sigismund Chapel in Cracow, Poland has the most spectacular sixteenth-century mausoleum north of the Alps. Built by Florentine masters in the 1520s, it shows reclining marble sculptures of King Sigismund the Old (ruled 1506–1548), who commissioned it, and of his son and daughter-in-law. The chapel, which adjoins the cathedral, was conceived in the grand Italian style, with medallions, ornate pilasters, and a coffered cupola roof. Equally remarkable and less well known are the sculptures of sleeping children erected in Polish churches to mourn dead infants. They are unique to Poland and executed with remarkable pathos. The child is shown at rest, sometimes with its hand supporting the chin, and accompanied by images of a skull, blighted tree, or hourglass but also with symbols of resurrection such as a flower, the figure of Christ, or the dolphins that carry the soul heavenwards. More than 330 of these child sculptures and reliefs have so far been identified in Poland, commemorating over 400 children.[13]

Faces mattered, since they were thought to provide a window into the soul. The peaceful expression of the children on the Polish tombs tells how they now rest on the bosom of the Almighty. But in most Central European art, the faces are different. They are often haggard, haunted, twisted, and sometimes deformed. We would expect grisly scenes of the Crucifixion with leering soldiers and a swooning Virgin or the faces of saints on their way to martyrdom to be gaunt and creased. But the wealthy clients who commissioned portraits of themselves surely must have counted on a more placid and flattering representation. If sixteenth-century German artists like the two Holbeins or Cranach obliged, there was often a twist—a creeping skeleton on the edge of the painting, a hidden skull, or a background landscape that dwarfed the sitter.[14]

A literary and artistic trope throughout the Middle Ages, death became in the fifteenth and sixteenth centuries a Central European preoccupation. The *Danse Macabre* or 'Dance of Death' was among the most popular subjects for not only panels and frescoes but also sculptures, tapestries, stonework in churches, and mummings or dumbplays. In print, Hans Holbein (the Younger)'s woodcut collection *Pictures of Death* (completed in Basle in 1525) was one of the best-selling books of the sixteenth century. But death also stalked the pages of literature and nowhere more intensely than in an anonymous fifteenth-century Polish version of the originally German *Dialogue of Policarp with Death*. Policarp describes his encounter with her (Death was almost always a 'she' or ungendered until Dürer reassigned her):

[She was] lean and pale and her yellow face shone like a wash basin. The end of her nose had dropped off; bloody dew was seeping from her eyes. There were no lips at her mouth. In her hand she carried a rattling scythe.[15]

Death in all its manifestations fused high and low culture in a single evocation that fascinated the full social spectrum, but for late medieval and Renaissance audiences it was also a spectacle acted out across the whole range of visual media.[16]

Historians often speak of the Renaissance north of the Alps as a pessimistic one, guided by a 'Darker Vision' of powerlessness, ruin, and moral decay. But it was underpinned by quite different sentiments. In its opening lines, the Polish *Dialogue of Policarp* gives us a glimpse of these:

Almighty God! Greater than all creation. Help me to compose this work, so that I can carefully unfold it for the extension of Your glory and for the improvement of mankind!

Man's baseness and the inevitability of death had as their counterpart the majesty of the divine. When meeting the Christ child on panels and altarpieces, ordinary mortals look away, unable to comprehend His perfection. But the faces of the child and Mary are always peaceful and at ease. They have the same tranquillity as the Polish child sculptures and reliefs, signifying that true repose will not be found in this world but only in the next, with God and the serene angelic host, where no one is blemished or troubled. The bleakness of Central European spirituality also included a message of hope.

Contemporaries were alert to the contrasts in style and content between Italy and Europe north of the Alps. Michelangelo (lived 1475–1564) thought the art of the north more devout, appealing 'to women, especially to the very old and the very young, and also to monks and nuns and to certain noblemen who have no sense of true harmony'. He was right to the extent that religious themes predominated in Central

European art. At the very least, the clients who commissioned artists usually wanted altarpieces in which they would figure in an attitude of pious devotion. But there was more to it than that. Central Europe *was* more devout—it had more wayside chapels, more people on pilgrimage, more chantries for reciting the mass, and more feast days than anywhere else in Europe. It also had more brotherhoods of lay people living in religious communes and more monastic houses that had adopted the contemplative worship shorn of ritual that the brotherhoods favoured.[17]

Piety underpinned more than just art but would go on to influence what the universities taught, eventually snuffing out the broad classical education that had been the starting point of the new curriculum. During the later Middle Ages, Central Europe had spawned universities. Prague, Cracow, Vienna, Erfurt, Heidelberg, and Cologne were fourteenth-century foundations. In the territory of the Holy Roman Empire, a further nine were founded in the course of the next century, more than in any other area in Europe. Hungary had no university, although its rulers made several attempts to establish one. Some Hungarians studied abroad, mainly at Vienna and Cracow, but it was perfectly possible to receive a higher education in Buda since there were schools there that offered a similar curriculum.[18]

Unlike in Italy where law and medicine predominated, the universities in Central Europe concentrated on the arts curriculum known as the *trivium*, or 'the three', which comprised Latin grammar, logic, and rhetoric. But from the late fifteenth century, the emphasis in Central European universities was firmly on rhetoric, which was about composing elegant Latin prose and verse, without being overworried about grammatical precision. Grammar and logic were now marginalized as, in the words of one contemporary critic, just 'babbling and clattering made up of inane noises, filling the day with obscure and ambiguous disputes or, should I say, puzzles'.[19]

To learn how to write, students were introduced to *litterae humaniores*, or 'worldly literature', so called to distinguish it from the 'divine literature' of the Bible and other religious texts. The masters who taught *litterae humaniores* were accordingly known as humanists. To begin with, they took their inspiration from Italy and classical Rome, spurred on by poets who had visited the peninsula and communicated their enthusiasm in the lecture hall. They wrote textbooks for their students and sent them to the printing press to be published. The problem was that printing gave a finality to the written word that was missing in the previous practice of reading out of manuscripts for dictation. So, humanists became increasingly involved in editing, chasing up manuscripts, and reconciling often very different texts. They wanted the versions that they communicated to be definitive.

Conrad Celtis (1459–1508) was Central Europe's first celebrity academic. Originally from Franconia, Celtis studied and lectured in Rome and northern Italy, after which he crossed Central Europe to teach at more than a dozen universities and cathedral schools. To inspire a new generation in classical literature, he founded in Cracow, Vienna, Buda, and Heidelberg 'sodalities', or learned societies, to foster literature and the arts. In between, he ransacked libraries looking for lost manuscripts, found several that he edited, and collected mistresses, to whom (anticipating Sinatra's 'It Was a Very Good Year') he later assigned in separate verses a particular phase in his life.[20]

But Celtis's time was already passing. The piety of Central Europe was transforming the university curriculum. Since many humanist teachers thought the odes of Horace and Catullus too erotic, the poetry of Ovid too effeminate, and the satires of Juvenal too lewd, the universities increasingly taught safe texts—the poetry of Virgil, the histories of Titus Livy, Cicero's speeches, and works of a thoroughly Christian character. The selection they chose for editing narrowed too. Even so, the humanist achievement in Central Europe was remarkable in demonstrating the textual errors in the Catholic Latin Bible, or Vulgate, and in furnishing editions of the classics that are still the basis of modern scholarship.

Humanism in Central Europe was moral and didactic. The editions that humanist scholars worked on were mainly intended for students. As one scholar explained, they served 'for the furthering of erudition and a better moral life' and as 'an aid to speech but also to improve the soul'. To boost the learning and moral sensibilities of their charges, lecturers and schoolteachers frequently wrote their own plays, modelled on classical comedies and tragedies, which they then had their students perform—often at wearying length so that the whole class had the chance to join in. A favourite was the reworking of the New Testament story of the Prodigal Son into the Prodigal Student, where the biblical phrase 'and wasted all his days in riotous living' was expanded to take up three-quarters of the play, during which the full repertoire of vices and moral snares was enacted.[21]

The first Prodigal Student drama was Gnapheus's *Acolastus* (1529). At a time of religious turmoil throughout Central Europe, Gulielmus Gnapheus (Willem van de Voldersgraft, 1493–1568) was unable to keep his views to himself. Banished from city after city, he moved from The Hague in Holland to Elbląg (Elbing) in Poland and thence to Königsberg on the Baltic, from where he was exiled again on account of his heretical beliefs, finally taking refuge on the Frisian coast at Norden. At every stop, he founded schools and wrote plays, often of a satirical and moralizing type, contributing to the foundation of humanist Latin writing in Prussia and Poland. One of his targets was the Polish astronomer Copernicus (1473–1543), the subject of his drama *The Foolish Sage* (*Morosophus*, 1541). At this time, most people thought Copernicus's sun-centred cosmology to be self-evidently wrong. So, Gnapheus made sure to include a peasant chorus that sung to Copernicus's 'noble stupidity'.[22]

Gnapheus's crime, for which he was arrested in Holland in 1523, was for his wife to be found in possession of a sausage during Lent. The crime was trivial, but the prosecution of it was not. For it was an early occasion when city magistrates undertook a public prosecution. Up until the early sixteenth century, accusations were mainly laid by the victim, in the manner of a private action. So, if a witch blighted crops with a spell, the victim sued her for compensation. The case was then heard as X versus Y, with the court determining culpability and the reparation due. But now, something new was happening in the law—

public prosecutors and representatives of the ruler were appearing as legal agents. This too was the work of the Renaissance, and its effect was keenly felt in Central Europe.[23]

As its name suggests, Roman Law was the law that had been followed in the Roman Republic and Empire, which the Byzantine emperor Justinian codified in the sixth century CE. It influenced the procedure of church courts during the Middle Ages, spilling over to affect lay jurisdiction and legal education in the Italian universities. Bits of it burrowed deep, so much so that when in the 1430s a townsman living in the Swiss Vaud was asked what he thought the law was, he recited several aphorisms taken from Roman Law texts. But it was not until the end of the fifteenth century that Roman Law began to influence the substance of the law in Central Europe and to alter the way people thought about it.[24]

Roman Law fitted in with the Renaissance interest in the classical tradition, but it was also scholarly, composed in elegant Latin, and thorough: indeed, everything a humanist might want. Given its Roman origins, it was thought especially applicable to the Holy Roman Empire. By around 1500, it had become the law of the higher imperial courts and was also being adopted in ducal courts and in the cities, where it made early inroads. In Poland and Hungary, its influence was less pronounced. Even so, the vocabulary of the law in Polish and Hungarian courts shifted to accommodate it, adopting the categories and distinctions of Roman Law as well as its stress on written proofs. The self-governing German or Saxon community in Transylvania embraced it almost in its entirety.[25]

Roman Law turned established legal conventions on their head. First, it was learned and lawyerly. It introduced a terminology that made it possible to think in terms, for instance, of intentionality— hence the distinction between premeditated murder and manslaughter done either while brawling or in anger or by negligence. New classifications separated the law of property from inheritance and the custodianship that a guardian had (and frequently abused). With a new vocabulary of ownership that distinguished possession from occupation, the mortgage now became legally practicable. Without Roman Law, modern-day house purchase would be impossible, since it allows the lender to concede physical possession of a property to the debtor. (It was the other way around in most medieval law, where the lender became the actual possessor of a property that had been pledged against a debt.) Critical to its operation were written proofs so that judges might examine the cases before them dispassionately and with proper regard for the language of contracts.[26]

Secondly, Roman Law reinforced the authority of rulers and magistrates. Previously, Central European courts had made little distinction between civil and criminal law: if someone harmed you, then you sued him (or her) for damages. Now, prosecutors took charge of all actions that fell within the criminal law, acting on behalf of the city, duke, or monarch, and they frequently demanded penalties other than monetary ones. If magistrates considered an offence to have been committed, they also took over civil actions launched by one individual against another, converting them into criminal proceedings. Accusations of sorcery often fell into this category, with terrible punishments as a consequence. The new Roman Law courts were not only in the business of judging crimes—they were now killing people too. Gnapheus in The Hague was lucky to escape with his life for the crime of his wife's sausage. The companion with whom he had shared his cell did not.

But most of all, the Roman Law magnified the sovereign or, as it called him, 'the prince'—unsurprisingly so, since most of it originated in the Roman Empire where the emperor's will had been supreme. Monarchs had long borrowed the classical Roman language of power, talking of themselves as seated on the highest throne, being the embodiment of the law, and divinely ordained. But they now found in the Roman Law a new range of formulas—'what pleases the prince has the force of the law', which allowed the prince to legislate 'by his own right' and 'by the fullness of his power'. By investing the prince with supreme authority, Roman Law allowed the ruler to revoke existing laws and make his own, publishing decrees that counted as fully valid legal instruments even though they overturned established principles.

Behind its glittering façade of marble statues, Italianate arcades, and earnest scholars, the Renaissance state born of Roman Law nourished despotism. This was not evident at first, but over the sixteenth and seventeenth centuries many Central European rulers rid themselves of diets and assemblies, often using the language of Roman Law in justification. East of the Elbe River, peasants and villagers who had never listed their rights in *Weistümer* increasingly found that they were disadvantaged in litigation and eased to the status of serfs. But the powers that rulers claimed were not only legal ones. Increasingly, too, they pried into consciences and conduct, demanding spiritual obedience to their own faith and conformity to their own moral codes. The religious Reformation completed the legal Renaissance, and in Central Europe its beneficiary was the ruler.

Luther's Reformation, the Badlands of Thuringia, and the Court Painter of Saxony

IT WAS IN THE MIDDLE OF THE AFTERNOON OF WEDNESDAY, 4 MAY 1521. The two covered wagons stumbled through the lanes in the Thuringian forest. They were near what are now called the Badlands after the blocks of volcanic rock that push up through the woodland floor creating structures that look more like South Dakota than the German heartland. Except for the coachmen, the party comprised clerics, dressed in monks' habits. Although it was a weekday, the monks had spent the morning in worship. Only a few hours before, their leader, Martin Luther (lived 1483–1546), had given a sermon in the market square of the nearby village of Möhra, where his uncle lived.

Luther was not only a monk but also a hunted man. At the imperial diet held just three weeks before in Worms, the emperor Charles V had condemned Luther to outlawry because of his heretical beliefs, which had recently earned him the pope's excommunication. Luther was now in the common expression *vogelfrei*, 'as free as a bird', which meant that he should henceforth live apart from human society, making the woods his refuge, but always in fear of ensnarement and death, for like a bird he lived outside the law. Luther was now on the run, heading for safety to the university town of Wittenberg, where he hoped his supporters might protect him.

The masked horsemen came for Luther just after the little party had passed the grim tower of Altenstein Castle, on the approach to the rock outcrop called the Ass's Head (Eselskopf). Led by the lord of Altenstein, Burckhardt von Wenckheim, soldiers put fetters on Luther and dragged him out of sight of his companions. Luther remained calm, for he knew that this was all a charade. Once out of view, Wenckheim unfastened Luther and put him in a horse-drawn carriage. An hour later, Luther was received in the hilltop fortress of the Wartburg. Stripped of his habit, he was given comfortable quarters under the name of 'Lord George'.

Luther's companions may have been in on the secret, but the coachmen were not. Once home, they confidently reported that Luther had been kidnapped by bounty hunters. For several months, Luther's whereabouts remained a mystery and it was only after a year that Luther left the safety of the Wartburg. He spent the intervening time translating the Greek New Testament into German. It was printed in Wittenberg in 1522 and went through more than seventy editions over the next four decades. His Old Testament followed in 1534. To make sure that his German matched everyday speech, Luther occasionally sneaked out of the castle to listen to people talking in the nearby streets and markets.

Luther's pantomime kidnapping and subsequent concealment were the work of Frederick the Wise of Saxony. Frederick was a cautious and hesitant ruler, a dabbler in theology, and a man of strong convictions. Besides being a monk, Luther was a professor at his university and Frederick felt bound to protect him. Otherwise, Frederick stayed loyal to the traditions of the Catholic faith, amassing a collection of twenty thousand relics, many of which he kept in expensive caskets or mounted on gold and silver monstrances. Only on his deathbed did Frederick take the Mass in both kinds, consuming the bread and the wine. (In Catholic practice, laymen took at this time only the bread and, even then, rarely.)[1]

The staged abduction was vital to Luther's survival and to the movement for religious reform, or Reformation, that he inspired. There had been plenty of heretics in the past, but they and their teachings had mostly been snuffed out by princes, rulers, and city governments. Most recently, in 1498, the moral reformer and prophet Savonarola had been hanged and burnt by the city council of Florence. Luther and his teachings survived because of Frederick the Wise and, after Frederick's death, his son John of Saxony. Without their support and protection, Luther would surely have been executed like John Hus had been a century earlier. Lutheranism would now be just another name to list beside the failed and almost forgotten heresies of French Catharism, Piedmontese and German Waldensianism, and English Wyclifism. Luther's and Lutheranism's survival owed much to the charade played out in the Thuringian Badlands.

Luther's protest had begun modestly enough, criticizing just one aspect of Catholic devotion, which was the sale of indulgences: bits of paper that promised the buyer that for a price they would be let off years in Purgatory. The Ninety-Five Theses on indulgences that Luther posted on the door of Wittenberg's castle church in 1517 as an invitation to debate were less theologically controversial than the 151 Theses that his dean had previously pinned up attacking the veneration of relics. In fact, the Ninety-Five Theses elicited little response at the time among Luther's fellow academics. No debate was held—not because the university authorities banned it (as some historians allege), but because no one found the subject interesting enough.[2]

What pushed Luther's criticisms to the forefront were the attacks of the Dominican friars. Because Dominicans were the main peddlers of indulgences, their theologians pounced on Luther. They soon had him, as they quaintly put it, 'obelisked' (meaning skewered). Since the trade in indulgences had papal authorization, they explained, Luther's criticism amounted to an attack on the pope. Luther had no wish to create divisions within the Church, but he was forced to harden his position. Pressed by his adversaries, he steadily rejected most Catholic teaching—papal supremacy in matters of religion, the veneration of saints, that good works opened the doors of heaven, and that the sacraments actually became Christ's body and blood when they were blessed.

Luther's message may be summed up in two watchwords: faith and scripture. First, salvation came not from actions but from faith. Mankind had been freed from sin by Christ's sacrifice on the cross. By putting faith in Him, the sinner was 'justified' or saved. As Luther put it in 1520:

Christ is full of grace, life, and salvation. The human soul is full of sin, death, and damnation. Now let faith come between them. Sin, death, and damnation will then be Christ's. And grace, life, and salvation will be the believer's.[3]

Secondly, anything not in the Bible lacked divine sanction, for it was there that God had unfolded His plan. Since the Bible did not include popes, Purgatory, or priestly celibacy, they were unnecessary to the Christian life. When facing Emperor Charles V just before his counterfeit kidnap, Luther unequivocally declared his belief in the authority of the Bible with the famous line, 'Here I stand!' Less well known are his words to a fellow reformer delivered a year or so later—'I tell you that unless you can cite clear words of Scripture for your doings, I will not listen to you, even though you have swallowed the Holy Ghost, feathers and all!'[4]

At a time when humanists were searching for the authentic versions of the classical works they were editing, and Roman lawyers were emphasizing the importance of written law, Luther's stress on the Bible fitted in with Renaissance ideas of textual authority. But Luther was no Bible thumper. He recognized that what the Bible said was not always applicable to the conditions of his own day. Even so, many of his followers had a less nuanced understanding. Taking biblical precepts literally, they repudiated infant baptism, declared the Mass to be only symbolic of Christ's presence, and pressed for a return to the communal egalitarianism of early Christianity.

Frederick the Wise and his son and successor after 1525, Duke John of Saxony, kept Luther safe, first in Wartburg and subsequently in Wittenberg. Living in what amounted to exile in Saxony, Luther wrote. His output over his lifetime was extraordinary, comprising in the modern collected edition 121 volumes, eighty thousand pages in all. Although much consisted of sermons, there were also pamphlets aimed at popular consumption and more than thirty hymns that are still sung today. A competent baritone vocalist, composer, and lute player, Luther introduced congregational singing to churches. Until then, only the priests and choir had sung. With communal prayers, the distribution of the sacraments to all adults, and long sermons, Luther transformed worship in church from a spectacle to an event that involved the whole congregation.

But in confinement, Luther was unable to control the religious forces his teaching had released. The former dean of his university, Andreas Karlstadt, who had previously written the theses against relics, preached as early as 1521 in ordinary layman's clothing, renounced all three of his doctoral degrees as vanities, and took a stern-looking fifteen-year-old as his wife. (The artist Cranach gives us a portrait of her.) Recommending a return to the Mosaic Law of the Old Testament with its ban on idols, Karlstadt began 'cleansing' churches of images, plasterworks of the Virgin, and frescoes. Preaching that the statues of saints were whores sent to deceive and that the churches which housed them were no better than brothels, Karlstadt launched a furious iconoclasm or destruction of images across the Holy Roman Empire.[5]

But Karlstadt's targets were also social ones. It was an affront to God, he explained, that there were so many beggars and he urged Christians to cancel the debts that the needy owed them. Other reformers went further, preaching that God's Kingdom should be made on earth, with the foundation of a New Jerusalem and social equality based on the common ownership of property. By feeding ideas of popular revolution and building on local resentments over rents, religious enthusiasts contributed to the massive uprising known as the German Peasants' War (1525). It was a brief but bloody episode that lasted just several months, although in Münster in Westphalia, rebellion flared once more in the 1530s. The cages in which the victorious city authorities displayed the bodies of the executed 'Münster prophets' still hang from the walls of the city's parish church.[6]

Luther counselled the lords to show mercy to the rebel peasants but left them in no doubt that his sympathies lay with the established order. With the peasants' defeat, the movement for religious reform was shorn of its radical edge, which now lay outside the mainstream of belief. This made it less objectionable to city magistrates, dukes, and

counts, who from the 1520s appointed increasing numbers of Lutheran clergy to their courts and to parish pulpits and took no action
to stem the tide of Luther's teaching. Importantly, too, they cracked
down on preachers who spread messages of social revolution and they
closed Catholic monasteries and convents that performed no obviously
useful purpose.

As far as Emperor Charles V was concerned, Lutheranism was a
contagion that should be expunged. Charles, who was Emperor Maximilian's grandson and already king of Spain, had been elected Holy
Roman Emperor in 1519. But for almost a decade, from 1521 to 1530,
he left imperial affairs in the hands of his brother, Archduke Ferdinand
of Austria, while he himself lingered in Spanish Castile, enjoying the
attentions of his frail but dazzlingly beautiful wife, Isabella of Portugal. Ferdinand was a realist. The Lutherans were a powerful caucus in
many of the provincial diets in the Austrian lands and so controlled the
purse strings at a time when money was needed to fend off the Turkish
challenge. Ferdinand's measures to stem the Lutheran advance were
half-hearted. After blustering that Luther's adherents should be burnt,
he backed down, imposing instead a few weeks in jail with only bread
and water. Even this penalty was seldom imposed.

The Lutherans in the Holy Roman Empire were by the late 1520s
increasingly well organized. Calling themselves Protestants (because
they protested the measures taken against them), they were a noisy faction in the imperial diet. Returning to the empire in 1530, Charles V
promptly summoned the Catholic lords and announced his intention
to go to war in defence of the Catholic faith. But his audience considered the suggestion risible. As they explained, Charles did not have the
cash—'and the sinews of war are money.' Even if he had, he would push
the empire into civil war, and the French and the Turks would surely
take the chance to invade. The mercenaries he recruited would probably
defect anyway, and finally:

> The subjects of the Christian princes could rebel and rise up against
> their masters, in which case they would have a war with their own

vassals. For these and other compelling reasons, the emperor cannot go to war with the Lutherans for the faith.[7]

Charles wisely backed down, hoping instead that a compromise religious formula could be found that would bridge divisions. Even so, the advice of the Catholic lords hints at the continued and strong appeal that the new faith had among ordinary people. Charles's Catholic allies feared that cracking down on Lutheranism risked a war between themselves and their increasingly Protestant subjects. Their misgivings were well grounded.

Protestantism was popular. Throughout Central Europe, it tapped into a long tradition of disdain for the Catholic clergy, whose alleged immorality publicists never ceased to lament, and a growing nationalism that fed on resentment of Italian popes. As early as 1521, one papal envoy reckoned that nine-tenths of Germans were Lutheran sympathizers—'as for the rest, even if they are indifferent to Luther, it is at least "Death to the Roman Curia".' Much was due to Luther himself. Pugnacious and tireless, he would often preach three times a day, and his writings and sermons were scabrous and funny, with *Mist*, *Dreck*, *Scheisse*, and *Arsch* (manure, filth, shit, and arse) recurrent expressions. So, the pope was 'the cuckoo that devours the Church's eggs and craps out cardinals'; Luther's own 'farts in Wittenberg will make the pope's nose curl', and, 'if you're not allowed to laugh in heaven, I don't want to go there.' But behind the humour, Luther hammered home a single message—faith, the Bible, and the uselessness or, in Luther's expression, 'indifference' of traditional Catholic observance as a route to salvation.[8]

Fewer than one in ten Germans were literate, so Luther had to make sure that what he published had oral currency. He wrote overwhelmingly in German, with the intention that his writings would be read out to the uneducated—many contained easy verses that could be memorized, and some were intended to be sung. And he sent them to the printing press so that they might be circulated. First developed in Mainz around 1440, the printing press using moveable type had by the end of the century spread to several hundred centres across Central Europe, making it possible for the first time to produce affordable books and pamphlets. Luther recognized its importance, describing the printing press as 'the best and greatest gift by which God advances the Gospel'. Most of Luther's writings appeared in quarto editions. With their pages folded over several times before cutting, they made up paperback pamphlets of sixteen or thirty-two sides that were easily transported and affordable, each costing about a third of a labourer's daily wage or the price of a hen. Between 1516 and 1546, the printing presses churned out more than three million items written by Luther.[9]

Visual imagery was important, and Luther soon recruited the court painter of Saxony, Lucas Cranach. Like Luther, Cranach was a busy man. Of five thousand or so Cranach originals, roughly one thousand paintings survive—four hundred by him personally, the rest being the product of his studio in Wittenberg, which he personally supervised. Cranach's main duties as court painter were to see to everything artistic that affected the court of Frederick the Wise and of his successors as dukes of Saxony. These ranged from selecting tapestries for the ducal palace and choreographing tournaments to producing an illustrated catalogue of Duke Frederick's favourite relics and designing cake moulds.

Luther and Cranach began their collaboration in 1520 when the artist opened a printing shop in Wittenberg to work alongside his studio and began printing Luther's works. Cranach incorporated Luther's writings in imagery that overwhelmed the reader with its mesh of woodcut illustrations and lozenges of text, which left no part of the page blank. Black-and-white drawings, passages from sermons, and verses for singing combined on a single sheet to press home Luther's message. With woodcuts frequently used as wallpaper in homes and taverns, Cranach's was the first multimedia propaganda campaign in Central Europe.

Cranach packaged Luther for popular consumption, starting off with his appearance. A slight man, with a bony face and deep-set eyes, Luther did not exude a natural authority. Jerky in his movements and with a restless look, he seemed like a man possessed. So, Cranach beefed him up in portraits, giving him the same stoutness and solidity as the naturally corpulent Saxon dukes, with whom he was often shown in portraits, standing shoulder to shoulder. When it came to works written by Luther, Cranach wrote Luther's name in big block letters or used the monogram 'DML' standing for Doctor Martin Luther. Cranach made Luther into a brand, but he also made Wittenberg the largest centre of printing in the Holy Roman Empire and its printers and his own press the richest.[10]

Cranach's method of illustration was to shock. As early as 1520, he drew his *Pope-Ass*, which depicted the pope as a deformed creature that had recently washed up in the Tiber, supposedly in a friar's habit. Giving the pope a scaly body, claws, breasts, and a donkey's head, with monsters poking from his thigh and rectum, Cranach used it as the frontispiece for Lutheran pamphlets. Luther's disciple, Philip Melancthon, had fun dissecting the image—the breasts standing for the pope's lustfulness, the claws for greedy church lawyers, the donkey's head for the Catholic Church's empty braying, and so on. For Luther's 1522 New Testament, Cranach illustrated the Book of Revelation with the pope depicted as the biblical Whore of Babylon. Riding a seven-headed monster, the whore bears in her hand the Cup of Abominations and is crowned with a papal tiara.[11]

Cranach's whore proved too much for Duke Frederick the Wise, who ordered the papal tiara to be removed for the next edition. It was briefly replaced by a blank square. Even so, the shocking illustration in the first edition became one of the standard motifs of Reformation publicists and certainly did nothing to halt the success of Luther's New Testament, which sold out almost at once. Between 1522 and 1525, forty-three new editions were printed: no fewer than eighty-six thousand copies in all. Again, they were cheap to buy. A bound copy cost no more than a pig; an unbound version only half that. But what sold most of all were the simplest and plainest of productions—Luther's hymns and his catechisms, or statements of faith, arranged in the form of short questions and answers.[12]

Luther inspired artists and authors across the Holy Roman Empire to communicate his message in words and pictures of their own. The master singer of Nuremberg, Hans Sachs, was one of these. A cobbler by trade who sang in a chorus guild in his spare time, Sachs composed during his lifetime six thousand songs and dialogues for public performance, several thousand of which had a biblical or religious theme. Most extraordinarily, he put large chunks of Luther's Bible into verse. Embracing Lutheranism several years before the city of Nuremberg officially accepted the Reformation, Sachs composed the elegy *The Wittenberg Nightingale* in 1523 comparing Luther to a nightingale who leads a flock of sheep to safety away from lions, snakes, wildcats, and wolves. Like many of Sachs's verses, it was illustrated with woodcuts that explained the allegory in simple visual terms.[13]

The woodcut and the pamphlet were almost exclusively German phenomena in Central Europe. Further east, illustrations were mostly confined to the title page, and printed works had a more earnest and solemn content. Even so, hymnbooks had a wide distribution, often being aimed (as in Bohemia) for family singing around the fireplace. Together with catechisms, they explained the new Protestant religion in simple terms. Overwhelmingly, too, they used the vernacular. The Bohemian lands already had Bibles written in Czech, translated by John Hus and his followers back in the early fifteenth century. These were now augmented by translations of Luther's Bible, often using the same woodcuts. The Habsburg king of Bohemia, Charles V's brother Ferdinand, was so alarmed that his subjects were reading the Bible for themselves without the direction of the clergy that he instructed the publication in Czech of Sebastian Münster's popular encyclopaedia *Cosmographia* (1493) in the hope of diverting their attention. Even so, he made sure that the Church footed the bill for the translation and printing.[14]

Luther's Reformation was not only a German Reformation but also a Central European one. It struck deep roots in Transylvania, among the nobility and mining communities in northern Hungary (now Slovakia), and in Poland. Polish historians, for whom the Catholic faith is bound up with national identity, have generally downplayed

Lutheranism in Poland, treating it as either a latecomer in an already competitive religious field or as an affair of German folk who lived mostly in cities. In fact, in the 1530s and 1540s Poland probably had the greatest density of Lutheran congregations in continental Europe, after the Holy Roman Empire and Denmark. It was at the forefront of the Central European Reformation.[15]

There was an early warning of Lutheranism's spread in Poland, when in 1521 a public burning of the reformer's books prompted a riot in Toruń, but the turning point came four years later. After a series of defeats by the Poles, in 1466 the Teutonic Knights had surrendered western Prussia to Poland, including the order's previous headquarters at Marienburg. Now, in 1525, the grand master Albrecht of Hohenzollern transformed what was left of the order's Prussian possessions into a Lutheran principality, which he placed for safety under Polish overlordship, and then married a Danish princess, thus inaugurating a Protestant dynasty. Secondly, in the city of Gdańsk a pro-Lutheran faction overthrew the governing council and undertook an ambitious programme of church reform. In both cases, King Sigismund of Poland (ruled 1506–1548) responded in measured fashion. He took no action against his Prussian vassal but continued to treat him as a fellow Christian ruler. Printers in the new Prussian capital of Königsberg continued to supply Lutheran texts not only in German but also in Polish, Ukrainian, and Old Prussian.[16]

With Gdańsk Sigismund was initially harsher. Occupying the city with troops in April 1526, Sigismund denounced the religious innovations of the councillors, but having ejected them and executed thirteen of the ringleaders for sedition, he left the city alone and Lutheran worship resumed. Sigismund had acted tough, but he knew that rooting out Lutheranism would push Poland into civil war. He was right. By the late 1540s, about half of the deputies in the Sejm were either Protestants or sympathetic to Lutheranism and they were often raucous in their denunciations of the Catholic Church. So, Sigismund confined his persecution to those who advertised insurrectionary opinions. When pressed, he was conciliatory. In a famous phrase, he replied to one Catholic stalwart—'Permit me to be king of both the sheep and the goats.' Tellingly, too, there was only one execution on purely religious grounds during Sigismund's reign and that was for attempting to convert people to Judaism.[17]

In the late 1520s and 1530s, Luther's Reformation captured an increasing number of dukes and counts, of which the grand master of the Teutonic Knights is just one example. In the Holy Roman Empire, they included many of the big beasts: the rulers of Saxony, Hesse, Württemberg, Pomerania, and (in 1549) Mecklenburg. To their number should be added the rulers of the Palatinate and Brandenburg whose sympathies lay with the Reformation, even though they kept their own convictions private. The only sizeable duchies not to give way were Bavaria and Austria. Charles V's Catholic advisers urged him to arrest the trend, by violence if necessary, foreseeing that otherwise 'the entire German nation . . . would fall into a state of still further disorder, confusion and decline and would finally come to destruction, ruin and doom.' But Charles put his trust in a General Council of the Church, which he hoped would find a compromise formula capable of restoring unity.[18]

It was an increasingly vain hope. The Church Council that eventually met at Trento (Trent) in 1545 promptly affirmed Catholic doctrines, which were inimical to most Protestants. In anticipation of a military showdown in the empire, Charles prepared detailed 'painted maps' showing in one contemporary description 'the location of towns as well as the distances between them, and rivers and mountains'. Although now lost, these constituted the first comprehensive maps ever made of the German lands. Charles also prepared the political ground. Instead of proclaiming a religious war, he moved in 1546 against the leading Protestant princes with the excuse that they had occupied territories to which they were not entitled. This divided the enemy and so prepared the way for Charles's stunning triumph over the leading Protestant princes at the Battle of Mühlberg in 1547.[19]

In victory Charles showed moderation. Instead of seeking to impose Catholicism by force, he put in place an interim religious agreement

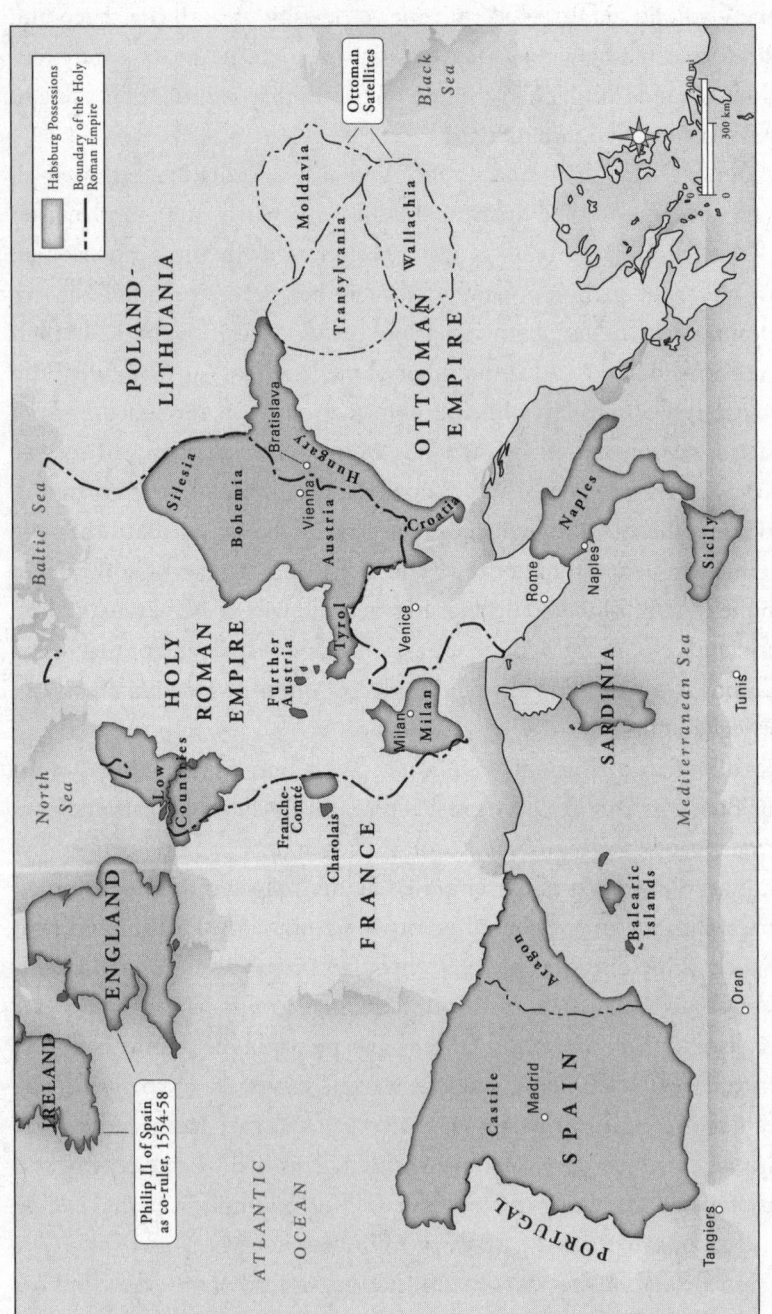

HABSBURG EUROPE c. 1550

that permitted some elements of Protestant worship in return for recognition of papal supremacy and that was applicable to both Protestants and Catholics alike. In effect, he established a separate scheme of faith for the Holy Roman Empire, albeit still under the nominal leadership of Rome. But neither side was willing to give ground, and both had misgivings about the power that victory had placed in Charles's hands. Consequently, the interim agreement was accepted only in those territories which Charles had occupied militarily. In the meantime, Charles's adversaries plotted his downfall, in league with the French king.

Charles's policy towards Protestantism rested on his conviction that, as a Habsburg, he should maintain the supremacy of the Catholic faith. As he explained at the imperial diet that had condemned Luther back in 1521, his forebears had always been 'defenders of the Catholic faith, its sacred ceremonies, decrees, and ordinances, and its holy rites, to the honour of God'. For this reason, he was compelled to condemn Luther to outlawry 'and to stake upon this course my dominions and my possessions, my body and my blood, my life and soul'. Dynasty brought obligations, and none of these was more important than to stand by the established Church.

But Charles's obligation to preserve the Catholic faith also derived from the office of emperor. Charles's advisers spoke grandiloquently of him as 'the greatest emperor since Charlemagne', appointed by God to be monarch of the whole world. He would bring peace to Christendom, they explained, so that 'the whole orb will be put under this very Christian prince and will receive Our Faith. So will be fulfilled the words of Our Redeemer, Let there be one flock and one shepherd.' For them, empire meant unity in the Catholic faith—a solution that left little room for religious dissent. Universalism, or the idea that Church, religion, and worldly power should map onto one another, compelled Charles to squeeze out doctrinal difference.[20]

But Charles's idea of empire was never less than capacious. It inspired him to lead crusades into North Africa, seek out coronation by the pope, and send off his sisters and daughters as spouses to most of Europe's leading families. In Central Europe, it led him to fight in 1546–1547 the war for religion that drew in combatants from across the Holy Roman Empire. In conducting it, he pushed across the Elbe into what is now Brandenburg, which was further east than any German monarch had campaigned for almost two centuries. In the geographical scope of his 'world empire', which reached through Spain to the Americas and the Pacific Ocean, in his promotion of the Habsburg dynasty, and in the power that he wielded in the Holy Roman Empire, Charles gave life to the old dreams of Emperors Frederick III and Maximilian I.

Charles's triumph in Central Europe lasted only a few years. Out-manoeuvred in 1552 by a Protestant 'league for liberty and freedom' and defeated militarily, he abandoned the interim agreement. By this time in a deep depression, Charles handed over the negotiation of a settlement to his brother, Ferdinand (after 1556, Emperor Ferdinand I). The peace deal Ferdinand struck at the diet of Augsburg in 1555 stated that in the territories of the Holy Roman Empire whoever was the local ruler would determine the religion of his subjects and whether they might be Catholics or Lutherans. If subjects disagreed, then they had the right to emigrate elsewhere. In 1553, he split the great empire he had accumulated down the middle, assigning the Habsburg lands in Central Europe to his brother, and Spain, the Netherlands, and the New World to his son Philip. Charles's 'world empire' was thus partitioned and, in Central Europe, the idea of Christian unity irrevocably abandoned.

The winners were the German princes. Whether Catholics or Protestants, they took charge of the religious organization in their territories, appointing councils and consistories of clergymen to impose the right religious beliefs, relayed through catechisms that parishioners were expected to recite and learn. Protestant rulers were usually the more energetic. Most presumed to be the 'highest bishop' (*summus episcopus*) in their territories, so they felt empowered to lay down elaborate schemes of faith for their subjects to follow. But Protestant and Catholic rulers alike were equally concerned that people should lead godly and moral lives, for the good of their souls. Across the Holy Roman Empire, they launched inspections of churches, schools, and universities, censored books, and instructed village elders to examine and report on the faith of countryfolk.

Most of all, they published ordinances or decrees that minutely regulated personal conduct. Bans on premarital sex, job shirking and vagrancy, gambling, and casting spells were as much the subject of these ordinances as injunctions to attend church, to take communion weekly, and in Protestant areas to go to Bible classes. Proclaimed from pulpits and read out in marketplaces, these ordinances dug increasingly deep into personal conduct, affecting the clothes people might wear, the alcohol on sale in taverns, the time villagers should be in bed, and the just wages to be paid to labourers. Over time, the language of the ordinances even affected everyday speech, generating different dialects: a Protestant so-called Meissisch idiom and a Catholic Upper German one. The difference between the two was so laden with religious associations that converts from one faith to the other often changed how they wrote.[21]

The outcome of the Reformation in Central Europe was not only religious but also political. To save souls and direct people heavenward, rulers and governments inflated their powers, demanding that subjects conform in their religious observance and moral conduct to their ordinances and decrees. It was a vast expansion of princely power that built on the legislative rights conveyed by Roman Law to rulers. Back in 1521, the duke of Saxony had rescued Luther and saved the Reformation from obliteration. In turn, Protestant princes had by their belligerence forced a settlement in 1555 which recognized Lutheranism as the religion in those territories with a Lutheran ruler. The Reformation now repaid its debt to the Holy Roman Empire's princes, enlarging their authority and expanding the scope of their power to reach into their subjects' lives.

CHAPTER 15

The Ottoman Turks and Central Europe's Long Frontier

EVERYONE KNEW THE TURKS WERE COMING. THEIR CAPTURE OF Constantinople in 1453 had sent a shockwave throughout Christendom. Aeneas Silvius, the future Pope Pius II, foresaw the Ottoman armies overrunning the Italian peninsula. He wrote from Graz in Styria shortly after receiving news of Constantinople's fall: 'We see the slaughter of the Greeks; next we expect the ruin of the Latins. The nearby house has been burned; now we await the fire. Who now lies between us and the Turks?' Fifty years later, a papal envoy to the imperial diet meeting at Nuremberg delivered an even more rousing address. He warned the assembly that the Turks' continued advance threatened Nuremberg itself. Where would the diet then convene, he asked—in Lübeck or perhaps in the Orkney Islands?[1]

The Ottoman advance through the Balkans and into Central Europe had begun in 1354, when the Turks overran Gallipoli on the European side of the Dardanelles (or Turkish Straits). Serbia fell in 1389, although fragments struggled on for a further half century; Bulgaria collapsed in the 1390s, and Bosnia vanished in the 1460s, falling, as was said at the time, 'like a whisper'. But the stark list of conquests hides the enormousness of the Ottoman achievement. At a time when most Christian armies had generally fewer than thirty thousand troops and could seldom advance more than several hundred kilometres from their mustering points, the sultan could raise armies of more than a hundred thousand men and march them fully supplied over 1,500 kilometres. The Ottoman army was also well equipped, with a solid infantry corps at its heart, supported by light and armoured cavalry, and with raiders whose task was to soften up the enemy and create panic in advance of the main assault. In 1521, the Turks took the great Hungarian fortress of Belgrade, prising open the gateway to Central Europe.

Yet, extraordinarily, the kingdom of Hungary almost survived. Its king, Louis II (ruled 1516–1526), was also ruler of Bohemia, and he was able to build on the battle tactics previously used by the Hussites, deploying tank units of armoured wagons and mobile cannons. With perhaps the most modern army in Christian Europe, he took on the Turks at Mohács in southern Hungary as they marched into his kingdom in August 1526. Catching the Turkish main army unawares as it prepared to bivouac, the Hungarian cavalry smashed the enemy's left flank and, wheeling round, advanced close enough to the centre to pepper Sultan Suleiman's cuirass with shot. Only the arrival of fresh Turkish troops saved the Ottoman host. Sheer numbers now decided the outcome, for however valiant and expertly commanded, an army of twenty-five thousand will seldom prevail against an enemy three times the size. In the ensuing rout, King Louis was tossed from his horse into a brook and either drowned or was trampled to death. Most of the kingdom's great lords perished with him.[2]

The Ottoman army marched into Hungary, but having sacked the capital, it withdrew on the approach of autumn. In the meantime, the kingdom's politics fell into mayhem. Because Louis II had died childless, the Hungarian diet claimed the right to choose his successor and elected as king the popular voivode of Transylvania, John Zápolya. In response, Charles V's brother, Archduke Ferdinand, marched into Hungary. Claiming inheritance by virtue of his marriage to the dead king's sister, Ferdinand recalled the diet, which duly elected him monarch. So, by the end of 1526 Hungary had two kings who could both claim the right of succession. Ferdinand also brought into line the subordinate kingdoms of Croatia and Slavonia in southeastern Hungary. To impose his will on the fractious Slavonian nobility, Ferdinand borrowed Spanish troops from his brother. This was the first occasion when Spanish forces fought for the Habsburgs in Central Europe and a harbinger of later, more brutal interventions.

Hungary collapsed into civil war. Since Ferdinand had the upper hand militarily, John Zápolya reluctantly allied in 1529 with the Ottoman Turks, becoming the sultan's vassal. The deal was confirmed on the former battlefield of Mohács, amid the ruin of war and the skulls of the dead. In support of Zápolya, the sultan now invaded Ferdinand's territories and in the same year put Vienna under siege. A three-way struggle began, pitting, on one side, the uneasy alliance of Zápolya and the Turks and, on the other, Ferdinand. An attempt by Zápolya to betray the sultan by coming to terms with Ferdinand, followed by Zápolya's death in 1540, led the next year to the Turkish occupation and garrisoning of the middle portion of the Hungarian kingdom.

Bit by bit, Hungary split in three—an eastern part made up mostly of Transylvania, which belonged to Zápolya's son, the infant John II Sigismund (lived 1540–1571); a crescent of land over which Ferdinand ruled that reached from Croatia and the Adriatic coast to the northeast of Hungary (now the westernmost part of Ukraine); and a broad central corridor, which lay in Turkish hands. Hungary's capital city of Buda became the seat of a Turkish pasha, or governor, while its principal church, the so-called Matthias Church, was converted into a mosque and its spire made into a minaret. As evidence that they were there to stay, the Turks moved the bodies of their holiest saints to Buda. The Turkish occupation of central Hungary would last for more than 140 years. The copper-domed shrine of the dervish poet Gül Baba still overlooks Budapest.

The Reformation added to political uncertainties and divisions. Besides Hungary, Ferdinand had also succeeded Louis II as king of Bohemia in 1526. Here, Lutheranism had radicalized Hussitism, fomenting a division between moderate and reformist wings and inspiring religious sectaries, who adopted even more extreme positions. But it was the sterner reformed faith of the Genevan theologian John Calvin that from the late 1530s won over the Hungarian countryside, replacing Lutheranism as the dominant Protestant faith there. Calvinism's stress on divine providence suited Hungarians as it explained their country's occupation by the Turks and Habsburgs. Calvinist preachers taught how the tribulations of the Hungarians were akin to those suffered by the Israelites in the Old Testament, on which account they, too, constituted a Chosen People. Calvinism and, unusually, Unitarianism also flourished in Transylvania under the care of godly noblemen and austere urban patricians. For a century and a half, the main church in Cluj in Transylvania, the massive St Michael's, was a Unitarian place of worship, where preachers denied Christ's divinity and taught that He was just a man.

Unitarian beliefs were plainly heretical, being akin to the Arianism that had flourished in Central Europe in the fourth and fifth centuries. Calvinists, too, trod on controversial ground, since unlike Catholics and Lutherans they rejected that Christ was physically or substantially present in the bread and the wine of the communion. Even so, the new faiths prospered, while in the eastern, Transylvanian part of the kingdom, the diet gave Calvinism and Unitarianism the status of official religions. In the Turkish-occupied area, there were no controls on religious observance whatsoever. The Ottoman pasha in Buda categorically affirmed in 1548 that 'all Hungarians and Slavs should be able to hear and receive the Word of God without any danger.' By the end of the century, if not before, three-quarters of parishes in the three divided parts of the Hungarian kingdom had in one shape or form become Protestant.[3]

The Ottoman invasion of Central Europe prompted unprecedented population flows. In the regions most exposed to warfare, the people fled northwards, abandoning homes where (in a contemporary verse) only 'black stones remain and leafless pines'. Their place was taken by newcomers from the south, who had either been displaced or were escaping from Ottoman rule. Many of these were stockbreeders from the mountainous hinterland of the Balkans, who sought out new pastures for their flocks in the overgrown fields of deserted lowland villages. Many, too, belonged to the Orthodox Church, adding to the complexity of religious affiliations. Strange mixes or syncretisms emerged at the points where religions overlapped, with Christian worship at dervish shrines, the Muslim veneration of Catholic saints, and rituals of blood brotherhood that cut across religious divisions.[4]

The frontier between the Ottoman Empire and the Habsburg parts of Hungary twisted six hundred kilometres from the Adriatic coast to the foothills of the Carpathians in what is now Slovakia and eastwards to the Transylvanian border. It was a hot frontier, where raiding was commonplace, with intermittent periods when whole armies intervened. By the middle of the sixteenth century, some eighty forts marked its length on the Habsburg side, rising to almost two hundred by the century's end, with garrisons of mercenaries mostly paid with money drawn from the other Habsburg lands. Hungary was made to pay too. Despite the loss of Transylvania and a further half of its territory to the Turks, Hungary was by the 1570s producing almost a million ducats a year in revenue. The Habsburgs knew how to tax.[5]

Even so, the troops on the Habsburg 'Military Frontier', as it was known, were frequently left unprovisioned. For upkeep, the garrisons relied on local resources on both sides of the frontier, often buying food and fodder from villages in Ottoman territory. They were not inclined to take harsh measures against their adversaries in case they interrupted supplies. Both sides also ran a lucrative trade in ransoms, using brokers to negotiate the release of captives and spies to establish a family's wealth. Encounters between Habsburg forces and Turkish troops, who were often as not local recruits, were frequently choreographed or fought by teams of champions drawn from the opposing armies. The later founder of the Jamestown colony in Virginia, Captain John Smith, who in the 1590s fought as a mercenary on the Habsburg side, recorded several of these duels, with the heads of slain warriors going as prizes to the victors.[6]

The greatest concentration of troops and fortresses lay in the two Hungarian border zones known as the Croatian and Slavonian (or Windish) Frontiers (Krabatische Gränitz, Windische Gränitz). By the 1590s, the two zones had altogether a hundred forts and blockhouses and accounted for a third of the garrison strength of the whole Military Frontier. Most of the strongholds were little more than stockades with at best several hundred troops apiece, but there were also much larger fortresses with garrisons of over a thousand men. These were typically built of stone and brick, often with a star-shaped ground plan, projecting bastions, and earth-backed walls. Mostly designed by Italian engineers, they were at the forefront of military architecture. Although not impregnable, they were easily capable of holding up an army for several weeks and disrupting the enemy's timetable. The new fortresses were deadly too: attacking troops had to reckon on a casualty rate of up to 30 per cent.[7]

Troops on the Habsburg Military Frontier fell into two categories. Salaried troops comprised mercenaries mainly recruited from the Holy Roman Empire. Some light-horse hussars and infantry drawn from among the local population were also paid. But the majority of troops were part-timers, who performed military duties and garrison service only when needed. They received in return a farmstead—there were plenty of abandoned fields for them to cultivate. Many of these irregulars were immigrants or *uskoks* (literally, 'escapers') from the Balkans who had moved to the relative shelter of the Military Frontier or into the adjoining 'no-man's-land' (*ničija zemlja*). They were supplemented by seminomadic shepherds, generically called Vlachs or Morlachs, who combined stock breeding and droving with military service. During the 1570s, there were in the two zones about three thousand frontiersmen in salaried units and three times as many unpaid, irregular troops, who both farmed and fought.[8]

The Habsburgs published regulations, protocols, and codes that laid down how troops on the frontier should conduct themselves, but they were just so much paper. Inspections of border fortresses reported rusting and fallen cannons, collapsed walls, and troops so rudely clad that they were unable to perform duties in winter. As one Habsburg officer reported in the 1570s, 'In some border forts, they go about like beggars, half naked and with their garments so badly torn that you can look in both from the front and the back.' The irregulars were particularly undisciplined, alternating military service with banditry. As one commentator with first-hand experience of their depredations reported, 'Although good soldiers, they are like all barbarian peoples, rough and wild . . . and they cannot survive long without brigandage and murder.'[9]

To tackle this, the Habsburg emperors who succeeded Ferdinand, Maximilian II and Rudolf II, opted for administrative refinements. They made the Croatian and Slavonian zones completely self-governing, taking them outside the jurisdiction of the local diets and bans, and centralizing authority on a committee that met in Graz in Styria under the loose oversight of the emperor's Imperial War Council in Vienna. They also began the process of converting irregular troops into paid soldiers, attached to specific forts, and so supposedly subject to greater military supervision. Even so, the bulk of the frontier troops remained part-time farmers. Not only were they defending their fields and thus more vigorous in combat, but they were also cheap, costing only a fifth of regular troops.[10]

The Habsburg Military Frontier that started in the Slavonian and Croatian zones was part of a border that extended across Hungary to Transylvania. On the way, it passed across the Hungarian Plain, where privileged communities of drovers or 'heyducks' (*hajdúk*) doubled up as herdsmen and border guards. But the Ottoman frontier in Central Europe ran further still. It looped around Transylvania and the neighbouring Romanian principalities of Wallachia and Moldavia, which like Transylvania counted as Ottoman vassal states, before running eastwards into the steppe country north of the Black Sea. For a thousand kilometres, the Ottoman frontier in Central Europe ran alongside the edge of Poland and Lithuania, until petering out east of Kyiv, beyond the lower reaches of the Dnieper River.

Whereas the frontier between Habsburg Hungary and Croatia and the Ottoman Empire was marked by a dense line of fortifications, there was nothing like this on the Polish and Lithuanian side. There were fortresses at strategic points on river crossings. But like Kamianets-Podilskyi above the Smotrych Canyon and Khotyn on the Dniester (both now in Ukraine), these were often sprawling and unsophisticated in their design, with tall stone walls that made them vulnerable to artillery fire. Responsibility for the defence of the frontier alternated on the Ottoman side between local Turkish commanders and agents of the Crimean khans, whose ancestors had embraced Islam in the early fourteenth century. The Crimean khans were descended from the Mongol-Tatars who had once dominated the steppe land. But from the fourteenth century onwards, the Mongol-Tatar Empire had fallen apart into quarrelling *ordas*, or courts, often colourfully mistranslated as 'hordes'.

The Tatar khans of the Great Orda of the Crimea were territorially ambitious. They dreamed of restoring the empire of Genghis Khan, but they were no match for the Ottoman sultan, who nibbled away at the Crimean ports and coastline and, after 1475, obliged the khans of the Crimea to acknowledge him as their overlord. The sultan now selected the khans and, although permitting some self-government, demanded that Crimea's relations with foreign powers be in the future directed by Istanbul. The Ottoman Empire also began advancing onto the steppe. By the end of the century, the swathe of land reaching from the mouth of the Danube to the Southern Bug River had been incorporated into the Ottoman provincial administration.

Ottoman Turks, their Crimean Tatar allies, and the rulers of Poland and Lithuania now confronted one another on the steppe land north of the Black Sea. After some negotiation in the late 1530s over fixing a border, the rival sides gave up, conceding that there would instead be an open space, almost a thousand kilometres wide, where no one officially ruled. The Turks called this space 'the wasteland', but for the Poles and Lithuanians it was 'the Wild Plain' (*dzikie pola*). According to one contemporary account, just the stretch from the last Lithuanian strongholds at Bratslav and Cherkasy to the Black Sea coast was a six days' journey, across an endless grassland uninterrupted by forests, marshes, or hills.[11]

But Lithuania was in trouble. The union with Poland had joined the two states at the top, but in all other respects Lithuania was independent, originally having its own government headed by a grand duke, who was chosen from the ruling dynasty, usually being the reigning king's prospective successor. But, from the middle of the fifteenth century, the offices of King of Poland and Grand Duke were combined, which meant that policy was made in Cracow and not in Vilnius. The consequence was to draw the Lithuanian nobility culturally westwards. They embraced Polish manners, took Polish wives, sent their sons to Polish schools, and adopted Polish as their main language, to such an extent that Lithuanian was reduced to the language of the peasantry. Institutionally, too, Lithuania mimicked Poland, having its own two-chamber diet, or Seimas, modelled on the Polish Sejm, with provincial assemblies, or Seimiks, that imitated the Polish regional diets, or Sejmiks.

Lithuania was swift to develop a modern administrative machine, with a busy chancellery in Vilnius that churned out letters in Latin, Polish, Ukrainian, Tatar, and Turkish (then written in Arabic script). But the actual reach of Lithuania's government was short. During the fourteenth and fifteenth centuries, the Lithuanian grand dukes had pushed eastwards across the steppe, laying claim to vast tracts of land. The borders they needed to control were consequently long and so were their communication lines. From Vilnius to Kyiv and Bryansk (now in Russia) was a distance of 700 kilometres, and to Lithuania's furthest outpost, at Dnipro (formerly Dnipropetrovsk) on the Lower Dnieper, more than 1,100 kilometres. On top of this, Lithuania was pushing into contested territory. To the south lay the Crimean Tatars, and to the east a still more formidable foe—Muscovite Russia.[12]

The tsars of Russia were intent on uniting all Orthodox believers under their sway, but they also aimed at winning access to the sea. Half of Lithuania's population was Orthodox, and Lithuania also stood in the way of the tsars' advance to both the Baltic and the Black Sea— so the grand duchy doubly earned Russian hostility. The first phase was played out in the opening decades of the sixteenth century when the tsars Ivan III (ruled 1462–1505) and Basil II (1505–1533) overran and captured a third of Lithuania's territory, including Smolensk. (Smolensk would change hands several more times, until finally falling to Russia in 1654.)

The second was fought after 1558, when Ivan IV 'the Terrible' (ruled 1547–1584) invaded the duchy of Livonia, seizing the city of Dorpat (Tartu, now in Estonia) and the port of Narva on the Gulf of Finland. A remnant of the lands once ruled by the Teutonic Order, the knights of the Livonian Order (formerly the Swordbrothers) who ruled the duchy had kept to their original vocation of praying and fighting, but they were mostly now old men. In 1561, the last master dissolved the order, embraced Protestantism, and made Livonia a vassal state of the Polish crown. In reward, King Sigismund II of Poland-Lithuania (ruled 1548–1572) gave the former master the fat prize of the duchy of Courland, which is now in Latvia. Courland went on to briefly become in the seventeenth century an imperial power, with colonies in the Caribbean and West Africa. Kunta Kinteh Island on the Gambia River was once Jacob or James Island, named in honour of Courland's duke.

The Lithuanian nobility had counted on King Sigismund giving them Livonia as compensation for the loss of Smolensk, but Ivan IV's invasion underlined the threat that Muscovy posed to their wider interests. In Lublin in 1569, a joint meeting of the Polish Sejm and Lithuanian Seimas agreed to a more complete merger of the two states. Henceforth, there was to be one 'Commonwealth' (*Rzeczpospolita*), and the two 'nations' (*narody*) would now constitute one people (*lud*) with a single parliament. Behind these fine-sounding aspirations were Lithuanian hopes for protection at home and for fancy Polish titles, and the Polish magnates' ambitions for big estates on the open spaces of the steppe. Since Poland would now be shouldering the defence of Lithuania, its most vulnerable southern part was incorporated into the Polish part of the Commonwealth.[13]

The acquisition of a large chunk of what is now Ukraine brought Poland directly onto the Wild Plain, the management of which now became the responsibility of the Polish government in Cracow (after 1596, Warsaw). But the Wild Plain was also, in an expression of the time, 'the trampled land'. Although both Poland and the Crimean khans were often at peace, having a mutual foe in Russia, there was a constant passage of Tatar freebooters and raiding parties across the

Wild Plain. Since the Ottomans had deprived the Crimean khans of their coastal cities, the khans increasingly relied on the trade in slaves for revenue and they did little to hinder Tatar war bands hunting for slaves. Most of the slaves were taken from Poland and Lithuania and from Russia, although the Tatars were busy, too, in the Caucasus, looking for Circassians and their fabled beauty. Their captives were then sold at the Crimean port of Kaffa—at any one time as many as thirty thousand slaves might be available for purchase in Kaffa's markets. Between 1500 and 1700, the Tatars captured and sold as slaves an estimated two million Poles, Lithuanians, and Russians.[14]

But the Wild Plain was not without a population of its own. In the fifteenth century, its peoples were mostly Tatar herders, but they were later supplemented by farmers coming from Poland and Lithuania, by merchants who wanted to avoid taxes, and by fishermen and drovers who doubled up as warriors and mercenaries. The people of the plain lived for the most part in fortified villages or in large camps called *Sichi*, but when safe to do so they travelled down the Dnieper River to hunt pine martens, net sturgeon, and gather honeycombs. Banditry was a lucrative sideline, and exposed merchant convoys yielded rich pickings. One visitor reported on the humble huts he found on the Wild Plain but noted that inside they were 'full of expensive silks, precious stones, sables and other furs, and spices'.[15]

From the late fifteenth century onwards, the armed bands operating on the Wild Plain were called Cossacks, after the Turkic *qazaq*, meaning 'freeman', but the term lacked precision, often being applied to anyone living on these open spaces of the steppe. During the sixteenth century, Cossack numbers were swollen by a new influx of peasants, who started farming otherwise empty and uncultivated land. According to one Lithuanian observer, they came 'in a great wave to the Dnieper and its tributaries; there are populous towns there and plenty of villages, where from childhood they swim, sail, fish, and hunt. Many of them are in flight from their parents, servitude and toil, or from punishment and iron shackles.'[16]

As this account suggests, one of the main reasons for peasants moving onto the Wild Plain was pressure from behind. On the territory of what had once been Lithuania but by the terms of the 1569 Union of Lublin was now part of Poland, avaricious magnates built huge agricultural estates worked by servile labour that exported grain along the Vistula, where it was bought up by Dutch merchants for onward shipment. Just one of these estates included in the 1590s no fewer than 1,300 villages, 100 towns, 40 castles, and 600 churches with a thousand priests. On their vast properties, Polish and Lithuanian magnates exercised an almost complete power, free of oversight or legal challenge. Accordingly, they frequently absorbed free peasant holdings into their domains, tying the occupants to the soil and making them perform onerous services. To avoid being made serfs, many peasants moved deeper onto the plain, adding to the flood of new migrants and to recruitment into Cossack war bands.[17]

The Cossacks were a problem for all their neighbours. Not only did they rob merchant convoys crossing the steppe land, but they also raided as far as Transylvania and Hungary. The Cossacks had their own fleet of *chaikas*, or 'seagulls', which attacked commercial shipping on the Black Sea and coastal ports, even reaching the suburbs of Istanbul. Historians often describe the *chaikas* as canoes, but they were in fact garishly painted, seafaring galleys, up to thirty metres long and armed with falconets or light cannon. But the Cossacks could be useful too. With a powerful infantry of musketeers and mobile wooden forts, they blocked the way to armies advancing on Poland and Lithuania from the south. On top of this, the Cossacks provided a reservoir of fighters whom Poland's kings might deploy across Central Europe and in their wars against Russia.[18]

At the heart of the recruitment of Cossacks was the so-called register—a list of Cossacks who served in the Polish army, although under their own commanders or hetmans. Entry onto the list entitled Cossacks to personal freedom, a wage, and exemption from taxes. In the steppe land, the first of these was of particular value, since Polish landowners often took over Cossack communities, converting them into villages of serfs. But to satisfy the magnates, the kings of Poland had to keep the register to just a few thousand Cossacks, since otherwise it would diminish the manpower on which the magnates' estates depended. So, most Cossacks were unregistered, even though they often fought as auxiliaries in the Polish armies.

Beyond this, free communities of Cossacks lived in the remoter parts of the Wild Plain, most notably the Zaporizhzhian Sich, which means 'the camp below the rapids', in this case of the Dnieper River. Although technically within the Kyiv province of Poland, the Zaporizhzhian Cossacks were a self-governing community or Cossack republic, with a population of about one hundred thousand persons who supported a military elite. Although authority nominally belonged to a Cossack council, the chief hetman held most power, but only for as long as he commanded the confidence of his warriors. Cossack government on the Lower Dnieper was, in one historian's words, 'dictatorship tempered by mob intervention'. The Zaporizhzhian Cossacks often joined in uprisings in Poland to extend the Cossack register.[19]

To begin with, the Cossacks were religiously diverse, but by the seventeenth century they had embraced a militant Orthodoxy. Their relations with the Polish kings were consequently ambiguous. On the one hand, they resented their Catholicism, but on the other, they wanted the freedoms and wages that came with the register and to expand the number of registered Cossacks. To force the hand of King Wladyslaw IV, the hetman of the Zaporizhzhian Cossacks Bohdan Khmelnytsky launched in 1648 a massive uprising which gathered support from Cossack communities across Ukraine. It swiftly degenerated into mayhem, in which Cossacks, aided by bands of peasants who resented the impositions put on them by their Polish landlords, indiscriminately murdered Jews, Catholic priests, and Polish noblemen.

Khmelnytsky aimed to establish a semi-independent hetmanate in eastern Ukraine and have the register swell to forty thousand Cossacks. But in 1651, the Polish king defeated his forces at Berestechko, in what was probably seventeenth-century Europe's largest land battle. Three years later, Khmelnytsky turned to Russia, putting the Cossacks at the tsar's disposal in return for Moscow paying for the upkeep of sixty thousand Cossacks belonging to the Zaporizhzhian Sich. From this point forward, the tsars treated Kyiv and the whole left bank of the Dnieper as belonging to them, after which they added to the title Tsar of All Russia the words 'and of Little Russia', this being their name for Ukraine. The 1667 Treaty of Andrusovo between Poland and Russia cemented Russian control of Kyiv and of a large chunk of eastern Ukraine.

The Zaporizhzhian Sich lay at the eastern end of the Ottoman frontier: a swathe of territory that wound almost two thousand kilometres from the Sea of Azov to Croatia and the Adriatic coast. It shared similar characteristics across its length, being the home of a militarized society of mostly irregular troops, who combined martial service with agriculture and a good deal of plundering. It was a place of religious fervour as well, where Croatian warriors consecrated their battle flags in churches and imagined themselves to be the heirs of the crusaders of the Middle Ages, and on the Hungarian frontier, where the drovers of the plain embraced a militant and apocalyptic Calvinism. The Cossacks' commitment to the Orthodox religion was equally uncompromising. In places, the gaps in authority and the absence of a strong parish organization allowed unusual varieties of belief to prosper. Besides Orthodoxy, the steppe land was also the home of Unitarians and Anabaptists (who believed in adult baptism), and even of Sabbatarians, who urged conversion to Judaism as the first step to embracing the true Christianity.[20]

Throughout its route, the frontier threw up heroes, too, who would be 'nationalized' over the succeeding centuries and made into Croatian, Hungarian, and Polish champions. But it was in Ukraine that the frontier would dig the most deeply into national culture through the poet, author, and artist Taras Shevchenko (1814–1861), who is feted today as Ukraine's greatest writer. Shevchenko's poem 'Haidamaky' ('Rovers', 1841) nostalgically reanimated a lost Cossack past, telling:

Of how they built the Sich,
Of how Cossacks on their longboats
Passed the Dnieper Rapids . . .
And how, having smoked their pipes
In Poland's blazing fires,
They came back home to banquet in Ukraine.

Shevchenko revels in the Cossacks' misdeeds—the consecration of knives as the preliminary to murder, feasting in blazing barns while smouldering corpses dangle from the rafters, the hammering of nails into skulls, and the casual killing of Jews, nobles, Poles, and Catholics. He has no time for Russians either, pejoratively describing them as *Moskvali*, or 'Muscovites', and as 'pot-bellied worthies', and he condemns Khmelnytsky for doing a deal with the tsar. For Shevchenko, Ukrainians should be brothers, united in the Orthodox faith but standing politically aloof from Moscow. More than any other writer, Shevchenko embedded the idea of the freebooting Cossack into Ukrainian national memory as both the symbol of a lost freedom and a metaphor for the precariousness of life on Central Europe's long frontier.[21]

CHAPTER 16

Toleration, the Magus, and the Alchemist as Emperor

M OST KINGDOMS IN EUROPE WERE DIVIDED BY RELIGION. There were two options available to rulers in confessionally divided countries. The first was to lay down what the correct faith was and crack down on those who believed differently; the second was toleration. The first of these came at tremendous cost, pushing the Low Countries and France into four decades of civil war and slaughter. The low point was reached in August 1572 when on the feast of St Bartholomew the French government launched an assault on the French Protestant leaders which rapidly became a general slaughter. Over several days, Catholic mobs murdered about three thousand Protestants in Paris and probably twice as many in the provinces. No stranger to violence, even Ivan the Terrible of Russia lamented the cruelty of the French ruler.[1]

One historian has recently observed that 'No sixteenth-century state willingly accepted or could easily imagine a peaceful co-existence of differing religious confessions.' Of course, much depends on what is meant by 'easily' or 'willingly'. Even so, the Central European experience was different to the West European. In large parts of the region, the second option of accommodation and compromise was experimented with in the sixteenth century. In some cases, it only came about because violence had failed, but in others it was embraced early on as a prudent and just solution to the problem of religious diversity.[2]

The 1555 Peace of Augsburg in the Holy Roman Empire had left it up to the ruler of the principality, duchy, or lordship to decide whether to adopt Lutheranism or Catholicism. Subjects were bound to follow, although they had the right to emigrate. The terms of the peace meant that most of the empire became Protestant, at least in name, since the only significant Catholic rulers left by this time were the rulers of Austria and Bavaria and the various bishops and abbots who had stuck with Rome. Even so, many of the subjects of Catholic rulers were Protestants and they often also controlled the diets. Although Calvinism was not recognized as a choice by the Peace of Augsburg, a few rulers switched to it from the 1560s onwards, most notably in the Rhine Palatinate and Kassel, while defiant Calvinist congregations also sprang up, mostly in the region of the Lower Rhine and Frisia.

In their territories, Protestant and Catholic rulers alike endeavoured to enforce religious conformity, publishing ordinances that told people what to believe and minutely regulated lives. But though rulers were generally tough when it came to gambling, swearing, idleness, and sexual misdemeanours, they held back from overvigorous enforcement of religious conformity, fearing resistance. On top of this, local communities of Catholics and Protestants often simply disregarded injunctions from above. They struck deals, sharing churches according to an agreed timetable and summoning the faithful with different peals of bells. Of course, there were disruptive episodes, when mobs interrupted services. But in much of the Holy Roman Empire, the violence was within Protestantism, with frequent confrontations between moderate Lutherans and more radical enthusiasts.

In large parts of Central Europe, both within and beyond the Holy Roman Empire, different religious communities peacefully coexisted. A German merchant visiting Vilnius in the 1580s observed:

In addition to the Lutherans, the city has all sorts of religions and sects, all of which have their churches and public observances, such as Catholics, Calvinists, Orthodox or Muscovites, Anabaptists, followers of Zwingli [a Swiss reformer], and Jews, who have their own synagogue and place of worship. Then there are also the heathens or Tatars, and all of the religions, congregations, and sects have freedom of conscience, in which no one is troubled.[3]

Bohemia and Moravia were similarly diverse. Besides Lutherans, Calvinists, and a scattering of Catholics, there were the many shades of belief into which Hussitism had dissolved—moderate Utraquists, whose rites were almost indistinguishable from Catholic practices; the Czech Brethren, who tried to re-create the utopian Christianity of the New Testament; and radical sects, who (depending upon the viewpoint of contemporaries) either practised an obsessive morality or gave themselves over to extremes of licentiousness. In 1548, King Ferdinand I expelled the Czech Brethren and sects from Bohemia, after which many went to neighbouring Moravia, where Ferdinand's edict did not apply. One Catholic observer later counted no fewer than twenty-five heretical sects in Moravia, including Demoniacs, who raved in divine ecstasy; Adamites, who taught that nakedness and promiscuity restored the innocence of the Garden of Eden; Manifestarians, who thought Christ and the devil to be physically present on earth, and so on.[4]

Accommodation was not just the way that local communities responded to religious diversity. Across Central Europe, rulers, diets, and city magistrates often mandated toleration. The earliest example is the Peace of Kutná Hora of 1485, in which the Bohemian diet gave religious freedom to Catholics and moderate Utraquists, although not to the Czech Brethren. With the advent of the Reformation, similar arrangements became more frequent. Perhaps the first of these was the Decision of Davos, allegedly from 1526 (the date is uncertain), which regulated religious affairs in a part of the Swiss Grisons. Clearly under some duress, the Catholic leaders of the Vier Dörfer commune agreed that 'everyone of either sex and whatever status is free to choose, embrace, and avow the Catholic or Protestant religion, as their conscience guides them.'[5]

The same principle was gradually extended to other parts of the Swiss Confederation. Most of the rural cantons remained Catholic, while the cities embraced Protestantism in the 1520s, usually under the influence of a persuasive local preacher—Ulrich Zwingli in Zurich, Joachim Vadian in St Gallen, and Johannes Oecolampadius in Basle, each of whom put his own theological stamp on Luther's teaching. Open conflict broke out between Protestant Zurich and the neighbouring Catholic canton of Schwyz in 1529 and 1531, but neither side was inclined to break the other—in any case, their troops preferred to fraternize rather than fight, famously sharing a meal of soup on what was supposed to be the battlefield.

The deal struck in 1531 to end the conflict anticipated the Peace of Augsburg of 1555 since it allowed the governments of the individual cantons to decide the religion. Disputes between and within cantons were hived off to special courts or 'parity commissions' which were made up of Catholics and Protestants in equal number. In cantons where there was a religious mix, a territorial division was allowed, so both Glarus and Appenzell cantons were eventually divided along confessional lines. Elsewhere, churches were shared, or (incredibly) the priest asked to hold two separate services so as to satisfy in turn Catholic and Protestant parishioners. Disputes were usually resolved amicably. Since the Swiss Confederation followed customary law rather than the black-and-white principles of Roman Law, there was more room for compromise and for arbitrated solutions.[6]

At the other end of Central Europe, in Transylvania, the complexity of religious beliefs also convinced the diet to allow toleration. 'For the sake of peace', the diet in 1564 recognized both Lutheranism and Calvinism as 'accepted religions', permitting followers to worship freely. Four years later, it extended toleration to Unitarians on the grounds that their ministers 'preached and pronounced the Gospel', and it mandated that 'nobody shall be troubled on account of his religion.' But Catholics were still harassed, with their churches periodically closed and clergy expelled. It was the same with Transylvania's Unitarians, whose leader (Ferenc Dávid) was jailed in 1572 for the invented crime of religious innovation. It was only in 1595 that Catholics, Unitarians, Lutherans, and Calvinists were formally recognized as equal in status and equally deserving of the right to worship freely. To their number, we should add the majority Orthodox population, whose rights were upheld in separate privileges.[7]

Even in the Catholic strongholds of Austria and Bavaria, toleration was the norm, if only because their rulers needed the consent of the mainly Protestant diets to gather taxes. Emperor Ferdinand I's son and successor, Maximilian II (ruled 1564–1576), obtained in 1568 a vote of 2.5 million ducats from the diets of Upper and Lower Austria in return for granting religious freedom to the provincial nobility. The extension of toleration to the so-called Inner Austrian duchies of Styria, Carinthia, and Carniola by Maximilian's brother, Archduke Charles, in 1578 yielded him 1.7 million ducats and the continuing financial commitment of their diets to buttress the Military Frontier. Meanwhile, Duke Albrecht V of Bavaria adopted, in his own words, a 'slippery and prevaricating' policy in religious affairs, meeting the demands of the Protestant leaders halfway in return for which the diet promised to repay his debts.[8]

In Bohemia, too, Emperor Maximilian II made concessions as a way of obtaining peace and subsidies from the diet. In 1575, he approved the joint statement of faith drawn up by Utraquists, Lutherans, and Czech Brethren, effectively guaranteeing religious freedom in Bohemia. The English adventurer Fynes Moryson, who journeyed through Bohemia in the 1590s, noted the 'great confusion of religions' across the kingdom: 'Yea, the same confusion was in all villages, and even in most of the private families, among those who lived at one table, and rested in one bed together.' It was the same in Poland, where by the 1560s about half the deputies to the Polish Sejm were Protestant. The French massacres of St Bartholomew's Day in 1572 prompted an urgent reappraisal in the Sejm, which affirmed in the following year the principle of comprehensive toleration—henceforth, religious differences were, in a contemporary description, to be fought 'with words rather than with the sword'.[9]

The resulting 1573 act of toleration was ill expressed. Its text left it uncertain whether toleration applied just to noblemen or to city folk and peasant tenants as well. But, despite its imperfections, it made Poland a magnet for missionary Czech Brethren from Bohemia, for Anabaptists on the run from oppression almost everywhere in Europe, and for their pacifist cousins called Mennonites, who moved after the 1530s from the Low Countries, eventually settling in large numbers in the Vistula delta. On top of these, there were the medley of sects that sprang from Unitarianism and from thinking too hard upon the mystery of the Trinity: Farnovians, who denied the Holy Spirit; Budneans, who refused to worship Christ; Sabellians, who thought of the Father, Son, and Holy Spirit as entirely separate entities, and so on. Loopholes in the act of toleration meant that Unitarians of all types continued to face intermittent, local persecution. Many found refuge in Ukraine, where religious control was weaker.

The toleration act explained its origins in 'the great dissidence in the affairs of the Christian religion in our country and to prevent any sedition for this reason among the people such as we clearly perceive in other realms'. Abroad, it was greeted as a masterstroke that had 'prevented civil war and preserved the kingdom in peace and quiet' and contrasted with the recent bloodshed in France and the Low Countries. For the imperial counsellor and general Lazarus von Schwendi (1522–1583), the Polish example showed that tolerance mandated from above was the 'only positive and possible way' of arranging religious affairs in divided communities.[10]

But compromise and toleration were not only a political choice. They were a philosophical one too, born of humanism and of the Renaissance interest in classical learning. Throughout Central Europe, humanists thronged the courts of rulers, educated the children of noblemen, served as librarians, diplomats, and churchmen, and maintained a busy correspondence. The most prolific writer of letters was surely Dantiscus (Jan Dantyszek, 1485–1548), the prince-bishop of Warmia in northeastern Poland. Almost seven thousand of his letters survive, sent to more than five hundred individuals, including popes, emperors, dukes, and city magistrates, in which he debated theological points, described haggling with Cornish sailors on a visit to England, and extolled the virtues of Gdańsk beer.

The classical texts that humanists read, edited, and discussed in their letters introduced ideas that were at odds with religious dogmatism.

For most classical writers, religion had consisted of walk-on gods who occasionally disrupted human lives by their meddling. In place of religious observance, they had emphasized civic virtues and an inclination to forbearance, courtesy, and moderation. Humanists picked up these ideas. They rejected what they called *alacritas* or 'hastiness' in judgement and urged instead openness in debate and a willingness to ponder alternatives in a considered and rational way. As the Dutch humanist Erasmus advised Luther, 'one gets further by courtesy and moderation than by clamour.'[11]

Humanists *thought* differently too. The late medieval logicians known as scholastics had seen everything in adversarial terms, as if the world should be understood in terms of propositions and counterpropositions that admitted no synthesis. Instead of the formulaic proofs of the logicians, humanists preferred the art of rhetoric and of persuasion—something their critics dismissed as 'chattiness'. They sought out a middle way between contending extremes and looked for the 'golden mean' that bridged rival beliefs, steering a way between (in one of the humanists' favourite texts) 'the deep sea and the dangerous coast'. This meant that they strove to reconcile and resolve differences and to look for what Catholics and Protestants had in common, not what divided them. As Lazarus von Schwendi wrote in the 1570s:

> God loves and blesses the one who follows moderate and conciliatory policies. But he will punish the one who in his own arrogance steps out of the middle way and conceives cruel and bloody schemes. . . . God will finally humble him and end his days in distress.[12]

But classical texts were not the only ones that scholars and humanists pillaged for meaning. There was at this time not much to distinguish the classical tradition from what we might call Occult learning. Indeed, Virgil's account in his *Eclogues* of the Sybil's prophecy of a new golden age showed that even the greatest of Latin poets had room for arcane knowledge. (It helped that the Sybil's prophecy might be read to foretell the birth of Christ.) Scholars seized upon ancient texts that combined Egyptian mythology, early Christian beliefs, and a debased form of Plato's philosophy. They believed them to originate from a certain Hermes Trismegistus (the Thrice-Powerful) who had lived at the time of Moses, but they were in fact products of the early first millennium, mostly originating in North Africa.

Alchemy brought together classical learning, the teachings of the mythical Hermes, and a developing interest in Jewish texts, especially the mystical Jewish Cabbala. Alchemy was not just about how to make gold but also touched upon astrology, angel summoning, and a personal voyage towards perfection. What made it so seductive was that its techniques were hidden in acrostics, number puzzles, secret alphabets, and obscure texts. Alchemy also had the appeal of a secret society. To fathom its concealed truths, the magus or adept had to go through stages of initiation, shedding his impurities in the same way that metal was refined in a furnace, until he became, in the words of one Polish alchemist, 'like Nature herself: true, plain, patient, constant etc, and that which is chief of all, religious and fearing God'. The idea survives in the word *laboratory*—a hybrid that brings together the Latin names for work and prayer (*labor, oratorium*).[13]

Implicit in alchemy and Occult knowledge was the unity of the cosmos. What played out in the heavens was replicated on earth so that macrocosm and microcosm worked in perfect harmony. Alexander the Great had, so it was believed, recovered the most important of Hermes' supposed texts, allegedly written on a slab of jade over Hermes' tomb. The inscription on the so-called Emerald Tablet rehearsed the principle of an undivided cosmos, starting as follows (in Sir Isaac Newton's translation):

> 'Tis true without lying, certain and most true.
> That which is below is like that which is above,
> And that which is above is like that which is below to do
>   the miracles of one only thing.

And as all things have been and arose from one by the
mediation of one:
So all things have their birth from this one thing by
adaptation.[14]

The meaning is thoroughly mysterious. Even so, the principle of 'as above, so below' is clear enough, sustaining the assumption of astrologers that the movement of the stars and constellations influenced human destinies. But if heaven and earth were truly one, as the Emerald Tablet averred, then it followed that invocations and manipulations of matter done on earth might alter the constitution of the heavens. If this could be achieved, then the earth itself must align with the changes to the cosmos, magnifying the magus's power. At the simplest level, the magus might capture an angel in a crystal ball and bid the spirit to do his work, and Abbot Trithemius of Sponheim explained around 1500 how to do this. But, of course, the magus might go much further. As the Emerald Tablet went on to promise: 'By this means you shall have the glory of the whole world and thereby all obscurity shall fly from you.'[15]

Alchemy was the pursuit of rulers across Central Europe, who built laboratories in their palaces, recruited magi to fill them, and collected arcane texts for their libraries. But the assumptions behind alchemy and the supposed unity of the cosmos inspired other activities. If the natural world consisted of microcosmic elements of the universe, then the study of plants and animals also gave a glimpse of the macrocosmic order—hence the interest of rulers in acquiring exotic plants and having their own menageries of leopards, ostriches, and even a dodo (as in the royal zoo in Prague). And if the material world was actually an expression of a universal principle, then by collecting unrelated objects and arranging them beside one another, the underlying unity of earthly things might be revealed. Out of this arose the passion for collecting that drove the construction of microcosms or 'theatres' of the world. Known as Wonder Chambers (*Wunderkammer*, Cabinets of Curiosities), they displayed alongside one another both the fabulous and the mundane—sea shells and narwhal tusks, medallions and lumps of classical statuary, and pinecones and pangolins.

The universe of the alchemists rested on a belief in the harmonious ordering of the cosmos and in the principles of unity and concordance, which drew apparent opposites into alignment. Its implications for religious belief were profound, for it suggested that the arguments of theologians were superficial and that they overlooked the larger, anterior truth which was common to all creeds. The alchemical tradition thus reinforced the humanist position that Christians should set aside their quarrels and search for a middle way of compromise and toleration. It was surely to this philosophical principle that Emperor Maximilian II subscribed. When challenged as to whether he was a Catholic or a Protestant, he answered simply that he was a Christian. For Maximilian, the differences between the two confessions mattered less than the essential truth embedded in the Christian message.

Maximilian II was a builder of zoos, gardens, and laboratories. The English magus John Dee rewarded the emperor's enthusiasm by dedicating to him his *Monas Hieroglyphica* (1564), which blended alchemy, astrology, and geometry to condense all knowledge in a single hieroglyph. In his court in Vienna, Maximilian also patronized the celebrated Milanese artist Giuseppe Arcimboldo (1527–1593). Arcimboldo's 'puzzle portraits' of heads painted as if they were composed of fruit, animals, branches, and leaves were once dismissed as a learned joke. Arcimboldo put Maximilian at the heart of his two portrait cycles, the *Four Seasons* and the *Four Elements*, with the emperor's head variously made up of garlands, tree stumps, a bonfire, bunches of grapes, and fishes and eels. But in so doing, the artist announced the emperor as master of the natural world, both presiding over and participating in its perpetual metamorphosis and transmutation. Just in case the message was missed, an accompanying three-hundred-line poem by Arcimboldo's collaborator, Giovanni Fauci, explained it.[16]

Maximilian's son and successor, Emperor Rudolf II (ruled 1576–1612), took everything a stage further. For long periods, he neglected the business of government, preferring instead the seclusion of Prague Castle. Rudolf presided over the Bohemian capital as an early modern Howard Hughes, often refusing to greet ambassadors and deputations of the diets, preferring instead the company of magi and artists, astrologers and alchemists. They filled his court, even setting up furnaces for their experiments in the castle gardens. Rudolf spent his time in conversation with them, as well as consorting with Jewish mystics and rabbis. As he confessed, their conversation often baffled him, for they were so deeply imbued with the mysteries of the cosmos as to be incomprehensible to the uninitiated.

Dwelling upon the profoundest mysteries of the universe and of human existence, Rudolf went into a deep depression. He feared for his life, constructing covered pathways in the castle grounds so that he might walk unobserved by any rooftop assassin. His laboratory experiments became more venturesome and dangerous, at one point singeing his beard, and he seems to have trespassed beyond the accepted conventions of Christian belief. Immediate members of his family had no doubt that Rudolf was involved in diabolic practices. His nephews wrote in 1606:

> His Majesty has now reached the stage of abandoning God entirely; he will neither hear nor speak of Him, nor suffer any sign of Him. Not only does he refuse to attend any sermon, public service, procession or the like, but he hates and curses all who participate in them. . . . His majesty is interested only in wizards, alchemists, Cabbalists and the like, sparing no expense to find all kinds of treasures, learn secrets, and use scandalous ways of harming his enemies. . . . He also has a whole library of magic books. He strives all the time to eliminate God completely so that he may in future serve a different master.

Three years later, a visiting Tuscan envoy partially confirmed their account. Noting that Rudolf had begun his reign well enough, he went on:

But Rudolf has ruined everything by taking up the study of art
and nature, with such increasing lack of moderation that he has
deserted the affairs of state for alchemists' laboratories, painters'
studios, and the workshops of clockmakers. . . . Disturbed in his
mind by some ailment of melancholy, he has begun to love soli-
tude and shut himself off in his palace as if behind the bars of a
prison.[17]

Rudolf's collection of treasures and secrets did not survive. Neglected by his successors, it fell victim to the Swedes, who plundered
Prague in 1648. A glimpse of its size is given in a list of objects the
Swedes stole from the castle: 470 paintings, 69 bronze figures, several
thousand coins and medals, 179 pieces of carved ivory, 50 objects of
amber and coral, 600 vessels of agate and crystal, 403 Indian curiosities,
185 items made of precious stone, uncut diamonds, and over 300 mechanical instruments. Other accounts put Rudolf's picture collection
alone at several thousand separate works.[18]

Rudolf's Correggios, Sprangers, Hieronymus Boschs, and Leon-
ardos may now all be dispersed or destroyed, and his alchemical pursuits dismissed as fantastical, but his legacy endures in astronomy.
Today, astronomy is highly mathematical with telescopes mounted on
satellites, while astrology is the stuff of cranks and fortune tellers. But
in the sixteenth and seventeenth centuries, there was no distinction
between the two. Copernicus in Poland did all the right calculations
to prove that the earth revolved around the sun, but he took his starting point from the alchemists, who posited that the perfection of the
sun made it impossible that it should revolve around the surly earth.
As Copernicus put it:

The Sun is rightly called the Lamp, the Mind, the Ruler of the Universe. Hermes Trismegistus names him the Visible God; Sophocles'
Electra calls him the All-seeing. So the Sun sits as upon a royal
throne ruling his children the planets, which circle round him.[19]

It was the same with the astronomers whom Rudolf recruited to his court. The Danish Tycho Brahe and the South German Johannes Kepler, whose observatories Rudolf funded, could not have been more different. Kepler came from a humble background and was hen-pecked at home, while Tycho Brahe's family owned a large chunk of Denmark. Besides his distinctive false nose (the result of a duelling accident), Tycho Brahe kept an elk in his lodgings as a drinking companion. But both were convinced that the movement of the stars influenced human affairs, and they both worked on horoscopes. Many hundreds of Kepler's projections survive, although it was one of Brahe's, foretelling Rudolf's murder by a monk, that left the emperor in despair.

Brahe and Kepler's collaboration in Prague only lasted a year, for Brahe died prematurely in 1601. But Brahe had by this time plotted the trajectories of more than a thousand stars. Kepler now converted Brahe's observations into ephemerides (predictions of planet and star positions), which he subsequently published in 1627 as *The Rudolphine Tables*. A work of incredible complexity, Kepler's tables demonstrated that celestial orbits were elliptical and proved the Copernican system that put the sun at the centre of the planets, which Tycho Brahe had doubted. It should be added that Brahe's observations were all by eye, since he had no telescope, and that Kepler worked without a calculating machine, even though the earliest of these was already in use. Kepler was instead the first to use logarithms as an aid to mathematics.[20]

Both Brahe and Kepler were Protestants, and they prospered in the tolerant environment of Rudolf's court. So did astronomical studies generally, even after Rudolf's death in 1612. Although the papal inquisition in Rome declared in 1616 that belief in the heliocentric system was heretical, after which the pope banned all books that explained it, heliocentrism continued to be fundamental to astronomy in Prague. The Jesuit university in Prague, the Clementinum, which Emperor Ferdinand I had founded in 1556 as a rival to the Hussite and Protestant university in the capital, continued to teach and investigate alternative cosmologies. Frescoes in the Clementinum's Old Mathematical Hall showed beside the conventional model of the heavens with the earth at its centre the different planetary systems of Copernicus and Brahe. Others depicted cherubs playing with telescopes, prisms, and globes.[21]

Rudolf's politics were wayward and erratic. Around 1600, he fell under the influence of a so-called Spanish faction at court, after which he sought to reimpose Catholicism in Hungary, even though he was already at war with the Turks. The policy backfired spectacularly when the Hungarian magnate Stephen Bocskai led a revolt against Rudolf with Ottoman backing—the sultan even sent Bocskai a crown, which the Hungarian prudently never wore. Outmanoeuvred and with his forces worsted on the battlefield, Rudolf abandoned his plans and, in 1606, conceded full religious toleration in Hungary.

Rudolf's mismanagement prompted in turn an attempt by his brother, Matthias, to replace him. To rally support, Matthias dished out charters of toleration to Upper and Lower Austria. Rudolf did the same in Bohemia, but it mattered not a jot, for Matthias convinced the Bohemian diet to depose Rudolf and elect him king instead. In the end, all that Rudolf was left with were the imperial crown and the grounds of Prague Castle, the gates of which were guarded on Matthias's orders by a band of trigger-happy musketeers. Rudolf's death in 1612 concluded a reign almost identical to Prospero's in Shakespeare's *The Tempest*, written just a year or two before:

> *The government I cast upon my brother*
> *And to my state grew stranger, being transported*
> *And rapt in secret studies.* (Act 1, Scene 2)[22]

Yet Rudolf's failure was not just personal. The humanist vision of a tolerant middle path was also giving way to solutions to religious difference that were predicated on coercion. Across Central Europe, a new generation of Catholic reformers were busy winning souls and, where persuasion failed, they were ready to use force. Starting in the 1560s, successive rulers of Bavaria and of the Inner Austrian duchies of

Styria, Carinthia, and Carniola closed Protestant churches, hounded preachers, and drove country folk into ponds for speedy baptism. Their preferred instruments were 'reform commissions': priests backed up by soldiers, who went from village to village to examine consciences, see that everybody knelt when the Angelus bell pealed, and give out certificates of conformity. In Central Europe, the Catholics were back, and their champions would lead it to civil war.

CHAPTER 17

Calendars, the Catholic Recovery, and Central Europe's Thirty Years' Civil War

B Y THE FIRST DECADE OF THE SEVENTEENTH CENTURY, PROTES-tantism looked triumphant in much of Central Europe. Where they were not already in control of the diets, Protestants had won rights of religious freedom. But Protestantism's gains were brittle. Resentment at its success intensified sectarian violence, with Catholic mobs disrupting services and attacking preachers. Protestants replied in kind, targeting objects of Catholic veneration. There was, it seems, a division of labour—Protestants mostly went for church property and furnishings, while Catholics homed in on worshippers. Throughout Central Europe, religious lines were hardening, and even places that had once been relatively peaceful, like Cracow and Vilnius, often descended into chaos. But what cemented rivalries in place was the calendar. As it turned out, when you worshipped proved more divisive than how you did.

In 1582, Pope Gregory XIII introduced the new 'Gregorian' calendar since the old Julian calendar, instituted by Julius Caesar in 46 BCE, had included too many leap years to be accurate. To make up for Caesar's original error, Gregory added ten days to the date. The adjustment made perfect astronomical sense. Poland embraced it at once, by royal decree, and most of the Habsburg lands in Central Europe followed. But in the Holy Roman Empire, the imperial diet rejected Rudolf II's bid to impose the new calendar and, by its own inaction, left the decision to individual cities and lords. Most Protestant areas stuck by the old calendar until the eighteenth century, even then adopting a variant of the Gregorian based upon Kepler's calculations. The Swedish calendar, followed along parts of Central Europe's Baltic shore, sought for a time to mix the Gregorian and Julian, so being at odds with everywhere else in Central Europe.[1]

For many, the change of calendar was confusing. As a group of Bavarian peasants complained, 'We have dues and rents to pay, but the fruit is not yet ripe. No shopkeeper or farmer knows when he should be in church. We go too late to market.' Other country folk pointed out that bears came out of their lairs on the old Candlemas Day (15 February) and not on the new, and that cattle stood in their stalls to salute Christ's birth only on the Christmas Eve of the Julian calendar. But because the pope had authorized the new calendar, many Protestants also suspected a trick or, at the very least, that the sale of printed concordances of dates was a crafty way of making money. In Hungary, popular resistance compelled the diet to impose in 1599 swingeing fines for nonobservance of the new calendar. Even so, throughout the seventeenth century many Protestants in both Hungary and Transylvania continued to use the old calendar in their private correspondence.[2]

Elsewhere, violence flared. It was most pronounced in mixed communities where Catholics following the Gregorian calendar had Protestant neighbours who kept to the Julian. With the introduction of the new calendar, the two religions celebrated Easter and Christmas on different days, which gave opportunities to disrupt processions and services and hurl accusations of blasphemy. Inspired by preachers who taught that the new calendar must necessarily hasten the Day of Judgement, Protestant gangs as far apart as Riga in Livonia and Augsburg in Bavaria ransacked Catholic churches on holy days in anticipation of the Apocalypse. Ten days later (eleven after 1700), their victims took their revenge. It was the same in parts of Poland and Lithuania where Orthodox believers kept to the old Julian calendar.

Switzerland split down the middle. Catholic cantons and cities embraced the Gregorian calendar, while their Protestant counterparts stuck by the Julian. Where cantons were mixed, the diet of the confederation took the easy course of leaving it to local communities to

decide. Over time, most fell behind the Gregorian, although a few
having adopted it moved back to the old since they were, as they explained, 'uncomfortable' with the new style. The remote Alpine valley
of Avers in the Grisons stuck by the Julian until 1812, and to this day
some villages in Appenzell celebrate two New Year's Days, with much
bell ringing and yodelling on each. But Appenzell is a charming exception. Everywhere else in Central Europe, a line had been drawn.
Whereas in the past, it had been possible to straddle religious divisions,
now a stand had to be taken. The middle course foundered on dates.[3]

The new calendar was part of a larger movement of reform within
the Catholic Church, known as the Counter-Reformation. Prompted
by the advance of Protestantism, popes and churchmen instituted a
thorough programme of change and renewal in the Catholic Church.
The Church Council that met at Trento between 1545 and 1563
pinned down the doctrines of Catholic belief, reaffirming traditional
elements while also making worship more participatory and instruc-
tional. Catholic churches now began to introduce elevated pulpits for
preaching and pews so that congregations might listen more com-
fortably. By order of the council, church interiors were brightened up
with opulent ceilings and gilt stuccowork. The council also promoted
communal acts of worship, like singing hymns in the local language.
Many of the new Catholic hymnbooks that circulated in Central Europe borrowed from refrains sung in the countryside and some even
included popular Protestant verses.[4]

New religious orders conveyed the messages of reformed Catholicism. The teaching and missionary order known as the Jesuits (or Society of Jesus) founded schools and universities, sustained beleaguered
congregations in areas of Turkish and Tatar occupation, and reached
out to Jews, Muslims, and even Gypsies. As confessors and educators,
they captured noblemen's souls, while their reputation for bibulous
hospitality did not make them unwelcome as neighbours. Bishops,
too, struggled over decades to improve the morals and learning of the
clergy, to found seminaries for the education of priests, to print in-
structional literature for congregations, and to inaugurate new local

saints and pilgrimage trails as a focus for popular devotion. In Poland, bishops, Jesuits, and preaching orders of friars, like the Capuchins, made significant gains. Although royal edicts published against heresy in the 1630s banned the construction of new Protestant churches and forced Unitarians to move eastwards, conversion to Catholicism was generally achieved peacefully. In the words of one Polish historian, unlike the kingdoms of Western Europe, Poland was 'a state without stakes'.[5]

By the close of the sixteenth century, Catholicism had a confidence and solidity that contrasted with the intemperate scrapping and bickering between the fissiparous branches of Protestantism. But Catholicism's most extraordinary gain, among the Orthodox communities in Poland and Lithuania, was also its most unexpected. Yielding a prospective windfall of as many as three or four million souls, it was very roughly the equivalent of the Catholic Church's entire haul in the New World. But whereas the Catholic Church had implanted itself in the Americas on the back of conquest and colonization, its new advance in Central Europe was obtained by negotiation and agreement. This, though, proved its weakness since, as it turned out, there were many among Rome's recent recruits who had no wish to be part of its flock.

The combined kingdom of Poland and duchy of Lithuania had a substantial Orthodox population, living very roughly where modern-day Ukraine and Belarus are today. By the 1580s, the Orthodox bishops there were seriously worried. Muscovite Russia pretended to leadership of the Orthodox world and its tsars aimed to bring the Orthodox congregations of Poland and Lithuania beneath the sway of their newly established patriarch in Moscow. Protestant missionaries, including Unitarians, were also founding churches in otherwise solidly Orthodox places. The Orthodox clergy were altogether incapable of rising to the challenge. Too many were ill-educated, and most were under the thumb of local landowners who dissuaded them from reforming religious practices.

In 1596, a group of Orthodox bishops did a deal with Rome. The union of Churches sealed at a church synod in Brest was based on an

offer that the popes had already made, albeit in vain, to the Greek and
Coptic churches in Constantinople and Ethiopia. In return for keeping
their liturgy and calendar, and the right of parish priests to marry, Orthodox bishops in Poland and Lithuania now recognized the authority
of the pope and accepted most Catholic doctrines, forming a separate
Union or Uniate Church (or Greek Catholic Church) in communion
with Rome. The bishops who accepted the union were given equal
status to Catholic bishops, which entitled them to a seat in the upper
house of the Sejm. But it was not the case that the Uniate bishops sold
out to the Catholics in return for privileges. As the bishops saw it, the
only way to save Orthodoxy was to infuse it with the spirituality and
superior organization of Counter-Reformation Catholicism.[6]

But the Uniate bishops failed to convince all Orthodox believers,
for whom the deal with Rome smacked of heresy. Even before the act
of union was sealed, staunchly Orthodox abbots and churchmen began excommunicating pro-union clergy for misbelief. The Orthodox
confraternities, or brotherhoods of laymen, which did most of the hard
work of funding churches, almshouses, choirs, and schools, also came
out against the union, as did almost all the provincial Orthodox nobles
in modern-day Ukraine. Although King Sigismund III of Poland and
Lithuania (ruled 1587–1632) tried to assuage Orthodox sensibilities,
relations between the Orthodox and Uniate communities were embittered by polemical denunciations, leading to riots and even the murder
of opponents.

But it was the Cossacks of what is now southern Ukraine who were
the most violent in their rejection of the Uniate Church. Even before
the union had been sealed, Cossack bands were raiding the property
of its known supporters. By the beginning of the seventeenth century,
Cossacks were guarding Orthodox churches and providing armed es-
corts for their clergy. Their commitment to the pure Orthodox religion
was unwavering. As one of their spokesmen put it at an Orthodox
Church synod meeting in 1628, the Cossacks had paid with their lives
for the Orthodox faith, and 'we are also prepared to secure it with our
blood or with the blood of those who would show disrespect for it or

betray it.' Two years later, what is now southeastern Ukraine dissolved
into a condition of rolling civil war, with rival bands looting churches
of both faiths.[7]

Where opposition was more muted, in what is now Belarus and
the western half of Ukraine, the Uniate Church made strong inroads.
Gradually, Uniate church interiors began to look more Catholic, often
dispensing with an iconostasis screen, so leaving the altar visible to the
congregation. Confession boxes (a recent Catholic innovation) and organs also began to appear, while in their outward appearance churches
increasingly copied the architectural styles of the Italian Baroque. Although services continued to be conducted in the Old Slavonic liturgy,
Latin became the language of Uniate scholarship and learning, especially in newly founded seminaries where the Uniate clergy were drilled
according to a largely Jesuit curriculum. There were overlaps, especially
in seventeenth-century Kyiv, where a new generation of educated Orthodox clergy seem to have only read Latin texts, including Protestant
works. But, with this exception, what is now Ukraine split culturally
in two. One part looked westwards to Rome and Latin Christianity,
while the other increasingly sought its inspiration from the Orthodox
Church of Moscow and Russia.[8]

The Uniate solution would be repeated among Ukrainian Orthodox congregations in Hungary in 1646 and among Romanian Orthodox believers in Transylvania in 1698, netting further souls for the
Catholic Church. But the Catholic recovery in Central Europe was not
just a matter of internal church politics. Powerful men were also lining
up in support of the Catholic faith and putting aside their policies of
compromise and delay. The dukes of Bavaria were among the first. In
the late 1550s, the young Duke Albrecht V of Bavaria affirmed that it
was his sovereign right to maintain his subjects 'in the true Catholic
faith, and Christian discipline and conduct'. Having stuffed his government with Catholic loyalists, he cracked down on negligent priests,
but his interest soon spread to the irritating statelet of Ortenburg. An
independent enclave of just a few square kilometres set on the edge
of Bavaria, Ortenburg's Lutheran count encouraged Protestants from

outside the principality to attend worship in his churches. In 1563, Albrecht V sent in his troops.[9]

The action was plainly illegal, and Albrecht was soon obliged to withdraw, but not before his men had raided the count's magnificent new Renaissance palace and seized his correspondence. This revealed that the count had been, if not quite conspiring with prominent Protestant noblemen in Bavaria against Albrecht, at least joining with them in disparaging the duke as a 'Pharaoh' and him and his Catholic ministers as 'heretics', 'buffoons', 'bloodsuckers', and 'bats flitting in the dusk'. Albrecht hauled the lot of them to court for treason. Although he eventually dropped the charges, it was enough to break resistance to his policies. As for the Bavarian diet, where Protestant noblemen held the purse strings, Albrecht simply postponed its sessions, rolling over taxes from one year to the next.[10]

Bavarian Wittelsbachs and Austrian Habsburgs were old rivals. But in the interests of a common front against Protestantism, Albrecht built bridges with his two Habsburg neighbours, the archdukes Ferdinand of the Tyrol and Charles of Styria, who were the brothers of Emperor Maximilian II (and so the uncles of Emperor Rudolf II). Already wed to a Habsburg princess, Albrecht promoted the policy whereby each generation of the two dynasties intermarried. Together with Archduke Ferdinand, Albrecht also built up a network of allies in the southwest of the Holy Roman Empire. The League of Landsberg was ostensibly aimed at keeping the peace, but Albrecht used it instead to hem in Protestant Württemberg and support the hard-pressed bishops of Franconia. By the 1570s, Albrecht was even planning to draw the Low Countries, now under Spanish military occupation, into the league, but this was too much for most of its members and the alliance broke up.[11]

Even so, the rapprochement between Habsburgs and Wittelsbachs was politically decisive, for it created a solid body of support for the Catholic Church that reached from Croatia to the border with Switzerland. It turned out to be biologically important too, for the marriage in 1570 of Duke Charles of Styria to Albrecht's daughter, Maria Anna of Bavaria, would produce the greatest Catholic champion of the seventeenth century and the man who would bring Protestantism in Central Europe to its knees—Charles and Maria Anna's son, Archduke Ferdinand of Styria or, as he would become, Emperor Ferdinand II (ruled 1619–1637).

Ferdinand of Styria was a product of the Counter-Reformation and of Catholicism's recovery in Central Europe. Schooled by Jesuits, he was uncompromising in his dedication to the Catholic faith, declaring that he would prefer 'to lose land and people rather than bring harm to religion'. But he also brought an ideological barrage of rights with him—the right of rulers to determine the religion of subjects, as granted by the 1555 Peace of Augsburg, and the right of monarchs to do as they wished according to the Roman Law principle that 'what pleases the prince has the force of the law'. Ferdinand was not only a Catholic ruler; he was in his own mind a complete sovereign as well, with a power that was unconstrained by the law. But he was a Habsburg too, convinced that it was his family's mission to spread the Catholic faith on a worldwide stage. As his Jesuit confessor explained, Ferdinand was foretold not only to rule Austria and Central Europe but also the whole globe, and to be advanced by the prayers of the faithful to heavenly glory. Ferdinand was dangerous.[12]

His mother had advised the young Ferdinand always 'to show his teeth', and he did not hold back. On coming of age in 1596, following the death of his father, Ferdinand let it be thought that he had agreed to maintain religious freedom in the Inner Austrian duchies of Styria, Carinthia, and Carniola. But although the festivities at his inauguration were lavish, with the deputies tucking down afterwards to a seventeen-course feast, Ferdinand's promises as duke were evasive. No sooner had the provincial diets voted him taxes than Ferdinand set his troops on Protestant preachers and congregations. When challenged, he appealed to Roman Law and to the ruler's right to legislate 'of his own volition' (*ex proprio motu*).[13]

Emperor Matthias, who had succeeded his brother Rudolf as emperor in 1612, was lukewarm in his commitment to Catholicism but steadfast in his promotion of the Habsburgs as rulers. Neither he nor his older brother Rudolf II had sons. Ferdinand of Styria was Matthias's closest relative, and Matthias did all he could to make him his successor. The noblemen attending the Bohemian and Hungarian diets knew Ferdinand's reputation, but Matthias cajoled and convinced them to back Ferdinand, often in private one-to-one conversations. When Ferdinand put in writing that he would uphold the principle of toleration, the two diets proclaimed him in 1617–1618 as king of Bohemia and Hungary, respectively, even though the ailing Matthias was still alive. As it turned out, in his future dealings with the Hungarians, Ferdinand would stick by his commitment, even though it offended his conscience and authority. Quite possibly, he might have kept his promise to the Bohemians too had not events worked out differently.[14]

Rudolf's grant of toleration in Bohemia, which Ferdinand had sworn to uphold, was ambiguous in its provisions. A dispute over the ownership of churches built on royal land rapidly escalated into violence. The leaders of the Bohemian Protestants suspected that the regency council in Prague, appointed to oversee the transition from Matthias to Ferdinand, was plotting to overturn the religious settlement. A heated meeting in Prague Castle famously led to two of the regents (along with a secretary) being hurled out of a high window. They survived their defenestration since they landed not on an asphalt carpark, as the space is today, but instead on soft ground, although Catholic commentators were swift to suggest the intervention of angels.

The coup launched by the Protestant leaders in Prague was supported by only a minority of Bohemian noblemen, but these now dizzily declared Ferdinand's previous election void. In Ferdinand's place, they elected a political madman as king, Frederick of the Palatinate, whose wizards and Calvinist clergy had convinced him that he was destined to fulfil a divine purpose, hitherto hidden in alchemical mysteries. Although Ferdinand succeeded as emperor by vote of the electors on Matthias's death in 1619, his position looked hopeless. The Moravian, Hungarian, and Transylvanian diets threw in their lot with the Bohemian rebels, while Upper and Lower Austria went into revolt. In a coordinated action, leaders of the Lower Austrian nobility joined with a Bohemian army to menace Vienna. Only the chance arrival of loyal troops saved the new emperor, for otherwise Ferdinand had no forces in the city except for the small garrison and a band of students, mustered under the dubious command of their professors.

But Ferdinand had several aces up his sleeve. His brother-in-law Maximilian of Bavaria was even more committed to the Catholic cause than he was, having signed in his own blood a personal vow of dedication to the Virgin. Ferdinand's fellow Habsburg and brother-in-law Philip III of Spain could also be counted on. With a largely Bavarian and Spanish army, Ferdinand invaded Bohemia in 1620, smashing Frederick of the Palatinate's forces outside Prague in a battle that lasted just two hours. In panic, Frederick fled Prague Castle, leaving behind a half-eaten meal and his entire correspondence. His letters were subsequently published at Maximilian of Bavaria's instruction, but edited to cast Frederick in the worst possible light—as one of a band of 'shameful, ungodly people who for long strove for the crown and to destroy the House of Austria and seize Catholic churches'.

Bohemia was now crushed. Forty-eight ringleaders of the rebellion were condemned to death, although one was dramatically reprieved on the scaffold. The 'theatre of blood', which took place in June 1622 on Prague's Old Town Square, was accompanied by a band of drummers whose task it was to drown out the final speeches of the victims. In Bohemia and Moravia, a far-reaching programme of reconversion was put in train. Rebels were fined or had their lands confiscated. On top of this, all who refused to become Catholics were forced into exile, again with loss of land, prompting the flight of about 150,000 persons. A new generation of Habsburg loyalists was installed in their place. The university, formerly a hotbed of religious radicalism, was put under Jesuit supervision.

In justifying his actions, Ferdinand turned once more to Roman Law, his reliance upon which is nowhere more clearly demonstrated than in the Renewed Constitution (*Vernewerte Landesordnung*) that he gave Bohemia in 1627. Despite its name, this amounted to the comprehensive reordering of the public law in the kingdom and the destruction of its historic institutions. The crown was now to be hereditary rather than elected, the role of the diets confined to approving the ruler's instructions, especially in regard to taxation, and the new constitution itself made subject to alteration by the monarch 'of his own volition'.[15]

In explaining the grounds on which he overturned Bohemia's historic constitution, Ferdinand made the presumption that all authority rested with him. The nobility and the diet did not possess rights of their own, except those that had been ceded to them by the monarch. This was pure Roman Law, for otherwise the traditional or customary law presupposed that ruler and diet had equal, autonomous, and separately generated rights. Since the Bohemians had risen against him, Ferdinand went on to explain, he was entitled to revoke the privileges that he and his predecessors had given them, for they had forfeited any right to enjoy them. Henceforth, Ferdinand reserved to himself and his heirs 'the power to enact laws and decrees, and everything devolving from the legislative power [*ius legis ferendae*—another Romanism] which belongs to Us, as the King, alone'.

But, of course, not all Bohemians were rebels, which led to Ferdinand's second Roman Law solution. The revolt, he explained, had taken place 'in a collective manner' (*in forma universitatis*), and so each was bound by the group decision. Consequently, all might be punished irrespective of their personal guilt, and most duly were. Although the contention that Bohemia now entered upon three centuries of 'Darkness' is the overstated claim of Czech nationalist historians, the historic kingdom effectively became a mere annex of the Austrian lands. In token of its subjection, even the Bohemian chancellery, which undertook much of the routine work of government there, was in 1624 moved from Prague to Vienna.

The war in Bohemia was the opening phase in a series of contests that are known collectively as the 'Thirty Years' War' (1618–1648). Each phase bore within it the seeds of future conflict, to such an extent that contemporaries considered the fighting to be a single period of warfare. The Thirty Years' War drew in most of Europe's principal powers—Spain and Portugal, the Netherlands, Sweden, France, and

THE HOLY ROMAN EMPIRE IN 1648

Boundary of the Holy
Roman Empire 1648

North Sea

Baltic Sea

Swedish
Pomerania

Mecklenburg

Prussia

Lüneberg
(Hanover)

Brandenburg

Berlin

POLAND

NETHERLANDS

Saxony

Hesse-
Kassel

Gotha

Dresden

Spanish
Netherlands

Saxe-Gotha

Silesia

Spanish
Netherlands

Prague

Bohemia

Moravia

Württemberg

Bavaria

HUNGARY

Lake
Constance

Vienna

FRANCE

Salzburg

Austria

SWITZERLAND

Tyrol

Styria

Savoy

Carinthia

Milan

VENICE

Carniola

Piedmont

OTTOMAN

TURKS

Adriatic
Sea

Tuscany

Papal
States

Mediterranean
Sea

Kingdom
of Two
Sicilies

0   150 mi

0   150 km

much of the Holy Roman Empire. For some, the motivation was religious, for others purely defensive, and for a few opportunistic. Beside the main theatre of conflict in the Holy Roman Empire were parallel contests—in the Low Countries and Catalonia, in Hungary and Transylvania, in Brazil and West Africa, and even as far off as Taiwan. The Thirty Years' War also spilled over into the Baltic, leading in the 1620s and 1630s to a triangular contest for regional hegemony that drew in Sweden, Poland, and Russia. This was a Central European civil war that became continental and even global. It was a harbinger of other, more modern conflicts, which started in Central Europe and had consequences for the whole world.

The first decade went well for Ferdinand. Frederick of the Palatinate's Protestant supporters were routed, and Ferdinand threw back a Danish invasion and overran Lutheran Mecklenburg. Confident in his victory, Ferdinand now repeated what he had done in Inner Austria and Bohemia, linking the principles of Roman Law to his assertion of Catholic religious supremacy. Claiming a double prerogative as both lawgiver and supreme judge, Ferdinand revisited the Peace of Augsburg of 1555, demanding that all ecclesiastical properties occupied by Protestants over the previous decades be returned to the Catholic Church.[16]

The Edict of Restitution of 1629 threatened to ruin many Protestant rulers in the empire who over the preceding decades had seized no fewer than two archbishoprics, thirteen bishoprics, and some five hundred monasteries and convents. Unsurprisingly, it released a new round of warfare, with the Lutheran king of Sweden intervening from the north to support the beleaguered Protestant cause. It was now that the war took on the character of comprehensive slaughter with, in one historian's powerful description, armies of mercenaries operating as if 'zombie-like murder collectives', robbing churches of their silver plate, torching homes, and torturing villagers into revealing their hidden wealth before hanging them anyway. On top of casual slaughter came dislocation, famine, and the plague. One Swabian shoemaker's diary recorded his frequent flights to the safety of Protestant Ulm. On one such occasion, in 1634, he noted:

There is distress and misery, starvation and death. There we lay on top of each other in great wretchedness. Then price increases and hunger broke in on us, after these the evil disease, pestilence. Many hundreds of people died during this year.[17]

In just a few months, the shoemaker lost his son, as well as three of his sisters and a brother. At the same time, a mercenary captain fighting on the emperor's side was close by in Bavaria. He left his own record:

> We stayed here eight days and plundered Landshut. As booty, I took a pretty girl and clothes worth twelve talers, and some linen . . . and back to Heidelberg, where we took the city again and besieged the castle for fourteen days, intending to blow it up. When everything was ready, with twenty-four tons of powder under the castle, an enemy army arrived, thirty-thousand strong . . . my son went off with a fine cow and sold it for eleven talers.

Altogether, in more than two decades of campaigning, the captain travelled over twenty-four thousand kilometres, from the Baltic to the Adriatic, wherever the money was best.[18]

Facing the prospect of a Protestant victory, Ferdinand backed down. In the Peace of Prague of 1635, Ferdinand made peace with the German Protestant leaders, effectively withdrawing the Edict of Restitution and surrendering Upper and Lower Lusatia (parts of Bohemia) to Saxony. In alliance with the Swedes, French forces now took the lead in maintaining the fight against Ferdinand, who increasingly depended on his cousins in Spain for troops and for cash to buy mercenaries. The war accordingly lost most of its religious character, becoming instead a political contest between France and the Habsburgs. The last year of the war saw a Swedish army occupy and loot Prague Castle—the site of the defenestration that had begun the conflict three decades earlier.

The Thirty Years' War claimed the lives of as many as seven million people in Central Europe. Most were civilians who fell victim to casual slaughter, famine, and disease or were killed by poison gas (made of henbane) and by dysentery from water that had been deliberately fouled. The Peace of Westphalia, which ended the conflict in 1648, was mostly concerned with nuts and bolts—where borders should be changed, whose rights to territory affirmed, and that the dukes of Bavaria should be allowed to keep the title of elector, originally conveyed upon them by a grateful Ferdinand II in 1623. It affirmed that the territorial rulers of the Holy Roman Empire might choose their own religion and admitted Calvinism as one option, but it allowed their subjects the right to practise their own beliefs too (within certain limits) and forbade conversion by force. In the future, disputes over church property and the extent of freedom of conscience would be for the courts to decide.

By the time the peace treaty was made, Ferdinand II had been succeeded by his son, Ferdinand III (ruled 1637–1657). In the discussions leading up to the peace treaty, Ferdinand III won an important religious exemption for the Habsburg lands, which meant that he was not obliged to permit freedom of worship in his territories. No sooner was the treaty agreed than Ferdinand sent in priests and friars, supported by military detachments, to root out what remained of Protestantism in Upper and Lower Austria. In just one small part of Lower Austria (the Manhartsberg, above Krems), a team headed by one of Ferdinand's counsellors recorded twenty-three thousand converts, whose names he entered into a register dedicated to Ferdinand III, 'the conqueror of heresy'. Where it survived, Protestant worship in Austria went underground—sometimes literally into cellars, but more often into the forests or the corners of fields. Recollection of persecution is etched on the Austrian landscape in names like 'Church in the Wood', 'Chapel Meadow', and 'Preaching Stone' (Waldkirche, Tempelwiese, Predigerstein).[19]

Silesia, a part of the Bohemian crownlands, had a separate status as a result of treaties of toleration that Ferdinand II had made over the course of the war with the elector of Saxony. But Ferdinand III ignored these, declaring: 'Religious life in Silesia has nothing to do with agreements, but rests entirely on the grace of the emperor and king.' Since Ferdinand III's grace did not extend to permitting Protestant worship, he began the reconversion of Silesia. Troops took over 650 Protestant church buildings, requisitioning them for Catholic use, and on Ferdinand's instruction 500 clergy were exiled. Only three churches were allowed to Silesia's Protestants, and Ferdinand laid down that they should be built of wood, without steeples. Taking him at his word, Protestants duly built the three largest timber-framed churches in all Europe, two of which are still standing.[20]

With the imposition of the Counter-Reformation in Silesia, a broad swathe of Central Europe was now made Catholic. The line of division split the region diagonally, with a northern and westerly part that stuck by Protestantism and a larger southern and easterly one that was now either Catholic or Uniate. For the Catholic Church, it was an extraordinary recovery that built on military victory, the tenacity of its champions, and their unscrupulous use of Roman Law and raw power to force through their will. Whereas at the start of the seventeenth century, Protestantism looked like it was on the brink of victory in Central Europe, fifty years later it was in retreat.

But the territorial rulers of the Holy Roman Empire were winners too. At Westphalia, they had acted and been respected as independent sovereigns, signing the agreement to end hostilities as if complete monarchs. True, the Holy Roman Empire endured, with an emperor and a central court for adjudicating disputes. But it was a shadow of what it had been under Charles V, when the emperor's command had carried across half of Europe. Ferdinand II had sought to renew the fusion of dynasty, Catholicism, and empire, building if not a worldwide empire then one that commanded all Central Europe. The Peace of Westphalia signalled the end of an ambition that had sustained the Habsburgs for almost two centuries. More and more, the Habsburg rulers would look to their own dominions, building up their own power in the Austrian and Bohemian lands and in Hungary, leaving the Holy Roman Empire rudderless.

CHAPTER 18

The Condition of the Countryside: Peasants, Gypsies, Jews, and Others

T HE FURTHER EAST FROM THE RHINE, THE GREATER WERE THE loads on the peasantry. This cannot be an exact statement, but it is a convenient one. In the more western parts of Central Europe, in the Rhineland, Franconia, Bavaria, and Swabia, and in the Austrian lands, there was a generally free peasantry. Some peasants were obliged to provide labour in lieu of rent for their lords, but these were regulated by custom, written down in *Weistümer*, and formally recalled at annual meetings. Closer to the Rhine, most peasants paid their dues in cash to absentee lords who had little interest in cultivating their own farmland. Although peasants complained about the chickens and eggs that they had to convey to their masters on feast days, seeing them as tokens of subjection, they were in most respects freemen.

Further east, lords were more directly involved in agriculture, maintaining large farms of their own and selling off their grain surpluses as cash crops on both domestic and international markets. This had not always been the case, since in the Middle Ages Central Europe's principal exports had been cattle and metal ores. But an upswing in cereal prices across sixteenth-century Europe made the commercial exploitation of Central Europe's grain attractive. Landowners east of the River Elbe were better placed to take advantage of the new market since peasant communities there had fewer written rights than their counterparts on the other side of the river. Their landlords accordingly found it easier to convert their cash rents into services and so deploy peasants as labour on their farms. On the open plains of what is now Poland and Ukraine, there was plenty of good farmland on which to grow grain.

Without *Weistümer* itemizing their obligations, peasants were generally powerless in litigation since under the influence of Roman Law most courts demanded written proof of exemptions and rights. The Roman Law worked in landlords' favour too. In courtroom disputes, when neither lords nor peasants could prove their case in writing, judges generally presumed in favour of the lord, invoking either his absolute ownership of things (*dominium*: another Romanism) or even the Roman law of slavery. Courts and landlords thus cooperated to convert peasants into serfs, bound to stay in the village in which they had been born and to perform increasingly onerous services. Since the landowning nobility usually controlled the local diets, peasant obligations were frequently written into law too, including prohibitions on their movement off the lord's land.[1]

A fault line cut through Central Europe dividing along the course of the Elbe River what German historians call landlordism (*Grundherrschaft*) in the west and serfdom (*Gutswirtschaft*, literally 'manorial economy', where the peasants laboured in their lords' fields) in the east. From 1500 onwards, peasant tenants in the eastern half of Central Europe had increasingly to help on the manor farms of their lords by ploughing, manuring, harvesting, threshing, and hauling to market, often for several days of the week. In Poland and Hungary, even landless cottagers had to work for the lord. The lords' farms were frequently big, too, swallowing up as much as a third or even a half of all arable land in parts of Poland, Pomerania, and Mecklenburg and in the duchies of Schleswig and Holstein.[2]

There was never any great consistency. East of the Elbe, peasants and lords often switched from labour services to rents and back again, depending upon where the economic advantage lay at the time. Proximity to roads and rivers was important too. For lords, there was no point coercing peasants to work in their fields if the fruits of their labour could not be transported for sale—far better to have rents paid in cash. Where labour was short, lords faced an unenviable choice. They could either demand more from the workforce, which might then abscond, or try to attract new settlers by offering greatly reduced rents and freedom from onerous services.

But serfdom was not all bad. Lords who aimed to make a profit from agriculture, rather than just collect rents as absentees, were more likely to invest in dams and irrigation and to pioneer innovations on the land, from new crop rotations to seed drills. In Holstein, lords frequently switched from cereal production to cattle herding, transforming their farms into highly efficient exporters of dairy products, with economic benefits that flowed downwards to the workforce. Elsewhere, lords encouraged peasants to amalgamate their strips into single plots and intensify production so that peasants, too, became exporters of grain. Peasant serfs in the north of the Holy Roman Empire, in Brandenburg and along parts of the Baltic coast, were generally better off than peasant freemen in Swabia.[3]

Landownership was complex everywhere. The assumption was that the fields belonged to the lords, which was why the peasants owed rent for cultivating them. But the common land beyond the village boundary belonged to no one. Peasants might graze cattle and flocks upon it, and use the acorn forests for their pigs, but not convert it to ploughland since that implied possession. Hillsides suitable for viticulture did not usually belong to the lord but to the community, which managed the vineyard terraces collectively, usually through special vintners' associations. Peasants might cultivate for their own profit the strips and fields which they held of the lord, but if they wanted more land of their own, then they were expected to rent it from other tenants or clear scrubland. Since there were seldom land registers, the extent of the scrub and the parts of it that had been brought into cultivation were frequently unclear.

Litigation between lords and their peasant tenants over rents, services, and boundaries was continuous throughout Central Europe. The first step for aggrieved communities or individuals was to petition the lord through the village court. Thereafter, the petition wound its way through the manor court to the county or district court, and in some cases into the royal or ducal administration. The legal process was slow and judicial outcomes uncertain, so when faced with a suit launched by their tenants, most lords sought to bargain. Stubborn landowners might at the very least expect anxious journeys down lonely country lanes, but in most of Central Europe relations between lords and peasants were marked by compromise rather than confrontation. Only occasionally did violence flare into open rebellions—in 1514 in Hungary, in 1525 in the southwest of the Holy Roman Empire, and in 1573 in Croatia. All were brutally suppressed. In their wake came ordinances and laws that confirmed the existing legal order, usually to the disadvantage of the peasantry.

The condition of the peasantry varied not only from west to east but also from place to place, even down to the individual village. Some peasants had substantial plots, of as many as a hundred hectares (250 acres), and incomes that exceeded those of many noblemen. In Hungary, wealthy rural folk were considered almost on a par with nobles and so entitled to attend meetings of the noble county assemblies, although they generally sat at the back. But many country-folk were landless, working as day labourers, usually on the farms of their better-off neighbours. Some lived in hovels, in hollows in the ground with tunnels to escape tax collectors, but most of the rural workforce lived in more salubrious accommodation. One Scottish observer noted in western Hungary tidy white-washed homes shaded by walnut and acacia trees, with neat fields beyond—'perhaps as good a picture of a rich and prosperous peasantry as one could find in any part of Europe'.[4]

Homes were mostly two-room buildings, with a kitchen and stove (but often without a chimney), larders, and a cellar. The second room was often set aside for special occasions, like birthing, dying, and receiving important guests, and piled high with linen and embroidery, which were as much marks of peasant wealth as a horse and carriage. Except in winter, interior accommodation was irrelevant except for sleeping and cooking, for daily life was spent either in the fields, beneath the eaves that fronted the farmhouse, or in the barn that villagers had chosen for drinking and card playing. Until the nineteenth century, clocks were rare and daily life was regulated by the church bell and the cockerel. Gardening was strictly for vegetables and herbs, so it was a sign of nobility to have soil to spare for flowers.

Much of village life was organized by the peasants themselves, who decided collectively the timetables for sowing and harvesting and how the fields were to be divided up. Village courts, composed of elders, allocated penalties for minor crimes. Since the cost of imprisoning an offender was burdensome, they usually imposed acts of public disgrace or stigmatization, like standing in the pillory or shaving a moustache or fines, beatings, and road repair. In Calvinist communities, the council of elders or presbytery of the local church often doubled up as a village court, shaming maldoers by making them confess their misdeeds to the congregation or wait in the church porch on a Sunday while parishioners filed past. More serious crimes usually went to the manor court at which officials of the lord presided.

Peasant communities were never self-sufficient, but the intermittent tasks that had to be performed could seldom sustain a livelihood. Itinerant groups filled the gaps, undertaking predominantly dirty jobs and working as tinkers, tanners, blacksmiths, entertainers, horse dealers, and hangmen. These tasks were often done by Gypsies, although the name is a catch-all that includes different groups. So, whereas the Roma and Sinti are both Romani speakers originally from northwestern India, the Jenish, who performed similar social and economic functions in Central Europe, are of distant German origin.

The Gypsies came to Europe in the last of the migrations from the east that had begun with the Goths back in the fourth century. They entered Central Europe not in a single wave but in ripples, from the late fourteenth century to the eighteenth century. Dark-skinned, often colourfully dressed, and speaking an unknown tongue, they were originally thought to be either Tatars, the Old Testament Philistines, or Egyptians (whence the name of Gypsy). The German word for Gypsy, *Zigeuner*, and its Central European variants (the Hungarian *cigány*, Czech *cikán*, Polish *cygan*, and Romanian *țigan*) probably originate in the Greek *athinganoi*, meaning 'untouchables'.

Gypsies call themselves *Roma* or 'men', but it was only in the late eighteenth century that scholars established the origin of their language in a variety of Sanskrit. Taking advantage of gaps in the rural economy, many Gypsies moved into predominantly low-status occupations, thereby confirming their identity as outsiders, on a par with forest folk like charcoal burners (with whom they were frequently included in legislation). Their difference often prompted wild allegations of child theft, polluting water supplies, and spying for the Turks, which sometimes spilled over into violence and murder.

Gypsies were mostly seminomadic, living in tents and shacks during the winter and travelling in the summer months. From the sixteenth century onwards, rulers and diets across Central Europe were increasingly concerned with rural disorder and with vagrancy as one of its causes. Clampdowns on tramps and beggars often targeted Gypsies as well. So, from one description from 1586 of the folk that were unwelcome in the Rhineland county of Nassau:

> Gypsies, tramps, masterless vagabonds, buskers with fiddles, zithers, and other stringed instruments, crooks, look-outs, fortune tellers, idle beggars, troublemakers, peddlers, and other riff-raff, who are bent on dirty-dealing, murder, robbery, theft, arson, and other misdeeds; and diviners, conjurors, gazers into crystal balls, and quacks who make out that they are doctors who can cure people and cattle but use illicit means to cheat poor people.[5]

In order to escape arrest, many Gypsies moved into the shadow of cities and onto large estates. Even so, local magistrates routinely neglected injunctions aimed at Gypsies, for they made no sense. The laws against vagrancy were undiscriminating and did not recognize that Gypsies had skills that were important to local communities. As a census from the 1760s of the Gypsy population in a part of what is now Slovakia indicates, most Gypsy households were headed by craftsmen, usually blacksmiths and carpenters, who often doubled up as musicians. Since there were other, less reputable people on the road, magistrates had enough to keep them occupied. In parts of Central Europe in the early eighteenth century, almost a tenth of the population comprised vagrants.[6]

Despite regulations prohibiting wanderers, Gypsies across much of Central Europe continued to roam in summer, without (it would seem) the local authorities doing much to stop them. In the principality of Transylvania, the diet passed laws that permitted Gypsies to travel in return for special payments and sought to organize their communities under the leadership of so-called voivodes who were responsible for tax collection and for maintaining order. Gypsy encampments outside city walls were commonplace and Gypsy craftsmen tolerated so long as they did not trespass upon the established rights of guildsmen. In parts of Transylvania, Gypsies moved onto the land and were rapidly absorbed into the peasantry.[7]

Poland and Lithuania were typical in enacting legislation that prohibited Gypsies from travelling under pain of banishment or imprisonment. But, as elsewhere in Central Europe, penalties were seldom enforced. Local Polish and Lithuanian lords gave guarantees of good behaviour so that Gypsies might visit fairs and markets untroubled and they actively recruited Gypsies to settle on their estates. Large Gypsy groups moved in particular to the extensive estates of the Radziwiłł lords in Lithuania. Comprising no fewer than two thousand towns and villages, the Radziwiłł lands were sufficient to accommodate itinerant companies of Gypsies as well as sedentary Gypsy craftsmen. On the Radziwiłł estate at Smarhoń, now in Belarus, the town hosted a bear-training academy, where bears were taught to dance in wooden shoes, presumably to support travelling Gypsy musicians.[8]

Central Europe was never built of homogeneous blocks of population. Besides the blurring of different linguistic and cultural groups in frontier regions, there was widespread immigration from abroad. In Poland, Hungary, Transylvania, and Bohemia, all the cities had large German populations, whose origins may be traced back to at least the thirteenth century. German merchants and patricians either controlled most of their governments or, as in Vilnius in Lithuania and Cluj in

Transylvania, joined in power-sharing arrangements whereby offices rotated among the different national groups. In the Transylvanian and Hungarian countryside, Romanian shepherds and labourers were recruited to fill gaps in the population, often setting up villages next to more established communities and following their own laws and religious observances. The Upper Tisza, in what is now western Ukraine near the city of Berehove, was a mosaic of settlements—Hungarian, Romanian, and Ukrainian, with a sprinkling of German landowners. Since the valley floor needed experts in drainage, there were even a few Flemings.[9]

Migration brought unexpected population movements. Between 1500 and 1650, many Scots settled in Poland, not only on the Baltic shore but also deep inland, as far as Lublin, Tarnów, and Cracow. The English traveller Fynes Moryson and the indefatigable Scottish adventurer 'Lugless' Willie Lithgow (so called because his brothers had cruelly cut off his ears, or 'lugs', in childhood) met them there at the beginning of the seventeenth century and reported them to be in the tens of thousands. In Lithgow's opinion, Poland was 'the mother and nurse for the youth and younglings of Scotland'. In fact, there were probably fewer than ten thousand Scots in Poland at any one time and they were mainly engaged in hawking mirrors, scissors, handkerchiefs, oranges, and other low-value goods, often on behalf of a small number of wealthy Scottish merchants resident in Cracow. By the end of the seventeenth century, most Scots had moved on, leaving almost no trace.[10]

In contrast to the Scots, Armenians in Central Europe were linked into the long-distance trade, since they were able to take advantage of a web of business contacts built up over centuries in the Balkans, Middle East, and Caucasus. There had been Armenians in Central Europe from at least the twelfth century. Their numbers were swollen by the destruction in the 1370s of the Armenian kingdom of Cilicia (now in southern Turkey) and, a century later, by the Turks' devastation of the Armenian merchant colony in Kaffa in the Crimea. In both Poland and Transylvania, Armenian refugees were welcomed and given rights of self-government, including their own courts of elders. The law code they followed in late medieval Lviv survives—a bizarre collection of obscure and irrelevant provisions that included rights of salvage on the high seas, the rules of kidnapping, and the penalties to be imposed on oxen that strangled one another.[11]

Armenians were predominantly merchants, and some would later use their wealth to buy both country estates and their way into the Polish and Hungarian nobility. Unlike Armenians, but in a manner similar to Gypsies and itinerant Scots, Jews at first undertook roles that traditional rural communities could not fill, working as tanners and dyers, repairing clothes and footwear, and peddling cheap and second-hand wares. Most countryfolk bartered goods, keeping their cash back for taxes and essential purchases, but Jews had money from the sale of goods, so they could put some of it into making short-term loans, free from the restrictions on usury that until the Reformation weighed down on Christian lenders. Like Gypsies, Jews were, in the historian Yuri Slezkine's inelegant but useful expression, 'service nomads' looking for economic gaps in an overwhelmingly agrarian economy.[12]

In most of Central Europe, the Jewish population was numerically insignificant. In the Holy Roman Empire (excluding Bohemia), it amounted to about 40,000 persons at the start of the eighteenth century, and in Hungary to 11,000, so in both cases Jews comprised well under 1 per cent of the overall population. But these figures are dwarfed by the Jewish population in Poland and Lithuania, where by 1720 Jews numbered 375,000 souls, or about 4 per cent of the population. They were, though, unevenly spread, with a preponderance in what is now western Ukraine, where in the eighteenth century they made up to a third and even a half of the population in several provinces.[13]

Previously living in the Rhineland, many Jews had dispersed across Central Europe in the later Middle Ages to avoid persecution. They had brought with them their blended language called Yiddish, which is a mix of High German, Aramaic, and Hebrew, written in Hebrew characters and from right to left. Most Jews were not city folk but, in the expression of the time, *Landjuden* (literally, 'Land Jews'), living in villages and small market towns—the fabled *shtetls* of the Polish and

Lithuanian countryside. The *shtetl*, which is a diminutive of the Yiddish *shtot*, or town, remains to this day a metaphor both for a lost world of neighbourliness and for the precariousness from which many Jews were happy to escape. It stares back at us in the paintings of Marc Chagall (1887–1985)—simple cottages lining muddy lanes, Torah-clutching rabbis in prayer shawls, fiddlers perched on rooftops, and magic cows with parasols.

In the Holy Roman Empire, 90 per cent of Jews lived in small settlements, but usually in insufficient numbers to have a cemetery or synagogue, so worship was done in private homes with whoever had the best voice serving as cantor. Most Jewish men, and many Jewish women too, were involved in trade of some sort, although the nature of their commerce differed from place to place. In Frisia, Jews were predominantly engaged in the cattle trade, operating slaughterhouses and butcheries; in Franconia, they pressed grapes and bottled wine, according to kosher rules but selling to Jews and non-Jews alike; in Swabia, they dealt in horses, and so on. If local guild regulations prohibited Jews from working as tailors, they might find a niche repairing clothes. Or, should the established guilds of gold- and silversmiths have a monopoly on the jewellery trade, Jews might instead develop a line in engraving and cutting gems.

Jews were vulnerable, not least because they were thought to have cash. Even when local regulations did not insist on Jews wearing a yellow tag or distinctive hats, their beards and women's headscarves often singled them out as targets. On top of this, local communities often turned on Jews in times of distress, blaming them for mishaps and economic downturns. For their own protection, some Jews clustered in cities, often behind gates, although in some places strict residential requirements obliged the construction of ghettoes, where several thousand Jews were crowded into a single street. Even so, expulsions were commonplace—from Berlin and Brandenburg in 1510 and, again, in 1573; from Regensburg in 1519 and from the whole of Bavaria in 1551; from Frankfurt in 1614, and so on. To these, we should add the frequent occasions when local magistrates either expelled the handful

of Jewish families living in mixed communities or imposed such intolerable conditions on their marriages and the number of children they
might have that Jews moved on.[14]

Jews looked for protection. They moved into Swabia and Franconia in the later Middle Ages precisely because the knights and counts
of the petty principalities there could keep a closer eye on them and
shield them from harm. Elsewhere, better-off Jews bought special privileges from rulers and great lords that relieved them of local restrictions
and bypassed residency requirements. A few obtained the status of
'court Jews' (*Hofjuden*), providing courts with luxury items and loans.
Their opportunities were enlarged when, as a consequence of defaults
and the ruination of commerce and currencies during the Thirty Years'
War, many established banks went bust, culminating in the liquidation
of the Fugger bank in 1657. From selling jewels and making high-
interest loans to rulers, Jews took over as the main bankers, funding
armies and courtly extravagances.

Court Jews kept rulers financially afloat. They also freed counts
and dukes in the Holy Roman Empire from having to negotiate with
their diets, providing a flow of cash that allowed rulers to bypass the
conditions that the diets frequently laid on new subsidies. On top of
this, court Jews had a network of business connections and kinsmen
that might be called upon to aid rulers in other ways—providing supplies for armies, delivering horses, running mints and buying up the
precious metals for their operation, and negotiating commercial treaties. So, when he decided that he needed tall grenadier guards, Frederick William I of Prussia turned to the court Jew Jacob Gompertz,
paying him on a sliding scale to comb Europe for the tallest.[15]

But despite their usefulness, court Jews occupied a precarious place.
They followed the high nobility in having grand townhouses, country
estates, and expensive mistresses, but they depended entirely on their
patrons. Sudden changes at the top often led to trumped-up charges
of fraud and embezzlement, the seizure of assets, and even death. Jews
were easy scapegoats, too, when rulers had to fend off complaints of
misgovernment, as well as a convenient resource for rulers to loot. The

wealthy Jewish families that survived often did so by integrating into the larger society, taking careers in the army, marrying into established families, and converting to Christianity.

Poland was a safer place to be. From the thirteenth century onwards, royal charters gave Polish Jews considerable rights of self-government and put Jews living in royally chartered cities under the ruler's personal protection. In both shtots and shtetls, Jews in Poland developed an astonishing range of communal institutions. Through their municipal councils, or kahals, Jewish communities funded schools, places of worship, hospitals, law courts, and even chimney sweeps. Set above the kahals was the so-called Council of the Four Lands (or three, or five—the title was never fixed), made up of kahal deputies and a college of rabbis, which decided problematic legal cases, regulated conduct, and apportioned the taxes that Jews paid in a lump sum to the royal treasury.

Jews saw themselves as more rooted in Poland than elsewhere. Their stories told how the Hebrew name for Poland, *Polin*, originated in a divine injunction *Poh lin*, meaning 'Dwell here', or stood for *poh lan Yah*, 'Here dwells the Lord.' Either way, the mistaken etymology convinced Jews that their settlement in Poland was part of a divinely ordained plan. As one rabbi explained as early as the fifteenth century, Poland was 'of old a refuge for the exiled children of Israel'. A century later, a rabbi in Cracow put it more bluntly: 'Perhaps we ought to prefer a piece of dry bread in peace in these lands . . . where the hatred of Jews has not taken the dimensions of that in German lands. May God allow this condition to continue until the coming of the Messiah.'[16]

The Polish Sejm imposed limits on Jewish commercial dealings with agencies of government, so there was less opportunity for court Jews to prosper in Poland. Instead, Jews looked to individual noblemen. In what is now Belarus and Ukraine, noble landowners encouraged the immigration of Jews both to rejuvenate their towns and villages and to provide additional income from rents and dues. Many went further, leasing out to Jews the right to collect taxes, to farm parts of the estate using peasant labour, and to open up new land for cultivation. But the most important right that Jews bought from lords was the monopoly on the sale of spirits. When cereal prices fell in the eighteenth century, landowners increasingly converted grain into vodka, selling off the right to its manufacture. As one of the greatest of eighteenth-century Polish magnates, Joseph Czartoryski, explained: 'In our country the vodka distilleries could be called mints because it is only thanks to them that we can hope to sell off our grain in years when there is no famine.'

By the eighteenth century, as many as a third of all Jews in Poland were occupied in some way with the trade in vodka and beer—Poles famously drank no fewer than three litres of beer a day, after which they moved on to spirits. Since lords generally outlawed home brewing and distilling, Jews had a captive market. Descriptions of taverns in the countryside were unfailingly bleak. As one early-nineteenth-century account put it:

> The inn is generally a miserable hovel . . . partitioned off in one corner of a large shed, serving as a stable and yard for vehicles; the entrance is under a low porch or timber; the floor is dirt; the furniture consists of a long table or two or three small ones in one corner, a bunch of straw, or sometimes a few raised boards forming a platform with straw spread over it for beds. . . . Here the Jew, assisted by a dirty-faced Rachel, with a keen and anxious look, passes the full day in serving out to the meanest customer beer and hay and corn; wrangling with and extorting money from intoxicated peasants. [Rachel is in this context a pejorative name for a Jewish woman.][17]

Resentment at the closeness of Jews' relationship with the lords and at what many thought to be Jewish exploitation of the peasantry fed into the massive uprising in what is now Ukraine, led by the Cossack Bohdan Khmelnytsky. (See Chapter 15.) Beginning in 1648, the revolt rapidly descended into chaos as Cossack bands slaughtered Polish noblemen, Uniate priests, and Jews. Several tens of thousands of

Jews were murdered and untold numbers sold into Tatar slavery. Surviving witness accounts describe the sadistic cruelty of the Cossacks and of the peasants who had joined their ranks, and of the deliberate destruction of synagogues and Torah scrolls. For Jews, the slaughter was all the more painful because, according to ancient prophecies, 1648 should have been the year of redemption when the dead were brought back to life.[18]

In the wake of the massacres, many Polish Jews turned inwards, embracing either the fatalism of what would much later be immortalized by Sholem Aleichem's 'Tevye the Dairyman', the model for Tevye in the Broadway *Fiddler on the Roof*, or the (faltering) confidence of the Old Testament Job that tribulation was a divine test, administered only to the faithful. Mystical movements sprang up in the wake of the slaughter, with rumours of a Messiah's arrival and of a new order that would see the legalism of traditional Judaism replaced by a more personal and prayerful religion, shorn of ceremony and rabbinical nit-picking. In the eighteenth century, these trends would produce the diffuse set of beliefs known as Hasidism, which taught God's immanence in all creation and that He should be joyfully celebrated, even with handstands and somersaults.

The Jewish population in Poland-Lithuania doubled in the century after 1650, but without an economic upswing to match the demographic surge. By around 1700, possibly as many as 20 per cent of Polish Jews were beggars, and modern Yiddish retains an abundant vocabulary of names by which to describe a beggar: *shnorer* or cadger, *luftmentsh* or a man with no obvious income, *medine yid* or a homeless scrounger, and a dozen more besides. The tide of war spilling over Poland and Lithuania in the second half of the seventeenth century increased hardship, sending periodic waves of poor Jews westwards, so reversing Jews' historic easterly movement. In the immediate wake of the Khmelnytsky revolt of 1648, between ten and fifteen thousand Jews travelled from Poland to the Holy Roman Empire. Thousands more followed in the succeeding decades, often in bands of fifty or a hundred at a time.[19]

The usual response of cities and governments was to move migrant Jews on, denying them the chance to settle. Until they could find a safe haven, often on the edges of existing Jewish communities, many Jews survived by begging. In the popular imagination, they joined the formless mass of undesirables, whom one ordinance described as

> tramps, vagabonds, foreign beggars and, in particular, Jewish ones, idlers, people who have no obvious occupation or make out that they were imprisoned by the Turks and now seek alms, and people who go around with bears, bags of tricks, and other entertainments. [Brunswick, c. 1700][20]

The landless, begging Jew highlighted rural impoverishment. Ordinances repeatedly conflated the Jewish beggar with the rural rabble and urged officials to crack down on both. Even so, governments and advisers across Central Europe were increasingly aware that indigent Jews were part of a larger problem that lay with the structure of economic relationships in the countryside. If Jews could be turned away from begging and peddling, then they might be made into useful subjects: indeed, their business skills might have a transforming or even 'alchemical' effect upon rural enterprises. But for this to happen, the economic landscape would first need to be transformed. The people who would seek to bring this about were the first political economists, known as the Cameralists. Virtually forgotten today, they would transform Central Europe.[21]

CHAPTER 19

Cameralism, Ottoman Endgame, and the Human Laboratory

B Y THE SECOND HALF OF THE SEVENTEENTH CENTURY, GOVERN-ments across Central Europe were increasingly aware that their economies were being left behind. Visitors to England, France, and the Netherlands saw the ships, manufactures, and populous cities, all of which were missing back home. As one of the earliest of these self-critical observers remarked, 'We are forever only giving foreigners occasion for hearty laughter. They are laughing at us, and they are right.' Or, as Philip von Hörnigk wrote in his *Austria over all (if she only wants to)* (1684), 'Nothing is sound with us, from head to foot. . . . Things are in such a condition that it is something like an Austrian miracle that everything has not yet gone to total ruin long ago.'[1]

Hörnigk belonged to the group of early economists known as Cameralists, or practitioners of 'treasury science'. (The word for treasury was at the time *Camera* or *Kammer*, literally meaning 'a chamber'.) Cameralism was the study of how states and institutions might maximize revenues so as to become rich, thus overcoming their economic backwardness. In Central Europe, Cameralists generally split down the middle. Some believed that the key to prosperity lay in developing manufactures and boosting exports, with the ruler taking the lead in founding factories, glassworks, and silk farms. Others looked to advance agriculture by the introduction of new crops and by 'impopulation', meaning moving people to cultivate land that was insufficiently exploited.

Despite their different stresses, Cameralists agreed that serfdom was a bad thing. It prevented labourers moving to new factories and farms,

hid inefficiencies in the rural economy, and was a cause of impoverishment. Far better a free peasantry, with farmers working plots that
they held as hereditary tenures, for they were then more likely to be
prosperous and content. If governments wanted to lift themselves out
of their self-imposed penury, one Cameralist explained, they should
heed 'the sighs and laments of a million peasants and craftsmen', for
it was on the fruits of their labour that the happiness of all rested. As
for vagrants and idlers, they should be set to work building roads and
canals, and Gypsies forced to become settled. For Cameralists, it did
not matter that their solutions trampled on the established rights of
individuals and the privileges of landlords. As one leading Cameralist
put it, 'Every tradition which has no justifiable basis should be abolished automatically.'[2]

Cameralists were strong on regulation. By their reckoning, people lacked knowledge, so they could seldom be trusted to make the
right decisions. A benevolent government, possessed of all the right
information, should decide for them instead. Accordingly, Cameralists
frequently advocated what amounted to 'a programme of total regulation'. Their regulations drilled deep, laying down the types of crop
and trees to be cultivated, where bridges and hospitals should be built,
what people should eat to keep them nourished, and so on. Some were
plainly absurd—that cripples be banned from marketplaces lest they
frighten women into miscarriages and so diminish the population or
that rulers install secret passages and loopholes in their palaces to check
up on their servants. The 'well-ordered state' to which Cameralists as-
pired was sometimes called the *Polizei-Staat*, which means 'regulated
state', although in many respects 'police state' would do equally well.[3]

Cameralists took over. They became the bureaucrats of rulers
across Central Europe, honing their administrative skills and increasingly influencing what should be taught at universities. Along with
law, Cameralism became part of the necessary training of future civil
servants, with professorships in cameral science established in 1721
in the Prussian universities of Halle and Frankfurt on the Oder. But
progress in implementing Cameralist policies was slow. Many rulers

were suspicious of innovation, and city guilds, noble landlords, and traditionalist clergymen were often obstructive. But in the 1720s a space unexpectedly opened up in Central Europe where Cameralism could be tested on what was almost literally a greenfield site. This was the Banat of Timişoara. To understand how this small territory, nestling on the edge of the southern Carpathians, became the Cameralist testing ground, we need to backtrack a little to the Ottoman occupation of Central Europe and how it ended.

In the decades following the 1648 Peace of Westphalia, the Habsburgs were fighting on two fronts. In the west, they faced the French king Louis XIV (ruled 1643–1715). As free with other men's lands as he was with their wives, as one wit put it at the time, Louis aimed to push France's border to the Rhine, annexing the German duchies and lordships that stood in his way. In 1681, the great Rhine fortress of Strassburg became Strasbourg, completing the French capture of Alsace and Franche-Comté (the County of Burgundy). Meanwhile, in the east, the Turks continued to harass the Military Frontier and to keep hold of most of Hungary. In 1658, Leopold I succeeded his father, Ferdinand III, as emperor and he spent most of his long reign at war (he died in 1705). But his plight was obvious. As one of his leading generals put it to him: 'Your army, Sire, is your monarchy; without it your dominions will yet fall a prey to the Turks, the French, or perhaps one of these days to the Hungarians. Your capital is a frontier town.'[4]

The western and eastern theatres of war were interlinked. Louis XIV supported rebellions against the Habsburgs launched from Transylvania, which was an Ottoman vassal state, sending money and what would now be called 'military advisers'. At critical moments, Louis XIV took advantage of Leopold's armies being occupied in the east to renew pressure in the west, forcing the emperor to abandon campaigns against the Ottomans and redeploy his resources from the Danube to the Rhine. But the Ottomans were too bold. In 1683, the sultan's chief minister, vizier Kara Mustafa, launched an invasion of the Habsburg lands and besieged Vienna. At the last minute, Habsburg forces, supported by a large Polish army, put the Ottoman forces to flight. Vienna was saved, for which Kara Mustafa paid with his life. On the sultan's orders, he was strangled by a silk scarf in the fortress of Belgrade.

In the wake of the victory at Vienna, Leopold pressed forward. Buda was reconquered in 1686 and Belgrade two years later. Transylvania's last independent prince, Michael II Apafi, submitted in 1692, subsequently abdicating in return for a handsome pension and a palace in Vienna. Leopold promised to maintain religious freedom both in Hungary and in the principality of Transylvania, but his understanding of toleration was not capacious. Protestants might only practice their religion out of sight, and they could not build new churches and were ineligible for public office. A failed rebellion led by the magnate Ferenc Rákóczi in 1703 signalled the end of opposition to Habsburg rule in both Hungary and Transylvania.

In 1699, Leopold had settled with the Turks at Karlowitz (Sremski Karlovci), now in northern Serbia, obtaining most of the historic kingdom in Hungary. The peace was signed in a marquee, the flaps of which had been opened on all four sides to symbolize its worldwide significance. Karlowitz was Central Europe's first modern treaty, too, with borders drawn in detail on more than four hundred maps, the depth of rivers plotted (to anticipate the erosion of their banks), and lines of cairns erected as markers on the ground. But it was all so much wasted effort, for the peace did not last.[5]

Rákóczi's fate had been settled in 1704 when in a combined operation British and Habsburg armies had smashed his French ally at Blenheim (Blindheim or Hochstatt) in Bavaria, leaving Rákóczi isolated. The Battle of Blenheim is feted as the victory of John Churchill, Duke of Marlborough, but it was also the triumph of the Habsburg general Eugene of Savoy, whose forces had in the nick of time arrived on the battlefield, outflanking the French. A master of deception and the witty barb, Eugene campaigned in the Habsburg service for more than five decades. With a mansion in Vienna and the still grander Belvedere summer palace on the city's outskirts, Eugene's successes in battle brought him spectacular rewards and the gratitude of a succession of Habsburg emperors.

Eugene foresaw the Eastern Question—that is, how the decline of the Ottoman Empire in Europe was to be managed. He rightly anticipated that Russia would seek a foothold in the Balkans and that the Habsburgs should move first to pre-empt Russian ambitions. So, Eugene convinced Emperor Charles VI to break the Treaty of Karlowitz and to begin a new campaign against the Turks in 1716. In short order, Eugene captured Timişoara and Petrovaradin in the last remaining parts of Ottoman Hungary, and went on the next year to capture Belgrade.

Eugene contemplated driving deep into the Balkans, even as far as Thessaloniki, but settled instead for an advantageous peace. The treaty concluded in 1718 at Passarowitz (Požarevac, now in Serbia) gave the Habsburgs a slice of western Wallachia called Oltenia, Belgrade and what is now northern Serbia, and the former Ottoman eyalet or province of Timişoara. A square of territory roughly the size of modern Belgium, the province of Timişoara was bounded by the Tisza, Mureş, and Danube Rivers. Following its conquest, it was known by a mistake of historical geographers (who confused it with a different place) as the Banat.[6]

Up until this point, the Habsburg administration had assigned the portions of Hungarian territory captured from the Turks to the descendants of their former owners. Where these could not be found, or proof of possession had been lost, the land was either absorbed into the crown estate or sold off. But Oltenia and most of Habsburg Serbia had never been part of Hungary. The government in Vienna accordingly designated these lands as the 'absolute domain' (*absolutum domanium*) of the crown and placed them under the Imperial Treasury and the Imperial War Council, headed by Eugene of Savoy. But it went further. Claiming military necessity, the government included the Banat in this arrangement, even though it had until the 1550s been a part of the kingdom of Hungary and plenty of Hungarian noblemen could assert a right of ancestral ownership to estates within it.[7]

Eugene of Savoy was given ultimate authority over this enormous space. Fortunately, the archive of the Imperial Treasury had a plan drawn up in the late 1680s that told him exactly what to do. The Habsburgs were never at a loss for long names, and the plan was the work of the 'Royal and Imperial Sub-Delegation of the Commission for Hungarian Affairs'. Meeting on some eighty separate occasions, the Sub-Delegation provided in its so-called *Work of Instauration* (*Einrichtungswerk*) a blueprint for how to modernize territories in Hungary that had been captured from the Turks. Some of its recommendations had already been adopted in the parts of Hungary that Leopold had captured in the 1680s and 1690s. Now, Eugene of Savoy entrusted his top general, Claude Florimund Comte de Mercy, a Lorrainer in Habsburg service, with implementing the *Work of Instauration* in the Banat through a dedicated commission and appointed him civil and military governor.

The *Work of Instauration* was a typically Cameralist project, predicated on top-down management and governmental intervention. The population of a conquered area should be expanded by immigration to increase productivity, new industries and crops should be encouraged, mines opened, hospitals built, sanitary and fire regulations drawn up, march routes and depots established to prevent troops plundering supplies, and modest dress codes and sensible eating habits enforced. Importantly, too, the *Work of Instauration* had little time for noble rights. As the commission's president explained: 'The numerous privileges of the nobility in respect of public burdens contradict the principles of all good government.'[8]

The Banat was a blank sheet and ideal for experimentation. In the Middle Ages, the Banat had been rich farming land, but warfare and neglect had resulted in the decay of riverbanks and dykes, leading to widespread flooding and endemic malaria (known as 'Banat fever'). Presiding above the swampland of the River Timiş lay the massive redoubt of Timişoara. With four great bastions, it resembled, according to one Turkish observer, nothing less than a giant tortoise (*kaplum bagea*) in the water. But the hinterland was waterlogged, and the population was sparse, with an average of just two persons per square kilometre. Most were Serbs and Romanians, whom Habsburg administrators often lumped together under the antique name of 'Illyrians' (as in Shakespeare's *Twelfth Night*). They were convinced that the Banat's ruin was mainly due to the primitiveness of the Illyrians, who were ignorant of agriculture, superstitious, and under the thumb of their ill-educated Orthodox clergy.[9]

The original *Work of Instauration* had put much store in racial health. So, in Hungary, it had recommended the immigration of Germans in order that 'the Hungarian blood, which is naturally inclined to revolution and disquiet, might be tempered with the German, and thereby brought to a constant trust and love of their natural, hereditary monarchy and nobility.' Under Eugene of Savoy's guidance, the same principle was applied in the Banat, with the difference that German settlers should squeeze out Illyrians. But at least they were to be shunted aside. Everyone else was to be moved out of the Banat completely, including 'unbelievers like heathens, Jews, Turks, Lutherans and Calvinists, and all types of heretics'. Here, the new order in the Banat far exceeded the *Work of Instauration*, which had envisaged the immigration of German Protestants into the empty parts of Hungary. Indeed, the Comte de Mercy, governor and head of the Banat Instauration Committee, had recruited German Lutherans to work on his private estates in Hungary.[10]

The population rise in the Banat was astonishing. From eighty thousand people in 1717 there were sixty years later no fewer than three hundred thousand. Unfortunately, they were not the sort of people Eugene of Savoy had wanted, for most were Serbs and Romanians from Oltenia and Habsburg Serbia, moving to the greater safety of the Banat. During Mercy's administration of the Banat (1722–1733), about ten thousand Germans were settled. A second wave in the middle decades of the century bought in a further forty thousand. Even so, Germans accounted for only an eighth of the Banat's overall population.[11]

The problem was that few Germans wanted to go there. The journey was long (two months by river and road from the collection points in Bavaria) and the prospects arduous. The Banat was, in one saying of the time, 'the grave of Germans'. Promises of land, a home, furniture, tax exemptions, and paid passage were insufficient to swell numbers, so the government in Vienna resorted to using the Banat as a dumping ground for criminals and undesirables. These were mostly poachers, alcoholics, and prostitutes, but they also included refugees from Habsburg Spain who were considered a drain on the imperial finances. Upon arrival, some convicts were put in workhouse prisons, and others made to build fortifications. The flow of deportees was never large, scarcely more than several hundred a year in the 1740s, but they hardly represented the strong German admixture that Eugene of Savoy had hoped would bolster the Banat's biological stock.[12]

Even so, Mercy and his successors as governor tried to push through the Cameral programme of the original *Work of Instauration*. To begin with, they rebuilt the city of Timişoara, replacing its bastions with massive star-shaped fortifications. Inside, they had the old city torn down and imposed a gridiron street plan with a formal square and parade ground. The design of Timişoara provided a pattern for new villages and towns, where houses were arranged in square blocks, on plots of an equal size, according to specific instructions:

It is the job of the engineer to lay out the primary streets, side-streets, a church square (always to be located in the middle of the village), chaplaincy, schoolhouse, and inn. Of equal importance is determining the location for a public well for each street, which will be dug in the following winter. Each house plot must measure seventy-five to a hundred *Klafters* in length and twelve to fifteen *Klafters* in width. All buildings are to be located on only one side of the plot; the house should be constructed in such a way that the gable wall faces the street and a minimum of nine *Klafters* of free space separates each neighbouring plot.[13] [A *Klafter* is the length of a man's outstretched arms: about 1.80 metres, or a fathom.]

Banat officials also numbered the homes, which was probably the first time in Central Europe that house-numbering was so comprehensively done. The strips of land that the newcomers were given to farm were similarly drawn on maps and given identifying codes. But the settlers were at least allowed to choose the street names, which often harked back to their place of origin—Palatine Street, Zweibrücken Street, Swabian Street, and so on.[14]

Mercy also began work draining the swamps and drove roadways across them to link settlements. In the process, he demolished Romanian and Serb villages that stood in the way of roads or occupied fields that German settlers might more profitably cultivate. Elsewhere, German newcomers took over Serbian and Romanian settlements, expelling their inhabitants. Recent historians often celebrate the Banat as an early and successful experiment in multiculturalism and colonial paternalism. In fact, the Banat was built upon policies that were more akin to apartheid, with the best land going to Germans while Serbs and Romanians were given separate zones of settlement on less fertile soil.[15]

The Banat remained overwhelmingly agricultural since, once drained, its fields were mostly good black earth, rich in nutrients. But Mercy and his successors were determined to build its industry and manufacturing. A start was made in the 1720s when Mercy succeeded in recruiting several hundred Tyrolean miners, whom he settled in the mountainous eastern part of the Banat to dig for copper and gold. Non-Germans, if they were thought to be useful, were also recruited—Italians as silkworm farmers, Armenians as leatherworkers, Bulgarians as cattle breeders, and so on. They settled in gridiron communities, whose names often promised a fresh start—New Arad, New Palanka, and for Spaniards, New Barcelona. Despite restrictions on their immigration, Jews came too, numbering several hundred in Timişoara by 1780, and bought up the monopolies on selling beer and spirits.

The Banat was, in one historian's words, a human laboratory. Many Cameralists thought of themselves as part of a bureaucratic elite, striving to maximize resources and improve the welfare of subjects. Most hid behind dull lists of statistics, minute descriptions of manufacturing processes, and manuals of forest management. But not a few thought in bigger terms about how to make states and regions work better and more productively. Typically, they regarded the entrenched privileges of the nobility as detrimental to economic efficiency and the happiness of peoples. They promoted instead meritocracy and saw themselves as a new mandarin elite: literally so. As one of Cameralism's chief exponents put it—'The most reasonable and wise constitution on our globe, which I unhesitatingly declare the Chinese to be, does not know hereditary nobility.' (Cameralists were fascinated by China, since they envied its production of fine silk and porcelain and its strong bureaucratic ethos.)[16]

The Banat was an ideal testing ground. Since it was crownland, it had no nobility. The rural workforce was accordingly free in the sense that peasant farmers were not tied to their lords' villages and so might move. They owed rent to the provincial government, for they were cultivating its fields, but ordinary dues and taxes were generally low. All this fitted with the principles outlined in the *Work of Instauration*, which had opposed the settlement of 'peasants who are bound to the soil, still less serfs,' preferring instead 'free tenants with the right of movement'. Even so, cash was in limited circulation, so peasants in the Banat often paid in produce. One official noted with disgust how a German settler at New Palanka had paid his tax 'with four hundred eggs and the same number of worms, and he hopes to send us more of the same!' More usually, peasants performed labour services. Though lighter than in Hungary and Transylvania, they often amounted to one day a week.[17]

Although a few crept in, Protestants were excluded from the Banat. During the middle decades of the eighteenth century, successive Habsburg rulers clamped down on Protestants in the Austrian duchies, often putting the children of Protestant parents into the care of Catholic religious orders and banishing the adults to Transylvania. At Vienna and Bratislava, officials combed through convoys of delinquents, sending Protestants to Transylvania and Catholics to the Banat. But the Banat remained multiconfessional. Back in the 1690s,

Emperor Leopold had, in return for their support in his war with the Turks, granted Orthodox Serbs the right to practice their religion unhindered, and Leopold's successors did not renege on his commitment. Along with tens of thousands of Serbs, the Serbian Orthodox patriarch of Peja (now in Kosovo) moved to southern Hungary, transferring his see to Sremski Karlovci. The same principle of toleration was extended to the Banat. Unlike Protestants, the Serbian Orthodox Church faced few impediments to worship there.

Even so, the Banat's governors cultivated the conspicuous Catholic piety that flourished throughout Habsburg Central Europe, with wayside shrines, choreographed processions of flagellants, plaster statues of the Virgin, and an abundance of feast days. The Comte de Mercy added to these by announcing that his name day should be a public holiday, but he also cultivated St John Nepomuk (died 1393) as the Banat's patron saint. Martyred by drowning in Prague's Vltava River, St John had become the saint of floods, whose intercession, Mercy hoped, would speed up the work of draining the swamps. More practically, he oversaw the construction of almost fifty new churches in the countryside and Timişoara. The Banat was intended not just as a defensive shield against the Turks but also, in one contemporary description, as 'the bulwark of Christendom against unbelievers'. To demonstrate the spiritual superiority of Christian belief, church architecture was monumental, with symmetrical façades outside, onion domes, and ornate interiors, crammed full of gilded images, stuccowork, and towering altarpieces.[18]

The Banat was the site of architectural competition, with religious orders and confessions vying to have the largest churches. Among these, the grandest were the new cathedral church built in Timişoara in the 1740s according to designs first drawn up in Salzburg and the massive pilgrimage shrine and basilica of Maria Radna. But Orthodox Serbs were not far behind, constructing their own cathedral in Timişoara in the same decade (although it took a further fifty years to complete the towers). Timişoara's Orthodox cathedral was not the first Orthodox church in Central Europe to be built in the Baroque style, for that prize belongs to the cathedral of Saints Cyril and Methodius in Prague, but it certainly counts among the earliest and, in terms of its location, the most unexpected.[19]

With its domes and cupolas, symmetrical façades, and monumental architecture, the Baroque style was pompous and grandiose. It suited the triumphalism of the Catholic Church, which had rolled back Protestantism's gains across a large part of Central Europe. But the Baroque was also the preferred style of emperors, kings, and magnates, by which they advertised their wealth and power. The Banat had no hereditary nobility. Its place was taken by officials, but as an aristocracy of talent they demonstrated their sway in much the same way, building palatial government offices, registries, and chancelleries, replete with ceremonial entrance halls, elegant staircases, and elaborately carved doorways. It was the same in the countryside, where schools, administrative buildings, and post offices copied the styles of a provincial nobility. In its secular architecture, the Banat was a showcase for the bureaucratic ideology of Cameralism.

In the second half of the eighteenth century, the Banat lost its singularity. Under Turkish pressure, Oltenia and Belgrade had been abandoned in the late 1730s. For reasons of military efficiency, Empress Maria Theresa now amalgamated the Banat's southern part into the Military Frontier. What remained she assigned in 1779 to Hungary, dividing the rump into counties and selling off the crownland to Hungarian noblemen and merchants. But although short-lived, the significance of the Banat should not be overlooked. It was an experiment in management from above that was driven by the ideas of Cameralism and the conviction that people might be administered and made into efficient producers. But behind the creation of the Banat lay a dangerous idea—that a docile, orderly, and controlled world might be born, presided over by an efficient apparatus of control.

CHAPTER 20

Bureaucrats, Sarmatians, and Little Landscapes

A NORWEGIAN ECONOMIST AND HIS WIFE HAVE PUBLISHED A list of bestsellers in the field of economics written before 1750. Top is Aristotle's *Economics*. Composed in the fourth century BCE, it is still available in paperback. Martin Luther's denunciation of usury (1524) is number three. But there, in the top ten, is an unfamiliar name—Veit Ludwig von Seckendorff (1626–1692), who was a government official in the duchy of Saxe-Gotha in Thuringia. Seckendorff's *German Princely State* (*Teutscher Fürsten-Staat*, 1656) is a thousand-page blockbuster that went through thirteen editions and was in continuous print for a century. Although only ever published in German, it was influential throughout Central Europe, shaping policy from the Banat to the Baltic.[1]

The *German Princely State* was a manual that combined the prescriptions of Cameralism with an exaggerated sense of the powers and responsibilities of government. It is addressed primarily to officials, who should, Seckendorff explained, make sure that commoners ate nutritious meals, had proper ventilation in their homes, wore unostentatious clothing, and avoided tobacco and hard liquor. His injunctions extended to the ruler. Seckendorff insisted that he should be busy, inspecting the countryside while out riding or hunting, not turning down invitations to lunch, and employing an army of accountants to prevent unnecessary waste. In taking Seckendorff's recommendations to heart, his employer, Duke Ernst of Saxe-Gotha (ruled 1640–1675), promptly froze Seckendorff's salary.

What made the *German Princely State* special was Seckendorff's new vocabulary and way of thinking. Much of what he wrote came from Roman Law, not least his assumption that the ruler had an almost unlimited right of command. But in the title of his book, Seckendorff introduced the unfamiliar word 'state' (*Staat*), and he linked it in the text to an equally novel term: 'territorial sovereignty', or *Landesobrigkeit*. Whereas previous writers had considered power as belonging exclusively to the ruler or ruling dynasty, Seckendorff thought of it as also adhering to the territory, which brought together the people who lived within its borders and made rulership possible. For Seckendorff, authority was vested first of all in the land, and only lent to the ruler, whose task was the coordination of the territory's people and resources for the benefit of the whole.

Seckendorff is seldom clear or consistent, but by fusing sovereignty and territory he introduced to Central Europe the idea of the modern state—a uniformly administered area, with fixed boundaries, and ruled by its own government and laws. Seckendorff acknowledged social hierarchy, and in an extended metaphor he described the state as 'a mystical body', with its members as the limbs and intestines. But his preferred term was 'subjects', or *Unterthanen*, pointing to the equal subordination of all to the whole. The word he used to describe the ruler is also telling. In keeping with the title of his book, Seckendorff acknowledged the name of prince, but he alternated it with the German *Regent*, suggesting a delegated and administrative role. It would not be until well into the next century that a German ruler would describe himself as the 'first servant of the state', but the idea was surely implicit in Seckendorff's great work.[2]

Seckendorff spent most of his career in the service of Duke Ernst, who ruled over the patchwork of disparate territories that is only known for short as Saxe-Gotha. The *German Princely State* suited Duke Ernst since he liked to be busy. Nicknamed 'the Pious', the duke was a prodigious meddler and an energetic Lutheran, who even learned a little Amharic in the hope of one day converting the Ethiopians to Protestantism. Indeed, Ernst's teacher, Abba Gorgoryos (c. 1600–1658), is probably the first sub-Saharan African in Central European history whose name we know. But despite its singularities, Ernst's reign as duke provides a lens through which we can observe the workings of the idea of the state on practical politics.[3]

The high point in the courtly calendar in nearly all of Central Europe was the festive taking of oaths of loyalty to the duke or ruler by noblemen and city magistrates. They did this every time a diet assembled. Indeed, the only purpose of many of the diets called in Saxe-Gotha was to have the oaths recited, in return for which the ruler solemnly promised to maintain all in their honours, lands, and liberties. If the diet had any controversial business to consider, it was dispatched with haste, since Duke Ernst controlled the agenda. His method will be familiar to committee-goers today. Much time was expended on trivia like the cash reserves of the school in Gotha, the upbringing of teenage nobles, the correct wearing of swords, and so on. Only after all this had been gone through were the more contentious matters reached. The assembled diet presented Ernst with their petitions. He promised to act upon them, but it is suggestive that the official record of the diet seldom discloses their content. Then, business moved to the final item—the year's taxes. For Ernst's first diet, held in 1641, only a brief note survives:

> The land tax due on Trinity Sunday and the drink tax due at Easter, the Feast of the Cross, and St Lucy's Day is agreed for a further six years, so from every sack of barley eighteen groschen will be paid and from every sack of malt thirteen groschen and six pennies. Vintners shall not pay the drink tax but give the tithe from their wine and brandy.

That was it. In less than a week, Duke Ernst had bored the diet into agreeing to taxes, for six years, without giving anything in return. When the time came in 1647 to reconvene the diet, it was the content of school textbooks that took first place on the agenda. As one commentator later observed of meetings of the diet in a neighbouring part of Saxony, they were 'a farce performed every six years, in which all the actors have to say is "Yes".'[4]

But at least Duke Ernst was still summoning a diet. From the middle years of the seventeenth century, ceremonies of homage in Saxe-Gotha mostly took place at separate events, independently of meetings of the diet, if only because the diet met so infrequently. When it did, commentators often found the event laughable. The overfed deputies just nodded through whatever was put to them, frequently falling asleep. From several days of debate, sessions of the diet were slimmed down to just a few hours of postprandial conversation. Anything important that was thought to need discussion was instead moved to smaller committees of the diet that met behind closed doors in the ruler's palace.

Seckendorff thought diets important. He enjoined the ruler to consult the diet and hear 'the honest opinion and deliberations of his subjects, and although he is not bound by them, he should not lightly reject them, but follow them instead, especially when they are based on good sense'. But diets took time, were expensive to arrange, and their discussions were often leaked to outsiders. So, Seckendorff advised the ruler to proceed where he could by committees, made up of delegates who were chosen by the diets. In fact, Seckendorff's solution was not unwelcome to the diet's members, who were frequently irked by having to listen to so much tedious business. Elsewhere in Central Europe, it was often the diets which took the lead in replacing full sessions with committees.[5]

Seckendorff favoured what we might nowadays call the interventionist or 'big state'. Its purpose was the common good and welfare, and Seckendorff's master, Duke Ernst, took his duties seriously. His colossal but austere palace in Gotha housed administrative offices and a school—even Seckendorff complained that parsimony seeped from its sparse furnishings. Duke Ernst was enthusiastic about health care, unleashing a corps of inspectors to check up on doctors, pharmacies, and midwives, and he cared about morals, appointing commissioners to crack down on 'disgrace and shame' (mostly fornication: adultery in Saxe-Gotha was a capital crime). He also instructed a thorough inventory of the population. Tabulating people by age, occupation, place of residence, income, and property, it was the first comprehensive census of its type in Central Europe. Seckendorff approved. His *German Princely State* has officials everywhere—measuring fields, numbering the books in libraries, listing the population in columns, and appearing unannounced from behind concealed doors.[6]

To fulfil the myriad of tasks necessary for the people's welfare, rulers like Duke Ernst needed a bureaucracy to match. Duke Ernst was lucky in his timing. By the second half of the seventeenth century, states across Central Europe were more capacious, with an administrative machinery that gave them the control he and Seckendorff wanted. In the aftermath of the Thirty Years' War (1618–1648), rulers had vastly expanded their tax-raising powers to pay for new armies, and they had grown their bureaucracies to match. Previously, military contractors or enterprisers had seen to the recruitment of troops in return for the right to raise local taxes. Now, it was the rulers who became the contractors and taxers, raising standing armies that were loyal to them as paymasters. Rulers needed troops to fend off the advances of Louis XIV of France as well as the Swedes, whose marauding from their Baltic strongholds continued into the 1650s. Even Saxe-Gotha, with a population that scarcely exceeded eighty thousand persons, had an army of eight thousand men.

Government in the sense of a civil service was still small. At Seckendorff's time, the central administration of Saxe-Gotha comprised just several dozen officials. But totting up the number of civil servants in the palace is too narrow a measure. As the idea of the state grew, it sucked into itself previously autonomous institutions, making them into agencies of state power. Throughout Central Europe, governments and rulers reformed the universities to churn out bureaucrats. They purged the cities of their independence, reducing their once argumentative councils to 'gentlemen, who just say amen', and they released state officials on the countryside. Englishmen are supposed to have hardly noticed the state until the First World War, when they received their first tax demands and call-up papers. By then, most Central Europeans had been living with it for two centuries or more.[7]

Across Central Europe, the *Amt*, or district office, was from the late seventeenth century onwards the main vehicle of state supervision. Previously recruited from among the provincial nobility, the district officer, or *Amtmann*, was now an appointee of government and usually a trained lawyer drawn from professional classes. In Protestant regions, many were the sons of clergymen. The range of duties they discharged was extraordinary—presiding over suits in civil cases; launching the prosecution of offenders; overseeing road and canal building; checking up on schools, flood defences, and poorhouses; supervising military recruitment, and so on. They drilled deep. Each year in the principality of Hesse-Kassel, they prosecuted about a third of the rural population for violation of the forest and pasturing laws.[8]

In the Holy Roman Empire, only Brandenburg and parts of Pomerania were without *Amt* officers, since the local nobilities there kept hold of appointments in the districts. Everywhere else, the *Amt* pressed forward. So, peasants frequently bypassed the manor courts held by their noble lords to litigate instead before the *Amtmann*. Not only did humbler folk consider him generally fairer, but his court also met at least weekly, providing speedier redress. Less pleasantly, *Amt* officials in Saxe-Gotha were responsible for following up accusations of witchcraft. During Seckendorff's time, they performed this duty with unhealthy enthusiasm, routinely torturing women into confession. In just five years, one *Amtmann* snared no fewer than thirty-eight witches, most of whom he had burnt. The big state is seldom a compassionate one.[9]

The state absorbed the nobility. Throughout Central Europe, noblemen had always filled the main offices of government, and this situation did not change. Rulers' households also grew, gathering hundreds of chamberlains, equerries, and privy councillors and even squads of honorary zookeepers, again drawn mostly from the nobility. Quite where the distinction between court and government service lay was never clear, for the ruler's personal business often overlapped with matters of state. Office space was seldom demarcated either, so the different functionaries collided in the corridors. Rulers across Central Europe built palaces, often modelled on Versailles or the Louvre in

Paris, the wings and floors of which accommodated both professional bureaucrats and courtiers, all vying for preferment in the ruler's and state service.

Along with palaces, household and governmental staff proliferated. Under Duke Ernst's successors in the main line of the house of Gotha, the number of officials working in the central offices of state and palace exploded into the hundreds. In the middle years of the eighteenth century, Duchess Louise Dorothea, the wife of Ernst's great-grandson, included among the sundry household staff who were there just 'for show' (in her words): 17 lord chamberlains, 12 chamberlains, a dozen pages, and 180 mounted guardsmen, dressed like playing cards. Since Duke Ernst's death, the number of governmental departments had doubled. As the duchess observed, 'Counting up the title holders, officials, and servants, who crowd around the throne, it would seem that nearly all the population of Gotha must be in one way or other dependent upon the court.'[10]

The same explosion in palace and governmental personnel is evident throughout Central Europe, but the court and civil service formed only one branch of state employment. Governments needed armies, and, with the decline of the military contractor, they took over the tasks of recruitment, drilling, provisioning, paying, and commanding. Saxe-Gotha had an army that was on paper large, but only because it leased regiments to its neighbours, effectively using its population as an export crop—a 'Holland Regiment' of troops recruited in Saxe-Gotha was continuously on the Dutch payroll from 1692 to 1806. Even so, the Saxe-Gotha officer corps was, like everywhere else in Central Europe, made up almost exclusively of noblemen. Many were from outside the duchy, drawn there by pay and prospects, with a few later moving into Prussian service. But others joined as ensigns and worked their way up the military hierarchy.[11]

Throughout much of Central Europe, the nobility adapted to the big state by becoming part of it. They became officials in government, servants in the ruler's household, and officers in the armed forces. Rulership had become bureaucratized and militarized, proceeding by paperwork, lists, commissions, and district officers. Noblemen were more closely associated with the ruler's person, serving him as chamberlains and generals, but they were still a part of the machinery of state. Many resented it, seeing in it a diminution of their status and liberty. They looked instead to England, where they observed a prosperous and free gentry and a squirearchy that was politically influential and not in state service. The fashionableness in eighteenth-century Central Europe of the English landscape park and fox hunting also embodied an aspiration.[12]

In large parts of the region, the state consumed the nobility. In Hungary and Poland, the nobility consumed the state. For Hungary, this cannot be a precise statement since the kingdom had little apparatus of government to be ingested. The Hungarian chancellery was a letter box in Vienna, which just referred matters to the ruler's privy council or to an overburdened and understaffed Hungarian regency council meeting in Bratislava, while the expansive Hungarian treasury apparatus had real teeth, but little appetite. So, for most of the time, the kingdom was rudderless. Diets met infrequently, roughly once every ten years, and on the back of the flimsy legislation they passed, some revenue was collected.

Real power lay with the county assemblies of noblemen. In the sixteenth and seventeenth centuries, the provincial Hungarian gentry had met in fields and barns, but by the eighteenth century they often had their own permanent county seats—opulent palaces that doubled up as dance halls, stuffed with officials and gilt Baroque splendour. The nobles in the counties were busy too. Meeting in full session several times a year, they regulated local affairs, organized the collection of taxes, and kept order in the countryside. When they were recalcitrant, the government in Vienna imposed its own version of the *Amtmann*—commissars, backed up by troops, who took over the county administration until such a time as the local noblemen fell into line.

In Saxe-Gotha, Seckendorff had made a metaphor of the mystical body of the state. In Hungary, too, noblemen spoke of 'the body of the kingdom' and, more abstractly, of 'membership of the Holy Crown'. But whereas Seckendorff had included all subjects in his description, in

Hungary the nobles believed that they alone constituted the community of the realm. City dwellers were only distantly associated with the body of the kingdom, as an appendage to it, for their rights were fewer than noblemen's, and country folk were entirely outside it. 'Rustics' (as rural labourers were called) were, in the contemporary estimation, failed Hungarians, whose forebears had been deprived of liberty because of their lack of martial courage and their repeated disobedience. The Hungarian nation was a nation of noblemen.

At times, Hungarian noblemen muttered about their descent from chieftains of the Huns, but the myth of Hunnic origins never caught on. It was different in Poland and Lithuania. There, the nobility loudly proclaimed its members' common ancestry in the ancient tribe of Sarmatians, who had wandered across the steppe land of what is now southern Ukraine in the centuries either side of Christ's birth. Even at the time, many Polish and Lithuanian noblemen knew the Sarmatian connection to be false, but it served to unite them in a shared conceit. Both Polish and Lithuanian nobles donned what they said to be Sarmatian dress, sporting sabres, hats with heron feathers, and long crimson coats that were held in place with gaudy silk sashes. They also cultivated so-called Sarmatian haircuts, shaving their heads except for a tuft on the scalp and wearing long moustaches.

Sarmatian styles spilled over to influence military dress, rendering it increasingly exotic. During the last decades of the sixteenth century, the Polish army began to deploy 'winged hussars'—armoured cavalrymen and lancers, draped in wolf and (usually fake) leopard skins, from whose saddles projected wooden-framed wings made of eagle and vulture feathers. The armour of commanders was also striking. In place of plate, they wore a leather jerkin, onto which they riveted semicircular steel scales that overlapped one another. The *karacena* battle dress was deliberately chosen since it was how Roman sculptors had depicted the original Sarmatian warriors. By adopting their scaly armour, Poles were claiming kinship with these lizardmen of antiquity.[13]

Sarmatianism both reflected and reinforced the exceptional rights claimed by noblemen in Poland and Lithuania. Although there were enormous variations of wealth among the nobility, noblemen considered themselves to be legally equal. All were part of the same privileged community, called the noble *szlachta*. (The name derives from the German *Geschlechter*, meaning 'kinsmen' or 'lineages.') Whether rich or poor, members of the *szlachta* stood in the same, immediate relationship to the monarch, as his vassals, and they had identical rights, at least on paper. Polish noblemen advertised these as their 'Golden Liberty'—their freedom from taxes and arbitrary arrest, and their right to serve the king in war. But, from the 1570s, Polish noblemen had another right that they all shared—to decide who should be their king.

The nobility's takeover of the succession followed a familiar pattern. For almost two centuries, ever since 1386, Poland and Lithuania had been ruled by the Jagiellon dynasty, so called after its first king, the Lithuanian Jogaila. Son had succeeded father, and whenever there was a break in the line, a brother had filled in. But in 1572, King Sigismund II died. Syphilitic, gout-stricken, and probably tubercular, Sigismund had failed to produce an heir with any of his three wives. By a cruel quirk of dynastic misfortune, Sigismund was also without brothers, cousins, uncles, and even great-uncles. He was completely the last male of his line. An attempt to fill the void with the French prince Henry of Valois failed—he lasted just six months in Poland before dashing back home to claim the crown of France.

Where biology and commitment failed, the Sejm and the *szlachta* stepped in. As a first step, the Sejm had in 1573 bound Henry of Valois to acknowledge the crown as elective, to govern with a council made up of members of the upper house, and not to make war or levy taxes without the Sejm's consent. With Henry gone, the Sejm went further still. Under pressure from the provincial Sejmiks, the Sejm now summoned every nobleman to Warsaw to vote on who should be king. In 1575, some ten thousand nobles met outside Warsaw and threw their weight behind the Transylvanian prince, Stephen Bathory, thus overturning the decision of the Sejm's upper house that had already voted Emperor Maximilian II as monarch in the hope that he would aid the kingdom in its wars with the Turks.[14]

From then on, all Poland and Lithuania's rulers would be chosen at Election Sejms, where possibly as many as one hundred thousand noblemen would debate and quarrel over the merits of the candidates, and where the monarch they chose would commit himself by oath to the so-called Henrician Articles that Henry of Valois had agreed to. From the 1570s onwards, the nobility's decisive role in choosing the monarch, and binding him to the articles, was feted as the cornerstone of noble freedom. As one nobleman later explained, 'On this basis of free election, the Poles have built this precious construct of Golden Liberty.' Another put it more cynically: 'To lose the right of free election would be to destroy our chief pillar of Liberty. It is Liberty's most profitable marketplace, at which whatever she needs, we succeed in bargaining for.'[15]

The Henrician Articles were Poland and Lithuania's first constitution—they regulated the succession, affirmed the central role of the Sejm in legislation, and bound the ruler to govern in accordance with the laws it made. Commentators struggled to find a word to describe the system of government that the articles had inaugurated. Some explained it as a 'mixed monarchy' or 'balanced power', where the two-chamber Sejm moderated royal rule. Others saw it as a perfect example of Aristotle's political model, since it brought together monarchy, aristocracy, and democracy, albeit one in which more than 90 per cent of the population was voiceless. Even so, all could agree that the best description was a republic (*Rzeczpospolita*): not in the sense of presidential government but of a 'public good' (the literal translation of the Latin *res publica*) or commonwealth, in which power was dispersed throughout the political community for the benefit of the noble nation.

Saxe-Gotha and Poland and Lithuania represent different poles in the story of state building in Central Europe. In the first, the state took over the nobility; in the second, the nobility took over the state. Much of Central Europe veered between the two extremes. In the Austrian lands, public power stayed divided, with the ruler periodically confronting the diets and nobility and hammering out a compromise position in the manner of a treaty, as if between two equally sovereign bodies. In Bavaria and Württemberg, the committees of the diet frequently proved obstructive, retaining a strong control of taxation and hemming in the ruler's capacity for independent action. In Mecklenburg, a single diet continued to meet, ignoring the division of the duchy among heirs. It blocked the establishment of a standing army, deposed one ruler as unfit, and declared most of the territory untaxable. It remained in place until 1918, lingering on, in one historian's words, as 'an antique fossil'.[16]

Despite this variety, throughout Central Europe the balance of power was shifting away from the nobility. The great lords, with estates often several thousand square kilometres in extent, remained influential both in government and in the localities, often having palaces in both the countryside and the capital. But most noblemen withdrew inwards, cultivating like Voltaire's Candide 'their own gardens'. They did so almost literally, embracing a genre of literature that extolled the countryside of their birth, fostering the loyalty to place that underpinned provincial noble identity. They compiled and commissioned 'castle books' that made much of old mounds of stones, listed the deeds of noble families, often reproducing word for word their most important charters, and described the flora and fauna of the countryside in laborious and loving detail.

The greatest of these antiquarian collectors was Johann Weichard von Valvasor (1641–1693) from the duchy of Carniola (Krain), now in Slovenia. Valvasor was a polymath of distinction and sufficiently renowned to be admitted to membership of the Royal Society in London. He also published an account in the society's journal of the mystery of Lake Cerknica in Carniola, which on account of its subterranean chambers filled and emptied over the year with bewildering speed. An enthusiast for hidden knowledge, Valvasor spent several years hunting ghosts and compiled a macabre typology of deaths and of the torments of hell (with illustrations). Valvasor was by his own account a successful alchemist 'without any fraudulence'. While working in Vienna in the 1660s, he made a tincture of gold from lead but, sadly for him, used up more gold in the preparation than the experiment yielded.[17]

Valvasor's greater achievement was his four-volume study, *The Glory of the Duchy of Carniola* (*Die Ehre dess Hertzogthums Crain*), which he published in 1689. Made up of 3,500 large folio pages with more than five hundred engravings, *The Glory of the Duchy* cost so much to print that it ruined Valvasor, obliging him to sell his castle and library at a knock-down price. The contents of the four volumes addressed the history, topography, folklore and folk customs, and the plants and wildlife of Carniola, based on Valvasor's own archival research, travels, and interrogation of the local population. Although he opposed the persecution of witches, Valvasor was a believer in witchcraft and he described how on Christmas Eve good spirits battled near Lake Cerknica with blood-sucking sorceresses. Valvasor also told that the local Slovene peasantry believed the squirrel-like dormice in their woods to be shepherded by the devil, who clicked, whistled, and screeched to drive them through the trees. (They were probably hearing an owl; the edible dormouse, or *glis glis*, remains a Slovene culinary delicacy.)

The antiquarian compilations of enthusiasts like Valvasor extolled the provincial landscape, or *Landschaft*—the countryside in which rural noblemen flourished and which, for many of them, was the horizon of their ambition. Rulers and dynasties might come and go, but the countryside with its ruins and fauna lived on. But Valvasor's age was passing. Already, authority in the countryside was passing from the gentleman to officials like Seckendorff, who saw the countryside as a resource to be inventoried and supervised. The provincial literature exemplified by the *Glory of the Duchy of Carniola* was superseded in turn by a new type of publication known as *Staatenkunde*—long lists of tables and repetitive prose that drily itemized the resources of the countryside, for the purposes of their better exploitation by a burgeoning apparatus of state control.

CHAPTER 21

The Prussian Way: Cemetery Marionettes and the Machine State

I N 1701, CENTRAL EUROPE HAD A NEW KINGDOM, THE FIRST since Emperor Frederick II had raised Bohemia to the status of a monarchy in 1212. This was the kingdom of Prussia. On 18 January that year, another Frederick, the margrave of Brandenburg and duke of Prussia, crowned himself king of Prussia in his audience chamber in the bleak Königsberg Castle on the Baltic coast. The ceremony and the festivities that went with it were probably the most expensive event in Prussian history. It took thirty thousand horses and eighteen hundred carriages just to convey Frederick, his family, and retinue from the Brandenburg capital of Berlin to Königsberg. To pay for his new crown, Frederick levied a special tax on all his subjects, and expended twice his annual income on the accompanying celebrations. It was a waste. The crown was never again used, since Frederick's successors did not bother with coronations. Even at the time, King Frederick's queen, who was crowned after him, found the event tiresome, snorting and sneezing snuff throughout its performance.[1]

How Prussia reached this point may be briefly told. Back in 1525, the grand master of the Teutonic Knights Albrecht of Hohenzollern had embraced Lutheranism, dissolved the order, and, to shore himself up politically, acknowledged the king of Poland as his overlord. Duke Albrecht (ruled 1525–1568) and his descendants adopted as their banner the black eagle, but it was surmounted with an S, in honour of the reigning king, Sigismund I of Poland, and with a crown around its neck, to remind Prussians that they were part of Sigismund's kingdom. But the Prussian Hohenzollern line had swiftly degenerated into insanity. With the Polish king's agreement, Brandenburg's rulers, who were the closest male heirs in the Hohenzollern line, succeeded to the duchy in 1618.

Brandenburg was a hotchpotch of territories. Reaching from the Lower Rhine to the Polish frontier, it had in the words of one of its fifteenth-century rulers 'been scraped and piled together by pilfering and grabbing'. But by deft diplomacy and by successively playing off the Swedes, Poles, and French, Brandenburg emerged from the Thirty Years' War as the second largest territory in the Holy Roman Empire, after the Habsburg lands of Austria and Bohemia. In 1657, the Brandenburg and Prussian ruler Frederick William manoeuvred the Polish king John Casimir into recognizing him as the duchy of Prussia's sovereign. But it belonged to his son to take the logical next step, converting sovereignty into kingship in 1701. Although Frederick's monarchy was just in Prussia, Brandenburg and the rest of the Hohenzollern lands in Central Europe were habitually now called the Kingdom of Prussia.[2]

Ever since 1613 the rulers of Brandenburg had been Calvinists, ruling over a largely Lutheran territory. But King Frederick demonstrated little Calvinist thrift, building palaces with opulent gilded and amber interiors, setting up statues to himself, and transforming Berlin with monumental architecture and paved streets. Frederick's grandson, Frederick II 'the Great' (ruled 1740–1786) would be dismissive of his achievements. King Frederick I had, he explained, mistaken vanity for greatness, and he had 'only desired the crown so hotly because he needed a superficial pretext to justify his weakness for ceremony and his wasteful extravagance.'[3]

King Frederick I's successor, King Frederick William I (ruled 1713–1740), likewise had no time for his father's excesses, except for tobacco and hard alcohol, which he consumed with vigour. Upon coming to power, King Frederick William promptly dismissed two-thirds of the royal household, including the royal chocolate cook and several castrato singers. In his youth, Frederick William had fought in 1709 against the French army of Louis XIV in the bloodbath of the Battle of Malplaquet, and he declared the day to have been the happiest in his life. But as ruler, Frederick William avoided war as much as he could, while doubling the size of his army to make it the fourth largest in Europe. Known even in his own lifetime as 'the sergeant king' since it was his habit to wear a sergeant's uniform, Frederick William applied all the latest military innovations, with daily parades, standardized weaponry, and bandsmen to keep up the troops' morale and pace. Frederick William's drill master instilled discipline with ferocious punishments and by having his troops learn to march in goose step.

The goose step at least served a purpose, since it showed at a glance whether the troops were marching in unison. But Frederick William's quest for abnormally large grenadiers was a pointless conceit, since the men were often disabled as a consequence of their height. Altogether, the king had several thousand of these giants, whom he personally drilled and tried to marry off to equally tall women. All had to be at least 188 centimetres high (6 feet 3 inches), but there were plenty who hit 213 centimetres (7 feet). In order to magnify their appearance, Frederick William gave them tall mitre caps and, we are told, deliberately dressed them in uniforms that were too small. Frederick William himself measured just 160 centimetres (5 feet 3 inches).[4]

Recruitment was vital to building up the Prussian army, but the cost of paying salaries and convincing men to enlist for life was an obstacle. So, in 1733, Frederick William abandoned piecemeal enlistment and embarked instead upon conscription. All men between sixteen and twenty-four were now drafted into their local or canton regiment and trained for two years, after which they became unpaid reservists, with annual refresher courses of several months' duration. Conscription transformed Prussia into a military state, where almost every man became in time a part-time soldier, obliged by law to wear military dress in church and on public occasions. Since new uniforms were issued annually, the previous year's military greatcoats were sold second hand, so almost the entire male population was soon wearing dark blue (*Dunkelblau*). As one wag observed at the time, it was hard to tell whether Prussia was a kingdom with an army, or an army with a kingdom.[5]

In Saxe-Gotha, the civil administration absorbed the nobility; in the kingdom of Prussia, the army swallowed it. King Frederick William made military service an obligation for all young noblemen, instructing his recruiters to be particularly alert to those who were 'good looking, healthy, and possess straight limbs'. By the mid-1720s, there was virtually no noble family in the Hohenzollern lands which had not at some point had a son in the Prussian officer corps. As it was, many of the twenty thousand or so noble or Junker families in the kingdom had insufficient land to pass on to all their heirs, so an army career made sense, but failure to serve was also a crime. The traditional social hierarchies were played out in the army, with noblemen serving as officers and their tenant peasants as the ordinary rank and file.[6]

Although noblemen predominated in the military bureaucracy and the administration of the royal estates, the civil service was the preserve of the urban middle class. During the late seventeenth and the eighteenth century, Prussia's rulers centralized the civil service, expanding it to fill the gap left by the kingdom's increasingly powerless diets, which had previously undertaken most of the work of tax assessment and collection. Even so, the civilian bureaucracy was small. Just three thousand civil servants looked after a population of 2.25 million, a ratio of 1:750. (In Britain, by contrast, the ratio was 1:500.) But the compromise with the nobility meant that noblemen continued as before to perform for free much of the daily routine of local administration, with the central administration only having a supervisory role.[7]

Although small, the civilian administration dug deep. Trained in cameral science at the universities of Königsberg and Halle, Prussian bureaucrats regulated through decrees issued in the name of the king that were read to church congregations every Sunday. When they were not instructing on everything from the upkeep of roads to food prices, they taxed. Most notoriously, the Prussian civil service employed some four hundred military veterans as 'sniffers' (*Schnüffler*), whose task was to smell out unlicensed coffee grinding. Several dozen officials also pounced on gentlemen in the street, pulling off their wigs to check that the insides bore the stamp showing that the wearers had paid the requisite tax on the headpiece.

King Frederick William was a brute, who terrorized even his friends because he thought it funny. He saw nothing odd in presiding over the public garrotting of a civil servant who had neglected his duties and, on the same day, kneeling to pray with his entire court before a group of Protestant refugees. His son and successor, Frederick II, was generous in his tribute to him. To keep his subjects happy and improve the army and administration, Frederick explained, his father had 'avoided war that he might not be disturbed in the pursuit of plans so excellent. By these means, he travelled silently towards grandeur, without awakening the envy of monarchs.' As it turned out, the young Frederick would be quite different.[8]

On 31 May 1740, Frederick II succeeded to the throne on the death of his father. On 16 December, he invaded the wealthy province of Silesia (then a part of Habsburg Bohemia), driving out the Habsburg forces there in just seven weeks. Frederick had no dynastic claim to Silesia, although he tasked his officials to find one. But the Habsburg possessions in Central Europe were vulnerable. In October 1740, Emperor Charles VI had died, leaving only a daughter, the young Maria Theresa (ruled 1740–1780). For almost four decades, Charles had sought to ensure the right of a female Habsburg to succeed him. First, he had in the so-called Pragmatic Sanction of 1713 unified the inheritance laws in all his lands to allow a woman ruler, declaring his territories to be 'separate and indivisible'. Second, he had convinced the leading sovereigns of Europe to endorse the arrangement, including Frederick William of Prussia, back in 1726. But this mattered not a jot to Frederick II. He correctly guessed that the international guarantees of the Pragmatic Sanction were paper thin and took his chance.

Frederick's seizure of Silesia led to three wars between Prussia and the Habsburgs (1740–1742, 1744–1745, 1756–1763), which spilled over into a global war fought between their respective allies. But Frederick held onto the province, incorporating it into Prussia, and earning for himself the sobriquet of 'the Great'. Not only did Frederick keep the Habsburgs in check, but he also withstood the international coalition that Maria Theresa organized against him, which drew in France, Russia, Sweden, Saxony, and most of the princes of the Holy Roman Empire. His only halfway reliable ally was Britain, which was fighting its own war with the French in North America. At critical moments, British loans were all Frederick had to keep Prussia financially afloat. Several times Frederick was saved from disaster either by his enemies' failure to follow up a victory or by the timely death of an adversary. But the price of survival was high. The war fought between 1756 and 1763 cost Frederick's army 120 generals, 1,500 officers, and 100,000 men.

Frederick's daring and Prussia's endurance were a challenge to all Central Europe. As well as fighting him, his enemies copied him. In the Habsburg lands, Maria Theresa introduced in 1770 a canton system of military recruitment modelled on the Prussian. It was accompanied by a massive statistical exercise that listed households, numbered homes, and forced all adults to carry identification cards. Other states followed, either adopting the same model of conscription (as in Baden) or, at the very least, enlarging their armies. Even the tiny county of Schaumburg-Lippe in the northwest of the empire, with a population of just 20,000 people, managed to field an army of 1,200 men.[9]

It was the same in administration. Starting in the 1740s, Maria Theresa began the centralization of government in the Habsburg lands, imitating Prussian administrative methods. Militarization and bureaucracy went hand in hand—necessarily so, since armies had to be paid for and civil servants were needed to collect and administer money. By the end of Maria Theresa's reign, roughly a half of all civil servants in Vienna were employed in the government audit and accounting departments. The smaller principalities followed. Best known for its episcopal palace, with its grand staircase and massive ceiling frescoes, the prince-bishop's Würzburg Residence was also a military and administrative hub, overseeing a civil service of three thousand officials. Today's pretty Würzburg, a UNESCO World Heritage Site, was in the eighteenth century one of Central Europe's most heavily governed territories.[10]

In seeking to keep up with Prussia, rulers became increasingly imitative of it. As a consequence, many of the ideas which we associate with the Enlightenment were transported through the Prussian connection to the rest of Central Europe. There they fused with Cameralism, the Roman Law tradition, and the ruler's established right to patrol the morals of subjects, to yield an expansive doctrine of state power. In Britain and North America, the Enlightenment tended towards the extension of popular sovereignty, curbs on government, and the enlargement of individual liberty and of the rights of the citizen. In Central Europe, the Enlightenment tended towards the reverse—towards regulation and the subjection of the individual to the common good, as the ruler understood it to be. As one of the main exponents of the Central European Enlightenment put it: 'All the duties of peoples and subjects may be reduced to the formula: to promote all the ways and means adopted by the ruler for their happiness, by their obedience, fidelity, and diligence.'

Enlightenment thinkers rejected tradition and religion as intellectual starting points. As one of Central Europe's earliest Enlightenment philosophers put it: 'Clear your mind of everything. Put aside everything you trust in, for prior belief is the source of all errors.' Instead, Enlightenment thinkers tried to base their philosophies on what could be known for sure and what might be deduced rationally from it. In considering the state and society, philosophers in Central Europe subscribed overwhelmingly to the theory of Natural Law. Natural Law theory rested on two principles, both of which fed into the Central European Enlightenment. The first was that society and sociability were implicit in the human condition. The second was that government existed for the benefit of society—kings did not rule because God had appointed them; their dominion was for a purpose that lay in the society of their subjects. From this, it followed that rulers should have as their goal the welfare of subjects.[11]

The most influential Central European philosopher of the eighteenth century went even further. Christian Wolff (lived 1679–1754) was a professor at the Prussian university of Halle and Frederick II's favourite German thinker. Wolff explained his understanding of Natural Law in thirty volumes that he wrote first in German and then translated into Latin to give them an international audience. At the heart of Wolff's philosophy was the *Glückseligkeit*, or 'bliss' of subjects. Good government should strive to this end by promoting subjects' peace, security, and material sufficiency. And in place of the natural sociability of mankind, Wolff posited the human drive towards 'completedness' (*Vollkommenheit*) and even perfection. It was the business of government to facilitate and direct this impulse, by 'doing everything that promotes the common good'.[12]

Frederick II was critical of philosophers' comprehensive solutions, affirming that it was his wish that 'in my territories everyone may pray and fornicate as they see fit.' For the Prussian philosopher Immanuel Kant, the idea that the state should intervene to make people happy according to its own definition of happiness amounted to 'the worst conceivable despotism'. Like the American Founding Fathers, Kant believed that it was government's duty to let individuals find their own happiness, providing it did not infringe on anyone else's. But the capacious philosophy of Natural Law became a bureaucrats' charter, justifying all manner of top-down interventions for the benefit of society and subjects alike. And presiding at the top of the administrative hierarchy was the ruler, whom Frederick II described as the chief civil servant or 'first servant of the state'.[13]

Habsburg officials found Natural Law theory compelling, publishing manuals of good governance that taught that the ultimate end of the state was the common good and general happiness, and that individuals were only free to the extent that the law allowed. The opening paragraphs of the most celebrated of these textbooks spoke of the state as a 'moral person' and explained that private interests should be limited by the public good and that the welfare of the parts should be considered secondary to the whole. Spurred on by her advisers, the Empress Maria Theresa was a prodigious meddler, publishing decrees on everything from the advertisements in apothecaries' shop windows to the correct blowing of horns, the design of tobacco pipes, and the qualifications needed to visit a library. Her interference in private lives extended to separating Protestant children from their parents in order to save their souls and unleashing a Chastity Commission on the streets of Vienna to crack down on immorality.[14]

But her son and successor, Emperor Joseph II (ruled 1780–1790), took matters a step further—regulating the use of candles in churches (to preserve beeswax), instructing coffins to have false bottoms so that they could be reused (to save on wood), forbidding the kissing of the corpse at funerals (to prevent contagion), and so on. Notoriously, in the early 1780s Joseph II closed down seven hundred monasteries and nunneries because he considered them not to perform any useful service. His decree, the Edict on Idle Institutions, terminated the vocations of fourteen thousand monks and nuns. In the 1770s, the last decade of her reign, Maria Theresa published roughly a hundred decrees a year. Under Joseph II, the number increased more than sevenfold. The compendium of his decrees, published at the end of his reign, runs to eighteen stout volumes.

It was the same elsewhere in Central Europe. Indeed, the prize for overregulation that historians so frequently award to Emperor Joseph II surely belongs to Karl Theodor of the Palatinate, who in just thirty-five years (1742–1777) published 120,000 decrees, including bizarre rules on the five acceptable ways to measure the length of a fish. By the end of the century, officials throughout Central Europe had lost track of what they were supposed to be doing and so they commissioned collections of decrees, with indexes and cross-referencing. Even the minor Swiss canton of Aargau, with a population of little more than one hundred thousand people in 1800, managed six hefty volumes of 'all the laws and decrees that are in force'. A few of the greater territories succeeded in weaving codes that brought the laws together in the hope of making them intelligible, starting in 1794 with the Prussian *General Land Law* (*Allgemeines Landrecht*). Running to nineteen thousand separate articles, the Prussian code was only slightly less unwieldy than the decrees it replaced.

In attempting to comprehend the size and power of the new apparatus of state in Central Europe, writers tried to find analogies. The new science of anatomy and the study of disease gave a range of possibilities, with commentators likening the state either to the perfect human body or to an overgrown and deformed organism. Others found in the laws of physics justification for organizing human affairs around a set of perpetual rules. The principles of geometry, already a feature of garden design and architecture, prompted writers to consider the state as a work of art. Gradually, though, one image prevailed—the idea of the machine.[15]

Until the eighteenth century, the largest machine familiar to people in Central Europe was the watermill. When moored to riverbanks, watermills could turn as many as half a dozen wheels, while mills sited beside streams often drove hammers, saws, and bellows as well as turning millstones. Massive though they were, watermills had nothing on steam pumps. Operating in northern Hungary from as early as the 1720s, the first steam engines were used to pump water from mines. But aristocrats also put them to work to power fountains or exhibited them as wondrous items in pavilions. With their pistons moving beams that sometimes stood fifteen metres high, the earliest so-called fire machines were objects of both terror and awe.[16]

Traditionally powered engines were also showing an increased sophistication and application. They had to. Even when assembled in blocks, the tall obelisks that were fashionable in landscape parks demanded a massive apparatus and network of pulleys to put them into position. Water-powered looms and spinning mules, installed across Central Europe in the last decades of the eighteenth century, were equally demanding of technical ingenuity. Successive publications celebrated their design and energy, prompting a flood of Central European engineers to Great Britain, to see at first hand the latest mechanical innovations and steal their plans.[17]

But the most exciting technical innovation of the eighteenth century was the automaton, which was a counterfeit human, powered by clockwork, who moved and acted as if a real person. There were automatons that served at table or banged tambourines or played the flute: albeit at an imperfect pitch, as one of Frederick II's advisers complained. A few were frauds, like the Turkish chess player, whose movements were secretly directed by a small person hidden inside the apparatus. Cheating aside, the most technically accomplished automata were the watchmaker Pierre Jaquet-Droz's mechanical children, constructed in the 1770s in the Hohenzollern principality of Neuenburg (Neuchâtel, now in Switzerland). Incredibly, Jaquet-Droz's 'child writer' could be programmed with up to forty characters to pen letters on the operator's behalf.[18]

From this, it was not hard to believe that automata might become human beings or that human beings were actually automata. The French philosopher and physician La Mettrie put it starkly in his *L'Homme-Machine* (*Man, the Machine*, 1748)—'The human body is a machine which winds itself up, a living picture of perpetual motion.' Exiled from France for denying the existence of the soul, La Mettrie was welcomed in Prussia by King Frederick II and installed in the royal palace of Sanssouci outside Berlin as one of Frederick's personal doctors. The writer Jean Paul (J. P. F. Richter, 1763–1825) built on La Mettrie's imaginings, conjuring up an image of society ladies replaced by machines who, too, could gossip and play cards. Jean Paul went further. He saw the entire bureaucratic apparatus of the state as one vast impersonal machine, presided over by people who act as automatons, 'in a vain attempt to at least appear like artificial machines, since unfortunately they cannot be natural machines.'[19]

But the most chilling vision was Bonaventura's, whose real name remains a mystery. In Bonaventura's *Nightwatches* (*Nachtwachen*, 1804), the narrator is a hallucinating night watchman who presides over the cemetery and its adjoining streets. His fevered brain sees marionettes who think they are human, and human beings who act as if marionettes. On one of his rounds, the watchman sneaks into a house, where he spies a creature working through papers at a desk:

At the start, I remained in doubt whether it was a human being or a mechanical figure, so very much was everything human in it erased . . . for everything passionate and sympathetic was extinguished on its cold wooden forehead and the marionette sat lifelessly erect. Now the invisible wire was pulled, and the fingers clicked, grasped the pen, and signed three papers in a row; I peered more acutely—they were death warrants.[20]

The watchman confounds the judge by showing him the adultery of his wife, which demands the death sentence too. But Bonaventura and Jean Paul were straws in the wind. Rulers, civil servants, magistrates, and university teachers saw the machine as an aspiration and not as a threat. Its rhythms and predictability showed what the state should be—a perfectly running clockwork of cogs and springs.

The most complete description of the state as a machine was given in 1758 by J. H. G. Justi, at that time a servant of the Danish king but soon to move to Prussian employment (where he ended up in jail for embezzlement):

A properly constructed state must be exactly analogous to a machine, in which all the wheels and gears are precisely adjusted to one another; and the ruler must be the foreman, the mainspring or the soul—if one may use the expression—which sets everything in motion.[21]

Justi was not alone. Frederick II likened the state to a pocket watch and, in a deliberately provocative piece (published in 1757 under a pseudonym), he wrote that 'our entire state is also really a machine . . . what gives it strength and movement is force.' The French politician and libertine the Comte de Mirabeau agreed that Frederick's Prussia was 'a great and beautiful machine . . . it has outstanding qualities: the spirit of order and regularity adheres to it.' During the second half of the eighteenth century, the machine metaphor became the usual way

of describing the state in Central Europe, squeezing out (and sometimes combining uneasily with) the older metaphor, going back to
Plato, that saw the state as analogous to the human body.[22]

In the seventeenth and early eighteenth centuries, the state had
absorbed the nobility, defanging its diets and making nobles into
the servants of government, provincial officials, and household staff.
Now, the state was swallowing society, through regulation, taxation,
and conscription, and converting subjects into the ratchets and wheels
of its apparatus. Its takeover of society and the substitution of human relationships with mechanical ones was the stuff of Bonaventura's
nightmares, but no less acutely felt at the time by other observers,
who decried its 'abstract rationalism', artificiality, and despotism. For
the influential German philosopher Johann Gottfried Herder (1744–
1803), the machine state replaced freedom with 'happiness in functioning as insensible cogs in a perfect machine'. On the one hand,
Herder explained, the machine state bound all to its service, but on the
other, it made society impossible by treating subjects as instruments,
with neither free will nor what he called *Sympathie*—the capacity to
create the social relationships upon which a community is founded.[23]

Across Europe, there had been developing in the eighteenth century what historians now like to call a 'public sphere' or 'civil society',
where subjects were free to exchange ideas and arrive at shared conclusions. In the Netherlands, France, and Britain, the public sphere was
highly developed and sustained by newspapers, periodicals, libraries,
salons, clubs, academies, and universities. Print and conversation lay
at its heart, as well as a spirit of egalitarianism that allowed women to
have a voice. In Central Europe, by contrast, the public sphere was
anaemic for most of the eighteenth century. This was partly on account
of the smallness of most of its cities, which meant that Central Europe
was slow to develop a middle class of readers, salon-goers, and conver-
sationalists. But it was also due to censorship which limited what could
be read and thus talked about, at least in public.

Censorship was ubiquitous, although uneven. In Frankfurt, an Imperial Book Commission lazily monitored books for sale at the annual

fair, occasionally organizing book burnings. In a few places, like Hamburg, Saxe-Gotha, and Saxony, there were almost no controls at all. But in Bavaria and the Habsburg lands, censorship was tough. A new Bavarian index of forbidden books, imposed in 1770, caught most French philosophers, anything smelling of Protestantism, books on magic and divination, and illustrated versions of Boccaccio's mid-fourteenth-century *Decameron*. But at least the list was small, running to no more than a hundred items. By contrast, in the Habsburg lands, Maria Theresa's censorship commission blacklisted almost five thousand works, banning anything that deviated from Catholic orthodoxy, was written by Voltaire or Rousseau, or was considered pornographic or contentious. As one acute observer put it, censorship made Austria a 'kingdom of the dead', where only old and venerable literature was allowed to circulate.[24]

In the Habsburg lands, theatre and concertgoing took the place of the literary salon, providing spaces where the educated and the fashionable could meet and converse, without trespassing into the controversial realms of politics and philosophy. Vienna's musical life was the most outstanding in Central Europe, supporting composers like Gluck, Haydn, and Mozart, and patronized by both the imperial court and great aristocratic families with palaces in the capital. It was in Vienna that audiences first learned to listen to music, rather than hearing it only as an accompaniment to firework displays and spectacular operatic performances. The theatre was less sophisticated, relying on imported French and Italian productions and on traditional farces featuring the harlequin 'Jack Sausage' ('Hanswurst'), where sexual innuendo combined with trouser-dropping to the amusement, we are told, of audiences of all ranks.[25]

Across a large part of Central Europe, the developing public sphere lived underground—almost literally so, in clubs and societies that met in secret, often in cask-lined cellars. The German philosopher Immanuel Kant found this entirely predictable. As he explained: 'The spirit of freedom is the effective cause of all secret societies. For it is a natural vocation of man to communicate with his fellows . . . secret societies would disappear if freedom were encouraged.' But there was more to it than that. Secret societies also picked up on the contemporary fascination with ancient Egypt, with knowledge hidden in hieroglyphs, rites of initiation as a preliminary to illumination, and a belief in hidden forces that only an adept could master. As the German playwright, poet, and novelist Johann Wolfgang von Goethe (1749–1832) observed, mesmerism and the belief that the human body might be influenced by magnets held by a master in a purple robe exemplified a widespread fascination with the performance of bogus mysteries.[26]

Freemasonry brought these trends together. In Central Europe, there was not one freemasonry but many, with the so-called Strict Observance the most popular—unsurprisingly so, since (unlike mainstream British freemasonry) it had several dozen degrees or grades, fancy titles that recollected the Knights Templar, and the conspiratorial appeal of being directed by 'Unknown Masters'. A few freemasonic groups, like the Rosicrucians, were dedicated to alchemy; others, like the Bavarian Illuminati, aimed to infiltrate government to promote a reforming agenda in politics. Beyond their love of passwords and secret ceremonies, what united freemasons was, in one contemporary description, their commitment 'to virtue, religion, peacefulness, welfare, and the pure joy of mankind'. But freemasons also saw themselves as members of a virtuous elite, distinguished by their moral rectitude, talent, and superior knowledge.[27]

Freemasonry had at its height more than four hundred lodges across the empire. The initiation of German rulers into the mysteries of the mason's craft—not least Frederick II of Prussia—gave it a respectability that outweighed the papal prohibitions of 1738 and 1751. It was the same in Poland, where King Stanisław Poniatowski (ruled 1764–1795) was also a freemason, along with (it would seem) the bishop of Poznań and the archbishop of Gniezno. By the 1780s, Warsaw had almost thirty lodges and a thousand freemasons. In the Habsburg lands, freemasonry's success was blunted by the outright opposition of Maria Theresa, who even sent in troops to break up lodge meetings. So, in 1780, Vienna had just six lodges with two hundred members in all. All this changed with Maria Theresa's death in 1780 and her son Joseph II's advent to power.[28]

Maria Theresa had never been happy with the Enlightenment, distrusting its questioning of religious precepts and of traditions. She remained unhealthily intolerant of difference, rounding up Gypsies for deportation and exiling Jews from Prague in 1745 and thirty years later from Vienna. When it came to negotiating with the Jewish bankers who kept her afloat, she did so from behind a screen. Her Criminal Code of 1768, the so-called *Nemesis Theresiana*, not only retained torture but also included gruesome diagrams showing the best instruments for inflicting pain during interrogation and how to use them properly. It was only under the influence of her son Joseph that she finally abolished torture in 1776.

Joseph was personally devout, but he was questioning of accepted institutions unless they could prove their worth and of bans on books and people. Starting after his mother's death in 1780, Joseph decreed freedom of worship and removed most of the disabilities on Jews and Protestants. It was the same with censorship. In the same year, Joseph II cancelled almost all restrictions on publishing and, in a masterstroke, replaced the bishop of Worms as head of the Imperial Book Commission in Frankfurt with the German distributor of the pornographic novel *Fanny Hill* (*Fille de joie*). All at once, Vienna and the main Habsburg cities had newspapers and periodicals over which people might converse, picking up and exchanging new ideas. Coffee shops were a favoured venue for discussion, swelling both in number and in size—there were in the 1780s no fewer than seventy in Vienna alone. Although Joseph II regarded freemasonry's rituals as mumbo-jumbo (*Gaukelei*), lodges burgeoned on the back of the new freedoms. By 1785, there were almost seventy lodges meeting across the Habsburg lands and seven hundred freemasons in Vienna alone.

But freemasonry in Central Europe could never act as the counterweight to government and the state, or as the foundation for a civil society and public sphere that might challenge the established order. The educated classes on which freemasonry drew for its membership were overwhelmingly employees of government. About a half of freemasons in the Berlin and Prussian lodges were either civil servants or army officers. Roughly the same proportion holds for the Habsburg lands too, where most of Maria Theresa's ministers were secretly freemasons, while in Bavaria nearly all the members of the duke's censorship commission belonged to the Illuminati. Even in far-off Transylvania, of the 279 freemasons listed between 1767 and 1790 as members of Sibiu's Three Water-Lilies Lodge, 86 were army officers and 110 were officials in the provincial administration.[29]

At first sight, freemasonry in Central Europe may seem to resemble what one historian has called 'a school of civic responsibility', and the lodges look like harbingers of a new public sphere and civil society that was separate to the state. But on closer examination, freemasonry was still tied to the state, drawing its membership from state employees serving in either the administration or the army. In their internal organization, the lodges even mimicked the bureaucracy, with the higher grades going in the main to the more important state servants. Freemasonry reinforced the bureaucratic, top-down management of society. But more than that, it added to the conviction that change was best introduced from above, by the masonic men of virtue who were now charged with operating the machine of state.[30]

CHAPTER 22

Dissecting Europe's Orang-utan: The Partitions of Poland and Lithuania

THE COMBINED KINGDOM AND GRAND DUCHY OF POLAND AND Lithuania had not kept up. By the eighteenth century, governments throughout Central Europe had massively expanded their armies and bureaucracies. They had disciplined their nobilities by pressing them into state service, tamed their countries' diets, and eliminated many of the obstacles that stood in the way of efficient management. Almost everywhere, legislation was now done by decree, not by agreement with the privileged orders. The French philosopher Montesquieu (1689–1755) saw this keenly. Across Europe, he explained, the 'intermediary powers' (*pouvoirs intermédiaires*) that had kept government in check and maintained a spirit of freedom had been either overthrown or diminished. Without the counteracting political power exercised by nobilities, city magistrates, and the clergy, monarchical despotism flourished.

In Poland and Lithuania, Montesquieu saw an exception. The combined state had preserved its historic constitution inherited from the Middle Ages, so much so that it gave 'an accurate idea of the Europe of bygone times'. Montesquieu described this mostly by reference to conditions on the land and to the oppression of serfs by their landlords, but (as Montesquieu also observed) its institutions were equally a throwback to the past. Uniquely in Central Europe, the nobility still held power in Poland and Lithuania. Its privileges, gathered in the course of the fifteenth and sixteenth centuries, not only remained intact but also had grown. So too had the powers of the Sejm, which the nobility dominated. As their representatives were

311

fond of explaining, they lived in a 'noble democracy' and had done for centuries.[1]

Back in the 1570s, the Sejm had gathered massive rights through the Henrician Articles, both controlling a large swathe of policy and, through the right of election, deciding on who should be monarch. Election Sejms, often attended by tens of thousands of noblemen, continued to be a feature of Polish and Lithuanian politics during the seventeenth and eighteenth centuries. Every time the massed noblemen met to choose a ruler, their deputies drew up fresh conditions to which they bound the successful candidate: to provide bursaries out of his own pocket so that noblemen's sons could study abroad; to repair the border forts; to pay for a Baltic fleet, and so on. Yet, the Sejm lived in constant dread of the monarch using what powers he had left to impose autocratic rule. So, the Sejm restricted the ruler's authority, depriving him of taxes, an army, and the capacity to have a foreign policy through the appointment of permanent ambassadors abroad.

But having disabled the king, the Sejm showed itself incapable of wielding power. Sejm procedures were never less than shambolic. Notoriously, a single deputy could void all the legislation approved by the Sejm by wielding his veto, usually by shouting out in the assembly, '*Nie poswalam!*' ('I don't allow it!'). In fact, he did not even need to be present, since it was enough that he registered his protest in writing. From the veto's first use in 1652 until the end of independent Poland and Lithuania in 1795, two-thirds of meetings of the Sejm were broken up either by a deputy's veto or by filibustering, when a group of deputies took it in turn to give day-long speeches, so blocking the passage of legislation. It was the same at the level of the provincial assemblies or Sejmiks, where the deputies wielded their power of veto with equal frequency and enthusiasm.

The 'free veto' (or *liberum veto*) was extolled by the Polish and Lithuanian nobility as the embodiment of their freedom. As the author of a popular treatise written at the start of the eighteenth century explained, 'The right of veto is the particular distinction of the Polish nobility and a pillar of its liberty.' He went on: 'Should it be removed, freedom will readily perish, and the nobility will be levelled in its rights with the nobility of other states, which live under absolute rule.' This was not entirely absurd. The ruler still had extensive powers of patronage and could build support among the nobility by giving away lucrative offices, chunks of royal land, and perhaps most importantly plum positions in the Church, over which the monarch had the right of appointment. Many noblemen feared that an unscrupulous ruler could buy himself a majority in the Sejm. As they saw it, the veto was a check that allowed a single virtuous deputy to stand in the way of a Sejm that had been bribed and manipulated by a devious monarch.[2]

Foreign commentators found Polish and Lithuanian politics bewildering. One French traveller summed up the opinion of many: 'The government of Poland, its constitution, the way they hold elections and run the diets is so absurd that the country cannot survive.' Yet, extraordinarily, it managed to do so. Poland and Lithuania weathered the crisis or 'Deluge' of the 1650s, when in the wake of Khmelnytsky's Cossack revolt, Russian, Swedish, Transylvanian, and Ottoman armies invaded their space. They endured, too, the disaster of the Great Northern War (1700–1721), when Poland and Lithuania were caught between the hammer of Charles XII of Sweden and the anvil of Russia's Peter the Great.[3]

The Deluge alone probably cost the kingdom and grand duchy a quarter to a third of their overall population, but the lessons of military defeat were soon forgotten. Not only had Poland and Lithuania survived, but just a few decades later, in 1683, King Jan Sobieski had also led his troops to a stunning victory against the Ottoman Turks outside Vienna. For most Polish and Lithuanian noblemen, Sobieski's achievement justified keeping everything the way it was. But they forgot the aftermath of Sobieski's campaign. With insufficient funds voted by the Sejm and with only antiquated artillery, Sobieski's advance north of the Black Sea faltered before the walls of the great redoubt at Kamianets-Podilskyi (now in western Ukraine). The Sejm was unwilling to fund an army more than twenty thousand strong or pay for its modernization, even though Poland and Lithuania's neighbours were increasingly mounting armies of a hundred thousand or more well-equipped troops.

When electing the ruler, the Sejm preferred foreign candidates. It was not just that they came with larger bribes, although this helped. To begin with, the nobility was convinced that a Swedish ruler, drawn from the house of Vasa, would help them bolster and then recover Poland's possessions in the Baltic province of Livonia. Pursuing this goal, the three Vasa kings, who ruled Poland and Lithuania from 1587 to 1668, dragged the kingdom and grand duchy into a succession of ultimately disastrous wars. But, from the end of the seventeenth century onwards, foreign powers were increasingly the choosers and not the chosen. So when Jan Sobieski died in 1696, two rival factions, backed respectively by the French on one side and the Habsburgs and Russians on the other, elected two different kings. The Habsburg and Russian candidate, the duke or elector of Saxony, won the day, since he was the first to march his troops into Cracow and Warsaw, while his French opponent sent a flotilla to bob uselessly on the Baltic outside Gdańsk.

The elector of Saxony, subsequently King Augustus II (1697–1706, 1709–1733), was big in every way except politically: as his dates indicate, he was even deposed for several years during his reign. Weighing in by the time of his death at 110 kilograms, Augustus II was strong enough to snap horseshoes in half with his bare hands. His munificence was legendary. Dresden owes its architectural splendours mainly to his patronage, but Augustus built palaces across Poland too, most notably in and around Warsaw. Augustus's sexual appetite was equally enormous. Although it is implausible that he sired more than three hundred bastards, it is a comment on Augustus II's reputation that the sum could still be believed. He died, typically enough, after a prolonged drinking bout. His final words were: 'My whole life has been an unceasing sin; God have mercy upon me.'[4]

Augustus II's death in 1733 was predictably followed by a split in the Election Sejm. The French-backed Stanisław Leszczyński, whose daughter was married to King Louis XV of France, won a majority. But Augustus II's son and heir, Augustus III, had the support of Empress

Anna of Russia, and her soldiers were the more numerous. Even so, a French fleet disembarked troops near Gdańsk to prop up Louis XV's candidate. It was the first time in history that French and Russian troops faced one another on the field, and it was a victory for the Russians. Leszczyński fled to France, where he (or more probably a ghost writer in his service) drafted a penetrating analysis of all that was wrong in his homeland, denouncing in over three hundred pages the misuse of the veto, the oppression of the peasantry, and the privileges of the nobility.

Leszczyński's *A Free Voice* (*Głos wolny*, 1743) was typical of a new and flourishing political literature in Poland that urged the thorough reform of the country's institutions. As one group of nobles explained to the French ambassador in 1732, the problem was that a weak Poland and Lithuania posed no threat and 'that the interest of Europe requires that Poland's present form of government should continue, lest any of the neighbouring princes annex it'. So, the country's antique constitution and Russia's overweening influence went unchallenged. Russian armies crossed its territory freely, treating the countryside in a favourite phrase of historians as a 'wayside inn'. On Augustus III's death in 1763, the inevitable followed. Fourteen thousand Russian troops gathered outside Warsaw on behalf of the new Russian empress Catherine the Great (ruled 1762–1796) to make sure that her candidate was elected, who just happened to be Catherine's former lover, Count Stanisław Poniatowski. He was, Catherine explained to Frederick II of Prussia, 'a pawn that suits our mutual interests'. Pathetically, Stanisław imagined that he might one day marry Catherine.[5]

At his coronation in 1764, Stanisław Poniatowski took the title of August to signify that he, like the Roman emperor Caesar Augustus, would restore the greatness of Poland and Lithuania. He had the backing of several of the most important magnate families, most importantly the Czartoryskis, who had over the preceding decades taken advantage of the political chaos to carve out statelets of their own, with their own mini armies, diplomats, and retinues of noble clients. The Czartoryskis supported the new king's attempts at reform and, under pressure from Catherine the Great, the religious guarantees he gave to Orthodox and Protestant believers—born Sophie of Anhalt-Zerbst, Catherine had been brought up a Lutheran and she had influential Protestant advisers.[6]

But this was too much for many noblemen, who perceived a double threat both to the Catholic religion and to liberty. In 1768, some ten thousand nobles, united in the so-called Confederation of Bar, took up arms against King Stanisław Poniatowski. In the confusion, peasant rebellions broke out across Poland and Lithuania, while Cossacks and Orthodox believers in Polish Ukraine recommenced their murderous rampages against the Catholic and Uniate clergy and Jews. Ingeniously, the confederates turned to the Genevan philosopher Jean-Jacques Rousseau for support. Rousseau duly penned a manifesto that took their side by recommending the preservation of 'national institutions which shape the genius, the character, the tastes and the manners of a people', among which he included a watered-down version of the veto. But even he confessed that 'it is hard to understand how a state so strangely constituted has been able to last so long.' As it turned out, it would not last much longer.[7]

Maria Theresa had survived the onslaught that followed her accession in 1740. After more than two decades of warfare, she had not recovered more than a strip of Silesia, but she had kept her throne. More than this, she had in 1745 contrived to have her husband, Francis Stephen of Lorraine, elected Holy Roman Emperor, giving her the title of empress. Maria Theresa bore Francis Stephen thirteen children who survived to adulthood. By her efforts, the Habsburg dynasty, which had in the 1730s seemed on the edge of extinction, was not only replenished but also, through the imperial connection, back at the centre of Central European politics. It was an astonishing recovery.

But beneath the homely façade she cultivated, Maria Theresa was predatory. Once she had formally made peace with Frederick II of Prussia in 1763, finally acknowledging Silesia's loss, Maria Theresa was alert for territories to compensate. The Ottoman Empire offered good pickings. Some of her less cautious advisers egged her on, pressing her to establish 'a true Roman Empire' by annexing Macedonia, Albania, and the Peloponnese, after which she would be known as Empress of the West. As it turned out, Maria Theresa's schemes for grabbing a part of the Ottoman lands yielded her a lesser prize—ten thousand square kilometres of desolate woodland on the edge of the Carpathians, which Austrian troops occupied in 1774. Lying between Transylvania and Poland, in what had previously been the Turkish satellite principality of Moldavia, the territory lacked at first a name, until it was decided to use the Polish name for 'land of the beech trees', or Bukovina, even though the majority population was Romanian.[8]

As early as the mid-1760s, Maria Theresa also had her eyes on Poland and she began having her court historians collect the evidence that parts of Poland actually belonged by right to Hungary. In fact, the proof was not hard to find since Hungary's kings had back in the fifteenth century pawned to Poland a chunk of land that now lies in the shadow of the High Tatra Mountains of Slovakia. Without thinking to redeem the pledge, the empress occupied the territory in 1769. Using the excuse that Polish troops regularly trespassed across the border onto Hungarian soil, Maria Theresa consented in 1770 to a fence for demarcation purposes between Austria and Poland, which just happened to enclose a hundred Polish villages and two salt mines.

Prussia was also eager to expand into Poland. The historic duchy of Prussia was divided from Brandenburg by a wedge of territory, in places up to four hundred kilometres wide. Until 1466, this had all belonged to the Teutonic Order, but following their defeat the knights had ceded it to Poland. For more than a century, Prussia's rulers had plotted its return and nibbled away at outposts, prompting Frederick II's observation that Poland should be eaten 'like an artichoke, leaf by leaf'. But Russia was the biggest player. For most of the century, Poland and Lithuania had counted as little more than a Russian protectorate, which Russia's rulers periodically stripped of land. In the 1660s, its rulers had in the wake of the Khmelnytsky revolt seized Poland's lands east of the Dnieper River, as well as the city of Kyiv on its west bank. They had fought with Sweden over Livonia, even though

318

THE PARTITIONS OF POLAND 1772–1795

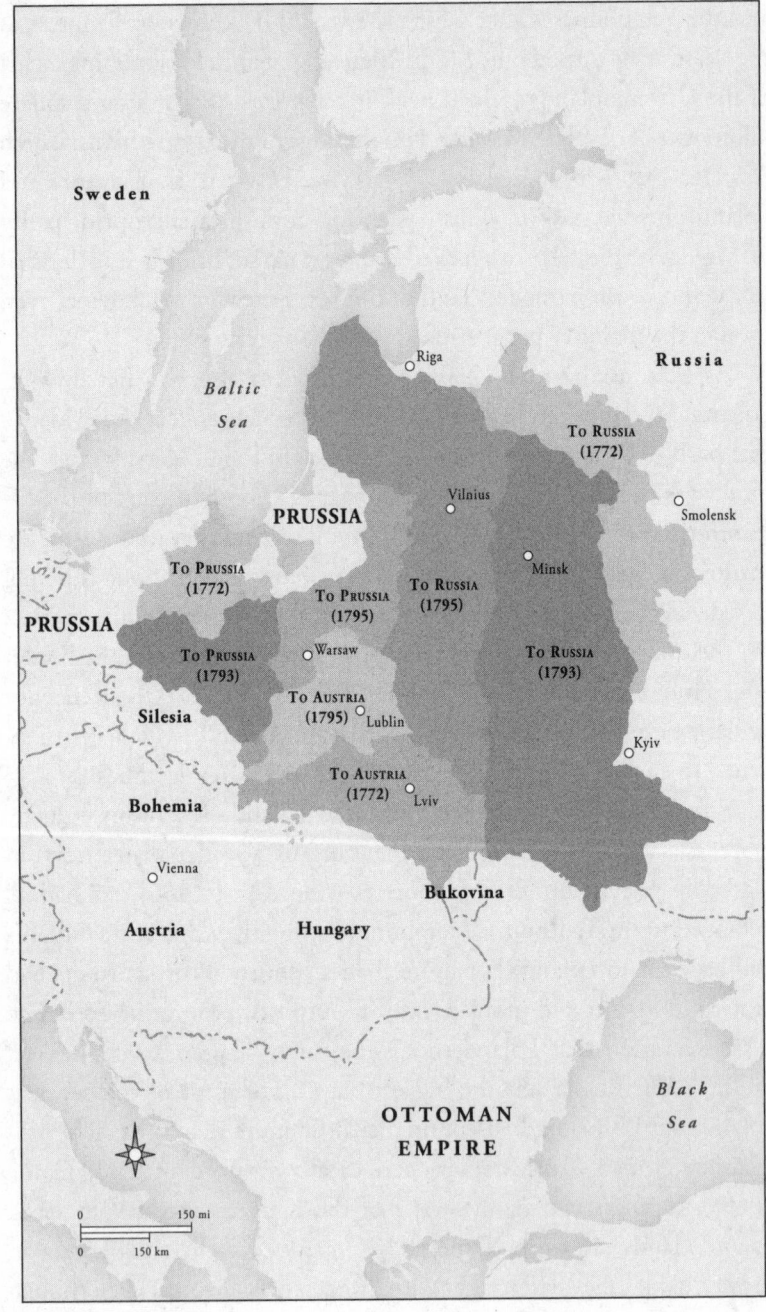

the duchy belonged conjointly to Poland and Lithuania. Now a part of Latvia, Courland too was a province that belonged to Poland, but from the 1730s onwards, the Russian ruler appointed its duke, without reference to Warsaw.[9]

Maria Theresa forced the pace. Not only was she carving out chunks of Polish territory adjoining the Hungarian border, but it was also plain that she had no intention of relinquishing them. In his palace in Potsdam, just outside Berlin, Frederick learned with consternation in February 1771 that Habsburg officials were now issuing passports in the area of occupation and redesignating Polish officials as Austrian subjects. He wrote to his ambassador in St Petersburg that any thought of keeping Poland and Lithuania intact was now hopeless. Maria Theresa meant to go off with a part. It was important that this 'should not affect the balance of power between Austria and Prussia, which is important for me and of interest to Russia as well'. Maria Theresa meanwhile protested that her intentions were pacific and that she had been misunderstood, but nobody believed her.[10]

The deal was done in the summer of 1772, in the aftermath of Russia's eventual suppression of the insurrectionary Confederation of Bar. Explaining that 'the spirit of faction, disorder, and internal strife' had made Poland and Lithuania ungovernable, Catherine the Great of Russia, Frederick II of Prussia, and Maria Theresa bit off altogether more than a quarter of Poland and Lithuania's territory and a third of its population. They did so, as their diplomats brazenly explained, in the interests of maintaining harmony in Poland and Lithuania and in a spirit of good neighbourliness. Frederick II took the corridor between Brandenburg and Prussia, which he renamed West Prussia; Catherine the Great received a swathe of eastern Lithuania, where it adjoined Russia's border; and Maria Theresa incorporated Lviv and southwestern Poland into the Habsburg realms, giving the new territory the archaic name of the Kingdom of Galicia and Lodomeria.[11]

Extraordinarily, the two decades following the partition of 1772 were remnant Poland and Lithuania's golden age. Literature, the arts, theatre, and education flourished. Warsaw was home to more than two hundred artists, of whom seventy were closely connected to the royal court. In the countryside, wealthy noblemen rebuilt their palaces in the now fashionable Palladian style with pillared porticos, modelled on English country houses. Albeit a puppet who reported to Catherine the Great in St Petersburg, King Stanisław Poniatowski proved himself an enlightened and thoughtful sovereign. He championed the reform of the universities and sponsored Poland's first newspaper, *The Monitor* (1765–1785). Appearing twice weekly, its editions railed against superstition, religious bigotry, and what it described as the new Polish passions for gossip and duelling.

King Stanisław was building on meagre foundations. Back in the 1740s, a Polish scholar had sought to rival Chamber's new encyclopaedia and steal a march on Diderot's seventeen-volume *Encyclopédie* by publishing his own compendium of knowledge, the *New Athens*. It affirmed the existence of giants and unicorns but dismissed pelicans as a hoax and the Copernican universe as deluded. The encyclopaedia's definition of a horse was disconcertingly straightforward—'a horse: as it is, all can see.' But, from the 1770s onwards, the ideas of the Enlightenment hit the shrunken kingdom, overturning many of the suppositions and pretensions, and much of the self-satisfied ignorance that had previously guided its politics and led it to disaster. Partly inspired by King Stanisław's example, influential noblemen in Poland and Lithuania finally recognized their country's political, social, cultural, and economic backwardness and decided that something had to be done.[12]

All of Central Europe was in awe of Montesquieu. His *Persian Letters* (pretending to be written by a bewildered visitor to France) were emulated to poke fun at time-worn institutions, while Montesquieu's *Spirit of the Laws* became the essential guide to political organization. Rather like Molière's shopkeeper who learned after forty years that he had been speaking prose, Central European writers discovered from Montesquieu that the bundle of customs and laws that guided the exercise of power was actually a 'constitution' (although they struggled at first to find an appropriate translation). But nothing was more persuasive than Montesquieu's prescription for liberty:

Constant experience shows us that every man invested with power
is apt to abuse it, and to carry his authority as far as it will go. . . .
To prevent this abuse, it is necessary from the nature of things that
power should be checked by power. (*Spirit of the Laws*, 11, 4.)

Montesquieu spent almost twenty years writing his *Spirit of the
Laws* and the completed text was by no means coherent. But what he
seemed to say was that in France the intermediary powers possessed
by the nobles and law courts restrained despotism, while in Britain
the separation of powers between the royal executive, the elected legislature, and the appointed judiciary preserved individual freedom,
making Britain constitutionally superior to the Republican Rome of
antiquity. Montesquieu knew full well that the British constitution
did not work like that, but it fitted his scheme of a balanced or mixed
constitution and made his remedy all the more persuasive.

In Poland and Lithuania, reformers took Montesquieu to heart.
From 1788 to 1792, a new Sejm met in more than 560 sessions, with
the right of veto suspended for its duration. There was much talking,
with no fewer than thirty-two thousand speeches and interventions.
But King Stanisław forced the pace, drafting a constitution and, on
3 May 1791, forcing it through a session of the Sejm packed for the
occasion with his own supporters. What he gave the Sejm was pure
Montesquieu, adopting wholesale his principle of a separation of powers. As the constitution explained:

Three distinct powers shall compose the government of the Polish
nation according to the present Constitution, namely: 1st. Legislative power in the Sejm; 2nd. Executive power in the King and
the Council of Ministers; 3rd. Judicial power, in the jurisdictions
existing, or to be established.[13]

The Constitution of 3 May is celebrated as the first modern constitution in European history and the second in the world (after the
United States Constitution came into force in 1789). Even so, it was

not as revolutionary as Stanisław and his supporters maintained. Besides Montesquieu, the Sejm deputies had feted his Genevan rival, Jean-Jacques Rousseau, talking of a constitution that empowered the nation and channelled its will. But the 'Polish nation' of 1791 was still the nobility, and its better-off members at that, for the constitution had removed the existing right of poor nobles to vote for Sejm deputies. Although the constitution talked of villagers and not serfs, it did not abolish the institution of peasant servitude. And, though religious toleration was affirmed, the constitution still made it a crime to convert from Catholicism, with unspecified penalties. In order to prevent the foreign manipulation of royal elections, the monarchy was declared hereditary, but there was no thought of instituting a presidency or bill of rights.

King Stanisław was delighted with his achievement. Believing the constitution had transformed Poland and Lithuania's prospects, he predicted that 'the eyes that see Poland today, and will see her in thirty years' time, will not recognize her.' Tragically, Stanisław was right, but in a way that he did not imagine. In St Petersburg, Empress Catherine nursed the double fear that a stable Poland and Lithuania would be better able to resist Russia's protective embrace, and that the new constitution was a cover for subversive ideas coming out of the 1789 French Revolution. There were misgivings in Berlin too. As the Prussian foreign minister asked: 'How can we defend our state against a numerous and well-ruled nation?' With Prussia's active support and the new Habsburg emperor Francis II's acquiescence, Catherine the Great invaded Poland and Lithuania in 1793. The new constitution was torn up and a second partition imposed that stripped the kingdom and grand duchy of a further three hundred thousand square kilometres of land. The next year, Tadeusz Kościuszko, a veteran of the American War of Independence, engineered a mutiny in the Polish army and declared the serfs freed. Wielding scythes, Kościuszko's peasant battalions scored an unexpected victory over the Russians at Racławice. It was too much for Poland's three neighbours. They forced King Stanisław's abdication and in 1795 took all that was left in a third and final carving up.[14]

Contemporary observers were split in their opinion over what had happened. The Scottish philosopher David Hume likened Poland and Lithuania's predatory neighbours to 'barbarians, Goths and Vandals', while the English writer and politician Horace Walpole described the partitioning powers as 'the most impudent association of robbers that ever existed'. Hume's fellow countryman Robert Burns gave his own verdict, in characteristic style, blaming Catherine the Great ('Auld Kate') for Poland and Lithuania's destruction and the humbling of King Stanisław ('Stanislaus'):

> *Auld Kate laid her hands on poor Stanislaus*
> *And Poland has bent like a bow:*
> *May the deil [devil] in her ass ram a huge prick o' brass!*
> *And damn her to hell with a mowe [fuck]!* (1792)

Even in Prussia, there were writers sympathetic to Poland and Lithuania who lamented the barbarity of the country's demise, the lost opportunities for political reform, and the assignment of its eastern part to Russian despotism. In the decades following Poland and Lithuania's erasure, a minor literary genre in Prussia looked back fondly to a past of picturesque costumes, outdoor dances to the music of the fiddle, and a centuries-long yearning for freedom.[15]

But most commentators reckoned Poland and Lithuania deserved their fate. The constitution was a shambles, the country lacked political stability, and the oppressions of its crude nobility were manifest. 'A miserable regime' had been Voltaire's verdict, and most Frenchmen concurred, citing (like Louis-Philippe, count of Ségur) 'the slavery of the peasants, the turbulent freedom of the nobility, oriental luxury without any of life's amenities . . . in the countryside habits that are still Sarmatian . . . an unbelievable pastiche of centuries past'. The German explorer and naturalist Georg Forster concurred, coining the term *polnische Wirtschaft*, or 'Polish economy', as a catch-all for what he defined as 'unspeakable filth, laziness, drunkenness, and sloppiness'. In Poland, he explained, even countesses combed the lice from their hair in public, and gentlemen blew their noses on their hands. The title of one pamphlet, published in 1780 in simultaneous French and German editions, summed up a wide swathe of opinion by likening Poland to a misshapen ape—'The Orang-utan of Europe, or Poland as it really is'.[16]

The partitioning of Poland and Lithuania was a disaster for Central Europe. Kingdoms had in the past been swapped between dynasties or had been taken over by foreign rulers. Hungry neighbours had nibbled away at their edges and, occasionally, gone off with whole provinces. But this was the first time a major state had been obliterated in its entirety and the map of Central Europe so comprehensively redrawn. The future British prime minister Lord Palmerston was forthright. Writing anonymously in 1839 (he was then foreign minister), Palmerston averred that the partitions were responsible for 'the most dangerous innovation in the international law of Europe, inasmuch as it has given a legal sanction to the acquisition by physical force in defiance of right, and in contempt of justice'. As Palmerston went on to observe, the chief beneficiary of this new lawlessness had in fact been Napoleon, who had showed an even greater contempt for established kingdoms, boundaries, and monarchs.[17]

Palmerston thought it fitting that having sown the storm, Russia should have reaped the whirlwind, being invaded by Napoleon in 1812 and losing Moscow to the flames. But in the longer term it was Russia that gained the most from the partitions, since it had won more than just territory. Previously, Russia's rulers had confined their ambitions to the Baltic shore and the Ottoman possessions around the Black Sea. By eliminating Poland and Lithuania, they had moved Russia's border almost six hundred kilometres westwards, to include both Minsk and Vilnius. Russia was now a Central European power and its salience in Great Power diplomacy a fact. In the wake of Poland and Lithuania's first partition, the Irish statesman and philosopher Edmund Burke had asked rhetorically, 'Poland was but a breakfast, where will they dine?' For Russia, it would ultimately be in Central Europe.[18]

CHAPTER 23

Napoleon and the Map of Central Europe

ROM 1792 TO 1815, CENTRAL EUROPE WAS ALMOST CONTINU-
ally at war. In 1803, the French Revolutionary Wars became the
Napoleonic Wars. But the conflict was uninterrupted and Central Europe was the cockpit. Britain was France and Napoleon's most steadfast
opponent, being at war almost without a break from 1793 to 1815. But
Britain's war was mostly naval. For fourteen years in all, the Habsburg
armies confronted French armies on land, and they bore the brunt of
the French and Napoleonic fury. Repeatedly defeated, the Habsburgs
in Vienna conceded both territory and prestige. The low point came in
1806, when the Holy Roman Emperor, the Habsburg Francis II (ruled
1792–1835), bowed to Napoleon and announced the empire's dissolution. The proclamation announcing his abdication rehearsed Francis's
titles, perversely including 'At all times Enlarger of the Empire', which
had been part of the monarch's style since the thirteenth century.

Two years before, in 1804, Francis had declared himself to be Emperor of Austria, which he intended to rival Napoleon's new title of
Emperor of the French. So, although the Holy Roman Empire was
abolished, Francis continued to carry an imperial handle, but now as
Emperor Francis I of Austria. It was a sleight of title that mattered not
a jot in the big power politics of the new century. The Habsburg possessions in Central Europe were squeezed and, on Napoleon's whim,
bartered and reassigned. Between 1797 and 1809, the Habsburgs were
stripped of their possessions in the Low Countries and Italy, and then,
bit by bit, of the Tyrol, much of Croatia and the Adriatic coast, and
chunks of Poland that the Habsburgs had previously won in the partitions. On top of this, between 1792 and 1815 the Habsburgs lost the

greatest number of troops fighting against the French, with altogether half a million men killed.

Militarily exhausted, Emperor Francis I made peace with Napoleon in 1809, assigning to Napoleon his eldest daughter as Napoleon's new bride and empress, and sending troops to support the French invasion of Russia in 1812. Francis was unusual in holding out against Napoleon for so long. The king of Prussia Frederick William II (ruled 1786–1797) had made peace with France as early as 1795. When his successor Frederick William III (ruled 1787–1840) rejoined the fray, in 1806, the Prussian armies were destroyed almost at once. Now it was Prussia's turn to lose territory. Napoleon gave half of Prussia to his allies, including most of the land it had previously stripped from Poland. By contrast, the rulers of Bavaria and Württemberg came to terms with Napoleon early on, marrying their daughters to, respectively, Napoleon's stepson and brother, in exchange for which Napoleon gave them swathes of formerly Austrian territory.

What happened in the two decades after 1792 was not just a war of armies but also a battle of ideas. France changed over this period from a constitutional monarchy to republicanism and revolutionary Jacobinism, and then to military dictatorship and empire. But there were some ideas that remained consistent—citizenship, constitutional government, and the sovereignty of the nation, on whose behalf Napoleon always claimed to be acting. France's governments routinely traduced each of these, but the vision and aspiration remained of a modern, law-governed state, based on citizens and not subjects. It was a potent ideological mix that challenged all of Europe's 'Old Regimes'.

Across Central Europe, responses were the same—a crackdown on the press and on anything that smelled of radicalism, revolution, and change. A new bout of censorship in the Habsburg lands caught Swift's *Gulliver's Travels* and Bunyan's *Pilgrim's Progress*. In Prussia, Frederick William III introduced the ingenious device of stripping publishers of their copyright if they printed anything that might be thought subversive, thus threatening their businesses with ruin. Secret societies were another target. As early as 1793, freemasonry was banned outright in

CENTRAL EUROPE IN 1810

the Habsburg lands and Hanover but lingered on under the cover of
reading clubs and chivalric societies. Elsewhere, governments overlooked freemasonry, since too many top bureaucrats were caught up
in it, but homed in instead on student fraternities, lest their pranks
corrupt the minds of future state officials.

Clearly, some genuine plotting was going on. A few Austrian and
Hungarian radicals, or 'Jacobins', opened channels to the French, but
most confined their activity to writing manifestos and vulgar ditties
that they privately circulated:

> *The people aren't just bog roll but can do their own
>   thinking.*
> *If you won't learn good manners, you'll be hanged like
>   a lout.*
> *Off to the guillotine, blood for blood.*
> *Had we a guillotine here, a lot of big men would pay.*

One of the earliest conspiracies uncovered by the police involved
the supposed distribution of proclamations by '100,000 specially
trained dogs', but even the authorities did not take it seriously. Another included the construction of a war machine of spikes mounted
around an axle, for use by peasants against mounted attack. Since the
conspirators had no contacts in the countryside, it was never built, let
alone tested. There was one execution in Vienna and seven in Hungary.
Most of those tried were either found not guilty or pardoned. The
long prison terms given to the remainder were soon recognized as unjust and commuted. In the Habsburg lands, the revolutionary Jacobin
threat was a phantom.[1]

It was much the same elsewhere in Central Europe. After a flurry
of enthusiasm in the first years of the French Revolution, heads soon
became wiser. Some learned the hard way. In 1796, a pastor's son on
the Swiss border greeted in his best clothes the arriving French troops
with a speech extolling republican virtues—the soldiers promptly di-
vested him of his pocket watch, boots, and waistcoat. In Mainz, several

hundred firebrands briefly founded a revolutionary republic in 1793, but it survived only for as long as it had the protection of the French army. Revolutionaries elsewhere on the west bank of the Rhine were noisy but few in number. Solemnly declaring a war against 'the tyrants of all countries, who have usurped the rights of the people,' the Cis-Rhenian (West Rhineland) revolutionaries fondly imagined that they could build a sister republic to France. Napoleon rudely disabused them of their hopes. Once he had occupied it militarily, Napoleon broke the west bank of the Rhineland into prefectures administered from Paris, finally annexing the region to France in 1801.[2]

The French Revolutionary Wars and Napoleonic Wars recast the map of Europe. As the British prime minister William Pitt the Younger presciently observed in 1805, upon hearing of Napoleon's victory at Austerlitz over the Austrians and Russia, 'Roll up that map, it will not be wanted these ten years.' (He also downed a glass of brandy to steady his nerves.) In the years after Austerlitz, the Low Countries, northwestern Germany, including Hamburg, Bremen and Lübeck, Tuscany and the Papal States, and the southwestern parts of the Habsburg Empire (rechristened Illyria) became parts of France. Beyond these, Napoleon aimed to build a cordon of compliant states, wherever possible ruled over by members of his own family. Elsewhere, as in Switzerland, he hoped to create mirror images of France, with centralized regimes, equal citizenship, and republican constitutions. Incorporation into France, client states, and government by dictators drawn from his own family would, Napoleon hoped, keep his unreliable Austrian, Prussian, and Russian allies at a distance and leave him free to deal with Britain.[3]

In the course of reordering Europe, Napoleon pulled Central Europe to pieces. In place of the Holy Roman Empire, Napoleon created in 1806 the Confederation of the Rhine, over which he appointed himself Protector with deliberately ill-defined powers. But whereas the Holy Roman Empire had comprised several hundred principalities and statelets, by a process of forced amalgamation the confederation had at its height only thirty-five. Several of these were ruled by Napoleon's kinsmen. So, the newly proclaimed Kingdom of Westphalia had

Napoleon's brother, Jerome, as its lazy and philandering sovereign; the Grand Duchy of Frankfurt had (after 1813) his stepson as duke, while Napoleon's brother-in-law and subsequently his nephew governed the new Duchy of Berg. Napoleon also made the existing dukes of Bavaria, Saxony, and Württemberg into kings, thus binding them close to him as the author of their royal titles.

Further east, Napoleon established in 1807 the Duchy of Warsaw, which he formed out of the territory taken by Prussia from Poland in the partitions, to which he later added a chunk of the Austrian Kingdom of Galicia and Lodomeria. Although under the nominal rule of the king of Saxony, the duchy was a satrapy of France. Its constitution was Napoleon's work—he dictated it, literally, and apparently at such speed that the king of Saxony could not keep up. The Polish statesman Adam Czartoryski, at the time in the service of Tsar Alexander I, imagined that the duchy would provide the starting point for a reconstituted Poland. But Napoleon's interest was troops, and he converted Polish hopes into cannon fodder. Between 1807 and 1813, the duchy supplied as many as 180,000 soldiers for Napoleon. Of these, 90,000 perished in Napoleon's catastrophic invasion of Russia in 1812. Extraordinarily, most of the survivors continued fighting for Napoleon even after his colossal defeat the next year at the Battle of Leipzig, when all his other allies had deserted him.[4]

The Duchy of Warsaw was typical of the cleft stick in which Napoleon was caught. He wanted to endow Central Europe with modern, constitutional states, where the people were not subjects but citizens. So, along with a constitution, the duchy received the French Napoleonic Code, which presumed legal equality and aimed in its 2,281 articles to be able to resolve all courtroom disputes. He pushed for the same in the Confederation of the Rhine, advertising his ambition to make the code 'the common law of a European confederation of states . . . one of the greatest legal changes ever undertaken, whose consequences for morals, trade, language etcetera cannot be reckoned'. In fact, most of the members of the confederation either failed to adopt the code or only introduced it piecemeal. Nevertheless, Napoleon's promotion of the code typifies his aim to forge a new empire, united to France not only by force of arms but also by shared values.[5]

But at the same time, Napoleon wanted soldiers, and his empire was, in a long-standing description, an *empire de recrutement* (recruiting empire). It was not just the Duchy of Warsaw that provided Napoleon with troops. The Confederation of the Rhine also contributed, providing by 1809 about one hundred thousand men. In the 1812 campaign against Russia, almost a quarter of Napoleon's army of six hundred thousand men was made up of troops taken from the Confederation of the Rhine, the Austrian Empire, and Prussia, while over half the horses that he deployed were also either bought or requisitioned in the confederation or the Warsaw duchy. Napoleon expected too that his allies would billet French troops, provide fodder and supplies for his armies, and pay tribute in the form of taxes.[6]

Napoleon's recruitment extended to Central European poets, playwrights, and authors, whom he tried to enlist on France's and his own behalf. He tempted them with the prospect of careers in a new superuniversity that he claimed to have planned in either Kassel or Jena, depending on his audience. To the young scholar of literature Jacob Grimm, he offered the post of Chief Librarian in Westphalia—Grimm took it. To the historian and biographer of Frederick II of Prussia, Johannes von Müller, he gave the office of Secretary of State in Westphalia, hoping that Müller would write an equally fulsome account of his own life—Müller accepted the job, but died before he could begin work. To the composer Beethoven, he dangled the office of Master of Music in Westphalia—but Beethoven received a better offer and stayed in Vienna. The playwright, poet, and novelist Johann Wolfgang von Goethe was easily won over. Summoned to Napoleon's presence in Erfurt in 1808, Goethe was flattered when the French emperor quoted from one of his books. For the rest of his life, Goethe extolled Napoleon's genius.

But Napoleon's empire was also an empire of plunder. French soldiers robbed and looted wherever they went. Notoriously, the French governor of Brunswick dined with visiting German dignitaries with food served on their own stolen tableware. Elsewhere, French officials inventoried works of art in palaces, churches, and formerly royal collections, selecting the best for the Louvre in Paris, renamed in 1802 the Napoleon Museum (Musée Napoléon). Smaller items, described at the time as 'lovely little things' (*petits objets charmants*), often went to adorn the outfits and apartments of Empress Joséphine (Napoleon's first wife). The duke of Brunswick lost seventy-eight paintings, including works by Raphael, Titian, Rembrandt, and Van Dyck, and Emperor Francis I surrendered more than four hundred. Napoleon even stripped St Mark's Basilica in Venice of its four bronze horses, which he later installed on top of the originally wooden Arc de Triomphe in Paris. (They were returned to Venice in 1815.)[7]

Napoleon knew that compromises and accommodations were necessary for the resources and conscripts that his ambition required. So, when the Swiss rebelled against the centralized Helvetic Republic that Napoleon had imposed on them in 1798, he gave way, publishing five constitutions in succession in the hope of winning the Swiss round. His efforts were in vain. Austrian and Russian armies arrived to help oust the French, with the Russian General Korsakov camping in 1799 on the outskirts of Zurich—the farthest point westward that Russian troops had yet advanced. Eventually summoning the Swiss leaders to Paris in 1803, Napoleon addressed them as a Corsican who had been 'born in a land of mountains and understands how mountain people think', and invited them to pen their own constitution. They promptly restored the old confederation, to which Napoleon acceded—he needed the Alpine passes safe from Swiss marauders.[8]

In places, Napoleon thought to cultivate not just French sympathies but also Frenchmen. The kingdom of Westphalia was home to the experiment. Made up of parts of Prussia, Hanover, Brunswick, Hesse, and a medley of minor territories, it was divided not only by former allegiances but also by legal customs, coinage, weights and measures, social structures, and even speech, since the various dialects were often mutually incomprehensible. Even the kingdom's name was a misnomer, plucked from a duchy only one-fifth the size of the kingdom that had previously belonged to the archbishopric of Cologne. As one historian has recently explained: 'It was as if a foreign power had conquered the United States and combined portions of New Jersey, New York, Ohio, and Pennsylvania into a new entity called the Kingdom of Chesapeake.'[9]

Napoleon's plan was to give Westphalia French laws, a French system of education and measurement, decimal coinage, a French style of government with a Council of State, a token parliament, and centrally appointed prefects and to force children to learn French at school. As one French minister condescendingly explained to a German professor in the new Westphalia: 'You will be forced to speak the French language, and I regard this obligation as a means of advancement for science and letters in Germany.' But Napoleon put it more diplomatically, declaring that 'all men of genius, all those who have attained distinction in the republic of letters, are French no matter in what country they may have been born.'[10]

Napoleon was too shrewd to push for complete Frenchification in Westphalia, and even within the historic boundaries of France he did not press it, still allowing some primary education in Breton and German. So, Westphalia's government newspaper, *Le Moniteur westphalien*, continued to be published in bilingual editions and the law courts conducted their business in both languages with the help of interpreters. In everyday speech, Westphalians frequently adopted French words but then made them conform to a German grammar and morphology. To ease exchange, an enterprising scholar published a 'Dictionary for Explaining and Putting into German the Foreign Expressions Adopted in Our Language'. The dictionary confirms that what Westphalians encountered in their daily lives was not French at all but a bastard tongue—*dejeuniren*: to breakfast; *monotonisch*: monotonous; *mensurabilitaet*: measurability, and so on. Extraordinarily, the almanac of the kingdom, a sort of official *Who's Who*, was only published in German—inevitably so, since Westphalia's civil servants were almost entirely German speakers.[11]

The example of the Illyrian Provinces further illustrates Napoleon's flexibility both with the boundaries of states and with the language of his subjects. The Illyrian Provinces, founded in 1809, were another Chesapeake. They comprised the Dalmatian littoral, which had formerly been Venetian; the previously Austrian lands of Carniola; Trieste, along with slivers of the Tyrol and Carinthia; parts of the Habsburg Military Frontier; and all Croatia west of Zagreb, which had hitherto been a Hungarian crownland. The idea behind the Illyrian Provinces was to give France control of commerce in the northern Adriatic, but the new political creation was a patchwork of torn-off strips, sewn together to make a slender skein of territory almost eight hundred kilometres long. It was remote, too, from France: it took a letter twenty days to go from Paris to Dubrovnik, and that was in the summer, whereas from Paris to Milan needed just three or four days.[12]

Even so, the Illyrian Provinces were treated as if a part of France. They were put under intendants reporting to a governor and split up into provinces and districts, with all major decisions taken in Paris. French currency was introduced which, on account of its unfamiliarity, led to the widespread forgery of banknotes. More happily, French ideas of citizenship and of equality before the law led to the abolition of noble privileges, the removal of guild monopolies, and the elimination of legal discrimination against Jews. In 1811, Napoleon extended smallpox vaccination to the provinces, integrating them into the programme that had been running in France for almost a decade. He also kept in place the cordon of quarantine camps, fumigation chambers, and baths of vinegar that ran across the Military Frontier and were Central Europe's first line of defence against epidemics spreading westwards from the Ottoman Empire.[13]

Yet although the provinces were a part of metropolitan France— and so administratively and jurisdictionally as French as Rouen or Bordeaux—there was no attempt to make Illyrians into Frenchmen. Italian and German continued as official languages. It was only on the parade ground that French was the exclusive language. Napoleon also instructed that there should be a weekly news digest in both Italian and Croatian. Printed in Zadar between 1806 and 1810, the *Regio Dalmata—Kraglski Dalmatin* was the first newspaper published in what would later be recognized as the Croatian language but was at the time called Dalmatian. After 1810, the *Regio Dalmata* was replaced by the *Télégraphe Officiel*, printed in Ljubljana in Carniola in four languages—French, Italian, German, and Dalmatian. In fact, what was said to be written Dalmatian did not cover the huge range of Slavonic dialects and languages spoken in the Illyrian Provinces, but it hardly mattered. Eighty to 90 per cent of the population was illiterate.[14]

For reasons of efficiency, Napoleon's governor of the Illyrian Provinces, Auguste de Marmont, went further. It was important that courts functioned and that orders were understood. Accordingly, he instructed that the Slavonic language spoken in the northern, upland parts of the Illyrian Provinces be standardized and no longer constitute what modern linguists call a 'dialect continuum' of diverging idioms and vernaculars. So, while the language of instruction in most secondary schools would be in French, elementary schools would continue to teach in the local language, which was now to be codified. Only later would students benefit from a superior education in French, ultimately progressing to Ljubljana's new lycée, which was itself modelled on and supervised by Napoleon's pet university, the Imperial University of Paris. Literacy was the first step in the making of citizens; French culture, the second.

The priest and schoolteacher Valentin Vodnik (1758–1819) enthusiastically embraced the project of linguistic codification. Encouraged by Marmont, Vodnik published language textbooks for children and exemplars of good style. To demonstrate the versatility of the language, he also wrote a cookbook, a manual for midwives, and an ode to Napoleon composed in the manner of the Roman poet Horace. Vodnik called the language in which he wrote Carniolan and he saw it as almost the counterpart of Valvasor's *The Glory of the Duchy of Carniola*—something little and provincial that was to be celebrated. Following Napoleon's defeat, Vodnik was vilified as a collaborator and in 1815 forced into retirement. But his legacy endured, contributing to the flourishing of a literature in the first half of the nineteenth century that was first known as Carniolan and then as Slovene.

Vodnik's work was typical of a new interest in language as a marker of identity and as a badge that demonstrated what a people was. Throughout Central Europe, scholars increasingly harked to the influential German philosopher Johann Gottfried Herder (1744–1803), who in the last decades of the eighteenth century had taught that a shared language and cultural traditions were the building blocks of national communities. As Herder put it: 'Has a nation anything more precious than the language of its fathers? In it dwells its entire world of tradition, history, religion, principles of existence; its whole heart and soul.' For Herder, the nation forged from language and freely expressing its soul in art and literature was natural and the opposite of the machine state, which he decried as an artificial construction that crushed everything into a deadly uniformity.[15]

Herder's vision inspired philologists, antiquarians, and historians across Central Europe to hunt out old manuscripts that contained the earliest examples of a so-called national language and evidence of its first literature. So, there was great excitement in Carniola when in 1807 scholars found during their trawls through the Court Library in Munich four parchment leaves from the tenth century on which there were some sentences that looked as if they might have been composed in something like early Carniolan. Other scholars working in Ljubljana and Carniola built on Vodnik's researches, gathering verses and ballads that were eventually published in the five-volume anthology the *Carniolan Bee* (*Kranjska čbelica*, 1830–1848).[16]

Carniolan scholars were industrious but hardly exceptional. As the Holy Roman Empire moved towards dissolution, German antiquarians published newly discovered biographies of Charlemagne, who had founded the empire a millennium before. Their reproach to the new German kings, dukes, and French placemen who made up the Confederation of the Rhine was both obvious and intended. They also edited medieval works like the *Nibelungenlied* and *Tristan*, which had previously been dismissed as inferior literary products, advertising them as the German equivalent to Homer's *Iliad*: in his *Ring* cycle, Richard Wagner would later render them into exemplars of German cultural achievement. But it was not just literary merits that were at stake. As the *Nibelungenlied*'s first editor explained, the poem also comforted 'the German soul' and was 'a true encouragement, during the fatherland's most shameful episode, and a high promise for the return of German sovereignty'.[17]

Where epics were missing, scholars supplied them, composing long poems, often in an archaic style, that mimicked Arthurian romances or the great authors of classical antiquity. James Macpherson's *Ossian*—a fabulous late-eighteenth-century confection of medieval Irish and Scots Gaelic verses, with a good deal of sheer invention—inspired a spate of similar forgeries. Some were skilfully done, like Václav Hanka's forgeries, published in appetizing morsels in Prague after 1817, which purported to be fragments of thirteenth-century Czech verse. Others were feebler affairs, like the Transylvanian 'Csík Chronicle' (*Csíki Krónika*), which pretended to show a direct line of descent from Attila's Huns to the Hungarians of the eastern Carpathians. But scholars and forgers were all playing the same game—discovering, imagining, and inventing a pristine language, historic descent, and literary tradition around which a people might coalesce and dignify itself with the name of nation.

Napoleon added to this. In Poland, Westphalia, and the Illyrian Provinces, he either exploited national sentiment or tried to manipulate new identities, the better to cultivate an affection for France, to make government more efficient, and to give him the troops on which his empire depended. Across Central Europe Napoleon had admirers, who welcomed his destruction of the old order and his promise of a continent united under the banner of liberty, law, and citizenship. But most people resented his war making, destructiveness, and dictatorial methods. In less than a year, the German composer Beethoven moved from idolization to loathing, dedicating in 1803 his third symphony, the *Eroica*, to Napoleon, and then, in 1804, scratching out the inscription in disgust at Napoleon making himself an emperor.

Nations find it difficult to coalesce around a single identity, for the criteria of belonging will always be disputed. It is much easier to say what a nation is not—and Germans learned from Napoleon that they were the very opposite of Frenchmen. For the patriotic Ernst Moritz Arndt, what moved him the most was the sight of castle ruins on the banks of the Rhine, shattered by French explosives. In his most famous anthem 'Where Is the German Fatherland?' Arndt answers:

> *This is the German's fatherland:*
> *Where rage wipes out the foreign dross,*
> *Where every Frenchman is called a foe,*
> *Where every German is called a friend.*
> *This shall it be,*
> *The whole of Germany it shall be.* (1813)

Others were just as intense, denouncing the humiliations inflicted by Napoleon on the German people and preaching an imminent moral regeneration that would replace the fallen Holy Roman Empire with a new German national state that would dominate Europe. As if to confirm that they were not French, Germans began renaming their cities, replacing the supposedly effeminate French or Latin *C* with the harder, more German *K*—so Coblenz and Cassel became Koblenz and Kassel, Cöln was renamed Köln (Cologne), and so on. Patriotic Germans also began rebuilding their cities, choosing the High Gothic style as best exemplifying German architectural traditions. The model was the great cathedral on the Rhine at Strasbourg, seized from the Holy Roman Empire by Louis XIV of France in 1681 and subsequently a focus for German nostalgia.[18]

Napoleon's gift to Central Europe was a set of interrelated ideas about the citizen and the state. The order of privilege was to be superseded by a society of merit—it just happened that Napoleon's relatives were the most meritorious. Subjects were to be made into citizens, each equipped with a kitbag of rights, and protected in all their daily encounters by the force of the law, communicated in a massive legal code. Citizens were also to be participants in the political process, even though in French practice this meant rigged plebiscites in which the failure to vote counted as a yes. The future Prussian chancellor Karl August von Hardenberg recognized the potency of these ideas: that they were 'so great and so universally acknowledged that the state which does not embrace them must either be forced to accept them or await its downfall.'[19]

Stripped of their French and Napoleonic origins, the ideas that Napoleon stood for would become liberalism, which had as its starting point the idea of the free citizen and of rights that adhere automatically to individuals rather than being the gifts of government. Liberalism necessarily included ideas of constitutionalism and the rule of law and was opposed to censorship as an infringement of the citizen's right to choose what to read. But Napoleon also unleashed modern nationalism on Central Europe. In some places, he did so directly, manipulating identities with the aim of instilling loyalty to him and feeding his recruiting empire. In others, his influence was more indirect and unintended, prompting an upsurge in national sentiment by the humiliations he inflicted. Napoleon released the genies of nationalism and of liberalism on Central Europe, but, unlike Napoleon, they could not be exiled. In the century following Napoleon's final defeat at Waterloo and his banishment to distant St Helena in 1815, they would pull Central Europe apart. Poland's fate of partition would become Central Europe's, and its map too would be changed.

The Gallant World of Tomcat Murr: Romanticism, the Grimms, and the Hanover Handbook

E. T. A. HOFFMANN'S *TOMCAT MURR* IS A PRODUCT OF THE European movement in arts and literature known as Romanticism. Romantic writers emphasized the self and the primacy of emotion or, as the English poet Wordsworth put it, 'the spontaneous overflow of powerful feelings'. In Central Europe, they were inspired by the *Sturm und Drang* (Storm and Stress) movement in German literature, led by Goethe's *The Sorrows of Young Werther* (1778), which is the story of an artist's unrequited love and hopeless ambition set against the backdrop of a stale society, at the end of which Werther kills himself. Whereas the Enlightenment had idealized disengaged enquiry, for Romantics the important things were love, art, companionship, and the cultivation of the self, even though they might lead to tragic consequences. Goethe himself put it simply: 'One ought, every day at least, to hear a little song, read a good poem, see a fine picture, and, if it were possible, to speak a few reasonable words.'[1]

Romantic writers inveighed against the regimentation and anomie brought about by capitalism and the growing apparatus of state government. Many looked back fondly to an imagined past of castles, unspoilt forests, and rustic crafts, which they contrasted with the spreading industrial cities. Romantic writers most often thought in terms of opposites—of authentic culture versus the artifice of modern civilization, of the natural community versus the modern society of classes, and of qualitative human bonds versus the quantitative relationships defined by usefulness and accountants' sums.

Romanticism lacks a set of core beliefs. It is not an ideology but instead an outlook—a way of thinking and, importantly too, a way of feeling. In its repudiation of the present, it may be both revolutionary and backward-looking. Romanticism's slipperiness meant that it could feed into all the main intellectual movements of the nineteenth century, from liberalism to conservatism, and from socialism to nationalism. In literature, as well, Romanticism inspired the realism of Balzac's novels, the Gothic horrors of the German *Schauerroman* (shudder novel), the fairy tales of the Grimms, and the fantastical imaginings of E. T. A. Hoffmann, of which his novel *Tomcat Murr* is just one example.

Published in two volumes in 1820–1822, *The Life and Opinions of the Tomcat Murr together with a fragmentary Biography of Kapellmeister Johannes Kreisler on Random Sheets of Waste Paper* purports to be the autobiography of a cat. But the cat wrote his life on the back of discarded paper that just happened to be the autobiography of the court musician Kreisler. The printer carelessly muddled the two accounts so that they ran into one another, often printing pages out of sequence, so that the text ends up at the same point in time as it begins.

The two fictional autobiographies of Murr and Kreisler are situated in the make-believe principality of Sieghartweiler, somewhere in the German south. Forced by Napoleon into the Confederation of the Rhine, the principality has been swallowed up into a larger one, but Prince Irenaeus is unaware of this—he continues to hold balls and disastrous firework displays, to rearrange his porcelain, and to convene his Council of Finance, even though all its members have to approve are minor items of household expenditure. For entertainment, the prince commissions elaborate devices and musical instruments from Murr's owner, Master Abraham, who is a Jewish magician, alchemist, and inventor.

Murr lives high up in Abraham's lodgings, behind the stove, but on venturing outside he finds a typically urban environment of sausage sellers, coiffed poodles, dangerous strays, and rooftop pigeons.

Although Murr composes poetry that, in keeping with the conventions of the time, extols his love for nature, it is Kreisler who ventures into it, joyfully describing the woodland glades, springs, and overgrown paths of the countryside, where he woos his amour. Murr's home is the attic, whose proximity to the heavens inspires him to elevated thoughts, as he describes them. Although praising the purity of love, in his own wooing of queen cats, Murr is inconstant, incestuous, and urgent, as toms are.

The fictional principality of Sieghartweiler was not restored after Napoleon's defeat. None of its companions among the 'real' little states were, for there was no appetite for a return to the extreme political fragmentation that had characterized the now defunct Holy Roman Empire. The Congress of Vienna, at which Napoleon's former adversaries assembled in 1814 to redraw the map of Europe, preserved most of the territorial amalgamations Napoleon had introduced, although there was some swapping of land. The kingdoms of Württemberg, Bavaria, and Saxony were maintained, and to their number was now added Hanover. The kingdom of Westphalia was, however, dissolved, with its western part being given to Prussia. The Duchy of Warsaw was rebranded as Congress Poland (in tribute to the Congress of Vienna) and made a self-governing part of Russia, moving the Russian border a further four hundred kilometres westward. But Austria, Prussia, and Russia could not agree what to do with Cracow, since it bordered all three states. So, it was made an independent republic, although under increasing Austrian control.

The architect of the new Europe worked out in the wake of Napoleon's defeat was the long-serving Austrian chancellor Metternich. Metternich is often criticized for preferring to stick by the status quo, but it was a status quo of which he was the author. He had at the Congress of Vienna ensured the return of monarchs, including to France, because he believed monarchy led to stability. Although still suspicious of France, he saw it as a counterweight to the Russian Empire. To keep both France and Russia in check, he worked for a strong Central Europe under Austrian leadership. So, Austria was given presidency of a union that brought together the German states, including Prussia, in what became known as the German Confederation. The congress rewarded Austria, too, with the area around Milan and with Venice and its hinterland, which now became the Kingdom of Lombardy-Venetia. Austria also received back most of the Kingdom of Galicia and Lodomeria, which Maria Theresa had previously stolen from Poland.

Like almost all the statesmen and politicians of Central Europe, Metternich feared a revolution from below. Even after Napoleon's defeat, he imagined that a secret 'Directing Committee' was still busy in Paris plotting the overthrow of monarchy and that isolated outbreaks of political violence were all part of a larger conspiracy. In fact, there was little dissent in the heartland of the Austrian Empire and most conspiracies there were invented by the police. It was different elsewhere. In the new Austrian kingdom of Lombardy-Venetia, insurrectionary movements flourished. The secret society known as the Carbonari, or 'charcoal burners', and its successor organization 'Young Italy' fomented rebellions and guerrilla warfare across the peninsula with the aim of freeing it from all foreign rule. By the early 1830s, Young Italy had at least sixty thousand members dedicated to insurrection and assassination, its own newspaper, and sister organizations in the German Confederation, France, Switzerland, and Poland. There were even a Young Tyrol, Young Ukraine, and Young Argentina.[2]

Congress Poland was a disaster. The Poles had inevitably been disappointed with Russian rule, which rode roughshod over the promises made to them at the Congress of Vienna. Congress Poland, they learned, was not after all to be the first step in the remaking of an independent Poland but a province of Russia. The great Polish magnate Adam Czartoryski, who had once served as Russian foreign minister, ended up in 1830 reluctantly on the side of a major uprising against Russian rule. The rebellion was crushed and Congress Poland fully absorbed into Russia. During the 1830s, tens of thousands of former army officers and Polish noblemen were transported—the lucky ones to serve in the Caucasus, the less fortunate to prison camps in Siberia. In anticipation of arrest, thousands more like Czartoryski and the young Fryderyk Chopin fled abroad.

In exile, Czartoryski made his riverfront Paris mansion, the Hôtel Lambert, a centre both for Polish culture and for international diplomacy aimed at restoring Polish self-rule. From the mansion's grand salons, Czartoryski sent out agents across Europe to gather support and glean any intelligence that might be used to discomfort Russia. Czartoryski filleted and passed on their reports to London and Paris, where they arrived in his trademark green dispatch boxes. Just twenty kilometres west of the Hôtel Lambert, in the city of Versailles, a second group of exiles, known as the Democratic Society, or Centralizacja, plotted the violent overthrow of Russian and Austrian rule over what had historically been the kingdom of Poland. Links between the Centralizacja and Young Italy only confirmed Metternich's opinion that dark forces were fomenting insurrection across Central Europe.

Metternich could do little to put an end to conspiracies hatched in France. But he used Austria's presidency of the German Confederation to push through censorship and the policing of universities across Central Europe. His targets were radical professors, whom he despised, and student clubs, particularly athletic associations and fraternities. Some of these societies did indeed combine games and rituals of membership with the promotion of a unified German state, but (as Metternich knew) the majority were harmless.

As it turned out, Tomcat Murr was admitted to a feline fraternity that met on the rooftop above his master's lodging. The company railed against 'Philistine' cats who had only the veneer of education, mewed student songs in Latin, and purred gallant verses that had, so Murr thought, been originally composed by Handel—

> *All too sharply barks the Pom,*
> *Far too loud the poodle,*
> *See the bold and valiant tom,*
> *Silencing that noodle!*

Murr received a sore head from drinking too much pickled herring juice and found himself fighting a duel. But that was it, and so it was for the majority of human students. At the Wartburg Festival of 1817, which was attended by several hundred students from German fraternities, speakers loudly denounced Napoleon's recent aggression and the rule of princes. But the sum of their achievement was to burn a cavalry corset, gentleman's wig, corporal's staff, and a pile of books as symbols of the old order. Few students signed the festival's radical manifesto for fear of compromising any future career they might have in state service. Although there were periodic flurries of protest, most fraternities stuck to what they did best, which was horseplay and drinking. Their conformity to the existing order is shown by the titles with which they honoured students who had drunk the most beer—in declining order of consumption, emperor, pope, king, and duke, with a final toast given to the local ruler.[3]

Even so, at Metternich's direction the governments of the German states cracked down on student activities, even to the extent of banning beam exercises and knee bending lest gymnastics be a cover for subversion. In private, Metternich confided that the student fraternities were 'no serious danger', but he still conjured up the prospect of them spawning a whole generation of revolutionaries. By taking the lead against the students, he could magnify both his own importance and Austria's leadership of the confederation. The impressionable King Frederick William III of Prussia (ruled 1797–1840) was so convinced by Metternich's warning that 'there is a very widespread conspiracy which aims at the overthrow of all German governments without exception' that he gave him access to all the Prussian police files, including, he promised, 'even the most secret'.[4]

Censorship was pervasive across much of Central Europe. Although it was only of the 'preliminary' variety, whereby editors had to submit copy in advance of publication to the censors, most newspapers reliably toed the line, printing only banal and feel-good items and government communiques. (Postpublication censorship was tougher since whole print runs might be confiscated.) For circulating

the proceedings of the Hungarian diet, Metternich gaoled the opposition Hungarian politician Louis Kossuth in 1837 on grounds of sedition since the deliberations of the deputies were regarded as official
secrets. Following the 1830 uprising, a tougher censorship regime was
imposed in what had been Congress Poland than anywhere else in
Central Europe. By requiring the censors to ban books of a 'metaphys-
ical' nature and all publications that described challenges to authority,
Tsar Nicolas I made it impossible to write about philosophy and history except in the most superficial terms.

But despite controls on the press, reading clubs, coffee houses, and
casinos proliferated. Of these, the casinos were probably the most important (and the least researched). Although they had gaming rooms
for roulette and billiards, they were modelled on the clubs of London's Piccadilly, and they only called themselves casinos since the name
of 'club' smacked of revolutionary Jacobinism. With police approval,
some casinos and reading societies took French, Italian, and English
newspapers where the members could read about what was truly going on in their country. But conversing too openly carried penalties.
Likewise in the salons, gossiping about politicians was allowed, but
talking politics was not. Visiting an elegant soirée of dogs, Tomcat
Murr encountered only the 'dullest most insipid chatter', and so fell
asleep in the corner. Many of his real-life contemporaries had similar
experiences. As one wrote of Vienna around 1820, 'If I was to characterize briefly the tone of society at that time, I would want to call it just
harmless: the conversation moved, without political cabals, in a fairly
uniform circle and great importance was placed on essentially insignificant things. . . . It was a struggle for superiority of elegance.' Another
put it bluntly—'The elements of animated discussion, of interesting
conversation, seem wanting in Austria.'[5]

Metternich had his exact opposite in King Ernest Augustus of Hanover. Metternich was a dandy, gossip, astute politician, and woman-
izer, who maintained complicated high-class liaisons throughout his
life. But instead of courting ladies, Ernest Augustus (lived 1771–1851)
preferred to ride them down on his horse, literally. The fifth son of

King George III of Britain, Ernest Augustus was an enthusiastic soldier with battle scars on his face and blind in his left eye from war wounds. Although educated in Hanover, he spent most of his life in England as the Duke of Cumberland and a member of the House of Lords. Choleric and opinionated, Ernest Augustus opposed both Catholic emancipation and the reform of the franchise. For a brief moment, it seemed likely that he would become prime minister when the Duke of Wellington resigned in 1829, but George IV (ruled 1820–1830) recalled Wellington just in time.

Ernest Augustus complained that he had been accused of every crime in the Ten Commandments. He was right, possibly because he had indeed committed them. Besides terrorizing women from his horse in Hammersmith, he was also allegedly complicit in the murder of a servant, in driving to suicide a husband whom he had cuckolded, in fomenting mutiny in the army, and in egregious discourtesies to highborn women. *The Times* in London was harsh in its portrait of Ernest, describing him as possessing 'a certain criminal blackness below the standard dye of aristocratic debauchery'. The diarist Charles Greville, who as Britain's top civil servant had plenty of disagreeable encounters with Ernest, was equally scathing:

> There never was such a man, or behaviour so atrocious as his—a mixture of narrow-mindedness, selfishness, truckling, blustering, and duplicity, with no object but self, his own ease, and the gratification of his own fancies and prejudices.[6]

Since 1714, Britain and Hanover had shared the same ruler, starting with Britain's King George I, otherwise known as Elector Georg Ludwig of Hanover (lived 1660–1727). The electorate had disappeared in the Napoleonic Wars, swallowed up in the kingdom of Westphalia. With Napoleon's defeat, Hanover was reconstituted, but this time as a kingdom, although still sharing its monarch with Great Britain. On the death of William IV in 1837, his niece Victoria (died 1901) succeeded as British sovereign, but Hanover did not recognize the right of female succession, so as the eldest male heir, Ernest Augustus became Hanover's king. Until the birth of Victoria's first child, in 1840, Ernest remained next in line to the British throne.

The kingdom of Hanover was a museum, frozen in time. A petty nobility of minor knights thronged the royal palace, parading at balls in their exclusive red gowns beneath a portrait of their absentee king. A lifeless diet met. Its upper house was the preserve of the nobles, and its lower chamber dominated by a so-called secretary-ocracy of state officials. The Hanoverian economy was predominantly agricultural and the landlords rapacious and unimaginative, seeking to increase profits by squeezing the peasantry rather than by innovating. Nearly all improvement—from the foundation of technical colleges to the introduction of merino sheep—came from the top and by government initiative.[7]

In 1816, George III had appointed his seventh son, Duke Adolphus of Cambridge, as his governor in Hanover. Adolphus was content to leave things as they were. But the 1830 revolution in Paris, which saw the Bourbon monarchy overthrown in favour of 'the people's king' Louis-Philippe, spilled over into Hanover. Duke Adolphus's first thought was to arrest potential troublemakers, but rioting in Göttingen and the flight of the garrison prompted him instead to promise a constitution which would guarantee the rights of citizens and empower the parliament. The 1833 constitution did exactly that, making all legislation dependent on parliamentary approval, limiting the governor's right to make law by decree, and guaranteeing freedom of the press and assembly.

This was the political inheritance into which Ernest Augustus stepped in 1837. Predictably, his first act was to abolish the constitution since he regarded it an unacceptable constraint on the natural rights of monarchy. When the diet protested, he trimmed its powers so that it met only every three years and might only discuss legislation with his consent. But what followed was extraordinary, for King Ernest Augustus rapidly proved himself to be an adept, benign, and diligent monarch. On his death in 1851, the Hanoverian newspapers praised 'his lively temperament' and 'sense of responsibility' which had won over his subjects' hearts. Even *The Times* in London grudgingly wrote that he had been 'an able and even a popular monarch', albeit by German standards.[8]

Outside Hanover's main railway station is a bronze equestrian statue of Ernest Augustus, paid for after his death in 1851 by the city's grateful citizens. It is fitting, for in the 1840s Ernest Augustus brought the railways to Hanover, funding them from the state budget. But he had no wish to have the railways scar his capital, so he ordered the primary junction between the kingdom's two main lines to meet outside Hanover at Lehrte, thus sparing the city centre (unlike in Prussian-ruled Cologne). He also introduced gas lighting and sewers, while maintaining a court of such parsimony that visitors to his palace thought they were being singled out for offence. When not dining frugally at home or recovering from a hangover (he drank excessively), Ernest Augustus travelled in an ordinary carriage from village to village, meeting his subjects, hearing their concerns, and often commanding immediate redress. Ernest Augustus was probably the most visible of all Central Europe's nineteenth-century sovereigns.[9]

Ernest Augustus was also responsible for planning one of the greatest engineering feats of the nineteenth century. Despite its name, the Ernst-August Stollen, built between 1851 and 1864, is not a cake but a forty-kilometre tunnel beneath the Harz mountains. Originally intended as a drainage sluice for the lead, iron, and zinc mines, it was broad enough to transport ores on railway trucks and to power machinery. The entire subterranean complex of passages and galleries connecting to the tunnel extended to more than 525 kilometres, at a depth below ground of up to 390 metres. It was an achievement that should have made the engineering mastermind behind it, Johann Christian Zimmermann, as renowned as Britain's Brunel, but tunnels lie invisible underground and so their architects go unsung.[10]

Zimmermann held the title of Oberbergrat, or Senior Councillor for Mines, and it was the Royal Hanoverian Mining Administration that oversaw the construction of the Ernst-August Stollen. Ernest

Augustus's Hanover was a bureaucratic state. Its reach was extensive and is nowhere better documented than in the 1846 *Court and State Handbook for the Kingdom of Hanover* (*Hof- und Staats-Handbuch für das Königreich Hannover*). The title betrays Ernest Augustus's method—to blend together the courtly and the state administration so that both were equally subject to his sovereign will. But into this vortex he also sucked what had hitherto been private interests and self-governing communities and corporations. The Royal Hanoverian Mining Administration is a typical example. It was headed by royal officials but relied on commercial investors. Businessmen provided the cash for the king's tunnel, but its design was left to Zimmermann. In return, the investors received positions in the mining administration, a say in decision-making, and fine titles, which they might wield as proof of their commercial probity.

An achievement of sorts in itself, the handbook listed eleven thousand state and court officials, including several thousand army officers and clergymen, who equally counted as civil servants. The reach of the bureaucracy was formidable—in schools, sanitation, forest administration, poorhouses, railways, and the postal service. Many of the people listed in the handbook have marks beside their name, recording a medal or some other award from the king. For Ernest Augustus, service to the king, kingdom, crown, or government was identical and the determiner of status. This confusion was characteristic of a wide swathe of Central Europe at the time, where monarchy was extending its reach through the administrative machine while still promoting itself as the focus of loyalty.

For all his idiosyncrasies, King Ernest Augustus was typical of Central European rulers in his belief that good government rested on a mix of paternalism, conservative politics, and economic intervention. So, although he encouraged industry and manufacturing, he opposed the construction of large factories, lest the concentration of the workforce ease the dissemination of radical ideas, and he obliged labourers to carry residence papers to stop them moving into the cities. He also kept a network of spies to check up on reading clubs and other associations. Since commercial banking was underdeveloped throughout Central Europe, Ernest also took the lead in financing big projects, founding in 1843 the government-owned Royal Hanoverian State Railways. In the last year of his reign, he joined Hanover to the free-trade Prussian customs union, boosting the kingdom's exports and manufacturing capacity.[11]

Ernest Augustus was the Romantics' archenemy. Officialdom, railways, enterprise, and the rewards of state service represented the opposite of what Romanticism stood for. (Unlike the artist William Turner, few Romantics could see beauty in a steam locomotive.) For Romantics, Ernest Augustus was a 'philistine', without aesthetic sensibilities, and the bureaucratic state he had created was typical of the desiccated administrative machine which they despised. In this respect, it is no accident that the fictional Kreisler in *Tomcat Murr* refuses an administrative position, preferring instead to embrace art, music, and eventually madness. It is perhaps no coincidence either that *Tomcat Murr*'s author, Hoffmann, should himself have been by day an assiduous bureaucrat in Berlin, while spending his nights in decadent amusement: he died in 1822, aged forty-six, of alcoholism and syphilis. Like Goethe's Faust, two souls heaved in Hoffmann's breast.

The confrontation between the Romantics and Ernest Augustus was immediate and notorious. Göttingen University's professors were also civil servants. They are listed in the Hanover handbook along with the grand titles and medals they had earned in state service— Court Councillor, Privy Councillor, Ecclesiastical Councillor, Knight of the Royal Order of Guelph, and so on. Upon coming to the throne in 1837, Ernest Augustus demanded that, as state officials, the professors swear an oath of allegiance to him. Seven refused, including the brothers Jacob and Wilhelm Grimm, on the grounds that they considered the king's recent abrogation of the constitution to be illegal. Ernest Augustus promptly sacked them from their posts and sent them into exile. When challenged, he dismissed complaints, observing that professors were seldom loyal: 'Like whores and dancers, they follow the money.'[12]

As it turned out, all the Göttingen Seven did follow the money, soon finding employment in other universities—Berlin University took the Grimms and Leipzig most of the others. Even so, their dismissal provoked an uproar throughout the German Confederation and indeed beyond. Even in distant Transylvania, the cause of the Göttingen Seven was reported and cast in terms of a struggle between constitutionalism and the royal forces of reaction. The Prussian press was more circumspect. Acknowledging the scholarly contribution of the sacked professors, the *Berlin Political Weekly* (*Berliner Politisches Wochenblatt*) reminded its readers of the duties of civil servants, upon which rested all orderliness and effective royal governance. The weekly had good reason to be cautious, since the Prussian king had also dismissed or suspended from office his fair share of troublesome academics.[13]

Jacob and Wilhelm Grimm are best known for their fairy tales, but their *Children's and Household Tales* (*Kinder- und Hausmärchen*, 1812, and many subsequent editions) was a work of profound scholarship. The third volume of the expanded second edition of 1819 is devoted entirely to footnotes and appendixes. In a reversal to the Harry Potter books, which were written for children and read by grown-ups, the Grimms' stories were aimed at an academic audience and drew a younger readership. Responding to popular demand, the Grimms published 'junior' editions, often changing the stories to make them less sexually loaded—so Rapunzel is not made pregnant by her prince, kings never wed their daughters, and beds are not introduced until a couple are married. But, knowing that children relish the gruesome, the Grimms kept the evil queen dancing to death in red-hot iron clogs, doves pecking out eyes, and toddlers on dinner menus.[14]

The Grimms built on Herder's idea that a shared language and culture were fundamental to a nation. They believed that folk tales embodied the mental architecture of a people and disclosed a collective way of thinking that had been passed across the generations. But whereas previous collectors of folk tales had been content simply to repeat what they had heard, the Grimms dug deeper and applied the latest methods of source criticism, footnoting, and cross-referencing to older myths upon which, they believed, German culture and identity were founded. This was a political project which aimed at teaching Germans who they were and promoting German unity and statehood. So, besides folk tales, Jacob Grimm (the more prolific of the two) researched and printed law codes from the Middle Ages, collected medieval verse and troubadours' songs, and examined in three volumes the impact of the forest on German sensibilities.

Back in 1780, Frederick the Great had reviled the German language as 'semi-barbarous', 'graceless', and 'unsubtle'. Johann Wolfgang von Goethe (1749–1832) had rescued the German language from obloquy by showing its versatility not only as a literary medium but also as a vehicle for communicating scientific research. The philosopher Immanuel Kant had similarly demonstrated the capacity of German in expressing metaphysics. Jacob and Wilhelm Grimm now went further, excavating the roots of the German language. Like the *Oxford English Dictionary*, the Grimm's German dictionary (*Deutsche Wörterbuch*) did not just explain a word but burrowed into its origins, history, and past uses, taking up as much as a hundred pages for the single word *Geist* (spirit). The brothers anticipated that the enterprise would take ten years and half a dozen volumes to complete. As it turned out, the first volume was sixteen years in the making. The thirty-second, which ends with *Zypressenzweig* (twig of a cypress tree), was only published in 1961, a century after Wilhelm's and Jacob's deaths. The complete set, with 320,000 entries, weighs in at a hefty eighty-four kilograms.

In Central Europe, language lay at the heart of the Romantic movement. It was seen not only as the means by which emotions were conveyed but also as how the individual was able to live in society with others. By examining the origins of words and the manner of their adoption and adaptation, the building blocks of that society were rendered visible. Society was defined by the language it used and the linguistic community was the nation, which Romantics saw as the most natural of all associations, for it rested on the primal act of speech. Language had evolved over time, so the nation it had forged was not only a linguistic community but a historical one too. Like verbs and

nouns, ruins and ancient forests were also part of the cultural landscape out of which the nation had come. So, when a Romantic artist
like Caspar David Friedrich (1774–1840) painted a blasted oak, a broken church, or a cross set on an eery hillside, he was not only trying
to record a scene or even communicate an emotion but also seeking to
glimpse the nation's soul.

Tomcat Murr knew a little of this. High up in his master's lodgings,
Murr pondered the relationships among languages, seeking to prove
that Cattish and Doggish were 'branches of the same tree, so that tomcat
and poodle, when inspired by a higher spirit, understood each other.'
To prove the common language, Murr investigated the linguistic properties of animal sounds to show their identical roots—'bow-wow—
miaow-miaow—yap-yap—snap—grrr—purr—huff-huff—hisss, and
so forth.' Yet the world of Tomcat Murr in sleepy Sieghartweiler could
not last. The logic of the linguistic community and of the language
nation was an overarching state that brought together all speakers of
the same tongue. The little principalities of the German Confederation
would have to give way to a united Germany and with it would perish
not just what remained of the fictional Sieghartweiler but also the Hanoverian state built by Ernest Augustus. The revolutions of 1848 were
the dress rehearsal for this next phase in Central Europe's history.

CHAPTER 25

1848 and the Coming of Revolution

THE REVOLUTIONS OF 1848 WERE ONE OF THOSE KNOTS IN Central European history when strands that had previously been developing in isolation became tangled—Romanticism and nationalism, citizenship and constitutionalism, conditions on the land, and the unhealed sore of the Polish partitions. Folly and genius also played a part, for personalities often proved as important in the making of the events of 1848 as deep structures and recurrent patterns. But so too did rumour. In the absence of a reliable press and of a sophisticated reading public, rumours quickly acquired credence. Reported in newspapers (often as 'there is no truth in the story that . . .'), they rehearsed both gossip, ancient calumnies, and dangerous misunderstandings.

Revolution first broke out with an insurrection in Austrian-ruled Galicia in 1846. Its architects intended uprisings in Prussian and Russian Poland to break out simultaneously. But the rebellion launched in Galicia by the Cracow branch of the Democratic Society (or Centralizacja) was thoroughly botched. In its first phase, patriotic ladies were supposed to infiltrate gala balls at which they would render Austrian army officers inattentive and so easily disarmed and overcome. Typically, the masterminds behind this ludicrous plot included several university professors, but since they were tardy in their recruitment, the plot was never even attempted. The parallel rising planned for Prussia was betrayed to the police before it could begin. The one that was supposed to break out in Russia fizzled out from a straightforward lack of support.[1]

Undeterred, on 18 February 1846, the ringleaders in Cracow precipitously announced a Polish national uprising, ignoring their own timetable. Within hours, bands of peasants had taken up arms, but against the conspirators and the nobility in general, whom they indiscriminately joined together as foes. A false rumour had told them that 'the Good Emperor' in Vienna demanded a show of their allegiance and was paying a bounty on the traitors' severed heads. In just three days, the peasants slew two hundred noblemen. For several weeks, wagons trundled before the local offices of the Austrian administration in Galicia bearing grisly cargoes. Austrian officers duly paid the 'head tax', thereby giving credence to the rumour that the emperor had commanded the massacre.[2]

But rumour worked the other way around too. Convinced by reports that forces loyal to the conspirators were massing in large numbers, Austrian officers kept their troops in the cities, leaving the countryside to the peasants. In all, about a thousand nobles were killed, more than four hundred manor houses torched, and scores of noble women raped. The future author of the novella *Venus in Furs*, the young Leopold von Sacher-Masoch, whose father was chief of police in Lviv in eastern Galicia, witnessed the pathetic collapse of the rebellion:

> I saw the insurgents arrive, some dead, some wounded, on an overcast February day, escorted by armed peasants. The insurgents lay upon miserable little carts, the blood ran down from the straw, and the dogs licked it up.

Even after order had been restored, many peasants in Galicia refused to perform the traditional labour services for their lords, reckoning that these would soon be abolished anyway as reward for their loyalty. As Metternich shrewdly observed, the rebels' aim to create a Polish democracy had overlooked the actual people. In the wake of the rising, he sent troops into the free republic of Cracow and annexed it, adding to the popular conviction that the whole rebellion had been contrived in Vienna.[3]

The 'Galician horrors' created a panic in Hungary, where many nobles feared the same fate. In 1831, during a cholera epidemic, peasants had slain Hungarian noblemen in Upper Hungary when it was rumoured that they were conspiring with Jews to contaminate the water supply. The Galician massacres forced a radicalization of Hungarian politics, with conservatives now competing with reformers to present the more liberal programme. All the old shibboleths now became targets—the political power of the nobles and their almost exclusive representation in the kingdom's diet, peasant serfdom, and the nobility's exemption from taxation. The radical journalist and politician Louis Kossuth put it starkly, 'We are on the brink of disaster . . . delaying the treatment will lead inevitably to death.'[4]

But it was events in France that set off the chain of revolutions that engulfed Central Europe in 1848. Under pressure from the streets, King Louis-Philippe abdicated in February and fled Paris, escaping to London under the alias of 'Mr Smith'. In Austria, people thought it entirely possible that Metternich would march on France. Just a few months before, he had threatened to intervene in Switzerland, where a constitutional quarrel between liberal centralizers and Catholic federalists had spilled over into a not-very-bloody civil war. The prospect of a war in France caused a collapse in bond prices in Vienna, since military intervention could only be paid for by a new bond issue which would in turn drag down the value of existing investments. As nervous bondholders cashed in their securities, the banks began to run out of money. The Saxon ambassador to Vienna witnessed the panic:

> The middle class is seething. Incredible rumours circulate. It looks like the state will go bankrupt. The pressure on the banks for currency was yesterday intense, so much so that they were putting on ten cashiers in place of two just to meet the demand. The coffeehouses are full of the latest news. The newspapers carrying reports from Paris are read out to groups of twenty or thirty people. It's certain that before long we'll be wading through torrents of blood. [5 March 1848][5]

Middle-class fears over savings had their counterpart in working-class worries over food and employment. Waterlogging of the land by rainfall had destroyed the potato crop in 1845, for the popular lumper potato was prone to blight. The next year, the harvest had failed, doubling grain prices and bringing starvation closer. As food prices swallowed up money that might have gone into buying finished goods, manufacturing suffered, and layoffs became commonplace. In 1847, bands of impoverished labourers routinely scoured the Central European countryside with sacks and baskets to raid fields. The more determined plundered granaries and wrecked distilleries since these were diverting an already thin crop.[6]

Close to France, the Grand Duchy of Baden first felt the impact of the revolution. A series of 'people's festivals', otherwise pleasant family events featuring music, fireworks, and hot-air balloons, became increasingly agitated, with radical speech making and petitions in favour of political reform. Rumours of gangs of French beggars crossing the border, of something stirring in the forest, and of mysterious drums beating in the distance added to tensions. At the beginning of March 1848, crowds massed in Mannheim and Karlsruhe presenting a potpourri of demands. The grand duke immediately installed a new reforming ministry, relaxed what little censorship remained in Baden, and promised a constitution. Baden set the pace.[7]

Across the German Confederation, rulers followed Baden's lead. Faced with copycat demonstrations, they appointed their own reform-minded governments and committed themselves to constitutional reform and the abolition of censorship. In most places, the transition from despotism to constitutional rule was effortless and achieved with little bloodshed. Hanover was probably the quietist. Since no one wanted King Ernest gone, it was enough for him to threaten abdication to restore order among his subjects. Berlin was the exception. Hearing a rumour that the army was marching in full force against them, crowds of protesters who had been camping out in the city zoo threw up barricades, provoking the city garrison into hand-to-hand fighting, which cost several hundred lives. King Frederick William IV (ruled 1840–1861) made concessions just in time, ditching his conservative ministers, presiding over a service of commemoration for the slain, and convening a National Assembly for all the Prussian provinces, elected on a broad franchise.

But the most conspicuous change was the flood of publications released by the ending of censorship. Whereas before there had been just nineteen newspapers in the Austrian Empire that published political news, in 1848 the number leapt to over three hundred. In Prussia, Hanover, and Württemberg, there was a jump of about 50 per cent. But the press was just one medium. Societies, pressure groups, and impromptu gatherings drafted public statements, manifestos, and petitions. Known collectively as 'addresses' (*Adressen*), some forty thousand were composed across the German Confederation in the wake of March 1848. Besides these, artists and illustrators introduced to Central Europe the political cartoon, hitherto almost unknown. They had plenty of targets—Frederick William IV's alcoholism, symbolized by a champagne bottle; Prussian generals depicted as angels of death; and royal mistresses bearing riding crops.[8]

The reformers were split down the middle between liberals who favoured constitutional and legal remedies and so-called democrats who were bent on a radical social transformation. The moderates formed societies and pressure groups to which they appended the prefix 'Civic' (*Bürger-*), while the democrats favoured the tag of 'People's' (*Volks-*). Although the democrats were the noisier, the moderates were the more numerous. In the south of the confederation, Catholic organizations of a broadly conservative complexion strengthened their numbers. In Baden alone there were several hundred newly formed 'Pius associations' (named after the then pope Pius IX), with tens of thousands of members and a ready-built organization of parishes, priests, and schools on which they could rely. Military veterans' clubs also articulated conservative sympathies, drawing on a broad base of popular support.[9]

It was the same in the countryside. In the spring of 1848, violence flared across much of Central Europe, but it was mainly fuelled by local grudges—high rents, scarcities of food, enclosure of common land, and falling wages. The protesters were mostly opportunistic, looking to exploit the breakdown in authority to seize the political agenda. The conservative character of their demands is evident in the thousands of petitions sent in by countryfolk to the Prussian diet over the summer of 1848—for a reduction in taxes on milling corn and on the sale of spirits, for the lifting of all controls on hunting, for the continued church supervision of education (there were very many of these), and for axing 'the army of officials, especially administrators', along with their generous pension entitlements. Once landlords and governments had promised to attend to these complaints, peasants and farm labourers returned to the fields. They were not interested in revolution. They simply wanted the old order to work properly and to meet what they considered their just expectations.[10]

By making concessions to the moderates and keeping the radicals at arm's length, Central Europe's rulers kept their thrones. The exception was King Ludwig I of Bavaria (ruled 1825–1848), who stood by the honour of his mistress, the Irish singer and dancer Lizzie Gilbert, otherwise known under the exotic assumed name of Donna Maria de los Dolores Porrys y Montez, or Lola Montez for short. Montez brought Ludwig down. After she had pulled out a pistol when confronting demonstrators in a Munich street, the police requested that they be allowed to enter the royal palace to search her for weapons. Coming on top of demands for a constitution, the insult was too much for the choleric Ludwig, who promptly abdicated in favour of his son, Maximilian II. With her lover no longer able to give her the royal title she sought, Montez abandoned the elderly man to seek out a living in the Australian outback.

Revolution hit Vienna on 13 March. A meeting in Vienna of the provincial diet of Lower Austria was the occasion for a preplanned riot. Troops shot into the crowd, provoking chaos across the capital. That evening, bands of ruffians ransacked shops, invaded the mansions of the well-to-do, and tore streetlights from the ground, after which they lit the gas jets at pavement level to release spouts of flame into the darkness. Now aged seventy-four, Metternich's influence as first minister was already waning. In February 1848, the Saxon ambassador was shocked by his physical decline:

> Ailing, stone deaf, he has shrunk to a shadow of his former self, captive to his own repertoire of stock phrases and rhetorical sleights, a childish old man, whose head is scarcely strong enough to weather the current storms.[11]

Only a few months before, Metternich had seemed resigned to disaster. 'I am an old physician', he told a visiting diplomat, 'and can distinguish between temporary and fatal diseases. We now face one of the latter. We'll hold on for as long as we can, but I have doubts about the outcome.' The chaos in Vienna's streets gave Metternich's enemies in the imperial household the opportunity they sought. Led by the emperor's sister-in-law, the Archduchess Sophie, they closed ranks, demanding his resignation. Metternich gave way but only after a long-winded oration in which he listed his accomplishments over a fifty-year career. Then, fleeing Vienna's Hofburg palace in the back of a laundry cart (but not disguised as a washerwoman, as some historians insist), he took the train from Vienna's Nordbahn railway station, heading for London. Looters had already set fire to his summer mansion in Vienna's outskirts. It burned behind him.[12]

Emperor Ferdinand (ruled 1835–1848) is a Habsburg mystery. He was a keen botanist and in later life a shrewd speculator on the stock market and in real estate, amassing a large personal fortune. But he was epileptic, an illness that was misunderstood at the time, had a cruelly misshapen skull, and gave off an air of boredom and idiocy, as if everything was too hard or bothersome for his intellect to master. In any other ruler, his bon mot, 'Governing is easy, it's signing my name that's difficult', might have been taken as evidence of a profound wit, but in Ferdinand's case it was seen as confirming his inadequacy as a monarch. (In fact, it was probably directed at the mountains of paperwork he was expected to sign off every day.)[13]

Faced with a succession of delegations and petitions from civic dignitaries, anxious professors, and ebullient radicals, Ferdinand's response was 'Tell the people that I agree to everything!' And so it was. Court heralds in bright tabards and ministers in sober frockcoats variously announced over the next few days a constitution, the summons of a parliament, and an end to censorship. Booksellers moved their stocks of previously banned books from cupboards into shop windows. On the evening of 15 March, Ferdinand rode around Vienna in an open carriage to rapturous applause. As the crowds thronged around him, the emperor tearfully asked them why they had not told him earlier what they wanted. That evening, he appeared on the balcony of the Hofburg palace in Vienna, again to rapturous applause.[14]

Restoring the genie of revolution to the bottle was another matter. Throughout the Austrian Empire, every institution—village councils, reading clubs, and even lunatic asylums—began composing constitutions and distributing manifestos. Individuals, too, printed handbills and posters, listing demands. Some petitions gathered as many as twenty thousand signatures or were launched at meetings where thousands were in attendance. Mobs worked up by the press harassed the real Count Frankenstein, the inventor of electrolysis and politically a conservative. They played *Katzenmusik* (literally 'caterwauling': normally done by screeching mistuned fiddles) outside his home in Graz in Styria, causing him either to kill himself or to die of a heart attack.[15]

Vienna dissolved into anarchy. Idlers and unemployed camped out in the city's Prater park as part of a hastily improvised poor relief and public works scheme—they typically spent the days shirking and the nights looting. The interior minister published in April a constitution for the non-Hungarian part of the Austrian Empire and then immediately rewrote it, since the news that the new imperial parliament was to have an upper house of lords and a lower house elected only by the wealthy set off a furious reaction on the streets. Ministries fell in rapid succession, each less capable than the one before of controlling events. In May, Ferdinand temporarily abandoned the capital for the safety of Innsbruck in the Tyrol. Power in Vienna passed into the hands of revolutionary committees, at the head of which stood an 'Academic Legion' of students, graduates, and professors, who made the university a powerhouse of radical speech making, violent demonstrations, and noisy addresses.

As part of his policy of concession, Ferdinand had in April 1848 given in to the demands of the Hungarian diet and agreed to the so-called April Laws. The April Laws amounted to a new constitutional settlement for Hungary (which is why the constitution published by the interior minister in Vienna had left Hungary out). It had been rushed through the Hungarian diet on the rumour that crowds of peasants were descending on Pest—they were, but only because it was market day. The April Laws made Hungary self-governing, although still united to the rest of the Habsburg lands through the person of the ruler. They additionally laid down freedom of the press, the abolition of serfdom in the countryside, merger with Transylvania, and legal equality, thus obliterating the special privileges of the nobility and creating a single class of citizen. A new ministry took over in Hungary, comprising all the talents—the reforming conservative Stephen Széchenyi, the charismatic journalist Louis Kossuth, and the ingenious lawyer Ferenc Deák. Their memory is recalled to this day in street names in every Hungarian town and village.

Stephen Széchenyi was Hungary's wealthiest aristocrat and, in the contemporary description, an 'Anglomaniac'. Having visited Great Britain, he was determined to make Hungary in its image. So, he founded the Hungarian Academy to cultivate science and the arts, the National Casino to give Pest the equivalent of one of London's Piccadilly clubs, a jockey club to encourage horse breeding, and the first permanent bridge across the Danube to link Pest and Buda, modelled on the town of Marlow's bridge across the River Thames. Acutely aware of Hungary's economic backwardness, he diagnosed its origin in the fossilized system of landownership, which, on the one hand, discouraged investment in agriculture and, on the other, kept most of the population in servitude. Scrap the 'nexus of subjection' (or *nexus subditelae*, as it was known at the time), and a modern Hungary might

be born. The April Laws rested on the same conceit—that a constitution which entrenched parliamentary sovereignty in a centralized
unitary state would miraculously produce a public sphere in which
citizens became *polgári*—a Hungarian word, which like the German
bürgerlich, conjured up an image not only of bourgeois prosperity but
also of courtesy, tolerance, and public spiritedness.

Hungary was simply not ready for this. Foreign visitors to
Bratislava, Pest-Buda (the two cities would only be united in 1873
as Budapest), and Cluj in Transylvania noted approvingly the coffee
houses, theatres, and elegant salon society. But the countryside was
locked in material and intellectual poverty, and it was here that most
of Hungary's population of thirteen million people lived. Noblemen
and 'rustics' often shared the same basic type of accommodation and
lodgings—wooden hovels, without glass windows, rusted cutlery and
earthenware crockery, and sparse interior furnishings. The only distinction between the two groups was that the nobleman might vaunt
his superior standing by having on the wall of his home an antique
coat of arms. Illiteracy was the norm—figures from western Hungary
suggest that only about 5 per cent of the rural population could write
their names.

Nor was Hungary Hungarian in the sense that the people there all
spoke Hungarian (or Magyar). Under 40 per cent of the population
had Hungarian as their first language. The rest spoke Romanian, German, and various Slavonic dialects that ran into one another but which
would in time stabilize as Croat, Serb, Slovak, Slovene, and Ukrainian.
The April Laws envisaged a unitary state, administered from Buda,
with a parliament elected on a franchise that favoured the better-off,
who were mainly Hungarian speaking. The official language would
also be Hungarian. Until the early 1840s, the official language in Hungary had been Latin. Although few could speak Latin fluently, it was a
universal medium that had privileged education rather than any single
language community. Croatian deputies to the new Hungarian parliament felt particularly aggrieved. Elegant Latin speakers, they were
now made voiceless. When they complained, the Hungarian politician

Kossuth offended them further by announcing that he could not find Croatia on the map.[16]

For most people living in Hungary, language and identity had not yet fused, but religion and identity had. Serbs and Romanians were mostly Orthodox or Uniate. (As discussed in Chapter 17, Uniates follow an Orthodox liturgy but recognize the authority of the pope.) They knew that they were different from the Hungarians who were Catholic and Lutherans. Croats, too, recalled their separate history and the independent statehood they had enjoyed before their kingdom had become a part of Hungary back in the twelfth century. As for Transylvania, Hungarian politicians had long demanded its merger with the 'mother-kingdom', considering its continued separation from Hungary to be part of a 'divide and rule' tactic on the part of Vienna. But only a third of the Transylvanian population was Hungarian, the rest comprising Germans, Romanians, and Ukrainians. These now began organizing to oppose unification.[17]

In Hungary, collective identities set people apart. In the German Confederation, they drew people together. The lead was given by Prussia, where as early as March 1848 King Frederick William IV had publicly donned the red, black, and gold colours that symbolized German unity and announced that 'Henceforth, Prussia is merged with Germany.' The other German states fell into line, joining Prussia in appointing deputies to a 'pre-parliament' in Frankfurt. The pre-parliament's job was to organize elections across the confederation, but its decision to admit all adult males as voters was miscommunicated and, in any case, it had to leave electoral administration to the existing governments since they alone had the capacity to organize them. The result was a squeezing of the franchise to exclude those who lacked 'independent means' (a suitably vague category) and the institution of a two-tier system, whereby local assemblies would appoint delegates, who would then in turn elect the deputies.

Although the voting was generally free of violence, it was by no means secret. Over several weeks in April and early May 1848, voters queued up before tables to announce their choice for delegate, while behind the scenes local bigwigs, priests, and officials decided on the list of suitable deputies. This was Germany's first election and, supposedly, a milestone in its development as a unified nation state, but it was an embarrassment. This was not just because the franchise had been chopped about and manipulated. In district after district, only about a quarter of accredited voters turned up, prompting earnest denunciations in the press of apathy and irresponsibility. But, as today's politicians soon learn, working people often have more pressing things to worry about than manifestos and elections.[18]

In May 1848, the elected deputies met at St Paul's Church (Paulskirche) in Frankfurt, the circular interior of which had been deemed most suitable for the new German National Assembly. Its pulpit was replaced by a chairman's podium, but the large balcony was left open to the public, who from above heckled the deputies and interrupted the proceedings with jeers and cheers. Of the 830 deputies (the number fluctuated on account of deaths, resignations, boycotts, and so on), the overwhelming majority were civil servants—administrators, government clerks, professors, judges, and state prosecutors. Among these were four of the original 'Göttingen Seven', including Jacob Grimm. Now a deputy from Prussia, Grimm would explain to the assembly how freedom trumped equality and how a motion differed from an amendment.[19]

The deputies set to work immediately, appointing in June a government under the nominal oversight of a regent, who would hold office until a permanent sovereign and new constitutional order had been decided. By choosing as regent the Archduke John, the deputies ingeniously squared monarchical tradition with change, for although John was a Habsburg, his wife was a postmaster's daughter and he conducted himself without aristocratic pretensions. The parliament's deputies now began drafting a constitution for a new Germany, which they hoped would somehow mesh with the constitutions of its member states. But, as the summer wore on, frustrated radicals resorted to enlisting the mob to press home their demand for a republic, with the result that Prussian and Hessian troops were needed to protect the assembly from assault.

The German Confederation included several million Slav speakers, principally in Bohemia, Moravia, Carniola, and Prussia, but these boycotted the elections. Invited to help in the preparations for the Frankfurt National Assembly, the Czech historian František Palacký sent his famous rebuke—'The object of your assembly is to establish a federation of the German nation in place of the existing federation of princes to guide the German nation to real unity . . . but I am not a German. I am a Bohemian, of Slavonic blood.' Instead, Palacký went on to organize a rival Pan-Slav Congress in Prague, which brought together more than three hundred self-appointed delegates from Bohemia, Moravia, northern Hungary, Croatia, and Serbia, as well as Poles, Ukrainians, the Russian anarchist Mikhail Bakunin, and the Slovene poet Stanko Vraz. Having no other language in common, the congress conducted its business in German. Even so, it boldly announced that a great historical moment had arrived when the Slavonic nations of Central Europe would fuse together in brotherhood and union.[20]

Throughout the German Confederation, governments, rulers, and newly convened parliaments urged on 'the unity of Germany'. But German unity could only come at the cost of tearing Central Europe apart. A new Germany for German speakers would have to include the Austrian lands, where a German population predominated, breaking up the Austrian Empire and leaving behind a Hungary that was already on the way to full independence. Meanwhile, a new Slav state looked as if it might fill the space of what remained of the Austrian Empire, bringing together Czechs, Poles, and Ukrainians, as represented at the Pan-Slav Congress, in a new Slavonic federation. It also seemed unlikely that the South Slavs attending the congress would settle for anything less than equal statehood. Already in Zagreb, the Ban, or governor of Croatia, was talking of war.

By June 1848, the comprehensive refashioning of Central Europe looked imminent, and the vision of the nation as the basis for all political life looked on the edge of fulfilment. But it was not to be yet. Despite the drama of protest, petitioning, and earnest debate, all that had happened was that the rulers of Central Europe had pulled their troops back to barracks and left the streets to the crowd and the debating chambers to political novices. Once the rulers and their generals had recovered confidence, they would march the troops out again and reimpose the old political order. The adage that '1848 was the turning point at which modern history failed to turn' would prove nowhere more applicable than in Central Europe.[21]

CHAPTER 26

The Revenge of the Generals and the Making of Nations

T HE TIDE TURNED FIRST IN THE AUSTRIAN EMPIRE. THE AUS-
trian generals were intent on restoring the status quo. Ignoring the
emperor and his ministers in Vienna, they launched in June 1848 an
assault on Prague, scattering the Pan-Slav Congress. Then, in October,
they turned on the revolutionary committees in Vienna, unleashing an
artillery barrage and storming the city. The left-wing deputy of the German National Assembly, Robert Blum, who was in Vienna to support
the revolution there, was captured during the assault. After a summary
trial, a military court condemned Blum to the gallows on grounds of
sedition, ignoring the immunity he had as a deputy of the assembly.

The Austrian generals were equally scornful of the imperial parliament that was meeting in Vienna. It had been in session since July
with some 380 representatives drawn from across the Austrian Empire,
except Hungary, which had its own diet. So far, the parliament had not
achieved much. It had declared serfdom abolished but had left unresolved the tricky matter of how landlords were to be compensated for
the loss of rents and services. The deputies sat in national blocs, bick-
ered (relations between Czechs and Germans were especially tense),
and indecorously exchanged blows in the street. The minutes of the
parliament survive, showing session after session wasted on procedural
points, interjections, and quibbles over who had said what.[1]

The fighting in the capital gave the generals the excuse to relocate
the imperial parliament to the insignificant city of Kroměříž (Kremsier)
in Moravia, where it continued in futile debate. Following the Austrian generals' lead, King Frederick William IV of Prussia authorized his

army to suppress the Prussian National Assembly in Berlin. In November 1848, the Prussian general Wrangel sat down in front of the theatre where the assembly was meeting, ordered the deputies to disperse, and watched in silence as they filed past him. The next month, King Frederick William published his own constitution for Prussia, ignoring the one that the parliament had been drafting. In short order, the Austrian imperial parliament and the Prussian National Assembly had both been muzzled. Of the four great representative bodies thrown up by the revolutions of 1848, only the German National Assembly in Frankfurt and the Hungarian parliament remained.

Frederick William's new constitution for Prussia was sufficiently reformist to give hope to the deputies in Frankfurt. Having laboriously completed their work on a German constitution, the assembly now voted him emperor. The deputies were hoping to use Frederick William's authority to buttress their own waning prestige, but the king dismissed the offer of this 'crown of dirt and clay' and 'the dog collar with which people want to chain me to the 1848 revolution'. The end came swiftly. In May 1849, the king withdrew the mandates of the Prussian deputies in Frankfurt. Austria, Saxony, and Hanover did the same, forcing the assembly's dissolution. Uprisings in support of the assembly erupted in Dresden, the Rhineland Palatinate, and Baden. They were brutally suppressed by Prussian and Saxon troops. 'Sleep, sleep, my child! The Prussian is walking around' is still a lullaby in Baden.[2]

In the Austrian Empire, the generals convinced Emperor Ferdinand to abdicate. He had agreed the April Laws with Hungary and had thus set Hungary on the path to independence, so in the generals' eyes he had to go. Ferdinand went gladly, resigning in December 1848, for he had better things to do in his greenhouses. Ferdinand's heir was his brother, Franz Karl, but as a moderate and modest man, the generals had no time for him either—nor, it would seem, had his wife, the Archduchess Sophie, who urged him to give up his rights. So, the generals installed as ruler Ferdinand's nephew, Franz Joseph, the son of Franz Karl and Sophie. Young, impressionable, and passionate about army uniforms and parades, Franz Joseph was a willing cipher. He would give them in return the war in Hungary for which they yearned.

Since the summer of 1848, Hungary had been in a state of civil war. The nationalities in the kingdom were bound to resist Hungarian claims to political hegemony, so Serbs, Romanians, Croats, Transylvanian Germans, and Slovaks took up arms against Hungarian rule. The Austrian generals spurred their leaders on, supporting the Ban of Croatia with money and supplies when he invaded Hungary in September 1848. The Hungarian government held out, ably led by Louis Kossuth. As finance minister, Kossuth did the impossible, floating a new paper currency which retained its value even though it was unbacked by bullion. Given responsibility for raising an army, Kossuth again surprised, eventually conjuring up two hundred thousand recruits and factories that churned out uniforms and munitions, as well as field hospitals and rest homes for the wounded.

Kossuth was a spellbinding orator who could hold audiences of both politicians and peasants mesmerised in speeches that lasted more than three hours. He was also a master of self-advertisement. Hungary's new banknotes bore his expansive signature, while the newspaper he started was boldly called *Kossuth's News*. Step by step, he widened the breach between Hungary and Vienna, making compromise impossible. Kossuth always claimed to be standing by the rights that Emperor Ferdinand had given to Hungary in the 1848 April Laws. But the April Laws had only given Hungary limited self-government, not the complete political independence for which Kossuth called. When the Ban of Croatia invaded Hungary in September 1848, the diet set up a committee of national defence to coordinate policy and appointed Kossuth its chairman. Kossuth led Hungary to disaster.[3]

In 1848, the Hungarian diet had agreed to move its sessions from Bratislava to Pest-Buda, from which point the city counted as the kingdom's capital—the main royal palace was there as well as the law courts, so the decision made sense. Pest-Buda now became the target of the imperial forces when they entered Hungary in December, forcing Kossuth to abandon the new capital and move the seat of government to Debrecen in the east. From there, Kossuth's generals waged war, pushing westwards to recover the capital, which changed hands in the spring of 1849, finally falling for good to the imperial forces in July. As the fighting intensified, Hungary's government became brutal, enacting decrees with retrospective force that imposed the death penalty for anything that fell within its capacious definition of treason.[4]

For most of the war, the Hungarian leaders claimed that they were only seeking to make good the April Laws granted by Ferdinand in 1848 and that their revolution was thoroughly lawful. It was not until April 1849 that the diet meeting in Debrecen formally declared Hungary's independence and deposed the 'perjured house of Habsburg', installing Kossuth as governor. The declaration, which was drafted by Kossuth, was sent to all the European capitals in the hope of rallying support for the Hungarian cause. But it was a sorry and unconvincing document that floridly rehearsed the crimes done to the Hungarians over three hundred years by the country's Habsburg rulers. It showed no sympathy for the aspirations of the various nationalities in Hungary, denouncing them as 'rebels', 'traitors', and 'bands of robbers'. As one Hungarian general subsequently observed, it was precisely because Kossuth's government had failed to accommodate the other national groups living in Hungary that they had all ended up on the Habsburg side.[5]

The Austrian and Hungarian armies were numerically an even match, although the Austrian side was the better trained and equipped. What tilted the military balance was Russia. To speed up Hungary's defeat, the young Austrian emperor Franz Joseph turned to Tsar Nicholas I, travelling to Warsaw to beg assistance in person. He found the railway journey comfortable and his host sympathetic. The tsar was alarmed that several thousand Poles were volunteers in the Hungarian army and that former leaders of rebellions against Russian rule in Poland were also among its generals and staff officers. The communiqué announcing the meeting of the two emperors duly presented the Hungarian uprising as threatening the peace of Europe with anarchy and as requiring an international response. The Russian offensive began in June; Hungary's generals surrendered in August.[6]

Hungary was now crushed. Its generals were hanged, and several thousand people sentenced to hard labour, which often amounted to a death sentence. Kossuth fled into exile. Military rule followed, after which Franz Joseph ordered the comprehensive integration of Hungary into the Austrian Empire. He replaced Hungary's old counties with districts administered directly from Vienna and for a few years even made German the official language. Centralization was matched by modernization. Franz Joseph ordered that Hungary's antique laws, frozen in a largely sixteenth-century form, be replaced by the up-to-date Austrian Civil Code. And, whereas the Hungarian parliament had dealt with the problem of peasant serfdom only superficially, blustering about the noble dignity that attached to all citizens, Franz Joseph pushed through the detailed changes that actually liberated the peasants, granting them freehold tenures on largely generous terms. Although generations of Hungarians have celebrated Kossuth as the emancipator of the peasants, their true benefactor was the young Franz Joseph.

The other parts of the Habsburg Empire in Central Europe had not rebelled against their sovereign with the same vigour as Hungary (although there had been risings in Habsburg-ruled northern Italy and a short-lived insurrection in Galicia). Even so, Franz Joseph brought the rest of the empire into line. Bit by bit, the Hungarian model was rolled out across the Austrian Empire. Franz Joseph ordered the provincial parliaments abolished, dismissed the puny parliament still meeting in Kroměříž, installed a regime of harsh censorship, arrested or exiled his critics, made German the language of administration and secondary education, and restored the privileges of the Catholic Church, including its right to censor religious publications. As a popular saying put it at the time, the empire was now governed by four armies—'a standing army of soldiers, a sitting army of bureaucrats, a kneeling army of priests, and a creeping army of informers'.[7]

By the beginning of the 1850s, it seemed as if Central Europe was back where it had been a decade before. The old regimes were again in power and the map of Central Europe had not, after all, been redrawn. But something had happened. The idea of the nation had been implanted in ordinary people's consciousness. Hitherto a rallying point mostly for poets, scholars, teachers, and antiquarians, nationalism was becoming a mass phenomenon. The events of 1848 had not only asked people to take sides but also generated new heroes. Men adopted their beards, women embroidered samplers with their sayings, and children composed verses in their honour.

The struggles of 1848 energized new communities and created new badges of belonging. Clothing was one way people showed to which national group they adhered. Czechs now distinguished themselves with elaborately buttoned jackets, and Slovenes with dormouse pelts. Germans preferred cloaks and broad hats, and certainly not the *Frack*, or jacket with tails, which was thought to symbolize political submissiveness since it was what a petitioner had to wear when meeting the ruler. Clothing was expensive and so in Hungary an alternative was found in facial hair, especially moustaches, of which one diligent observer noted no fewer than twenty-three varieties. Each denoted a different national affiliation, he explained, including the 'Slav catfish' style. Adventurous patriots also flaunted cockades in the national colours, even at the cost of arrest and imprisonment.[8]

Nationalism was not just a political posture but also an everyday event. It was, in the famous description of the nineteenth-century French historian Ernest Renan, 'a daily plebiscite'—a people's continuous affirmation of their wish to live in a community. But nationalism was not only a conversation among the living but also a communion with the past. So, when it came to dress, patriots invoked history in the form of folk costumes. Most of the outfits they chose were invented and had little to do with genuine traditions. The gaudy Kalocsa pattern used on embroidered shirts and blouses in Hungary (and still sold to tourists in Budapest) was taken from a design originally used in Serbian-populated villages in the south of the country. In Bavaria, photographers and artists concocted a supposedly historical style or promoted homemade items submitted by seamstresses in competitions for the best-dressed couple in the district. As for a German dress, there was little consensus, although the fashions of the Black Forest and hunting jackets were thought the most authentically national, with 'costume societies' (*Trachtenvereine*) advertising the various styles.[9]

Nationality was embedded in everyday semiotics—namely, a system of signs that gave out messages telling who a person was, to which group they belonged, and how they should be classified. Within this scheme, alcohol occupied a high place as a marker of kinship and distinction. Hungarians, in particular, were convinced not only of the merits of Hungarian wine but also that good wine was a sign both of nobility and of Hungarianness. Wishing to restore what he called the 'ancient glory' of Hungarian wine, Széchenyi ruled that Pest's National Casino should stock in its cellar 'forty-four kinds of Hungarian wine and twelve kinds of foreign wine'. He also specified in one of his wills (Széchenyi was a prolific will writer) that his heart be cut out after his death, pickled in a distillation of Hungarian wine, and exhibited in the National Museum.

Other nations drank differently. Hungarian commentators explained that the German preferred beer, and the Slovak downed spirits made of potato or plum. The Slovak's dedication to hard liquor was not only a supposedly national characteristic but also one of the ways Hungarians explained the backwardness and poverty of Slovak rural life. (English writers made the same connection between poteen and penury in Ireland.) Even when drunk, the different nations were supposed to exhibit their own characteristics. So, the Hungarian became maudlin and boastful, the Slovak feigned wisdom, the German chattered and knocked things over, the Romanian grumbled and was violent, and the Ukrainian mumbled to himself and was vengeful.[10]

Classification extended to sexuality, with patriots devising taxonomies of womanhood in which their own women came out the cleanest and most beautiful. For the patriotic Serb Jakov Ignjatović, who had been brought up in Hungary, Serbian women stood out among those of all other nationalities 'like a poppy in bloom among ears of corn'. Put a Serbian woman next to a German one, he explained, and it was like putting a tiger next to a lamb. Slovak writers were equally proud of their womenfolk, denouncing Hungarian women as overweight, because 'the Hungarian is an admirer of fat women, the same way he likes to see baked bread on his table in great quantities.' Slovak women should be kissed differently too, one writer explained, 'from brow to chin, then across the face from ear to ear, and both times the lips meet, soul meets soul'.[11]

Taverns were another signifier of belonging. In mixed communities, national groups kept to different hostelries, some of which also served dishes named after national heroes or in the national colours. Adam Mickiewicz's national epic *Pan Tadeusz* (1834) itemized the Polish cuisine—beetroot soup, forest mushrooms, white cheeses, and the sauerkraut and pork dish known as *bigos*. Hungarians, meanwhile, celebrated red pepper, which by the 1840s was considered thoroughly national, along with paprika chicken and the thin peppery stew called *gúlyás* (whence today's goulash). Despite its strong regional variations, German cuisine was the benchmark against which all other nations measured their culinary excellence, since it was universally held to embody the German temperament—in one contemporary description, 'gross, coarse, greasy, massive, and incoherent'.[12]

Coffee houses, which spread rapidly across Central Europe in the nineteenth century, were also marks of affinity. They were gendered in the sense that they were masculine environments—women tended to keep to outdoor 'garden' cafés or places that advertised *Kaffee und Konditorei* (coffee and cakes). But along with casinos, of the type Széchenyi had brought to Pest, coffee houses were increasingly nationalized. In Sibiu in Transylvania, there were separate casinos for Hungarians, Germans, and Romanians. In Chernivtsi in the Bukovina, where Jews predominated as consumers, coffee houses advertised their distance from the divisive politics of national identity by adopting neutral 'imperial' names—Black Eagle, Café Habsburg, and Kaiser Café.[13]

The nation was signalled in dress, alcohol, food, coffee houses, ideas of womanhood, and the etiquette of kissing. But it could be heard too. Classical music originated in Central Europe. The courts of rulers and palaces of aristocrats vied for musicians and, from the late eighteenth century onwards, for composers. In Mozart's Vienna, and in Haydn's Eszterháza in Hungary, the four-movement orchestral symphony and the solo-instrument concerto triumphed over the contemporary fashion for catchy tunes, mostly taken from Italian opera, that played against a backdrop of conversation and card playing. Music was no longer wallpaper but something to be heard and attended to, in silence—just to make sure, Prussian grenadiers patrolled concert audiences in Berlin. And compositions were no longer occasional, to be performed just a few times and then forgotten, as had been the fate for almost a century of J. S. Bach's *St John's Passion*. Composers wrote works to last, in the hope that they would become part of a historical repertoire—in short, become 'classical'.

Composers were feted and no longer treated as tradesmen who should sup with the servants. By the early decades of the nineteenth century, they had become stars. The novelist and mistress of Fryderyk Chopin, George Sand (Amantine Dupin), complained light-heartedly of the composer's reputation: 'in a period of two hours, with a couple of flourishes of the hand, he put six thousand and several hundred francs in his pocket, and applause, encores, and the flutterings of the most beautiful women in Paris—the rascal.' Other composers cultivated celebrity. While performing piano solos, Franz Liszt had fake faints, being carried offstage and then staggering back to resume playing. He selected his mistresses for effect too—the dancer Lola Montez (before she went off with King Ludwig I of Bavaria), a married Saxon duchess, and the cigar-smoking Carolyne zu Sayn-Wittgenstein.[14]

Audiences had long associated music with national difference—so, in an old French saw, 'Spain sobs, Italy wails, Germany bellows, and Flanders howls.' But music now became self-consciously national, with composers advertising tunes and melodies as unique to the nation. Chopin was among the first, distilling in his mazurkas, polkas, and sonatas popular folk melodies from the Polish countryside. Chopin claimed to have learned these in his childhood, but they were probably taken from a printed collection of Polish folk songs.

Even so, they became the rallying call of Polish nationalism at a time when most other expressions of cultural identity were banned in Prussian and Russian Poland. They were, as the German composer Robert Schumann remarked at the time, 'cannon concealed among flowers'.[15]

The association of music with the nation was even more explicit in the works of Richard Wagner and the Czech composer Bedřich Smetana. Both incorporated in their works what they claimed to be folk melodies but which were clearly of wider provenance than just their homelands—Smetana's famous melody in *Ma Vlast* (*My Homeland*) celebrating Prague's Vltava River is also found in the Israeli national anthem, and both probably derive from a sixteenth-century Italian madrigal. Importantly, too, Smetana and Wagner fused music with legend. Smetana took themes from the earliest medieval Czech chronicles, which he set to stirring anthems, while Wagner plundered the Central European and Scandinavian repertoire of myths to create the seventeen-hour-long fusion of epics in his 'Ring of the Nibelung'. In their operas, both composers also chose settings that evoked an imagined national past—turreted castles, mountain crags, primordial forests, and cavalcades of jolly medieval craftsmen.

It did not matter that the orchestral music, piano concertos, and opera stories were not national at all, but either confected, manipulated, or part of a larger European musical canon—the bagpipe drone of Chopin's mazurkas is hardly unique to Poland. The aim of composers was to present audiences with (in Wagner's words) 'an image of their true nature', out of which a new artistic identity might arise that glorified the nation. Wagner's Festival Hall in Bayreuth and the so-called Provisional Theatre in Prague, where Smetana was director, were the musical factories that would cultivate Germans and Czechs and regenerate them with new national sensibilities.[16]

Operas, symphonies, and recitals were for the better-off. But their melodies passed down the social hierarchy, being sung around tables in taverns and performed by bands in parks, outdoor cafés, and assembly rooms (*Reduten*). They were also part of the repertoire of the new dance halls which sprang up in the first decades of the nineteenth century, each often capable of accommodating thousands of paying guests—up to eight thousand at a time in the (original) Vienna Odeon, founded in 1845. Programmes in popular venues were usually medleys—a mix of folk ballads, waltzes, and marches. But many included works of an overtly political and nationalist content, like Liszt's 'Among the Mountains' ('*A hegyek között*'), which was dedicated to the generals who had fought for Hungary in 1848–1849; Kornél Abrányi's 'Don't Cry, My Homeland' ('*Ne sírj, hazam*'), recollecting the exiled Kossuth; and Chopin's 'Polonaise', celebrating Poland's struggle for independence.[17]

Choirs were the great vehicles for the popularization of music and the dissemination of national melodies and lyrics. They spread by the use of lithography in printing sheet music, which made it for the first time affordable, and by increasingly furious competitions that sometimes meant that every choir had to receive first prize. In mixed neighbourhoods in Bohemia, the different German and Czech national communities fielded separate choirs, which were often linked to local gymnastic associations, which are better thought of as militias in waiting. Throughout Central Europe, repertoires were unashamedly national and patriotic. German choirs sang 'The Watch on the Rhine', Czechs sang Josef Tyl's 'Where Is My Home?', and Hungarians sang Sándor Petőfi's 'National Song'. Material was updated in dedicated monthlies and weeklies and in new anthologies bearing such titles as 'The Ringing of Bells', 'Musical Leaves', and, for Czechs, 'A Wreath of Patriotic Songs Woven for Homeland-Loving and Self-Sacrificing Girls'.[18]

National belonging was not a matter of fact but of decision. Although his mother was German, Kossuth chose to be Hungarian, but his uncle became a notable Slovak patriot. Many, however, had no obvious grounds for embracing a single affiliation. One soldier at the beginning of the twentieth century wrote his diary in four different languages—German for regimental matters, Slovene when thinking about his girlfriend, Serbian for songs he recalled, and Hungarian for his sexual fantasies. Others changed what they said they were according to circumstance and financial advantage, or they were indifferent, often conversing in several languages or in a blended argot. Even among educated city folk, when writing in a hurry (as for instance on postcards) they might mix words or grammars, moving (as in Styria) from German to Slovene and back again.[19]

How people identified was something impressed by neighbours, parents, friends, and the workplace. But government and the bureaucracy were also involved. In the Austrian Empire, the first steps were taken in 1849 to itemize the linguistic communities to which people might be said to belong. Nine were identified—German, Hungarian, Italian, Romanian, Polish, Czech, Ukrainian, Slovene, and Croatian (although Croatian might be written in both Latin and Cyrillic script to accommodate Serbs). These nine then became the official languages in which teaching might be conducted in schools and the empire's laws published. But the nine languages bore little relation to the medley of languages and dialects that were actually in use. Most obviously, Slovak was not included, since it was thought close enough to Czech not to merit a category of its own. But Yiddish, Friulian, Dalmatic, Hutsul, Wind (or Windisch), Lemko, Pulsch, Armenian, Gypsy Romani, and Szlonzok were also left out.[20]

The first Austrian censuses had been primarily interested in identifying who might be recruited to the army and how many horses they had. But from 1880, Austrian censuses also had a box in which the responsible head of the household had to write in the 'language of daily use' (*Umgangssprache*) on behalf of his family and servants. Again, it was the same nine languages, except that Czech was now hyphenated with Slovak and Moravian. The Hungarian census, which was held separately in 1881, was more accommodating, with categories for Romani speakers, Armenians, and mutes. Later Hungarian censuses directed the public to eight named categories, although allowing them to write in an affiliation from a subsidiary list. Officials conducting the census advised people who described what they spoke as Saxon, Swabian, Yiddish, Landler, or just 'our language' (*unsere Sprache*) to call it 'German'.[21]

In Habsburg Central Europe, censuses forced people into predetermined linguistic categories, effacing the intermediate identities which made nationality fuzzier and so more permeable. Friulian, Lemko, and Hutsul barely survive today, although Hutsul can be heard spoken in Michael Cimino's film *The Deer Hunter* (1978), which was partly filmed in Cleveland. Migrants from Carniola carried Wind or the Windisch language to Ohio, where its memory survives even though the community news sheet is now published in English. The last speaker of Dalmatic died in 1898. Such is often the fate of languages and of the badges of belonging that do not appear on approved government lists.

Outside the Habsburg lands, most censuses were unconcerned with nationality, simply presuming that the populations were German or that what they spoke was unimportant. (Only in 1905 were Frisian and Danish speakers separately identified in Schleswig-Holstein.) Prussia was different not only in the sheer scale of the information it gathered but also in categorizing the population by 'mother tongue' (*Muttersprache*). Starting with the censuses of 1858 and 1861, Prussian administrators included besides German a medley of other linguistic options—Czech, Moravian, Wendish, Polish, Kashubian, Masurian, Lithuanian, Frisian, and so on. But the raw results were then aggregated in the final count. All Slav speakers, including Wends, Kashubs, and Masurians, were joined together as Polish; Frisian, Dutch, and Yiddish speakers were classified as German; and in some aggregations, Lithuanians were made into Germans too, since demographers were convinced that they would soon become Germans anyway.[22]

The purpose of the Prussian censuses was not to give a snapshot of the linguistic make-up of the kingdom. It was driven by policy and intended to show where non-Germans predominated and where the Germanization of the population through schooling, expulsion, and forcible resettlement should be intensified. But it yielded one of the most extraordinary visual representations of its kind: *The Linguistic Map of the Prussian State based on the 1861 Census*. The map shows Prussia as having at its core a solid body of beige-coloured German speakers but threatened on its eastern flank by an undifferentiated red block of Polish speakers. Even so, an inset map reassures the reader that Germans were in the overwhelming majority, not only in Prussia but also throughout Central Europe, including Flanders, the Netherlands, and most of Switzerland. A slightly paler wash includes Scandinavia, Denmark, and England, on the grounds that these countries were reliably 'Germanic'.[23]

The Linguistic Map of the Prussian State illustrates dilemmas already evident in Ernst Moritz Arndt's song, 'Where Is the German's Fatherland?' (1813):

> *Is it Prussia, is it Swabia?*
> *Is it where the vines blossom on the Rhine?*
> *Is it where the seagull moves on the Jutland coast?*
> *Oh no! No! No!*
> *His fatherland must be bigger!*
> [And so on, for a further eight verses.]

But how extensive should the fatherland be? Should it be the 'little Germany' of Prussia and the smaller states of the German Confederation or the 'big Germany' which also drew in the German-speaking parts of Austria? Or could it be part of a new superstate, which combined the German Confederation with all of the Austrian Empire? This was certainly Franz Joseph's ambition in the early 1850s, since he reckoned that in such an 'empire of seventy million' he would inevitably play the leading role. Or might not the Germans fulfil what some already saw as their historic destiny, expanding the frontier of Germany into the 'wildernesses' of the east? To Arndt's still unresolved question, Bismarck would provide one answer.

CHAPTER 27

Bismarck, Khuen-Héderváry's Croatia, and the Presumption of the Law

THE EXAMPLE OF OTTO VON BISMARCK (LIVED 1815–1898) will be welcome to parents who fear their teenage children are taking not so much a gap year as a gap life. Brought up not in historic Prussia (as commonly thought) but in Prussian Pomerania, Bismarck had an unsettled youth, abandoning his university studies and unsuccessfully starting on several careers. In between, he terrorized his neighbours with drunken brawls and reckless behaviour with shotguns and practised such japes as setting squirrels loose in women's bedrooms. His youthful affairs principally involved the daughters of wealthy parents, whom he hoped would be able to pay off his debts.

Bismarck only married in his early thirties and his wife, the shy Johanna von Puttkamer, taught him to be serious and to consider a career in public service. Under her guidance, Bismarck embraced Pietism, a form of Lutheranism that stresses prayer and the inner light of faith, shorn of the paraphernalia of ritual observance. Bismarck's letters to Johanna cannot fail to move the reader:

> I did not marry you to have a society wife for others, but in order
> to love you in God and according to the requirements of my own
> heart, to have a place in this alien world that no barren wind can
> cool, a place warmed by my own fireplace, to which I can draw
> near while it storms and freezes outside.[1]

The Bismarck that comes over in his correspondence with Johanna hardly squares with the many hundreds of stern bronze statues and stone 'Bismarck towers' that once honoured his memory. (Most have now been destroyed, either melted down during the Second World War or pulled down more recently.) A chance wax-cylinder recording by Thomas Edison also confirms the recollection of contemporaries that the supposedly stirring orator had a voice that was, in fact, squeaky and faltering.[2]

Notwithstanding Johanna's influence on him, Bismarck remained a gluttonous, hard-drinking oaf for the rest of his life—eventually, even his doctor refused to treat him, recommending instead that he consult a veterinarian. Railway staff had a hard job collecting up all the empty bottles of beer that Bismarck let roll into corners during his train journeys. Visitors to London today may care to admire the benches on the Thames Embankment just east of Westminster Bridge. It was on one of these that in 1885 Bismarck slept off a hangover while on his way to the British Foreign Office.

The Bismarck ancestral home was a draughty, rat-ridden farmhouse with tumbledown stables. But Bismarck counted as a nobleman or Junker. So, once he had resolved on a career in public service, it proved easy for him to work his way up the political ladder, moving up from the local office of commissioner for dykes to a member of the Prussian provincial diet. His timing was good and so were his political alliances, for he backed the conservative cause in the revolution of 1848. Having made his mark as an ardent royalist, Bismarck was King Frederick William IV's choice in 1851 to become Prussian representative at meetings of the committee of the German Confederation. Bismarck took the job eagerly. As he later put it to his friend, the American historian John Motley, he had found the 'House of Phrases' (as he described the Prussian diet) full of 'uncommonly childish and excited politicians' where 'people talk nonsense.'[3]

The committee met in Frankfurt with the Austrian delegate in the chair, which was the arrangement agreed at the Congress of Vienna in 1815. As a mark of his superior status, only the Austrian might smoke at meetings. Upon joining the committee, Bismarck promptly lit a cigar, using the Austrian's matches. Misunderstood at the time as a breach of etiquette, it was an overt challenge to the political order. Up until this point, the German Confederation had rested on a balance between Austria and Prussia. From now on, Bismarck worked to tilt the scales to Prussia's advantage, undermining Austria's influence among the smaller states in the confederation and isolating Austria diplomatically. He also urged Prussian neutrality when in 1859 the sly French emperor Louis-Napoleon III lured the young Franz Joseph into a hopeless war that saw the Habsburgs lose Lombardy and Milan to the new kingdom of Italy.

The rise of Prussia and its eventual transformation into the German Empire was by no means a foregone conclusion. Prussia had been humiliated militarily by the first Napoleon, had failed at the Congress of Vienna (1814–1815) to annex Saxony, and had settled into a docile foreign policy, always nervously looking over its shoulder at neighbouring Russia. Its free-trade zone, or customs union (*Zollverein*), which it rolled out across much of the German Confederation after 1834, was not an underhand bid for Central European mastery, as historians often suggest. Prussia was territorially fragmented, with its parts scattered, and goods passing from one part of the kingdom to another often had to pay swingeing tariffs as they crossed state boundaries. Additionally, the customs union benefited the weaker neighbouring states, since they made a disproportionate profit on goods coming from outside the union, making them less vulnerable to a Prussian takeover.

But Prussia's economic rise was inexorable. The Ruhr Valley, the bulk of which Prussia had received in 1815 in compensation for Saxony, proved to be an unexpected powerhouse of coal and steel. Railways spread both opportunities and wealth, harnessing, as one early entrepreneur excitedly put it, 'the triumphant car of technological progress to smoking colossuses'. But the first Prussian attempts to build locomotives were disappointing—they either blew their gaskets or only moved on downhill lines. The technology had, instead, to be imported from the Stephenson yards in Newcastle. Even so, by joining the railway race late (a full decade behind Great Britain and Belgium), Prussia was able to leapfrog to the six-wheel 2-2-2 locomotive, which coped better with steeper inclines and so had less need for cuttings and detours. Between 1850 and 1870, the mostly state-owned Prussian railway network expanded tenfold to more than five thousand kilometres of track.[4]

Bismarck has left behind enough speeches for historians to find inconsistencies in his thinking. He wavered between policies, and the only personal ambition he disclosed was to drink in his lifetime ten thousand bottles of champagne. But by the early 1860s (if not before) he had arrived at some sort of plan. Anticipating that the new Prussian king William I (ruled 1861–1888) would soon call upon him to head a new ministry, Bismarck visited London in the summer of 1861 to gauge international opinion. There he met the Conservative British politician Benjamin Disraeli, to whom he explained in the fluent English he had learned at university:

> I shall soon be compelled to undertake the conduct of the Prussian government. . . . As soon as the army shall have been brought into such condition as to inspire respect, I shall seize the first best pretext to declare war against Austria, dissolve the confederation, subdue the minor states, and give national unity to Germany under Prussian leadership. I have come here to say this to the Queen's ministers.

But Bismarck did not say this just to Disraeli. Also in the room was the Austrian ambassador.[5]

As they left the meeting, Disraeli observed to the Austrian envoy, 'Take care of that man, he means what he says.' But back in Vienna, Emperor Franz Joseph ignored Disraeli's reported advice, thinking Bismarck's words to be bluster. Within less than five years, Franz Joseph had been tricked into going to war with Prussia and been thoroughly trounced. It did not take much. The Austrians thought they had their army hidden in Bohemia, but Bismarck's private banker Gerson von Bleichröder telegraphed the factors there to ascertain the purchase price of fodder. Where the cost was highest, there was the Austrian army. It helped, too, that the Prussian army was equipped with breech-loading rifles rather than with the Austrians' much clumsier muzzle-loading muskets. Outmanoeuvred and outgunned, the Austrian army collapsed in just seven weeks over the summer of 1866.

Bismarck dissolved the German Confederation and annexed to Prussia most of the territory north of the River Main. The kingdom of Hanover was abolished in 1866 and its last king, George V (lived 1819–1878), the son of Ernest Augustus, went into exile. Liechtenstein, previously a member state of the confederation, declared its independence and neutrality. Squeezed between Austria and Switzerland, it was too remote for Bismarck to worry about. Luxembourg also squeaked its way to independence. In the hands of an enemy, its massive fort—the so-called Gibraltar of the North—posed a threat to all its neighbours. By international agreement, the duchy was declared neutral on condition that its duke dismantle the fort. It took sixteen years of work to demolish it.

Five years after defeating Franz Joseph, Bismarck fulfilled the 'Little German' solution. Reckoning that France would soon take arms against the enlarged Prussian state, Bismarck diplomatically isolated the French emperor Louis-Napoleon III and then picked a fight with him. In the summer of 1870, the Prussian armies led by General von Moltke destroyed their French adversaries at Metz and Sedan, and Louis-Napoleon was captured. Bismarck, King William I of Prussia, Moltke, and the vanquished emperor met in a weaver's cottage near Sedan. After shaking hands, Napoleon went into captivity and the others marched on Paris. Four months later, in January 1871, Bismarck choreographed the proclamation of William I as German emperor in the Palace of Versailles's Hall of Mirrors. As well as first minister of Prussia, Bismarck now became chancellor of the new German Empire.

But the new empire that Bismarck had forged was one that left out the Germans of the Austrian lands—some ten million persons, as against the forty million Germans living in the new German Empire. To that extent, Bismarck provided a political solution and not an answer to the problem of German nationhood. Back in the early nineteenth century, Arndt had asked where the German's fatherland lay—

So name the great land to me!
Certainly, it must be Austria,
Rich in victory and honours.

Without Austria, Bismarck's Germany was appreciably smaller than Arndt's imagined German fatherland. For the time being, the omission was put on hold, to return with a vengeance in the two decades after 1918.

Germans (or at least most of them) had been united under Prussia. The Austrian Empire, meanwhile, split in two. Franz Joseph's absolutist rule collapsed in the 1860s, weighed down by military failure and a mountain of debt. The bankers would not lend to a sovereign who was answerable to no one. Anselm Rothschild put it bluntly—'No constitution, no money.' Step by step, Franz Joseph was forced to embrace constitutional rule. He tried at first a fake constitution, at the centre of which was an unelected parliament made up of his aristocratic chums. When this failed to convince the bankers, he went the full way, establishing in 1861 an elected parliament, or Reichsrat, for the whole Austrian Empire, made up of representatives sent by the diets of the provinces and smaller parts of the empire.[6]

The Hungarian politicians refused to play along. A Hungarian parliament met in 1861, but its members spent most of their time debating how best to translate 'indignation' from Latin into Hungarian. They refused point blank to send representatives to the Austrian parliament. In the opinion of most Hungarians, the 1848 April Laws had given Hungary independence and were still valid. So, they opposed any bid to merge their country into a mega-state with a Viennese central parliament. Behind the scenes, a few connived with Bismarck. In August 1866, a force of fifteen hundred exiles organized by the former Hungarian general George Klapka briefly invaded Hungary in support of the Prussians.[7]

Franz Joseph was desperate for a deal, for with Hungary still unsettled his influence abroad was diminished. The trick was to arrive at a solution which kept Hungary in the Habsburg orbit while giving it the freedoms previously conveyed in the April Laws. The dexterous Hungarian lawyer Ferenc Deák had the answer. Hungary would be given complete home rule but would pool military matters and foreign policy with the rest of the empire. The Settlement agreed by Franz Joseph in 1867 did exactly that. Hungary became self-governing, with its own parliament and government in Pest-Buda (after 1873, Budapest). It remained linked to the rest of the Austrian Empire through the person of the ruler and by 'common ministries' of foreign affairs and war, plus a third ministry of finance that provided the money for the other two.

The Settlement (or Compromise, *Ausgleich*) of 1867 was an ingenious solution. It kept the empire together while still dividing it in half. Hungary was one part, and all the rest the other: Bohemia, Polish Galicia, the Tyrol, Bukovina, and so on. Because the non-Hungarian part had no obvious name, it went by the monstrous official title of 'The Lands and Kingdoms Represented in the Reichsrat'. Since nobody had time for such a mouthful, it was informally called Cisleithania, meaning 'the lands on this side of the Leitha'—the Leitha was the river which then divided Hungary from Austria. In view of Hungary's new status, the empire was also renamed 'the Austro-Hungarian Empire' (Austria-Hungary, for short). Franz Joseph was duly crowned in 1867 as Hungary's king and he appointed a new Hungarian ministry.

Germany, Cisleithania, and Hungary were constitutional states in the sense that constitutions governed their public life and enumerated to varying degrees the rights belonging to citizens. All three also had recognizable parliaments. In Germany after 1871 and in Austria from 1907, all adult males had an equal vote, although in Hungary fewer than 10 per cent were eligible. Germany and Cisleithania were federal. The new German Empire kept in place the former diets of a dozen of the formerly independent German states, and Cisleithania continued to be divided up into provinces with their own governments and diets. In Hungary, the principle of the unitary state prevailed, with a central government and parliament in Budapest. Even so, Croatia retained its parliament, or Sabor, which met in Zagreb. But although there were parliaments, the regimes in Germany, Cisleithania, and Hungary were not parliamentary. In Central Europe, power remained where it had always been: with the monarch and the state bureaucracy.

The civil service set the pace. Throughout Central Europe, government ministers were mostly bureaucrats. Having worked their way up the administration, they saw themselves responsible to the ruler and not answerable to parliaments. In both Cisleithania and Hungary, it was entirely possible for the monarch to suspend the parliament or to ignore it entirely and rule through a government of bureaucratic placemen. The parliaments themselves were dominated by lawyers and state administrators (the two overlapped), who balanced their obligations to the government with the duties they owed to their political parties and constituents. It was only in the 1890s that civil servants in Germany were made to take leave of office when elected to the German parliament, or Reichstag; before this time, they were generally expected to toe the government line, supporting its legislative proposals. In Hungary, about a half of the deputies serving in the 1880s were either current or former civil servants and local government officials.[8]

Constitutions were supposed to hem in the ruler and his servants, but there were plenty of ways around them. The governments in Berlin, Budapest, and Vienna reserved to themselves all sorts of emergency powers, which meant that budgets could be enacted without parliamentary scrutiny or approval. On top of this, whole swathes of government business operated without constitutional checks, most notably military and foreign policy matters, which were considered to belong to the sovereign's prerogative. As one Prussian deputy explained approvingly to the German Reichstag in 1910, the emperor's right of command meant that 'he must always be able to say to any lieutenant, "Take ten men and close down the parliament!"' His advice was met with stormy applause.[9]

Nothing better exemplifies the power of the executive and civil service than what constitutional historians call 'the presumption of the law'. In nineteenth-century Britain, France, and the United States, the presumption of the law lay with the citizen. Where the law was silent, the citizen was free. As the 1789 French Declaration of the Rights of Man put it, 'Nothing may be prevented which is not forbidden by law, and no one may be forced to do anything not provided for by law.' But throughout Central Europe, the opposite principle applied. Where the law was silent, 'administrative discretion', or *freie Verwaltung*, prevailed, which meant that the government and bureaucracy might fill in the gaps with decrees, which bypassed the parliaments altogether. Indeed, administrative discretion was often built into the legislative process. So, laws were left ill-framed and vague, with the intention that ministerial decrees would in time flesh them out.[10]

In filling the gaps in the law, ministries of the interior were the most solicitous, regularly issuing instructions that were injurious to freedom. Since the law did not specifically allow their free operation, societies and assemblies were obvious targets, with officials imposing restrictions on how they might assemble and conduct their meetings. And because the law said nothing about behaviour on the street, police chiefs issued directives on manners, including in Hungary such nonsenses as a prohibition on flirting with well-born ladies. Since the regulations had no legislative basis other than the right of state agencies to enact and enforce them, they could not be appealed against in courts of law.[11]

Laws against socialists in Cisleithania were left deliberately vague. Socialism was not forbidden of itself, but political associations that police chiefs or the interior ministry considered 'contrary to the law' or 'seditious' were, which meant that their members were liable to fines and imprisonment on grounds that were often arbitrary. The 1870 Vagabond Law gave local officers in Cisleithania wide discretionary powers to deport from their areas individuals who were unable to demonstrate a means of support, which they used against strikers and political agitators. Since political meetings were generally allowed only if the participants were invited, organizers had to go through the laborious business of sending letters to members and logging participants in advance. Other inconveniences included the obligation to alert the police two days in advance that a meeting had been planned, which gave the authorities time to ban it on a technicality.[12]

Sometimes, government decrees were kept secret, so citizens were unaware that they were committing offences until the decrees were retrospectively published in special collections of 'hitherto uncirculated decrees'. Or the published decrees came with exclusions that were not advertised. At least in Germany, most 'police notices' were ostentatiously displayed (as they still are) to announce both the regulation and the scope of the policeman's power, including the famous notice in Baden 'It is permitted to travel on this road.' The English comic novelist Jerome K. Jerome in *Three Men on the Bummel* (1900) found German police notices absurd, akin to the German habit of numbering trees, but they disclosed the extent to which personal freedoms existed only as islands in an unregulated sea of bureaucratic power.

With a population of just over two million in 1860, the kingdom of Croatia shows in microcosm the political tensions, ambiguities around nationhood, and habits of bureaucratic management that underpinned developments throughout nineteenth-century Central Europe. Officially known as 'the Kingdom of Croatia, Slavonia, and Dalmatia', Croatia was a doll inside a doll, since it belonged within the larger Hungarian kingdom as a subordinate or, in Croatian eyes, equal part. And, despite the kingdom's official title, Dalmatia was not part of Croatia at all, since it lay in Cisleithania and was governed from Vienna, right through to 1918.

On top of this, a third of Slavonia along with a chunk of Croatia formed until 1881 a part of the Austrian Military Frontier, which was administered by the War Ministry in Vienna. Croatia's government was headed by a governor, who held the historic title of Ban. But the emperor in Vienna (in his capacity as king of Hungary) appointed the Ban on the advice of the Hungarian prime minister, without reference to the Croatian Sabor, or parliament. To add to these humiliations, there was no separate coronation of the Croatian king in Zagreb, but whoever was crowned king of Hungary automatically became king of Croatia.

Nor were Croats sure of where their destiny lay. One group, which looked to the creative but venomous Croatian bishop Josip Strossmayer (lived 1815–1905), saw Croats as a branch of the South Slavs and promoted unification with the neighbouring Serbs, but under Croatian leadership. It was to this end that Strossmayer founded in Zagreb in 1866 a specifically *Yugoslav* (or South Slav) Academy of Arts and urged reconciliation between the Catholic and Orthodox Churches. Others, who gathered in the so-called Party of Rights, looked in the opposite direction, towards a fusion of Croatia with Dalmatia and the Slovene parts of Cisleithania, and later on with Bosnia. But the abolition of the Military Frontier in 1881 made almost three hundred thousand Serbs into citizens of Croatia. Croatian politicians increasingly feared being 'swamped' by Serbs and, ultimately, being brought into a Serb-dominated South Slav state.

Relations with Hungary were never less than strained. In 1868, Croatian and Hungarian politicians had made their own constitutional settlement, or *Nagodba* (literally, 'agreement'). The deal gave Croatia rather less than home rule, for considerable powers were reserved to joint offices in Zagreb that reported to the Hungarian government in Budapest. The financial terms worked out in the *Nagodba* were not ungenerous. Although most tax revenue went to the joint offices, these kept it in Croatia to support big economic and infrastructural projects. Even so, many Croats were convinced that Hungary was going off with Croatian money. The Habsburg occupation of Ottoman Bosnia in 1878 magnified tensions. Hungarians feared a fresh admission of Slavs into Austria-Hungary that would upset the delicate balance of national groups there, but many Croats saw Bosnians as compatriots in waiting, who would tilt the demographic scales in their favour.[13]

The joint offices in Zagreb were staffed by Croats on permanent contracts and by Hungarians on secondment. Attempts to make the Croats learn Hungarian were a cause of bitter controversy. On top of this, it was never agreed whether the joint offices were actually Croatian or Hungarian institutions. Of course, they were both—the clue was in the word *joint*. But when in 1883 a middle-ranking official thought to put up inscriptions in Hungarian as well as Croatian on the coats of arms hanging before the buildings of the joint offices, mayhem followed. Riots erupted in Zagreb, the Ban resigned, and the emperor in Vienna imposed martial law. Order was only restored when the general in charge ordered writing in any language to be removed from the coats of arms.[14]

It was into this chaos that Franz Joseph parachuted the young Charles Khuen-Héderváry (lived 1849–1918) as Croatia's new Ban. Khuen-Héderváry was in every way the opposite of Bismarck. He was a superaristocrat who could trace his descent back to the twelfth century. He could even boast that one of his estates still had the stump of a poplar tree which had survived the Mongol-Tatar invasion of 1241. Spare, elegant, and wearing the most fashionable of beards, Khuen-Héderváry was married to Margaret Teleki de Szék, the astonishingly beautiful daughter of one of Transylvania's top aristocrats. But Khuen-Héderváry also patronized learned societies, was a keen geologist and student of heraldry, and had managed in his youth to notch up three law degrees. Importantly, too, he had estates in Slavonia, spoke flawless Croatian, and when in Croatian company insisted upon being known not as Charles (Károly) but as Dragutin. Khuen-Héderváry was, he proudly proclaimed, both a Hungarian and a Croat.[15]

Khuen-Héderváry shared with Bismarck a single-minded ruthlessness. Croatia had its own parliament, or Sabor. It did some good work, removing legal restrictions on Jews and Protestants, improving the quality of teacher training, legislating to remove the last encumbrances on the peasantry, and endeavouring to make the work of the law courts transparent. But the small single-chamber Sabor of just a hundred or so deputies was also a noisy critic of government policy. Newspapers published the deputies' speeches verbatim, noting too whenever a speaker was applauded or hissed. Khuen-Héderváry was determined to bring it into line.

As it was, the Sabor was elected on a narrow franchise. Only 2 per cent of the population had the vote and ballots were cast in public, so everyone could see. Khuen-Héderváry manipulated the qualification for the vote, ensuring that it went only to the wealthy and to civil servants. The government newspaper made clear the obligations of officials, whose conduct at the polls was monitored:

> All higher officials who have an influence on political events are fully responsible for upholding the official opinions, and if they do not agree with the direction the government wishes to take, they are required to forfeit their positions or to keep their own opinions private. This is a matter they must settle with their own conscience.[16]

About a half of the electorate were bureaucrats and a similar proportion of the deputies were civil servants too. Added to this, Khuen-Héderváry used his power as Ban to appoint unelected officials and churchmen to the legislature, where they made up a third of its membership. Croatia's parliament was not a check on the government; it was the government. With no sharp distinction between parliament and executive, legislation and government decree became increasingly synonymous, with the second becoming the more numerous. Journalists joked that 'the laws are missing, but we have instead a whole legion of decrees.'[17]

To diminish the opposition, Khuen-Héderváry had the police harass troublesome deputies and used local officials to fix the register of voters. He also made controversial concessions to the Serbs over the use in public of the Cyrillic alphabet and of the Serbian colours to ensure the support of Serb deputies in the Sabor. Between 1884 and 1901, the government party fixed and won five elections in a row. Even so, at the end of 1898 Khuen-Héderváry almost lost control over the Sabor. Complaints in the Sabor over the amount of money allocated to the joint ministries threatened to derail the budget. But Khuen-Héderváry's placeman in the Sabor, a university professor and so a government employee (Josip Pliverić), spelled out the Sabor's powerlessness with direct reference to the presumption of the law:

It is basic to the public law of Hungary and Croatia and in all the
textbooks that governments have the right in the absence of law to
issue decrees.

In short, if the budget was not passed, the government would imple-
ment it willy-nilly by decree. Rather than persist in its opposition, the
Sabor did as it was told and approved the budget.[18]

Khuen-Héderváry is the villain of Croatian historians, whom
they blame for hindering Croatia's democratic development and
for advancing a colonial policy that made Croatia into a satrapy of
Hungary. Yet, modern Zagreb is his achievement. Over two decades,
Khuen-Héderváry oversaw the building of Zagreb's Lower Town on
what had hitherto been meadows, with monumental architecture arranged on a grid plan intersected by a U shape of parkland—the so-
called Green Horseshoe. Most of the hard work he left to the Zagreb
city council, but the neoclassical design of Zagreb's oversized railway
station owed much to his intervention, and he promoted exchanges
and visits between Hungarian and Croatian architects.[19]

The 1896 celebrations in Budapest to commemorate the one-
thousandth anniversary of the Hungarians' entry into Central Europe
gave Khuen-Héderváry the platform on which to celebrate his rule
and Croatia's place in Austria-Hungary. In the centre of the exhibitions, four pavilions displayed Croatian textile manufacture, forest
management, art and culture, and alcohol production (with tots of
wine, beer, and brandy on sale). The most magnificent of the four was
the so-called Art Pavilion, which was a gallery made of iron and ma-
sonry, with an overarching glass canopy modelled on London's Crystal
Palace. At the end of the celebrations, Khuen-Héderváry instructed
that the pavilion be disassembled and transported to a plot on Zagreb's
Green Horseshoe, to act as a permanent gallery and showcase of Croatian artistic achievement. With its six-hundred-square-metre floor, the
Art Pavilion was small by most Central European standards, but it was
the largest space of its type south of the Danube and an advertisement
for Croatian cultural superiority among the South Slavs.[20]

Khuen-Héderváry's governorship ended in 1903 in much the same way it had begun—with riots over the flying of the Hungarian flag over the offices of the new railway station. But his achievement was typical of the bureaucratic regimes that dominated Central Europe in the last decades of the nineteenth century. In the monumental architecture they sponsored, in urban design, in draining marshes, in overseeing the details of peasant emancipation, and in the nitty-gritty of compiling new land registers (a necessary concomitant to reassigning property to the peasants), they showed the reach and benefits of government administration. Bureaucrats got things done. As the weekly *Railway Magazine: Voice of the Club of Austrian Railway Officials* reminded readers in its January 1895 editorial: constitutional disputes seethed, ministers came and went, and parties rose and fell, but railway officials kept to the task, pushing the lines outwards, staying within budget, and creating a truly integrated network. In short, bureaucratic rule triumphed over the bickering of politicians and parties.[21]

But the success of bureaucratic management came at a price that was larger than the fate of just parliaments and political parties. The bureaucratic state operated without scrutiny and was responsible only to itself and, in Austria, to the ten-volume civil service manual. With the presumption of the law on its side, it ate into society, subverting the personal freedoms that constitutions were designed to protect. As one of Hungary's greatest historians lamented in the immediate wake of the First World War:

The state became our pride, to which we offered up and sacrificed every freedom and high ideal. We made it into a monster, which gobbled up and consumed everything. . . . The old liberal principles of individual freedom, free choice, to do as one wished, and open competition were in complete contradiction to the monstrous growth of state power.[22]

CHAPTER 28

Assimilation, Biology, and the Skull Measurers

THE NEW HUNGARIAN GOVERNMENT INSTALLED IN 1867 started off liberal enough, but within just a few years it embarked upon a ruthless policy aimed against Hungary's national minorities. Slovaks, Romanians, Serbs, Germans, and Ukrainians made up more than a half of Hungary's population. To keep them politically powerless, successive Hungarian governments adopted the strategy of 'Magyarization'. They closed down cultural foundations belonging to the national minorities, manipulated the franchise to exclude their representatives, and arrested their politicians on trumped-up charges. But Magyarization was not just about discrimination. Its aim was to compel the national minorities to give up their separate identities and to become Hungarians. As one enthusiast put it, 'We shall just keep on at it until there is not a Slovak left.'[1]

Education was the key to Magyarization. Since Hungarian counted as the official language, it was made the vehicle of instruction in all but a handful of secondary schools and in more than two-thirds of elementary schools. University education was exclusively in Hungarian and any professional career depended upon the school-leaving certificate, or Matura, which required examinations to be sat in Hungarian. The consequence of these measures was to render the emerging middle class almost entirely Hungarian speaking. For non-Hungarians, social advancement depended upon becoming Hungarian and, to ease the transition to a new identity and status, the interior ministry made adopting a Hungarian name both cheap and free of the usual bureaucratic hassle.

Hungarians looked back to the War of Independence fought in 1848–1849 as the high point in a centuries-long struggle for statehood. They did not grasp that it had failed on account of a Hungarian chauvinism which had pulled the country into a bloody civil war with the minority nationalities. Ignoring the lesson, Hungarian politicians pressed on with Magyarization. They would pay the price after 1918, with the breakup and partition of Hungary and the assignment of more than two-thirds of its space to states run by the nations they had previously held in thrall.

In the newly united Germany, national minorities also faced policies aimed at their assimilation. In Schleswig-Holstein (the two provinces were united in 1866), new regulations forced Danes to learn German at school and deported to Denmark those who failed to serve in the army. It was the same in Alsace and the slice of Lorraine seized from France in 1871. All but a handful of schools switched to teaching in German, officials put up turrets on the sides of public buildings to make them look more German, and the police cracked down on such marks of French sympathy as bouquets of blue, white, and red flowers. Most of the population spoke a German dialect, called *Elsässerditsch*, but the heavy-handed policy of Germanization made Alsatians treasure their own separate identity. As a badge of belonging, Alsatian womenfolk now donned the *coiffe* or *Schlupfkapp*, even though its enormous butterfly wings had been headgear only previously worn around Strasbourg.[2]

Prussian and (after 1871) German policy towards the Poles was never consistent, but it also tended towards assimilation. Numbers mattered. Since the concentration of Poles in the east made their presence a threat, successive governments tried to weaken Polish identity and make Poles into Germans, mainly through schooling. Bismarck's 'cultural war' (*Kulturkampf*) against the influence of the Roman Catholic Church in the new Germany struck hard in the 1870s. Bismarck regarded the Catholic Church as backward-looking and loyal not to the new Germany but to the pope in Rome, but for Poles the Catholic faith lay at the heart of their national identity.

Bismarck's anti-Catholic and anti-Polish policies eased in the 1880s. At the very least, he needed the votes of the handful of the Polish deputies who sat in the fractious German parliament (Reichstag). Bismarck was ousted as chancellor (or first minister) by the new German emperor Wilhelm II (ruled 1888–1918) in 1890, but his successor continued a moderate course. German Prussians now took up the cudgels. Fearing that Poles would eventually outnumber them in Prussia, the premier German Prussian organization, the Eastern Marches Association (Deutscher Ostmark Verein), pushed for a renewed policy of Germanization. The government fell into line. During the 1890s, it renamed Polish towns to make them sound German, banned church sermons in Polish, released funds so that Polish farmsteads could be bought up and given to Germans, and invented new posts in the provincial bureaucracy just for Germans. By 1900, Poznań (Posen) had more civil servants per head of population than anywhere else in Germany.

In 1905, forty thousand Polish schoolchildren went on strike in opposition to Germanization in education—their parents were fined, and the ringleaders put in state orphanages. But most Poles avoided confrontation. They founded their own banks to buy up agricultural land, set up over a thousand lending libraries to preserve their cultural heritage, and used the burgeoning German economy to embed themselves in commerce and industry. By 1900, Polish breweries were among the largest in Germany. All of this was held together by the idea of 'organic work' (*praca organiczna*): to preserve their identity, Poles needed to cultivate their own cultural and economic assets. So, they should learn their literature at evening classes, found agricultural cooperatives to share resources, and keep up with the latest industrial innovations.

Hungary and the German Empire were on one side of the spectrum, pursuing policies that aimed to make state and nation coincide. The other half of the Habsburg empire, Cisleithania, was different. It was a multinational state, where the individual nationalities had extensive rights in respect of language use and cultural activities. In language policy, the key was the word *Landesübrig*: 'as ordinarily spoken in the locality'. But the words *locality* and *ordinarily* were imprecise, giving plenty of grounds for disputes, litigation, and angry confrontations. In the Habsburg crownland of Görz-Gradisca on the Adriatic coast (and now split between Italy and Slovenia), there was no agreement on whether German, Italian, or Slovene were 'ordinarily spoken' and whether the railway station should be called Görz, Gorizia, or Gorica, and if all three of these, which should be written first. So, it was left without a name.[3]

Cisleithania had a structure of higher administrative courts that managed disputes between members of the national groups. In order to maintain a rough balance, the courts generally came down on the side of whichever party was in the minority. But conflict and rivalry marked relations, as the different national groups vied for local supremacy. In villages, towns, and cities, each had their own separate fire brigades (they raced to put down fires first), veterans' associations, hunting clubs, athletics societies, and savings banks. But education was a battleground, with angry disputes over which languages should be taught and where. In Prague, the university split down the middle into German and Czech sections; only the botanical garden remained common to both, since the names of the plants were written in Latin.

Contests occasionally spilled over into real violence, especially when migration from the countryside into the cities upset traditional balances. More usually the national groups kept apart, living in separate quarters, the boundaries of which were marked by statues, monuments, and shop signs. So, in Prague, the name of the central square and boulevard was changed in 1850 from Horse Market to St Wenceslas Square, after the premier Czech saint. He was given a newer and larger statue at the top of the square in the 1890s and was joined there by the new National Museum, which was relocated from a nearby palace. Germans in Prague made the Lesser Quarter on the west bank of the River Vltava into their space, clustering around the statue of Field Marshal Radetzky, hero of the Napoleonic Wars and of the counterrevolutionary struggle in 1848. In the Bohemian countryside, different hiking trails kept Czechs and Germans apart.[4]

National rivalries dug deep into politics. The Cisleithanian parliament, or Reichsrat, established in 1867 was rent by division. Step by step, conservative politicians widened the franchise in the Cisleithanian part of Austria-Hungary, eventually to include by 1907 all adult males. By so doing, they hoped to outflank their liberal opponents, who relied overwhelmingly on middle-class votes. But with mass democracy also came mass nationalist parties and an increasingly embittered politics. Even trivial matters such as the provision of Slovene classes in a Styrian school provoked noisy interventions in the parliament, with MPs throwing inkpots in protest. The new socialist parties, which emerged on the back of democracy, scoffed at nationalism, declaring it to be 'false consciousness', of no more relevance than hair colour, but they duly split into German and Czech wings. So too did their trade union allies. But in the background, something even nastier was stirring. This was biology.

Central Europe was now at the forefront of the world's scientific advance, particularly in the fields of organic chemistry, optics, and electricity. Some of this was due to its many universities, in part the product of the region's previous political divisions and of the eagerness of minor rulers to make a name for themselves by founding a university. By 1900, there were nineteen universities in the German Empire, and a further ten in Austria-Hungary. But much also depended on the method of higher education in Central Europe, which put research and publication at the heart of scholarship and encouraged students to think for themselves by presenting papers at seminars instead of just taking notes in lectures. Universities were alert to the commercial possibilities of research while businesses set up research laboratories stuffed with graduates to translate academic theory into fertilizers, mothballs, electric dynamos, industrial dyes, and aspirin.

Biology was a latecomer. Back at the end of the eighteenth century, the philosopher Immanuel Kant had observed that although the laws of physics and of the universe had been transformed, he could not imagine 'a Newton who would make comprehensible even the generation of a blade of grass according to natural laws'. A century later, the study of botany and zoology had been transformed. In Moravia, the German monk Gregor Mendel (1822–1884) worked out in his monastery's garden the principles of genetics by watching the germination of pea plants. It helped that Mendel had studied physics at the universities of Brno and Vienna, so could transform his observations into mathematical formulas. In Berlin and Würzburg, scientists identified the cell as the building block of all organic material, and in the 1870s Robert Koch isolated the single-cell microbe as the main vector of disease.[5]

Charles Darwin never visited Central Europe. Unknown to him, German scholars had already proposed the basic principles of evolution in what they then called 'the transmutability of species'. But Darwin swept all before him, not least because his theory of evolution squared with contemporary ideas of human progress and material improvement. Just seven months after *The Origin of Species* was first published in 1859, a German publisher rushed out a translation. Follow-up research done at Jena on sponges and siphonophores (translucent creatures that float in the sea but which are made up of identical cells) confirmed the broad outlines of Darwin's theory.[6]

Darwin's popularity spilled out of the library and laboratory. A survey conducted in 1899 of reading habits among the German working class showed books on Darwinism holding four places in the top ten most read publications. Darwin's appeal rested on his idea of species in competition, which slotted in well with the conviction that nations were locked in eternal battle. As one prolific Austrian historian explained, 'In nature only one law rules, which is no law, the law of the stronger, of violence.' To give Germans the edge in this zero-sum contest, another much-read enthusiast recommended the introduction of polygamous breeding colonies, where sturdy German men would join together with equally strapping German women in brief but fecund marriages that were solemnized according to ancient rites.[7]

When it came to applying Darwinism, Hungarians had more mixed feelings. Ideas of hierarchy and survival justified Magyarization, but the assimilation of Slavs and Romanians by education and name-changing threatened dilution of the original Hungarian type. Comparisons between the cultures, character, and physiology of Hungary's different national groups became the subject of much condescending and earnest scholarship. So, for instance, one contemporary account announced that Transylvanian Romanian women 'have weak frames, they are slender with finely-cut faces; they are pretty but soon grow old; they are very industrious'. Slovaks were 'simple, religious, gentle, humble, and quiet, but often deceitful, obstinate, and, when heated, quarrelsome'. By contrast, the typical Hungarian merited the following description:

> The stature middle sized; the skull larger than middle sized; the head short and low; the sharp-featured face broad and oval. . . . The neck and the trunk are of a medium length and breadth; the chest broad in front and arched outwards on the sides. The navel lies high; the hollow of the pelvis is large, high, deep, of moderate width. . . . He moves in a composed manner, with an elegant position of the body, and his whole appearance shows strength and activity.[8]

This nonsense acquired fresh importance at the time of the 1896 millennium celebrations of the Hungarian conquest, a year-long extravaganza of patriotic make-believe. With so many statues and portraits of ancient heroes planned, journalists and politicians demanded that scholars identify the archetypal Hungarian face. A first attempt was unfortunate since the assembled faces were thought to resemble criminals, but thereafter a two-volume work with diagrams and photographs of noses and smiles yielded a more pleasing Hungarian self-image. In similar fashion, anthropologists collected skeletons to establish the 'median type of the true Hungarian', listed the skin, eye, and hair colour of more than fourteen thousand Hungarian children, and measured the height of recruits into the army, finding to their consternation that Hungarians were on average smaller than other nationalities.[9]

Ethnography, or the study of peoples, was popularized in museums and in travelling exhibitions, which put on view Africans, Maoris, Fuegians, and Inuit people in reconstructed habitats, sometimes along with zebras, monkeys, and ostriches. Most of the poor souls soon succumbed to disease and despair. But this was not just entertainment masquerading as instruction. German scientists subjected the group of Africans from Togo who were exhibited at the 1896 Berlin Trade and Colonial Fair to rigorous (and misguided) measurement, recording in painstaking detail the length of their arms, size of their earlobes, breadth of their shoulders, and so on. They then fed the results into existing research to see where their subjects sat in the global taxonomy of species. As for the Togolese, they were subsequently taken to appear in the Budapest Zoo.[10]

In Hungary, the same minute examination of physical characteristics focused on the measurement of skulls gathered from across Central Europe. At the forefront of skull measuring, or craniometry, was Aurél Török, who pioneered its study, inventing special equipment to gauge tiny distances. In more than six hundred pages, Török's *Elements of Systematic Craniometry* (*Grundzüge einer systematischen Kraniometrie*, 1890) explained 5,371 measurements, made more than one hundred thousand potential relations between points of the human skull, and came to no conclusions. It was the same with research done elsewhere. Upon investigation, even the most basic distinction between long-headed and short-headed skulls showed little correlation with peoples and nations. The most that the skull measurers' regression graphs, logarithms, and mean scores achieved was to advance the science of statistics. Craniometry was a dead end.

Other avenues of investigation proved equally disappointing. The study of blood groups and antigens threw up few coincidences with national types, while 'national psychology' (*Völkerpsychologie*) was seldom compelling in its investigations into how different nations sneezed, spat, or imitated animal sounds. It was the new science of bacteriology that breathed fresh life into biology. The role of microbes in spreading tuberculosis, cholera, typhoid, and diphtheria had been established by

1900. But the aetiology of typhus remained mysterious, although its link to insanitary conditions was correctly guessed at. Both the popular imagination and bureaucratic procedures identified outsiders as particularly likely to carry typhus. On the Prussian border and railways to Berlin, migrants were strictly controlled by marshalling them into segregated carriages and then making them pass through crowded disinfection centres.[11]

Bacteriology was also misunderstood as supporting evolutionary principles by showing organisms in microscopic competition and demonstrating how easily a host might be subdued by just a few tiny parasites. Popular vampire novels spoke to the same theme—of a single virus polluting society by the admixture of bad blood that could only be eliminated by the carrier's death. Whole social groups now began to be defined as pathogenic. They were imagined as invading the healthy body of the nation, contaminating it with alcoholism, mental illness, and moral depravity. Prostitutes were frequent targets, since they were thought not only to spread venereal disease but also to pass on to their descendants a corrupted sexuality as well as the physical deformities associated at that time with prostitution—a cleft palate, irregular teeth, and misshapen reproductive organs. From the 1870s, police forces across Central Europe were busy registering prostitutes, obliging medical checks, and cracking down on unlicensed streetwalkers.[12]

The stakes were high. In one popular account of the phenomenon of degeneration, the consequences were laid bare—'a people's moral collapse, psychological atrophy, and in the last stage, because the supreme degenerate, the true idiot, is incapable of reproduction, the people's extinction.' Across Central Europe, scientists and learned societies joined in the larger European and North American craze for eugenics, promoting it as the way of preserving and strengthening the national community through the control of what was called 'pathological heredity'. As the botanist and, later, professor of genetics in Prague Artur Brožek explained in 1912—'If society has the right to punish its members by death, it certainly has the right to isolate those members who are the ailing parts of its body for the period of their fertility.' It was, however, only in the 1970s that Czech and Slovak doctors embarked upon the mass sterilization of Gypsy people.[13]

Race brought these disparate scientific trends together. Germany and Austria-Hungary were both colonial powers. From the 1850s onwards, German missionaries, businessmen, and journalists had pushed governments to found colonial outposts abroad and to support German commercial ventures that were already carving out independent territories in the Pacific. But it was only in the mid-1880s and after much hesitation that Bismarck entered the 'Scramble for Africa', establishing German colonies in Togo, the Cameroons, German East Africa (now Tanzania, Burundi, and Rwanda), and German South-West Africa (now Namibia). By 1900, Germany's overseas empire comprised more than 2.5 million square kilometres, with an indigenous population of fourteen million people and almost thirty thousand settlers.

Austria-Hungary's empire was closer to home. In 1878, Franz Joseph occupied Bosnia-Herzegovina, which had previously been a part of the slowly disintegrating Ottoman Empire, finally annexing it in 1908. He did so to prevent it falling under Russian influence, but once incorporated in the Austro-Hungarian Empire, Bosnia-Herzegovina took on the aspects of a colonial and civilizing venture. As an article tellingly entitled 'On the Degeneration of the People of Bosnia-Herzegovina' explained, Balkan society had been 'cut off from civilization for centuries', with the consequence that syphilis and skin diseases had become endemic. The Austro-Hungarian mission in the Balkans was first marked by sanitation laws, the introduction of sanitary inspectors, and a roundup of prostitutes. In support of their theories, Austrian physicians claimed to have identified among the Bosnian Muslim population a new variant of syphilis and a narrowing of the pelvis in Muslim women, which was thought to originate from moving about on all fours. Ventures to colonize and civilize often start by identifying female differences.[14]

Race (*Rasse*) had previously been a loose term, used indiscriminately for breeds of cattle and dogs, language groups, and even religious denominations (hence 'the Catholic race'), as well as for the peoples belonging to the so-called main variants in which humankind was thought to be arranged—Caucasian, Mongolian, African, Native American, and Aboriginal Australian. European colonialism and German overseas ambitions pushed race to the forefront as a marker of biological difference and as a way of cataloguing the world. But the racial science of the late nineteenth century not only separated peoples but also arranged them along a scale, according to where they were thought to lie on the evolutionary map, with 'woolly-haired' (*wollhaarige*) black people at the bottom and straight-haired Indo-Germans or Aryans (principally white Europeans) at the top.

Race underpinned the German colonial experience. Ideas of racial hierarchy justified the brutal subjugation of 'lesser' African peoples as part of a Darwinian struggle between species for survival. In German South-West Africa, the advance of German settlers into the hinterland prompted in 1904 a revolt by the Herero and Nama peoples. It was put down in a brutal war that lasted four years and claimed possibly as many as a hundred thousand Africans' lives. Most died from a deliberate policy of driving Hereros into the waterless Namib desert. But this was a war waged on biological grounds. As one German officer put it at the time: 'Our Lord has made the law of nature such that only the strong of the world have a right to continuity, while the weak and purposeless will perish in favour of the strong.' A colonial administrator on secondment from Berlin was even more forthright: 'To secure the peaceful settlement of whites in the face of a native tribe that is absolutely incapable of culture and given to robbery may require nothing less than its annihilation.'[15]

The Herero genocide was deliberate. It came with a vocabulary that talked of 'extermination' and a 'final solution' (*endgültige Lösung*) and was explained in Berlin by repeated reference to the German nation's need for 'living space' (*Lebensraum*). But there were fears too that relations between soldiers and settlers and African women might lead to contamination. So, laws passed in the colony in 1905 first outlawed mixed marriages as 'race shaming' and then punished all sexual relations, with any offspring being given a separate racial category. The skull measurers were active as well, decapitating corpses and sending off some three hundred African heads for examination in Berlin, but only after they had been defleshed by imprisoned African women. In German South-West Africa racial science moved onto the killing fields.[16]

Ideas of race, hierarchy, and biology coalesced in antisemitism. During the late eighteenth and early nineteenth centuries, many Jewish *maskilim* (young scholars trained in the interpretation of the Old Testament) embraced the Jewish Enlightenment, or *Haskalah*. The Haskalah was a project that cut two ways. On the one hand, it sought to revive Judaism by producing new Hebrew editions and German translations of sacred texts. On the other, it urged Jews to discard their isolation from the larger society and integrate with it. For the influential Jewish philosopher Moses Mendelssohn (lived 1729–1786), religion should be a matter of private practice. A person's belief should not be an obstacle to social integration, but neither should it be a matter in which the state intervened.

The Haskalah was knocking at an open door. From the 1780s onwards, governments throughout Central Europe began removing the barriers that had prevented Jews from entering the professions or kept them in ghettoes. As part of this process, they required Jews to shave their beards and adopt surnames that were other than just 'son of . . .'. The intention behind these measures was never altruistic but aimed instead at rendering Jews 'useful' (as Emperor Joseph II explained), by exploiting their talents, conscripting them into the army, and making them easier to tax by fixing their names. But progress was slow, and plenty of obstacles remained preventing Jews from entering the higher ranks of the civil service and officer corps. Complete emancipation was only achieved in Baden in 1862, in Württemberg in 1864, in Austria-Hungary in 1867, and in Germany in 1871. In Russian-occupied Poland, by contrast, policy moved in an entirely different direction: towards pushing Jews out of commerce and the professions, restricting their movement and where they could live, and creating the conditions in which murderous pogroms might take place.

New architecture symbolized Jewish hopes. Across Central Europe, Jews rebuilt synagogues in a 'Moorish' style, with ornate domes, brightly coloured tiles, and horseshoe windows. Their design harked back to Arabic rule in medieval Spain, which many Jews imagined had been a time of accord between Jews and the society around them. Inside, prayers were delivered in German (or Hungarian), the rabbis dressed as if they were Protestant clergymen, and congregations sung to the sound of organs. Music and hymns added to the impression of assimilation so that, in the words of the Austrian novelist Joseph Roth (1894–1939), 'any Protestant blundering into a Jewish temple would have to admit that the difference between Jews and Christians is not all that great.'[17]

Integration seemed to work. During the second half of the nineteenth century, Jews migrated in increasing numbers from the countryside and shtetls into the cities. By 1900, 5 per cent of Berlin's population was Jewish. But in Vienna, Jews made up just under 10 per cent of the total, in Budapest and Cracow almost a quarter, and in Lviv a third or more. Many Jews made successful careers in the professions. By the turn of the century, more than a half of lawyers and doctors in Vienna and Budapest were Jewish. Throughout Central Europe, Jews were also important owners of art galleries and newspapers, patrons of charities, bankers, and industrialists. In Vienna, Jews were prominent in literature, music, and science, and in Berlin in the expressionist art of the Berlin Secession. Jewish athletes from Central Europe won nine gold medals at the first Olympic Games, held in 1896. A generation later, Jewish women would go on to win some of Central Europe's earliest beauty contests.[18]

But Jewish society was far from homogeneous. In the Galician countryside, the Haskalah made slow progress, blocked by inward-looking traditions of Hasidism that were resistant to change. The Yiddish language, which disciples of the Haskalah denounced as an archaic 'jargon', flourished, even going through its own Renaissance to become a vehicle for experimental literature and new theatre productions. And the Jews that migrated to the cities were not all bent on social integration but instead on maintaining their older cultural traditions. With their long beards, fur hats, and caftans, only speaking Yiddish, Polish, or Russian, and with their wives dressed in *sheitels* (modesty wigs), they were a common sight on the streets of Vienna's Leopoldstadt suburb. The German Jewish writer Jakob Wassermann recalled in 1921 his perplexity on encountering them:

> If I saw a Jew from Poland or Galicia . . . I certainly didn't feel a sense of brotherhood or even relatedness. . . . In everything he said and breathed, he was a total stranger to me, and when there was no human-individual symbiosis, I even found him repulsive.[19]

Antisemitism was a prejudice waiting to happen. Jews had historically been imagined as an alien other, defined by their different religion, dress, diet, and occupations. But now they were insiders, with a foothold in the middle class and a place on the Olympic podium. Yet, the influx of rural Jews was a reminder that they too were newcomers, who only one or two generations before had lived on the edge of society. But at least Jews with caftans were conspicuous. The integrated Jews, supposedly hiding their Jewishness behind business suits and new surnames, were invisible and so imagined as all the more dangerous. 'Amphibious', 'slippery', 'cunning', and 'chameleon-like' were the descriptions that most commonly attached to upwardly mobile Central European Jews.[20]

For much of the nineteenth century, Jews had been identified through their religion. But with the arrival of race as a marker of belonging, Jews were now viewed as a racial group, with characteristics that could not be effaced by baptism or by assuming the trappings of bourgeois culture. Their place on the racial tree was disputed, with some authors putting them near the top and others including them in a list of 'degenerate breeds'. But as newcomers, they were all biologically suspicious. Medical experts pronounced that the shape of the Jewish body made it vulnerable to tuberculosis, while the hurried pattern of Jewish life heightened Jews' nervousness, which was thought to be a precondition of diabetes. But syphilis was considered the most Jewish of diseases. In the so-called Jewish nose, antisemites saw evidence of the syphilitic infection that destroyed the septum, while the smell that attached to the breakdown of the body in late-stage syphilis was declared the 'Jewish stench'.[21]

In fact, statistics from the time demonstrated that Jews were less likely to suffer from tuberculosis and syphilis than other groups and that the incidence of diabetes among Jews was not especially high. Even so, the association of Jews with disease had been made. From being carriers of disease, Jews now became a disease. Antisemites explained how they infected the whole society, either by contaminating it with their own immorality or by implanting their genetic make-up within it, so hastening its decomposition (*Zersetzung*—a favourite word of antisemites). The images they conjured up were crudely sexualized, so Jews were portrayed either as pimps trafficking so-called Aryan women or secretly bent on the seduction of non-Jewish virgins with the aim of Hebraicizing civilization.

Antisemitism has historically been as multifaceted as its target—sometimes homing in on Jewish difference, sometimes identifying Jewish acculturation as a threat. In Central Europe, there was no single antisemitism but a cluster of assumptions, which expressed itself differently according to time and place. In Russian Warsaw, it was primarily a religious and economic phenomenon, partly aroused by the Catholic Church and partly by agitation over Jewish commercial competition. In Berlin, it was more social and fought out over invitations to the salons, and in Vienna it was highly political, with right-wing Christian Socials baiting Jewish socialists. In Hungary, it was directed mostly against new migrants from Galicia and Russian Poland—and often backed by established, middle-class Jews. Even so, antisemitism's new virulence shocked many Jews. In 1897, the Hungarian Jewish journalist and politician Theodor Herzl described its impact on the Jews of Bohemia:

> They clung closely to the German nation—too closely, as it seems.
> Then, suddenly, they began to be shaken off. Suddenly they were

called parasites. . . . All at once they were no longer Germans but Jews. It was a transformation without any transition, abrupt like an awakening from a dream.

Out of Herzl's despair, deepened by the antisemitism he saw in France, sprang Zionism and Herzl's vision of a new Jewish destiny in Palestine. As Herzl concluded, the Jews 'are a people—the enemy makes us one without our volition'.[22]

As it turned out, few Jews went to Palestine, then a part of the Ottoman Empire. By 1914, only about sixty thousand Central European Jews had moved there, mainly from Russian Poland to escape persecution. Most preferred to emigrate to the United States, where more than two million Jews had settled by the time of the First World War. They were part of one of the largest migrations in human history, which saw more than six million people move from Central Europe to North America between 1870 and 1914. Remittances sent home and remigration (possibly as many as a quarter or a third of all migrants returned to Central Europe) brought new wealth to large parts of the region. Most people went to America in search of material benefits and to escape poverty; only Jews were in flight from racial intolerance and they stayed.[23]

Because of its incoherence, antisemitism was easily colonized by language and ideas that borrowed from racial science, bacteriology, and sexual fantasies. Of all racial prejudices, antisemitism was the premier 'scavenger ideology', taking ideas from elsewhere and rearranging them into a new context. But its political impact was still muted. The antisemitic gutter press might have had a broad readership, but it seldom translated into votes for avowedly antisemitic parties. Except in Russian-occupied Poland, there was as yet no antisemitic legislation in Central Europe, nor quotas put on membership of the professions, nor obstacles put in the way of Jews becoming MPs or even government ministers. But the basis for antisemitism's synthesis into an all-embracing doctrine of difference had been laid and, in German South-West Africa, one possible solution to alterity had been found.[24]

CHAPTER 29

1914–1918: The War Against Central Europe

CENTRAL EUROPE HAD SINCE THE MIDDLE AGES STOOD FOR backwardness and battlegrounds. It had been fought over by empires and overrun by Frenchmen, Swedes, Russians, and Turks. Napoleon had prostrated its armies and the revolutions of 1848 had shown the weakness of its regimes and the malleability of its borders. Mid-nineteenth-century visitors wrote disapprovingly of Central Europe's sleepy cities, the guilds' stranglehold on commerce, the persistence of servile relations in the countryside, and the frequency of toll stations. Vienna elicited admiration for its theatres and museums, but even then was compared to a brothel, overseen by an intrusive police. Berlin had regularity in its street plan, several fine palaces, and a pleasant countryside, but visitors still thought it a barracks, while Pest was found to be not much more than a horse market, with its new buildings resting on mudflats.[1]

Among visitors to Central Europe, two images prevailed. The first was the peasant, with his shabby clothing and oafish behaviour, but never less than subservient to those he thought his betters. The second was the official, forever demanding papers. Tourism on the Rhine gave travellers a taste of Central Europe, but it was packaged in comfortable steam launches with (as today) predictable stopping places. Woe betide the more adventurous traveller who thought to venture into the Tyrolean Alps or Bohemian Forest, for hikers were suspicious and likely to be arrested under the vagrancy laws. The further east they strayed, visitors found flea-ridden accommodation, broken roads, and, in Hungary, the injunction to keep baggage in sight and pistols to hand.[2]

415

CENTRAL EUROPE IN 1914

Austro-Hungarian Empire

NORWAY

SWEDEN

North Sea

DENMARK

Baltic Sea

Königsberg

Vilnius

Gdańsk

Hamburg

Minsk

NETHERLANDS

Hanover

Berlin

GERMANY

Wrocław

Warsaw

RUSSIA

BELGIUM

Weimar

LUXEMBOURG

Frankfurt

Prague

Bohemia

Lviv

Galicia

Kyiv

Strasbourg

Chernivtsi

FRANCE

LIECHTENSTEIN

Vienna

River

Budapest

Bukovina

SWITZERLAND

AUSTRIA

HUNGARY

Cluj

Zagreb

Croatia

Belgrade

ROMANIA

Bosnia

Bucharest

ITALY

Sarajevo

Danube

SERBIA

Black Sea

MONTENEGRO

BULGARIA

ALBANIA

GREECE

OTTOMAN EMPIRE

Mediterranean Sea

0   300 mi
0   300 km

The unification of Germany changed how people saw Central Europe. Suddenly, there was a new power on the Continent. Western governments anxiously noted the astonishing growth of the German economy. Between 1890 and 1913, German iron and steel production more than quadrupled to a level that exceeded British, French, and Russian production combined. Over the same period, Germany's percentage of world manufacturing production went up by a half, second only to the United States, whereas everywhere else in Europe showed a proportional decline. Germany's birth rate, too, outstripped its neighbours, growing by 60 per cent between 1871 and 1911: France's growth over the same period was below 9 per cent. The new Germany was not only a European power but a global one too, with colonies in Africa and in the Pacific. Joining the colonial race late, it threatened the existing order.

Western opinion struggled to come to terms with Germany's rise, but it imagined the worst. In France and Britain, a new genre of invasion fiction typified anxieties. Its literary high point was Erskine Childers's *Riddle of the Sands* (1903), where intrepid Englishmen discover a German invasion plot hatched in Frisia, but the most popular iteration was William Le Queux's *The Invasion of 1910* (1906). Serialized in the *Daily Mail* (then with a readership of more than a million), Le Queux buttressed his story of a surprise German attack with convincing maps of German deployments around Sheffield and Potters Bar. The attack is eventually repulsed, at least in Le Queux's original account. But a pirated German version left out the last two hundred pages, so concluding with the German capture of London.[3]

The German Navy League gave some substance to these imaginings. Established by the Imperial Naval Office in Berlin in 1897, the league's aim was to convince the German parliament to vote more money for warships. Foreign observers anxiously watched the league's membership shoot up to more than a million Germans by 1910. They invariably reported its meetings to be made up of frothing nationalists, but the reality was quite different. The league's propaganda in its three thousand branches was mainly given over to lantern slides of cruisers and lectures on Africa, with the occasional exhibition of battleship gun turrets. But the league's big draw was its pioneering use of cinema. Often projected at meetings using high-resolution, 68-millimetre film, performances showed ships at sea, impressions of distant countries, and comedies imported from North America. Afterwards, excited children had the chance to buy sailor suits at knock-down prices. The German Navy League was Central Europe's first Disney films, with themed merchandise. It was not a conspiracy for world conquest.[4]

The same misapprehension attached to the German emperor Wilhelm II (William II, ruled 1888–1918). At a time when monarchs were taciturn and even tongue-tied, Wilhelm was loquacious, bombastic, and given to pipe dreams that he was only too happy to regale. At a dinner with King Leopold II of Belgium in 1904, Wilhelm proposed without any prior discussion with his officials that, should Belgium take Germany's side in any future war with France, he would reward Leopold with the title of King of Burgundy. Leopold was so shocked that on leaving the table he put his helmet on backwards. That was the problem. People took Wilhelm's bluster seriously and believed him when he talked of invading France, China, Central Africa, Brazil, the Middle East, Cuba, Puerto Rico, or wherever else the latest flight of fantasy took him. As one historian has put it, Wilhelm II was like a Tourette's tic in the heart of the German state.[5]

In trying to understand Germany, sober scholars turned to history. The new German Empire had, they declared, made an incomplete transition to the late nineteenth century—*belated* was their favourite word. German traditions of deference muted both opposition and press, while behind the scenes, they alleged, the old nobility still pulled the strings. Even though the name of Junkers only attached to Prussia, it now became a term of abuse for all German aristocrats and 'Junkerdom' the code word for German conservatism and expansion. The Junkers' continued influence meant, so critics alleged, that Germany's development into a modern constitutional state was lagging. Accordingly, Germany remained an autocratic empire, with only the veneer of democratic accountability.

Critics of Central Europe's governance were barking up the wrong tree. Germany was not a threat to peace, but its ally was. In 1879, Germany and Austria-Hungary had settled their differences in the face of the common Russian threat to the east. But Austria-Hungary was a declining power. In 1912–1913, the new states of the Balkans had grabbed most of what was left of the Ottoman Turkish Empire in southeastern Europe and had then fought each other over the spoils. Austria-Hungary had dithered, even though the Balkans counted as its backyard, where it might have been expected to show leadership and influence. By its irresolution, Austria-Hungary seemed to have become the new 'sick man' of Europe, threatening the whole balance of power.[6]

But even worse, Austrian statesmen knew their empire was in decline and were increasingly determined to do something about it. Serbia was their target, for it had grown enormously in just two years at the expense of the Ottoman Empire, more than doubling in size. Serbia's politicians were known to be casting greedy eyes on Habsburg Bosnia and the Serb-populated parts of southern Hungary. Austrian diplomats now began talking excitedly of a showdown between Slavs and Teutons, and of a Darwinist struggle for survival in the Balkans that would usher in what they hoped would be a 'totally new epoch'. By picking on Serbia, they began the chain of military events that would lead to ruin and dragged Austria-Hungary's German ally into the catastrophe.

The countdown to war began in June 1914 when Serbian terrorists murdered Franz Joseph's nephew Franz Ferdinand, the heir to the throne of Austria-Hungary, in the Bosnian capital of Sarajevo. The gunmen had been armed by a branch of the Serbian security forces, operated with the tacit approval of part of Serbia's government, and were not dissuaded in their mission by Russian diplomats, who knew what they were up to. Now was the moment for the 'blank cheques', when Wilhelm II gave the Austrian government his guarantee of support for tough measures against Serbia, and President Poincaré of France promised the Russian tsar his unconditional backing should he go to war in Serbia's defence.[7]

The two cheques were decisive. They gave Austria-Hungary and Russia the confidence to go to war and transformed what had originally been a local dispute into a general European war. Although Britain's obligations to Russia and France were far from exact, its statesmen knew that a failure to back its allies would jeopardize both Britain's reputation abroad and its future influence on the world stage. With an overseas empire that accounted for more than a fifth of the world's landmass, Britain's decision to go to war made the conflict a global one. By the end of the first week of August 1914, most of Europe and much of the world were at war.

For all their expert war-gaming and theorizing, German military planners were stuck in past. They still held to the principle of enveloping—of manoeuvring behind the enemy to cut him off and surprise him from behind, and they could muster all sorts of examples, from Hannibal to Napoleon, in support of their strategy. But almost at once, the German strategy of enveloping and smashing the French stalled on the Marne River, just east of Paris. Blocked by unexpected British and French advances, the German armies fell back eighty kilometres to the Aisne River, to positions they would hold for the next four years. By October 1914, the German military mastermind Helmut von Moltke (the younger) was despairing, writing in his diary: 'Our operations just aren't progressing and all our hopes . . . are betrayed. There will be no knock-out blow. The campaign is bogged down like a stagnant swamp.'[8]

The war in the west settled down into a war of attrition, fought along a 750-kilometre front from Nieuport on the English Channel to the Swiss border. It was not all a war of trenches, for in the northern sectors the water table was too high, so trenches soon flooded. German theorists called it 'positional warfare' (*Stellungskrieg*), but it was everywhere a war of mud, fought from shell holes, concrete blockhouses, and barbed-wire entanglements that stretched up to eight kilometres behind the front line. German casualties were enormous—by the end of 1914, they had at least 240,000 men killed and 800,000 wounded, out of a total army strength of 4 million. True, they had made gains in the west, capturing all but a sliver of Belgium and 10 per cent of French territory, including almost a quarter of its industrial belt. But these gains could only be kept if France, Britain, Russia, and (from 1915) Italy were decisively defeated.

After 1914, German strategy in the west relied on wearing the enemy down. Allied strategy rested on the hope of *la percée*, or breakthrough, but mostly settled for *grignotage*, or nibbling away. Where they could, the German commanders lured the Allied armies into ambushes, but these invariably turned into prolonged engagements, with appalling casualties on both sides. In defending the fortress of Verdun in 1916, the French lost almost four hundred thousand men in what became known as the 'blood pump' (*Blutpumpe*) or 'bone crusher' (*Knochenmühle*) on the River Meuse, but the Germans lost only slightly fewer. To draw the Germans away from the French and Verdun, the British fell into the trap of the Somme—a four-and-a-half-month battle that claimed altogether six hundred thousand French and British dead and wounded. But German losses were huge too, amounting to four hundred thousand men. Unable to sustain further casualties, the German armies in the west fell back to the heavily reinforced Hindenburg Line.

Positional warfare in trenches and bunkers suited the German high command. Since field fortifications could be held with fewer men, they had a reserve for deployment in the east. Here, the line ran twice the distance of its western counterpart, allowing for greater mobility and for the type of enveloping actions that were impossible in Belgium and France. Germany's armies had scored immediate successes there, defeating the Russians in two engagements in August and September 1914 (the Battles of Tannenberg and the Masurian Lakes), after which they rolled over a swathe of Russian Poland. But before they could drive further eastwards and take Warsaw, the German generals on the spot, Paul von Hindenburg and Erich Ludendorff, were distracted by the collapse of their Austro-Hungarian ally. (Warsaw would eventually be captured in August 1915.)

It is not true that the Austro-Hungarian high command mislaid an army in August 1914 on account of shambolic mobilization and deployment, for the generals always knew where it was: they had simply sent it to the wrong place. But, in September 1914, a part of the Austro-Hungarian army did manage to lose a battle in Galicia without the enemy even being present. Fearing that they were about to be attacked by Russian Cossacks, a regiment on the way to shore up Lviv began carelessly shooting, slaughtering its own side and setting off a panic. A platoon commander recorded the aftermath:

> Our hearts cringed at the sight of the rifles thrown away by cowardly and base soldiers. . . . Overturned wagons, carts with scattered cargoes of sacks, wine, rum and schnapps barrels, boxes of hardtack, thousands of loaves of bread all lay in piles on the ground. . . . The corpses of horses and men lay in ditches to the side of the streets.[9]

The same military insufficiency was replicated everywhere else on the Austro-Hungarian side—the dress swords that tripped up officers, the yellow gaiters that made them a target for snipers, the tin lids that had to serve as shovels, the saddles that were designed for dressage and not for campaigning, and the trains that had to run at 'maximum parallel graphic', or no faster than the slowest train in the sector, meaning at times a speed of just five kilometres per hour. Austria-Hungary had over decades underspent on its armed forces and only one man in twenty had in peacetime done military service. Neglect showed.

By the end of 1914, the Russians had captured most of Galicia and were within striking distance of Cracow. Then came the Italian declaration of war in May 1915, which forced the deployment of Austro-Hungarian troops to the Alps, and in the summer of 1916 a crushing Russian offensive, which convinced Romania to enter the war against Austria-Hungary. To withstand the Russians, the Austro-Hungarian armies depended on German reinforcements, which had to be rushed from the siege of Verdun to support their ally. In return for their help, the German commanders took increasing control of the Austro-Hungarian army, stiffening it with their own officers and subordinating it to their own strategic goals.

With German support, the Austro-Hungarian armies recovered their poise. Conscription brought under arms some three million men and swept up even those with medical exemptions, who were deployed in special units such as the Hungarian 'intestinal ailments battalion'. Army divisions were fitted out with proper supporting trains and field batteries, with the Škoda works in Plzeň in Bohemia producing super-heavy 'Big Bertha' howitzers. Austro-Hungarian scientists, working with Ferdinand Porsche at Austro-Daimler, designed six-cylinder aero-engines, four-wheel-drive armoured cars, and the first working helicopter. In aerial combat, Austria-Hungary had a decent complement of aces, not least the monocled Godwin von Brumowski, with thirty-five confirmed kills. Brumowski's most startling achievement was to bomb in 1916 a military review attended by the tsar near Khotyn (now in Ukraine), after which he shot down several of the Russian fighters sent to intercept him. Incredibly, Brumowski's monocle was not for show but to correct his poor eyesight, and his biplane was an antiquated Albatros B.1, of pre-war vintage.[10]

But it was another larger-than-life military man that saved Austria-Hungary. Photographs of the German field marshal August von Mackensen (lived 1849–1945) invariably show him extravagantly whiskered and scowling, sporting an otter-skin busby with an oversize death's head badge. Despite his forbidding appearance, Mackensen was suave, approachable, and liked by his men since he had risen through the ranks—his knightly 'von' was an award for service, not part of a hereditary title. For almost four years, Mackensen had served as an adjutant to Wilhelm II, where he had learned the importance of protocol and how to smooth ruffled feathers. In the task of overhauling the Austro-Hungarian army, Mackensen was an obvious choice, since he was the best man to charm its preening generals and the 'oyster-loving' Hungarian staff officers.[11]

In the spring of 1915, Mackensen took command of the German Eleventh Army based east of Cracow as well as having operational control of two Austro-Hungarian armies. He promptly overran Russian-occupied Galicia, recapturing Lviv and the strategic redoubt of Przemyśl. Then, turning northwards, Mackensen made a coordinated attack with German forces on the Russian centre, obliging the enemy to retire up to four hundred kilometres eastwards. Russian losses were enormous—a million dead and wounded, and a further million taken prisoner. As they retreated, the Russians burnt down the villages they were abandoning and deported more than three million civilians into the interior, but they seldom provided any relief for the refugees, who were left to starve either on the roads or in improvised shelters. German commanders on the spot were appalled by their enemy's brutality to its own people.[12]

Mackensen had never attended a military academy, so he had not been indoctrinated in the groupthink of envelopment. His preferred method was the reverse—to concentrate his forces and hit a single spot to achieve a breakthrough, with minimum losses to his men. Artillery, guided by spotter planes, played a vital tactical role in Mackensen's plans, wearing down the enemy in preparation for an assault, first by heavy mortar fire and then by flat-trajectory rounds aimed at bunkers. A Russian commander described what it was like to face Mackensen:

The Germans plough up the battlefields with a hail of metal and level our trenches and fortifications, the fire often burying the defenders of the trenches in them. The Germans expend metal, we expend lives.[13]

After his victories in Russian Poland, Mackensen was sent south by the German high command into the Balkans to coordinate the German and Austro-Hungarian offensive against Serbia. Here, he had to work not only with Austro-Hungarian commanders but also with Germany's Turkish and Bulgarian allies. It was a delicate assignment, as much political as military, but the strategic benefits were enormous. With Serbia out of the way, there would be a direct overland connection between Austria-Hungary and Germany's other ally, Ottoman Turkey, along the axis of the Orient Express railway.[14]

Mackensen's invasion of Serbia proceeded at lightning speed, starting with an amphibious landing at Belgrade. Despite valiant resistance, the city fell on 11 October 1915. Six weeks later, with the Serbian army in tatters and retreating into the mountains of Albania, the campaign was over. The Serbs had taken almost 100,000 casualties and a further 150,000 men were prisoners. On top of this, the Serbs had abandoned their entire artillery park and forty-two locomotives. Total losses for the Germans and their allies amounted to 67,000 men. Mackensen had pulled off a military masterstroke—defeating a seasoned enemy, on its home turf, in unfamiliar terrain, in less than two months. Never less than generous, Mackensen put up in Belgrade a monument dedicated to the 'Serbian heroes'.[15]

The original plan called for Mackensen to march south and capture the Greek port of Thessaloniki, but Romania's invasion of Transylvania in August 1916 forced a change of priorities. While a German army cleared the Romanians from Transylvania, 'Army Group Mackensen' moved through Bulgaria to overrun Romania's eastern seaboard and encircle Bucharest. Mackensen rode into the capital on a white horse on 6 December 1916. It was his birthday—he was now sixty-seven years old. With Mackensen's defeat of Romania, the German and Austro-Hungarian armies commanded a space of more than half a million square kilometres of enemy territory, running along the edge of Central Europe from Riga on the Baltic to the Danube Delta.

German and Austro-Hungarian troops entering Russian Poland were mostly appalled by the monotonous poverty they confronted—'all grey, dirty grey' (*Schmutziggrau*) was one soldier's description. Even so, a paternalist condescension prevailed. The soldiers found the peasants to be altogether simple, given to frequent worship in church and melancholy singing, but good with their hands. Steam bathhouses were bewildering, particularly since the countryfolk were otherwise filthy and verminous, and typhus was endemic: a fifth of German medical officers in Russian Poland died of it. But for most observers it was the absences that counted—of roads, bridges, sanitation, and education. The term that they came up with was *Unkultur*, meaning the complete absence of recognizable culture.[16]

German and Austro-Hungarian occupation policy had civilization as one of its goals: to bring the east into the twentieth century through 'German Work' (*Deutsche Arbeit*). This was no empty slogan, for the occupation armies dedicated huge efforts to infrastructure, building more than four hundred bridges and for the first time spanning the wide Bug River. They set up schools and theatres, organized newspapers, founded museums, brought agricultural fertilizers, regulated prostitution, and dug sewers. An album dedicated to the German Work in the east itemized its achievements—comprehensive land registers, a functioning judiciary, forty-one hospitals built and five mental asylums, and the modernization of a people who were 'a century behind' the occupiers in terms of their level of cultural achievement. To prove the point, the album included a statistical appendix that counted the number of vaccinations administered against typhus and the bubonic plague.[17]

To understand the people better, scholars in uniform investigated their speech and isolated Belarusian, or as they called it, 'White Ruthene', as a distinct language. Having discovered the Belarusians, they founded in 1915 the first ever Belarusian-language schools, sponsored a Belarusian press, and set up a permanent exhibition in Vilnius of Belarusian folk culture. Belarusians today partly owe their sense of belonging to the German pioneers who told them who they were and gave them some of their earliest history lessons. But this was no altruistic endeavour on the occupiers' part. By advancing Belarusian nationhood, the German occupation regime sought to detach from Russia a population estimated at the time at one million people.[18]

Hand in hand with the civilizing impulse came the practical need of *Verkehrspolitik*, or logistics. In the occupation zones, military commanders plundered resources and ordered whole populations to be registered, photographed, and given identity cards. They routinely regulated all social movement, demanding that homes be kept unlocked and visitors logged. From 1916 onwards, all adults in occupied Europe became liable for compulsory work service, enforced by fines and long jail terms. As the occupying troops seized the harvests, either for themselves or for shipment to Germany or Austria-Hungary, food shortages and malnutrition spread, causing in places a doubling of the death rate. New taxes hit the pockets of the poor—on matches, dogs, bicycles, salt, and the sale of eggs and other essentials, together with bans on private fishing and keeping pigeons for food (since they could also be used to send secret messages).

Across Central Europe, occupied or otherwise, military-bureaucratic rule triumphed. On the eve of the war, the government of Austrian Cisleithania invoked its right to rule by decree. The parliament was not sitting, and it would not be recalled until 1917, so the executive had a free hand, publishing over the next three years no fewer than 154 emergency laws and more than five hundred ministerial decrees. Martial law was immediately imposed in a half of Cisleithania and many crimes brought within the jurisdiction of military courts, including any criticism of the emperor. Along with the courts, the civil service became the instrument of the army high command, tasked with fulfilling military needs. With every crisis of production, its tentacles plunged deeper into the economy and society, pulling more and more beneath the supervision of centralized offices and of committees appointed by the War Ministry.[19]

Top-down management also characterized the German wartime economy. A central Raw Materials Section bought up and requisitioned resources and allocated them to several hundred cartels of mostly private companies, contracting them to produce finished goods at specified prices. Meanwhile, the War Ministry oversaw the munitions supply, closing down smaller factories and centralizing production. But it was never enough. Even before the war, there was insufficient manpower to sustain Germany's burgeoning economy. With more than seven million men in arms, labour shortages became critical. Compulsory service for men up to the age of sixty, the recruitment of women into the workforce, and forcing prisoners of war into the factories and fields still left huge shortfalls in production and on people's plates.

The head of the German armed forces, Field Marshal Hindenburg, pushed to put the economy on a total war footing, with every adult directly involved in the effort. But, by 1916, the same sort of deprivation experienced in the occupied territories was also hitting the German and Austro-Hungarian heartlands, with widespread rationing and a burgeoning black market. The basic ration in Austria was by 1916 just two hundred grams of bread per day, and per month two hundred grams of coffee and beet sugar alike and a hundred grams of cooking fat. Offal became a delicacy. As supplies faltered, long queues gathered outside bakeries and butcher's shops. At weekends, city folk went foraging and raiding in the countryside and fighting with vigilante gangs of farm labourers. Shortages were made worse by strikes which intensified in January 1918, when a million German workers downed tools.

For Germany and Austria-Hungary, 1918 was the turning point that turned the wrong way. The year before, Russia had collapsed into revolution and civil war. In the Treaty of Brest-Litovsk, agreed with Bolshevik Russia in March 1918, Germany and Austria-Hungary took almost the whole of what is now Belarus and Ukraine. Hindenburg had imagined that with a victory in the east, he could stiffen the Western Front with troops drawn from the east and smash the French and British once and for all, before their new American allies arrived on the front. But the last German offensive, launched in March 1918, stalled. One by one, its frontal assaults either foundered or missed their objectives. An Allied counterattack in August 1918 breached the Hindenburg Line. From there, it was open country all the way to the German border.

In Germany and Austria-Hungary, the domestic and military fronts collapsed simultaneously. Both were connected. The First World War was the first literate war, where the postal service connected families at home and serving soldiers. Together with the words 'Write again soon', letters from home conveyed anxieties over shortages of food and fuel, long working hours, and illnesses. Letters sent by serving troops were subject to strict military and police censorship, not only to conceal details of military operations but also to maintain morale and quash rumours. So, the most shocking letters sent by fathers and sons at the front were those that no longer bore the stamp of the field post but of a provincial or city post office, a sign that the sender had deserted.[20]

Even before the offensives of 1918, the German front in the west was buckling. Troops simply refused to fight and either walked home, lurked in shell holes or woodland, or went over to the enemy. The German definition of desertion was exacting, since it required proof of the intention to abscond, so the German military authorities preferred the catch-all description of 'shirking' (*Drückbergerei*), which included refusing orders, self-harm, and hiding, as well as prolonged absence without leave. By this looser measure, they estimated that there were by the last months of the war up to a million shirkers on the Western Front (out of a field army of 3.6 million men). On top of this, hundreds of thousands of troops gave up and surrendered to the enemy. By the autumn of 1918, as much as a third of the German army on the Western Front had either vanished or withdrawn from combat. A coded message sent by a Bavarian private to his parents in the middle of October 1918 summed up the mood of desperation: 'The situation is bad. Everyone is running away. If there is no armistice, get your hands on as much cash as possible.'[21]

It was the same in Austria-Hungary, where (depending on definition) somewhere between a hundred thousand and a million men had deserted by the end of the war. In the Austro-Hungarian countryside, some deserters and draft dodgers formed their own quasi-military units of so-called Green Cadres, robbing food transports, derailing trains, feasting in barns, and taking over whole villages. All in all, there were probably about a hundred thousand renegades, with large concentrations in Moravia, Galicia, northern Hungary, and Croatia. Many assumed the historic guise of bandits, sporting feathered hats, pistols, bandoliers, and scimitars, and they prided themselves on robbing from the rich to give to the needy, among whom they obviously included themselves. As they overran increasingly wide swathes of the country-side, the bandits made large parts of Austria-Hungary ungovernable.[22]

Writing during the war, the great German sociologist Max Weber (1864–1920) extolled bureaucracy as the most accomplished form of government. With a technical superiority over every other form of power, it constituted the purest type of authority:

> The fully developed bureaucratic apparatus compares with other organizations exactly as a machine is to the non-mechanized forms of production. Precision, speed, unambiguity, knowledge of the files, continuity, discretion, unity, strict subordination, reduction of friction and of material and personal costs—these are raised to the optimum point in the strictly bureaucratic administration. . . . Trained bureaucracy is superior on all these points.[23]

Weber was talking about an ideal type. But against any benchmark, the failure of the militarized bureaucratic regimes in Germany and Austria-Hungary was stark. Both had bent the economy and society into their service by regulation, requisition, interference, and coercion. They had built on a centuries-long tradition of officialdom and meddling. But they had not won the war; nor, in the end, had they shown themselves even capable of keeping people fed. War had pumped up the Central European tradition of bureaucratic rule. But bureaucracy had not brought the frictionless efficiency imagined by Max Weber, only disintegration and chaos. When the supreme test had come, the bureaucratic state had failed.

In its place, the peoples of Austria-Hungary now increasingly vested their hopes in new national states, and the idea of the nation became the focus for loyalty and expectation. Supported by Allied propaganda, nationalist politicians in Austria-Hungary trumpeted the cause of a South Slav state that brought together Serbs, Croats, and Slovenes, and for a union of Czechs and Slovaks. In Germany, by contrast, social-ism seemed the answer, but there were several socialisms on offer—the moderate, trade-union-backed, democratic socialism of the German Socialist Party, and the revolutionary socialism of the shop stewards who had led the strikes of January 1918 and looked to Bolshevik Russia for inspiration. Realizing the inevitability of defeat, the German general Ludendorff and what was left of Wilhelm II's shattered government sought a deal with the moderates, hoping to forestall revolution by speeding to peace. By the time they learned on 8 November of the Western Allies' impertinent demands, it was too late.

On 9 November 1918, the German government announced Wilhelm II's abdication—it took the emperor almost three weeks to confirm it, by which time he was in exile in the Netherlands. On 11 November, Franz Joseph's successor Emperor Karl (1916–1918) relinquished his involvement in public life (he did not formally abdicate, imagining that popular demand would see him eventually restored). The next day, what was left of the imperial parliament in Vienna declared 'German Austria' a republic, imagining that it would soon merge with Germany. By this time, nothing remained of the old Austro-Hungarian Empire. New national committees of self-appointed local worthies had taken power in Prague, Cracow, Lviv, and elsewhere, claiming that they were now the legitimate governments, while a new ministry in Budapest under the 'Red Count' Michael Károlyi had announced an independent Hungary. In little more than a century, the boundaries of Central Europe had been pulled apart by Napoleon, the Congress of Vienna in 1815, and Bismarck. Now they were to be redrawn once more.

CHAPTER 30

Violence, the City, and 'The Blue Angel'

IN THE FORTNIGHT BETWEEN 29 SEPTEMBER AND 13 NOVEMBER 1918, delegates of the defeated powers signed the instruments of their surrender. Bulgaria was the first, concluding an armistice in a former orphanage in Thessaloniki that had been turned into a military headquarters. A week later, Ottoman Turkey exited the war, capitulating on board a British battleship in the Aegean Sea. On 3 November, the Austro-Hungarian forces in Italy formally surrendered in a suburban villa outside Padua. Then, on 11 November, it was the turn of Germany, whose representatives had to concede to humiliating terms in a railway carriage near Compiègne. The German negotiator Walter Rathenau was convinced that the Allies aimed at no less than 'the destruction of German life, now and for all times' and foresaw his homeland eventually becoming a backwater of Asia.[1]

Hungary was last. Having declared Hungary an independent republic, its politicians were bound to make a separate peace. A first meeting with the Allies in Belgrade, led by the prime minister Michael Károlyi, went badly. Károlyi blamed everyone but the Hungarians for the war and continued his windy speech even though the flickering of the kerosene lamps in the requisitioned building prevented him from reading his notes. The French general d'Espèrey cut him short: 'In this war you were on the side of the Germans, thus your responsibility is equal to theirs, and your punishment will be equal to theirs.' Just before midnight, on 13 November, the Hungarian government agreed an end to hostilities and put the country's fate in the Allies' hands. It was Hungary's first international act as a sovereign republic.[2]

By recognizing the national committees that had set themselves up in Central Europe as governments, the Allies determined the broad shape of Central Europe's new states. But the new regimes ignored Allied calls not to carve out their own state boundaries in advance of the peace conference that was due to meet in Versailles. Instead, they continued the fighting in the hope that military gains on the ground would be translated into international borders. Over the course of 1919, Czechs and Poles fought over Silesia; Hungarians battled Czechs and Slovaks for possession of Slovakia; Romanian forces invaded Hungary, reaching Budapest, and Polish armies broke into Soviet Russia and (the briefly independent) Ukraine with the aim of restoring Poland's ancient boundaries. When the venture stalled outside Kyiv, the Polish strongman Józef Piłsudski turned on Lithuania, depriving the new republic of its capital, Vilnius.

The Versailles Conference of 1919–1920 reordered Central Europe, but in its attempt to balance principle with expediency it did so at the expense of an enduring peace. On the one hand, it sought to create states whose boundaries were congruent with nations. On the other, it wanted these states to be economically and politically viable lest they be later picked off by a resurgent Germany and Russia. The compromise was a cordon of middle-sized states that were not national at all but multinational. Czechoslovakia and Yugoslavia were, as their names suggest, mixes of peoples who felt little kinship for one another. But their respective national committees had convinced the Allies that they were genuinely popular creations and, by the time the conference was in session, they had their administrators and armies in place.

As the loser of the war, Germany was made to suffer, forfeiting more than 10 per cent of its European territory, including Alsace and Lorraine, all its overseas colonies, its navy and most of its army, while being saddled with financial reparations that could never be paid. The American president Woodrow Wilson had promised a 'just peace', but to most Germans the terms imposed at Compiègne and elaborated on at Versailles seemed thoroughly unjust. So, when it came to determining Germany's boundaries, the right of 'self-determination' and of nations to live in their own states was ignored. Czechoslovakia held onto the area of German settlement along its western rim known as the Sudetenland. Gdańsk, which was almost entirely German, became a 'free state' under international supervision and in a customs union with Poland since, without it, Poland would have had no viable port. On top of this, the Allies firmly rejected any idea that Germany and Austria might unite, lest this create a superstate, whereas their interest was to cut Germany down in size.

Hungary lost the most, since the national principle worked against it. The Allied negotiators in Paris assigned to Hungary's neighbours all areas of so-called mixed settlement (a loose term, mostly used to Hungary's disadvantage). The Trianon treaty of 1920 gave Transylvania and a strip of land to its west to Romania. Southern Hungary and Croatia went to Yugoslavia, northern Hungary to Czechoslovakia, and bits of Hungary's western borderland to Austria. By the terms of Trianon, Hungary lost more than two-thirds of its pre-war population and territory, while more than three million Hungarians now lived beyond its new boundaries. Tough border controls left families not only divided but also unable to meet.

The statesmen who drew up the settlement at Versailles recognized the limitations of their work. Altogether, about a third of the population of Central Europe constituted national minorities, trapped in states where the dominant nation was not their own. So, the peacemakers impressed special treaties upon the new states, obliging them to good conduct towards their minorities. The new governments signed the treaties and promptly disregarded them, leaving large swathes of their populations resentful and disaffected. As the British ambassador in Prague noted in 1922, the consequence of Czechoslovakia's insensitive policy towards its German minority 'can only be to intensify bitterness, to weaken the state, and to foster the growth of the cancer which will eventually bring it to destruction'. His observation was prescient.[3]

In the wake of its surrender, Germany dissolved into civil war. With Berlin threatened by revolutionary communists, or 'Spartacists', and Munich now run by far-left lunatics who thought it sensible to

abolish all money, Germany's politicians temporarily moved the seat
of the parliament to provincial Weimar. (It moved back to Berlin in
August 1919.) 'Weimar' became the shorthand for the republican experiment that the new parliament set in motion and for the losses and
humiliations it asked Germans to endure. Although celebrated nowadays for its exciting cultural innovations, Weimar Germany was at the
time seen as the bastard child of the Western Allies' determination to
humble a nation. It never recovered from the reputation of its birth.

The Versailles settlement brought peace but did not alter the inclination to political violence. The troops might have been physically
demobilized, but many had failed to do so psychologically or even
sartorially. In the absence of affordable civilian clothing, veterans continued to wear uniforms and, in winter, army greatcoats. Their ragged
outfits are a feature of the works of the German artists Otto Dix and
Georg Grosz. They also clustered around paramilitary formations. Of
these, the most infamous were the German Freikorps units, which in
the first years of peace acted as hired muscle while also pursuing their
own private wars against Jews, socialists, and rival racketeers. The
earliest Nazi Brownshirts, who from 1921 fought their own vicious
war against political rivals, were khaki-shirted because they wore old
military uniforms.

But the paramilitaries were not (as often portrayed) entirely bent
on overthrowing the political system. They were frequently a part of
the established order, for across Central Europe political parties and
organizations often had their own military wings. In Austria, socialists, conservative Catholics, and fascists maintained private armies
that battled out their differences on the streets. When not fighting
each other, the Austrian paramilitaries practised assassination, claiming more than eight hundred victims in the 1930s. It was the same
in Hungary. Once he had suppressed a communist-led insurrection
in 1919, the head of the new 'counterrevolutionary' government,
Miklós Horthy, a former admiral in Habsburg employ, recruited his
own army of veterans and set them to work against the communists.
Having murdered possibly as many as two thousand leftists, Horthy

gaoled seventy-five thousand communist sympathizers and pushed a further hundred thousand into exile abroad. Although political violence declined in Hungary in the 1920s and 1930s, it was always an undercurrent, fuelled by a nationalist press that ceaselessly inveighed against 'international Bolshevism', 'international Jewry', and 'international feminism'.[4]

Poland had emerged in 1918 from the ruins of the German and Austro-Hungarian Empires. But although recognized as a state by the Allies and the peacemakers in Versailles, its borders were left uncertain and it took six wars in just three years to establish Poland's new boundaries. In attempting to re-create the Polish state as it had existed before the partitions of the late eighteenth century, the new republic swallowed up too much. The acquisition of large chunks of what are now western Belarus and western Ukraine brought with them sizeable national minorities, accounting for five million people in a population of just over thirty million. Of these, the largest were Ukrainians. Claiming to act on their behalf, Ukrainian nationalists launched a war of terror, demanding their own independent state. Their preferred methods were sabotage, bombings, and murder. In the second half of 1930 alone, the Polish police recorded no fewer than two thousand 'incidents' involving Ukrainian insurgents. The 'pacification' that followed, undertaken by units of the police and army, was violent and indiscriminate, prompting Ukrainian separatists to commit new outrages.[5]

Across Central Europe, democratic politics buckled. Governments either abolished political parties altogether or rigged elections to ensure that only MPs supportive of the regime were returned to parliament. In Poland's parliament, a 'Non-Partisan Bloc for Supporting the Government' held the upper hand after 1928, while in Austria a 'Fatherland Front' and in Romania a 'National Renaissance Front' became monopoly parties, working to fulfil the government's agenda in rubber-stamp legislatures. The transition to authoritarian rule was hastened by the economic depression, which rolled over Central Europe after 1929, culminating in the collapse in 1931 of the region's largest lender, the Vienna-based Creditanstalt bank. To shore up the tottering state finances, governments increasingly resorted to rule through emergency decrees that bypassed the parliamentary process.

In Germany, weak and fractious coalitions hastened the parliament's demise. The government increasingly resorted to rule by decree against a backdrop of urban violence and six million unemployed, which amounted to a third of Germany's workforce. By the beginning of 1933, the veteran field marshal and now president Paul von Hindenburg had just two options left—either dispense with parliamentary politics altogether and inaugurate a presidential dictatorship or hand over the government to the man who commanded the most seats in the parliament. He chose the second course and made Adolf Hitler chancellor. Within three months, Hitler had destroyed what little was left of German democracy.[6]

Czechoslovakia was exceptional in maintaining a democratic character for most of the interwar years, but its democracy was flawed. Back in 1918, the leading Czech politicians had promised 'to make of the Czechoslovak Republic a kind of Switzerland', with Slovakia and the new state's eastern part of Ruthenia having their own governments. (Ruthenia had before 1918 been a part of Hungary.) Among Ukrainian-speaking Ruthenians there was even a vote on a federal union, but bizarrely only involving Ruthenians living in the United States: it was too hard to organize a referendum in the Carpathians, so a ballot among Ruthenian immigrants living in Pennsylvania had to suffice. But the new Czech leadership made it clear from the start that the German minority, which amounted to almost a quarter of Czechoslovakia's population, should expect no favours. As the incoming Czechoslovak president Tomáš Masaryk (in office 1918–1935) disdainfully noted shortly after his inauguration, the Germans were 'immigrants and colonists'. The new Czechoslovakia was to be the national state of the Czechs and Slovaks or, as Masaryk preferred to think of them, the Czechoslovaks.[7]

Despite the promises of a federal state, Czechoslovakia was centralized in Prague and the five main Czech political parties dominated its politics. These carved out between them not just the ministries but also the trade unions and most of the local administration, including hospital and school boards, charitable institutions, banks, businesses that relied on state contracts, and insurance companies. Professional and social advance rested on having the right party card. Party bosses maintained a firm hand over their MPs, replacing deputies who stepped out of line with more biddable party members. The heads of the main parties met in an unofficial cabinet, called 'the five' (*pětka*), which decided on the legislative programme and constituted Czechoslovakia's effective government, dismissing and appointing prime ministers at will. No government appointed by the five was ever censured, nor any of the bills they sponsored lost.[8]

The monopoly of power held by the five bred complacency and an unwillingness to adapt to changing circumstances. As the Czechoslovak economy faltered in the 1930s and the demands of the German and Slovak minorities became more vociferous, the government's countermeasures were increasingly oppressive. Censorship, already operating in the 1920s, became routine. The ministry of the interior demanded that all local government appointments (including elected mayors) have its approval, so blocking Germans from office, while decrees increasingly took the place of parliamentary legislation. Even before the German invasion of March 1939, Czechoslovakia had become an openly authoritarian and antisemitic state, where most political parties were banned, and Jews excluded from the professions and universities.[9]

The eclipse of democracy in interwar Central Europe may be explained several ways. The new states of Central Europe had been carved out of empires. The parts that were now welded together to make states came with different currencies, laws, political parties, and institutions of local government and were embedded in different economic networks. Pulling these together required extensive and sensitive management, of the type that young democracies and unseasoned politicians find difficult. Parliaments, which were usually elected by proportional vote, were split into many small parties (no fewer than thirty-six in the case of Poland), with little understanding of the give-and-take needed to build lasting coalitions. Under these circumstances, it was easy to resort to authoritarian solutions. In addition, the glue that held the disparate parts together was not a shared experience over time but the fantasy of the nation. In the absence of other bonds, national belonging was the sole reference point, prompting demonstrations of chauvinism and of the politics of exclusion.

Nationalism is predicated on difference, yet the cultural experience of Central Europe in the interwar years was remarkably uniform. Building on tensions evident before the war, the same anxieties and expectations were manifest throughout the region. Historians use the term 'modernization' as a shorthand for these strains, but at the time the more usual expression was 'Americanization'. Urban design, factory production lines, consumption, and entertainment were thought to have become more American in style, at the expense of traditional patterns and norms. Shellac 78-rpm records, the motor car, and lines of high-kicking Tiller girls were the symbols of this transformation, and Chicago the most frequent city of comparison.[10]

Transported to Central Europe after the First World War, jazz music embodied the new American modernity. It was exotic, cosmopolitan, and edgy, partly because of its association with negritude—and many jazz bands in the early 1920s used blackface to exploit the connection. Its pace matched urban lives. As one critic wrote, the jazz musician was the 'troubadour of today', and the 'tenor of the streets' was the 'tenor of the west'. The music of the jazz band 'clatters to the same beat as the typewriters which the clientele left behind two hours before, its song is the shout of the boss, made rhythmical, and its dance is around the golden calf. The jazz band is the extension of workplace by other means.' Describing Prague in the 1920s, the Czech poet and musician Emil František Burian was enthusiastic: 'Lots of people walk around me in the street full of dirt and noise. The bars are drunk with the phosphorescence of girls and the smoke of cool guys. . . . Yes, all this is today. Beautiful, modern, eternally jazzy today.'[11]

Tempo mattered. In what is still one of the most influential analyses of the twentieth-century city, the German sociologist Georg Simmel

(1858–1918) contrasted urban rhythms with the slow pace of village life and highlighted the way the metropolis intensified nervous stimulation through the rapid and constant change of external and internal sensations. For Simmel, the city overloaded the nerves with visual, auditory, and nose-turning stimuli: glaring billboards, the noise of traffic, and the stench of crowded tenements. Its assault on the senses forced either a sensory withdrawal and what Simmel called a 'blasé' attitude of world weariness or an aggressive search for personality by which individuals established a sense of self through cultivating an extreme idiosyncrasy and caprice in an otherwise crowded and anonymous urban space. In Germany's capital, Simmel's students explored the twin themes of a teasing of the senses and a cult of egocentricity, yielding two master tropes of the interwar years: 'Babylon Berlin' and 'Bohemian Berlin'—the one standing for the city's sensuality, the other for the overfashioning of personality.[12]

Simmel's description of the city concluded that it was the task of the sociologist 'neither to condemn nor to pardon, but only to understand'. The same detachment shaped the style of the German artistic movement known as the *Neue Sachlichkeit*. Normally translated as 'New Objectivity', Neue Sachlichkeit more properly means 'new matter-of-factness', where (in a contemporary description) objects were shown as they were: 'neither impressionistically relaxed, nor expressionistically abstract . . . but unswervingly faithful to positive palpable reality'. In the art and cartoons of Otto Dix and Georg Grosz, reality may be shown with a cynical and cruel eye. So, Dix's *Metropolis* (*Grosstadt*, 1928), a three-panel painting mimicking an altarpiece, included war amputees being pushed aside by leggy coquettes, while Grosz homed in on the social inequalities of Berlin and the physical violence that sustained them. But Neue Sachlichkeit artists were also concerned with integrating into their work the everyday tokens of mass consumption: toothpaste and soap, eggs and potted plants, sewing machines, stockings that sagged, and factory production lines. Their lack of explicit ideological commitment offended leftists, who railed against their 'paralysed minds'.[13]

The Neue Sachlichkeit cut across media. In music and drama, it produced the *Zeitoper*, or 'topical opera', which dealt with contemporary social dilemmas and favoured a repertoire of popular songs and jazz tunes, sometimes supported by on-stage gramophones. The underworld chic of Bertolt Brecht's *The Threepenny Opera* (*Die Dreigroschenoper*, 1928) is typical of the genre with its stark portrayal of working-class lives, rakish glamour, and street melodies. In architecture, the Neue Sachlichkeit yielded the high modernism of the super-dense housing estate, with accommodation arranged in cubes and packaged in clean lines and plate glass. The architects of Neue Sachlichkeit built for the megacity, although their legacy is mostly visible today in the design of nineteen-sixties' student dormitories and halls of residence.

Expansive in its mission to portray life as it really was, Neue Sachlichkeit overlapped with Dadaism. Dada was self-avowedly nihilistic, triumphant both in its repudiation of all conventions and in the meaninglessness of its slogan, *Bevor Dada da war, war Dada da* (Before there was Dada, there was Dada). Even so, Neue Sachlichkeit artists enthusiastically embraced its techniques of photomontage and collage as a way of displaying the mundane. But Neue Sachlichkeit's triumph was in cinematography. In its lean footage of street scenes, powerplants, locomotives, and nightlife, it showed life as the lens saw it. Neue Sachlichkeit's greatest cinematic achievement was surely Walther Ruttmann's *Berlin: The Symphony of the Metropolis* (*Metropolis. Die Sinfonie der Grossstadt*, 1927), which compressed twenty-four hours of city life into just sixty minutes, starting with locomotives rushing commuters to the centre and production lines bottling milk, and passing on to the printing of newspapers, doors revolving with office workers, telephones ringing, dogs fighting over scraps, and a fairground roller coaster.

The machine embodied the possibilities of technology and Max Brand's opera *Maschinist Hopkins* (first performed 1929) made the mechanized factory an almost religious space. For Brand, the production line's switches substituted for holy relics and the workplace's bells rang as if on church steeples, while huge wheels turned and talked to one another in a half light. Brand's stage directions are explicit:

Factory floor at night . . . Despite its sober atmosphere, the setup
of the main switchboard and its construction should appear symbolic, resembling an altar. It is completely dark in the hall. . . . The
glass background is gleaming softly and the fantastic outline of the
machines, increased through the shiny effect of the main switch,
suggest the merging of a factory floor and a temple.[14]

But the city and modern machinery more commonly generated
anxieties. Released in the same year as Ruttmann's *Berlin*, Fritz Lang's
Metropolis (1927) conveyed a dystopic vision. Regimented workers toil
glumly beneath ground, pulling levers and dying in explosions, while
above them the gilded children of capitalist bosses disport themselves
in pleasure gardens. The plot is laboured but ends on a happy note of
reconciliation as worker and capitalist shake hands. With its fusion of
cubist and futurist motifs, Gothic backdrops, and soft socialism, *Metropolis* has acquired a reputation that is perhaps larger than it deserves.
Even so, its representation of the city as a place of anonymity, enslavement, and inequality became a literary and cinematic commonplace in
the interwar years.

For many Central European authors, the city was a monster that
devoured lives and corrupted sensibilities. It was, in the commonest
contemporary description of Budapest, 'sinful': a place of financial in-
trigue and bartered bodies, supposedly presided over by Jewish pimps
and profiteers. In the writings of Liudas Vasaris, Kaunas, the capital
of interwar Lithuania, was equally disreputable. He described it as no
more than a hole in the ground, with a central square 'full of potholes
and a bow-backed cobble street full of skewed wooden slums with
leaky roofs that seem to be buried in the earth'. In a common trope
of interwar Lithuanian literature, Vasaris also shows Kaunas's women
to be temptresses who make visitors listless with their empty entertainments, eroticism, and repetitive dancing. The Polish Jewish writer
Bruno Schulz found his home city of Drohobych (now in Ukraine)
equally repellent. Its oil wealth had made Drohobych rich, but in
dreamlike sequences Schulz reveals its tawdriness as evening draws on:

The carefree crowds of chattering passers-by stroll past the shop windows—those dirty grey squares filled with shoddy goods, tall wax dummies, and barber's dolls. Showily dressed in long-laced gowns, prostitutes have begun to circulate. . . . They advance with a rapacious step, each with some small flaw in her evil corrupted face; their eyes have a black, crooked squint, or they have harelips, or the tips of their noses are missing.[15]

Whereas Neue Sachlichkeit art and cinema had depicted man and technology in harmonious combination, most Central European authors and artists saw the machine as a disembodied artifice, which imposed its own unnatural rhythms on the workforce and daily life. The mechanized combat of the First World War deepened anxieties, for it seemed that human beings were not just the raw material of destruction but might also be psychologically rebuilt to become killing machines. Bertolt Brecht explained the phenomenon in his *Man Equals Man* (*Mann ist Mann*, 1926), where the narrator warns the audience that 'Tonight, you will see a man reassembled like a car, leaving all his individual components as they are.' Expressionist writers found technology an easy target for their agitated prose, describing its scarring of the landscape, the shriek of its sirens, and the madness of its tempo, while neoromantic authors championed the silent beauty of nature, contrasting it with the noise and mediocrity of mass production. As the poet Rilke wrote:

See the machine roll,
wreak its revenge, maul,
warp and distort us.[16]

The machine might not only be a deforming monster but also take on human characteristics. The mechanical human had always held a fascination for Central European writers and readers, which the fantasies of Romantic and Gothic authors had prolonged—hence Bonaventura's marionettes and the eighteenth-century fashion for wind-up mannequins.

The earliest robots in twentieth-century fiction were the creation of the Hungarian author Frigyes Karinthy in 1916. In a sequel to *Gulliver's Travels*, Karinthy describes a race of mechanical creatures dwelling on a distant island which had over several tens of thousands of years perfected itself and learned to communicate through musical notes. They are benign, but having learned via a video feed (!) that human civilization has been destroyed by war, we are left in no doubt that they will inherit the world. The cinematic successors to Karinthy's kindly robots are, by contrast, bent only on destruction, threatening the world with death rays until, in Harry Piel's *Master of the World* (*Der Herr der Welt*, 1934), they ultimately settle for the role of maintenance engineers.[17]

Karinthy's and Piel's robots look like machines, but between their two appearances we are confronted by mechanized replicants that seem and act like human beings, while intent upon destroying them. The earliest of these does not strictly qualify as a replicant, being more a biological freak, but is illustrative of the genre. In 1919, the Hungarian Mihály Kertész (the later Michael Curtiz of *Casablanca* and *White Christmas* fame) directed a film version of *Alraune*. The film is now lost, but the novel on which the plot draws survives. It tells how a mad professor accomplishes the physical union of a prostitute with a mandrake plant, out of which is generated a sexually obsessive young woman, who drives the professor to suicide and then turns into a vampire. A variant on the same theme is *The Cabinet of Dr Caligari* (*Das Kabinett des Dr Caligari*, 1920), which has a hypnotist who, doubling up as director of a mental asylum, puts a patient in a trance, rebuilding him as a murderer in much the same way Brecht would later describe in his metaphor of a reassembled car.

The automatons of Karel Čapek's play *R.U.R.* are more conventionally engineered. Premiered in Prague in 1920, *R.U.R.* stands for 'Rossum's Universal Robots' and Čapek was the first to use the Czech word for work, *robota*, to mean a mechanical creature. Čapek's robots are made of organic tissue, but they are expressionless and move with mechanical precision. Helena, a beautiful visitor to the island factory where they are built, urges that the robots be given the same rights as humans. Under her spell, the manufacturer gives consciousness to the robots, after which they embark on a global rampage, killing all humans. Just in time, Helena is replicated, but her emotions are also passed on to the copy. The robot Helena goes on to repopulate the world, presumably in her own image. Čapek's influence on modern sci-fi from *Blade Runner* to *Westworld* is obvious.

Maria in Fritz Lang's *Metropolis* performs an analogous role. The real Maria preaches the politics of patience and gradualism to the workers, but a mad scientist makes a perfect copy of her and instructs her to destroy the city. Dancing in the dress of the Whore of Babylon (a page taken from an illustrated Bible works here as an intertitle), the replicant drives the leaders of the city into a frenzy of violence as they lust for her favours. She then goes on to rouse the workers, who break the underground engines, causing a flood. Believing their children to have perished in the rising water, the workers turn upon the mechanical Maria and burn her as a witch. The real Maria then returns with the children, whom she has saved, and the mayhem ends.

In *Alraune*, *R.U.R.*, and *Metropolis*, there is a clear crossover with another cinematic and literary trope of Central Europe's fin-de-siècle and interwar years—the woman who brings ruin. As seducer, vampiress, criminal, hypnotic dancer, bluestocking, and spy, the deadly female stalked fiction and cinema after the First World War, playing on male anxieties about the 'New Woman', whose economic independence challenged masculine assumptions. To explain the phenomenon of the New Woman and its consequences for male psychology, directors turned to Sigmund Freud and the science of psychoanalysis, portraying women's rise in overtly sexual terms and coupling it to men's fears of disempowerment, impotency, and castration.

In Central European representations of womanhood, there were always several types of dangerous females. One was the 'intersexual' who had moved into a previously male career, either as a university teacher or a bus driver, so depriving men of jobs. The intersexual's hair was invariably close cut, often into a pageboy, or *Bubikopf*; she wore male fashions, and, in a contemporary description, her intellect was 'so superior . . . that she becomes troublesome.' Opposing the intersexual woman was the femme fatale: the super-sexualized nightclub chanteuse and hostess, who morphed into the prostitute, parading her body with the tokens of seduction and performing for money. Cabaret was her stalking ground.[18]

Central European cabaret was a broad category that ranged from ticketed variety shows to drinking dens with or without a stage. It was distinguished by its fast-moving repertoire, which was held at the time to mirror 'our nervous, precipitate age, which finds no repose for long and prolix entertainments'. Performances by dancing girls, acrobats, and comedians were interspersed with songs, satirical sketches, and short plays. Budapest's cabaret prided itself on its high literary content, Warsaw's on its mimicry and political satire, and Prague's on its jazz. But Berlin's cabaret remains the most famous, on account of its edgy overlap with criminality, nude dancing, the hatred felt for it by the Nazis, and Christopher Isherwood's Sally Bowles.[19]

Celly de Rheydt, Anita Berber, and Valeska Gert were the most notorious performers on the Berlin cabaret stage because of their naked performances, pornographic repertoire, and ostentatious drug taking. But the most celebrated entertainer of the time is the celluloid Lola Lola in the Berlin production of *The Blue Angel* (*Der blaue Engel*, 1930). Played by Marlene Dietrich in her film debut, Lola is a singer in the cheap 'Blue Angel' bar who seduces, betrays, and drives to death a brittle, middle-aged schoolteacher. His emasculation and ruin are shown in unsparing detail against the sound of Lola's voice, which becomes husky and androgynous as the film reaches its conclusion. In an obvious nod to Freud, the eggs which the teacher received on his marriage to Lola are smashed on his head at the moment of his cuckoldry.[20]

Lola presides carelessly over the teacher's ruin, her pale face and skinny legs recalling the 'white death' of tuberculosis. But Lola does not just stand for moral infection and decay. She is also an assemblage of clichés and fetish objects—frilly underwear, corsets, see-through skirts, and stockings. In this respect, she is as contrived and artificial as the Dada montages of workers built out of fragments of industrial plant. Lola's signature song boasts that she is *eingestellt* for love—which may be translated in this context as 'tuned', 'pre-set', or even 'programmed'. In the English version of the song (released simultaneously with the German), Lola apologizes, 'I was made that way, I can't help it.' Explaining her inbuilt desires, she goes on to describe her sexuality as an unstoppable mechanical instrument, akin to a self-playing piano:

> *They call me naughty Lola,*
> *The wisest girl on earth,*
> *At home my pianola*
> *It works for all its worth*
> *The boys all love my music, I can't keep them away,*
> *So my little pianola keeps working night and day.*

In *The Blue Angel*, apprehensions and anxieties collide, laying uniquely bare the subterranean male psychology of interwar Central Europe— the New Woman and female sexuality, emasculation, human mechanization, and the city as a place of shallow and seductive entertainments.

The Blue Angel has been eclipsed in the popular imagination by Bob Fosse's *Cabaret* (1972), featuring Liza Minnelli as an upmarket Sally Bowles in interwar Berlin. In the final scene, as the film dissolves into a medley of female and transvestite limbs, the mirror wall showing the audience fills with swastika arm bands and flailing fists. But Nazi Germany did not only ban and destroy. Its cultural policy also accommodated existing trends but twisted them to serve its task of rebuilding the national community. So, Josef Goebbels's propaganda ministry promoted through the supple Marika Rökk a new and wholesome image of womanhood. It redefined jazz as 'swing', and even let some expressionist art briefly survive, to the extent that it was considered visually 'Nordic'. Women, while never banished to the kitchen and motherhood, were made less threatening by a broader definition of the national community that overlooked differences of gender. Nazi rule rebranded technology as an agent of material improvement and a symbol of 'German inventiveness' and 'German enterprise'.

Cabaret too was cleansed by making it more akin to American-style vaudeville revues. Kick lines of girls became demonstrations of physical fitness or of military precision, on which account the performers were sometimes put in army uniforms. Some nude dancing continued on condition that it served aesthetic purposes, but political jokes of any type were dangerous, including even the suggestion of a walking impediment, since it might be thought to be aimed at Goebbels's limp. Cabaret continued in Germany right through to the 1940s, but only as the most anaemic of entertainments. Allied bombing did the rest, reducing the number of Berlin venues to just two by 1944.[21]

But in manufacturing a wholesome, collective culture for Germans, the Nazis deliberately counterposed German Jews, attributing vices to them so as to leave the racial nation unblemished. Everything that had been wrong with Weimar culture was now blamed on Jews, from the class rivalries that had spilled over into street fights to the moral sickness, licentiousness, and sexual ambiguity with which interwar cabaret had been associated. The expungement of Jews from what was seen as the cultural and moral life of the German nation, and the responsibility loaded on them for the decadence of the interwar years, foreshadowed Nazi plans for their complete eradication. As Goebbels himself remarked in 1933, the Nazi takeover was not just a political revolution but also a cultural one that affected every aspect of life, and 'this revolution will carry on to the extreme end. . . . It will stop at nothing.'[22]

CHAPTER 31

The Second World War, Ordinary Central Europeans, and Industrial Murder

T HE GRANDEST SET OF ROOMS IN THE BRITISH FOREIGN OF-
fice in London is its Locarno Suite. The suite is named after the
treaties of 1925, which Europe's statesmen negotiated in Locarno in
Switzerland and signed off in London. The statesmen hoped that the
Locarno treaties would (as their texts proclaimed) bring about a 'relaxation of the tension between nations', but far from reducing tensions,
the treaties stoked them. Although the treaties guaranteed the existing state borders in western Europe, they fatally left open the map of
Central Europe, noting only that it should not be changed without
discussion. The German foreign minister Gustav von Stresemann was
delighted. As he wrote to his ambassador in Washington, the Locarno
treaties not only guaranteed that the French scheme to annex parts of
Germany failed but also opened up for Germany 'new possibilities in
the East'.[1]

The Locarno Suite is a monument to failure. The treaties signed
there signalled that Britain and France were now withdrawing diplomatically from Central Europe, leaving the region to work out its
own future. The French tried to keep some residual influence through
the 'Little Entente' they had built with Romania, Czechoslovakia,
and Yugoslavia (1920–1921). But the French entente treaties were
vague in their commitments, binding the French government only
to 'consult' with its allies in the event that they were attacked. The
French politicians trusted that the newly formed League of Nations
would act as a forum for ironing out differences. But when the crisis
came in September 1939 with the German invasion of Poland, all

the league could think to debate was the standardization of railway level crossings.[2]

British policy was nimbler. It avoided treaties, since to be meaningful they came with obligations that could be awkward. Britain's statesmen preferred the sort of give-and-take and timely concession that had guided British diplomacy in Europe since the nineteenth century. This was called at the time 'appeasement', a word that has since become synonymous with selling out. Nowadays, a better term might be 'conflict management'. The advent of Hitler to power in Germany in 1933 had little effect on British policy. The British envoy (later foreign minister) Lord Halifax was happy to hold out the prospect of a major readjustment of Central Europe's boundaries—he mentioned to Hitler in 1937 that Gdańsk, Czechoslovakia, and Austria might need to be rearranged, but only 'through the course of peaceful evolution and that methods should be avoided that might cause far-reaching disturbance'.[3]

As the British foreign minister Anthony Eden acidly noted at the time, Halifax's 'peaceful evolution' probably meant something quite different to Hitler, and so it proved. Hitler forced the pace. Having sent troops into the demilitarized Rhineland in 1936, he annexed Austria in 1938, on both occasions without French or British intervention. Czechoslovakia followed. The Czech politicians realized too late that their disregard for the sizeable German minority in the Sudetenland had left them vulnerable. British diplomats had little time for the Czech politicians or for Czechoslovakia, considering the first 'pig-headed' and 'inferior Slavs', and the second 'a modern and very artificial creation with no real roots in the past'. They much preferred dealing with the eloquent Sudeten German politician Konrad Henlein, whom they thought had real grievances and was 'moderate and reasonable'.[4]

After much international brinksmanship, the leaders of France, Britain, Germany, and Italy concluded at Munich in September 1938 the agreement that gave the Sudetenland to Germany. The British prime minister Neville Chamberlain returned home to a hero's

welcome on the balcony of Buckingham Palace, since people believed
him to have brought peace with Germany by resolving (in his words)
'a quarrel in a faraway country between people of whom we know
nothing'. The cession to Germany of a territory that was 90 per cent
German-speaking was equitable to the extent that it conformed to the
principle that states and nations should have the same boundaries. But
it was calamitous too, for it convinced Hitler that the Western powers
would not oppose him. As he later remarked, 'Our enemies are little
worms. I saw them at Munich.'[5]

Once the principle of self-determination for German speakers was
applied to multinational Czechoslovakia, the country was bound to
dissolve into fragments. Poland and Hungary helped themselves to
bits of the carcass on behalf of their respective national minorities, and
rump Slovakia declared independence. For three days in March 1939,
an independent microstate called Carpathian Ukraine (Karpats'ka
Ukrayina) ruled the easternmost tip of Slovakia. Its leaders solemnly
debated the design of a new postal stamp and bank notes, until Hungarian troops scattered them and annexed the country. But it was
Germany that took the lion's share of Czechoslovakia. On 15 March,
Hitler seized what was left of Bohemia and Moravia, making it a
German 'protectorate', even though he had promised that he had no
further territorial ambitions on the crippled state.

British and French policy now somersaulted. In London, the ex-
citable Romanian ambassador Viorel Tilea warned the foreign minister Lord Halifax on 17 March 1939 that Romania had just received
an ultimatum from Germany and that 'it was by no means to be
excluded that the German Government would make an almost immediate thrust upon Romania.' In fact, no such ultimatum had been
sent, but in the wake of Hitler's occupation of Bohemia and Moravia,
Tilea's warning scared the British government into action. Over the
next fortnight, Britain joined by France gave guarantees to Poland,
Greece, and Romania that it would maintain their independence.
Winston Churchill was appalled by the Polish guarantee. As he later
recalled, 'Great Britain advances, leading France by the hand, to guar-

antee the integrity of Poland—of that very Poland which with hyena appetite had only six months before joined in the pillage and destruction of the Czechoslovak State.' In September 1939, Hitler did indeed challenge Poland's independence, overrunning it in alliance with the Soviet Union. Britain and France stood by their guarantee, declaring war on Germany.[6]

The origin of the Second World War in Poland was no accident. Poland's condition in the eighteenth century had made it the focus of rivalries. Its partition and dissolution in the eighteenth century were widely acknowledged as 'the greatest political crime which stains the history of modern Europe'. But even with its restoration after 1918, Poland's position was precarious. British and French politicians saw Poland as a keystone in the diplomatic arch that was supposed to hold back Germany and Soviet Russia. But for their counterparts in Berlin and Moscow, Poland was a parvenu, an 'occasional state' (*Saisonstaat*) scarcely twenty years old in 1939, which had usurped territory that had from the late eighteenth century onwards been Russian and German. For Germans, long nurtured in the belief that Slavs occupied a lower level of civilization, the loss of territory to Poland was galling. As one of the first Germans to cross the Polish border on 1 September 1939 remarked, now was the time to avenge his homeland's 'sullied honour'.[7]

Polish military resistance was strong. In less than a month, the German invaders had suffered fifty thousand casualties, more than they would lose in the next year's fighting in France. But the Poles were outnumbered and from 17 September they also had to contend with a Soviet invasion in the east. At the end of the month, the German and Soviet governments agreed on a demarcation line, partitioning Poland again, with brutal consequences. The eastern part of Poland now became part of the Soviet Union, where Stalin commenced the slaughter of all those whom he thought likely to challenge communist rule. The rest was either incorporated directly into Germany or made into the German-run General Government, which became, in propaganda minister Goebbels's description, 'a dumping ground for dross: Jews, the sick, and idlers'. Even so, the General Government was only intended as a temporary measure. Starting in 1940, a 'General Plan for the East' (*Generalplan Ost*) was gradually put together which foresaw the whole space between the Gulf of Finland and the Crimea becoming a region of German settlement, based upon cosy farmsteads. Two-thirds of the existing population were to be shunted into Siberia and the cities rebuilt so that they looked like chocolate-box versions of medieval Würzburg.[8]

Of course, to fulfil the General Plan for the East, the Soviet Union had first to be removed. Hitler began its dismantling in June 1941, when the largest invasion force ever mounted in the history of warfare assailed the three-thousand-kilometre Soviet border, catapulting the Soviet Union into the Second World War. Just under four million men, mostly Germans but supported by allied Finnish, Hungarian, Romanian, and Slovak troops, pushed their way eastwards. By the end of the year, they had reached the tram lines on the outskirts of Moscow and Leningrad (St Petersburg). Instead of just 'living space' (*Lebensraum*) in the east, long a German nationalist fantasy, Hitler had acquired, in his own words, 'a giant space' (*Riesenraum*), and he had a clear idea of what to do with it. As he explained to his top generals and officials in July 1941: 'This giant space must obviously be pacified as soon as possible. This is done best when everyone who looks out of place [*schief*] is shot dead.'[9]

The problem was that there were already a lot of people in Central Europe who might be thought to look out of place—communists, teachers and lawyers who might organize resistance to German rule, Slavs who lacked fair complexions and so were racially dubious, Jews, homosexuals, alcoholics, congenitally disabled people, and so on. Hitler had already commenced the destruction of all these groups, first within Germany, and later in Austria, Czechoslovakia, and Poland. Gypsies were among the earliest victims, transferred in 1933 to concentration camps or to the compound at Berlin-Marzahn, where the skull measurers and experts in racial science set to work on them. Over the next dozen years, the Nazis would murder more than twenty thousand German and Austrian Gypsies. Altogether, somewhere between one hundred thousand and three hundred thousand Central European Gypsies perished in the Roma Holocaust, or 'Devouring' (*Porajmos*).[10]

The same violence followed against Poles. Starting in September 1939, 'anti-intelligentsia actions' (*Intelligenzaktionen*) led over the next six months to the murder of more than sixty thousand army reservists, lawyers, doctors, and teachers. A further three million Poles were conscripted for labour in the enlarged Germany and a quarter million children with supposedly German features taken from their parents and given to German families. In the General Government, a reign of terror was unleashed, with random shootings of civilians and the destruction of all cultural and educational institutions and many churches. Polish industry was dismantled and shipped westwards; only the mines and a little agriculture survived. With food supplies dwindling, rationing broke down, forcing Poles to rely on the extensive black market. For those still with jobs, the average monthly wage bought just a kilogram of black-market butter. But this hardly mattered to the German authorities, who regarded Poles as an expendable resource. As the governor-general Hans Frank explained to visiting Nazi bosses in December 1939:

> This area is in its entirety booty of the German Reich. . . . The area must be subjected to economic utilization as a whole, and it should benefit the German people with its entire economic value.[11]

But the group that was pre-eminently out of place in what had been Poland was the Jews. Here, German policy in occupied Central Europe intersected with antisemitism, to yield a murderous combination.

Until 1933, German antisemitism had been a minority faith. Before Hitler came to power, most ordinary Nazis were not strongly antisemitic; nor was German society. It was for this reason that the Nazi leadership in the late 1920s and early 1930s played down their anti-Jewish propaganda, directing their venom instead at communists and casting their ideological net wide to capture most shades of political opinion. It was only after Hitler became chancellor in 1933 that the

454 THE MIDDLE KINGDOMS

fanatical antisemitism of the Nazi leadership became evident, played out daily to households through the now ubiquitous medium of the wireless and rehearsed by enthusiasts in schools, workplaces, youth organizations, and summer camps. Germans learned to be antisemites.[12]

Even so, antisemitism did have a head start in Germany. Though many Germans were tolerant of Jews, they did not regard them as members of the national community but as outsiders, who were racially dissimilar to them. To that extent, the poison of racial biology had done its work. The sense that Jews were somehow different allowed Germans to overlook and adjust to the increasingly brutal behaviour of the Nazi leadership, even though the victims were known to them and might even have been friends and neighbours. The ambiguities attending everyday encounters are neatly summed up in one memoir. A boy when Hitler came to power, Horst Krüger recollects the Jewish families he had known in his childhood, who had fled his Berlin suburb:

> The Katzensteins and the Schlicks and the Wittkowskis had moved away. No one had really noticed in fact. They were our good Jews. . . . Ludwig Marcuse lived three houses away from us, and he too had left in 1933. Nobody noticed any of this.[13]

Elsewhere in Central Europe, antisemitism was fuelled by social conflict. The farther east, the more belated the breakthrough from an agricultural to an industrial and manufacturing economy. Jews who lived on the land, but not off it, were among the first to move into the new business sector, setting up factories, investing in enterprises, and making up the bulk of the professional classes. In Hungary and much of Transylvania, Poland, Slovakia, and to an extent Austria, being Jewish and being middle class were synonymous. Antisemitism was the way non-Jews expressed their frustration at being, as they saw it, blocked from social advance by Jewish intruders. Of course, there were plenty of poor Jews too, living a precarious existence in small towns and shtetls or on the edges of cities, but antisemitism does not trade in nuance.[14]

The 'quota', or *numerus clausus* (literally, 'closed number'), was the antisemites' cudgel—to reduce Jewish access to higher education to the same proportion as there were Jews in the overall population, with the aim of squeezing Jews out of the professions. Hungary was the first country to adopt a Jewish quota at universities, in 1920. It was rescinded eight years later but reimposed in 1938. In Transylvania, students set their own quotas, physically blocking Jewish students from attending lectures. Most Polish universities introduced their own quotas in the 1930s, while also forbidding Jewish medical students from dissecting non-Jewish cadavers and obliging Jews to sit separately in lecture theatres on so-called ghetto benches. Even before the German occupation in March 1939, the Czechoslovak government had banned all Jewish attendance at universities.[15]

Germany had no monopoly on antisemitism. It was endemic to large parts of Central Europe, with its most fanatical exponents in the region's east. In the extermination of Central European Jewry, many Poles, Hungarians, Lithuanians, Ukrainians, Romanians, Czechs, and Slovaks would prove eager accomplices: rounding up Jews, providing the logistical support for murder, and conducting their own brutal outrages. The most notorious of these was at Jedwabne, in what is now northeastern Poland, where in July 1941 local Poles killed about four hundred Jews in a day-long rampage, slashing throats, stamping on babies, and finally murdering the survivors in a barn that they deliberately set on fire. In an unexpected intervention, a nearby German military post saved a handful of Jews from death by sheltering them from the mob.[16]

Jedwabne was just one of many outrages perpetrated by self-appointed local executioners across a wide swathe of Central Europe after 1939. In roughly 250 places in what had been Poland, groups of Poles and Ukrainians joined in pillaging Jewish homes and businesses and in murdering their occupants. In many towns and villages, there was a history of anti-Jewish violence and, under the cover of the German invasion, acts were reprised, often following a choreography recalled from previous occasions. Macabre carnivals were played out so that middle-class Jews were made to clean the streets and rabbis had their beards set on fire. Particular violence was shown to women, whom their captors often paraded naked and raped in public. The horrors later enacted in the death camps, where women were also subjected to public acts of sexual abuse, suggest that male anxieties about female sexuality contributed to antisemitic violence.[17]

There were in the General Government about two million Jews. The initial plan, as proposed by the Nazi police chief Reinhard Heydrich, was to move them to 'concentration points' near railway lines so that they might be ready 'for further measures'. But there were too many Jews and the 'further measures' were not specified, so the governor-general Hans Frank ordered the construction of several hundred ghettoes, parts of cities and towns where the Jews were, literally, walled in. Nazi planners in Berlin imagined that the inmates would either starve to death or, if they were to be moved, sent across the border into the zone of Soviet occupation or to some overseas territory, ideally one with a harsh climate.

By invading the Soviet Union, the Germans had to accommodate a further two and a half million Jews. From the very first, the occupation authorities committed straightforward murder, deploying 'task forces' (*Einsatzgruppen*) behind the lines to kill off Jews, usually with the help of units recruited from the local population. By the end of 1941, the task forces had overseen the murder of about a million Soviet Jews, most notoriously at Babyn Yar in Kyiv, where thirty-four thousand Jews were murdered in just two days in September 1941. Killing now became the solution, not just in the territory of the Soviet Union but throughout occupied Central Europe. As the governor-general of occupied Poland learned on visiting Berlin at the end of 1941, the idea of moving Jews farther to the east or to new settlements was a fantasy: 'So, liquidate them yourself,' he was told.[18]

But it was a local initiative that started events leading to the first extermination camp. The Łódź ghetto in what had been Poland was already overcrowded and scheduled to receive a new wave of Jews from Germany and Bohemia. During the autumn of 1941, the governor of the Łódź region, Arthur Greiser, obtained the consent of the head of the Nazi SS terror organization, Heinrich Himmler, to 'evacuate' Jews from Łódź and nearby to make way for the incomers. A 'special unit' (*Sonderkommando*) that had been gassing the mentally disabled with exhaust fumes was available close by. Greiser now moved it to a secluded manor house at Chełmno and scaled up its operation, beginning in December 1941, with the aim of emptying the Łódź ghetto. Within six months, the unit had murdered almost one hundred thousand people, mostly through carbon monoxide poisoning in mobile death vans.

Although the method of gassing changed, Chełmno provided the blueprint and Nazi policy swung behind it, becoming formalized at the Wannsee Conference of January 1942. Instead of death by starvation or by shooting, Jews were now to be transported to dedicated plants, processed as if on a production line, and industrially murdered in dedicated gassing facilities. Over the course of the year, Nazi officials led by Himmler devised a system of spokes and hubs, with the ghettoes feeding human beings to extermination centres. But as the Nazis' genocidal mania grew, the camps ended up taking Jews from further afield. The largest, at Auschwitz-Birkenau, murdered Jews from across occupied Europe. Where transportation was difficult, Jews continued to be killed on the spot—in just the autumn of 1942, some three hundred thousand Jews were shot in Nazi-occupied Ukraine.

For much of Central Europe, the first years of the Second World War were a 'phoney war', fought elsewhere. Only in 1941 did Romania, Slovakia, and Hungary side definitively with Nazi Germany and declare war. The collapse of Yugoslavia following the German invasion of April 1941 added the Nazi puppet state of Croatia to the list of belligerents. Germany's new allies contributed troops to its war effort and endured considerable losses on the Eastern Front and in operations against partisans in the Balkans. Even so, for several years the war was for many Central European civilians just a distant noise. Extraordinarily, in 1943 Baedeker even published a new red hardback guide—to the General Government. For the traveller who could be bothered with the paperwork for an entry permit, the General Government's countryside offered 'numerous lovely excursions' to woods and chateaus, parks with open-air concerts, and tidy villages that the guide assured the reader were now 'clean of Jews' (*Judenrein*).[19]

Poland was the obvious exception to this false calm. Its civilian population endured a ruthless German occupation that lasted in some places for more than five years. On top of the murder of three million Polish Jews, Germans killed a further three million non-Jewish Poles in reprisal actions, by starvation and disease, and following round-ups of suspected sympathizers. In a final act of butchery, German SS units killed at least thirty thousand civilians in Warsaw in August 1944. Meanwhile, in the countryside, the numerous Polish Home Army waged a war of sabotage, train derailments, guerrilla warfare, and intelligence gathering. One in eight trains destined to support the German armies on the Eastern Front with the Soviet Union was either destroyed or substantially held up by Home Army operations, while almost a half of the high-grade intelligence received in Britain out of German-occupied Europe came from Polish sources.[20]

The Home Army was just one part of an enormous underground network of resistance in Poland that revived the nineteenth-century tradition of 'Organic Work'. In 1940, Himmler had recommended that Poles receive no more education other than how to count to five hundred, to sign their name, and to obey Germans. So, Poles set up clandestine schools that undertook the teaching of as many as a million children at a time and reconstituted universities that had been closed, not only giving lectures but also conducting examinations and awarding degrees. Secret theatres and concert venues operated in cafés and private apartments and, incredibly, Warsaw's main public library still managed between 1940 and 1942 to provide more than two million readers with 3.5 million books. Also, many non-Jewish Poles contributed to the resistance by rescuing Jews, providing safe houses and escape routes out of the ghettoes, and forging new identity papers, always at incredible personal risk. The award given by the state of Israel to the 'Righteous among Nations', namely, non-Jews who helped Jews during the Holocaust, counts more Poles among its recipients than any other nation. Courage, too, does not trade in nuance.[21]

When it came to his Central European allies, Hitler preferred dealing with conservative strongmen, rather than with zealots whose enthusiasm might jeopardize the war against the Soviet Union. So he kept in power Hungary's regent Admiral Miklós Horthy, and in Slovakia the Catholic priest Jozef Tiso—no ordinary cleric, Tiso was hanged for war crimes in 1947. In Romania, Hitler backed General Antonescu against the fanatical Iron Guard, even though the Iron Guard was favoured by Himmler and the SS. But Croatia was a loose cannon in Nazi schemes. Here, power fell into the hands of the Ustaša, or Croatian Revolutionary Movement, and its genocidal leader, Ante Pavelić, who sought to purify Croatia by murdering its Serbs, Jews, and Gypsies. Even seasoned German officers were appalled by Pavelić's savagery and the brutal blundering of his government.

By 1944, the German armies were in retreat on the Eastern Front, having been blocked first at Stalingrad and then at Kursk. By the summer, Soviet armies had reached the outskirts of Warsaw and overrun the easternmost part of Slovakia. In August, Romania's twenty-two-year-old king Michael led a coup against Antonescu and switched sides to join the Allies. The Hungarian regent had previously sought to do the same, but his efforts had been clumsy. The British diplomats that his agents negotiated with in Istanbul turned out to be German plants and his secret radio links to the Allies were insecure—every time he contacted the Allies, German planes buzzed the palace. In March 1944, the Germans occupied Hungary and when in October Regent Horthy tried to change sides, Hitler had him arrested and installed a pro-Nazi government. Slovakia too was occupied by German troops in August 1944, following a mutiny by part of the Slovak army.

Central Europe now felt the full brunt of the war. Until 1944, the Hungarian government had an understanding with the Western Allies. Unlike neutral Switzerland, whose Messerschmitt fighter planes shot down British and American aircraft entering its air space, the Hungarian air force did not take on Allied bombers destined for German targets, in return for which Hungary was spared air raids. But with the German occupation in March 1944, the strategic bombing of Hungary commenced, with six hundred or more aircraft often involved in single operations. To confuse aerial communications and anti-aircraft batteries, Hungarian American pilots countermanded Hungarian orders, speaking the language fluently.

By the end of 1942, the pace of mass slaughter had slackened in Central Europe. Four and a half million Jews had been killed by this time, and the Nazis found it increasingly difficult to squeeze more victims from the territory they occupied. The governments of Germany's satellites also resisted further deportations since they wanted to use Jews as labour and in some cases faced domestic opposition to what was now known to be murder. The German military occupation of Slovakia and Hungary in 1944 led to a final frenzy as Slovak and Hungarian Jews were rounded up and sent to the death factories in former Poland, mostly to Auschwitz. More than four hundred thousand Hungarian Jews were killed along with ten thousand Slovak Jews, which was all that was left by this time of Slovakia's Jewish population.

The rounding up of Jews could not have been done without the active involvement of a part of the local population: informers, police, military auxiliaries, and volunteers. In what had been Poland, denunciation by neighbours and the collaboration of the Polish 'blue police' possibly sent as many as two hundred thousand Jews to their deaths. Elsewhere, brigades of Lithuanian and Ukrainian auxiliary troops escorted Jews to their murder or killed them in local actions. In Hungary and Slovakia, which had their own governments, the state gendarmeries were complicit in deporting Jews. Indeed, in Hungary the identification, marshalling, and entrainment of Jews to Auschwitz was overseen by twenty thousand Hungarian police and agents of the ministry of the interior and local county offices, who reported to just two hundred German officials. In Berehove, the rounding up of Jews and their imprisonment in the local brickyards, from which they were soon sent to Auschwitz, was conducted almost entirely by Hungarian gendarmes, who often robbed and beat the captives. To speed the pace of murder, Hungarian Nazis belonging to the Arrow Cross movement also killed as many as nine thousand Jews in the last months of 1944.[22]

The mass murder of Central Europe's Jews depended on local complicity, but it needed a bureaucracy for its administration. In Germany, a double bureaucracy made up of civil servants on the one side and party functionaries on the other vied for power, numbering several million people in all (although, of these, many party functions were only part-time). Few were directly involved in slaughter, since the administration of the death camps was parsimonious—apart from camp guards, the murder factory at Belzec was run by no more than twenty to thirty officials. But all were touched by the experience of living in a murderous racial state—checking the genealogy of office underlings, cataloguing scientific papers that reported medical experiments on captives, arranging for the disposal of the property of the dead, and so on. Nor were bureaucrats just the mindless automatons they pretended to be after 1945. Many were actively engaged in finding solutions to problems, in anticipating requirements, and in jostling to exceed expectations.

The civil servants made extermination a series of technical challenges—from the legal definition of what a Jew was to the winding up of Jewish businesses whose owners had been killed. Established routines and the artificial vocabulary of the bureaucrat cushioned what was really going on. Killing and murder were never spoken of, but only 'evacuation', 'resettlement', and 'deportation'. For performing their duties, the civil servants received the rewards of office as if their tasks were entirely unexceptional—a new uniform, minor promotions, and medals.

The administration of the railways is illustrative of the bureaucratic ethos that made murder possible. Some two thousand trains belonging to German Reich Railways (Deutsche Reichsbahn) conveyed about three million Jews to their deaths. Each train had to be separately commissioned and paid for by Himmler's staff according to passenger numbers. The rate was based on second-class fares (even though

the passengers were crammed into wagons) and worked out according
to kilometre distance. The railway administration charged Himmler's
office half fare for children under ten, and those under four went for
free. Trains with more than four hundred people qualified as holiday
excursions and were eligible for further reductions. Only the guards
were counted as return fares.[23]

More than thirty years later, a film crew interviewed the railway
timetabler, Walter Stier, who wrote the train schedules from the ghettoes to the death camps:

> **Question:** Did you know that, for example, Treblinka
>   meant killing or . . .
> **Stier:** For heaven's sake, no. How should we know that? I
>   never was in Treblinka, I was never in such a . . . I
>   did not get out of Cracow, I am from Warsaw. . . .
>   I was always sitting at my desk, right?[24]

The adoption of everyday routines also characterized the deportation of Hungarian Jews to Auschwitz in 1944. The Hungarian county
administration had responsibility for moving Jews first to ghettoes and
then to collection points from where they would be entrained to their
deaths. Local government officials were appointed to wind up Jewish
businesses and property. They did so by following standard arrangements in respect of bankruptcy, itemizing possessions and stock, and
sealing the premises with wax tags. In many cases, they appointed
administrators over businesses that were thought useful to the war
effort so that they might continue trading. Valuables were either left
in company safes, which were also sealed, or handed over to finance
officers from the county, who inventoried them. The police pursued
missing items, while museum staff inspected confiscated objects that
were thought to have historical or artistic importance. Accountants
balanced the cost of compensating owners whose property had been
temporarily assigned to ghettoes against the value of Jewish property

seized. It did not matter whether the officials were fanatical antisemites
or not, the organizational routines took over.[25]

Almost a million Jews perished in the death camp at Treblinka
(now in northeastern Poland). Interviewed shortly before his death in
1971, Franz Stangl, the camp commandant, explained his actions by
his commitment to work:

> I had to do my job as well as I could. That is how I am. . . . My
> professional ethos was that if something wrong was going on in the
> camp I had to find it out. That was my profession; I enjoyed it. It
> fulfilled me.[26]

The master planner behind the destruction of Europe's Jews was Adolf
Eichmann. An Israeli court tried him for war crimes in 1962, sen-
tencing him to death. Eichmann claimed throughout his trial that he
was only obeying orders, and he appealed to the German Enlightenment philosopher Immanuel Kant for vindication. He had lived out
his whole life, Eichmann explained, according to Kant's definition of
duty, so that his own will had conformed to the legal precepts of the
state he served. The presiding judge was astonished at Eichmann's misunderstanding of Kant.[27]

However imperfectly Eichmann understood Kant, his appeal to
the philosopher is telling. The Holocaust was born of intellectual
trends and moral predispositions that were rooted not just in the German past (as is often maintained) but also in Central European history.
Ideas deriving from the Enlightenment that the state was an agent
of human betterment and that a professional bureaucracy might treat
individuals as mindless cogs or as anonymous numbers were taken to
industrial perfection. The intended result was a radically different and
'better' society, which united race and nation in a state that was now
purged (in a commonplace trio of the time) of 'vermin, lice, and Jews',
and so made virtuous. The urge to accomplish this new society made
many ordinary Central Europeans into murderers.

The imagined society of the future was born of nineteenth-century national romanticism, shaped by the language of racial science and biological difference, and infected by the idea of death as a euthanizing instrument of cleansing. But the ambition for change was intensified by the frustrations of nation-building and made brutal by the experience of war. For all its longing to re-create an illusionary past of homogeneous national communities in tune with the land and its past, the new society was also highly modern in its choice of the factory production line and of bureaucratic routines as the preferred instruments of annihilation. In Nazi-run Central Europe, the Neue Sachlichkeit's milk-bottling plants and great revolving wheels were repurposed for human destruction. Railway timetables, busy civil servants with schedules and quotas, workers with levers to pull, and scientists with chemical apparatus: the mechanical ingredients of the Holocaust in Central Europe were as everyday as the Central Europeans who made it happen.

CHAPTER 32

Mátyás Rákosi, Stalinist Central Europe, and Its Discontents

T HE YOUNG MÁTYÁS RÁKOSI (1892–1971) LOVED LONDON. The son of a Jewish shopkeeper in southern Hungary, he had made his way there via Hamburg in 1913. Already a socialist, Rákosi had immediately joined the Communist Club in London's Fitzrovia, whose Hungarian members had found him accommodation and a job as a shipping clerk. Rákosi spent his free time in pastry shops, joining in Suffragette demonstrations (he was hit on the head in one clash with police), visiting art galleries, and reading in the great library of the British Museum. He soon moved to the London suburb of Islington to be near an Irish girlfriend whom he wooed with apricots sent by post from his home near Subotica, in what is now Serbia. With war imminent, Rákosi hastened home to enlist in the Austro-Hungarian army. He would not see London again until June 1946, when he visited as Hungary's deputy prime minister and head of the Hungarian Communist Party. This time he ate at Claridge's.[1]

Rákosi's service in the First World War was short. Deployed against Russia, he was captured in 1915 and made a prisoner. Three years later, he was a fanatic, inspired by what he had seen of the revolution in Russia. When he returned to Hungary, it was as a so-called people's commissar of the communist government that took power in the country in March 1919. Communist rule in Hungary was chaotic and brutal—it did not help that the communist leader, Béla Kun, had a nervous breakdown and stayed in bed for most of its duration. Rákosi took charge first of trade policy and then of the communist security apparatus. He soon learned how to kill, being implicated in more than forty political murders.

Hungary's first communist experiment lasted fewer than five months. By August 1919, Rákosi was on the run, first to Vienna and then to Moscow. For five years, he lived in the Soviet Union, where he worked for the international communist organization known as the Comintern. In 1924, he returned under an alias to Hungary to take charge of its fledgling Communist Party. But most of the party's members were on the police payroll and he was soon betrayed and arrested. Sentenced to eight years in gaol, when the term expired in 1934 he was retried and condemned to life imprisonment. Prison was not so bad. Rákosi was allowed to read and even to hold party meetings with fellow communist prisoners, and he reckoned the food better than what he had been used to in Moscow.

On 30 October 1940, the guards instructed him to put on a suit. Rákosi expected to be executed, but instead he was escorted to a black limousine with diplomatic number plates. The car raced from the prison in Szeged to the Soviet border. Unknown to Rákosi, the Hungarian government had done a deal with Moscow whereby he would be released in exchange for the battle standards that the Russian army had captured at the end of the Hungarian War of Independence in 1849. Shortly after crossing into the Soviet Union, Rákosi saw crowds of (doubtless coerced) farm labourers and factory hands bearing banners of welcome. A week later, he stood next to Joseph Stalin in Moscow's Red Square as the Soviet leader reviewed the great military procession commemorating the 1917 Russian Revolution. But when he began to look for his old friends in Moscow, he was met with shrugs and evasion. Nearly all had been killed in Stalin's purge of imagined rivals and traitors and their names obliterated.

The Soviet Union joined the Second World War in 1941, fighting alongside the Allies to defeat Nazi Germany. Rákosi did not serve on the front line but stayed in Moscow, where he headed up the Hungarian Communist Party in exile and ran the 'Kossuth' radio station that broadcast Soviet and communist propaganda to Hungary. In 1942, he married a lawyer and fellow Communist from Yakutia in eastern Siberia, Feodora Kornyilova. For the rest of their married life, she reported back to the secret police, or NKVD (later KGB), on her husband. Since Kornyilova was a judge in the Soviet Supreme Court, Rákosi doubtless repaid the favour. (Kornyilova died in 1980 in a small flat in Moscow, living off a widow's pension.) As soon as it was safe, Rákosi returned to Hungary under Soviet protection. There he learned that his father, brother, and sister had all been murdered in Nazi concentration camps.

By the time of Germany's surrender in May 1945, the Soviet Union was in possession of a large chunk of Central Europe, reaching from the Elbe River, just fifty kilometres east of Hamburg, to the Austrian border with Yugoslavia. Everything east of this line lay in Stalin's hands. But Stalin wavered over what to do with Central Europe. At times, he treated it as loot, either requisitioning factories wholesale or founding joint ventures through which an occupied state provided the investment capital and the Soviet Union took whatever was produced. At others, Stalin seemed willing to allow some measure of political and economic independence, with the countries of Central Europe becoming so-called People's Democracies, holding a midway position between market capitalism and communism. But soon after the Hungarian Soviet economist Eugen Varga published in 1946 a work of theory to explain how hybrid economies might actually work, Stalin closed down Varga's institute and its journal.[2]

Rákosi was alert to these changes. Stalin had chosen him to lead Hungary's Communist Party and he had close contact with the Soviet leader, even holidaying with him on the Black Sea. But where he could, he forced the pace. The first stage, which Rákosi had completed by early 1946, was for Communists to take control of the ministry of the interior and use the police and security service to threaten rival politicians. Then, Rákosi destroyed step by step the other parties, either forcing their dissolution or weakening their electoral base by founding bogus parties that stole their programmes. Rákosi called this 'salami tactics', slicing away at the opposition bit by bit. In 1947, he destroyed the Smallholders Party, Hungary's largest party, intimidating its leadership with false accusations and using Soviet troops to kidnap its chief secretary. The next year, the Social Democrats folded, meekly voting to fuse with the Communists.[3]

In the elections of 1945 and 1947, the communists had done badly, scraping just a fifth of the vote. But with the rival parties out of the way, Rákosi called a new election in May 1949 in which only Communist-approved candidates were allowed to stand. A reign of terror now descended on Hungary, administered by a hundred-thousand-strong secret police force, with as many as two hundred thousand Hungarians held in labour camps and two thousand killed. At Stalin's prompting, Rákosi also 'uncovered' a plot within the party to hand Hungary over to the West. In the autumn of 1949, he purged the party, more or less at random, and sent a wave of previously loyal communists either to prison yards or to the gallows.

Although the pace of change differed, Hungary's experience was typical throughout Central Europe. The communist takeover happened faster in Croatia and Slovenia, where Soviet troops and home-grown communist brigades intimidated their rivals into silence, restoring the previously failed state of Yugoslavia. In Romania, the communists had seized power by the end of 1946. Even so, anti-Communist insurgents continued to fight on in the mountains of Transylvania until well into the 1970s. In Poland, the Communists took power in stages between 1945 and 1947 in conditions that amounted to open warfare, as the remnants of the Home Army fought the Soviet army for control. In Czechoslovakia, the tempo was slacker, since the Communists hoped to win power through the ballot box in genuinely free elections. This was not a pipe dream, since in the first post-war election the Communist Party had won almost 40 per cent of the vote. But tired of delay, early in 1948 Stalin ordered the Czechoslovak Communists 'to resolve the question of power'. Having provoked a cabinet crisis, the Communists brought their supporters onto the streets to demand a communist government; 'action committees' seized control of ministries, and police and armed vigilantes began rounding up opponents. A fraudulent election held in May 1948 sealed the communist victory.[4]

In Western Europe, politicians and journalists lamented the crushing of democracy in Central Europe. But Central Europe's experience with democracy in the interwar years had been only partial and, in most cases, short-lived. On top of this, it had just been through German and Nazi occupation and rule, and half a dozen years of warfare, culminating in the invasion of Soviet troops. The total number of deaths in Central Europe (Germany and Austria, Czechoslovakia, Hungary, and Poland) amounted during the war years to fifteen million people, or one in eight of the population. The raw figures hide the trauma of conflict: the comprehensive destruction of whole cities (80 per cent of Warsaw was flattened), the children orphaned, and the women gang-raped. The middle class in large parts of Central Europe had been systematically obliterated by the Nazi and Soviet conquerors. In Poland, a quarter to a third of all teachers were murdered, and a half of all doctors. In Hungary, where many doctors were Jewish, the number of physicians working in Budapest fell from 4,800 in 1939 to 2,200 in 1944. The destruction of populations is not a good starting point for democratic transformation.

The violence did not end with Hitler's squalid suicide in April 1945, nor with Germany's surrender. Soviet occupation troops often behaved barbarically and in Poland anti-Jewish pogroms resumed. In May 1946, a mob in Kielce in southern Poland killed forty Jews who had survived the Holocaust, injuring an equal number. It was just one of many outrages against Jews that flared across Poland in 1945–1946, claiming the lives of between five hundred and fifteen hundred Jewish Poles. Elsewhere, government measures to restore property and businesses to Jewish owners or their next of kin prompted outbreaks of violence. Across Central Europe, the accusation was revived that Jews were murdering Christian children, sometimes with the macabre twist that they were kidnapping them for secret medical experiments.[5]

Wartime agreements among the Allies redrew the map of Central Europe—for the third time in thirty years. Poland was shunted

CENTRAL EUROPE IN 1945

westwards. The Soviet Union kept its gains from 1939 and Poland was compensated with East Prussia, Silesia, and most of Pomerania. Romania recovered northern Transylvania, which Hitler had given to Hungary in 1940. Further Soviet gains included the Prussian city of Königsberg (renamed Kaliningrad), the northern Bukovina which was now absorbed into the Soviet Ukraine, all three of the Baltic states, and the easternmost part of Czechoslovakia. On top of this, Germany and Austria were carved up into occupation zones. Russian power, which had in the late eighteenth and nineteenth centuries wavered on the edge of Central Europe, was now firmly planted in its heart. In the Soviet occupation zone of East Germany alone, wedged between West Germany and Poland, there were no fewer than half a million Soviet troops. In 1952, the Soviet hold on the new communist state of East Germany was literally cemented into place by a new fortified border with West Germany; nine years later, the Soviets extended the demarcation line to Berlin, dividing the city in half with a wall.

At a meeting held in Potsdam in July 1945, the Allied leaders agreed that all existing German minorities should be deported to Germany. In fact, most Germans had fled westwards anyway to avoid the Soviet advance, while the Polish and Czechoslovak governments had already begun what were called at the time 'displacement actions'. Altogether, twelve and a half million Germans either moved of their own accord or were forcibly ejected, often in harsh conditions, travelling in the backs of lorries or in unheated cattle trucks. Well over half a million Germans died. In Transylvania and the Romanian Banat, some eighty thousand Germans, men and women alike, were rounded up as Nazi collaborators and sent to labour camps in the Soviet Union, where a quarter perished of neglect and disease.[6]

But it was not just Germans who were on the move. Hungarians were expelled from Czechoslovakia, Yugoslavia, and Transylvania and the Banat; Slovaks from Hungary; Poles from the new Soviet republics of Ukraine, Lithuania, and Belarus; and Ukrainians, Belarusians, and Lithuanians from Poland. Apart from Germans, some seven million people were uprooted across Central Europe, either pushing the

wreckage of their former lives in carts or on bicycles or thrown into
the backs of lorries with a single suitcase. Some minorities survived
this onslaught. About 1.6 million Hungarians remained in Romania,
and roughly half a million apiece in Czechoslovakia and Yugoslavia.
Even so, these massive population flows gave Central Europe a con-
gruence between state and nation that had been previously missing.
States and nations now more or less coincided, removing one of the
sources of friction that had long bedevilled relations between governments and peoples and had contributed to Central Europe's political
instability.[7]

Massacre, genocide, invasion, antisemitism, and forced deportation: Central Europe had over a decade been assailed by a pack of
apocalypses. Lives were cheapened or deemed worthless, bodies treated
as commodities to be bartered, and cruelty was normal. Visiting a refugee camp in Germany in 1946, the former First Lady Eleanor Roosevelt
observed:

> You can measure the extent of damage done to cities, you can re-
> store water supplies, gas and electricity, and you can rebuild the
> buildings needed to establish a military government. But to gauge
> what has happened to human beings, that is incalculable.[8]

Under these conditions of extreme degradation, politics was unlikely to work through channels of compromise and accommodation.
It became instead as violent and murderous as the personal experiences
of most Central Europeans. Rákosi and the communist bosses who
took power in Central Europe after the Second World War had the
advantage of Soviet backing, but in the brutal world of the 1940s they
excelled because they were the most brutal politicians.

No sooner were they in power than the communist regimes of
Central Europe copied the Soviet economic model, inaugurating
ambitious five-year plans and building huge industrial plants, often
using out-of-date designs and machinery. Their immediate goal was
'socialism', by which they meant the threshold to the workers' para-

dise of communism. But in the 1950s, the majority of the population in Central Europe still lived on the land. The communists needed to create the working class in whose name they always claimed to be ruling. So, labourers from the countryside became a new industrial proletariat, initially housed singly in barracks and visiting their families only briefly at weekends. (The working week was generally six 10-hour days.) In the countryside, governments forced through the collectivization of agriculture, making peasants amalgamate their plots and pool their animals and equipment. Resistance was intense, and collectivization had to be abandoned in Poland in the late 1950s as too socially disruptive.

All this was supposed to lead to an upsurge in economic performance and incomes. But instead of doubling (as Rákosi had boasted in 1948), incomes fell, by more than a fifth in just three years. The command economy, with civil servants laying down targets, was no substitute for the market, despite its imperfections. Shortages, even in basic agricultural foodstuffs, were routine and manufactured goods distinguished by their shoddiness. Bureaucrats in ministries applied only the most rudimentary accountancy measurements to enterprises, checking inputs against outputs, and (in a contemporary criticism) treating prices as 'mere bookkeeping units'. And all they had to rely on were the optimistic figures given them by factory bosses, so the overall performance of the economy was a mystery to them. Government statisticians made up sums to fit the five-year plans but, from the 1960s onwards, relied for harder facts on the guesses of the Economist Intelligence Unit in London, which told them quarter by quarter just how their economies were doing, from the provision of fertilizers to refrigerators per household.[9]

Communist bureaucracies were the reverse of what bureaucracies were supposed to be. They were not knowledgeable and the decisions they made were not rational ones but guided by ideology. Promotion was not on merit but by favour. At every level, from the party's central organs down to its local administration, communist bosses kept lists of (mostly) party loyalists who were eligible for office in ministries and local government and to oversee hospitals, the police, state enterprises, and factory production. In Poland in the mid-1950s, there were no fewer than 160,000 'names', each of whom presumed to a well-paid post, often in a specialist role for which he, or occasionally she, had no expertise. As the party's elite, the names (or nomenklatura, a Russian term) had privileged access to shops where Western goods were on sale in the otherwise almost worthless local currency. They drove chrome-heavy Buick lookalikes, called Volgas, and their wives wore furs.[10]

The economies of communist Central Europe survived the first few years, since governments raised cash by confiscating the assets of formerly private businesses and then plundering the state-owned savings banks and insurance companies. Thereafter, governments became increasingly dependent on loans, first from the Soviet Union, and then from Western governments and bankers. By the mid-1950s, Rákosi's Hungary had debts of close to half a billion US dollars. Much of what was borrowed went on servicing existing debts or was ploughed into capital-hungry but underperforming state enterprises. Of course, these liabilities seldom featured on the five-year plans, which instead reported bumper harvests and steady industrial growth.[11]

Communist self-congratulation was nowhere more evident than in the leadership cult, borrowed from Stalin's Soviet Union. The head of the party was feted as a visionary and inspiration, whose selfless dedication to the working class had brought it prosperity and peace. Poems praised his greatness and his name graced factories, schools, streets, and the new collective farms. On May Day and other communist feast days, processions in cities bore aloft the leader's portrait. Shops kept 'communist corners' in which his photograph was displayed next to Stalin's, sometimes with a selection of his printed speeches. Perhaps mischievously, Hungarian shop assistants crowned piles of women's underwear with Rákosi's photograph, while one butcher in Budapest carved his bust in lard. The theatre, too, rehearsed the leader's praises. In the nauseating *The Promise* (*Az ígéret*, 1952), which has as its theme a family moving into a new housing block, the young daughter hangs

Rákosi's portrait on the wall and asks her mother, 'Comrade Rákosi lives with us too, doesn't he?'[12]

There were people who believed all this, who dangled their babies at Rákosi, wrote him admiring letters, and were sufficiently shocked by any criticism of the regime to report the delinquency. Generally, they were not members of the working class, in whose name the Communist Party claimed to act. Communist Party members belonged overwhelmingly to the professional and managerial classes. Between 85 and 95 per cent of the 'names' in Hungary and Poland had university degrees or the vocational equivalent. Among ordinary party members, the same imbalance was evident. Whereas the Polish middle class in the 1950s and 1960s made up just a quarter of the overall Polish population, white-collar employees constituted about a half of party members. To put it another way: in Poland in 1968, fewer than 13 per cent of industrial workers and farmers were party members, but 40 per cent of engineers and 41 per cent of teachers were.[13]

From the late 1940s onwards, keen observers noticed the emergence of a new communist aristocracy of power that united bureaucrats, intellectuals, and others in a 'new class', a 'new elite', or even a 'new nobility'. The new elite was self-perpetuating, conferring privilege and place to newcomers on the basis of their suitability. Suitability came in several forms. First was the political, in the sense of a doctrinaire commitment to the communist mission. Second was intellectual, either by membership of the traditional academic professions of historian, philosopher, or writer, or by belonging to the new technical or managerial class. Finally, there was the social, comprising 'glamour personalities', like the ballerinas, actors, and dubiously wealthy whose posturing and fantastical self-fashioning Philip Roth satirized in *The Prague Orgy* (1985).[14]

Most ordinary Central Europeans stood outside this gilded world. They were uncommitted to communism, suspicious of its blustering certainties, and not so much compliant as disengaged, mechanically performing empty rituals of loyalty. As the Czech playwright Václav Havel famously explained in 1978:

The manager of a fruit-and-vegetable shop places in his window, among the onions and carrots, the slogan: 'Workers of the world, unite!' Why does he do it? What is he trying to communicate to the world? . . . That poster was delivered to our greengrocer from the enterprise headquarters along with the onions and carrots. He put them all into the window simply because it has been done that way for years, because everyone does it, and because that is the way it has to be. . . . He does it because these things must be done if one is to get along in life.[15]

When not gesturing to the party, Central Europeans retreated into domesticity, cultivating their own gardens—literally so, for it was a widespread ambition to have a summer house and allotment on the edge of the city. Most married young, had their families early, and were divorced by forty. The party kept them docile with the tokens of Western luxury—fashion magazines, washing-up liquid, and oranges.

Complacencies were often broken. Wage cuts and shortages prompted strikes and occasionally riots. The response of the party was usually to arrest the ringleaders and drop a few concessions to the rank and file. The larger danger was when a rift among the elite prompted more widespread unrest, leading to a crisis that threatened the whole edifice of communist power. This happened most spectacularly in Hungary in 1956, with a split in the party between reformers and the more doctrinaire Communists, mirroring the political crisis in the Soviet Union that followed Stalin's death in 1953. Reformers looked to the veteran Communist Imre Nagy and conservatives to Rákosi. Rákosi played a typically dirty game, discrediting his rival with smears and having him ejected from the party.

But in February 1956, the Soviet leader Nikita Khrushchev gave his 'secret speech' in Moscow to a congress of the Soviet Communist Party, outlining Stalin's crimes and betrayals. The speech was not so secret since it circulated in summaries among local party organizations throughout the Soviet Union and Central Europe. Never less than loyal to Stalin and to his memory, Rákosi was (correctly) presumed guilty by implication of the same excesses as his master. Under pressure from Moscow, the Hungarian party bosses forced Rákosi from office in June 1956—he duly made his way to the Soviet Union, where he ended up managing a wallpaper factory in Kirghizstan in Soviet Central Asia. Right up to his death in 1971, Rákosi believed that he would shortly be recalled to power in Hungary.

The regime was buckling. Students forced the pace. As potential members of the new elite, they had a vested interest in making the system work and in pushing through the changes they thought necessary for its improvement. The students were backed by former politicians whom Rákosi had ousted, several actors, and the Hungarian Writers' Union, which was an elite club of hack authors. Student demonstrations beginning on 23 October led to mass protests and to shooting. Reformers in the party prevailed upon Imre Nagy to head up a new government, but he was unable to halt the escalating chaos. In the cities, mobs murdered party members and secret policemen, while local committees took charge in the countryside, blocking the movement of food supplies. In factories, newly elected workers' councils sacked managers.

The first cabinet meeting of the Nagy government, held on 28 October 1956, showed a curious disconnect with reality. Sensibly enough, the politicians discussed food shortages, but their conversation soon became bogged down in the movement of individual trains and the size of railway shunting yards. Next, it was shop opening hours, the revision of school textbooks (would tearing out pages be enough?), the repair of broken windows, and the dates of national holidays. There was no estimation of Hungarian military preparedness nor any appreciation of the Soviet Union's strategic dilemma. Only a year before, the Soviets had formally welded together their satellites in Central Europe into the military alliance known as the Warsaw Pact. The chaos in Hungary jeopardized the Soviet Union's security and the integrity of the new alliance. For the Soviet leadership, it was a test too far.[16]

Khrushchev explained the situation bluntly to a meeting of Soviet party bosses in the Kremlin on 31 October 1956:

We should take the initiative in restoring order in Hungary. If we depart from Hungary, it will give a great boost to the Americans, English, and French—the imperialists. They will perceive it as weakness on our part and will go onto the offensive. . . . Our party will not accept it if we do this.[17]

On 4 November, Soviet tanks rolled into Budapest to put down the revolution. They encountered short-lived but massive popular resistance in working-class districts of the capital, where some fifteen thousand fighters took up arms or hurled petrol bombs. The same day, the Soviet leadership announced a new puppet Hungarian government, to be led by one of the victims of Rákosi's earlier purges, János Kádár. By the end of the month, Kádár was in charge, imposed on a defeated population by Soviet arms. He would run Hungary for more than thirty years. As one of his first acts, Kádár had Nagy arrested, tried for treason, and hanged.[18]

Communist governments throughout Central Europe kept bountiful supplies of pornography stacked in warehouses. At times of crisis, they distributed it to middlemen for sale on the streets. They did so now in Hungary, cynically reckoning that a man was never more harmlessly engaged than when thumbing through a dirty magazine. But this was a lesson of sorts too. To continue in power, the Communists needed to cater to the population's more basic needs. High-minded propaganda was no substitute for leakproof housing, denim jeans, and televisions. Kádár was among the first to embrace the 'new course', as it was called at the time, freeing up the economy and borrowing recklessly abroad to buy fancy imports from the West. At the time, it was called 'goulash socialism', meaning communism spiced with consumerism. As popular expectations rose, it would over the next thirty years become 'refrigerator socialism', 'car socialism', and even 'weekend cottage socialism'.[19]

Even so, the problem of elites and power was unresolved. Properly functioning democracies allow for intergenerational churn, with different groups alternating in power and freeing up space for younger newcomers. In communist Central Europe, power, bureaucracy, and privilege were intertwined, leading to blockages in promotion, an ageing managerial elite, and intellectual conformity. Having got their hands on the spoils of the system, managers and party functionaries were unwilling to let go. Occasionally, a dynamic new leader would burst through, like Nicolae Ceauşescu in Romania in 1965, but having briefly re-energized communist rule, he let the Romanian Communist Party slip back into its old ways. Ceauşescu was at least pragmatic enough to keep censorship and the secret police in place, toughening up both as his reign went on. In Czechoslovakia in the late 1960s, a new leader abandoned both, provoking the next great crisis in Central European communism.

CHAPTER 33

Communist Central Europe and Its Collapse

UNLIKE KÁDÁR IN HUNGARY, THE CZECHOSLOVAK COMMUNIST leaders shunned reform, presiding over a sclerotic economy based upon big industrial enterprises run by politically committed but inept bureaucrats. The Czechoslovak Communist Party itself was equally dinosaurian. Purges in the early 1950s had brought in a new elite of loyalists, but they had held onto all the top and middle-ranking positions, blocking the way for younger people. Graduates struggled to find the jobs they thought they deserved, while in workplaces middle-aged managers made the decisions, sidelining their younger and better-qualified colleagues.[1]

Among young people, disaffection was intense. As the Czechoslovak party youth organization noted in 1965, in typically wooden prose:

> Unlike the first post-war generation of young people, for which so-cialism was an ideal in the first place . . . today's younger generation sees socialism as an objective and contradictory reality, divested of illusions.[2]

In other words, young people were now seeing communism for what it was. Disenchanted working-class youngsters showed their estrange-ment through the widespread adoption of Beatles-style haircuts and in rock and roll music. By 1965, there were a thousand amateur bands in Czechoslovakia, churning out cover versions of songs by the Rolling Stones and the Byrds. Until reel-to-reel tape recorders became afford-able in the mid-1960s, enthusiasts used discarded X-ray plates that

480

could be cut into circles and grooved to make them into recordable discs. With a centre hole made by a cigarette end, the X-ray plates spun eerily on turntables, still showing on their surfaces the ghostly images of ribcages, skulls, and broken femurs.

The communist authorities in Czechoslovakia derided the 'long-hairs' as hooligans and regularly set the police to work with hair clippers and the promise of a night in the cells. Party propaganda consistently equated long hair with nihilism and lamented that many young people showed 'a lack of concern about social events expressed by their tatty and repellent appearance . . . and a tendency to consume excessive amounts of alcohol'. But the party's cultural warriors were unable to keep magazine writers and even radio and television producers in line. Editors and journalists stoked young people's appetites with stories about Western bands, clip programmes, portraits of musicians with not just mopheads but shoulder-length hair, and items on the latest fashion trends. It was a portent of what was about to happen in politics, where the party would soon also lose control of the media.[3]

Communist censorship could not cope with the main outlet for criticism favoured by more intellectually minded younger people—the theatre and cinema. The censors did not understand irony, let alone surrealist film and absurdist drama. So, they banned Věra Chytilová's film *Daisies* (*Sedmikrásky*, 1966), in which two girls embark on a wild spree of destruction, drunkenness, and tricking older men, on the grounds that it showed a wasteful attitude towards food, evidently disregarding its playfulness. (The film concludes with a dedication 'to those who get upset over a bed of lettuce that's been stomped on.') But Miloš Forman's *The Firemen's Ball* (*Hoří, má panenko*, 1967) was allowed, even though it was a barely concealed allegory of communist Czechoslovakia, where nothing works properly, plans fail disastrously, and the prizes for the tombola are all stolen.

Czech theatre built on the avant-garde of the interwar years, with productions of plays that either had no plot or were woven together from unrelated sketches or monologues, often performed in venues so crowded that the barrier between stage and audience was no longer obvious. They rarely confronted the regime directly, but audiences read them as works of contemporary criticism. Václav Havel's *The Garden Party* (*Zahradní slavnost*, 1963) and *The Memorandum* (*Vyrozumění*, 1965), both of which explore the language of bureaucracy, resonated with audiences who were used to the laboured officialese of communist rule, even though the two plays developed themes that belong to an older Czech literary tradition and were no less cruel in their characterization of middle-class platitudes. Absurdist drama did not challenge the regime, but audiences reacted as if it did, establishing its reputation as a vehicle for political dissent.[4]

In 1968, communist rule collapsed almost overnight in Czechoslovakia. By hitching demands for greater autonomy to a broadly reformist agenda, the Slovak branch of the Czechoslovak Communist Party broke the dead hand of the Prague leadership. With the approval of the new Soviet leader Leonid Brezhnev, the Slovak Alexander Dubček took over as head of the Czechoslovak Communist Party in January 1968. Dubček began a purge of the old guard but was unable to control the forces he had released. As Dubček's younger supporters took over in ministries and party organizations, they began pushing for a thorough renewal of society and for popular participation in the making of policy.

Certainly, no one was talking openly of a capitalist restoration or of ending the party's monopoly on power. But behind the scenes, economists were already starting to model how unemployment could be managed and a command economy switched to a market one. Meanwhile in lecture rooms, radical left-wing visitors from Western Europe held forth on Leon Trotsky, Antonio Gramsci, and Herbert Marcuse, whose writings on Marxism were at odds with almost all the basic tenets of Soviet and Central European communism. They even found time to picket the American embassy in Prague in protest at the war in Vietnam. What was happening in Czechoslovakia began to converge with student protest in both North America and Western Europe, enlarging its international significance.[5]

By the spring of 1968, the government had relaxed almost all censorship in Czechoslovakia and handed over the chief censor's office to a literary magazine as its headquarters. Censorship now worked the other way around, with the East German government banning the importation of Czechoslovak newspapers. Television programmes highlighted the dire state of the economy, giving some real figures for a change, and exposed the misdeeds of previous generations of Czechoslovak Communists. In Moscow, the Soviet leadership anxiously advised Prague of the growing influence of what it called 'anti-party elements' and watched with astonishment as the Czechoslovak press published increasingly radical programmes and manifestos. In July 1968, a meeting of Soviet and Central European communist leaders delivered to their Czechoslovak comrades what amounted to an ultimatum. Its opening paragraph was warning enough:

> The development of events in your country evokes deep anxiety in us. It is our deep conviction that the offensive of the reactionary forces, backed by imperialism, against your party and the foundations of the socialist system in the Czechoslovak Socialist Republic threatens to push your country off the road of socialism and thus jeopardizes the interests of the entire socialist system.[6]

Dubček's response was far from reassuring. He replied that the abolition of censorship had popular support, that the Czechoslovak party was testing out a new and different style of political leadership, and that although there were people trying to discredit the party and its leading role, they did not amount to a challenge to the international communist system. The result was predictable. In August 1968, Soviet-led Warsaw Pact forces invaded Czechoslovakia, deploying more than half a million men and six thousand tanks. Despite an earlier warning from Kádár about the ruthlessness of the Soviet leadership ('Do you really not know the kind of people you're dealing with?'), Dubček was shocked, complaining bitterly: 'That they should do this to me after I have dedicated my whole life to cooperation with the Soviet Union.' Dismissed from office, Dubček spent the next two decades working as a forestry inspector.[7]

The period of liberalization known as the 'Prague Spring' lasted just eight months—from January to August 1968. The communist restoration, or 'normalization', as it was called, went on for two decades. It partly rested on a deal. As the Czechoslovak president explained in his 1970 New Year's address, 'normality' promised 'a better tomorrow' for the people of Czechoslovakia in return for their acceptance of the leading role of the Communist Party and of the alliance with the Soviet Union. But there were plenty of party members who had already seen the way the wind was blowing. Once earnest reformers, they now lined up on the side of the hardliners. A purge of the party in 1970 gave them the chance to grab privileges and beg preferment. Once in power, they mouthed the rhetoric of change while returning Czechoslovakia to centralized, bureaucratic rule under the rigid hand of communist ideology.[8]

The reimposition of communist rule had immediate consequences for culture. When theatres reopened after the invasion, they only offered a safe repertoire of undemanding plays. Of more than 400 writers publishing in Czechoslovakia before August 1968, the communist authorities allowed only 170 to continue working. They sacked academics from the universities, closed down journals, and pulped reference books that had entries on authors whose writings were no longer acceptable. Special lists spelled out who might or might not be employed—for the 'unsuitable', only casual work was on offer. Czechoslovakia became 'normal', or as Václav Havel put it, 'calm as a morgue or a grave'. He was right in more than one way—heavy rock music was now banned and only saccharine 'soft pop' allowed.[9]

Czechoslovaks had been tamed by tanks, and Hungarians first killed on the streets and then bought off with goulash, but as many dictatorial regimes have learned to their cost, Poland was effectively ungovernable. From the mid-1950s to the 1980s, Polish politics followed a familiar course—a reformer would take over, promising to re-energize the economy but failing to do so, after which illegal strikes would force him from office, to be replaced by another reformer. The Communist Party still had some life in it, with a membership of several million people. But most of these were only members because their jobs depended on party patronage. More telling were surveys that periodically asked students whether they considered themselves to be Marxists: for 1958, 1978, and 1983, the scores were 2 per cent, 3 per cent, and 2 per cent.[10]

Even if the two million card-carrying party members were sincere Communists, they were numerically insignificant compared to the Catholic Church in Poland, which could count on thirty million churchgoers out of a population of thirty-five million. The Church had real influence. In 1976, the Catholic primate of Poland, Cardinal Wyszyński, successfully blocked amendments to the constitution that might have been harmful to Polish Catholics, openly condemned police violence, and intervened on behalf of political prisoners. Wyszyński also joined forces with Poland's three million small farmers to push for state-provided welfare and pensions. Since the private agricultural sector produced 75 per cent of Poland's food supply, the Church had a powerful political ally. Throughout the 1950s and 1960s, when most nonparty organizations were banned, Catholic discussion groups continued to meet, maintaining the tradition of intellectual opposition.

In 1978, the College of Cardinals in Rome elected Wyszyński's close colleague, the bishop of Cracow Karol Wojtyła, as pope. Taking the name of John Paul II, the new pope toured Poland in 1979, where he was seen by as many as thirteen million ecstatic Poles. Often preaching from the back of a truck (the first of his many popemobiles), John Paul spoke as popes are supposed to, urging reconciliation, charity, and spiritual renewal, but he also spelled out the need for Poles to found their own alternative society. In so doing, Pope John Paul consciously summoned the ghosts of previous political oppressions, when Poles had embarked on 'organic work', setting up their own educational, cultural, and political institutions, independent of the state. It was an overt challenge to communist rule.

In fact, by 1979 many Poles were already doing what Pope John Paul was urging them. Three years before, strikes and demonstrations across Poland had resulted in scores of arrests and hundreds of dismissals.

Since unemployment did not officially exist in Poland, sacked workers could not rely on public funds for support. Activists now founded action committees to give them material help and legal advice. But they went further, publishing accounts of their work and giving printed updates on cases. In an audacious move, their published statements carried the names and addresses of the authors, baffling the secret police who suspected that they were being led into a trap. One offended official took the most prominent of these organizations, KOR, or the Committee for the Defence of the Workers (*Komitet Obrony Robotników*), to court for libel. The judges found in the official's favour and ordered KOR to publish an apology in its next update, so lending a curious stamp of legal approval to its publicity.

The leader of KOR, Jacek Kuroń, explained his strategy bluntly: 'Do not set party committee offices on fire, build your own committees.' Many people did and possibly as many as two million Poles were engaged in some way with the work of KOR and its sister organizations—distributing leaflets, raising money, attending meetings, and bringing up grievances in the workplace. But most of all, they were readers of its literature and of Poland's increasingly powerful underground press. The figures are astonishing. Between 1977 and 1980, some thirty clandestine publishing houses in Poland produced about 160 books and 80 magazines, as well as textbooks for the 'flying university', which gave secret degree-level lectures and classes in Warsaw, Cracow, Gdańsk, and Wrocław. The underground press also targeted the working classes, publishing the fortnightly *Robotnik* (*Worker*), relaying legal rights, news updates, and guides on how to set up trade unions. *Robotnik* had a print run of twenty thousand and an estimated readership of five times that.[11]

Printing was mainly done in private flats on mimeographs, using stencils. But storing paper and distributing copy involved more conspicuous activity. It is a measure less of police assiduity than of the volume of printed underground literature that between 1976 and 1979 the police managed to confiscate 440,000 separate items. But the independent newspapers had their revenge. In February 1977, Censor

C-36 of the Cracow office smuggled to Sweden seven hundred pages of secret directives that exposed the workings of Polish censorship—for instance, that the export of meat to the Soviet Union should never be mentioned, that the Soviet Union must not be held responsible for massacres of Poles in the Second World War, that there was no alcoholism in Poland nor any censorship, and so on, including a list of authors and books whose existence might never be acknowledged. Published clandestinely in both full and condensed versions of thousands of copies apiece, *The Black Book of Polish Censorship* confirmed what most Poles had always suspected: the entire edifice of communist power was built on lies, evasions, and stupidity.[12]

The Polish Communist leader Edward Gierek came to power in 1970 with a plan to revitalize the economy by investing in new technology and industry, to be paid for through Western loans. Gierek imagined that the credits would pay for themselves through increased productivity and exports. In less than a decade, Poland's foreign debt shot up from a billion US dollars in 1971 to more than twenty-five billion in 1979, but after an initial boom, industrial growth stalled. By the late 1970s, Poland's entire export earnings were going on servicing its debt, leaving no room for further investment or for the purchase of consumer sweeteners to keep the workforce happy. Polish economists drily reported that the inflow of Western capital had exceeded the economy's capacity to absorb it. The state audit office had a different explanation. Managers were simply looting funds, it reported, using the cash that should have gone into investment to buy themselves foreign holidays, gold watches, cars, and works of art.[13]

Gierek's rule followed the usual course. To balance the books, Gierek increased prices, prompting strikes throughout the summer of 1980. This time, the strikers did not riot or attack party offices. Encouraged by the KOR leadership, they occupied the factories and set up strike committees to press home their demands. A new trade union organization called 'Solidarity' (Solidarność) led the way. Founded in the shipyards of Gdańsk by the electrician Lech Wałęsa, Solidarity forced Gierek to give way on prices, to recognize the right to found and belong to trade unions, to make Saturday a rest day, and to broadcast Catholic Sunday Mass over state radio. The link with the Catholic Church was vital. With portraits of Pope John Paul II presiding over union meetings, Solidarity laid claim to leadership not only of the workplace but also of the moral life of the nation. By the end of 1980, it had more than eight million members.

Behind the scenes, hardliners in the Communist Party were planning a coup—literally. They replaced Gierek with a bland nobody and, early in 1981, moved the defence minister General Wojciech Jaruzelski to the post of prime minister. Jaruzelski had form, having ten years before ordered the army to fire on strikers. While Soviet and Warsaw Pact forces mustered on Poland's borders, Jaruzelski began the militarization of local and central government, appointing generals to civilian office in several of the main ministries and as mayors in cities. In October 1981, Jaruzelski took over as Communist Party leader, while still holding the offices of defence minister and prime minister. Two months later, the hardliners struck. The army seized power, martial law was declared, and a Military Council of National Salvation led by Jaruzelski took over as Poland's government. In the early hours of 13 December, Poles woke to tanks on the streets, military checkpoints, the telephone lines cut, and (perhaps most shockingly) a nervous army captain in regimental dress reading the news on state television.

The defiance shown by Poles during the 1970s owed much to what was happening in West Germany. The Polish Communist Party was indissolubly linked to the Soviet Union and the Soviet Union posed as the guarantor of Poland's territorial integrity. Communism and national self-interest were to that extent conjoined. Until the early 1970s, West Germany had demonstrated an aggressive posture towards both the Soviet Union and the new Poland. The government in the West German capital of Bonn had refused to recognize the new borders in the east, instead labelling the parts of pre-war Germany that were included in the new Poland as 'under temporary Polish administration'. West German politicians had led noisy campaigns for the reincorporation of these lost parts in a newly enlarged Germany. One-fifth of West Germans were refugees from the east and they were a powerful electoral constituency. In an eccentric but menacing piece of theatre, the West German chancellor Konrad Adenauer was solemnly invested in 1958 as an honorary knight of the Teutonic Order, stoking Polish fears of a renewed German war of conquest in the east.[14]

On top of this, West Germany's de-Nazification had been superficial. The German chancellor between 1966 and 1969, Kurt Kiesinger, was a former well-placed Nazi Party member, while recommissioned veterans of the Second World War led the new West German army that was officially founded in 1955. (It had existed for several years before this as part of the police and border service.) A government-led propaganda campaign in the late 1940s and 1950s cast communists and Slavs in general as just the latest wave in a series of Asiatic invaders from the east, starting with the Huns. If all this sounds like Nazi propaganda, it is probably because it was—masterminded by much the same team as had led Josef Goebbels's propaganda operations before 1945. To show that it was earnest in its defence of the West, the West German government arrested and gaoled several thousand Communists on either trumped-up or dubious charges, finally banning the Communist Party of Germany in 1956.[15]

For many Poles and some West Germans, too, the Bonn government looked not entirely dissimilar to the regime it had replaced. But in the 1970s two things happened. After twenty years of conservative Christian Democrat rule, the rival Social Democrats took power under Willy Brandt in 1969. Brandt reversed the Christian Democrats' combative policy towards the Soviet Union and communist Central Europe in favour of negotiation and the strengthening of political and economic ties. As a first step in West Germany's 'new eastern policy' (*Neue Ostpolitik*), Brandt recognized in 1970 the separate East German communist state and the boundaries of the new Poland. Trade and loans followed, cementing relations between West Germany and Poland, but more important was the relaxation of entry controls, which meant that Poles increasingly visited West Germany for seasonal employment. By the 1980s there may have been as many as a million Poles working in West Germany.

Secondly, West Germany became the motor of the Common Market (later the European Economic Community and European Union). Not only did it have the largest economy within the Common Market, but its model of economic management also provided the blueprint for the Common Market's future development. Known by the clumsy name of 'Ordo-Liberalism', the German model was based on a free market operating within a tight regulatory framework, generous welfare provision, and a strong banking infrastructure to curb inflation and government overspending. By the 1970s it looked as if West Germany had not only abandoned its historic claims against Poland but also become the driving force in what was seen at the time as Europe's up-and-coming economic superpower. For Poles, West Germany was no longer a threat but a beacon of prosperity, democracy, and good neighbourliness.

The confidence felt by Poles to take on their communist government was replicated across Central Europe. Even in East Germany, otherwise a bastion of orthodoxy, protesters in the 1970s and 1980s organized demonstrations against the industrial degradation of the environment, human rights abuses, and the absence of housing that forced young people (among them the twenty-four-year-old Angela Merkel) to squat in abandoned buildings. In an unusual twist, East Germany also produced an overtly Stalinist opposition, whose members castigated the ideological softness of the East German leadership. Using the same mimeograph production methods as the Polish dissidents, the Stalinist underground press urged factory workers to found trade unions that genuinely looked after their interests, railed against price rises, rejected out of hand the leadership of the Soviet Union, and gave the frequencies for Radio Tirana in super-Stalinist Albania. In 1981, the East German government ordered a roundup of the Stalinists, giving jail terms to a dozen of the leaders.[16]

A curious semantic shift followed. The Cold War had divided Europe down the middle. From 1945 onwards, there was a Western

Europe and an Eastern Europe. The two halves met on a barbed-wire border. But from the late 1970s onwards, writers and academics began to refer to an intermediate zone between the two. They called this Central Europe, or *Mitteleuropa*. It was a name that had fallen out of fashion for four decades, surviving only in the context of the one-hour-ahead-of-GMT 'Central European Time' (which included Italy and Spain) and of the surprisingly comfortable 'Mitropa' sleeper service on East German railways. But the newly revived 'Central Europe' had nothing to do with the historic Central Europe which, despite its haziness, was a broad term with expansive and expandable borders that almost always included Germany. This was a much narrower creature that only included the slice of Central Europe that sat between West Germany and the Soviet Union.

The Central Europe label prospered, but attempts to describe Central Europe's unifying characteristics faltered. For a few writers, it was demonstrated in the shape of post boxes or in a popular preference for spirits over wine or 'in the heavy smell of boiled cabbage, stale beer, and the soapy whiff of overripe water melons'. Others talked vaguely of a 'kingdom of the spirit', of the problems of 'small nations' (as if Poland was in any way small), and of Central Europe's 'flourishing diversity' or proposed some sort of moral superiority born of suffering that made Central Europe the true repository of the ideals for which Western Europe claimed to stand. Or they boasted the literary effervescence that had attended the loosening of restrictions in Prague in 1968 as evidence of the region's intellectual weightiness, contrasting it favourably with Paris, where (as the Czech novelist Milan Kundera scolded) 'during dinner parties, people discuss television programmes, not reviews.'[17]

Definition was impossible not only because cultural boundaries are pervious but also because the idea of the new Central Europe was grounded in current politics. Central Europe was a codeword for Poland, Czechoslovakia, and Hungary being left to go their own independent way, without the danger of Soviet tanks intervening. It was a programme, dressed up in the language of exceptionalism and metaphor.

It would continue to be so, becoming in the 1990s a trope that stood for the anteroom to membership of the prosperous Common Market and European Union. When Central European journalists, politicians, and novelists spoke of Central Europe in the late twentieth century they had in mind either a 'Get Out of Soviet Jail' card or a debutante's ticket to the ball.

By the mid-1980s, communist Central Europe had reached an impasse. Its regimes were discredited, its economies bankrupt, and its populations sullen. It was only the possibility of Soviet intervention that kept its governments in place. After 1968, the Soviet leader Leonid Brezhnev had advanced the doctrine that the Soviet Union had the right to keep its satellites in the communist bloc by military means if necessary. The Soviet invasion of Afghanistan at the end of 1979 showed that this was not an empty threat—likewise the mustering of Soviet troops on the Polish border in 1981. But in 1985, a new Soviet leader took over, the fourth in just three years. On a damp morning in March that year, the freshly appointed head of the Soviet Communist Party, Mikhail Gorbachev, met the heads of the Central European communist countries for his predecessor's funeral in Moscow. There and then, he told them that the Brezhnev doctrine was dead and that they were on their own.[18]

It took time for the message to sink in, but by 1989 the regimes in Poland and Hungary were in headlong retreat. Their every concession prompted demands for more of the same, until the bargaining between government and opposition leaders boiled down to the real nitty-gritty: the Communists' immunity from prosecution for past crimes and the preservation of their pension entitlements. Poland was the first to throw off communism. A wave of strikes forced General Jaruzelski to hold a partially free election in June 1989. Solidarity candidates won in a landslide, although because of the way the vote was structured, they still did not command a majority of seats in the Polish parliament. But Solidarity's victory could not be denied. In August, Jaruzelski appointed as Poland's new prime minister the Solidarity MP Tadeusz Mazowiecki and charged him with forming a new government. Instead of sending in tanks, as a former generation of Soviet leaders would surely have done, Gorbachev sent Mazowiecki a telegram of congratulation.

Over the next four months, communist governments across Central Europe fell like dominoes. In Hungary in June 1989 Imre Nagy, the executed Communist leader who had led the 1956 revolution, was solemnly reburied in Budapest in a ceremony attended by more than one hundred thousand people and watched by millions on state television. Everyone knew that along with Nagy communism was being buried too. Over that summer, the Hungarian Communist Party agreed to hold multiparty elections and changed its name to the Hungarian Socialist Party. Former Communists busily advertised their democratic credentials and commitment to freedom, slyly reckoning that they had a good chance in the elections scheduled for 1990. They were to be disappointed.[19]

East Germany, Czechoslovakia, and Romania resisted the trend. At the time, commentators foresaw a two-speed Central Europe split between new democracies and hardline communist regimes. In fact, the Communists had no heart for a struggle. A massive outflow of East Germans through the now open Hungarian border together with demonstrations in Leipzig and East Berlin brought down the veteran East German communist leader Erich Honecker in October 1989. Nobody believed his successor would last long. In a characteristic display of bureaucratic bungling, around seven p.m. on 9 November the East German interior minister in a televised news conference misread his brief and declared the border with West Germany to be open, with immediate effect. Only that day, East German border guards had received renewed instructions 'to arrest and, if necessary, eliminate anyone crossing the border'. At Berlin's Bornholmer Street checkpoint on the Berlin Wall, Colonel Harald Jäger confronted thousands of East Germans pressing to be allowed through to the West. He looked glumly at his pistol and its twelve rounds of ammunition. At eleven thirty p.m., he gave the order to open the gate.[20]

The Czechoslovak Communists tried to tough it out. But the Prague police, having beaten up student protesters on 17 November, announced that evening that they were no longer minded to do the regime's dirty work. Five days later, the head of the army said the same. So, demonstrations went unchallenged, drawing in hundreds of thousands of people who, after hearing speeches, jingled their keys— the traditional way of announcing closing time in pubs. On 24 November, the entire Czechoslovak government resigned, after which the opposition took power. Meanwhile a revolution in Timişoara in Romania's Banat spilled over first of all into Transylvania and then, on 21 December, onto the streets of Bucharest. Rather than suppress the demonstrators, the army mutinied. On Christmas Day, the Romanian dictator Nicolae Ceauşescu was shot by a hastily gathered firing squad. Four days later, the Czechoslovak parliament elected Václav Havel as president of Czechoslovakia.

A Hungarian election poster from the early 1990s showed in rear view the caricatured thick neck of a Soviet army officer, with the caption COMRADES, IT'S OVER. Back in the 1970s and 1980s, communist propagandists when challenged over the shortcomings of their Central European regimes often rehearsed the mantra 'Yes, we have our failings, but we have our achievements as well.' Even then, it was not at all obvious what those achievements were. Under communist rule, Central Europe had become a wasteland of rusting factories, environmental degradation, and barren farms sitting on rich agricultural soil. Its population had been scarred by political violence and corrupted by the moral compromises necessary for survival. Effacing Communism's legacy would take more than sticking posters on walls.

CHAPTER 34

Post-Communism: Slavoj Žižek and the Lesson of Laibach

'**B**LISS WAS IT IN THAT DAWN TO BE ALIVE. BUT TO BE YOUNG was very heaven.' So wrote William Wordsworth on witnessing the French Revolution in 1789, but 1989 does not have its poets. The initial euphoria of pulling down the Berlin Wall soon passed, and the keys that had clinked in Prague to signify to the communist regime that its time was up were restored to pockets. As with any great event, a hollowness soon prevailed, exemplified by the inflow of luxury Western goods that might be admired but not bought, by cheap pornography in pocket-size editions (the easier to hide from wives and girlfriends), and by sensationalist revelations in a new tabloid press of the misdoings of former communist bosses.

The year 1989 lacks, too, any debate on its fundamental meaning analogous to the heavyweight sparring between Edmund Burke and Thomas Paine over the French Revolution. Central Europeans largely saw 1989 as an act of repudiation—an alien imposition had been toppled and the nations formerly under Soviet domination were now free to resume the independent course which communism had disrupted. But Central Europeans also expected that their lives would improve materially and that Western living standards would soon be theirs. As the philosopher George Steiner sneered: 'Video-cassettes, porno-cassettes, American-style cosmetics and fast foods, not editions of Mill, de Tocqueville or Solzhenitsyn, were prizes snatched from every West Berlin shelf by the liberated. The new temples to liberty (the 1789 dream) will be McDonald's and Kentucky Fried Chicken.'[1]

With Central Europe making both a political and aspirational leap westwards, West European observers saw the ideological validation of their own system. State socialism had failed, and an axiomatic truth was about to be proved—free market economics and democratic politics made people wealthier, happier, and more fulfilled. With every embrace of the norms of Western capitalism, the newly freed peoples of Central Europe supposedly confirmed capitalism's superiority and moral worth. In apparent further proof, the West European Left, which had always proclaimed its distance from Soviet-style communism, collapsed into self-doubt and recrimination. The Communist Party of Great Britain abolished itself in 1991, while the Italian Communist Party changed its name to advertise its latest democratic turn. Elsewhere in Western Europe, communist front organizations dedicated to 'world peace' fell apart.

Poets may seldom have celebrated the changes, but musicians did. Communist Central Europe had permitted a wide variety of musical genres, had welcomed bands from the West, and had sponsored its own lookalike musicians. 'Do you like Dean Reed?' was a baffling question often put to Western visitors to communist Central Europe in the 1970s. Reed was in fact an American émigré to East Germany. Having failed to make his name as a singer in the United States, Reed now performed to sell-out audiences as communism's answer to Elvis Presley. (Reed killed himself in 1985.) The old regimes had not, however, permitted lyrics that were critical of communism and the Soviet Union or which might be associated with controversial lifestyles. Punk was out, but so too was much Czech 'tramp music', which in its lyrics promoted the freedom of the wanderer and of nights spent around campfires.[2]

In the wake of 1989, punk, hip-hop, and eventually gangsta rap became available throughout Central Europe. But the most conspicuous genre was folk music. The communist authorities had promoted folk ensembles in the 1980s as a harmless diversion, organizing inter-village competitions, in which the participants paraded in traditional folk dress, usually designed for the occasion. Now these events were live-streamed on prime-time television, eventually having their own dedicated television channels. But they no longer just promoted an image of rustic simplicity—their purpose was to lend authenticity to the nation by revealing its musical and sartorial inheritance.

Czechoslovakia split up peacefully in 1993 in a row between politicians over the pace of economic reform. The disintegration of Yugoslavia was longer and bloodier, with a succession of civil wars that lasted from 1991 to 1999. Wars waged mostly by Serbian paramilitaries in Slovenia, Croatia, and Bosnia, and Serbia's own eventual implosion and loss of the province of Kosovo in 1999, led to three hundred thousand deaths and prompted massive refugee movements. A new word entered the lexicon—*etničko čišćenje*, or 'ethnic cleansing', meaning the forcible expulsion from a territory of civilians who belonged to the wrong ethnic or national group. Out of this cauldron came Turbofolk.

Turbofolk originated in Serbia around 1990 but soon spread to neighbouring Croatia. Still popular, it combined traditional folk rhythms with synthesized music and a style of singing (or trilling) that derived from melismatic chants in the Orthodox liturgy (where a single syllable is carried through many notes). It also built on Turkish, Albanian, and Gypsy elements, often with an accompaniment of horns and accordions. Its lyrics were typically banal, being either love ballads or songs of material aspiration—

> *Coca-Cola, Marlboro, Suzuki,*
> *Discotheques, guitars, and bouzouki;*
> *That's life, it's not an ad.*
> *It's us and why we're so glad.*

But the message lay with the medium. Belted out by silicon-bosomed divas, Turbofolk cultivated an aggressive masculinity in which women played the part of submissive wives and wailing girlfriends, and it glorified a tribal culture of lawlessness and loot. It helped that the most prominent Serbian female singer of Turbofolk, Ceca, was married to Arkan, a career criminal who had been responsible for some of the most egregious war crimes in the early 1990s. In 1991, Ceca appeared in battle fatigues to urge on the Serbian militias fighting in Croatia. Turbofolk was the anthem of ethnic cleansing.[3]

Turbofolk was, however, just one variant in a wave of popular music with its origins in folk that swept both the Balkans and Central Europe in the 1990s. In Hungary, 'dance houses' (tánchízak), in which folk music ensembles played to audiences, often in private homes, had a pedigree that went back to the 1970s, and they generally remained free of the excesses of Turbofolk. In Romania and Poland, however, the type of loud, synthesized music that blasted out at weddings and expensive parties provided the basis for new genres of folk. Romanian manele blended R&B with Gypsy rhythms and traditional songs, often sung ungrammatically and accompanied with older dance forms. Polish Disco Polo mixed folk rhythms with Italian disco beat to create, in one description, a 'new nightclub music, Polish style'. But whereas Turbofolk and manele eschewed complex messages, lyrics in Disco Polo songs often harked to Polish traditions of liberality and extravagant hospitality and of a historic 'Golden Liberty', although one now mostly conceived in terms of the right to drunkenness.

Folk music, with its roots in what were understood to be national traditions, stood apart from rock music, which was more cosmopolitan in its reach and often communicated its lyrics in English, transcending national boundaries. Many Central European rock groups had been at the forefront in their criticism of communist rule and their music helped to define the dissident underground—most notably, the Prague band Plastic People of the Universe, and in Warsaw the pro-Solidarity Perfect. Rock bands maintained a role in public criticism after 1989, not least in the former Yugoslavia. The most important of these bands, as well as the most critically acclaimed, was (and remains) the Slovene group Laibach.

Laibach was founded in the Yugoslav republic of Slovenia in 1980 and was promptly banned from performing. For a start, its posters were offensive—one depicted a black cross in a circle, which to sensitive Yugoslav politicians seemed suspiciously close to a swastika;

another showed a knife-wielding assailant gouging out his victim's eyes. On top of this, the band's name recalled the old German, and subsequently Nazi, name for the Slovenian capital Ljubljana. Banned from domestic venues, Laibach toured abroad, building its international reputation. The communist authorities gave way, not only in Yugoslavia but elsewhere in communist Central Europe too. Laibach's provocatively named Occupied Europe tour of 1983–1985 took in Budapest, Wrocław, Warsaw, and Cracow, as well as Ljubljana and Belgrade, with additional performances in London, Amsterdam, Brussels, and Hamburg.

Laibach may be described as Freddie Mercury meets the Nazi cinema of Leni Riefenstahl. Moustached and frequently bare-chested, the lead singer growls lines in German, English, and (less so today) Slovene. The accompaniment often comprises clashing drums, trumpet blasts, traditional musical instruments, and sound collages that blend politicians' speeches with dogs barking and martial anthems. The band members frequently wear uniforms that unmistakably hark back to the Third Reich or they march in hunting costume. Multimedia scene sets mimic the tropes of fascist architecture, with video projections of black crosses, military aircraft, and death heads.

Laibach continues to perform, most sensationally by reworking *The Sound of Music* musical before a perplexed North Korean audience in 2015. But however the band is described—post-punk, avant-garde, Dadaist, industrial, or art rock—it has managed to outlive communism, the violent collapse of Yugoslavia, and the first decades of post-communism. Laibach has as its unofficial spokesman the celebrated Slovenian philosopher Slavoj Žižek, and his interpretations of Laibach's oeuvre have lent the band both a fashionable reputation and intellectual weight. Žižek may not always be right in what he says about the band, but he comes from the same philosophical milieu of late-stage Slovenian communism, with its potpourri of psychoanalysis, classical German metaphysics, and soft Marxism.

Laibach's music and production rest on two principles. First, the artist should criticize not by ironic imitation but by taking on the identity of his oppressor, subverting his power by affirming it. So, Laibach's embrace of the motifs of fascism aims to eviscerate totalitarianism's ambition for absolute control. Laibach's music, with its rasping excesses, is intended to do auditory violence that reproduces 'regime noise', so also depriving totalizing propaganda of its monopoly on the senses by becoming a 'recuperator of subversion'. As Laibach's 1982 manifesto put it, 'All art is subject to political manipulation except that which speaks the language of the same manipulation.'[4]

Secondly, Laibach is alert to the totalitarian potential of culture, which it defines in a broad sweep as including management science, Nazi kitsch, the noise of the factory floor, and the rhythms of popular music. So, the band reinterpreted the Austrian pop song 'Life Is Life' by Opus with lyrics that harked to fascist themes of 'blood and soil' ('The feeling of the people is the feeling of the land') to demonstrate that even the trite original might be transformed into militant, mobilizing music. Released in 1988, Laibach's cover versions of songs from the Beatles' *Let It Be* album recontextualized the line 'Get back to where you once belonged' to interrogate the latest, vicious turn in Yugoslavia's national politics.

Laibach showed no enthusiasm for the changes that took place in Central Europe with the collapse of communism. Their 1992 album *Kapital* communicates the consequences with a repeated knocking and intervening clunks and screams, hinting at the workplace uniformity of global capitalism and at the social alienation and anomie of consumer culture. At a time when the demise of state socialism was being celebrated and the virtues of the market extolled, Laibach proposed 'The economy is death' and entitled the album's opening track 'Decade Null'. Laibach's use of repetitive techno rhythms also spoke to a new totalitarianism under the aegis of the liberal, consumer state, since as the band explained, 'Disco rhythm stimulates automatist mechanisms and co-forms the industrialization of consciousness according to the model of totalitarianism.'[5]

Laibach and Žižek are hard to follow. Their obscurity often looks like obfuscation, intended to conceal half-baked ideas. Their importance and enduring fascination lie not with the details of their philosophies but with their repudiation of the new market system that came in the 1990s. For both Laibach and Žižek, the changes after 1989 did not constitute a liberation but instead a new cultural and economic order, imposed from above. As much as the global communism that it had replaced, global capitalism needed a set of illusions about itself to sustain its primacy. The Western model had replaced un-freedom with more of the same, being only, as Laibach explained, 'a polite expression for developed totalitarianism'.[6]

Laibach and Žižek were right in their analysis, at least to the extent that the extravagant promises made on behalf of global capitalism were not kept. Not only did the 1990s see a decline in living standards throughout much of Central Europe, but also the consensual deal that had kept West Germany prosperous and quiet was also discarded. The welfare underpinning of German Ordo-liberalism was abandoned in favour of free market neoliberalism, but the political consensus, which left power with a small group of elites, was maintained. The new German order was then transferred via the European Union (EU) to the member states which had previously been under communist rule.

It was not supposed to have happened in this way, but the economic recklessness of West German politicians made it almost inevitable. In July 1990, the conservative Christian Democrat–led government in Bonn abolished the East German mark and replaced it with the West German mark. Most savings and wages in the old East Germany were converted at parity. Intended to prevent a migration flow from east to west in search of higher salaries, the generous exchange rate also bought votes for Chancellor Helmut Kohl's Christian Democrats in what were now known as Germany's 'five new states' (or Länder). Whereas everywhere else in formerly communist Central Europe, governments devalued their currencies as they embraced market reform, the old East Germany effectively revalued its currency. The outcome was predictable—many workers were simply not worth what they were being paid, so they were sacked. By the mid-1990s, 15 per cent of the formerly

East German workforce was officially unemployed and an even larger proportion was on short-time working or retraining schemes, or prematurely retired. Altogether 90 per cent of jobs in manufacturing were lost.[7]

Western politicians and economists were also too optimistic about East German industry, half believing older communist propaganda about its strength. The British historian Norman Stone was more accurate when he advised Margaret Thatcher in 1990 that by unifying with East Germany, West Germany was simply inheriting 'twelve enormous Liverpools' (then a byword for broken industry). Politicians in Bonn gave a government-appointed Trust, or Treuhand, responsibility for the privatization of East German state assets: twelve thousand separate businesses in all. The Treuhand initially valued these at 600 billion West German marks. In the event, the revenue from sales was just over 70 billion. This was despite the Treuhand having already restructured and slimmed the businesses to make them commercially attractive. About three-quarters of the businesses bought went to West German firms or foreigners. Workforce cooperatives were introduced only in agriculture, as a means of replacing collective farms.[8]

The Treuhand was set up to prevent the fire sale of state assets, but it became the chief arsonist, pursuing a policy of sell or burn. With swathes of its manufacturing and service sector destroyed, 80 per cent of economic activity in the former East Germany depended on capital flows from West Germany, which was unsustainable. Little attempt was made, therefore, to introduce in East Germany social market conditions. In wage negotiations, the new employers sidelined the trade unions and disregarded national agreements in favour of local settlements that were less advantageous to the workforce. New jobs often came without social insurance, and agencies administered vacancies, paring back benefits. East Germany became the pioneer of flexible working, 'mini-jobs', and if not quite zero-hour contracts then at least contracts with only a few guaranteed hours (which kept workers off the unemployment statistics). In return, East Germans received retraining and motivational seminars that were intended, among other things, to cure them of their sloppy work habits and, for women, their poor make-up technique.[9]

But it was not just in East Germany that German politicians sponsored neoliberal and laissez-faire approaches to the economy. In West Germany, too, the traditional safety nets were weakened, with cuts introduced in the early 2000s to pensions, unemployment benefits, and healthcare provisions. The consensus with the trade unions that had given them a voice in determining national wage levels was similarly bypassed so that most German workers now bargained directly with employers. The privatization introduced in East Germany was also carried westwards, with denationalization of the post and telecommunications, parts of the national grid, and hospitals.[10]

By 1990, Germany was the big hitter in the European Community (European Union after 1993). Its prescriptions shaped European policy towards the formerly communist states of Central Europe, and they too were distinguished by a neoliberal agenda that emphasized labour flexibility, marketization, and a diminished role for the state. Even before their accession to the EU in 2004, the formerly communist countries of Central Europe were obliged through the 'convergence criteria' contained in the EU's Maastricht Treaty (1992) and the Stability and Growth Pact (1996) to privatize most state industry, cut back on welfare programmes, and embrace a programme of balanced budgets and fiscal austerity. Their governments did so with gusto, even to the extent of adding to neoliberal policies by privatizing pensions, cutting corporate taxes, and introducing flat-rate income tax.[11]

The benefits were soon there on paper. New ratings registered the successes of the Central European economies—the Open Market Index, the Global Competitiveness Index, and the Ease of Doing Business Index. In the first ten years after the end of communism, GDP per head doubled and foreign direct investment soared to roughly US$20 billion a year in the Czech Republic and Hungary and to more than US$30 billion in Poland. But the wealth was spread unevenly, with most going to the cities and into the bank accounts of a new class of *biznesmeni*. High-rise suburbs and rural communities saw little improvement in living standards. The growing inequality of the 1990s was summed up in the expression *Polska dwóch prędkości*—'two-speed Poland', referring to the divide on motorways between the numerous rear-engine Fiat 126s, which stuck to the slow lane, and the new elite's Audis and BMWs which swished sleekly past them.[12]

Critics of neoliberal reforms predicted that the hardships of transformation would force its abandonment. But after a challenging first decade, the fruits began to show. Wealth trickled down instead of trickling away, with the result that average wages across Central Europe rose by as much as a half in the period 2000 to 2007. Front-loading washing machines replaced tubs, second-hand VW Golfs took the place of Fiat 126s, and there was a proliferation of high-street travel agencies. Part of this was the result of a takeoff in manufacturing. German car giants moved production to the formerly communist countries of Central Europe to take advantage of its skilled but cheap workforce. By the early 2000s, Slovakia was producing more cars per head of population than anywhere else in the world. The old Škoda works in the Czech Republic was also turned around by Volkswagen into the manufacturer of the world-beating Octavia model. But much depended too on home-grown businesses that exported ceramics, cosmetics, flat-pack furniture, domestic lighting, and so on, some of which was repackaged to conceal its origin. Tourism flourished in the wake of the renovation of city centres.

The consumer boom of the 2000s had weak foundations. Back in the 1990s, Western companies had used their capital to buy up and regenerate businesses. In the new decade, they bought private debt in the form of mortgages and, later, credit cards and personal loans. Inexperienced Central Europeans borrowed, often in foreign currencies, and the lenders paid little heed to their customers' ability to repay. Central European borrowers were the classic 'thin files' of the subprime mortgage market—individuals with no credit history and only a few details of salary and outgoings. In a notorious advertisement for mortgage loans, shown on Hungarian television in 2007, a young couple explain to a female broker that their income is small.

She puts her hands over her ears and la-la-las. A voice tells us that the Raiffeisen Bank gives mortgages based on the value of the property and not on the applicant's income, and that approval of a purchase takes only ten days.[13]

Even without the worldwide financial crash of 2007–2008, the Central European economy was a bubble waiting to burst. In the wake of the banking crisis, businesses without reserves went bust and mortgagers faced ruin as currency fluctuations made it hard to repay loans denominated in Swiss francs or euros. Hungary was the worst affected as a million Hungarians had taken out foreign-denominated loans, the instalments on which now went up by a third. In 2011, the Hungarian government took over the banks' loan books and converted the money owed into Hungarian forints at a rate advantageous to borrowers, but only on condition that they paid off the outstanding balance at once. For two-thirds of mortgaged households, this was an impossibility.

International institutions, most notably the International Monetary Fund (IMF) and European Union, were the only organizations with the financial heft and reputation to prevent a larger economic collapse. By extending emergency loans and stand-by credit facilities to governments, the IMF and EU allowed recapitalization of the banks, while also substituting for the decline in foreign investment flows. The EU alone, under its 2010 European Financial Stability Facility, set aside a trillion euros to bail out Europe's most troubled economies. The price, however, was high—a renewal of the austerity regime that forced governments to balance budgets, reduce welfare programmes, cut public sector employment and salaries, and eliminate many collective bargaining arrangements. Wages once again plummeted, and unemployment rose to 10 per cent of the workforce in Poland and Hungary and 15 per cent in Slovakia.

Growth rates, having fallen precipitously between 2007 and 2009, recovered after 2010, but the message was clear—the economies of Central Europe depended on the European Union. The problem was that the funds the European Union disbursed not only came with conditions attached but were, as a matter of routine, also misspent.

The principal sources of EU funding in the formerly communist countries of Central Europe were (and are) agricultural subsidies and convergence money, of which the second went mostly on big infrastructure projects. The EU allocated cash without checking that it was being properly spent, lest it be accused of infringing on state sovereignty or weakening the principle of subsidiarity (whereby issues are decided at the level closest to their resolution). Because the farm subsidy programme of the European Union was skewed towards larger enterprises, businessmen aided by politicians amassed large quantities of subsidy-rich farmland, either by driving out smaller producers or by fixing auctions of state-owned land that was left over from the time of communist collective farming.[14]

Throughout the European Union, infrastructural funds intended for large-scale building projects were embezzled. In 2013, EU commissioner Cecilia Malmström put the annual figure of European money lost to corruption at 120 billion euros and estimated that 20 to 25 per cent of the value of public contracts was lost to fraud. Italy was responsible for a good part of this, but politicians and businessmen in the Czech Republic, Hungary, Romania, and Slovakia were also implicated. The usual trick was to fix the bidding and procurement process so that inflated tenders were accepted in return for a kickback. Sometimes, the projects were themselves dummies and intended only for soliciting EU money. Private consultancies managed the bids for contracts or infrastructural grants, writing out the tenders or applications and fielding follow-up questions, in return for which they expected a slice of the proceeds.[15]

By the 2010s, the scale of corruption in Central Europe was so great that political commentators began to talk of 'state capture'—that the institutions of government had been taken over by corporate interests and even organized crime. There was some truth in this. Most of the money stolen through procurement rackets went into buying luxury goods and fancy foreign villas, but a part of it fed back into criminal activity. It also sustained several political parties in power. By making corrupt deals, party bosses received in return financial support for their organizations and built up networks of dependency, which they then mobilized against political rivals and opposition media outlets. Putin in Russia pioneered the technique, and his acolytes in Central Europe copied it using EU cash.

The countries of Central Europe today are democracies and their elections are not rigged. Governments in power manipulate the media (many media outlets are either state-owned or depend for their advertising revenue on businesses with party links) and they misuse state resources for election purposes, but they do not organize the systematic stuffing of ballot boxes. Although turnout in elections tends to be low by West European standards (generally, between 50 and 60 per cent), Central Europeans are alert to political trends and have no hesitation in demonstrating, often for months, against abuses of power, corruption, and environmental degradation. Even so, opposition protest is still channelled peacefully and through the ballot box, not waged by street-fighting paramilitaries.

Throughout Central Europe, elections are relatively free and fair. Not only do governing parties lose but the party system in much of the region also shows considerable volatility. On average, political parties in Central Europe have a life span of ten to fifteen years, for electorates are unforgiving of economic downturns and scandals, holding the parties (in one commentator's expression) 'hyper-accountable'. As 'tainted but experienced' and 'uncorrupted but inexperienced' parties vie for votes, and as the newcomers themselves become tarnished, parties rise, fall, and vanish with often bewildering speed. Having lost the protection of government, politicians in declining parties face the possibility of prosecution and imprisonment for their previous abuses of office. At the very least, they should expect a visit by the tax police.[16]

Politicians in Central Europe have every incentive to hang onto power. Many endeavour to do so by building up a coalition of dependants through targeted welfare payments and by expanding the number of businesses and agencies that rely on state patronage. But politicians have not been averse to using a language that builds on the tropes and metaphors of the past in order to mobilize popular support. A few have resorted to familiar antisemitic codewords: 'cosmopolitan elements', 'international finance capitalism', and 'hidden, global forces', tapping into a residual but enduring antisemitism. Others, taking advantage of the migration crisis from the Middle East, have appealed to their country's historic role in the defence of Christian civilization and as a bulwark against invasion from the alien east, installing razor-wire fences on their state's borders as proof of their patriotic credentials. Anti-gay rhetoric, espoused by ruling parties in parts of Central Europe, is another way of rallying support among an electorate that tends to be culturally conservative. In Poland alone, almost a hundred towns and cities were by 2022 so-called LGBT-free zones, where the local authorities had officially declared all public activity by gays and nonbinary people to be 'unwelcome'. Opinion polls suggest that measures of this sort enjoy increasing popular support.[17]

In 2012, Laibach performed in the Turbine Hall of the Tate Modern in London. Its vast space was also host to Damien Hirst's *For the Love of God*: a platinum skull encrusted with diamonds which was on display as part of a Hirst exhibition. In the centre of the Laibach stage was the band's trademark, the mounted head of a deer with antlers. The juxtaposition of the two was coincidental but stands as a metaphor for the condition of today's Central Europe. On the one side, there is the glitzy but essentially hollow promise of what Žižek has called 'abundance capitalism'. On the other, there is a totem of the instinctual and tribal. Laibach and Žižek have long railed against the tyranny of global capitalism, although without saying what should replace it and how. But for the time being, Central Europeans look like remaining busy shoppers, bustling in global capitalism's marble malls. Long may they do so, for the alternative is unlikely to be that they start reading Tocqueville and Solzhenitsyn but that they could succumb to forces that are darker and more elemental than the innocent employment of hunting for bargains.

Conclusion

IF REGIONS HAVE BIRTH CERTIFICATES, THEN CENTRAL EUROPE'S is the gospel book of Otto III, from around 1000 CE, which shows the crowned emperor receiving the gifts of the Catholic Christian world—Rome, France, the German lands, and the lands of the Slavs. Central Europe, which was then still a space ruled by German and Slav chieftains, had been brought into the fold of the Catholic Church and the orbit of the Roman emperor, joining there Italy and the French kingdom. The gospel book celebrates Christianity's enlargement, the majesty of the emperor who sat at its earthly head, and Central Europe's inclusion in the comity of peoples that belonged to the restored Roman Empire and to the Catholic faith. (See Chapter 4.)

Over the next centuries, Wends, Hungarians, Old Prussians, Lithuanians, and even Cuman nomads would be melded into the new Central Europe. Their leaders might object to the authority claimed by the Roman emperor, challenging his commands, but they all submitted equally to the Catholic faith. In 1274, at the Church Council meeting at Lyons, the preacher and Dominican friar Humbert of Romans (d. 1277) reviewed the historic achievement of Catholic Christianity. It had prevailed, he explained, over persecution, heresy, and the assaults of the heathen. Along with the Poles and Hungarians, worshippers of idols had been brought to the faith so that the only barbarians left to threaten Christendom were the Mongol-Tatars.[1]

But the change that Humbert noted was not just a religious one. In its social organization and cultural expressions, Central Europe had adapted to patterns that were typical throughout most of Western Europe. By the thirteenth century, it had knights and noblemen with coats of arms, city folk with legal rights, villages that were increasingly self-regulating, and enthusiastic crusaders bent on war against the unbeliever. With new stone castles and walled cities, the physical landscape of Central Europe had changed too. During the later Middle Ages, the other markers of West European civilization would be grafted onto Central Europe—universities, parliaments or diets, the first commercial banks and exchanges, and an energetic engagement among theologians with the identity of the Antichrist.

It was the same after 1500. There is not one of the distinguishing currents of West European civilization that is missing from Central Europe. Renaissance and Reformation, the Catholic recovery or Counter-Reformation, Enlightenment, Romanticism, industrialization, and modern nationalism manifested themselves with an energy equal to anywhere in Western Europe. Central Europe experienced too the same highs and lows as the countries to its west—religious conflict provoked by the advance of Protestantism, the international chaos caused by Louis XIV and Napoleon, the curbing of liberty in the wake of the French Revolution, the 1848 revolutions, interwar authoritarianism, and two world wars. It went through the same processes of discovering the modern state in the eighteenth century, the nation in the nineteenth, and the nation state in the twentieth. In the making of the modern state and nation, Britain and France may have had the chronological edge, but Central Europe was not slow to catch up.

In the second half of the twentieth century, most of Central Europe was captured by the Soviet Union and brought for the first time into an entirely new orbit. It never rested easily in its communist setting. From 1956 onwards, Central Europe's puppet governments were forced into accommodations and concessions that both weakened their power and bankrupted their economies. Almost without resistance, they surrendered in 1989, leaving Central Europe to find its way back to Western Europe. The return has not been an easy one and 'the transition', as economists and political scientists call it, that was first thought likely to last just a few years has gone on for more than three decades. As it turned out, communism was far more destructive to economies and to political and business ethics than most specialists had imagined.

Yet, Central Europe was never just a reflection of Western Europe or an appendage that uncritically copied its trends. At times, it launched events—most notably the Reformation, which began with Martin Luther and was protected by German princes for long enough to gain a foothold across Western and Central Europe. More often, it embraced currents coming from Western Europe and gave them either a twist of its own or a new intensity. In the art and architecture of the Renaissance, Central Europe fused Italian and northern Gothic styles, overlaid with a deep spirituality. In the politics of religion, it was the site of the most destructive and prolonged religious war in European history, and yet for a time distinguished by its toleration of religious difference. In the economic exploitation of the countryside, large parts of Central Europe, from Holstein eastwards, experienced varieties of serfdom that were largely missing in Western Europe. Central Europe's confrontation with modernity in the form of the city, mechanization, and female empowerment lent its interwar culture a unique tension, agitation, and inventiveness.

Among these trends, there are several which, taken together, point to the region's singularity. The first of these was the explosion of diets, assemblies, self-governing communities, and local autonomies that guided the region's medieval development. The circumstances that gave rise to these were varied—the pattern of settlement and colonization, the flatness of the feudal pyramid throughout Central Europe, and the emergence of powerful and often numerous nobilities. To counter invasion and challenges to their authority, rulers were forced to co-opt the nobles, extending their rights and embedding dialogue into the practice of government. These processes have their parallels in Western Europe, but in Central Europe they dug deeper, creating not only powerful diets that negotiated with the ruler as an equal but also provincial assemblies of noblemen that resisted attempts to centralize authority on the person of the monarch. Cities and villages were equally

conscious of their freedoms, maintaining their own independent institutions and rehearsing their own laws.

From the sixteenth century onwards, popular institutions were in
retreat across Central Europe. Only in Poland and Lithuania, Hungary, Switzerland, and Cossack Ukraine did they survive much beyond
the mid-seventeenth century. Power moved instead upwards, to rulers
and governments. The underpinnings of this takeover rested on Roman Law and on the rights of sovereigns to patrol the religion and
morals of subjects. It was intensified by the philosophy of Natural Law,
by the precepts and prescriptions of Cameralism, and underpinned by
bureaucracies that swallowed up nobilities and converted their once
noisy diets into pliant committees. The modern state to which these
impulses gave rise was highly regulatory and intrusive, empowered by
the presumption that it had the right to legislate by decree. As modern
states tend to, the states of Central Europe accumulated powers that
they were unable to discharge effectively.

Central Europe was from the sixteenth century onwards the seat
of empire. The most lasting of these was the Habsburg empire. Its rulers were after 1438 the sovereigns of the Holy Roman Empire, lending the Habsburgs an ambition for world monarchy that merged into
older dreams of Austrian exceptionalism. The Habsburgs confronted
the Ottoman Turkish Empire along the long Military Frontier that
marked Central Europe's edge. At the end of the eighteenth century,
Habsburgs, the tsars of Russia, and the Hohenzollern kings of Prussia, and later emperors of Germany, divided up between them the
joint monarchy of Poland and Lithuania, moving Russia's European
border decisively westwards. Having outlived the French Empire of
Napoleon, the three empires went on to partition the rest of Central
Europe.

In Western Europe, the state preceded the nation. State boundaries identified where nations were, and governments through their
control of the army, bureaucracy, and education forced nations into
being within the spaces of their states. It was different in Central Europe, where nations crystallized without states to give them definition.

Romantic writers identified nations by language, history, and lore, and the marks of nationhood were seized upon by peoples. But there were plenty of places in Central Europe where nations overlapped and shared the same space. The incongruity of state and nation prompted drastic revisions of boundaries within Central Europe. Having been torn apart by Napoleon, Central Europe was threatened with a new round of changes in 1848, was rebuilt by Bismarck, and comprehensively dismantled and reorganized in the wake of both world wars. All of this was done in the service of the national idea. Where people did not fit, their new twentieth-century masters either killed them or loaded them into cattle trucks. Stalin put it simply around 1946. Referring to the trapped Hungarian minorities in the states of Central Europe, he observed, 'The Hungarian problem is only one of boxcars.'[2]

In Central Europe, nations were not only delineated by the Romantics' vision of language and legend but also thought to be biological units. In the late nineteenth century, the vocabulary of disease and of the laboratory infected discourses of nationhood. It led to the nonsenses of skull measuring, plans for breeding colonies, and diagrams illustrating racial hierarchies. By 1900, racial science had spilled over into genocide in Germany's African colonies and into ideas of a natural struggle for survival that legitimized war. Antisemites increasingly marked out Jews as biologically and racially different and blamed them for the immorality and failures of Central Europe during the interwar years. In the Holocaust, the apparatus and ethos of bureaucracy, technology and automation, and the idea of the exclusivist racial state combined to make Central Europe the home of the death factory.

In the wake of the Second World War, forced expulsions and the redrawing of borders created a correspondence between state and nation that had been previously missing in Central Europe. The iron grip of the Cold War kept national rivalries in check and lent the illusion of permanence to state boundaries. The territorial status quo was brutally upset after 1991 when, in the former Yugoslavia, Serbian-backed forces sought to unite to Serbia the parts of Bosnia and Croatia where Serbs were in the majority. They did not succeed. The peace concluded in 1995 reaffirmed the principle that borders should not be changed except by agreement. The understanding was that in the case of a state breaking up, like the former Yugoslavia, its previous internal boundaries should become the new state borders.[3]

In the wake of the war in former Yugoslavia, European Union and North Atlantic Treaty Organization (NATO) membership was rolled out across Central Europe, binding its member states into international treaties, economic relationships, and legal obligations that seemed to make it impossible that nationalist rivalries might ever again tear the region apart. On top of this, the new states were all democracies—they had to be as a precondition for membership in the European Union. Once in the European Union, some states retreated from their commitments, and their democracies were, and remain, often flawed by political corruption, government control of the media, and dangerous sloganizing. But their governments have without exception committed themselves to good relations with their neighbours and to the peaceful resolution of differences. It helps that there is not much left for them to quarrel over.

The challenge to the new Central Europe lies at its edge. There, state building has been imperfect, leading to political anomalies: the enclave of Kaliningrad, formerly Königsberg, wedged between Poland and Lithuania but a part of Russia, and the unrecognized microstate of Transnistria, a sliver of territory that Russian-backed separatists seized from the Republic of Moldova in 1992. Both Kaliningrad and Transnistria are run by criminals on Moscow's payroll. Further east, Belarus is a dictatorship led by a maverick despot, whose grip on power rests with the security forces. In the Balkans, Bosnia remains divided between rival statelets, while Serbian politicians are unreconciled to the loss in 1999 of the province of Kosovo, now an independent state with an Albanian population. Kaliningrad, Transnistria, Belarus, Bosnia, and Serbia form an arc of instability that runs along Central Europe's eastern border.

But the principal threat is from Russia. From the eighteenth century onwards, Russia had always been a factor in Central European politics—partitioning Poland and Lithuania, sending its armies west-wards to defeat Napoleon, invading Hungary in 1849, taking on Germany in two world wars, and occupying most of the region after 1945. For a few decades after the collapse of the Soviet Union in 1991, it looked as if Russia had been squeezed out of the region's affairs except as a provider of cheap gas and a source of dirty money. Then, in 2022, Russia invaded Ukraine, starting the largest war in Europe since 1945. Cities that had been fought over in the Second World War, like Kharkiv, Dnipro, Mariupol, and Odesa, and more or less forgotten ever since, became once again notorious as targets for missiles and the places of mass graves. Russia's attempt to overturn borders that had been settled following the Soviet Union's collapse in 1991 has challenged the idea that the map of Central Europe is indelibly drawn. In this respect, Russia's contested annexation of Ukrainian Crimea in 2014 may be the harbinger of future, more brutal seizures.

For Central Europe, threats have always come from all directions, but historically those coming from the east have been the most terrible. Huns, Goths, Avars, Hungarians, Mongol-Tatars, Ottoman Turks, and Cossack and Crimean raiders have all broken into Central Europe on its eastern flank, bringing with them murder and rapine. Medieval scribes had a name for the invaders—they were the dogmen, who had escaped from the Caucasus where Alexander the Great had once enclosed them. Today's dogmen may lack the imaginary snouts and tails of their forebears, but with their rocket launchers, tanks, and drones, they are just as terrible and no less subversive of the ideals for which Otto III's gospel book stands.

Acknowledgements

Simon Winder of Penguin Books first suggested this book to me more than twenty years ago, but at the time I lacked the confidence to take it on. I am no more confident today, but, for over three decades, I have had the words 'Central Europe' in my academic handle and, now that I am retired, can postpone the challenge no longer.

The book was mostly written during the lockdown and completed at the time Russia invaded Ukraine. If the lockdown has taught us anything, it is that books which are not online or hidden behind expensive paywalls do not exist. Some of the gaps in my reading are simply due to all the libraries in London being closed at the time I was writing a particular chapter. The war in Ukraine has influenced content too, not least my decision to give the country greater prominence in the text as a part of Central Europe. It has also meant that the final text reads more gloomily than earlier drafts.

I am most grateful to the librarians at University College London (UCL) who throughout the pandemic kept the servers running so that I could access from home most academic journals and some books. My editors, Brian Distelberg of Basic Books and Simon Winder at Penguin, went through the manuscript, highlighting gaps, infelicities, and muddled paragraphs. Eva Hodgkin at Penguin appraised the text minutely, correcting my grammar and suggesting improvements. Their interventions have improved the finished work immensely.

The final editing and production of this book was led by Hachette in New York. I am most grateful to Melissa Veronesi for managing the business of production and to Christina Palaia for her most thorough and thoughtful copyediting.

Adam Gauntlett at Peters, Fraser and Dunlop has done as agents should—reading through the proposal, making suggestions as to how the book should be shaped, occasionally nudging me, but always giving me the maximum encouragement and support. I am lucky to have him to represent me.

Rebecca Haynes at UCL's School of Slavonic and East European Studies (SSEES) read through the first draft and Thomas Lorman at SSEES checked the second. Both are walking encyclopaedias of Central Europe's history and were fast to point out errors and silliness. Richard Butterwick-Pawlikowski of SSEES made sure that what I wrote on Poland and Lithuania was more or less right, and Tim Beasley-Murray of UCL confirmed that what I had said about Slavoj Žižek was not entirely obtuse. Doubtless errors and misinterpretations remain. They are my fault.

Three friends and colleagues died during the pandemic, although not of it. With all three, I had often discussed the problems of Central European history and the ingredients that make it special: Trevor Thomas, who for several decades taught Habsburg history at SSEES; János Bak of the Central European University in Budapest, and George Schöpflin, formerly of SSEES and more recently a Fidesz MEP for Hungary. I shall miss their conversation, companionship, and insights.

I have often been grumpy when writing this book, frustrated by being stuck at home by the pandemic and worried that I had taken on too much. Ann has supported me throughout the endeavour, with patience, strength, and love. This book is dedicated to her.

Ramsgate, Kent
February 2023

Further Reading

MOST HISTORY BOOKS ABOUT CENTRAL EUROPE ARE NATIONAL HISTORIES. Of these, probably the most accessible are in the Cambridge 'A Concise History of' series—for Austria (Steven Beller), the Baltic States (Andrejs Plakans), Germany (Mary Fulbrook), Hungary (Miklós Molnár), Poland (Jerzy Lukowski and Hubert Zawadzki), and Romania (Keith Hitchens). For Czech history, see Derek Sayer, *The Coasts of Bohemia: A Czech History* (Princeton, 1998), and for Ukraine, Serhii Plokhy, *The Gates of Europe: A History of Ukraine* (London, 2016). For Slovenia, see Oto Luthar, *The Land Between: A History of Slovenia* (Frankfurt a/M and Oxford, 2008).

Several recently published national histories deserve special mention: Robert Frost, *The Oxford History of Poland-Lithuania, 1385–1569* (Oxford, 2015) and Richard Butterwick, *The Polish-Lithuanian Commonwealth: Light and Flame* (New Haven and London, 2020). Like buses, you can wait a lifetime for something on the Holy Roman Empire only for three to arrive in quick succession: Joachim Whaley, *Germany and the Holy Roman Empire*, 2 vols. (Oxford, 2012); Peter H. Wilson, *The Holy Roman Empire: A Thousand Years of Europe's History* (London, 2016); and Barbara Stollberg-Rilinger, *The Holy Roman Empire: A Short History* (Princeton, 2018).

For the Habsburgs, see Steven Beller, *The Habsburg Monarchy, 1815–1918* (Cambridge, 2018), and Pieter M. Judson, *The Habsburg Empire: A New History* (Cambridge, MA, and London, 2016). Both of these deal predominantly with the nineteenth and early twentieth centuries. For the earlier period, see R. J. W. Evans, *The Making of the Habsburg Monarchy, 1550–1700* (Oxford, 1979), and Martyn Rady, *The Habsburgs: The Rise and Fall of a World Power* (London, 2020).

Histories of Central Europe as a region are few. A start was made by the University of Washington Press with its East Central Europe series, notably Jean W. Sedlar, *East Central Europe in the Middle Ages, 1000–1500* (Seattle, WA, and London, 1993); Joseph Rothschild, *East Central Europe Between the Two World Wars* (Seattle, WA, and London, 1974), and Paul Robert Magocsi, *Historical Atlas of East Central Europe* (Seattle, WA, and London, 1993).

More specific works as they relate to each chapter of the present book are as follows:

INTRODUCTION. CENTRAL EUROPE, THE DOGMEN, AND THE OAK WOODS OF BEREHOVE

Andrew Runni Anderson, *Alexander's Gate, Gog and Magog, and the Inclosed Nations* (Cambridge, MA, 1932).

Asghar Seyed-Gohrab, Faustina Doufikar-Aerts, and Sen McGlinn, eds., *Embodiments of Evil: Gog and Magog* (Leiden, 2011).

Hugo Gryn, with Naomi Gryn, *Chasing Shadows* (London, 2000).

David Gordon White, *Myths of the Dog-Man* (Chicago and London, 1991).

CHAPTER 1. THE ROMAN EMPIRE, THE HUNS, AND THE *NIBELUNGENLIED*

Walter Goffart, *Barbarian Tides: The Migration Age and the Later Roman Empire* (Philadelphia, 2006).

Peter Heather, *Empires and Barbarians* (London, 2009).

The Nibelungenlied, trans. A. T. Hatto, rev. ed. (London, 1969).

E. A. Thompson, *The Huns*, rev. ed. (Oxford, 1996).

Herwig Wolfram, *The Roman Empire and Its Germanic Peoples* (Berkeley, Los Angeles, and London, 1997).

CHAPTER 2. THE FRANKS AND CHARLEMAGNE: THE VIEW FROM LAKE CONSTANCE

Johannes Fried, *Charlemagne* (Cambridge, MA, 2016).

Patrick J. Geary, *Before France and Germany: The Creation and Transformation of the Merovingian World* (New York and Oxford, 1988).

Janet L. Nelson, *King and Emperor: A New Life of Charlemagne* (London, 2019).

W. Vogler and J. C. King, eds., *The Culture of the Abbey of St Gall: An Overview* (Stuttgart and Zurich, 1991).

J. M. Wallace-Hadrill, *The Long-Haired Kings* (Toronto, Buffalo, and London, 1982).

CHAPTER 3. AVARS AND SLAVS: DESTRUCTION AND CONVERSION

Averil Cameron, *Byzantine Matters* (Princeton, 2014).

Florin Curta, *Southeastern Europe in the Middle Ages, 500–1250* (Cambridge, 2006).

Walter Pohl, *The Avars: A Steppe Empire in Central Europe, 567–822* (Ithaca, NY, 2018).

Martyn Rady, 'The Slavs, Avars, and Hungarians', in *The Cambridge History of War*, vol. 2, ed. D. A. Graff and A. Curry (Cambridge, 2020), 133–150.

A. P. Vlasto, *The Entry of the Slavs into Christendom: An Introduction to the Medieval History of the Slavs* (Cambridge, 1970).

CHAPTER 4. THE RETURN OF THE HUNS, SLAVE STATES, AND THE SHAPING OF CENTRAL EUROPE

Nora Berend, Przemysław Urbańczyk, and Przemysław Wiszewski, *Central Europe in the High Middle Ages: Bohemia, Hungary and Poland c. 900–c. 1300* (Cambridge, 2013).

C. A. Macartney, *The Magyars in the Ninth Century* (Cambridge, 1930).

Henry Mayr-Harting, *Ottonian Book Illumination: An Historical Study*, 2nd ed. (London, 1999).

Michael McCormick, *Origins of the European Economy: Communications and Commerce, A.D. 300–900* (Cambridge, 2001).

Timothy Reuter, *Germany in the Early Middle Ages, c. 800–1056* (London and New York, 1991).

CHAPTER 5. THE MAKING OF THE HOLY ROMAN EMPIRE AND CENTRAL EUROPE'S WILD EAST

Robert Bartlett, *The Making of Europe: Conquest, Colonization, and Cultural Change, 950–1350* (London, 1993).

Eric Christiansen, *The Northern Crusades: The Baltic and the Catholic Frontier 1100–1525* (London and Basingstoke, 1980).

John B. Freed, *Frederick Barbarossa: The Prince and the Myth* (New Haven and London, 2016).

Helmold of Bosau, *The Chronicle of the Slavs*, ed. F. J. Tschan (New York, 1966). (Written c. 1170.)

Len Scales, *The Shaping of German Identity: Authority and Crisis, 1245–1414* (Cambridge, 2012).

CHAPTER 6. THE MONGOL-TATARS, NEW CITIES, AND NEW KNIGHTS

Pál Engel, *The Realm of St Stephen: A History of Medieval Hungary, 895–1526* (London, 2001).

Erik Fügedi, *Castle and Society in Medieval Hungary, 1000–1437* (Budapest, 1986).

Piotr Górecki, *A Local Society in Transition: The Henryków Book and Related Documents* (Toronto, 2007).

Martyn Rady, *Nobility, Land and Service in Medieval Hungary* (Basingstoke and New York, 2000).

Martyn Rady, János M. Bak, and László Veszprémy, eds., *Anonymus and Master Roger* (Budapest and New York, 2010).

CHAPTER 7. DYNASTIC CHANGE, CHARLES IV OF BOHEMIA, AND THE PROPHETS OF THE ANTICHRIST

Barbara Drake Boehm and Jiří Fajt, eds., *Prague: The Crown of Bohemia, 1347–1437* (New Haven, 2005).

Thomas A. Fudge, *The Magnificent Ride: The First Reformation in Hussite Bohemia* (Aldershot, 1998).

Stephen E. Lahey, *The Hussites* (Leeds, 2019).

Balázs Nagy and Frank Schaer, eds., *Autobiography of Emperor Charles IV; and, His Biography of St Wenceslas* (Budapest, 2001).

František Šmahel, *The Paris Summit, 1377–1378: Emperor Charles IV and King Charles V of France* (Prague, 2015).

CHAPTER 8. COUNCILS, DIETS, AND THE CONFUSION OF THE LAWS

Julia Burkhardt, 'Procedure, Rules and Meaning of Political Assemblies in Late Medieval Central Europe', *Parliaments, Estates and Representation* 35, no. 2 (2015): 153–170.

F. L. Carsten, *Princes and Parliaments in Germany: From the Fifteenth to the Eighteenth Centuries* (Oxford, 1959).

Kenneth J. Dillon, *King and Estates in the Bohemian Lands 1526–1564* (Brussels, 1976).

Antonio Marongiu, *Medieval Parliaments: A Comparative Study* (London, 1968).

Stephen Werbőczy, *The Customary Law of the Renowned Kingdom of Hungary*, ed. János M. Bak, Péter Banyó, and Martyn Rady (Budapest and Idyllwild, CA, 2005).

CHAPTER 9. CITIES, VILLAGES, AND FREEDOMS: FROM FRISIA TO TRANSYLVANIA

T. H. Aston and C. H. E. Philpin, eds., *The Brenner Debate: Agrarian Class Structure and Economic Development in Pre-Industrial Europe* (Cambridge, 1985).

Clive H. Church and Randolph C. Head, *A Concise History of Switzerland* (Cambridge, 2013).

Béla Köpeczi and B. Kovrig, eds., *History of Transylvania*, 3 vols. (Boulder, 2001–2002).

Horst Haider Munske, Nils Århammar, Volker F. Faltings, Oebele Vries, Jarich F. Hoekstra, Alastair G. H. Walker, and Ommo Wilts, eds., *Handbook of Frisian Studies* (Tübingen, 2001).

Ioan-Aurel Pop and Thomas Nägler, eds., *The History of Transylvania*, 2nd ed., 3 vols. (Cluj, 2018).

CHAPTER 10. OLD PRUSSIA, THE ADVENTURES OF HENRY BOLINGBROKE, AND THE UNION OF POLAND AND LITHUANIA

Darius Baronas and S. C. Rowell, *The Conversion of Lithuania: From Pagan Barbarians to Late Medieval Christians* (Vilnius, 2015).

Liliya Berezhnaya and Heidi Hein-Kircher, eds., *Rampart Nations: Bulwark Myths of East European Multiconfessional Societies in the Age of Nationalism* (New York, 2019).

F. L. Carsten, *The Origins of Prussia* (Oxford, 1954).

Eric Christiansen, *The Northern Crusades: The Baltic and the Catholic Frontier, 1100–1525* (London, 1980).

Desmond Seward, *The Monks of War: The Military Religious Orders* (London, 1972).

CHAPTER 11. MERCHANTS, THE HANSEATIC LEAGUE, AND THE FUGGERS

Philippe Dollinger, *The German Hansa* (London and Basingstoke, 1970).

Richard Ehrenberg, *Capital and Finance in the Age of the Renaissance: A Study of the Fuggers and Their Connections* (New York, 1928).

Donald J. Harreld, ed., *A Companion to the Hanseatic League* (Leiden and Boston, 2015).

József Laszlovszky, Balázs Nagy, Péter Szabó and András Vadas, eds., *The Economy of Medieval Hungary* (Leiden and Boston, 2018).

Greg Steinmetz, *The Richest Man Who Ever Lived: The Life and Times of Jacob Fugger* (New York, 2015).

CHAPTER 12. THE DRAGON IN THE CHINA SHOP AND THE HABSBURG IMAGINATION

Gerhard Benecke, *Maximilian I, 1459–1519: An Analytical Biography* (London, 1982).

Imre Takács, Zsombor Jékely, Szilárd Papp, and Györgyi Poszler, eds., *Sigismund Rex et Imperator: art et culture au temps de Sigismond de Luxembourg. Catalogue d'exposition* (Mainz, 2006).

Marie Tanner, *The Last Descendants of Aeneas: The Hapsburgs and the Mythic Image of the Emperor* (New Haven, 1992).

Pierre Terjanian, ed., *The Last Knight: The Art, Armor, and Ambition of Maximilian I* (New York, 2019).

Mark Whelan, *Sigismund of Luxemburg and the Imperial Response to the Ottoman Turkish Threat, c. 1410–1437* (PhD thesis, University of London, 2014).

CHAPTER 13. CENTRAL EUROPE'S RENAISSANCE, ROMAN LAW, AND THE LIBRARY OF THE RAVEN KING

Thomas DaCosta Kaufmann, *Court, Cloister and City: The Art and Culture of Central Europe 1450–1800* (London, 1995).

Erwin Panofsky, *The Life and Art of Albrecht Dürer*, 5th ed. (Princeton, 2005).

Gerald Strauss, *Law, Resistance, and the State: The Opposition to Roman Law in Reformation Germany* (Princeton, 1986).

Marcus Tanner, *The Raven King: Matthias Corvinus and the Fate of His Lost Library* (New Haven and London, 2009).

Malcolm Vale, *A Short History of the Renaissance in Northern Europe* (London and New York, 2020).

CHAPTER 14. LUTHER'S REFORMATION, THE BADLANDS OF THURINGIA, AND THE COURT PAINTER OF SAXONY

Alister E. McGrath, *Luther's Theology of the Cross: Martin Luther's Theological Breakthrough*, 2nd ed. (Malden, MA, 2011).

Natalia Nowakowska, *King Sigismund and Martin Luther: The Reformation Before Confessionalization* (Oxford, 2018).

Steven Ozment, *The Serpent and the Lamb: Cranach, Luther, and the Making of the Reformation* (New Haven and London, 2011).

Geoffrey Parker, *Emperor: A New Life of Charles V* (New Haven and London, 2019).

Martyn Rady, *The Emperor Charles V* (London and New York, 1988).

CHAPTER 15. THE OTTOMAN TURKS AND CENTRAL EUROPE'S LONG FRONTIER

Paul Robert Magocsi, *A History of Ukraine* (Seattle, 1996).

William H. McNeill, *Europe's Steppe Frontier, 1500–1800* (Chicago and London, 1964).

Stanko Guldescu, *The Croatian-Slavonian Kingdom 1526–1792* (The Hague and Paris, 1970).

Serhii Plokhy, *The Cossacks and Religion in Early Modern Ukraine* (Oxford, 2001).

Gunther E. Rothenberg, *The Austrian Military Border in Croatia, 1522–1747* (Urbana, 1960).

CHAPTER 16. TOLERATION, THE MAGUS, AND THE
ALCHEMIST AS EMPEROR

R. J. W. Evans, *Rudolf II and His World: A Study in Intellectual History* (Oxford, 1984).

E. Fučíková, ed., *Rudolf II and Prague: The Court and the City* (Prague, London, and New York, 1997).

Howard Louthan, *The Quest for Compromise: Peacemakers in Counter-Reformation Vienna* (Cambridge, 1997).

Peter Marshall, *The Mercurial Emperor: The Magic Circle of Rudolf II in Prague* (London, 2007).

Regina Pörtner, *The Counter-Reformation in Central Europe: Styria 1580–1630* (Oxford, 2001).

CHAPTER 17. CALENDARS, THE CATHOLIC RECOVERY,
AND CENTRAL EUROPE'S THIRTY YEARS' CIVIL WAR

Olaf Asbach and Peter Schröder, eds., *The Ashgate Research Companion to the Thirty Years' War* (London and New York, 2014).

Robert Bireley, *Ferdinand II, Counter-Reformation Emperor, 1578–1637* (Cambridge, 2014).

Paul Shore, *Narratives of Adversity: Jesuits on the Eastern Peripheries of the Habsburg Realms (1640–1773)* (Budapest and New York, 2012).

Janusz Tazbir, *A State Without Stakes: Polish Religious Toleration in the Sixteenth and Seventeenth Centuries* (New York, 1973).

Peter Wilson, *Europe's Tragedy: A New History of the Thirty Years' War* (London, 2010).

CHAPTER 18. THE CONDITION OF THE COUNTRYSIDE:
PEASANTS, GYPSIES, JEWS, AND OTHERS

Viorel Achim, *The Roma in Romanian History* (Budapest and New York, 2004).

Markus Cerman, *Villagers and Lords in Eastern Europe, 1300–1800* (Basingstoke and New York, 2012).

Gershon David Hundert, *Jews in Poland-Lithuania in the Eighteenth Century* (Berkeley and Los Angeles, 2004).

Lech Mróz, *Roma-Gypsy Presence in the Polish-Lithuanian Commonwealth* (Budapest and New York, 2015).

Antony Polonsky, *The Jews of Poland and Russia, 1350–1881* (Liverpool, 2019).

CHAPTER 19. CAMERALISM, OTTOMAN ENDGAME, AND THE HUMAN LABORATORY

Michael Hochedlinger, *Austria's Wars of Emergence: War, State and Society in the Habsburg Monarchy 1683–1797* (London, 2003).

Irina Marin, *Contested Frontiers in the Balkans: Habsburg and Ottoman Rivalries in Eastern Europe* (London and New York, 2013).

Derek McKay, *Prince Eugene of Savoy* (London, 1977).

Marten Seppel and Keith Tribe, eds., *Cameralism in Practice: State Administration and Economy in Early Modern Europe* (Woodbridge, 2017).

Andre Wakefield, *The Disordered Police State: German Cameralism as Science and Practice* (Chicago and London, 2009).

CHAPTER 20. BUREAUCRATS, SARMATIANS, AND LITTLE LANDSCAPES

W. H. Bruford, *Germany in the Eighteenth Century: The Social Background of the Literary Revival* (Cambridge, 1935).

Jerzy Lukowski, *Disorderly Liberty: The Political Culture of the Polish-Lithuanian Commonwealth in the Eighteenth Century* (London and New York, 2010).

Oto Luthar, *The Land Between: A History of Slovenia* (Frankfurt and Oxford, 2008).

Henry Marczali, *Hungary in the Eighteenth Century* (Cambridge, 1910).

Felicia Roşu, *Elective Monarchy in Transylvania and Poland-Lithuania* (Oxford, 2017).

CHAPTER 21. THE PRUSSIAN WAY: CEMETERY MARIONETTES AND THE MACHINE STATE

Derek Beales, *Joseph II*, 2 vols. (Cambridge, 1987–2009).

Christopher Clark, *Iron Kingdom: The Rise and Downfall of Prussia, 1600–1947* (London, 2006).

James Van Horn Melton, *The Rise of the Public in Enlightenment Europe* (Cambridge, 2001).

Robert A. Minder, *In the Footsteps of the Freemasons in Vienna: A City Guide* (Vienna, 2021).

Barbara Stollberg-Rilinger, *Maria Theresa: The Habsburg Empress in Her Time* (Princeton and Oxford, 2022).

CHAPTER 22. DISSECTING EUROPE'S ORANG-UTAN:
THE PARTITIONS OF POLAND AND LITHUANIA

Richard Butterwick, *The Constitution of 3 May 1791: Testament of the Polish-Lithuanian Commonwealth* (Warsaw, 2021).

Richard Butterwick, *The Polish-Lithuanian Commonwealth 1733–1795: Light and Flame* (New Haven and London, 2020).

Jerzy Lukowski, *Liberty's Folly: The Polish-Lithuanian Commonwealth in the Eighteenth Century, 1697–1795* (London, 1991).

Jerzy Lukowski, *The Partitions of Poland 1772, 1793, 1795* (London, 1999).

Adam Zamoyski, *The Last King of Poland* (London, 1997).

CHAPTER 23. NAPOLEON AND THE MAP OF CENTRAL EUROPE

F. M. Barnard, *Herder's Social and Political Thought: From Enlightenment to Nationalism* (Oxford, 1965).

Jaroslav Czubaty, *The Duchy of Warsaw, 1807–1815: A Napoleonic Outpost in Central Europe* (London and New York, 2016).

Joep Leerssen, *National Thought in Europe: A Cultural History*, 3rd ed. (Amsterdam, 2014).

Sam A. Mustafa, *Napoleon's Paper Kingdom: The Life and Death of Westphalia, 1807–1813* (Lanham, MD, 2017).

Adam Zamoyski, *Phantom Terror: The Threat of Revolution and the Repression of Liberty, 1789–1848* (London, 2014).

CHAPTER 24. THE GALLANT WORLD OF TOMCAT MURR:
ROMANTICISM, THE GRIMMS, AND THE HANOVER HANDBOOK

Tim Blanning, *The Romantic Revolution* (London, 2010).

E. T. A. Hoffmann, *The Life and Opinions of the Tomcat Murr*, trans. Jeremy Adler (London, 1999).

Ruth Michaelis-Jena, *The Brothers Grimm* (London, 1970).

Wolfram Siemann, *Metternich: Strategist and Visionary* (Cambridge, MA, 2019).

John Wardroper, *Wicked Ernest: The Truth About the Man Who Was Almost Britain's King* (London, 2002).

CHAPTER 25. 1848 AND THE COMING OF REVOLUTION

George Barany, *Stephen Széchenyi and the Awakening of Hungarian Nationalism, 1791–1841* (Princeton, 1968).

Sir Lewis Namier, *1848: The Revolution of the Intellectuals*, rev. ed. (Oxford, 1992).

Thomas Nipperdey, *Germany from Napoleon to Bismarck, 1800–1866* (Princeton, 1996).

Mike Rapport, *1848: The Year of Revolution* (London, 2009).

R. John Rath, *The Viennese Revolution of 1848* (New York, 1969).

CHAPTER 26. THE REVENGE OF THE GENERALS AND
THE MAKING OF NATIONS

Istvan Deak, *The Lawful Revolution: Louis Kossuth and the Hungarians, 1848–1849* (New York, 1979).

Jason D. Hansen, *Mapping the Germans: Statistical Science, Cartography, and the Visualization of the German Nation, 1848–1914* (Oxford, 2015).

Alexander Maxwell, *Patriots Against Fashion: Clothing and Nationalism in Europe's Age of Revolutions* (Basingstoke and New York, 2014).

Tara Zahra, 'Imagined Noncommunities: National Indifference as a Category of Analysis', *Slavic Review* 69, no. 1 (2010): 93–119.

Adam Zamoyski, *Chopin: Prince of the Romantics* (London, 2010).

CHAPTER 27. BISMARCK, KHUEN-HÉDERVÁRY'S CROATIA,
AND THE PRESUMPTION OF THE LAW

Ágnes Deák, *From Habsburg Neo-Absolutism to the Compromise, 1849–1867* (Boulder and Highland Lakes, 2009).

Celia Hawkesworth, *Zagreb: A Cultural and Literary History* (Oxford, 2007).

László Péter, *Hungary's Long Nineteenth Century: Constitutional and Democratic Traditions in a European Perspective*, ed. M. Lojkó (Leiden and Boston, 2012).

Jonathan Steinberg, *Bismarck: A Life* (Oxford, 2011).

A. J. P. Taylor, *Bismarck: The Man and the Statesman* (London, 1955).

CHAPTER 28. ASSIMILATION, BIOLOGY, AND THE SKULL MEASURERS

David Olusoga and Casper W. Erichsen, *The Kaiser's Holocaust: Germany's Forgotten Genocide and the Colonial Roots of Nazism* (London, 2011).

Peter Pulzer, *The Rise of Political Anti-Semitism in Germany and Austria* (Cambridge, MA, 1988).

Marius Turda, *Eugenics and Nation in Early 20th Century Hungary* (Basingstoke and New York, 2014).

Peter Watson, *The German Genius: Europe's Third Renaissance, the Second Scientific Revolution and the Twentieth Century* (London, 2010).

Paul Weindling, *Epidemics and Genocide in Eastern Europe, 1890–1945* (Oxford, 2010).

CHAPTER 29. 1914–1918: THE WAR AGAINST CENTRAL EUROPE

Maureen Healy, *Vienna and the Fall of the Habsburg Empire: Total War and Everyday Life in World War I* (Cambridge, 2004).

John Horne, ed., *A Companion to World War One* (Chichester and Malden, MA, 2010).

Vejas Gabriel Liulevicius, *The German Myth of the East: 1800 to the Present* (Oxford, 2009).

Manfred Rauchensteiner, *The First World War and the End of the Habsburg Monarchy, 1914–1918* (Vienna, Cologne, and Weimar, 2014).

Alexander Watson, *Ring of Steel: Germany and Austria-Hungary at War, 1914–1918* (London, 2014).

CHAPTER 30. VIOLENCE, THE CITY, AND 'THE BLUE ANGEL'

Peter Gay, *Weimar Culture: The Outsider as Insider* (London, 1969).

Robert Gerwarth, *The Vanquished: Why the First World War Failed to End* (London, 2016).

Peter Jelavich, *Berlin Cabaret* (Cambridge, MA, and London, 1993).

Michael H. Kater, *Culture in Nazi Germany* (New Haven and London, 2019).

Siegfried Kracauer, *From Caligari to Hitler: A Psychological History of the German Film*, rev. ed. (Princeton and Oxford, 2004).

CHAPTER 31. THE SECOND WORLD WAR, ORDINARY CENTRAL EUROPEANS, AND INDUSTRIAL MURDER

Zygmunt Baumann, *Modernity and the Holocaust* (Cambridge, 1989).

David Cesarani, *Final Solution: The Fate of the Jews 1933–1949* (London, 2017).

Norman Davies, *Europe at War, 1939–1945* (London, 2006).

Jan T. Gross, *Neighbours: The Destruction of the Jewish Community in Jedwabne, Poland* (Princeton, 2001).

Halik Kochanski, *The Eagle Unbowed: Poland and the Poles in the Second World War* (London, 2012).

CHAPTER 32. MÁTYÁS RÁKOSI, STALINIST CENTRAL EUROPE, AND ITS DISCONTENTS

Anne Applebaum, *Iron Curtain: The Crushing of Eastern Europe 1944–1956* (London, 2012).

Csaba Békés, János Rainer, and Malcolm Byrne, eds., *The 1956 Hungarian Revolution: A History in Documents* (Budapest and New York, 2002).

Martin Mevius, *Agents of Moscow: The Hungarian Communist Party and the Origins of Socialist Patriotism, 1941–1953* (Oxford, 2005).

László Péter and Martyn Rady, eds., *Resistance, Rebellion and Revolution in Hungary and Central Europe: Commemorating 1956* (London, 2008).

Hugo Service, *Germans to Poles: Communism, Nationalism and Ethnic Cleansing After the Second World War* (Cambridge, 2013).

CHAPTER 33. COMMUNIST CENTRAL EUROPE AND ITS COLLAPSE

Siobhan Doucette, *Books Are Weapons: The Polish Opposition Press and the Overthrow of Communism* (Pittsburgh, 2017).

Timothy Garton Ash, *The Uses of Adversity: Essays on the Fate of Central Europe* (Cambridge, 1989).

Joseph Rothschild and Nancy M. Wingfield, *Return to Diversity: A Political History of East Central Europe Since World War II*, 4th ed. (Oxford, 2008).

Bernard Wheaton and Zdeněk Kavan, *The Velvet Revolution: Czechoslovakia, 1988–1991* (Boulder, 1991).

Kieran Williams, *The Prague Spring and Its Aftermath: Czechoslovak Politics, 1968–1970* (Cambridge, 1997).

CHAPTER 34. POST-COMMUNISM: SLAVOJ ŽIŽEK AND THE LESSON OF LAIBACH

Daphne Berdahl, *On the Social Life of Postsocialism: Memory, Consumption, Germany* (Bloomington, 2010).

Ivan Krastev and Stephen Holmes, *The Light That Failed: A Reckoning* (London, 2019).

Bálint Magyar, *Post-Communist Mafia State: The Case of Hungary* (Budapest and New York, 2016).

Alexei Monroe, *Interrogation Machine: Laibach and NSK* (Cambridge, MA, and London, 2005).

Abbreviations

DRMH	Decreta Regni Mediaevalis Hungariae
MGH	Monumenta Germaniae Historica
MGH Auct. Ant.	Auctores Antiquissimi
MGH Capit.	Capitularia Regum Francorum
MGH Const.	Constitutiones et acta publica imperatorum et regum
MGH Fontes iuris	Fontes iuris Germanici antiqui in usum scholarum separatim editi
MGH Ldl.	Libelli de lite imperatorum et pontificum
MGH LL	Leges (in folio)
MGH Poetae	Poetae Latini medii aevi
MGH SS	MGH Scriptores (in folio)
MGH SS rer. Germ.	MGH Scriptores rerum Germanicarum in usum scholarum
MGH SS rer. Germ. N.S.	MGH Scriptores rerum Germanicarum, Nova series
OeSta/HHStA	Austrian State Archive, Haus-, Hof- und Staatsarchiv, Vienna
RI	*Regesta Imperii*
RTA	*Deutsche Reichstagsakten*
SEER	*Slavonic and East European Review*

Notes

INTRODUCTION: CENTRAL EUROPE, THE DOGMEN, AND THE OAK WOODS OF BEREHOVE

1. E. Ann Matter, 'The Soul of the Dog-Man: Ratramnus of Corbie Between Theology and Philosophy', *Rivista di Storia della Filosofia* 86 (2006): 43–53; MGH SS 11, 9.

2. For 'they ate the bodies', see *The Book of Ser Marco Polo, the Venetian*, ed. H. Yule, vol. 1 (Cambridge, 1871), 276. See further, *The Greek Alexander Romance*, ed. Richard Stoneman (London, 1991), 186–187.

3. Eizo Matsuki, 'The Crimean Tatars and Their Russian-Captive Slaves', *Mediterranean World* 18 (2006): 171–182; Dagmar Klímová-Rychnová, 'Kulturní zázemí epiteta "Tataré-Psohlavci"', *Český lid* 55, nos. 2–3 (1968): 109–120.

4. Dana Rehn, 'Going to the Dogs: The Foreign and Renaissance Other in German Renaissance Prints', *Otherness: Essays and Studies* 5, no. 2 (2016): 111–150.

5. The original Latin text is given in Tibor Neumann, *Bereg megye hatóságának oklevelei* (Nyíregyháza, 2006), no. 223 (1476).

CHAPTER 1. THE ROMAN EMPIRE, THE HUNS, AND THE *NIBELUNGENLIED*

1. The original Latin list known as the *Laterculus Veronensis* is given in Theodor Mommsen, *Verzeichniss der Römischen Provinzen* (Berlin, 1863), 491–493.

2. Tilmann Bechert, 'Bevölkerung und Gesellschaft der römischen Provinz Germania Inferior', *Antike Welt* 14, no. 1 (1983): 46–57; J. J. Wilkes, 'The Roman Danube: An Archaeological Survey', *Journal of Roman Studies* 95 (2005): 124–225; Anett Firnigl and Miklós Nagy, 'Using Colors at the Roman Villas of Balaton Upland', *Óbuda University e-Bulletin* 8, no. 2 (2018): 39–46.

3. For the Hungarian Plain, see János Tokai, 'Római császárkori erődrendszer a Barbaricumban', *Tisicum. A Jász-Nagykun-Szolnok Megyei Múzeumok Évkönyve* 15 (2006): 69–75; László Selmeczi, 'Ördögárok mondái

Biharban', *A Debreceni Déri Múzeum Évkönyve 2000–2001*, Debrecen 2001, 183–190.

4. Tacitus, *Germania*, 33, trans. H. Mattingly and J. B. Rives (London, 2009), 50.

5. Tacitus, *Histories*, 1.79, trans. C. H. Moore, *Histories*, vol. 2 (London and New York, 1925), 133; for 'a robber horde', see K. W. Arafat, *Pausanias' Greece: Ancient Artists and Roman Rulers* (Cambridge, 1996), 190.

6. Pliny the Elder, *Natural History*, 16.6, trans. J. Healey (London, 1991), 207; Zoë M. Tan, 'Subversive Geography in Tacitus' *Germania*', *Journal of Roman Studies* 104 (2014): 181–204.

7. For the early German languages, see Peter von Polenz, *Geschichte der deutschen Sprache*, 10th ed. (Berlin and New York, 2009), 1–30.

8. K. S. Painter, 'Booty from a Roman Villa Found in the Rhine', *Minerva* 5, no. 1 (1994): 22–27.

9. E. A. Thompson, *The Huns* (Oxford, 1948), 24–29.

10. Jan den Boeft et al., eds., *Philological and Historical Commentary on Ammianus Marcellinus XXXI* (Leiden and Boston, 2018), 11–29.

11. Herwig Wolfram, *The Roman Empire and Its Germanic Peoples* (Berkeley, Los Angeles, and London, 1997), 88–89.

12. MGH Auct. Ant. 9, 475.

13. *The Gothic History of Jordanes*, trans. C. C. Mierow (Princeton, 1915), 102; Leopold Kretzenbacher, *Kynokephale Dämonen sudosteuropäischer Volksdichtung* (Munich, 1968), 21, 34. See also Monika Kropej, *Supernatural Beings from Slovenian Myth and Folk Tales* (Ljubljana, 2012), 202.

14. E. A. Thompson, *The Huns* (Oxford, 1948), 148–149.

15. For the Huns as ruling a state, see Hyun Jin Kim, *The Huns, Rome and the Birth of Europe* (Cambridge, 2013), especially 17–42.

16. 'The flocks are gone': see Michael P. McHugh, *The Carmen de Providentia Dei Attributed to Prosper of Aquitaine* (Washington, DC, 1964), 261. See also, Helmut Bender, 'Archaeological Perspectives on Rural Settlement in Late Antiquity in the Rhine and Danube', in *Urban Centers and Rural Contexts in Late Antiquity*, ed. Thomas S. Burns and J. W. Eadie (East Lansing, 2001), 185–198.

17. Martyn Rady, 'Recollecting Attila: Some Medieval Hungarian Images and Their Antecedents', *Central Europe* 1, no. 1 (2003): 5–17; Martyn Rady, 'Attila and the Hun Tradition in Hungarian Medieval Texts', in *Studies on the Illuminated Chronicle*, ed. J. M. Bak and L. Veszprémy (Budapest, 2018), 127–138; for the Walther legend and its Polish version, see Marion Dexter Learned, 'Origin and Development of the Walther Saga', *Proceedings of the Modern Languages Association* 7, no. 1 (1892): 131–195.

CHAPTER 2. THE FRANKS AND CHARLEMAGNE: THE VIEW FROM LAKE CONSTANCE

1. The best introduction to Arian theology remains John Henry Cardinal Newman, *The Arians of the Fourth Century* (London, 1908), 201–235 (first published in 1833). Quotation from P. Schaff, ed., *Nicene and Post-Nicene Fathers*, 1st series, vol. 3 (New York, 2007), 97.

2. For early Arian influence in Central Europe, see Herwig Wolfram, 'Vulfila, Bishop and Secular Leader', in *Arianism: Roman Heresy and Barbarian Creed*, ed. G. M. Berndt and R. Steinacher (London and New York, 2016), 131–144 (143); Edit B. Thomas, 'Arius-Darstellung. Eine römerzeitliche Ziegelritzeichnung aus Kisdorog in Pannonien', *A Szekszárdi Béri Balogh Ádám Múzeum Évkönyve*, nos. 4–5 (1975): 77–116.

3. J. M. Wallace-Hadrill, *The Frankish Church* (Oxford, 1983), 17–36.

4. Wolfgang H. Fritze, 'Universalis gentium confessio. Formeln, Träger und Wege universalmissionarischen Denkens im 7. Jahrhundert', *Frühmittelalterliche Studien* 3 (1969): 78–130 (96); Kuno Meyer, *Selections from Ancient Irish Poetry*, 2nd ed. (London, 1913), 51.

5. For 'performed no services', see Ferdinand Lot, *The End of the Ancient World and the Beginning of the Middle Ages* (New York, 1961), 354–356; J. M. Wallace-Hadrill, *The Long-Haired Kings* (Toronto, Buffalo, and London, 1982), 195, 209.

6. MGH SS 1, 64.

7. 'Royal Frankish Annals', sub 749, given in *Carolingian Chronicles*, trans. B. W. Scholz (Ann Arbor, 1972), 39; Florence Close, 'Le sacre de Pépin de 751? Coulisses d'un coup d'État', *Revue belge de philologie et d'histoire* 85, nos. 3–4 (2007): 835–852.

8. MGH SS 1, 11.

9. *Urkundenbuch der Abtei Sanct Gallen*, ed. H. Wartmann, vol. 1 (Zurich, 1863), 2–10, 37, 42, 47, 69, etc.

10. For the origin of Charlemagne's name, see Alessandro Barbero, *Charlemagne: Father of a Continent* (Berkeley, Los Angeles, and London, 2004), 413; as a military genius, Bernard S. Bachrach, *Charlemagne's Early Campaigns (768–777)* (Leiden, 2013), 99.

11. Quotation from MGH SS 30. 2, 794; for enslavement, see MGH SS 1, 37. See also Richard Hodges, 'Charlemagne's Elephant', *History Today*, December 2000, 21–27.

12. MGH Capit. 1, 145–146; Janet L. Nelson, *King and Emperor: A New Life of Charlemagne* (London, 2019), 291; Thomas Haye, *Päpste und Poeten. Die mittelalterliche Kurie als Objekt und Förderer panegyrisher Dichtung* (Berlin and New York, 2009), 120.

13. MGH SS 1, 45.

14. Walter Ullmann, *The Carolingian Renaissance and the Idea of Kingship* (London, 1969), 7, 22.

15. Henry Mayr-Harting, 'Charlemagne, the Saxons, and the Imperial Coronation of 800', *English Historical Review* 111, no. 444 (1996): 1113–1133.

16. Ernst Tremp et al., *The Abbey Library of St Gall* (St Gallen, 2020), 15.

17. For the gnawing, see MGH Poetae 2, 271; see further, Jennifer M. Feltman, 'Charlemagne's Sin, the Last Judgment, and the New Theology of Penance at Chartres', *Studies in Iconography* 35 (2014): 121–164; Janet L. Nelson, 'Women at the Court of Charlemagne: A Case of Monstrous Regiment?', in Nelson, *The Frankish World, 750–900* (London, 1992), 223–242; Johannes Fried, *Charlemagne* (Cambridge, MA, and London, 2016), 515.

CHAPTER 3. AVARS AND SLAVS: DESTRUCTION AND CONVERSION

1. For Frankochorion, see György Györffy, 'Das Güterverzeichnis des griechischen Klosters Szávaszentdemeter (Sremska Mitrovica) aus dem 12. Jahrhundert', *Studia Slavica* 5 (1959): 9–74 (10–14); Gyula Moravcsik, *Az Árpád-kori magyar történet bizánci forrásai*, 2nd ed. (Budapest, 1988), 168.

2. C. Mierow, ed., *The Gothic History of Jordanes* (Princeton, 1915), 59.

3. M. Mielnik-Sikorska et al., 'The History of Slavs Inferred from Complete Mitochondrial Genome Sequences', *PLoS ONE* 8, no. 1 (January 2013): 1–11.

4. Angus Maddison, *Contours of the World Economy, 1–2030 AD* (Oxford, 2007), 232.

5. Martyn Rady, 'The Slavs, Avars and Hungarians', in *The Cambridge History of War*, ed. D. A. Graff and A. Curry, vol. 2 (Cambridge, 2020), 133–150 (139–140).

6. *The Fourth Book of the Chronicle of Fredegar*, ed. J. M. Wallace-Hadrill (London and Edinburgh, 1960), 39–40.

7. *Einhard and Notker the Stammerer: Two Lives of Charlemagne*, trans. D. Ganz (London, 2008), 27, 87; *The Russian Primary Chronicle*, ed. and trans. S. H. Cross (Cambridge, MA, 1930), 141.

8. For shepherding peoples, see Arnold J. Toynbee, *A Study of History*, vol. 3 (Oxford, 1934), 22; Helen D. Donoghue et al., 'A Migration-Driven Model for the Historical Spread of Leprosy in Medieval Eastern and Central Europe', *Infection, Genetics and Evolution* 31 (2015): 250–256; Jesper L. Boldsen, 'Leprosy in the Early Medieval Lauchheim Community', *American Journal of Physical Anthropology* 135 (2008): 301–310.

9. For the Avar origin of the treasure, see Falko Daim et al., eds., *Der Goldschatz von Sânnicolau Mare* (Mainz, 2015).

10. *Carolingian Chronicles*, trans. Bernhard Walter Scholz (Ann Arbor, 1972), 111–122; György Dénes, 'A bolgárok hódításai és telepítései a Kárpát-medencében a magyar honfoglalás előtt', in *Néprajz—Muzeológia*, ed. A. Tóth (Miskolc, 2012), 52–64 (57–58).

11. Erwin Herrmann, *Slawisch-germanische Beziehungen im südostdeutschen Raum* (Munich, 1965), 219–221.

12. Marvin Kantor, *Medieval Slavic Lives of Saints and Princes* (Ann Arbor, 1983), 65, 111.

13. Kantor, *Medieval Slavic Lives of Saints and Princes*, 65.

14. Eric J. Goldberg, *Struggle for Empire: Kingship and Conflict Under Louis the German, 817–876* (Ithaca and London, 2006), 286–288.

15. For the Glagolitic in Croatia, see Julia Verkholantsev, *The Slavic Letters of St. Jerome* (DeKalb, IL, 2014), 34–62.

16. For 'men of a different language', see Anthony Kaldellis, *Hellenism in Byzantium: The Transformations of Greek Identity and the Reception of the Classical Tradition* (Cambridge and New York: 2007), 357.

CHAPTER 4. THE RETURN OF THE HUNS, SLAVE STATES, AND THE SHAPING OF CENTRAL EUROPE

1. Norbert Kersken, 'Nationale Geschichtsschreibung im östlichen Mitteleuropa', *Mediaevalia Historica Bohemica* 4 (1995): 148–170.

2. 'Nithard's Histories', 3 (830), in *Carolingian Chronicles*, ed. Bernhard Walter Scholz (Ann Arbor, 1972), 131.

3. Rudolf Schieffer, 'Ludwig der Fromme. Zur Entstehung eines karolingischen Herrscherbeinamens', *Frühmittelalterliche Studien* 16, no. 1 (1982): 58–73; Courtney M. Booker, *Past Convictions: The Penance of Louis the Pious and the Decline of the Carolingians* (Philadelphia, 2009), 50.

4. Latin text in Courtney M. Booker, 'The Public Penance of Louis the Pious', *Viator* 39, no. 2 (2008): 1–20 (18).

5. For the slicing up of the empire, see 'Nithard's Histories', 7 (839), in Scholz, *Carolingian Chronicles*, 139.

6. C. A. Macartney, *The Magyars in the Ninth Century* (Cambridge, 1930), 71.

7. Peter B. Golden, *An Introduction to the History of the Uralic Peoples* (Wiesbaden, 1992), 258–260.

8. Péter Király, 'A magyarok népneve a történeti forrásokban és a szomszédos népek névhasználatában', *Életünk* 35, no. 1 (1997): 94–127 (114–115).

9. S. MacLean, ed., *History and Politics in Late Carolingian and Ottonian Europe: The Chronicle of Regino of Prüm and Adalbert of Magdeburg* (Manchester and New York, 2009), 232.

10. Archdeacon Thomas of Split, *History of the Bishops of Salona and Split*, ed. D. Karbić et al. (Budapest and New York, 2006), 63; MGH SS 1, 54, 77. See also Timothy Reuter, *Germany in the Early Middle Ages c. 800–1056* (London and New York, 1991), 128.

11. For Henry's character, see Widukind of Corvey, *Deeds of the Saxons*, ed. B. S. Bachrach and D. Bachrach (Washington, DC, 2014), 57–58 (1.39).

12. Liudprand of Cremona, *The Embassy to Constantinople*, 10 (1.5); Márton Tősér, 'Az arkadiopolisi csata—az utolsó kalandozó hadjárat, 970', *Hadtörténelmi Közlemények* 117, no. 2 (2004): 595–611.

13. Andrzej Buko, *The Archaeology of Early Medieval Poland* (Leiden and Boston, 2008), 195–196.

14. Michael McCormick, 'New Light on the "Dark Ages": How the Slave Trade Fuelled the Carolingian Economy', *Past and Present* 177 (2002): 17–54 (44).

15. *Quellen zur deutschen Volkskunde*, ed. V. von Geramb and L. Mackensen, vol. 1 (Berlin and Leipzig, 1927), 12. For Poland, see Marek Jankowiak, 'Dirhams for Slaves. Investigating the Slavic Slave Trade in the Tenth Century' (paper delivered to the Medieval Seminar, All Souls College, 27 February 2012).

16. Michael McCormick, *Origins of the European Economy: Communications and Commerce, A.D. 300–900* (Cambridge, 2001), 763; Alice Rio, *Slavery After Rome, 500–1100* (Oxford, 2017), 105n100.

17. Undine Ott, 'Europas Sklavinnen und Sklaven im Mittelalter', *WerkstattGeschichte*, nos. 66–67 (2014): 31–53 (49); Mateusz Bogucki, 'Forged Coins in Early Medieval Poland', *Polish Numismatic News* 8 (2009): 209–236.

18. Adelbert Davids, ed., *The Empress Theophano: Byzantium and the West at the Turn of the First Millennium* (Cambridge, 1995), 54–55.

19. Andreas Ranft, ed., *Der Hoftag in Quedlinburg 973. Von den historischen Wurzeln zum Neuen Europa* (Berlin, 2006), 4–5, 21, 24.

20. Gerd Althoff, *Otto III* (University Park, PA, 2003), 105, 125.

21. György Györffy, *István király és műve* (Budapest, 1977), 137; for Byzantine religious influence in Hungary, see Gyula Moravcsik, 'The Role of the Byzantine Church in Medieval Hungary', *American Slavic and East European Review* 6, nos. 3–4 (1947): 134–151; for the burying alive, see the curious conclusion of the Anonymus Chronicle (c. 1200) given in Martyn Rady, 'The *Gesta Hungarorum* of Anonymus, the Anonymous Notary of King Béla: A Translation', *SEER* 87, no. 4 (2009): 681–727 (727).

CHAPTER 5. THE MAKING OF THE HOLY ROMAN EMPIRE AND CENTRAL EUROPE'S WILD EAST

1. David Bachrach, 'Toward an Appraisal of the Wealth of the Ottonian Kings of Germany, 919-1024', *Viator* 44, no. 2 (2013): 1–28.

2. MGH Const. 1, 632–633; MGH SS 16, 347.

3. Claudia Moddelmog, 'Stiftung oder Eigenkirche? Der Umgang mit Forschungskonzepten und die sächsischen Frauenklöster im 9. und 10. Jahrhundert', in *Gestiftete Zukunft im mittelalterlichen Europa*, ed. W. Huschner and F. Rexroth (Berlin, 2008), 215–243.

4. For 'many loathsome acts of adultery', see MGH Ldl. 1, 584; for the churches as their own, see Susan Wood, *The Proprietary Church in the West* (Oxford, 2006), 855.

5. See here Hans Delbrück, *Ueber die Glaubwürdigkeit Lamberts von Hersfeld* (Cologne, 1873).

6. Anon., 'Life of the Emperor Henry IV', 7, given in *Imperial Lives and Letters of the Eleventh Century*, ed. Theodore E. Mommsen and Karl F. Morrison (New York, 2000), 117; I. S. Robinson, *Henry IV of Germany, 1056–1106* (Cambridge, 2000), 230–231.

7. Eike von Repgow, *The Saxon Mirror*, ed. Maria Dobozy (Philadelphia, 1999), 133 (III. 65).

8. Wilhelm Kohl, *Das Bistum Münster* (*Germania Sacra* 37, no. 1) (Berlin and New York, 1999), 394–395.

9. John B. Freed, 'The Origins of the European Nobility: The Problem of the Ministerials', *Viator* 7 (1976): 211–241.

10. John B. Freed, *Frederick Barbarossa: The Prince and the Myth* (New Haven and London, 2016), 100.

11. Len Scales, *The Shaping of German Identity: Authority and Crisis, 1245–1414* (Cambridge, 2012), 234.

12. See here the website EBIDAT—Die Burgendatenbank (www.ebidat .de/ebidat.html).

13. MGH SS rer. Germ. 33, 60; Eric Christiansen, *The Northern Crusades: The Baltic and the Catholic Frontier 1100–1525* (London and Basingstoke, 1980), 17.

14. Helmold of Bosau, *The Chronicle of the Slavs*, ed. F. J. Tschan (New York, 1966), 45–49; Dmitrij Mishin, 'Ibrahim Ibn-Ya'qub At-Turtushi's Account of the Slavs from the Middle of the Tenth Century', *Annual of Medieval Studies at CEU* 25 (2019): 184–199. For the Pomeranian dog, see Hans Räber, *Enzyklopädie der Rassenhunde*, vol. 1 (Stuttgart, 2001), 514–515.

15. P. F. Kehr, *Urkundenbuch des Hochstifts Merseburg*, vol. 1 (Halle, 1899), 75–77. See also Mihai Dragnea, 'Crusade and Colonization in the Wendish

Territories in the Early Twelfth Century: An Analysis of the So-Called Magde-burg Letter of 1108', *Mediaevalia* 42 (2021): 41–61.

16. MGH SS 12, 850; Robert Bartlett, 'The Conversion of a Pagan Soci-ety in the Middle Ages', *History* 70, no. 229 (1985): 185–201.

17. Wincenty Kadłubek, *De origine et rebus gestis Polonorum*, ed. A. Muł-kowski (Cracow, 1864), 208.

18. For Albrecht's title, see Lutz Partenheimer, *Albrecht der Bär. Gründer der Mark Brandenburg und des Fürstentums Anhalt*, 2nd ed. (Potsdam, 2016), 130, 307. For nobles in Albrecht's service, see O. Von Heinemann, *Albrecht der Bär. Eine quellenmassige Darstellung seines Lebens* (Darmstadt, 1864), 224–226; for population figures, see Charles Higounet, *Les Allemands en Europe centrale et orientale au Moyen Age* (Paris, 1989), 105–106.

19. Helmold of Bosau, *Chronicle of the Slavs*, 236.

20. Kyra T. Inachin, *Die Geschichte Pommerns* (Rostock, 2008), 17–18.

CHAPTER 6. THE MONGOL-TATARS, NEW CITIES, AND NEW KNIGHTS

1. Cosmas of Prague, *The Chronicle of the Czechs*, ed. János M. Bak and Pavlína Rychterová (Budapest and New York, 2020), 181–183 (bk. 2, chap. 10); D. Kunčer, ed., *Anonymi Descriptio Europae Orientalis* (Belgrade, 2013), 133–148.

2. Kunčer, *Anonymi Descriptio Europae Orientalis*, 139, 146, 148; C. C. Mierow, ed., *The Deeds of Frederick Barbarossa by Otto of Freising* (New York, 1953), 66, 175; G. W. Leibnitz, *Alberici monachi Trium fontium Chronicon* (Leipzig, 1698), 556.

3. Balázs Nagy, 'The Towns of Medieval Hungary in the Reports of For-eign Travellers', in *Segregation—Integration—Assimilation: Religious and Ethnic Groups in the Medieval Towns of Central and Eastern Europe*, ed. D. Keene et al. (Farnham and Burlington, VT, 2009), 169–178.

4. C. C. Mierow, ed., *The Deeds of Frederick Barbarossa by Otto of Freising* (New York, 1953), 67. See also MGH Ldl. 3, 463.

5. Cosmas of Prague, *Chronicle of the Czechs*, 27 (bk. 1, chap. 5); Eduard Mühle, *Die Piasten. Polen im Mittelalter* (Munich, 2011), 59.

6. Christian Lübke, *Arbeit und Wirtschaft im östlichen Mitteleuropa. Die Spezialisierung menschlicher Tätigkeit im Spiegel der hochmittelalterlichen Toponomie in den Herrschaftsgebieten von Piasten, Premysliden und Arpaden* (Stuttgart, 1991), 9. For the German lands, see Bruno Krüger, *Die Kietzsied-lungen im nördlichen Mitteleuropa* (Berlin 1962).

7. S. A. M. Adshead, *Central Asia in World History* (Basingstoke and New York, 1993), 61.

8. For the English envoy, see Gabriel Ronay, *The Tartar Khan's Englishman* (London, 1978).

9. Martyn Rady, 'The Mongol Invasion of Hungary', *Medieval World*, November/December 1991, 39–46.

10. MGH SS 17, 394. For a contemporary account of the Mongol-Tatar occupation of Hungary, see *Anonymus and Master Roger*, ed. J. M. Bak, M. Rady, and L. Veszprémy (Budapest and New York, 2010), 132–228. For evidence of destruction, see Mária Vargha, 'Traces of Destruction: The Archaeological Remains of the Mongol Invasion of Hungary', *Acta Archaeologica Carpathica* 52 (2017): 235–258; József Laszlovszky et al., 'Contextualizing the Mongol Invasion of Hungary in 1241–42', *Hungarian Historical Review* 7, no. 3 (2018): 419–450.

11. Martyn Rady, *Nobility, Land and Service in Medieval Hungary* (Basingstoke and New York, 2000), 28.

12. Martyn Rady, 'The Title of New Donation in Medieval Hungarian Law', *SEER* 79, no. 4 (2001): 638–652.

13. J. F. Willems, ed., *Oude Vlaemsche Liederen* (Ghent, 1848), 35–37.

14. For Poland and the Black Death, see Ole J. Benedictow, *The Complete History of the Black Death* (Woodbridge, 2021), 585–603.

15. Martyn Rady, 'The German Settlement in Central and Eastern Europe During the High Middle Ages', in *The German Lands and Eastern Europe*, ed. Roger Bartlett and Karen Schönwälder (Basingstoke and New York, 1999), 11–47.

16. Karl Lachmann, *Die Gedichte Walthers von der Vogelweide*, 8th ed. (Berlin, 1923), 37. See also Edwin H. Zeydel, *Ruodlieb: The Earliest Courtly Novel* (Chapel Hill, 1959), 27.

17. Benedykt Zientara, 'Die deutschen Einwanderer in Polen vom 12. bis zum 14. Jahrhundert', *Vorträge und Forschungen* 18 (1975): 333–348.

18. Zoltán Tóth, 'La boucle de Kigyóspuszta', *Archaeológiai Értesítő* 71 (1943): 174–184, and plate 32.

CHAPTER 7. DYNASTIC CHANGE, CHARLES IV OF BOHEMIA, AND THE PROPHETS OF THE ANTICHRIST

1. For dynastic failure, see Martyn Rady, 'Foreword', in *Social and Political Elites in Eastern and Central Europe (15th–18th Centuries)*, ed. C. Luca et al. (London, 2015), ix–xv (xi).

2. MGH SS 25, 350; H. Pabst, *Annalen und Chronik von Kolmar* (Berlin, 1867), x.

3. Armin Wolf, *Die Entstehung des Kurfürstenkollegs 1198–1298* (Idstein, 1998), 50–54.

4. Barbara Reynolds, *Dante: The Poet, the Thinker, the Man* (London and New York, 2006), 234–242.

5. Quotation from Dante, *Paradiso*, 30.137, in *The Divine Comedy*, ed. R. Kirkpatrick (London, 2012), 467.

6. Jürgen Dendorfer, 'Der König von Böhmen als Vasall des Reiches?', in *Friedrich Barbarossa in den Nationalgeschichten Deutschlands und Ostmitteleuropas*, ed. K. Görich and M. Wihoda (Cologne, Weimar, and Vienna, 2017), 229–284 (232–246); Volker Press, 'Böhmen und das Reich in der frühen Neuzeit', *Bohemia* 35, no. 1 (1994): 63–74.

7. Jean Froissart, *Chronicles*, ed. G. Brereton (London, 1978), 89–90; *Fontes rerum Bohemicarum*, J. Emler, vol. 4 (Prague, 1884), 514 (Beneš of Weitmil).

8. David Charles Mengel, 'Bones, Stones, and Brothels: Religion and Topography in Prague Under Emperor Charles IV (1346–78)' (PhD thesis, Notre Dame, IN, 2003), 267–324.

9. Julia Verkholantsev, *The Slavic Letters of St Jerome: The History of the Legend and Its Legacy* (DeKalb, IL, 2014), 78–79.

10. G. Dobner, ed., *Monumenta Historica Boemiae*, vol. 2 (Prague, 1768), 79–282.

11. The text of the 1356 Golden Bull is given in English translation in *A Source Book for Mediaeval History*, ed. O. J. Thatcher and E. H. McNeal (New York, 1905), 284–298.

12. Hans Hubert Hofmann, 'Karl IV. und die politische Landbrücke von Prag nach Frankfurt am Main', in *Zwischen Frankfurt und Prag* (Munich, 1963), 51–74. For Charles's itinerary, see Eberhard von Holtz, *Itinerar Kaiser Karls IV (1346–1378)* (Berlin, 2013), http://www.regesta-imperii.de /fileadmin/user_upload/downloads/ri_viii_itinerar.pdf.

13. Len Scales, 'Wenceslas Looks Out: Monarchy, Locality, and the Symbolism of Power in Fourteenth-Century Bavaria', *Central European History* 52 (2019): 179–210.

14. Paul Crossley and Zoë Opačić, 'Prague as a New Capital', in *Prague: The Crown of Bohemia, 1347–1437*, ed. B. Boehm and J. Fajt (New Haven and London, 2005), 59–73.

15. Eleanor Janega, 'Jan Milíč of Kroměříž and Emperor Charles IV: Preaching, Power, and the Church of Prague' (PhD thesis, University College London, 2015), 71–72.

16. I. Hlaváček and Z. Hledíková, eds., *Protocollum visitationis archidiaconatus Pragensisannis 1379–1382* (Prague, 1973), discussed in Eleanor Janega, 'Suspect Women: Prostitution, Reputation, and Gossip in Fourteenth-century Prague', in *Same Bodies, Different Women: 'Other' Women in the Middle Ages*

and the Early Modern Period, ed. C. Mielke and A. Znorovszky (Budapest, 2018), 40–69.

17. Mengel, 'Bones, Stones, and Brothels', 211–262.

18. Eleanor Janega, 'Jan Milíč of Kroměříž and Emperor Charles IV: Preaching, Power, and the Church of Prague' (PhD thesis, University College London, 2015), 8–63.

19. For plague pits, see Mark Whelan, 'From Chronicles to Plague Columns: The Black Death in Bohemia', *The Friends of Czech Heritage Newsletter* 23 (2020): 7–9.

20. Jan Hus, *De Ecclesia. The Church*, ed. D. S. Schaff (New York, 1915), 140–141; Pavlína Cermanová, 'Constructing the Apocalypse: Connections Between English and Bohemian Apocalyptic Thinking', in *Europe After Wyclif*, ed. J. P. Hornbeck and M. Van Dussen (New York, 2017), 66–88.

21. *RTA*, 3 (Munich, 1877), 255–264 (in German and Latin versions); Maria E. Dorninger, 'Liebe und Erotik in mittelalterlichen Handschriften. Geschichten und Bilder (in) der Bibel', in *Liebe und Erotik im Mittelalter*, ed. Ulrich Müller (Salzburg, 2006), 4–27, online resource.

22. David Short, 'The Broader Czech (and Slovak) Contribution to the English Lexicon', *Central Europe* 1, no. 1 (2003): 19–39 (20); Thomas A. Fudge, 'Žižka's Drum: The Political Uses of Popular Religion', *Central European History* 36, no. 4 (2003): 546–569.

23. Franz Machilek, 'Hus und die Hussiten in Franken', *Jahrbuch für fränkische Landesforschung* 51 (1991): 15–37; Ferdinand Seibt, 'Hus und wir Deutschen', *Kirche im Osten* 13 (1970): 74–103 (79–82); Martyn Rady, 'Jiskra, Hussitism and Slovakia', in *Confession and Nation in the Era of Reformations*, ed. E. Doležalová and J. Pánek (Prague, 2011), 77–90 (87–89); Rebecca Haynes, *Moldova: A History* (London, 2020), 24–25.

24. Alexandra Kaar, 'Embargoing "Heretics" in Fifteenth-Century Central Europe: The Case of Hussite Bohemia', *Journal of Medieval History* 46, no. 4 (2020): 478–497.

CHAPTER 8. COUNCILS, DIETS, AND THE CONFUSION OF THE LAWS

1. *Monumenta Medii Aevi Historica res gestas Polonias illustrantia*, vol. 1 (Cracow, 1874), 56, 73, 61, 86, 107, etc.

2. Cosmas of Prague, *The Chronicle of the Czechs*, ed. J. M. Bak and P. Rychterová (Budapest and New York, 2020), 179 (2.8).

3. *Urkunden-Buch des Landes ob der Enns*, vol. 2 (Vienna, 1856), 399–401.

4. Quotation from MGH Const. 2, 609; for Bohemia, see H. Jireček, *Svod Zákonův Slovanských* (Prague, 1880), 488–492; for Hungary, see DRMH, 1, 158–171; for Bavaria, see Karl Bosl, 'Aus den Anfängen der Landständischen

Bewegung und Verfassung. Der Vilshofener Vertrag von 1293', in *Wirtschaft, Geschichte und Wirtschaftsgeschichte*, ed. Wilhelm Abel et al. (Stuttgart, 1966), 8–27; for the Tyrol, see Hannes Obermaier, 'Tiroler Landrecht', in *Eines Fürsten Traum. Meinhard II.—Das Werden Tirols* (Dorf Tirol and Innsbruck, 1995), 131–133. For the Statute in Favour of the Princes, see MGH Const. 2, 211–213, 418–420.

5. MGH Const. 2, 420; *The Liber Augustalis or Constitutions of Melfi*, ed. J. M. Powell (New York, 1971), 11.

6. MGH Const. 3, 50; MGH LL 2, 341.

7. Quotation from *RTA*, 1, 34.

8. Martyn Rady, 'Hungary and the Golden Bull of 1222', *Banatica* 24, no. 2 (2014): 87–108.

9. For Poland, see Maurice Michael, ed., *The Annals of Jan Długosz* (Chichester, 1997), 510–511 (1452); for violence in Hungary, see *Codex epistolaris saeculi decimi quinti*, ed. Anatol Lewicki, vol. 3 (Cracow, 1894), 158; for bishops, see Heinrich Schoppmeyer, 'Die Entstehung der Land-stände im Hochstift Paderborn', *Westfälische Zeitschrift* 136 (1986): 249–310 (266).

10. For peasant participation more generally, see F. L. Carsten, *Princes and Parliaments in Germany: From the Fifteenth to the Eighteenth Centuries* (Oxford, 1959), 424–425. For cities, see Gabriele Annas, *Hoftag, Gemeiner Tag, Reichstag. Studien zur strukturellen Entwicklung deutscher Reichsversammlungen des späten Mittelalters*, vol. 1 (Göttingen, 2004), 93–94.

11. Peter Štih, *The Middle Ages Between the Eastern Alps and the Northern Adriatic* (Leiden and Boston, 2010), 380–407.

12. Christopher Nicholson, 'The Bohemian Diet in the Jagiellonian Period (1471–1526)', in *Between Worlds: The Age of the Jagiellonians*, ed. Florin Ardelean et al. (Frankfurt, 2013), 140–156; Martyn Rady, 'Rethinking Jagiełło Hungary', *Central Europe* 3, no. 1 (2005): 3–18; Michael, *Annals of Jan Długosz*, 529.

13. *RTA*, 2, 452; *RTA*, 9, 599–603; Annas, *Hoftag, Gemeiner Tag, Reichstag*, 1: 165–167.

14. For membership of the imperial diet in 1521, see Karl Zeumer, *Quellensammlung zur Geschichte der deutschen Reichsverfassung in Mittelalter und Neuzeit*, 2nd ed. (Tübingen, 1913), 313–317.

15. Eberhard Isenmann, *Die deutsche Stadt im Mittelalter 1150–1550*, 2nd ed. (Cologne, Weimar, and Vienna, 2014), 310–311; Beat Kümin, 'Rural Autonomy and Popular Politics in Imperial Villages', *German History* 33, no. 2 (2015): 194–213.

16. Anna Sucheni-Grabowska, 'The Origin and Development of the Polish Parliamentary System', in *Constitution and Reform in Eighteenth-Century Poland*, ed. Samuel Fiszman (Bloomington and Indianapolis, 1997), 13–50.

17. Kenneth J. Dillon, *King and Estates in the Bohemian Lands 1526–1564* (Brussels, 1976), 21.

18. Julia Burkhardt, 'Procedure, Rules and Meaning of Political Assemblies in Late Medieval Central Europe', *Parliaments, Estates and Representation* 35, no. 2 (2015): 153–170.

19. Stephen Werbőczy, *Tripartitum* (1517), 1. 3. 6 (DRMH, 5, 51).

20. Jan Łaski, *Commune incliti Poloniae privilegium* (Cracow, 1506). For confusion of the laws, see Jan Herburt de Fulstein, *Statuta Regni Poloniae in ordinem alphabeti digesta* (Zamość, 1597), *praefatio* (unpaginated).

CHAPTER 9. CITIES, VILLAGES, AND FREEDOMS: FROM FRISIA TO TRANSYLVANIA

1. John Watts, *The Making of Polities: Europe, 1300–1500* (Cambridge, 2009).

2. Quotation from Karl Mollay, ed., *Das Ofner Stadtrecht. Eine deutschsprachige Rechtssammlung des 15. Jahrhundert aus Ungarn* (Budapest, 1959), 67.

3. Dagmer M. H. Hemmie, *Ungeordnete Unzucht. Prostitution im Hanseraum (12.–16. Jahrhundert)* (Cologne, Weimar, and Vienna, 2007), 157.

4. Eberhard Isenmann, *Die deutsche Stadt im Mittelalter 1150–1550*, 2nd ed. (Cologne, Weimar, and Vienna, 2014), 314–326. Quotation from Julius Weizsäcker, *Der Rheinische Bund 1254* (Tübingen, 1879), 139.

5. For the spread of Magdeburg law in Central Europe, see now the interactive website Das Magdeburger Recht. Baustein des modernen Europa at Magdeburg-law.com.

6. Ulrich Falk, 'Der Wald der Konsilien. Rechtsgutachten in der Gerichtspraxis der frühen Neuzeit', *Rechtshistorisches Journal* 20 (2001): 290–310.

7. Quotation from Thomas Maissen, *Geschichte der Schweiz* (Baden/Schweiz, 2010), 30.

8. Quotation from *Sammlung Schweizerischer Rechtsquellen*, series 3: Luzern, vol. 2.2, *Vogtei Willisau*, ed. August Bickel (Basle, 2002), 73.

9. George Cushing, 'Hungarian Cultural Traditions in Transylvania', in *Historians and the History of Transylvania*, ed. László Péter (Boulder and New York, 1992), 113–131.

10. For the Orthodox population, see Ioan-Aurel Pop, *'De manibus Vallacorum scismaticorum': Romanians and Power in the Mediaeval Kingdom of Hungary* (Frankfurt a/M, 2013), 389–391.

11. Ştefan Pascu, *Voievodatul Transilvaniei*, vol. 3 (Cluj-Napoca, 1986), 553.

12. György Székely, 'Huszitizmus és a magyar nép', *Századok* 90 (1956): 331–367 (332–335, 341–343).

13. Henrik Marczali, *A magyar történet kútfőinek kézikönyve* (Budapest, 1902), 271.

14. Joseph Bedeus von Scharberg, *Die Verfassung des Grossfürstenthums Siebenbürgen* (Vienna, 1844), 21–26. See also Martyn Rady, 'Voivode and Regnum: Transylvania's Place in the Medieval Kingdom of Hungary', in *Historians and the History of Transylvania*, ed. László Péter (Boulder and New York, 1992), 87–101.

15. W. J. Buma and W. Ebel, eds., *Das Fivelgoer Recht* (Göttingen, 1972), 75–135; MGH Fontes iuris 12 (Lex Frisionum), 65–98; for mummified corpses, see Thomas de Cantimpré, *Bonum Universale de apibus* (Douai, 1627), 120.

16. Johannes A. Mol, 'Gallows in Late Medieval Frisia', *Amsterdamer Beiträge zur älteren Germanistik* 64, no. 1 (2007): 263–297.

17. Henry Koehn, *Sylt. Ein Führer durch die Inselwelt*, 5th ed. (Berlin and New York, 1975), 68; for Frisian 'insolence' in refusing to pay imperial taxes, see Rolf H. Bremmer, *An Introduction to Old Frisian* (Amsterdam and Philadelphia, PA, 2009), 143.

18. Oebele Vries, 'Das Friesische im Mittelalter', in *Handbook of Frisian Studies*, ed. H. H. Munske (Tübingen, 2001), 538–550.

19. Peter Blickle, *Kommunalismus. Skizzen einer gesellschaftlichen Organisationsform*, vol. 2 (Munich, 2000), 71–85.

20. Clemens Bergstedt et al., *Die Mark Brandenburg im späten Mittelalter* (Berlin, 2011), 293.

21. Adolf Stölzel, *Die Entwicklung der gelehrten Rechtsprechung*, vol. 1 (Berlin, 1901), 503; Fritz Kern, *Kingship and Law in the Middle Ages* (Clark, NJ, 2005), 179 (first published in 1956).

22. Walther Maas, 'Zur Entwicklung der polnischen Agrarstruktur vom 15. bis 18. Jahrhundert', *Vierteljahrschrift für Sozial- und Wirtschaftsgeschichte* 20, nos. 3–4 (1928): 490–498.

23. Ladislas Reymont, *The Peasants: Autumn* (New York, 1925), 58; Sheilagh Ogilvie, 'Communities and the "Second Serfdom" in Early Modern Bohemia', *Past and Present* 187 (2005): 69–119 (111–112).

24. '. . . ne muge a bethe ni a bedde, a uidse ni a ueine, a uueie ni a uuetere ni a glede ise, a huse ni a godeshuse, bi fiure ni bi sinre wiuue wesa.' Cited in Rolf H. Bremmer, 'The Orality of Old Frisian Law Texts', *Amsterdamer Beiträge zur älteren Germanistik* 73, no. 1 (2014): 1–48 (12).

25. Thomas S. B. Johnston, 'The Old Frisian Law Manuscripts and Texts', in *Handbook of Frisian Studies*, ed. Horst Haide Munske (Tübingen, 2001), 571–587.

26. Martyn Rady, 'Core and Periphery: Eastern Europe', in *National Histories and European History*, ed. Mary Fulbrook (London, 1993), 163–182 (168–170).

27. Hermann Wiessner, *Sachinhalt und wirtschaftliche Bedeutung der Weistümer im Deutschen Kulturgebiet* (Baden and Vienna, 1934), 45.

28. Edgar Melton, '*Gutsherrschaft* in East Elbian Germany and Livonia, 1500–1800', *Central European History* 21, no. 4 (1988): 315–349.

CHAPTER 10. OLD PRUSSIA, THE ADVENTURES OF HENRY BOLINGBROKE, AND THE UNION OF POLAND AND LITHUANIA

1. The illustrations for the Czech manuscript are in the British Library (Add. MS 24189) and available digitally. See www.bl.uk/manuscripts/.

2. Alan V. Murray, 'The Saracens of the Baltic: Pagan and Christian Lithuanians in the Perception of English and French Crusaders to Late Medieval Prussia', *Journal of Baltic Studies* 41, no. 4 (2010): 413–429.

3. Maciej Miechowita (Matthias de Mechow), *Tractatus de duabus Sarmatiis* (Cracow, 1518, unpaginated), 2. 1. 3; for cannibalism, see K. Höhlbaum, ed., *Die jüngere livländische Reimchronik* (Leipzig, 1872), 1–2.

4. Jos Schaeken, 'Observations on the Old Prussian Basel Epigram', *International Journal of Slavic Linguistics and Poetics* 44–45 (2002–2003): 331–342.

5. M. Fischer, ed., *The Chronicle of Prussia by Nicolaus von Jeroschin* (London and New York, 2010), 63. See also Christopher Hartknoch, *Dissertationes Historicae de variis rebus Prussicis* (Frankfurt and Leipzig, 1679), 109–179.

6. J. A. Brundage, ed., *The Chronicle of Henry of Livonia* (New York, 2003), 91–92.

7. Andreas Lorck, *Hermann von Salza. Sein Itinerar* (Kiel, 1880).

8. Harald Zimmermann, *Der Deutsche Orden in Siebenbürgen*, 2nd ed. (Cologne, Weimar, and Vienna, 2011), 191.

9. *RI* V, 1, 1n1598.

10. Gregory Leighton, 'Did the Teutonic Order Create a Sacred Landscape in Thirteenth-Century Prussia?', *Journal of Medieval History* 44, no. 4 (2018): 457–483.

11. Seweryn Szczepański, 'Old Prussian "Baba" Stones: An Overview of the History of Research and Reception', *Analecta Archaeologica Ressoviensia* 10 (2015): 313–363; Anon., *Gottesidee und Cultus bei den alten Preussen* (Berlin, 1870), 71.

12. S. C. Rowell, 'Unexpected Contacts: Lithuanians at Western Courts, c. 1316–c. 1400', *English Historical Review* 111, no. 442 (1996): 557–577 (564).

13. Werner Paravicini, *Die Preussenreisen des europäischen Adels*, vol. 1 (Sigmaringen, 1989), 147–150.

14. Hartmut Kugler, 'Die Livländische Reimchronik des 13. Jahrhunderts', *Latvijas Zinâtòu Akadçmijas Vçstis* 9 (1993): 22–30 (25); Jürgen Wolf, 'König Artus in Preussenland', in *Neue Studien zur Literatur im Deutschen Orden*, ed. A. Mentzel-Reuters and B. Jähnig (Stuttgart, 2014), 79–92.

15. Lucy Toulmin Smith, ed., *Expeditions to Prussia and the Holy Land Made by Henry Earl of Derby* (London, 1894). See also, F. R. H. Du Boulay, 'Henry of Derby's Expeditions to Prussia', in *The Reign of Richard II*, ed. Du Boulay and C. M. Barron (London, 1971), 153–172.

16. 'They stood five weeks': *Scriptores rerum Prussicarum*, ed. T. Hirsch et al., vol. 2 (Leipzig, 1863), 643.

17. *Scriptores rerum Prussicarum*, ed. T. Hirsch et al., vol. 3 (Leipzig, 1866), 448.

18. Crimes done by knights are given in detail in *Lites ac res gestae inter Polonos Ordinemque Cruciferorum*, vol. 1, ed. T. Działyński (Poznań, 1855).

19. Maurice Michael, ed., *The Annals of Jan Długosz* (Chichester, 1997), 347.

20. Michael, *Annals of Jan Długosz*, 467.

21. Paul Srodecki, 'Der Traktatenstreit zwischen dem Deutschen Orden und dem Königreich Polen auf dem Konstanzer Konzil', *Schweizerische Zeitschrift für Religions- und Kulturgeschichte* 109 (2015): 47–65 (60).

22. Nora Berend, *At the Gate of Christendom: Jews, Muslims and 'Pagans' in Medieval Hungary, c. 1000–c. 1300* (Cambridge, 2001), 163–171; Paul Srodecki, 'The Use of the "Christian Outpost": Propaganda to Legitimise the Conquest of Galicia-Volhynia Under the Two Last Piast Kings of Poland, 1323–1370', *Colloquia Russica* 2 (2012): 114–119.

23. Paul Srodecki, 'Der Traktatenstreit zwischen dem Deutschen Orden und dem Königreich Polen auf dem Konstanzer Konzil', *Schweizerische Zeitschrift für Religions- und Kulturgeschichte* 109 (2015): 47–65 (54, 60).

24. Janusz Tazbir, 'From Antemurale to Przedmurze, the History of the Term', *Odrodzenie i reformacja w Polsce* 61, no. 2 (2017): 67–87.

25. *Joannis Długosz Senioris Opera Omnia*, ed. A Przezdziecki, vol. 14 (Cracow, 1878), 360 (Annales, 12:1462); *The Correspondence of Erasmus: Letters 1523 to 1524*, ed. R. A. B. Mynors and A. Dalzell (Toronto, Buffalo, and London, 1992), 104; Niccolò Machiavelli, *The Discourses*, 2. 8, ed. B. Crick (London, 2003), 297–298.

26. Andreas Angyal, *Die slawische Barockwelt* (Leipzig, 1961), 70; Stephen Werbőczy, *Tripartitum*, Serenissimo principi (DRMH 5, 12–13).

CHAPTER 11. MERCHANTS, THE HANSEATIC LEAGUE, AND THE FUGGERS

1. Peter Spufford, *Handbook of Medieval Exchange* (London, 1986), xxxvi; Joseph A. Amato, *On Foot: A History of Walking* (New York, 2004), 42–71.

2. Marcus Pitcaithly, 'Piracy and Anglo-Hanseatic Relations, 1385–1420', in *Roles of the Sea in Medieval England*, ed. R. Gorski (Woodbridge, 2012), 125–145; David K. Bjork, 'Piracy in the Baltic, 1375–1398', *Speculum* 18, no. 1 (1943): 39–68.

3. Johannes Müller, 'Das spätmittelalterliche Strassen- und Transportwesen der Schweiz und Tirols', *Geographische Zeitschrift* 11, no. 3 (1905): 145–162; Magdolna Szilágyi, 'Medieval Roads in Transdanubia', *Hungarian Archaeology*, Summer 2012, www.academia.edu/2489482/Medieval_Roads _in_Transdanubia._The_Methods_and_Potentials_of_their_Historical_and _Archaeological_Investigations.

4. Sándor Takáts, 'A magyar malom', *Századok* 41 (1907): 150.

5. Eberhard Isenmann, *Die deutsche Stadt im Mittelalter 1150–1550*, 2nd ed. (Cologne, Weimar, and Vienna, 2014), 774.

6. Aloys Schulte, *Geschichte der Grosser Ravensburger Handelsgesellschaft 1380–1530*, vol. 1 (Stuttgart and Berlin, 1923), 60; Paul Simson, *Der Artushof in Danzig* (Gdańsk, 1900), 315–322.

7. Philippe Dollinger, *The German Hansa* (London and Basingstoke, 1970), 412.

8. Klaus Friedland, 'The Hanseatic League and Hanse Towns in the Early Penetration of the North', *Arctic* 37, no. 4 (1984): 539–543.

9. Edda Frankot, '*Of Laws of Ships and Shipmen': Medieval Maritime Law and Its Practice in Urban Northern Europe* (Edinburgh, 2012), 147–148.

10. Karl Koppmann, *Das Seebuch* (Bremen, 1876), especially 52–54; Christian Peplow, 'Überlegungen zur alltäglichen Navigationspraxis der hansischen Seeschifffahrt im Ostseeraum des Spätmittelalters', *Jahrbuch der Deutschen Gesellschaft für Schiffahrts- und Marinegeschichte* 18 (2015): 10–30; Philippe Dollinger, *The German Hansa* (London and Basingstoke, 1970), 145.

11. Eliyahu Ashtor, *Levant Trade in the Middle Ages* (Princeton, 1983), 156.

12. For what follows, see Martyn C. Rady, 'The Hungarian Copper Trade and Industry in the Later Middle Ages', in *Trade and Transport in Russia and Eastern Europe*, ed. M. McCauley and J. E. O. Screen (London, 1985), 18–44.

13. For the earliest history of liquation in Central Europe, see Wolfgang von Stromer, *Oberdeutsche Hochfinanz* (*Vierteljahrschrift für Sozial- und Wirtschaftsgeschichte*, Beihefte 55–57, 1970), 137–144.

14. Zoltán Batizi, 'Mining in Medieval Hungary', in *The Economy of Medieval Hungary*, ed. J. Laszlovszky et al. (Leiden and Boston, 2018), 166–181 (176).

15. Richard A. Goldthwaite, 'The Medici Bank and the World of Florentine Capitalism', *Past and Present* 114 (1987): 3–31; Raymond de Roover, *The Medici Bank: Its Organization, Management, Operations, and Decline* (New York and London, 1948), 59–62.

16. Andreas Hauptmann et al., 'The Shipwreck of Bom Jesus, AD 1533: Fugger Copper in Namibia', *Journal of African Archaeology* 14, no. 2 (2016): 181–207.

17. Ulinka Rublack and Maria Hayward, eds., *The First Book of Fashion: The Books of Clothes of Matthäus and Veit Konrad Schwarz of Augsburg* (London, 2015).

18. Österreichische Nationalbibliothek, MSS, HAN Cod. 10906 (*Was der Buchhalten sei, auch von Dreierlei Buchhalten*, 1555).

19. A. C. Littleton and B. S. Yamey, eds., *Studies in the History of Accountancy* (Homewood, IL, 1956), 224–225; Valentin Groebner, 'Inside Out: Clothes, Dissimulation, and the Arts of Accounting in the Autobiography of Matthäus Schwarz, 1496–1574', *Representations* 66 (1999): 100–121 (114).

20. Criminal cases involving Ulin Fugger are given in Max Jansen, *Die Anfänge der Fugger* (Leipzig, 1907), 168–169. For the early history of the family, see Mark Häberlein, *The Fuggers of Augsburg: Pursuing Wealth and Honor in Renaissance Germany* (Charlottesville, VA, and London, 2012), 9–30.

21. Greg Steinmetz, *The Richest Man Who Ever Lived: The Life and Times of Jacob Fugger* (New York, 2015), 18–19.

22. Jansen, *Die Anfänge der Fugger*, 57. Quotation from Richard Ehrenberg, *Das Zeitalter der Fugger*, 3rd ed., vol. 1 (Jena, 1922), 89.

23. Christoph Bellot, 'Zur Augsburger Fuggerkapelle', in *Humanismus und Renaissance in Augsburg*, ed. G. M. Muller (Berlin, 2010), 445–490 (487–488); *Denkwürdigkeiten von Hans von Schweinichen*, ed. H. Osterley (Breslau, 1878), 77.

24. Steinmetz, *Richest Man Who Ever Lived*, 29.

25. Steinmetz, *Richest Man Who Ever Lived*, 45–46; Jacob Strieder, *Die Inventur der Firma Fugger aus dem Jahre 1527* (Tübingen, 1905), 44–45.

26. Ehrenberg, *Das Zeitalter der Fugger*, 145.

27. Ján Novak, 'Die Bedeutung der Wasserenergie für die Entwicklung des Bergbaus in Europa in die Epoche des Feudalismus', *Technikatörténeti Szemle* 8 (1975–1976): 237–42 (239); Rady, 'The Hungarian Copper Trade and Industry', 23–25. For the Newcomen pump, see Jacob Leupold, *Theatrum Machinarum Hydraulicarum*, vol. 2 (Leipzig, 1725), 94–96.

28. Irena Gieysztorowa, 'Research into the Demographic History of Poland', *Acta Poloniae Historica* 18 (1968): 5–17; J. C. Russell, 'Late Ancient and Medieval Population', *Transactions of the American Philosophical Society* 48, no. 3 (1958): 1–152 (123–129).

29. For city populations, see Isenmann, *Die deutsche Stadt im Mittelalter*, 62.

CHAPTER 12. THE DRAGON IN THE CHINA SHOP AND THE HABSBURG IMAGINATION

1. František Palacký, *Geschichte von Böhmen*, vol. 3, part 1 (Prague, 1845), 419–423.

2. *Die Klingenberger Chronik*, ed. A. Henne (Gotha, 1861), 208–209.

3. János Thuróczy, *Chronicle of the Hungarians*, ed. Frank Mantello (Bloomington, 1991), 43–52.

4. *Codex Diplomaticus Hungariae ecclesiasticus ac civilis*, ed. G. Fejér, vol. 10, part 4 (Buda, 1841), 682–694.

5. *RTA*, 8, 373: noted by Mark Whelan, 'Sigismund of Luxemburg and the Imperial Response to the Ottoman Turkish Threat, c. 1410–1437' (PhD thesis, University of London, 2014), 42.

6. *Sopron szabad királyi város története*, ed. J. Házi, vol. 1, part 2 (Sopron, 1923), 54; Balázs Nagy, 'Ceremony and Diplomacy: The Royal Summit in Buda in 1412', in *The Jagiellonians in Europe: Dynastic Diplomacy and Foreign Relations*, ed A. Bárány (Debrecen, 2016), 9–18.

7. Klaus H. Feder, 'Die ritterliche ungarische Gesellschaft vom Drachen', *Zeitschrift der Österreichischen Gesellschaft für Ordenskunde* 36 (1999): 1–20.

8. Whelan, 'Sigismund of Luxemburg', 94.

9. Veronika Novák, 'Sárkány a porcelánboltban: Luxemburgi Zsigmond és a párizsi ceremóniák', in *Francia–magyar kapcsolatok a középkorban*, ed. A. Györkös and G. Kiss (Debrecen, 2016), 253–269.

10. Based on Ferencz Toldy, *A magyar történeti költészet Zrínyi előtt*, part 1 (Vienna, 1850), 21–22.

11. J. H. Wylie and W. T. Waugh, *The Reign of Henry V*, vol. 3 (Cambridge, 1929), 9–10.

12. Norman Simms, 'The Visit of King Sigismund to England, 1416', *Hungarian Studies Review* 17, no. 2 (1990): 21–29.

13. Whelan, 'Sigismund of Luxemburg', 53.

14. Theodor von Sickel, 'Zur Geschichte der Siegel Kaiser Sigismund's', *Anzeiger für Kunde der Deutschen Vorzeit* (new series) 19 (1872): 14; Bettina Pferschy-Maleczek, 'Der Nimbus des Doppeladlers: Mystik und Allegorie im Siegelbild Kaiser Sigmunds', *Zeitschrift für Historische Forschung* 23, no. 4 (1996): 433–471. See also Len Scales in *English Historical Review* 124 (2009): 944–946.

15. Karl-Friedrich Krieger, *Die Habsburger im Mittelalter* (Stuttgart, 2004), 171.

16. Heinrich Koller, *Kaiser Friedrich III* (Darmstadt, 2005), 81–82, 251–253; Oswald von Wolkenstein, *Songs from a Single Eye: Oswald von Wolkenstein*, trans. Richard Sieburth (New York, 2019), 19–20.

17. Ralf Mitsch, 'Die Gerichts- und Schlichtungs-Kommissionen Kaiser Friedrich III', in *Das Reichskammergericht. Der Weg zu seiner Gründung und die ersten Jahrzehnte seines Wirkens (1451–1527)*, ed. B. Diestelkamp (Cologne, Weimar, and Vienna, 2013), 7–77 (58); Ralf Mitsch, *Das Kommissionswesen unter Kaiser Friedrich III* (Mannheim, 2000), 640–680.

18. Peter Moraw, 'The Court of the German King and of the Emperor at the End of the Middle Ages, 1440–1519', in *Princes, Patronage and the Nobility: The Court at the Beginning of the Modern Age c. 1450–1650*, ed. R. G. Asch and A. M. Birke (Oxford, 1991), 103–137 (118).

19. For the heraldic manuscript, see OeSta/HHStA, HS W84.

20. For manuscript editions, see Christoph J. Hagermann, *Geschichtsfiktion im Dienste territorialer Macht. Die Chronik von den 95 Herrschaften des Leopold von Wien* (Heidelberg, 2017), 9.

21. P. Terjanien, ed., *The Last Knight: The Art, Armor, and Ambition of Maximilian I* (New York, 2019), 17–37.

22. Duncan Hardy, *Associative Political Culture in the Holy Roman Empire: Upper Germany, 1346–1521* (Oxford, 2018), 247.

23. For 'either a nothing', see Rebecca Boone, 'Empire and Medieval Simulacrum: A Political Project of Mercurino di Gattinara, Grand Chancellor of Charles V', *Sixteenth Century Journal* 42, no. 4 (2011): 1027–1049 (1032).

CHAPTER 13. CENTRAL EUROPE'S RENAISSANCE, ROMAN LAW, AND THE LIBRARY OF THE RAVEN KING

1. Antonius Bonfinius, *Decades Rerum Hungaricarum*, 4. 3 (Leipzig, 1771), 577.

2. *Mátyás király levelei*, ed. Vilmos Fraknói, 2 vols. (Budapest, 1893–1895), 1:51, 1:124, 2:5, 2:56, 2:87, 2:105, 2:298.

3. András A. Deák, 'Az esztergomi reneszánsz vízgép históriája', *Hidrológiai Közlöny* 88, no. 3 (2008): 13–22 (15–16); László Zolnay, *A középkori Esztergom* (Budapest, 1983), 190.

4. Antonius Bonfinius, *Decades Rerum Hungaricarum*, 4. 7 (Leipzig, 1771), 646–647.

5. For much of what follows, see Martyn Rady, 'The Corvina Library and the Lost Royal Hungarian Archive', in *Lost Libraries: The Destruction of Great*

Book Collections Since Antiquity, ed. James Raven (Basingstoke and New York, 2004), 91–105.

6. M. G. Kovachich, *Scriptores rerum Hungaricarum minores*, vol. 1 (Buda, 1798), 347; József Teleki, *Hunyadiak kora Magyarországon*, vol. 5 (Pest, 1856), 511.

7. Csaba Csapodi, *The Corvinian Library: History and Stock* (Budapest, 1973), 57–61; Ireneo Affò, *Memorie di Taddeo Ugoleto* (Parma, 1781), 30–31.

8. Quotation from László Kontler, *Millennium in Central Europe: A History of Hungary* (Budapest, 1999), 126. See also Pál Engel, *Realm of St Stephen: A History of Medieval Hungary, 895–1526* (London and New York, 2001), 320. For Handó, see Dániel Pócs, 'The Codices of György Handó', *Hungarian Historical Review* 8, no. 3 (2019): 508–572.

9. Ana Maria Gruia, 'Fashionable Stove Tiles in Slovakia and Slavonia During the Fifteenth Century' in *Slovakia and Croatia: Historical Parallels and Connections*, ed. Veronika Kucharská et al. (Zagreb and Bratislava, 2013), 316–328.

10. Jürgen Soenke, 'Die Wesererrenaissance', *Burgen und Schlösser* 10, no. 2 (1969): 33–37; Michael Baxandall, *The Limewood Sculptors of Renaissance Germany* (New Haven and London, 1980).

11. Quotation from Jan Bialostocki, *The Art of the Renaissance in Central Europe* (Ithaca, NY, and Oxford, 1976), 85, cited in Thomas DaCosta Kaufmann, *Court, Cloister and City: The Art and Culture of Central Europe 1450–1800* (London, 1995), 48; Peter Burke, *Hybrid Renaissance: Culture, Language, Architecture* (Budapest and New York, 2016), 11–42.

12. Jan Piet Filedt Kok, 'Antwerp Mannerism', *Burlington Magazine* 148, no. 1237 (2006): 287–289.

13. Jeannie Łabno, 'Child Monuments in Renaissance Poland', *Sixteenth Century Journal* 37, no. 2 (2006): 351–374.

14. For faces, see Michael Baxandall, *Painting and Experience in Fifteenth-Century Italy* (Oxford, 1972), 58–59.

15. Czesław Miłosz, *The History of Polish Literature*, 2nd ed. (Berkeley, 1983), 21–22. See also the online selection at www.staropolska.pl 'Conversations of a Master with Death', translated by M. J. Mikoś. For Dürer's regendering of Death, see Christine Welch, 'Images of Death in Art and Literature', in *Death, Burial, and Remembrance in Late Medieval and Early Modern Europe, c. 1300–1700*, ed. P. Booth and E. C. Tingle (Leiden and Boston, 2021), 272–299 (283).

16. Seeta Chaganti, 'Danse Macabre and the Virtual Churchyard', *Postmedieval: A Journal of Medieval Cultural Studies* 3, no. 1 (2012): 7–26.

17. For Michelangelo, see James Snyder, *The Renaissance in the North* (New York, 1987), 6. For brotherhoods and reformed monasteries, see László Mezey, 'A Devotio moderna a dunai országokban', *Egyetemi könyvtár évkönyvei* 5 (1970): 223–237; G. Sarbak, 'Die ungarische Pauliner und die Devotio Moderna', in *Wessel Gansford (1419–1489) and Northern Humanism*, ed. F. Akkerman et al. (Leiden, New York, and Cologne, 1993), 170–179.

18. James H. Overfield, *Humanism and Scholasticism in Late Medieval Germany* (Princeton, 1984), 4–9.

19. Quotation is from Rudolph Agricola (c. 1443–1485), given in Johannes Rivius, *Libellus, de ratione docendi* (Louvain, 1550), 77.

20. Lewis W. Spitz, *The Religious Renaissance of the German Humanists* (Cambridge, MA, 1963), 81–109.

21. 'For the furthering of erudition': see Spitz, *Religious Renaissance*, 32–33.

22. Gulielmus Gnapheus, *Morosophus. Ein törichter Weise*, ed. Hans-Dieter Hoffmann (Frankfurt a/M, 2010), 9–24; more generally, Jacqueline Glomski, *Patronage and Humanist Literature in the Age of the Jagiellons* (Toronto, Buffalo, and London, 2007).

23. For the sausage, see H. Babucke, *Wilhelm Gnapheus, ein Lehrer aus dem Reformationszeitalter* (Emden, 1875), 5.

24. J.-F. Poudret and Jeanne Gallone-Brack, eds., *Les Sources du droit du Canton de Vaud. A: Coutume. 1: Enquêtes* (Lausanne, 1972), 125.

25. Martyn Rady, *Customary Law in Hungary: Courts, Texts, and the Tripartitum* (Oxford, 2015), 152–156.

26. Georg Dahm, 'On the Reception of Roman and Italian Law in Germany', in *Pre-Reformation Germany*, ed. G. Strauss (London and Basingstoke, 1972), 282–315 (308–311).

CHAPTER 14. LUTHER'S REFORMATION, THE BADLANDS OF THURINGIA, AND THE COURT PAINTER OF SAXONY

1. Dirk Syndram et al., eds., *Kurfürst Friedrich der Weise von Sachsen (1463–1525)* (Dresden, 2014).

2. Alister E. McGrath, *Luther's Theology of the Cross: Martin Luther's Theological Breakthrough*, 2nd ed. (Malden, MA, 2011), 22–27.

3. Alister E. McGrath, *Theology: The Basics*, 4th ed. (Chichester, 2017), 12.

4. Cited in Roland H. Bainton, 'Thomas Müntzer: Revolutionary Firebrand of the Reformation', *Sixteenth Century Journal* 13, no. 2 (1982): 3–16 (9).

5. For a probable portrait of Karlstadt's wife, Anna von Mochau, see Alejandro Zorzin, 'Ein Cranach-Porträt des Andreas Bodenstein von Karlstadt', *Theologische Zeitschrift* 70 (2013): 4–24.

6. Quotation from *The Essential Carlstadt*, ed. E. J. Furcha (Walden, NY, 2019), 122–123.

7. Valentin von Tetleben, *Protokoll des Augsburger Reichstages 1530*, ed. H. Grundmann (Göttingen, 1958), 151.

8. Erwin Iserloh, Joseph Glazik, and Hubert Jedin, *Reformation and Counter-Reformation* (London, 1980), 76; Terry Lindvall, *God Mocks: A History of Religious Satire* (London and New York, 2015), 88–89.

9. Mark U. Edwards Jr., *Printing, Propaganda, and Martin Luther* (Berkeley, 1994), 14–39.

10. Ulinka Rublack, *Reformation Europe* (Cambridge, 2017), 78–83.

11. Bobbi Dykema, 'The Ass in the Seat of St Peter: Defamation of the Pope in Early Lutheran Flugschriften', in *Character Assassination Throughout the Ages*, ed. M. Icks and E. Shiraev (New York, 2014), 153–171.

12. Steven Ozment, *The Serpent and the Lamb: Cranach, Luther, and the Making of the Reformation* (New Haven and London, 2011), 107.

13. *Die Welt des Hans Sachs* (Exhibition Catalogue, Nuremberg, 1976), 4–6; Rosemarie Bergmann, 'Hans Sachs Illustrated: Pamphlets and Broadsheets in the Service of the Reformation', *RACAR: revue d'art canadienne / Canadian Art Review* 17, no. 1 (1990): 9–16, 89–91.

14. *Kozmografia česká* (Prague, 1554). See Mirjam Bohatcová, 'The Book and the Reformation in Bohemia and Moravia', in *The Reformation and the Book*, ed. J.-F. Gilmont (Aldershot, 1998), 385–409.

15. Natalia Nowakowska, 'Forgetting Lutheranism: Historians and the Early Reformation in Poland', *Church History and Religious Culture* 92, nos. 2/3 (2012): 281–303.

16. Tobias Stich, *Buchdruck im Konfessionellen Zeitalter. Die Drucke der Offizin Osterberger in Königsberg* (Munich, 2014), 18–19.

17. Natalia Nowakowska, *King Sigismund and Martin Luther: The Reformation Before Confessionalization* (Oxford, 2018), 115.

18. Howard Louthan, *The Quest for Compromise: Peacemakers in Counter-Reformation Vienna* (Cambridge, 1997), 15.

19. James D. Tracy, *Emperor Charles V, Impresario of War: Campaign Strategy, International Finance, and Domestic Politics* (Cambridge, 2002), 213.

20. Martyn Rady, *The Emperor Charles V* (London and New York, 1988), 51.

21. Ute Lotz-Heumann and Matthias Pohlig, 'Confessionalization and Literature in the Empire, 1555–1700', *Central European History* 40, no. 1 (2007): 35–61 (46).

CHAPTER 15. THE OTTOMAN TURKS AND CENTRAL EUROPE'S
LONG FRONTIER

1. T. M. Izbicki et al., eds., *Reject Aeneas, Accept Pius: Selected Letters of Aeneas Sylvius Piccolomini (Pope Pius II)* (Washington, DC, 2006), 315; Norman Housley, 'Christendom's Bulwark: Croatian Identity and the Response to the Ottoman Advance', *Transactions of the Royal Historical Society* (sixth series), 24 (2014): 149–164 (151).

2. For Hungarian state capacity before Mohács, see Martyn Rady, 'Fiscal and Military Developments in Hungary During the Jagello Period', *Chronica* (Szeged), 11 (2011): 85–98.

3. Géza Kathona, *Fejezetek a török hódoltsági reformáció történetéből* (Budapest, 1974), 50.

4. Catherine Wendy Bracewell, *The Uskoks of Senj: Piracy, Banditry, and Holy War in the Sixteenth-Century Adriatic* (Ithaca and London, 1992), 19–36; Wendy Bracewell, 'Ritual Brotherhood Across Frontiers in the Eastern Adriatic Hinterland, Sixteenth to Eighteenth Centuries', *History and Anthropology* 27, no. 3 (2016): 338–358.

5. István Kenyeres and Géza Pálffy, 'A Habsburg monarchia és a magyar királyság had- és pénzügyigazgatásának fejlődése a 16–17. században', *Századok* 152, no. 5 (2018): 1033–1076 (1038–1051).

6. Géza Pálffy, 'Ransom Slavery Along the Ottoman–Hungarian Frontier in the Sixteenth and Seventeenth Centuries', in *Ransom Slavery Along the Ottoman Borders*, ed. G. Dávid and P. Fodor (Leiden, Boston, and Cologne, 2007), 35–83; John Smith, *Travels and Works of Captain John Smith*, ed. E. Arber, vol. 2 (Edinburgh, 1910), 839.

7. Gustav Bayerle, 'One Hundred Fifty Years of Frontier Life in Hungary', in *From Hunyadi to Rákóczi: War and Society in Late Medieval and Early Modern Hungary*, ed. J. M. Bak and B. K. Király (New York, 1982), 227–242 (236).

8. Nataša Štefanec, 'Demographic Changes on the Habsburg-Ottoman Border in Slavonia (c. 1570–1640)', in *Das Osmanische Reich und die Habsburgermonarchie*, ed. M. Kurz et al. (Munich and Vienna, 2005), 551–578.

9. Gunther Erich Rothenberg, 'Antemurales Christianitatis: The Austrian Military Border in Croatia 1522–1749' (PhD thesis, University of Illinois at Urbana-Champaign, 1958), 41, 56. For 'In some border forts', see *Stephan Gerlachs dess Aeltern Tage-Buch*, ed. David Ungnad (Frankfurt a/M, 1674), 305. For 'Although good soldiers', see Johann Weikhard von Valvasor, *Die Ehre dess Herzogthum Crains*, vol. 4 (Nuremberg, 1689), 75.

10. For the early administration of the frontier, see Rainer Egger, 'Hofkriegsrat und Kriegsministerium als zentrale Verwaltungsbehörden der

Militärgrenze, *Mitteilungen des Österreichischen Staatsarchivs* 43 (1993): 74–93 (76–79).

11. Michael J. Polczynski, 'The Wild Fields: Power and Space in the Early Modern Polish-Lithuanian/Ottoman Frontier' (PhD thesis, Georgetown University, 2016), 74. For a description of the Wild Plain, see Michalon Lituanus, *De moribus Tatarorum, Litvanorum et Moschorum* (Basle, 1615), 2.

12. For the Lithuanian chancellery, see now *The Lithuanian Metrica: History and Research*, ed. Artras Dubonis et al. (Boston, 2020).

13. For the terms of the Union of Lublin, see Richard Butterwick, *The Polish-Lithuanian Commonwealth: Light and Flame* (New Haven and London, 2020), 14–15.

14. Dariusz Kołodziejczyk, 'Slave Hunting and Slave Redemption as a Business Enterprise: The Northern Black Sea Region in the Sixteenth to Seventeenth Centuries', *Oriente Moderno* (new series) 25, no. 1 (2006): 149–159; Brian L. Davies, *Warfare, State and Society on the Black Sea Steppe, 1500–1700* (Abingdon and New York, 2007), 24.

15. Serhii Plokhy, *The Gates of Europe: The History of Ukraine* (London, 2015), 77, citing Michalon Lituanus, *De moribus Tatarorum, Litvanorum et Moschorum*, 36.

16. Michalon Lituanus, *De moribus Tatarorum, Litvanorum et Moschorum*, 36.

17. Linda Gordon, *Cossack Rebellions: Social Turmoil in the Sixteenth-Century Ukraine* (Albany, NY, 1983), 40.

18. For Cossack warfare, see Robert I. Frost, *The Northern Wars: War, State and Society in Northeastern Europe, 1558–1721* (London and New York, 2000), 50.

19. Gordon, *Cossack Rebellions*, 87.

20. George H. Williams, 'Protestants in the Ukraine During the Period of the Polish-Lithuanian Commonwealth', *Harvard Ukrainian Studies* 2, nos. 1–2 (1978): 41–72, 184–210.

21. *The Complete Kobzar: The Poetry of Taras Shevchenko*, trans. Peter Fedynsky (London, 2013), 148–239; Andrew Wilson, *The Ukrainians: Unexpected Nation*, 3rd ed. (New Haven and London, 2009), 90–95.

CHAPTER 16. TOLERATION, THE MAGUS, AND THE ALCHEMIST AS EMPEROR

1. Figures given in Arlette Jouana, *The St Bartholomew's Day Massacre: The Mysteries of a Crime of State* (Manchester, 2007), 135, 143; Robert Payne and Nikita Romanoff, *Ivan the Terrible* (New York, 1975), 354.

2. Eamon Duffy, *Fires of Faith: Catholic England Under Mary Tudor* (New Haven and London, 2009), 79.

3. *Die Reisen des Samuel Kiechel*, ed. K. D. Haszler (Stuttgart, 1866), 102, noted in David Frick, *Kith, Kin, and Neighbors: Communities and Confessions in Seventeenth-Century Wilno* (Ithaca and London, 2013), 1.

4. R. J. W. Evans, *The Making of the Habsburg Monarchy* (Oxford, 1979), 10; for a contemporary survey of heretical belief, see J. G. Hering, *Compendieuses Kirchen- und Ketzer-Lexicon* (Schneeberg, 1731, and many later editions).

5. P. D. Rosi da Porta, *Historia Reformationis Ecclesiarum Raeticarum*, vol. 1 (Chur, 1771), 146.

6. Randolph C. Head, 'The Swiss Reformations: Movements, Settlements, and Reimagination, 1520–1720', in *The Oxford Handbook of the Protestant Reformations*, ed. U. Rublack (Oxford, 2016), 167–185 (181); Thomas Maissen, 'Disputatio de Helvetiis, an Natura Consentiant. Frühneuzeitliche Annäherungen an die schweizer Konsensbereitschaft', *Traverse* 9, no. 3 (2001): 39–55 (42–43).

7. *Erdélyi országgyűlési emlékek*, ed. S. Szilágyi, vol. 2 (Budapest, 1876), 231, 343, and vol. 3 (Budapest, 1877), 472.

8. Michael Doeberl, *Entwickelungsgeschichte Bayerns*, vol. 1 (Munich, 1908), 408–410.

9. David R. Holeton, 'Fynes Moryson's Itinerary: A Sixteenth Century English Traveller's Observations on Bohemia, Its Reformation, and Its Liturgy', in *The Bohemian Reformation and Religious Practice*, ed. Z. V. David and D. R. Holeton, vol. 5, part 2 (Prague, 2005), 379–411 (391); Peter J. Klassen, *Mennonites in Early Modern Poland and Prussia* (Baltimore, 2009), 15.

10. Lazarus von Schwendi, 'Bedencken an Kayser Maximilianum II', given in Johann Christian Lünig, *Europäische Staats-Consilia, oder curieuse Bedencken*, vol. 1 (Leipzig, 1715), 336–353 (347–349); Howard Louthan, *The Quest for Compromise: Peacemakers in Counter-Reformation Vienna* (Cambridge, 1997), 114–115. For the text of the Warsaw Convention, see Norman Davies, *God's Playground: A History of Poland*, rev. ed., vol. 1 (Oxford, 2005), 126.

11. Ross Dealy, *The Stoic Origins of Erasmus' Philosophy of Christ* (Toronto, 2017), 338–339; A. G. Dickens and Whitney R. D. Jones, *Erasmus the Reformer* (London, 2000), 118.

12. Horace, *The Complete Odes and Epodes*, 2. 10, trans. D. West (Oxford, 1997), 64; Howard Louthan, *The Quest for Compromise: Peacemakers in Counter-Reformation Vienna* (Cambridge, 1997), 23.

13. Quotation from Michael Sendivogius, given in S. J. Linden, ed., *The Alchemy Reader: From Hermes Trismegistus to Isaac Newton* (Cambridge, 2003), 176.

14. King's College Library, Cambridge, Keynes MS 28, fol. 2 r–v (spelling adjusted).

15. For Trithemius's method of conjuring angels, see the translation in Francis Barrett, *The Magus or Celestial Intelligencer*, book 2, part 4 (London, 1801), 131–140. Barrett's edition carries a warning to the reader.

16. Thomas DaCosta Kaufmann, 'Arcimboldo's Imperial Allegories', *Zeitschrift für Kunstgeschichte* 39, no. 4 (1976): 275–296.

17. R. J. W. Evans, *Rudolf II and His World: A Study in Intellectual History* (Oxford, 1984), 45, 84.

18. Karl Vocelka and Lynne Heller, *Die Lebenswelt der Habsburger. Kultur und Mentalitätsgeschichte einer Familie* (Graz, Vienna, and Cologne, 1997), 98.

19. Stanisław Mossakowski, 'The Symbolic Meaning of Copernicus' Seal', *Journal of the History of Ideas* 34 (1973): 451–460 (459).

20. Antonín Švedja, 'Science and Instruments', in Fučiková et al., *Rudolf II and Prague*, 618–619.

21. Pavel Chadima and Martin Šolc, 'Astronomy and Musaeum Mathematicum at Clementinum College in Prague', *Acta Universitatis Carolinae. Mathematica et Physica* 46 (Suppl., 2005): 173–183.

22. For Rudolf's final days in Prague, see Gertrude von Schwarzenfeld, *Rudolf II. Ein deutscher Kaiser am Vorabend des Dreissigjährigen Krieges*, 2nd ed. (Munich, 1979), 256–259.

CHAPTER 17. CALENDARS, THE CATHOLIC RECOVERY, AND CENTRAL EUROPE'S THIRTY YEARS' CIVIL WAR

1. Roscoe Lamont, 'The Reform of the Julian Calendar', *Popular Astronomy* 28 (1920): 18–32.

2. Felix Stieve, *Der Kalenderstreit des sechzehnten Jahrhunderts in Deutschland* (Munich, 1880), 29; János Cikkei Herepei, *Adattár xvii. századi szellemi mozgalmaink történetéhez*, vol. 3 (Budapest and Szeged, 1971), 86.

3. Felix Maissen, 'Der Kalenderstreit in Graubünden (1582–1812)', *Bündner Monatsblatt*, nos. 9–10 (1960): 253–273.

4. Anthony Ruff, 'Catholic Reformation Hymnody', in *Hymns and Hymnody: Historical and Theological Introductions*, ed. M. A. Lamport et al., vol. 2 (Cambridge, 2019), 78–90.

5. For the Jesuits in Central Europe, see Paul Shore, *Narratives of Adversity: Jesuits on the Eastern Peripheries of the Habsburg Realms (1640–1773)* (Budapest and New York, 2012). For Poland, see Janusz Tazbir, *A State Without Stakes: Polish Religious Toleration in the Sixteenth and Seventeenth Centuries* (New York, 1973).

6. Mikhail Dmitriev, 'The Religious Programme of the Union of Brest in the Context of the Counter-Reformation in Eastern Europe', *Journal of Ukrainian Studies* 17, no. 1 (1992): 29–43.

7. Serhii Plokhy, *The Cossacks and Religion in Early Modern Ukraine* (Oxford, 2001), 129.

8. Liudmila V. Charipova, *Latin Books and the Eastern Orthodox Clerical Elite in Kiev, 1632–1780* (Manchester and New York, 2006), 158; Andrew Wilson, *Belarus: The Last European Dictatorship*, 2nd ed. (New Haven and London, 2021), 48–53.

9. Dieter Albrecht, *Maximilian I. von Bayern 1573–1651* (Munich, 1998), 37.

10. Michael Doeberl, *Entwickelungsgeschichte Bayerns*, vol. 1 (Munich, 1908), 414.

11. Maximilian Lanzinner, 'Der Landsberger Bund und seine Vorläufer', in *Alternativen zur Reichsverfassung in der Frühen Neuzeit?*, ed. V. Press (Munich 1995), 65–79.

12. Guilielmus Lamormaini, *Ferdinandi II. Romanorum Imperatoris Virtutes* (Antwerp, 1638), 189.

13. Robert Bireley, *Ferdinand II, Counter-Reformation Emperor, 1578–1637* (Cambridge, 2014), 33; August Dimitz, *Geschichte Krains*, vol. 3 (Ljubljana, 1875), 271.

14. For Matthias's negotiations, see Bernd Rill, *Kaiser Matthias. Bruderzwist und Glaubenskampf* (Graz, Vienna, and Cologne, 1999), 287.

15. The text of the Renewed Constitution is given in C. A. Macartney, *The Habsburg and Hohenzollern Dynasties in the Seventeenth and Eighteenth Centuries* (New York, 1970), 39–45.

16. Michael Frisch, *Das Restitutionsedikt Kaiser Ferdinands II. vom 6 März 1629* (Tübingen, 1993), 100–129.

17. Sigrun Haude, 'The Experience of War', in *The Ashgate Research Companion to the Thirty Years' War*, ed. O. Asbach and P. Schröder (London and New York, 2014), 257–268 (262). For 'murder collectives', see Simon Winder, *Germania: A Personal History of Germans Ancient and Modern* (London, 2010), 175.

18. *Peter Hagendorf—Tagebuch eines Söldners aus dem Dreissigjährigen Krieg*, ed. J. Peters (Göttingen, 2012), 51–53.

19. Mark Hengerer, *Kaiser Ferdinand III (1608–1657). Eine Biographie* (Vienna, Cologne, and Weimar, 2012), 294–295.

20. Małgorzata Morawiec, 'Die schlesischen Friedenskirchen', in *Der Westfälishe Friede*, ed. H. Duchhardt (Munich, 1998), 741–756.

CHAPTER 18. THE CONDITION OF THE COUNTRYSIDE: PEASANTS, GYPSIES, JEWS, AND OTHERS

1. For the law of slavery, see David M. Luebke, *His Majesty's Rebels: Communities, Factions, and Rural Revolt in the Black Forest, 1725–1745* (Ithaca and London, 1997), 177.

2. Jerzy Lukowski, 'The Peasantry of Poland-Lithuania on the Eve of the French Revolution', *History of European Ideas* 12, no. 3 (1990): 377–393.

3. Carsten Porskrog Rasmussen, 'Innovative Feudalism: The Development of Dairy Farming and *Koppelwirtschaft* on Manors in Schleswig-Holstein in the Seventeenth and Eighteenth Centuries', *Agricultural History Review* 58, no. 2 (2010): 172–190; Karin Friedrich, *Brandenburg-Prussia, 1466–1806* (Basingstoke and New York, 2012), 60.

4. John Paget, *Hungary and Transylvania*, vol. 1 (Philadelphia, 1850), 177.

5. *Corpus Constitutionum Nassovicarum*, ed. A. F. Rühle von Lilienstern, vol. 1 (Dillenburg, 1796), 509.

6. Péter Tóth, 'Kóborlás és letelepedés (A magyarországi cigányok feudális kori történetéhez)', *Levéltári Évkönyv* 7 (1994): 17–26.

7. Béla Kéri Nagy, 'A cigányok évezredes vándorútja a távoli keletről a Kárpát-medencébe', *Gyökerek. A Dráva Múzeum tanulmánykötete*, ed A. Mészáros (Barcs, 2007), 11–37 (15–16); Balázs Szűk, 'Adalékok az erdélyi cigányságnak a 14. század végétől 1893-ig terjedő történetéhez', *Művelődés* 65 (April 2012): 26–29.

8. Lech Mróz, *Roma-Gypsy Presence in the Polish-Lithuanian Commonwealth* (Budapest and New York, 2015), 281–283; Heinrich von Brandt, *Aus dem Leben des Generals der Infanterie*, vol. 1 (Berlin, 1863), 487.

9. István Szabó, *Ugocsa megye* (Budapest, 1937), 38, 48, 247–256, 286.

10. Waldemar Kowalski, *The Great Immigration: Scots in Cracow and Little Poland, Circa 1500–1660* (Leiden and Boston, 2016), 7–24; A. Francis Steuart, *Papers Relating to the Scots in Poland, 1576–1793* (Edinburgh, 1915).

11. Fabian Wittreck, 'The Old Armenian Lawcode of Lemberg', in *Diaspora, Law and Literature*, ed. K. Stierstorfer and D. Carpi (Berlin, 2017), 155–170.

12. Yuri Slezkine, *The Jewish Century* (Princeton and Oxford, 2004), 4–39.

13. J. Friedrich Battenberg, *Die Juden in Deutschland vom 16. bis zum Ende des 18. Jahrhunderts* (Munich, 2001), 10; Győző Ember, 'Magyarország lakossága a xviii. században', *Somogy megye múltjából. Levéltári évkönyv* 20 (1989): 33–68 (52–54); Stefan Plaggenborg, 'Maria Theresa und die böhmischen Juden', *Bohemia* 39, no. 1 (1998): 1–16; Gershon David Hundert, *Jews in Poland-Lithuania in the Eighteenth Century* (Berkeley and Los Angeles, 2004), 23–29.

14. Diethard Aschoff, 'Judenkennzeichnung und Judendiskriminierung in Westfalen bis zum Ende des Alten Reiches', *Aschkenas* 3, no. 1 (1993): 15–47.

15. F. L. Carsten, 'The Court Jews: A Prelude to Emancipation', *Leo Baeck Institute Yearbook* 3, no. 1 (1958): 140–156 (145).

16. Gershon David Hundert, *Jews in Poland-Lithuania in the Eighteenth Century* (Berkeley and Los Angeles, 2004), 7–8; Antony Polonsky, *The Jews in Poland and Russia: A Short History* (Oxford, 2013), 11.

17. Cited in Hillel Levine, 'Gentry, Jews, and Serfs: The Rise of Polish Vodka', *Review (Fernand Braudel Center)* 4, no. 2 (1980): 223–250.

18. Ada Rapoport-Albert, 'A Reevaluation of the "Khmelnytsky Factor": The Case of the Seventeenth-Century Sabbatean Movement', in *Stories of Khmelnytsky: Competing Literary Legacies of the 1648 Ukrainian Cossack Uprising*, ed. A. M. Glaser (Stanford, 2015), 47–59 (49–50).

19. Anna Shternshis, 'Beggars and Begging', in *YIVO Encyclopedia of Jews in Eastern Europe*, https://yivoencyclopedia.org/article.aspx/Beggars _and_Begging; Christoph Kühn, *Jüdische Delinquenten in der frühen Neuzeit* (Potsdam, 2008), 35–37.

20. Günther Heinrich von Berg, *Handbuch des Teutschen Policeyrechts*, 2nd ed., vol. 1 (Hanover, 1802), 286.

21. Jonathan Karp, *The Politics of Jewish Commerce: Economic Thought and Emancipation in Europe, 1638–1848* (Cambridge, 2008), 102–103.

CHAPTER 19. CAMERALISM, OTTOMAN ENDGAME, AND THE HUMAN LABORATORY

1. Martyn Rady, *The Habsburg Empire: A Very Short Introduction* (Oxford, 2017), 61.

2. Johann August Schlettwein, *Grundwahrheiten der gesellschafftlichen Ordnung* (Giessen, 1777), 4; T. C. W. Blanning, *Joseph II and Enlightened Despotism* (London, 1970), 3.

3. For 'a programme of total regulation', see Keith Tribe, *Strategies of Economic Order: German Economic Discourse, 1750–1950* (Cambridge, 1995), 21.

4. *Memoirs of Prince Eugene of Savoy, written by himself* (London, 1811), 77.

5. John Stoye, *Marsigli's Europe 1680–1730: The Life and Times of Luigi Ferdinando Marsigli, Soldier and Virtuoso* (New Haven and London, 1994), 177–191.

6. Martyn Rady, 'Controverse istorico-istoriografice privind toponimul Banat', in *Identitate si Cultură. Studii privind istoria Banatului*, ed. Victor Neumann (Bucharest, 2009), 18–24.

7. For 'absolute domain' and *domanium*, see Official Langer, *Serbien unter der kaiserlichen Regierung 1717–1739* (Vienna, 1889), 5.

8. János J. Varga, 'Die Notwendigkeit einer neuen Einrichtung Ungarns nach die Türkenzeit', in *Einrichtungswerk des Königreichs Hungarn (1688–1690)*, ed. J. Kálmár and J. J. Varga (Stuttgart, 2010), 9–83 (68).

9. Irina Marin, *Contested Frontiers in the Balkans: Habsburg and Ottoman Rivalries in Eastern Europe* (London and New York, 2013), 15; Matthias Bel, *Compendium Hungariae Geographicum* (Bratislava and Košice, 1779), 257.

10. William O'Reilly, 'Divide et impera: Race, Ethnicity and Administration in Early 18th-Century Habsburg Hungary', in *Minorities in Europe*, ed. G. Hálfdanarson and A. K. Isaacs (Florence, 2003), 77–103 (79); *Feldzüge des Prinzen Eugen von Savoyen*, vol. 16 (Vienna, 1891), 162; László Szita, 'A lutheránus németség bevándorlása és településtörténete Tolna megyében a xviii. században', *Tolna Megyei Levéltári Füzetek* 5 (1996): 5–23.

11. Franz Griselini, *Versuch einer politischen und natürlichen Geschichte des Temeswarer Banats*, vol. 1 (Vienna, 1780), 196.

12. Stephan Steiner, *Rückkehr Unerwünscht. Deportationen in der Habsburgermonarchie der Frühen Neuzeit und ihr europäischer Kontext* (Vienna, Cologne, and Weimar, 2014), 314. For 'grave of Germans', see Felix Milleker, *Die erste organisierte Kolonisation unter Mercy. 1722–1726* (Vršac, 1923), 7.

13. Timothy G. Anderson, 'Cameralism and the Production of Space in the Eighteenth-Century Romanian Banat: The Grid Villages of the Danube Swabians', *Journal of Historical Geography* 69 (2020): 55–67 (61), citing a decree of 1772.

14. Colin Thomas, 'The Anatomy of a Colonization Frontier: The Banat of Temesvar', *Austrian History Yearbook* 19, no. 2 (1984): 2–22 (12–13).

15. Robert Born, 'Bollwerk und merkantilistisches Laboratorium. Das Temeswarer Banat in der Planungen der Wiener Zentralstellen (1716–1778)', in *Grenzregionen der Habsburgermonarchie im 18. und 19. Jahrhundert*, ed. H.-C. Maner (Münster, 2005), 37–49 (45).

16. Ere Pertti Nokkala, 'The Machine of State in Germany—the Case of Johann Heinrich Gottlob von Justi (1717–1771)', *Contributions to the History of Concepts* 5, no. 1 (2009): 71–93 (82). For laboratory, see Michael Hochedlinger, *Austria's Wars of Emergence: War, State and Society in the Habsburg Monarchy 1683–1797* (London, 2003), 228.

17. *Einrichtungswerk des Königreichs Hungarn (1688–1690)*, ed. J. Kálmár and J. J. Varga (Stuttgart, 2010), 131; Jenő Szentkláray, *Mercy kormányzata a temesi bánságban* (Budapest, 1909), 107.

18. Official Langer, *Serbien unter der kaiserlichen Regierung 1717–1739* (Vienna, 1889), 63.

19. Rodica Vârtaciu-Medeleţ, *Barock im Banat. Eine europäische Kulturlandschaft* (Regensburg, 2012), 87–135.

CHAPTER 20. BUREAUCRATS, SARMATIANS,
AND LITTLE LANDSCAPES

1. Erik S. Reinert and Fernanda A. Reinert, 'Economic Bestsellers Published Before 1750', *European Journal of the History of Economic Thought* 25, no. 6 (2018): 1206–1263.

2. For the body metaphor, see V. L. von Seckendorff, *Teutsche Reden* (Leipzig, 1691), 321.

3. *Dictionary of African Biography*, vol. 1 (Oxford, 2012), 493–494.

4. Friderich Rudolphi, *Gotha Diplomatica*, vol. 1 (Frankfurt a/M. and Leipzig, 1696), 103–105; Percy Stulz and Alfred Opitz, *Volksbewegungen in Kursachsen zur Zeit der Französischen Revolution* (Berlin, 1956), 153.

5. V. L. von Seckendorff, *Teutscher Fürsten-Staat* (Frankfurt and Leipzig, 1703), 63, 73; Ulrich Lange, 'Der ständestaatliche Dualismus—Bemerkungen zu einem Problem der deutschen Verfassungsgeschichte', *Blätter für deutsche Landesgeschichte* 117 (1981): 311–334.

6. Andreas Klinger, 'Veit Ludwig von Seckendorff's "Fürsten Stat" and the Duchy of Saxe-Gotha', *European Journal of Law and Economics* 19 (2005): 249–266.

7. A. J. P. Taylor, *English History 1914–1945* (Oxford, 1965), 1; Ronald G. Asch, 'Estates and Princes After 1648: The Consequences of the Thirty Years' War', *German History* 6, no. 2 (1988): 113–132 (125).

8. Stefan Brakensiek, *Fürstendiener—Staatsbeamte—Bürger. Amtsführung und Lebenswelt der Ortsbeamten in niederrheinischen Kleinstädten (1750–1830)* (Göttingen, 1999), 132.

9. August Beck, *Ernst der Fromme*, vol. 1 (Weimar, 1865), 441.

10. Eduard Vehse, *Geschichte der Höfe des Hauses Sachsen*, vol. 2 (Hamburg 1854), 12–43; Jenny von der Osten, *Luise Dorothee. Herzogin von Sachsen-Gotha 1732–1767* (Leipzig, 1893), 13–14.

11. More generally here, Christopher Storrs and H. M. Scott, 'The Military Revolution and the European Nobility, c. 1600–1800', *War in History* 3, no. 1 (1996): 1–41.

12. Ronald G. Asch, 'Staatsbildung und adlige Führungsschichten in der Frühen Neuzeit', *Geschichte und Gesellschaft* 33, no. 3 (2007): 375–397 (395–396).

13. Richard Brzezinski, *Polish Winged Hussar 1576–1795* (Oxford, 2006), 19–25; Jan K. Ostrowski et al., *Land of the Winged Horseman, 1572–1764* (New Haven and London, 1999), 208–209.

14. Felicia Roşu, *Elective Monarchy in Transylvania and Poland-Lithuania, 1569–1587* (Oxford, 2017), 76.

15. Jerzy Lukowski, *Disorderly Liberty: The Political Culture of the Polish-Lithuanian Commonwealth in the Eighteenth Century* (London and New York, 2010), 16.

16. Michael North, *Geschichte Mecklenburg-Vorpommerns* (Munich, 2015), 55.

17. Cathie Carmichael, 'The Fertility of Lake Cerknica', *Social History* 19, no. 3 (1994): 305–317; August Dimitz, *History of Carniola*, vol. 4 (Cleveland, 2013), 25–32.

CHAPTER 21. THE PRUSSIAN WAY: CEMETERY MARIONETTES
AND THE MACHINE STATE

1. Christopher Clark, 'When Culture Meets Power: The Prussian Coronation of 1701', in *Cultures of Power in Europe During the Long Eighteenth Century*, ed. H. Scott and B. Simms (Cambridge, 2007), 14–35.

2. '. . . mit dem stegrayf und den henden zu haufen gekrazt': Cordula Nolte, *Familie, Hof und Herrschaft. Das verwandtschaftliche Beziehungs- und Kommunikationsnetz der Reichsfürsten am Beispiel der Markgrafen von Brandenburg-Ansbach (1440–1530)* (Ostfildern, 2005), 45.

3. Christopher Clark, *Iron Kingdom: The Rise and Downfall of Prussia, 1600–1947* (London, 2006), 73.

4. Matthew McCormack, 'Tall Histories: Height and Georgian Masculinities', *Transactions of the Royal Historical Society* 26 (2016): 79–101.

5. Peter H. Wilson, 'Social Militarization in Eighteenth-Century Germany', *German History* 18, no. 1 (2000): 1–39.

6. Clark, *Iron Kingdom*, 98–99.

7. Eckhart Hellmuth, 'Der Staat des 18. Jahrhunderts. England und Preußen im Vergleich', *Aufklärung* 9, no. 1 (1996): 5–24 (15–16).

8. T. C. W. Blanning, 'Frederick the Great and Enlightened Absolutism', in *Enlightened Absolutism: Reform and Reformers in Later Eighteenth-Century Europe*, ed. H. M. Scott (Basingstoke, 1990), 265–288 (266–267).

9. Peter H. Wilson, *German Armies: War and German Politics, 1648–1806* (London and Bristol, PA, 1998), 282.

10. P. G. M. Dickson, 'Monarchy and Bureaucracy in Late Eighteenth-Century Austria', *English Historical Review* 110, no. 436 (1995): 323–367 (337); for Würzburg, see *Würzburger Hof- und Staats-Kalender für das Jahr 1800* (Würzburg, 1800).

11. Quotation from Christian Thomasius, *Ausübung der Vernunfft-Lehre* (Halle, 1705), 16.

12. Eckhart Hellmuth, *Naturrechtsphilosophie und bürokratischer Werthorizont* (Göttingen, 1985), 35.

13. Kurt Bayertz and Thomas Gutmann, 'Happiness and Law', *Ratio Juris* 25, no. 2 (2012): 236–246.

14. Joseph von Sonnenfels, *Grundsätze der Policey, Handlung und Finanzwissenschaft, Abgekürzet vom Hofrathe Moshammer* (Munich, 1787), 13–14.

15. Heinz Duchhardt, *Barock und Aufklärung*, 4th ed. (Munich, 2007), 82–84.

16. Stefan Körner, *Nikolaus II. Esterházy (1765–1833) und die Kunst. Biografie eines manischen Sammlers* (Vienna, Cologne, and Weimar, 2013), 142.

17. Walter Endrei, 'A nyugat-európai ipari forradalom textilipari találmányainak elterjedése', *Technikatörténeti Szemle* 8 (1975–1976): 147–152.

18. See here the 'Jaquet Droz Corporate Movie', Jaquet Droz, YouTube video, 17:49, 5 December 2011, www.youtube.com/watch?v=Wof WNcMHcl0.

19. Julien Offray de la Mettrie, *Machine Man and Other Writings*, ed. A. Thomson (Cambridge, 1996), 7; Roger M. Michalski, 'Creon's Secretaries: Theories of Bureaucracy and Social Order in 18th and Early 19th Century Prussia' (PhD thesis, University of Michigan, 2009), 158–159.

20. Gerald Gillespie, ed., *The Nightwatches of Bonaventura* (Chicago and London, 2014), 15–16.

21. Cited in Ere Pertti Nokkala, 'The Machine of State in Germany—the Case of Johann Heinrich Gottlob von Justi (1717–1771)', *Contributions to the History of Concepts* 5, no. 1 (2009): 71–93 (72).

22. Johann Volkna, *Politisches deutsches Glossarium* (Utopia, 1757), 137–138; Barbara Stollberg-Rilinger, *Der Staat als Maschine. Zur politischen Metaphorik des absoluten Fürstenstaats* (Berlin, 1986), 62, 65.

23. Alan Patten, '"The Most Natural State": Herder and Nationalism', *History of Political Thought* 31, no. 4 (2010): 657–689; Henry Jacoby, *The Bureaucratization of the World* (Berkeley, Los Angeles, and London, 1973), 44–46.

24. Quotation from Norbert Bachleitner, *Die literarische Zensur in Österreich von 1751 bis 1848* (Vienna, Cologne, and Weimar, 2017), 50; J. N. Fritz, *Catalogus verschiedener Bücher* (Munich, 1770); *Catalogus Librorum a Commissione Aulica Prohibitorum* (Vienna, 1762, with supplements); for 'kingdom of the dead', see Johann Pezzl, *Skizze von Wien*, 4th ed., vol. 2 (Vienna, 1803), 5.

25. *Letters of Lady Mary Wortley Montagu*, vol. 1 (London, 1769), 96.

26. Immanual Kant, *Kant: Political Writings*, ed. Hans Reiss, 2nd ed. (Cambridge, 1991), 85–86; Klaus H. Kiefer, *'Die famose Hexen-Epoche'. Sichtbares und Unsichtbares in der Aufklärung* (Munich, 2004), 199.

27. Ludwig Abafi, *Geschichte der Freimaurerei in Österreich-Ungarn*, vol. 2 (Budapest, 1891), 238.

28. For Poland, see Norbert Wojtowicz, 'Freemasonry in Poland, Formerly and Today', *La Heroldo*, September 2003, 22–26.

29. Thomas Şindilariu, 'Die Freimaurerloge St. Andreas zu den drei Seeblättern in Hermannstadt (1767–1790)', *Zeitschrift für Siebenbürgische Landeskunde* 25, no. 2 (2002): 218–227 (226). For the Prussian lodges and their membership, see Karlheinz Gerlach, *Die Freimaurer in Alten Preussen*, 2 vols. (Innsbruck, Vienna, and Bozen, 2009–2014).

30. Margaret C. Jacob, *Living the Enlightenment: Freemasonry and Politics in Eighteenth-Century Europe* (New York and Oxford, 1991), 12, 20.

CHAPTER 22. DISSECTING EUROPE'S ORANG-UTAN: THE PARTITIONS OF POLAND AND LITHUANIA

1. Mark Hulliung, *Montesquieu and the Old Regime* (Berkeley, Los Angeles, and London, 1976), 85–87.

2. Jerzy Lukowski, 'Machines of Government: Replacing the Liberum Veto in the Eighteenth-Century Polish-Lithuanian Commonwealth', *SEER* 90, no. 1 (2012): 65–97 (72).

3. Jerzy Lukowski, 'Political Ideas Among the Polish Nobility in the Eighteenth Century (to 1788)', *SEER* 82, no. 1 (2004): 1–26 (2).

4. *The Cambridge History of Poland*, ed. W. F. Reddaway et al., vol. 2 (Cambridge, 1941), 24.

5. 'Un sujet . . . convenable à nos intérêts réciproques.' Cited in Frank Spencer, *The Fourth Earl of Sandwich: Diplomatic Correspondence, 1763–1765* (Manchester, 1961), 34.

6. Jerzy T. Lukowski, 'Towards Partition: Polish Magnates and Russian Intervention in Poland During the Early Reign of Stanislaw August Poniatowski', *Historical Journal* 28, no. 3 (1985): 557–574.

7. Richard Butterwick, *The Polish-Lithuanian Commonwealth 1733–1795: Light and Flame* (New Haven and London, 2020), 109; Jean-Jacques Rousseau, *Considerations on the Government of Poland and on Its Proposed Reformation* (1772), chaps. 1 and 3.

8. Rebecca Haynes, *Moldova: A History* (London and New York, 2020), 72–73; for 'empress of the west', see Karl A. Roider, *Austria's Eastern Question 1700–1790* (Princeton, 1982), 137.

9. Jerzy Lukowski, *The Partitions of Poland: 1772, 1793, 1795* (London and New York, 1999), 17.

10. *Politische Correspondenz Friedrich's des Grossen*, vol. 30 (Berlin, 1905), 467, 483; *Politische Correspondenz Friedrich's des Grossen*, vol. 31 (Berlin, 1906), 442.

11. Christoph Koch, *Table des Traités entre la France et les puissances étrangères*, vol. 2 (Basle, 1802), 316–317.

12. David M. Althoen, 'That Noble Quest: From True Nobility to Enlightened Society in the Polish-Lithuanian Commonwealth, 1550–1830' (PhD thesis, University of Michigan, 2000), 178.

13. Richard Butterwick, *The Constitution of 3 May 1791: Testament of the Polish-Lithuanian Commonwealth* (Warsaw, 2021), 119 (adjusted).

14. Butterwick, *Polish-Lithuanian Commonwealth 1733–1795*, 255; for Catherine the Great's fears, see Simon Dixon, *Catherine the Great* (London, 2009), 309.

15. Robert F. Arnold, *Geschichte der Polenlitterateur*, vol. 1 (Halle, 1900), 249–256; see also David Pickus, 'German Writers, Power and Collapse: The Emergence of *Polenliteratur* in Eighteenth-Century Germany', in *The Germans and the East*, ed. C. Ingrao and F. A. J. Szabo (West Lafayette, 2008), 78–88.

16. K. Morvand, *L'Orang-Outang d'Europe, ou le Polonais tel qu'il est* (1780); Anon., *Der Orang-Outang in Europe oder der Pohle nach seiner wahren Beschaffenheit* (Berlin, 1780); Jacek Kordel, 'Zur Entstehung des Begriffs "polnische Wirtschaft"', *Przegląd Historyczny* 111, no. 4 (2020): 878–902 (882); *Georg Forster's sammtliche Schriften*, ed. G. Gervinus, vol. 7 (Leipzig, 1843), 306; for Ségur, see John Stanley, 'French Attitudes Toward Poland in the Napoleonic Period', *Canadian Slavonic Papers / Revue Canadienne des Slavistes* 49, nos. 3/4 (2007): 209–227 (212).

17. Anon., *Persia and Affghanistan: Analytical Narrative* (London, 1839), 68.

18. Jerzy Lukowski, *The Partitions of Poland: 1772, 1793, 1795* (London and New York, 1999), 83.

CHAPTER 23. NAPOLEON AND THE MAP OF CENTRAL EUROPE

1. Martyn Rady, *The Habsburg Empire: A Very Short Introduction* (Oxford, 2017), 69–70.

2. *Die Mainzer Republik II. Protokolle des Rheinisch-deutschen Nationalkonvents mit Quellen zu seiner Vorgeschichte*, ed. Heinrich Scheel (Berlin, 1981), 501; for the pastor's son, see Joachim Whaley, *Germany and the Holy Roman Empire*, vol. 2 (Oxford, 2012), 583.

3. J. Holland Rose, *William Pitt and the Great War* (London, 1911), 549–550.

4. Jaroslav Czubaty, *The Duchy of Warsaw, 1807–1815: A Napoleonic Outpost in Central Europe* (London and New York, 2016), 195; John D. Stanley, 'Napoleon's Last Allies: The Poles in 1814', *Polish Review* 61, no. 3 (2016): 3–31.

5. Cited in Beatrix Langner, *Jean Paul. Meister der zweiten Welt* (Munich, 2013), 402.

6. Gabriel Hanotaux, 'L'Empire de recrutement: la terre contre la mer: 1806–1810', *Revue des Deux Mondes* 34, no. 4 (1926): 824–863 (852); Paul L. Dawson, *1812 Campaign Preparations and Logistics*, April 2013, www.napoleon-series.org/military-info/battles/1812/Russia/c_1812_logistics.pdf.

7. Dorothy Mackay Quynn, 'The Art Confiscations of the Napoleonic Wars', *American Historical Review* 50, no. 3 (1945): 437–460.

8. Jonathan Steinberg, *Why Switzerland?*, 2nd ed. (Cambridge, 1996), 9.

9. Sam A. Mustafa, *Napoleon's Paper Kingdom: The Life and Death of Westphalia, 1807–1813* (Lanham, MD, 2017), 4–5.

10. Mustafa, *Napoleon's Paper Kingdom*, 204; *La Correspondance Napoléon Ier, publiée par ordre de l'Empereur Napoléon III*, vol. 1 (Paris, 1858), 322.

11. J. H. Campe, *Wörterbuch zur Erklärung und Verdeutschung unserer Sprache aufgedrungenen fremden Ausdrücke* (Brunswick, 1813); *Hof- und Staats-Handbuch des Königreichs Westphalen* (Hanover, 1811).

12. Frank J. Bundy, 'The Administration of the Illyrian Provinces of the French Empire 1809–1813' (Master's thesis, University of Omaha, 1966), 87–88.

13. Michael Bennett, *War Against Smallpox: Edward Jenner and the Global Spread of Vaccination* (Cambridge, 2020), 168; Gunther E. Rothenberg, 'The Austrian Sanitary Cordon and the Control of the Bubonic Plague: 1710–1871', *Journal of the History of Medicine and Allied Sciences* 28, no. 1 (1973): 15–23.

14. Jelena Lakuš, 'Reading Societies and Their Social Exclusivity: Dalmatia in the First Half of the 19th Century', *Libellarium* 1, no. 1 (2008): 51–74. The earliest four-language version of the *Télégraphe Officiel* was printed on 28 July 1810. See further, *Mémoires du Maréchal Marmont*, 3rd ed., vol. 3 (Paris, 1857), 435.

15. Isaiah Berlin, *Three Critics of the Enlightenment: Vico, Hamann, Herder*, 2nd ed. (Princeton, 2013), 208–300.

16. Darko Dolinar, 'Slovene Text Editions, Slavic Philology and Nation-Building', *European Studies* 26 (2008): 65–78.

17. Joep Leerssen, *National Thought in Europe: A Cultural History*, 3rd ed. (Amsterdam, 2014), 129.

18. Leerssen, *National Thought in Europe*, 80, 210.

19. Thomas Nipperdey, *Germany from Napoleon to Bismarck 1800–1866* (Princeton, 1996), 20.

CHAPTER 24. THE GALLANT WORLD OF TOMCAT MURR: ROMANTICISM, THE GRIMMS, AND THE HANOVER HANDBOOK

1. Quotation from Thomas Carlyle, *Wilhelm Meister's Apprenticeship and Travails*, vol. 1 (New York, 1882), 255.

2. For the Directing Committee, see *Memoirs of Prince Metternich*, ed. R. Metternich, vol. 5 (London, 1882), 241; Alan Sked, *Metternich and Austria: An Evaluation* (Basingstoke and New York, 2008), 21–23.

3. Konrad H. Jarausch, 'The Sources of German Student Unrest 1815–1848', *Historical Social Research / Historische Sozialforschung*, no. 24 (Suppl., 2012): 80–114 (85–92).

4. *Memoirs of Prince Metternich*, ed. R. Metternich, vol. 3 (London, 1881), 287; Wolfram Siemann, *Metternich: Strategist and Visionary* (Cambridge, MA, and London, 2019), 597.

5. Alice M. Hanson, *Musical Life in Biedermeier Vienna* (Cambridge, 1985), 113; for English newspapers, see C. Allix Wilkinson, *Reminiscences of the Court and Times of King Ernest of Hanover*, vol. 1 (London, 1886), 66.

6. *The (London) Times*, 20 November 1851; *The Greville Memoirs*, ed. H. Reeve, 3rd ed., vol. 1 (London, 1875), 180.

7. Heide Barmeyer, 'Hof und Hofgesellschaft in Hannover im 18. und 19. Jahrhundert', in *Hof und Hofgesellschaft in den deutschen Staaten im 19. und beginnenden 20. Jahrhundert*, ed. K. Möckl (Boppard am Rhein, 1990), 239–273.

8. *The (London) Times*, 20 November 1851; *Ernst August, König von Hannover, und seine Zeit. Ein Gedenkbuch für jeden Hannoveraner* (Quedlinburg and Leipzig, 1852), 84–85.

9. See here, C. Allix Wilkinson, *Reminiscences of the Court and Times of King Ernest of Hanover*, 2 vols. (London, 1886).

10. Georg Müller, *Dr. Phil. Johann Christian Zimmermann 1786–1853. Eine ungewöhnliche Karriere im Oberharzer Bergbau* (Clausthal-Zellerfeld, 2012).

11. K. Mlynek, ed., *Geschichte der Stadt Hannover*, vol. 2 (Hanover, 1994), 320–326.

12. Carl Ernst von Malortie, *König Ernst August* (Hanover, 1861), 119–120.

13. *Erdélyi Híradó*, 19 December 1837, 406–407; *Berliner Politisches Wochenblatt*, 30 December 1837, 302.

14. Maria Tatar, *The Hard Facts of the Grimms' Fairy Tales*, 2nd ed. (Princeton and Oxford, 2003), 3–38.

CHAPTER 25. 1848 AND THE COMING OF REVOLUTION

1. Iryna Vushko, *The Politics of Cultural Retreat: Imperial Bureaucracy in Austrian Galicia, 1772–1867* (New Haven and London, 2015), 212.

2. Moritz von Sala, *Geschichte des polnischen Aufstandes vom Jahre 1846* (Vienna, 1867), 309.

3. For rumours of the number of insurgents, see Moritz von Sala, *Geschichte des polnischen Aufstandes vom Jahre 1846*, 221; for Sacher von Masoch, see Larry Wolff, *The Idea of Galicia: History and Fantasy in Habsburg Political Culture* (Stanford, 2010), 143; for Metternich's 'eine Demokratie ohne Volk', see Heinrich von Srbik, *Metternich. Der Staatsman und der Mensch*, vol. 2 (Vienna, 1925), 151.

4. Gabor Pajkossy, 'Kossuth and the Emancipation of the Serfs', in *Lajos Kossuth Sent Word . . . Papers Delivered on the Occasion of the Bicentenary of Kossuth's Birth*, ed. L. Péter, M. Rady, and P. Sherwood (London, 2003), 71–80 (76).

5. C. F. Vitzthum von Eckstädt, *Berlin und Wien in den Jahren 1845–1852. Politische Privatbriefe*, 2nd ed. (Stuttgart, 1886), 75.

6. Manfred Gailus, 'Hungerunruhen in Preussen', in *Der Kampf um das tägliche Brot: Nahrungsmangel, Versorgungspolitik und Protest 1770–1990*, ed. M. Gailus and H. Volkmann (Opladen, 1994), 176–199.

7. Joachim Eibach, 'Gerüchte im Vormärz und März 1848 in Baden', *Historische Anthropologie* 2, no. 2 (1994): 245–264; Ralph C. Canevali, 'The "False French Alarm": Revolutionary Panic in Baden, 1848', *Central European History* 18, no. 2 (1985): 119–142.

8. W. A. Coupe, 'The German Cartoon and the Revolution of 1848', *Comparative Studies in Society and History* 9, no. 2 (1967): 137–167.

9. Thomas Nipperdey, *Germany from Napoleon to Bismarck, 1800–1866* (Princeton, 1996), 548–549.

10. James J. Sheehan, *German History, 1770–1866* (Oxford, 1989), 644. For peasant petitions and the 'army of officials', see *Stenographische Berichtung über die Verhandlungen der zur Vereinbarung der preussischen Staats-Verfassung berufenen Versammlung*, vol. 1 (Berlin, 1848), 243. More generally, see James F. Harris, 'Rethinking the Categories of the German Revolution of 1848: The Emergence of Popular Conservatism in Bavaria', *Central European History* 25, no. 2 (1992): 123–148.

11. C. F. Vitzthum von Eckstädt, *Berlin und Wien in den Jahren 1845–1852. Politische Privatbriefe*, 2nd ed. (Stuttgart, 1886), Appendix ('Stimmen der Presse'), 29 February 1848.

12. For 'I am an old physician', see James J. Sheehan, *German History, 1770–1866* (Oxford, 1989), 657; Friedrich Rückert, *Liedertagebuch 1848– 1849* (Göttingen, 2002), 478.

13. Horace Rumbold, *The Austrian Court in the Nineteenth Century* (London, 1909), 111.

14. William H. Stiles, *Austria in 1848–49*, vol. 1 (New York, 1852), 110–111.

15. *Grazer Zeitung*, 7 July 1848.

16. László Péter, *Az Elbától keletre. Tanulmányok a magyar és kelet-európai történelemből* (Budapest, 1998), 75.

17. Heinrich Friedjung, *Österreich von 1848 bis 1860*, 4th ed., vol. 1 (Stuttgart and Berlin, 1918), 48.

18. Theodore S. Hamerow, 'The Elections to the Frankfurt Parliament', *Journal of Modern History* 33, no. 1 (1961): 15–32.

19. *Stenographische Berichte über die Verhandlungen der deutschen constituirenden Nationalverfassung*, ed. F. Wigard, vols. 1–2 (Frankfurt, 1848), 1:166, 1:737, 2:971, 2:1310.

20. B. Trencsényi et al., eds., *A History of Modern Political Thought in East Central Europe*, vol. 1 (Oxford, 2016), 255; J. P. Jordan, *Aktenmässiger Bericht über die Verhandlungen des ersten Slavenkongresses in Prag* (Prague, 1848).

21. G. M. Trevelyan, *British History in the Nineteenth Century, 1782–1901* (London, 1922), 292.

CHAPTER 26. THE REVENGE OF THE GENERALS AND THE MAKING OF NATIONS

1. *Verhandlungen des Österreichischen Reichstages nach der stenographische Aufnahme*, 5 vols. (Vienna, 1848–1849).

2. The lullaby was first published in December 1849, in Stuttgart.

3. For Kossuth's handling of the April Laws, see László Péter, 'Introduction', in *Lajos Kossuth Sent Word . . . Papers Delivered on the Occasion of the Bicentenary of Kossuth's Birth*, ed. L. Péter, M. Rady, and P. Sherwood (London, 2003), 1–13 (9).

4. Tamás Katona, 'Csány László erdélyi főkormánybiztos', *Zalai Gyűjtemény* 30 (1990): 221–254 (246–247).

5. General Klapka, *Memoirs of the War of Independence in Hungary*, vol. 1 (London, 1850), liv. For the text of the declaration, see Lajos Kossuth, *Írások és beszédek 1848–1849-ből*, ed. T. Katona (Budapest, 1987), 378–398; in English translation in Henry W. De Puy, *Kossuth and his Generals* (Buffalo, 1852), 202–225.

6. *Wiener Zeitung*, 1 May 1849, 1235.

7. Viktor Bibl, *Von Revolution zu Revolution* (Vienna, 1924), 229.

8. Alexander Maxwell, 'The Handsome Man with Hungarian Moustache and Beard', *Cultural and Social History* 12 (2015): 51–76 (63, 73).

9. For Renan, see Michael Billig, *Banal Nationalism* (London, 1995), 95; Bärbel Kleindorfer-Marx, 'Idee, mediale Vermittlung und Rezeption des Volkstrachten-Festzugs 1895 in München', *Bayerische Jahrbuch für Volkskunde 2017* (Munich, 2017), 117–139 (122–124); Alasdair Brooks and Natascha Mehler, 'Kilts and Lederhosen: The Historical Archaeology of Nationalism in Scotland and Bavaria', in *The Country Where My Heart Is: Historical Archaeologies of Nationalism and National Identity*, ed. A. Brooks and N. Mehler (Gainesville, 2017), 3–34.

10. Martyn Rady, 'Politics and the Nation: Coffee and Alcohol', 2019, https://www.academia.edu/40639207/POLITICS_AND_THE_NATION_COFFEE_AND_ALCOHOL. See also Alexander Maxwell, 'National Alcohol in Hungary's Reform Era: Wine, Spirits, and the Patriotic Imagination', *Central Europe* 12 (2014): 117–135.

11. Jak Ignjatovic, *Der Serbe und seine Poesie* (Bautzen, 1866), 18–20; Alexander Maxwell, 'Nationalizing Sexuality: Sexual Stereotypes in the Habsburg Empire', *Journal of the History of Sexuality* 14, no. 3 (2005): 266–290.

12. For Adam Mickiewicz, see *Pan Tadeusz or the Last Foray in Lithuania*, trans. G. P. Noyes (London and Toronto, 1917), 70, 116–117, 244, 306; for Hungarian cuisine, see John Paget, *Hungary and Transylvania*, vol. 2 (Philadelphia, 1850), 261; for German, see W. Beatty-Kingston, *Music and Manners: Personal Reminiscences and Sketches of Character*, vol. 2 (London, 1887), 30.

13. H. Braun, ed., *Czernowitz. Die Geschichte einer untergangenen Kulturmetropole*, 2nd ed. (Berlin, 2005), 9.

14. For Sand on Chopin, see Adam Zamoyski, *Chopin: The Prince of the Romantics* (London, 2010), 205.

15. Tad Szulc, *Chopin in Paris: The Life and Times of the Romantic Composer* (New York, 1998), 98. For 'Spain sobs', see Tim Blanning, *The Triumph of Music: Composers, Musicians and Their Audiences, 1700 to the Present* (London, 2008), 236.

16. For Wagner, see Benjamin Curtis, *Music Makes the Nation: Nationalist Composers and Nation Building in Nineteenth-Century Europe* (Amherst, NY, 2008), 57.

17. Krisztina Lajosi, 'Hungarian Choral Societies and Sociability in the Nineteenth Century', in *Choral Societies and Nationalism in Europe*, ed. K. Lajosi

and A. Stynen (Boston and Leiden, 2018), 206–224. For the Vienna Odeon, see Derek B. Scott, *Sounds of the Metropolis: The Nineteenth-Century Popular Music Revolution in London, New York, Paris, and Vienna* (Oxford, 2008), 45.

18. Karel Šima, T. Kavka, and H. Zimmerhaklová, 'Choral Societies and the Nationalist Mobilization of Czechs in the Nineteenth Century', in Lajosi and Stynen, *Choral Societies and Nationalism in Europe*, 187–205.

19. Oto Luthar, 'The Slice of Desire: Intercultural Practices Versus National Loyalties', in *Understanding Multiculturalism: The Habsburg Central European Experience*, ed. Johannes Feichtinger and Gary B. Cohen (New York and Oxford, 2014), 161–173 (166–167); Karin Almasy, 'Postkartengeschichte(n). Der unterschätzte Quellenwert von handschriftlichen Spuren auf Postkarten', in *Bildspuren—Sprachspuren. Postkarten als Quellen zur Mehrsprachigkeit in der späten Habsburger Monarchie*, ed. K. Almasy et al. (Bielefeld, 2020), 75–99.

20. Rok Stergar and Tamara Scheer, 'Ethnic Boxes: The Unintended Consequences of Habsburg Bureaucratic Classification', *Nationalities Papers* 46, no. 4 (2018): 575–591.

21. *Az 1881. évi elején végrehajtott népszámlalás*, vol. 1 (Budapest, 1882), 222–223; *Az 1891. évi elején végrehajtott népszámlalás*, vol. 1 (Budapest, 1893), 1. 115; Ágoston Berecz, *The Politics of Early Language Teaching: Hungarian in the Primary Schools of the Late Dual Monarchy* (Budapest, 2013), 25.

22. Statistisches Landesamt Schleswig-Holstein, *Die Bevölkerung der Gemeinden in Schleswig-Holstein 1867–1970* (Kiel, 1972), 259. Jason D. Hansen, *Mapping the Germans: Statistical Science, Cartography, and the Visualization of the German Nation, 1848–1914* (Oxford, 2015), 36.

23. Richard Boeckh, *Sprachkarte vom Preussischen Staat nach den Zählungs-Aufnahmen von 1861* (Berlin, 1864).

CHAPTER 27. BISMARCK, KHUEN-HÉDERVÁRY'S CROATIA, AND THE PRESUMPTION OF THE LAW

1. Jonathan Steinberg, *Bismarck: A Life* (Oxford, 2011), 114.

2. See here, 'Otto von Bismarck's Voice in 4 Languages (1889)', Fadi Akil, YouTube video, 0:45, March 11, 2021, www.youtube.com/watch?v =8xTnZ0u3cG0. Bismarck recites comic verses in English, Latin, German, and French.

3. *Bismarck's Table-Talk*, ed. C. Lowe (London, 1895), 64–65.

4. Mike Clarke, 'The First Steam Locomotives on the European Mainland' (paper presented at First Early Railways Conference, Durham, 1998), www.mikeclarke.myzen.co.uk/Prussian%20Blenkinsop%20engine.pdf; Eric Dorn Brose, *The Politics of Technological Change in Prussia: Out of the Shadow of Antiquity, 1809–1848* (Princeton, 1993), 210.

5. Steinberg, *Bismarck*, 174.

6. For Rothschild, see Steven Beller, *The Habsburg Monarchy, 1815–1918* (Cambridge, 2018), 108.

7. For indignation, see Martyn Rady, *Customary Law in Hungary: Courts, Texts, and the Tripartitum* (Oxford, 2015), 224.

8. Ákos Szendrei, 'Országgyűlési képviselők párthovatartozása és társadalmi háttere a dualizmuskori Debrecenben, Nagyváradon és közös vonzáskörzeteikben', *Aetas* 31, no. 1 (2016): 76–94 (92).

9. Cited in László Péter, 'The Hungarian Diætalis Tractatus and the Imperial Constitutional Systems: A Comparison', *Central Europe* 6, no. 1 (2008): 47–64 (53).

10. Rady, *Customary Law in Hungary*, 235–236.

11. Martyn Rady, 'Nonnisi in sensu legum? Decree and Rendelet in Hungary (1790–1914)', *Hungarian Historical Review* 5, no. 1 (2016): 5–21.

12. Jakub S. Beneš, *Workers and Nationalism: Czech and German Social Democracy in Habsburg Austria, 1890–1918* (Oxford, 2016), 25–26.

13. For the internal administration of Croatia, see *Hof- und Staats-Handbuch der Österreichisch-Ungarischen Monarchie für 1892* (Vienna, 1892), 960–982.

14. R. W. Seton-Watson, *The Southern Slav Question and the Habsburg Monarchy* (London, 1911), 98–99.

15. László Heka, 'Khuen-Héderváry Károly horvát bán és magyar miniszterelnök a horvátok szemében', *Forum. Acta Juridica et Politica* 6, no. 1 (2016): 45–58 (47).

16. Cited in Stjepan Matković, 'Parliamentary Elections at the Turn of the Nineteenth Century in Croatia', *Parliaments, Estates and Representation* 22, no. 1 (2002): 193–200 (197).

17. *Agramer Zeitung*, 22 July 1896, 1.

18. *Agramer Zeitung*, 19 December 1898, 2.

19. Dragan Damjanović, 'In the Shadow of Budapest (and Vienna)—Architecture and Urban Development of Zagreb in the Late Nineteenth and Early Twentieth Centuries', *Zeitschrift für Osteuropa-Forschung* 67 (2018): 522–551. For a recent Croatian re-evaluation of Khuen-Héderváry, see Željko

Holjevac, 'Mítosz és valóság között. Khuen-Héderváry Károly (1849–1918) horvát bán', in *Szorosadtól Rijekáig. Tanulmányok Bősze Sándor emlékére*, ed. L. Mayer and G. Tilcsik (Budapest, 2015), 177–184.

20. *Az ezeréves Magyarország és a milleniumi kiállitás*, ed. Gyula Laurencic (Budapest, 1896), 141–144.

21. *Eisenbahn-Zeitung. Organ des Club österreichischer Eisenbahn Beamten*, 6 January 1895, 1–2; see further, Waltraud Heindl, *Josephinische Mandarine. Bürokratie und Beamte in Österreich*, vol. 2 (Vienna, Cologne, and Graz, 2013), 283.

22. Gyula Szekfű, *Három Nemzedék. Egy hanyatló kor története* (Budapest, 1920), 239, 259. For the Austrian manual, see Waltraud Heindl, *Josephinische Mandarine. Bürokratie und Beamte in Österreich*, vol. 2 (Vienna, Cologne, and Graz, 2013), 277–278.

CHAPTER 28. ASSIMILATION, BIOLOGY, AND THE SKULL MEASURERS

1. Hugh Seton-Watson and Christopher Seton-Watson, *The Making of a New Europe: R. W. Seton-Watson and the Last Years of Austria-Hungary* (London, 1981), 33.

2. Detmar Klein, 'Folklore as a Weapon: National Identity in German-Annexed Alsace, 1890–1914', in *Folklore and Nationalism in Europe During the Long Nineteenth Century*, ed. T. Baycroft and D. Hopkin (Leiden and Boston, 2012), 161–191.

3. Peter Haslinger, 'How to Run a Multilingual Society: Statehood, Administration and Regional Dynamics in Austria-Hungary, 1867–1914', in *Region and State in Nineteenth-Century Europe*, ed. J. Augusteijn and E. Storm (London, 2012), 111–128 (123).

4. The name of the square was changed from Rossmarkt to Wenzelsplatz or Václavské náměstí in January 1850, not in 1848 (as commonly maintained). See *Die Geissel. Tagblatt aller Tagblätter*, 15 January 1850, 47.

5. For Kant (*Critique of Judgement*, 1790), see Thomas Teufel, 'The Impossibility of a "Newton of the Blade of Grass" in Kant's Teleology', in *The Life Sciences in Early Modern Philosophy*, ed. O. Nachtomy and J. E. H. Smith (Oxford, 2014), 47–61 (48).

6. Robert J. Richards, 'The German Reception of Darwin's Theory, 1860–1945', in *The Darwin Encyclopedia*, ed. Michael Ruse (Cambridge, 2013), 235–242.

7. Peter Watson, *The German Genius: Europe's Third Renaissance, the Second Scientific Revolution and the Twentieth Century* (London, 2010), 428; 'In nature', see Richard Weikart, 'Progress Through Racial Extermination: Social Darwinism,

Eugenics, and Pacifism in Germany, 1860–1918', *German Studies Review* 26, no. 2 (2003): 273–294 (277); for breeding colonies, see Willibald Hentschel, *Mittgart. Ein Weg zur Erneuerung der germanischen Rasse* (Leipzig, 1906).

8. Antony Herrmann, 'The Ethnography of the Population', in *The Millennium of Hungary and Its People*, ed. J. Jekelfalussy (Budapest, 1897), 390–411 (402, 405, 408).

9. Emese Lafferton, 'The Magyar Moustache: The Faces of Hungarian State Formation, 1867–1918', *Studies in History and Philosophy of Biological and Biomedical Sciences* 38 (2007): 706–732.

10. *Deutschland und seine Kolonien im Jahre 1896*, ed. G. Meinecke (Berlin, 1897), 205–216; *Vasárnapi Újság*, 30 August 1896, 575.

11. Paul Weindling, *Epidemics and Genocide in Eastern Europe, 1890–1945* (Oxford, 2010), 67.

12. For the physical characteristics of prostitutes, see Dóra Vargha, 'A bűn medikalizálása', *Budapesti Negyed* 47–48 (2005): 166–198 (181).

13. For 'moral collapse', see William Hirsch, *Genie und Entartung* (Berlin and Leipzig, 1894), 334–335; for Brožek, see Michal Šimůnek, 'Eugenics, Social Genetics and Racial Hygiene: Plans for the Scientific Regulation of Human Heredity in the Czech Lands, 1900–1925', in *Blood and Homeland: Eugenics and Racial Nationalism in Central and Southeast Europe, 1900–1940*, ed. M. Turda and P. J. Weindling (Budapest and New York, 2007), 145–166 (147); Sarah Marks, 'The Romani Minority, Coercive Sterilization, and Languages of Denial in the Czech Lands', *History Workshop Journal* 84 (2017): 128–148.

14. Emil Mattauschek, 'Einiges über die Degeneration des bosnisch-herzegowinischen Volkes', *Jahrbücher für Psychiatrie und Neurologie* 29 (1908): 134–148; Brigitte Fuchs, 'Orientalizing Disease: Austro-Hungarian Policies of "Race", Gender, and Hygiene in Bosnia and Herzegovina, 1874–1914', in *Health, Hygiene and Eugenics in Southeastern Europe to 1945*, ed. Christian Promitzer et al. (Budapest and New York, 2011), 57–85.

15. For 'Our Lord', see Benjamin Madley, 'From Africa to Auschwitz: How German South West Africa Incubated Ideas and Methods Adopted and Developed by the Nazis in Eastern Europe', *European History Quarterly* 35, no. 3 (2005): 429–464 (436); for 'To secure the peaceful settlement', see Paul Rohrbach, *Deutsche Kolonialwirtschaft. Südwest-Afrika* (Berlin-Schöneberg, 1907), 352.

16. For the *Vernichtungsbefehl*, see Jeremy Sarkin, *Germany's Genocide of the Herero: Kaiser Wilhelm II, His General, His Settlers, His Soldiers* (Cape Town, 2011), 102; for *endgültige Lösung*, see Georg Hartmann, *Die Zukunft Deutsch Südwestafrikas* (Berlin, 1904), 21.

17. Quotation from Joseph Roth, *The Wandering Jews* (London, 2001), 22; Michael Brenner, *A Short History of the Jews* (Princeton and Oxford, 2010), 201–205.

18. Louise O. Vasvári, 'Böske Simon, Miss Hungaria and Miss Europa (1929): Beauty Pageants and Packaging Gender, Race, and National Identity in Interwar Hungary', *Hungarian Cultural Studies* 12 (2019): 193–238.

19. Brigitte Hamann, *Hitler's Vienna: A Dictator's Apprenticeship* (New York and Oxford, 1999), 338.

20. Roth, *Wandering Jews*, 122.

21. Jay Geller, *The Other Jewish Question: Identifying the Jew and Making Sense of Modernity* (New York, 2011), 99–112.

22. Menaghem Z. Rosensaft, 'Jews and Antisemites in Austria at the End of the Nineteenth Century', *Leo Baeck Institute Yearbook* 21, no. 1 (1976): 57–86 (68).

23. Figures are for Permanent Legal Residence. Given in US Department of Homeland Security, *2008 Yearbook of Immigration Statistics* (Washington, DC, 2009). For remigration, see Mark Wyman, *Round-Trip to America: The Immigrants Return to Europe, 1880–1930* (Ithaca and London, 1993).

24. For 'scavenger ideology', see George L. Mosse, *Toward the Final Solution: A History of European Racism* (Madison, 2020), 210 (first published in 1978).

CHAPTER 29. 1914–1918: THE WAR AGAINST CENTRAL EUROPE

1. For British views of Central Europe, see William F. Bertolette, 'British Identity and the German Other' (PhD thesis, Louisiana State University, 2012), 143–183; Dimitrios Kassis, *Descriptions of Germany in British Travel Literature* (Newcastle upon Tyne, 2020).

2. For hiking in the Tyrol and Bohemia, see *Provinzial-Gesetzsammlung von Tyrol und Vorarlberg für das Jahr 1816*, vol. 3, part 2 (Innsbruck, 1823), 359–360; *Sammlung der im Landesgesetz- und Regierungsblatte nicht erhaltenen Normalien* (Prague, 1855), 315. For pistols, see John Murray and Sons, *Handbook for Travellers in Southern Germany* (London, 1837), 353.

3. Mark Hewitson, *Germany and the Modern World, 1880–1914* (Cambridge, 2018), 298.

4. Marco Althaus, 'Die Flottenlobby mit dem Propaganda-Kino', *Politikakommunikation*, May 2012, 36–37.

5. John C. G. Röhl, *Wilhelm II: Into the Abyss of War and Exile, 1900–1941* (Cambridge, 2014), 309; for the Tourette's tic, see Christopher Clark, *Prisoners of Time: Prussians, Germans and Other Humans* (London, 2021), 115.

6. Alma Hannig, 'Austria-Hungary, Germany and the Balkan Wars: A Diplomatic Struggle for Peace, Influence and Supremacy', in *The Wars of Yesterday: The Balkan Wars and the Emergence of Modern Military Conflict, 1912–13*, ed. K. Boeckh and S. Rutar (New York and Oxford, 2018) 113–136 (123–124).

7. Sean McMeekin, *The Russian Origins of the First World War* (Cambridge, MA, and London, 2011), 42–57.

8. Helmut von Moltke, *Erinnerungen Briefe Dokumenten 1877–1916* (Stuttgart, 1922), 389.

9. Alexander Watson, *The Fortress: The Great Siege of Przemysl* (London, 2019), 37.

10. Christopher Chant, *Austro-Hungarian Aces of World War I* (Oxford, 2002), 50–54. Curiously, Nicholas II's diary has only a fleeting reference to this encounter. See *Dnevniki imperatora Nikolaya II, 1894–1918*, vol. 2, ed. S. V. Mironenko (Moscow, 2013), 220. I owe this reference to the kindness of Robert Service.

11. For 'Oyster Hungarians', see Manfred Rauchensteiner, *The First World War and the End of the Habsburg Monarchy, 1914–1918* (Vienna, Cologne, and Weimar, 2014), 759.

12. Peter Gatrell, *A Whole Empire Walking: Refugees in Russia During World War One* (Bloomington and Indianapolis, 1999), 19–32.

13. Robert T. Foley, *German Strategy and the Path to Verdun: Erich von Falkenhayn and the Development of Attrition, 1870–1916* (Cambridge, 2005), 149.

14. Sean McMeekin, *Berlin–Baghdad Express: The Ottoman Empire and Germany's Bid for World Power* (Cambridge, MA, 2010), 288.

15. Richard L. DiNardo, 'Modern Soldier in a Busby: August von Mackensen, 1914–1916', in *Arms and the Man: Military History Essays in Honor of Dennis Showalter*, ed. M. S. Neiberg (Leiden and Boston, 2011), 131–167 (151).

16. Vejas Gabriel Liulevicius, *The German Myth of the East: 1800 to the Present* (Oxford, 2009), 135–137; *Erinnerungsblätter deutscher Regimenter: 3. Kgl. Sächs. Husaren-Regiment Nr. 20* (Dresden, 1932), 110–129.

17. *Der Land Ober Ost. Deutsche Arbeit in den Verwaltungsgebieten Kurland, Litauen und Bialystok-Grodno* (Stuttgart and Berlin, 1917).

18. Hermann Bieder, 'Weissrussland unter deutscher Militärverwaltung im Ersten Weltkrieg', *Studia Białorutenistyczne* 9 (2015): 217–235; *Führer durch die Ausstellung Wilnaer Arbeitsstuben* (Vilnius, 1916), 9–12.

19. Joseph Redlich, *Österreichische Regierung und Verwaltung im Weltkriege* (Vienna, 1925), 120–241.

20. Maureen Healy, *Vienna and the Fall of the Habsburg Empire: Total War and Everyday Life in World War I* (Cambridge, 2004), 135–141. For literate war, see Jiří Hutečka, '"There Is Nothing New Out Here!" A Case Study of Communication Strategies and Gender Dynamics in the First World War Family Correspondence', *Theatrum Historiae* 21 (2007): 167–193 (168–169).

21. Alexander Watson, *Ring of Steel: Germany and Austria-Hungary at War, 1914–1918* (London, 2014), 537 (adjusted). Benjamin Ziemann, *Violence and the German Soldier in the Great War: Killing, Dying, Surviving* (London, 2013), 93–156.

22. For figures, see Li Gerhalter and Ina Markova, 'Geschlechterspezifische Un_Ordnungen in Österreich 1914–1920', *zeitgeschichte* 48, no. 4 (2021): 481–504 (492); Rauchensteiner, *First World War*, 981; Hannes Leidinger and Verena Moritz, *Der Erste Weltkrieg* (Vienna, Cologne, and Weimar, 2011), 64. See further, Jakub S. Beneš, 'The Green Cadres and the Collapse of Austria-Hungary in 1918', *Past and Present* 236 (2017): 207–241.

23. Max Weber, *Economy and Society*, ed. G. Roth and C. Wittich, vol. 2 (Berkeley, Los Angeles, and London, 1978), 971–972.

CHAPTER 30. VIOLENCE, THE CITY, AND 'THE BLUE ANGEL'

1. Fritz Klein, 'Between Compiègne and Versailles: The Germans on the Way from a Misunderstood Defeat to an Unwanted Peace', in *The Treaty of Versailles: A Reassessment After 75 Years*, ed. M. F. Boemeke et al. (Cambridge, 1998), 203–220 (203).

2. Bogdan Krizman, 'The Belgrade Armistice of 13 November 1918', *Slavonic and East European Review* 48, no. 110 (1970): 67–87 (78–79).

3. Mark Cornwall, 'National Reparation? The Czech Land Reform and the Sudeten Germans 1918–38', *Slavonic and East European Review* 75, no. 2 (1997): 259–280 (272).

4. Robert Gerwarth, 'Fighting the Red Beast: Counter-Revolutionary Violence in the Defeated States of Central Europe', in *War in Peace: Paramilitary Violence in Europe After the Great War*, ed. J. Horne and R. Gerwarth (Oxford, 2012), 52–71.

5. Alexander J. Motyl, 'Ukrainian Nationalist Political Violence in Inter-War Poland, 1921–1939', *East European Quarterly* 19, no. 1 (1985): 45–55.

6. Eberhard Kolb, *Deutschland 1918–1933. Eine Geschichte der Weimarer Republik* (Munich, 2010), 187.

7. Joseph Rothschild, *East Central Europe Between the Two World Wars* (Seattle and London, 1977), 80.

8. Peter Heumos, 'Konfliktregelung und soziale Integration. Zur Struktur der Ersten Tschechoslowakischen Republik', *Bohemia* 30 (1989): 53–70.

9. Peter Bugge, 'Czech Democracy 1918–1938—Paragon or Parody?', *Bohemia* 47 (2006–2007): 3–28.

10. Egbert Klautke, 'The Urban Jungle: Americanism and the Jazz Age in Weimar Germany', in *Constructing America /Defining Europe*, ed. J. Verheul et al. (Leiden and Boston, 2020); for Tiller girls, see Egbert Klautke, *Unbegrenzte Möglichkeiten. Amerikanisierung in Deutschland und Frankreich (1900–1933)* (Wiesbaden, 2003), 264–266.

11. For troubadours, see Michael J. Schmidt, 'Visual Music: Jazz, Synaesthesia and the History of the Senses in the Weimar Republic', *German History* 32, no. 2 (2014): 201–223; for Burian, see Brian Locke, '"The Periphery Is Singing Hit Songs": The Globalization of American Jazz and Interwar Czech Avant-Garde', *American Music Research Center Journal* 12 (2002): 25–55 (28).

12. For a new translation by John D. Boy of Simmel's 'The Metropolis and the Life of Spirit' (*Die Grosstädte und das Geistesleben*), see *Journal of Classical Sociology* 21, no. 2 (2021): 188–202. See further, Dietmar Jazbinsek, 'The Metropolis and the Mental Life of Georg Simmel', *Journal of Urban History* 30, no. 1 (2003): 102–125.

13. Siegfried Kracauer, *From Caligari to Hitler: A Psychological History of the German Film*, rev. ed. (Princeton and Oxford, 2004), 166.

14. Quotation from Frank Mehring, 'Welcome to the Machine! The Representation of Technology in Zeitopern', *Cambridge Opera Journal* 11, no. 2 (1999): 159–177 (163).

15. Bruno Schulz 'The Street of Crocodiles', in *The Fictions of Bruno Schulz*, trans. C. Wieniewska (Basingstoke and Oxford, 2012), 75.

16. Rainer Maria Rilke, *Selected Poems*, trans. S. Ransom and M. Sutherland (Oxford, 2011), 203.

17. Frigyes Karinthy, *Utazás Faremidóba* (Budapest, 1916).

18. Lynne Frame, 'Gretchen, Girl, Garçonne? Weimar Science and Popular Culture in Search of the Ideal New Woman', in *Women in the Metropolis: Gender and Modernity in Weimar Culture*, ed. K. von Ankum (Berkeley, Los Angeles, and London, 1997), 12–40.

19. Peter Jelavich, *Berlin Cabaret* (Cambridge, MA, and London, 1993), 24.

20. Erika Hughes, 'Art and Illegality on the Weimar Stage: The Dances of Celly de Rheydt, Anita Berber and Valeska Gert', *Journal of European Studies* 39, no. 3 (2009): 320–335.

21. Jelavich, *Berlin Cabaret*, 228–257.

22. Jelavich, *Berlin Cabaret*, 243.

Notes to Chapter 31

CHAPTER 31. THE SECOND WORLD WAR, ORDINARY CENTRAL
EUROPEANS, AND INDUSTRIAL MURDER

1. Jonathan Wright, 'Locarno: A Democratic Peace?', *Review of International Studies* 36, no. 2 (2010): 391–411.

2. For level crossings, see Norman Stone, *World War One: A Short History* (London, 2007), 187.

3. Cited in Elisabeth Barker, *Austria 1918–1972* (London and Basingstoke, 1973), 106.

4. Vit Smetana, *In the Shadow of Munich: British Policy Towards Czechoslovakia from the Endorsement to the Renunciation of the Munich Agreement (1938–1942)* (Prague and Chicago, 2008), 44–45; Mark Cornwall, 'The Czechoslovak Sphinx: "Moderate and Reasonable" Konrad Henlein', in *In the Shadow of Hitler: Personalities of the Right in Central and Eastern Europe*, ed. R. Haynes and M. Rady (London and New York, 2011), 206–226.

5. For 'little worms', see Richard Overy, *The Origins of the Second World War*, 3rd ed. (Abingdon and New York, 2008), 122.

6. Paul D. Quinlan, 'The Tilea Affair: A Further Inquiry', *Balkan Studies* 19 (1978): 147–157; Winston S. Churchill, *The Second World War*, vol. 1 (Boston, 1948), 311.

7. Leo Leixner, *Von Lemberg* (Munich, 1942), 10. For 'the greatest political crime', see Lord Macaulay, *History of England*, vol. 8 (New York, 1876), 141.

8. Czesław Madajczyk, 'Einleitung', in *Vom Generalplan Ost zum Generalsiedlungsplan*, ed. C. Madajczyk (Munich, 1994), v–xxi (v–vii); for Goebbels's description, see *Die Tagebücher von Joseph Goebbels*, ed. E. Fröhlich, vol. 8 (Munich, 1998), 406 (5 November 1940).

9. Saul Friedländer, *Das Dritte Reich und die Juden*, 2nd ed. (Munich, 2006), 582.

10. Sybil H. Milton, '"Gypsies" as Social Outsiders in Nazi Germany', in *Social Outsiders in Nazi Germany*, ed. R. Gellately and N. Stoltzfus (Princeton and Oxford, 2001), 212–232.

11. 'Extracts from Journal and Office Records of Hans Frank, Governor General of Poland, 1939–1944', Office of US Chief of Counsel, PS-2233, Harvard Law School Library, Nuremberg Trials Project.

12. Oded Heilbronner, 'German or Nazi Antisemitism?', in *The Historiography of the Holocaust*, ed. D. Stone (Basingstoke and New York, 2004), 9–23.

13. Horst Krüger, *The Broken House: Growing Up Under Hitler*, trans. S. Whiteside (London, 2021), 6–7.

14. See Peter G. J. Pulzer, *The Rise of Political Anti-Semitism in Germany and Austria* (New York, London, and Sydney, 1964), 293–294.

15. Yehuda Slutsky et al., 'Numerus Clausus', in *Encyclopaedia Judaica*, ed. M. Berenbaum and F. Skolnik, 2nd ed., vol. 15 (Chicago, 2007), 339–343; Natalia Aleksiun, 'Jewish Students and Christian Corpses in Interwar Poland: Playing with the Language of Blood Libel', *Jewish History* 26, nos. 3–4 (2012): 327–342.

16. Jan T. Gross, *Neighbours: The Destruction of the Jewish Community in Jedwabne, Poland* (Princeton, 2001). The number of Jews killed at Jedwabne is contested.

17. John-Paul Himka, 'The Lviv Pogrom of 1941: The Germans, Ukrainian Nationalists, and the Carnival Crowd', *Canadian Slavonic Papers/Revue canadienne des slavistes* 53, nos. 2–4 (2011): 209–243.

18. Frank's cabinet report, 16 December 1941, given in 'Extracts from journal and office records of Hans Frank, Governor General of Poland, 1939–1944', Office of US Chief of Counsel, PS-2233, Harvard Law School Library, Nuremberg Trials Project.

19. Jane Caplan, *'Jetzt judenfrei.' Writing Tourism in Nazi-Occupied Poland* (London, 2012).

20. Halik Kochanski, *The Eagle Unbowed: Poland and the Poles in the Second World War* (London, 2012), 234–236.

21. For Himmler, see Helmut Krausnick, 'Denkschrift Himmlers über die Behandlung der Fremdvölkischen im Osten (Mai 1940)', *Vierteljahrshefte für Zeitgeschichte* 5, no. 2 (1957): 194–198.

22. Jan Grabowski, *Hunt for the Jews: Betrayal and Murder in German-Occupied Poland* (Bloomington, 2013), 3; Martyn Rady, 'Ferenc Szálasi, "Hungarism" and the Arrow Cross', in *In the Shadow of Hitler: Personalities of the Right in Central and Eastern Europe*, ed. R. Haynes and M. Rady (London and New York, 2011), 261–277; Regina Fritz and Catherine Novak-Rainer, 'Inside the Ghetto: Everyday Life in Hungarian Ghettos', *Hungarian Historical Review* 4, no. 3 (2015): 606–640.

23. Ronald J. Berger, 'The "Banality of Evil" Reframed: The Social Construction of the "Final Solution" to the "Jewish Problem"', *Sociological Quarterly* 34, no. 4 (1993): 597–618.

24. Walter Stier, transcript of the Shoah interview by Claude Lanzmann, 1978–1981, United States Holocaust Memorial Museum, https://collections.ushmm.org/film_findingaids/RG-60.5064_01_trl_en.pdf.

25. Gyula Sáfár, 'A Békés megyei zsidó vagyon sorsa 1944-ben', in *A holokauszt Békés megyei történeteiből*, ed. A. Erdész and T. Kovács (Gyula, 2014), 87–99.

26. Gitta Sereny, *Into That Darkness: An Examination of Conscience* (New York, 1983), 162, 229.

27. Hannah Arendt, *Eichmann in Jerusalem: A Report on the Banality of Evil* (London, 1977), 135–137.

CHAPTER 32. MÁTYÁS RÁKOSI, STALINIST CENTRAL EUROPE, AND ITS DISCONTENTS

1. Tom Lorman, 'Rákosi in London', *Journal of the Islington Archaeology and History Society* 3, no. 3 (2013): 14–15; *Délmagyarország*, 22 June 1946, 1.

2. For Varga, see Kyung Deok Roh, 'Rethinking the Varga Controversy, 1941–1953', *Europe-Asia Studies* 63, no. 5 (2011): 833–855.

3. Paul Lendvai, *One Day That Shook the World: The 1956 Hungarian Uprising and Its Legacy* (Princeton, 2008), 30–34.

4. For anti-Communist fighters in Transylvania, see Dorin Dobrincu, 'Rezistenţa armată anticomunistă din Munţii Făgăraş—versantul nordic', *Anuarul Institutului de Istorie George Bariţiu: Series Historica* 46 (2007): 433–502.

5. Hugo Service, *Germans to Poles: Communism, Nationalism and Ethnic Cleansing After the Second World War* (Cambridge, 2013), 215–221; Levente Orosz, 'Antiszemitizmus Erdélyben a holokauszt után', *Tanulmányok a Holokausztról*, ed. R. Braham (Budapest, 2019), 237–256.

6. Gwénola Sebaux, '(Spät-) Aussiedler aus Rumänien', in *(Spät-) Aussiedler in der Migrationsgesellschaft* (Bundeszentrale für politische Bildung, Informationen zur politische Bildung, 340, 2019), online resource.

7. For figures of deportees, see Joseph B. Schechtman, 'Postwar Population Transfers in Europe: A Survey', *Review of Politics* 15, no. 2 (1953): 151–178.

8. *The Eleanor Roosevelt Papers*, vol. 1, part 1 (Charlottesville and London, 2010), 254.

9. For 'bookkeeping units', see Ota Šik, *Plan and Market Under Socialism* (Abingdon and Oxford, 2018), 32 (first published in 1967). For the role of the Economist Intelligence Unit, I am indebted to the late Alan Smith.

10. Maciej Tymiński, 'Local Nomenklatura in Communist Poland: The Case of the Warsaw Voivodship (1956–1970)', *Europe-Asia Studies* 69, no. 5 (2017): 709–727.

11. Étienne Forestier-Peyrat and Kristy Ironside, 'The Communist World of Public Debt (1917–1991): The Failure of a Countermodel?', in *A World of Public Debts: A Political History*, ed. N. Barreyre and N. Delalande (Cham, 2020), 317–345 (325).

12. Balázs Apor, *The Invisible Shining: The Cult of Mátyás Rákosi in Stalinist Hungary, 1945–1956* (Budapest and New York, 2017), 166.

13. David S. Mason, 'Membership of the Polish United Workers Party', *Polish Review* 27, nos. 3–4 (1982): 138–153; Gil Eyal and Eleanor Townsley, 'The Social Composition of the Communist Nomenklatura: A Comparison of Russia, Poland, and Hungary', *Theory and Society* 24, no. 5 (1995): 723–750.

14. Ivan Volgyes, 'Social Change in Communist Eastern Europe: Hungary in a Comparative Perspective', *Comparative Southeast European Studies* 32, no. 6 (1983): 334–343; for the new noblemen, see George Konrad and Ivan Szelenyi, *The Intellectuals on the Road to Class Power* (New York and London, 1979), 190.

15. Václav Havel et al., *The Power of the Powerless: Citizens Against the State in Central-Eastern Europe*, ed. John Keane (London and New York, 2015), 27–28.

16. For the cabinet meeting of 28 October 1956, see C. Békés et al., eds., *The 1956 Hungarian Revolution: A History in Documents* (Budapest and New York, 2002), 273–283.

17. C. Békés et al., *1956 Hungarian Revolution*, 307.

18. Zsuzsanna Vajda and László Eörsi, 'Saints of the Streets: The Participants in 1956', in *Resistance, Rebellion and Revolution in Hungary and Central Europe: Commemorating 1956*, ed. L. Péter and M. Rady (London, 2008), 227–237.

19. Joseph Rothschild and Nancy M. Wingfield, *Return to Diversity: A Political History of East Central Europe Since World War II*, 4th ed. (New York and Oxford, 2008), 164.

CHAPTER 33. COMMUNIST CENTRAL EUROPE AND ITS COLLAPSE

1. Kieran Williams, *The Prague Spring and Its Aftermath: Czechoslovak Politics, 1968–1970* (Cambridge, 1997), 6.

2. Filip Pospíšil, 'Youth Cultures and the Disciplining of Czechoslovak Youth in the 1960s', *Social History* 37, no. 4 (2012): 477–500 (479).

3. Quotation from Pospíšil, 'Youth Cultures', 477–500 (493).

4. Robert B. Pynsent, 'Václav Havel: A Heart in the Right Place', *East European Politics and Societies and Cultures* 32, no. 2 (2018): 334–352.

5. Jan Kavan, 'Czechoslovakia 1968: Revolt or Reform? 1968—a Year of Hope and Non-Understanding', *Critique* 36, no. 2 (2008): 289–301.

6. Richard Lowenthal, 'The Sparrow in the Cage', *Problems of Communism* 17, no. 6 (1968): 2–28 (16–17).

7. Fred H. Eidlin, *The Logic of 'Normalization': The Soviet Intervention in Czechoslovakia* (Boulder and New York, 1980), 72.

8. Williams, *Prague Spring*, 40–41.

9. Barbara Day, *Trial by Theatre: Reports on Czech Drama* (Prague, 2019), 204–205.

10. Janina Frentzel-Zagorska, 'The Dominant Political Culture in Poland', *Politics* 20, no. 1 (1985): 82–98 (97).

11. Siobhan Doucette, *Books Are Weapons: The Polish Opposition Press and the Overthrow of Communism* (Pittsburgh, 2017), 34–51.

12. J. L. Curry, ed., *The Black Book of Polish Censorship* (New York, 1984).

13. Krzysztof Lesiakowski, 'Professional Negligence, Mismanagement and Malpractice: Polish Companies in the Light of Supreme Audit Office Materials in the Years 1976–1980', *Studiae Historiae Oeconomicae* 34 (2016): 149–165.

14. Jost Hermand, *Kultur im Wiederaufbau. Die Bundesrepublik Deutschland 1945–1965* (Munich, 1986), 242.

15. Patrick Major, *The Death of the KPD: Communism and Anti-Communism in West Germany, 1945–1956* (Oxford, 1998), 262–292.

16. *Der Spiegel*, no. 35 (1981), online resource; *Der Rote Stachel—Sammelflugblatt der KPD/Marxisten-Leninisten, Sektion DDR*, October 1979.

17. Norman Davies and Roger Moorhouse, *Microcosm: Portrait of a Central European City* (London, 2003), 6; Milan Kundera, 'The Tragedy of Central Europe', *New York Review of Books* 31, no. 7 (26 April 1984), https://www.nybooks.com/articles/1984/04/26/the-tragedy-of-central-europe/.

18. Matthew J. Ouimet, 'National Interest and the Question of Soviet Intervention in Poland, 1980–1981: Interpreting the Collapse of the Brezhnev Doctrine', *SEER* 78, no. 4 (2008): 710–734 (734).

19. Author's personal conversation with Deputy Prime Minister Imre Pozsgay, October 1989.

20. Hans-Hermann Hertle, *Der Fall der Mauer. Die unbeabsichtigte Selbstauflösung des SED-Staates* (Opladen, 1996), 182–183.

CHAPTER 34. POST-COMMUNISM: SLAVOJ ŽIŽEK AND THE LESSON OF LAIBACH

1. 'The State of Europe: Christmas Eve 1989', *Granta 30: The New Europe*, 2 February 1990, https://granta.com/the-state-of-europe-christmas-eve-1989/.

2. Tom Dickins, 'Folk-Spectrum Music as an Expression of Alterity in "Normalization" Czechoslovakia (1969–89): Context, Constraints and Characteristics', *SEER* 95 (2017): 648–690. For Reed, see Reggie Nadelson, *Comrade Rockstar: The Story of the Search for Dean Reed* (London, 2004).

3. Robert Hudson, 'Songs of Seduction: Popular Music and Serbian Nationalism', *Patterns of Prejudice* 37 (2003): 157–176; Robert Rigney, 'The Resurgence of Turbofolk', *New Presence*, no. 2 (2011): 111–123; Rory Archer, 'Assessing Turbofolk Controversies: Popular Music Between the Nation and the Balkans', *Southeastern Europe* 36 (2012): 178–207.

4. Alexei Monroe, *Interrogation Machine: Laibach and NSK* (Cambridge, MA, and London, 2005), 69, 235.

5. Monroe, *Interrogation Machine*, 239.

6. Marc De Kesel, 'Act Without Denial: Slavoj Žižek on Totalitarianism, Revolution and Political Act', *Studies in East European Thought* 56 (2004): 299–334; Simon Paul Bell, 'Laibach and the NSK: An East-West Nexus in Post-totalitarian Eastern Europe' (PhD thesis, Anglia Ruskin University, 2014), 190.

7. Daphne Berdahl, *On the Social Life of Postsocialism: Memory, Consumption, Germany* (Bloomington, 2010), 93.

8. M. Kaser, 'Post-Communist Privatization: Flaws in the Treuhand Model', *Acta Oeconomica* 48 (1996): 59–76. For Norman Stone's advice, see Adam Burgess, *Divided Europe: The New Domination of the East* (London, 1997), 28.

9. Daphne Berdahl, *On the Social Life of Postsocialism: Memory, Consumption, Germany* (Bloomington, 2010), 96–98.

10. Ben Gook, 'Backdating German Neoliberalism: Ordoliberalism, the German Model and Economic Experiments in Eastern Germany After 1989', *Journal of Sociology* 54 (2018): 33–48.

11. Ada Madariaga, 'The Politics of Neoliberalism (in Europe's Periphery)', *Comparative European Politics* 17 (2019): 797–811.

12. Philipp Ther, *Europe Since 1989: A History* (Princeton and Oxford, 2016), 113, 143.

13. The advertisement is available on www.youtube.com/watch?v=Oj Xl61uKq8c ('Raiffeisen Bank TV-Ad: Easy [Sub-prime] Loans in Hungary, 2007', Dominik Schnitzer, YouTube video, 0:34).

14. Matt Apuzzo, 'Populist Politicians Exploit EU Aid, Reaping Millions', *New York Times* (New York edition), 3 November 2019, A1.

15. For Malmström's estimates, see '€120 Billion Lost to Corruption in EU Each Year', *EUobserver* (online edition), 6 March 2013.

16. Tim Haughton and Kevin Deegan-Krause, 'Hurricane Season: Systems of Instability in Central and East European Party Politics', *East European Politics and Societies and Cultures* 29 (2015): 61–80.

17. Council of Europe Commissioner for Human Rights, *Memorandum on the Stigmatisation of LGBTI People in Poland* (CommDH2020/27) (Strasbourg, 2020).

CONCLUSION

1. J. D. Mansi, *Sacrorum Conciliorum Nova*, vol. 24 (Venice, 1780), cols. 110–112.

2. US Department of State, *Foreign Relations of the United States, 1955–1957*, vol. 25: *Eastern Europe* (Washington DC, 1990), 494.

3. Martyn Rady, 'Self-Determination and the Dissolution of Yugoslavia', *Ethnic and Racial Studies* 19, no. 2 (1996): 379–390.

Index

MARTYN RADY is Masaryk Professor Emeritus of Central European History at University College London. A leading expert on Central Europe, he is the author of *The Habsburgs: To Rule the World*, *The Habsburg Empire: A Very Short Introduction*, and other books on Hungarian and Romanian history. He lives in Gloucestershire, UK.